WILLIAM QUAN JUDGE
1851-1896

ECHOES OF THE ORIENT

The Writings of William Quan Judge

COMPILED BY DARA EKLUND

VOLUME II

POINT LOMA PUBLICATIONS, INC.
P.O. Box 6507
San Diego, California 92106

Printed in the United States of America by

STOCKTON TRADE PRESS, INC.
Commerce, California

PUBLISHER'S NOTE

With this second volume of *Echoes of the Orient*, Point Loma Publications, Inc., is pleased to continue its cooperation with the compiler in the production of the writings of William Q. Judge, and takes this occasion to thank those who have contributed generously to the continuing of this project.

We trust that this volume will be received with appreciative attention from a growing number of readers.

FOREWORD

Our first volume of Judge's collected writings focused on *The Path* magazine, edited and founded by him; our second, comprises his contributions to several Theosophical journals. In *The Irish Theosophist* we see his influence on his native Ireland where he helped to kindle the Irish Literary Renaissance. In Europe H.P.B. welcomed his valuable articles in her *Lucifer* magazine. As an outcome of W. Q. Judge's trip to India in the summer of 1884, *The Theosophist* printed several accounts of his lectures there. These summaries are included along with several articles contributed to that chief organ of the Society. It should be noted, however, that in this volume no attempt has been made to arrange the material in strict chronological sequence except within the context of each chapter.

The Path magazine material not to be found in Volume One embraces miscellaneous articles, news items, and a few editorial statements; and these are included here. "Answers to Questioners" and dialogues, such as "The Stream of Thought and Queries," are grouped with *The Theosophical Forum* extracts. It is in these extracts that Mr. Judge's gift as a teacher shines most vividly in his simple yet cogent answers to questioning students. Most correspondence from *The Path* will be reprinted in a later volume devoted to Mr. Judge's letters.

A report of *The Theosophical Congress* held at *The World's Parliament of Religions* (Chicago World's Fair) was compiled in book form by the American T.S. in 1893. As this report is accessible only in a few major Theosophical libraries, we are reprinting here the contributions of W. Q. Judge, who acted as chairman of the advisory council to this Parliament on behalf of Theosophy.

I am greatly indebted to Boris de Zirkoff for helpful suggestions and valuable source material and photographs; to Helen Todd and Emmett Small of Point Loma Publications for editorial assistance; to Lina Psaltis, Irene Ponsonby and Nicholas Curtis Weeks for proofreading; to Seetha Neelakantan and Joy Mills for placing the Adyar Theosophical archives at my disposal; and to several centers of the Theosophical Movement and independent students for their warm wishes and encouragement.

Love of and practical devotion to Theosophy is the living flame which will keep William Quan Judge's teachings in print for this suffering world.

Dara Eklund, Compiler.

Los Angeles, California
October 22, 1979

DEDICATION

To Dr. Henry A. Smith who passed away as this work embodying the teachings of one of his favorite Theosophists, was being set up.

TABLE OF CONTENTS

SECTION I

From "The Irish Theosophist"

SECTION II

From "Lucifer"

SECTION III

From "The Theosophist"

SECTION IV

World's Parliament of Religions

SECTION V

Selections from "The Path"

SECTION VI

SECTION VII

SECTION VIII

SECTION IX

SECTION X

SECTION XI

Faces of Friends

ILLUSTRATIONS

FROM "THE IRISH THEOSOPHIST"

Æ: George William Russell
1867-1935

"The Irish Theosophist"

[Running through five volumes, from October 15, 1892, through September 15, 1897, *The Irish Theosophist* was a magazine "devoted to Universal Brotherhood, Eastern Literature and Occult Science." Founded by D. N. Dunlop, it fostered articles and essays by the noted authors of the Irish Literary Renaissance. *The Canadian Theosophist*, Vol. III, No. 4, June 15, 1922, pp. 57-58, printed a colorful description of Mr. Dunlop, stating that after a number of years in America, he went to England with the Westinghouse Company. He became an influential businessman in London, as Secretary for the British Amalgamated Manufacturers' Association. The account says, "Mr. Dunlop began in Ireland with the Dublin Group, which was responsible, as may be read in Ernest Boyd's volume on *Ireland's Literary Renaissance*,[1] for much that is most valuable in that movement. He contributed to *The Irish Theosophist*, as did his wife, Eleanor Dunlop . . ." He was also on the Executive Council of the T.S. in England and Wales, finally resigning due to disenchantment with the uncharitable attitude of officials towards members who disagreed with their policies.

Among the members of the Dublin Group was George William Russell, known by the pen name "Æ". The Dublin Lodge, T.S. had been founded by Charles Johnston in 1886, and Æ was introduced into it a year or so later by his fellow poet W. B. Yeats. Æ's first meeting with W. Q. Judge was during the latter's visit to Dublin in 1892. Judge became a 'spiritual Hero,' loved and supported by that Lodge without a dissenting voice. Believing that the cycle had ended with W.Q.J.'s passing, and fearing the T.S. would become a "nursery of the Black Art." Æ resigned to form *The Hermetic Society*. Later he wrote to his friend, Captain P. G. Bowen, of "that great and wise man, William Q. Judge whose very memory seems to have been forgotten by present day Theosophists. I think he was a true adept in that sacred lore . . ."[2]

Fortunately, the Theosophic world seems to be rousing itself to a more harmonious acknowledgement of Judge than existed at the dawn of this century when Æ felt the T.S. had reached its twilight zone.

---

[1] New York, John Lane Co., 1916.

[2] Originally written Oct. 17, 1892, this letter was quoted from *The Aryan Path*, December 1935, pp. 722-26.

For further appreciation of how much Judge meant to the Dublin Circle we quote from tributes published in the month following his death.—*Compiler*.]

Tributes to *W. Q. Judge*

[*The Irish Theosophist*, Vol. IV, April 15, 1896, No. 7, pp. 121-23]

W. Q. J.

O hero of the iron age,
Upon thy grave we will not weep,
Nor yet consume away in rage
For thee and thy untimely sleep.
Our hearts a burning silence keep.

O martyr, in these iron days
One fate was sure for soul like thine:
Well you foreknew but went your ways.
The crucifixion is the sign,
The meed of all the kingly line.

We may not mourn—though such a night
Has fallen on our earthly spheres
Bereft of love and truth and light
As never since the dawn of years;
For tears give birth alone to tears.

One wreath upon thy grave we lay
(The silence of our bitter thought,
Words that would scorch their hearts of clay),
And turn to learn what thou hast taught,
To shape our lives as thine was wrought.

ABOUT 9 a.m. on Saturday, the 21st of last month, our beloved leader left us. As we go to press no details are to hand. Meantime we cannot let this issue appear without a few words from one or two who knew that heart, thought by many to be "something else."—EDITOR, *Irish Theosophist*.

The claim of William Q. Judge upon us is impersonal and universal, for it is the claim of work, and of work only.

Not the man then, but his work. The Work was his ideal. He valued men and women only by their work and the spirit in which it was done; he held right thought to be the best work of all; he worked with anyone who was wishful or willing to do work in any real sense, whether such persons were enemies or friends.

Slowly, under the moulding touch of time and suffering, his character evolved before the eyes of the community whose estimate is the estimate of twenty years' experience and is not to be shaken. If there be little said about him as an occultist, it is because such men, in such relations, leave no visible, material traces. Of them it may be said, in the language of paradox: They are known to be what they are because they are unknown; they are recognized because they are misunderstood; they are honored in the inner world because they are dishonored in the outer world; they have suffered that other men may rejoice; hatred is their portion because they have loved much; sorrow is their lot until that day when the whole world shall rejoice. Such men, in their unrecorded deeds, wear the likeness of the rootless Root, the unevolved Evolver, in the sense that, being themselves obscure, they are the source of greatness in others. Themselves silent, they are the cause of eloquence in others. Theirs are the thoughts which spur others to great deeds. Theirs is the quietness which overcomes everything, just as water, the softest thing, overcomes all hardness. They, and they alone, come into this world of ours with one idea, one ideal, which they carry out along a hundred lines with unwavering purpose, never pausing, never resting, never changing, knowing no alteration of mind, no lesser deity than the One Self, no other service than the service of that Self hidden in humanity; childhood, youth and manhood sees them pursuing the same changeless purpose, and when the wearied body falls and dies and the fire-soul frets through the frail, ethereal casing, these men, these Egos cannot rest in the grave of the ether: they know no heaven; Death itself cannot stay them; the blissful life of the spheres cannot give them pause; they return—they, the disembodied and free, turn from the free and glorious starry airs, they take again the fetters of the body, and for what? For what end? Only for this; that they may work, and serve the Self eternal.

J.

It is with no feeling of sadness that I think of this withdrawal. He would not have wished for that. But with a faltering hand I try to express one of many incommunicable thoughts about the hero who has departed. Long before I met him, before even written words of his had been read, his name like an incantation stirred and summoned forth some secret spiritual impulse in my heart. It was no surface tie which bound us to him. No one ever tried less than he to gain from men that adherence which comes from impressive manner. I hardly thought what he was while he spoke; but on departing I found my heart, wiser than my brain, had given itself away to him; an inner exaltation lasting for months witnessed his power. It was in that memorable convention in London two years ago that I first glimpsed his real greatness. As he sat there quietly, one among many, not speaking a word, I was overcome by a sense of spiritual dilation, of unconquerable will about him, and that one figure with the grey head became all the room to me. Shall I not say the truth I think? Here was a hero out of the remote, antique, giant ages come among us, wearing but on the surface the vesture of our little day. We, too, came out of that past, but in forgetfulness; he with memory and power soon regained. To him and to one other we owe an unspeakable gratitude for faith and hope and knowledge born again. We may say now, using words of his early years: "Even in hell I lift up my eyes to those who are beyond me and do not deny them." Ah, hero, we know you would have stayed with us if it were possible; but fires have been kindled that shall not soon fade, fires that shall be bright when you again return. I feel no sadness, knowing there are no farewells in the True: to whosoever has touched on that real being there is comradeship with all the great and wise of time. That he will again return we need not doubt. His ideals were those which are attained only by the Saviours and Deliverers of nations. When or where he may appear I know not, but I foresee the coming when our need invokes him. Light of the future æons, I hail I hail to thee!

Æ.

"It is a cry of the soul," were the words in which he summed up the meaning and purpose of the theosophical movement when initiating us in 1888. There was nothing of the maudlin sentimentalist about him. Clear, simple and powerful are all his utterances, for the strong light of soul shone through all he did and said. One more has been added to the long list of the world's crucified saviours. It is almost like presumption to essay an appreciation in words of great souls like these. We cannot measure, weigh, or sound their depths. How inadequate, then, any attempt of the kind. We can but point to the work achieved even in these few years and realize dimly that we have entertained angels unawares; that the Great Ones of the earth have been among us and we knew them not.　　　　F. J. D. [Fred J. Dick]

Meditation, Concentration, Will

[*The Irish Theosophist*, Vol. I, July 15, 1893, pp. 97-98]

These three, meditation, concentration, will, have engaged the attention of Theosophists perhaps more than any other three subjects. A canvass of opinions would probably show that the majority of our reading and thinking members would rather hear these subjects discussed and read definite directions about them than any others in the entire field. They say they must meditate. They declare a wish for concentration, they would like a powerful will, and they sigh for strict directions, readable by the most foolish theosophist. It is a western cry for a curriculum, a course, a staked path, a line and rule by inches and links. Yet the path has long been outlined and described, so that any one could read the directions whose mind had not been half-ruined by modern false education, and memory rotted by the superficial methods of a superficial literature and a wholly vain modern life.

Let us divide Meditation into two sorts. First is the meditation practiced at a set time, or an occasional one, whether by design or from physiological idiosyncrasy. Second is the meditation of an entire lifetime, that single thread of intention, intentness, and desire running through the years stretching between the cradle and the grave. For the first, in Patanjali's Aphorisms will be found all needful rules and particularity. If these are studied and not forgotten, then practice must give results. How many of those who reiterate the call for instruction on this head have read that book,[1] only to turn it down and never again consider it? Far too many.

The mysterious subtle thread of a life meditation is that which is practiced every hour by philosopher, mystic, saint, criminal, artist, artisan, and merchant. It is pursued in respect to that on which the heart is set; it rarely languishes; at times the meditating one greedily running after money, fame, and power looks up briefly and sighs for a better life during a brief interval, but the passing flash of a dollar or a sovereign recalls him to his modern senses, and the old meditation begins again. Since all theosophists are here in the social whirl I refer to, they can every one take these words to themselves as they please. Very certainly if their life meditation is fixed low down near the ground, the results flowing to them from it will be strong, very lasting, and related to the low level on which they work. Their semi-

---

[1] *The Yoga Aphorisms of Patanjali*, An interpretation by William Q. Judge, New York, 1889.

occasional meditations will give precisely semi-occasional results in the long string of recurring births.

"But, then," says another, "what of concentration? We must have it. We wish it; we lack it." Is it a piece of goods that you can buy it, do you think, or something that will come to you just for the wishing? Hardly. In the way we divided meditation into two great sorts, so we can divide concentration. One is the use of an already acquired power on a fixed occasion, the other the deep and constant practice of a power that has been made a possession. Concentration is not memory, since the latter is known to act without our concentrating on anything, and we know that centuries ago the old thinkers very justly called memory a phantasy. But by reason of peculiarity of the human mind the associative part of memory is waked up the very instant concentration is attempted. It is this that makes students weary and at last drives them away from the pursuit of concentration. A man sits down to concentrate on the highest idea he can formulate, and like a flash troops of recollections of all sorts of affairs, old thoughts and impressions come before his mind, driving away the great object he first selected, and concentration is at an end.

This trouble is only to be corrected by practice, by assiduity, by continuance. No strange and complicated directions are needed. All we have to do is to try and to keep on trying.

The subject of the Will has not been treated of much in theosophical works, old or new. Patanjali does not go into it at all. It seems to be inferred by him through his aphorisms. Will is universal, and belongs to not only man and animals, but also to every other natural kingdom. The good and bad man alike have will, the child and the aged, the wise and the lunatic. It is therefore a power devoid in itself of moral quality. That quality must be added by man.

So the truth must be that will acts according to desire, or, as the older thinkers used to put it, "behind will stands desire." This is why the child, the savage, the lunatic, and the wicked man so often exhibit a stronger will than others. The wicked man has intensified his desires, and with that his will. The lunatic has but few desires, and draws all his will force into these, the savage is free from convention, from the various ideas, laws, rules, and suppositions to which the civilized person is subject, and has nothing to distract his will. So to make our will strong we must have fewer desires. Let those be high, pure, and altruistic; they will give us strong will.

No mere practice will develop will *per se*, for it exists forever, fully developed in itself. But practice will develop in us the power to call on that will which is ours. Will and Desire lie at the doors of Meditation and Concentration. If we desire truth with the same intensity that we had formerly wished for success, money, or gratification, we will speedily acquire meditation and possess concentration. If we do all acts small and great, every moment, for the sake of the whole human race, as representing the Supreme Self, then every cell and fibre of the body and inner man will be turned in one direction, resulting in perfect concentration. This is expressed in the New Testament in the statement that if the eye is single the whole body will be full of light, and in the *Bhagavad Gîtâ* it is still more clearly and comprehensively given through the different chapters. In one it is beautifully put as the lighting up in us of the Supreme One, who then becomes visible. Let us meditate on that which is in us as the Highest Self, concentrate upon it, and will to work for it as dwelling in every human heart.

WILLIAM Q. JUDGE

The Closing Cycle

[*The Irish Theosophist*, Vol. III, January 15, 1895, pp. 54-56]

In the November number the "expiring Cycle" is referred to by Mr. Sinnett, and members are rightly warned not to be so absurd (though that is my word) as to think that after 1897 "some mysterious extinguisher will descend upon us."

Who is the person who gave out the concrete statement that 1897 was to be the close of a cycle when something would happen? It was H. P. Blavatsky. There is not the slightest doubt about it that she did say so, nor that she fully explained it to several persons. Nor is there any doubt at all that she said, as had been so long said from the year 1875, that 1897 would witness the shutting of a door. What door? Door to what? What was or is to end? Is the T.S. to end and close all the books?

Nothing is more plain than that H. P. Blavatsky said, on the direct authority of the Masters, that in the last twenty-five years of each century an effort is made by the Lodge and its agents with the West, and that it ceases in its direct and public form and influence with the twenty-fifth year. Those who believe her will believe this; those who think they know more about it than she did will invent other ideas suited to their fancies.

She explained, as will all those who are taught (as are many) by the same Masters, that were the public effort to go on any longer than that, a reaction would set in very similar to indigestion. Time must be given for assimilation, or the "dark shadow which follows all innovations" would crush the soul of man. The great public, the mass, must have time and also material. Time is ever. The matter has been furnished by the Masters in the work done by H. P. Blavatsky in her books, and what has grown out of those. She has said, the Masters have said, and I again assert it for the benefit of those who have any faith in me, that the Masters have told me that they helped her write the *Secret Doctrine* so that the future seventy-five and more years should have some material to work on, and that in the coming years that book and its theories would be widely studied. The material given has then to be worked over, to be assimilated for the welfare of all. No extinguisher will fall therefore on us. The T.S., as a whole, will not have the incessant care of the Masters in every part, but must grow up to maturity on what it has with the help to come from those few who are "chosen." H. P. Blavatsky has clearly pointed out in the *Key*,[1] in her conclusion, that the plan is to keep the T.S. alive as an active, free, unsectarian body during all the time of waiting for the next great messenger, who will be herself beyond question. Thereby will be furnished the well-made tool with which to work again in grander scale, and without the fearful opposition she had without and within when she began this time. And in all this time of waiting the Master, "that great Initiate, whose single will upholds the entire movement," will have his mighty hand spread out wide behind the Society.

Up to 1897 the door is open to anyone who has the courage, the force, and the virtue to TRY, so that he can go in and make a communication with the Lodge which shall not be broken at all when the cycle ends. But at the striking of the hour the door will shut, and not all your pleadings and cryings will open it to you. Those who have made the connection will have their own door open, but the public general door will be closed. That is the true relation of the "extinguisher" as given by H. P. Blavatsky and the Master. It seems very easy to understand.

"Many are called but few are chosen," because they would not allow it. The unchosen are those who have worked for themselves alone; those who have sought for knowledge for themselves without a care about the rest; those who have had the time, the money, and the ability to give good help to Masters' cause, long ago defined by them to be work for mankind and not for self, but have not used it thus. And sadly, too, some of the unmarked and unchosen are those who walked a long distance to the threshold, but stopped too long to hunt for the failings and the sins they were sure some brother pilgrim had, and then they went back farther and farther, building walls behind them as they went. They were called and almost chosen; the first faint lines of their names were beginning to develop in the book of this century; but as they retreated, thinking indeed, they were inside the door, the lines

---

[1] *The Key to Theosophy*, 1889, London.

faded out, and other names flashed into view. Those other names are those belonging to humble persons here and there whom these proud aristocrats of occultism thought unworthy of a moment's notice.

What seems to me either a printer's error or a genuine mistake in Mr. Sinnett's article is on page 26 [Nov. 15, 1884 issue], where he says: "will be knowledge generally diffused throughout the *cultured classes.*" The italics are mine. No greater error could seem possible. The cultured classes are perfectly worthless, as a whole, to the Master-builders of the Lodge. They are good in the place they have, but they represent the "established order" and the acme of selfishness. Substitute *masses* for *cultured classes,* and you will come nearer the truth. Not the cultured but the ignorant masses have kept alive the belief in the occult and the psychic now fanned into flame once more. Had we trusted to the cultured the small ember would long ago have been extinguished. We may drag in the cultured, but it will be but to have a languid and unenthusiastic interest.

We have entered on the dim beginning of a new era already. It is the era of Western Occultism and of special and definite treatment and exposition of theories hitherto generally considered. We have to do as Buddha told his disciples: preach, promulgate, expound, illustrate, and make clear in detail all the great things we have learned. That is our work, and not the bringing out of surprising things about clairvoyance and other astral matters, nor the blinding of the eye of science by discoveries impossible for them but easy for the occultist. The Master's plan has not altered. He gave it out long ago. It is to make the world at large better, to prepare a right soil for the growing out of the powers of the soul, which are dangerous if they spring up in our present selfish soil. It is not the Black Lodge that tries to keep back psychic development; it is the White Lodge. The Black would fain have all the psychic powers full flower now, because in our wicked, mean, hypocritical, and money-getting people they would soon wreck the race. This idea may seem strange, but for those who will believe my unsupported word I say it is the Master's saying.

Three Great Ideas

[*The Irish Theosophist,* Vol. III, February 15, 1895, p. 173]

Among many ideas brought forward through the theosophical movement there are three which should never be lost sight of. Not speech, but thought, really rules the world; so, if these three ideas are good let them be rescued again and again from oblivion.

The first idea is, that there is a great Cause—in the sense of an enterprise—called the Cause of Sublime Perfection and Human Brotherhood. This rests upon the essential unity of the whole human family, and is a possibility because sublimity in perfectness and actual realization of brotherhood on every plane of being are one and the same thing. All efforts by Rosicrucian, Mystic, Mason and Initiate are efforts toward the convocation in the hearts and minds of men of the Order of Sublime Perfection.

The second idea is, that man is a being who may be raised up to perfection, to the stature of the Godhead, because he himself is God incarnate. This noble doctrine was in the mind of Jesus, no doubt, when he said that we must be perfect even as is the father in heaven. This is the idea of human perfectibility. It will destroy the awful theory of inherent original sin which has held and ground down the western Christian nations for centuries.

The third idea is the illustration, the proof, the high result of the others. It is, that the Masters—those who have reached up to what perfection this period of evolution and this solar system will allow— are living, veritable facts, and not abstractions cold and distant. They are, as our old H. P. B. so often said, *living men.* And she said, too, that a shadow of woe would come to those who should say they were not living facts, who should assert that "the Masters descend not to this plane of ours." The Masters as living facts and high ideals will fill the soul with hope, will themselves help all who wish to raise the human race.

Let us not forget these three great ideas.

WILLIAM Q. JUDGE

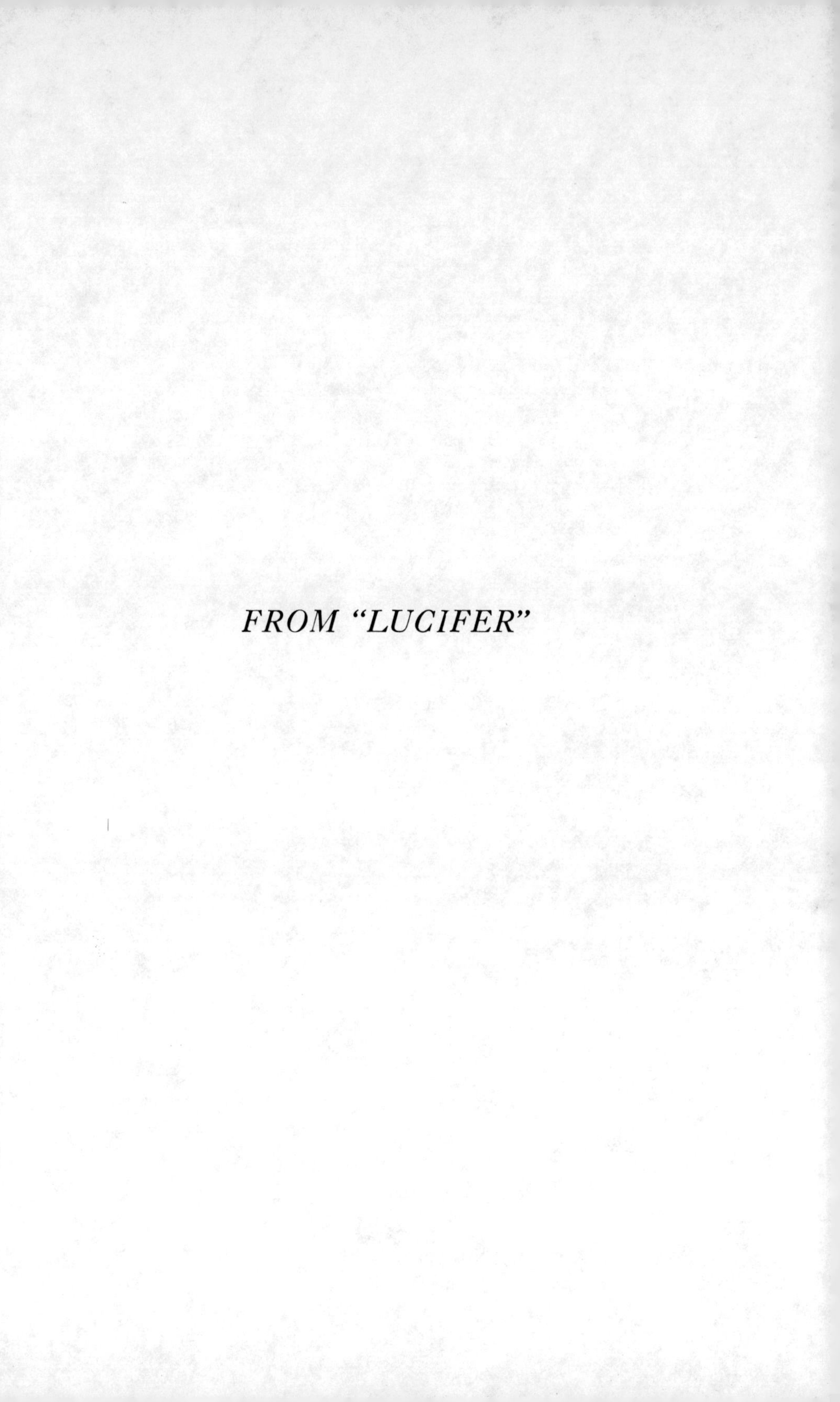# FROM "LUCIFER"

COMPILER'S NOTE

[*Lucifer* was started by H. P. Blavatsky in September, 1887. Contrary to the common use of this name, H.P.B. chose for her title a concept of "Lucifer" existing prior to the Christian age. She refers to the "Light-bringer . . . . the pale morning star, the precursor of the full blaze of the noon-day sun."[1] While Mr. Judge did not contribute many articles during her life, the tributes to H.P.B., published in *Lucifer* following her death, are stirring reminders of his unfailing dedication to his teacher and her work for humanity.—*Comp.*]

[*Answer by Correspondence to an Astrological Question,
Lucifer, Vol. III, September, 1888, pp. 68*]

Over the ambitious signature of "Magus" a correspondent asks in your July issue, "What is planetary influence and how does it act on man?" "Nemo" in his reply answers other questions but fails to answer this one.

Not being myself a Magus I will not assume to fully describe planetary influence, since to do so would lead us into realms quite beyond our comprehension. But we will get a better idea of the subject by recollecting that the ancients always considered the "ambient"—or entire heavens—at birth, as being that which affected man, and that planets were only the pointers or indices showing when and where the influence of the "ambient" would be felt. The modern astrologers, following those great leaders, but unable to grasp the enormous subject, reduced the scheme to the *influences of planets*. They have thus come to leave out, to a great extent, influences cast by powerful stars, which often produce effects not to be sought for under planets: "When such stars have rule nor wise nor fool can stay their influence." The planets were held, rightly as I think, to be only foci for "the influence of the whole ambient," having however a power of their own of a secondary nature exercisable when the ambient influence was weak.

When London was burnt a mighty star—not a planet—had rule, and Napoleon was prefigured by a star also, his fall being due in fact to the aspect of the heavens *as a whole*, and not to the ruling of Wellington's significator. A slight accident might have thrown the power

---

1 [See her introductory article, "What's in a Name," *Lucifer*, Sept. 1887, in *Blavatsky Collected Writings*, Vol. VIII, pp. 5-13, for the full scope envisioned for her magazine.—*Comp.*]

of the latter out of the horary field. Similarly, the cyclic vicissitudes of this globe will not be shown by any planetary scheme, but by certain *stars* that fix the destiny of poor Earth. When they have their day and term the wise man will be unable to rule his own stars or any other.

WILLIAM Q. JUDGE

"Yours till Death and after, H.P.B."

[Lucifer, Vol. VIII, June 1891, pp. 290-92]

Such has been the manner in which our beloved teacher and friend always concluded her letters to me. And now, though we are all of us committing to paper some account of that departed friend and teacher, I feel ever near and ever potent the magic of that resistless power, as of a mighty rushing river, which those who wholly trusted her always came to understand. Fortunate indeed is that Karma which, for all the years since I first met her, in 1875, has kept me faithful to the friend who, masquerading under the outer *mortal* garment known as H. P. Blavatsky, was ever faithful to me, ever kind, ever the teacher and the guide.

In 1874, in the City of New York, I first met H.P.B. in this life. By her request, sent through Colonel H. S. Olcott, the call was made in her rooms in Irving Place, when then, as afterwards, through the remainder of her stormy career, she was surrounded by the anxious, the intellectual, the Bohemian, the rich and the poor. It was her eye that attracted me, the eye of one whom I must have known in lives long passed away. She looked at me in recognition at that first hour, and never since has that look changed. Not as a questioner of philosophies did I come before her, not as one groping in the dark for lights that schools and fanciful theories had obscured, but as one who, wandering many periods through the corridors of life, was seeking the friends who could show where the designs for the work had been hidden. And true to the call she responded, revealing the plans once again, and speaking no words to explain, simply pointed them out and went on with the task. It was as if but the evening before we had parted, leaving yet to be done some detail of a task taken up with one common end; it was teacher and pupil, elder brother and younger, both bent on the one single end, but she with the power and the knowledge that belong but to lions and sages. So, friends from the

HELENA PETROVNA BLAVATSKY
1831-1891

Picture sent by H.P.B. to Epes Sargeant, Esquire.

first, I felt safe. Others I know have looked with suspicion on an appearance they could not fathom, and though it is true they adduce many proofs which, hugged to the breast, would damn sages and gods, yet it is only through blindness they failed to see the lion's glance, the diamond heart of H.P.B.

The entire space of this whole magazine would not suffice to enable me to record the phenomena she performed for me through all these years, nor would I wish to put them down. As she so often said, they prove nothing but only lead some souls to doubt and others to despair. And again, I do not think they were done just for me, but only that in those early days she was laying down the lines of force all over the land and I, so fortunate, was at the center of the energy and saw the play of forces in visible phenomena. The explanation has been offered by some too anxious friends that the earlier phenomena were mistakes in judgment, attempted to be rectified in later years by confining their area and limiting their number, but until some one shall produce in the writing of H.P.B. her concurrence with that view, I shall hold to her own explanation made in advance and never changed. That I have given above. For many it is easier to take refuge behind a charge of bad judgment than to understand the strange and powerful laws which control in matters such as these.

Amid all the turmoil of her life, above the din produced by those who charged her with deceit and fraud and others who defended, while month after month, and year after year, witnessed men and women entering the Theosophical Movement only to leave it soon with malignant phrases for H.P.B., there stands a fact we all might imitate —devotion absolute to her Master. "It was He," she writes, "who told me to devote myself to this, and I will never disobey and never turn back."

In 1888 she wrote to me privately:—

"Well, my *only* friend, you ought to know better. Look into my life and try to realize it—in its outer course at least, as the rest is hidden. I am under the curse of ever writing, as the wandering Jew was under that of being on the move, never stopping one moment to rest. Three ordinary healthy persons could hardly do what *I have* to do. I live an artificial life; I am an automaton running full steam until the power of generating steam stops, and then—good-bye! * * * Night before last I was shown a bird's-eye view of the Theosophical Societies. I saw a few earnest reliable Theosophists in a death struggle with the world in general, with other—nominal but ambitious—Theosophists. The former are greater in numbers than you may think, and *they prevailed*, as you in *America will prevail*, if you only remain staunch to the Master's programme and true to yourselves. And last night I saw .:. and now I feel strong—such as I am in my body— and ready to fight for Theosophy and the few *true* ones to my last breath. The defending forces have to be judiciously—so scanty they are—distributed over the globe, wherever Theosophy is struggling against the powers of darkness."

Such she ever was; devoted to Theosophy and the Society organized to carry out a program embracing the world in its scope. Willing in the service of the cause to offer up hope, money, reputation, life itself, provided the Society might be saved from every hurt, whether small or great. And thus bound body, heart and soul to this entity called the Theosophical Society, bound to protect it at all hazards, in fact of every loss, she often incurred the resentment of many who became her friends but would not always care for the infant organization as she had sworn to do. And when they acted as if opposed to the Society, her instant opposition seemed to them to nullify professions of friendship. Thus she had but few friends, for it required a keen insight, untinged with personal feeling, to see even a small part of the real H. P. Blavatsky.

But was her object merely to form a Society whose strength should lie in numbers? Not so. She worked under directors who, operating from *behind the scene*, knew that the Thesosophical Society was, and was to be, the nucleus from which help might spread to all the people of the day, without thanks and without acknowledgement. Once, in London, I asked her what was the chance of drawing the people into the Society in view of the enormous disproportion between the number of members and the millions of Europe and America who neither knew of nor cared for it. Leaning back in her chair, in which she was sitting before her writing desk, she said:—

"When you consider and remember those days in 1875 and after, in which you could not find any people interested in your thoughts, and now look at the wide-spreading influence of theosophical ideas—however labelled—it is not so bad. We are not working merely that people may call themselves *Theosophists*, but that the doctrines we cherish may affect and leaven the whole mind of this century. This alone can be accomplished by a small earnest band of workers, who work for no human reward, no earthly recognition, but who, supported and sustained by a belief in that Universal Brotherhood of which our Masters are a part, work steadily, faithfully, in understanding and putting forth for consideration the doctrines of life and duty that have come down to us from immemorial time. Falter not so long as a few devoted ones will work to keep the nucleus existing. You were not directed to found and realize a Universal Brotherhood, but to form the nucleus for one; for it is only when the nucleus is formed that the accumulations can begin that will end in future years, however far, in the formation of that body which we have in view."

H.P.B. had a lion heart, and on the work traced out for her she had the lion's grasp; let us, her friends, companions and disciples, sustain ourselves in carrying out the designs laid down on the trestle-board,

by the memory of her devotion and the consciousness that behind her
task there stood, and still remain, those Elder Brothers who, above the
clatter and the din of our battle, ever see the end and direct the forces
distributed in array for the salvation of "that great orphan—Humanity."

WILLIAM Q. JUDGE, F.T.S.

H. P. B. at Enghien

[*Lucifer*, Vol. VIII, July, 1891, pp. 359-61]

In the spring of 1884 H.P.B. was staying in Rue Notre Dame des
Champs, Paris, and in the house were living Col. Olcott, Mohini M.
Chatterji and the writer. Part of the time Bertram Keightley was also
there. As always since I have known H. P. B. during the past seventeen years, she was there as elsewhere engaged daily with her writing,
save for an occasional drive or visit. Many visitors from all classes
were constantly calling, and among the rest came the Countess
d'Adhémar, who at once professed a profound admiration for H.P.B.
and invited her to come to the Château owned by the Count at Enghien,
just outside the city, including in her invitation myself and Mohini
Chatterji. Bertram Keightley was also invited for a few days. The invitation was accepted and we all went out to Enghien, where H.P.B.
was given two large rooms downstairs and the others slept in rooms
on the upper floors. Every convenience was given to our beloved
friend, and there she continued her writing, while I at her request
carefully read over, sitting in the same room, *Isis Unveiled*, making
indices at the foot of each page, as she intended to use it in preparing the *Secret Doctrine*.

A lake was at one side of the house and extensive grounds covered
with fine timber hid the building from the road, part being a well-kept
fruit and flower garden. A slight description of the rooms is necessary.
Wide stairs led up to the hall; on one side, which we may call the
road front, was the billiard room, the high window of which opened
upon the leaden roof of the porch; the dining room looked out at the
back over the edge of the lake, and the drawing room opened from it
on the other side at right angles to the side of the billiard room. This
drawing room had windows opening on three sides, so that both garden
and lake could be seen from it. In it was the grand piano at the end
and side opposite the dining room door, and between the two side

windows was a marble slab holding ornaments; between the windows at the end near the piano, was the fireplace, and at that corner was one of the windows giving a view of the lake. Every evening it was the custom to spend some time in the drawing room in conversation, and there, as well as in the dining room, took place some phenomena which indeed were no more interesting than the words of H.P.B., whether those were witty, grave or gay. Very often Countess d'Adhémar's sister played the piano in a manner to delight even H.P.B., who was no mean judge. I remember well one melody, just then brought out in the world of Paris, which pleased her immensely, so that she often asked for its repetition. It was one suggestive of high aspiration and grandiose conceptions of nature. Many lively discussions with the Count on one side and H.P.B. on the other had taken place there, and often in the very midst of these she would suddenly turn to Mohini and myself, who were sitting listening, to repeat to us the very thoughts then passing in our brains.

Count d'Adhémar did not ask for the production of phenomena, but often said that could he and a few of his friends be convinced about Theosophy perhaps much good would result in France. Some of us desired in our hearts that in the home of such kind friends phenomena might occur, but none suggested it to H.P.B. But one day at dinner, when there were present the Count and Countess, their son Raoul, H.P.B., Mohini, the Countess' sister, myself, and one other, the strong and never-to-be-forgotten perfume which intimate friends of H.P.B. knew so well as often accompanying phenomena or coming of itself, floated round and round the table, plainly perceptible to several and not perceived either before or afterwards. Of course many sceptics will see nothing in this, but the writer and others well know that this of itself is a phenomenon, and that the perfume has been sent for many miles through the air as a message from H.P.B. or from those hidden persons who often aided in phenomena or in teachings. At this dinner, or at some other during the visit, we had all just come in from the flower garden. I had plucked a small rosebud and placed it upon the edge of the tumbler between myself and the Countess' sister who was on my left, H. P. B. being seated on my right. This lady began to tallk of phenomena, wondering if H. P. B. could do as related of the Indian yogis. I replied that she could if she would, but did not ask her, and added that she could make even that small rosebud bloom at once. Just then H. P. B. stretched her hand out towards the rose, not touching it, and said nothing, continuing at once her conversation and the dinner. We watched the bud until the end of the meal and saw that it grew in that space of time much larger and bloomed out into a rose nearly full grown.

On another evening after we had all been in the drawing room for some time, sitting without lights, the moon shining over the lake and all nature being hushed, H. P. B. fell into a thoughtful state. Shortly she rose and stood at the corner window looking over the water, and in a moment a flash of soft light shot into the room and she quietly smiled. Reminding me of this evening the Countess d'Adhémar writes in this month of June:—

"H. P. B. seemed wrapped in thought, when suddenly she rose from her chair, advanced to the open window, and raising her arm with a commanding gesture, faint music was heard in the distance, which advancing nearer and nearer broke into lovely strains and filled the drawing room where we were all sitting. Mohini threw himself at H.P.B.'s feet and kissed the hem of her robe, which action seemed appropriate outcoming of the profound admiration and respect we all felt toward the wonderful being whose loss we will never cease to mourn."

This astral music was very plain to us all, and the Count especially remarked upon its beauty and the faintness of it as it sank away into the unknown distance. The whole house was full of these bell sounds at night when I was awake very late and others had retired. They were like signals going and coming to H. P. B.'s room downstairs. And on more than one occasion as we walked in the grounds under the magnificent trees, have they shot past us, sometimes audible to all and again only heard by one or two.

The lead roof of the portico was a place where after dinner we sometimes sat, and there on some of those delightful evenings we were joined by the Countess Wachtmeister, who afterwards did so much for the comfort of H. P. B. at Würzburg and other places. Many chats were held there about occultism. In one of these we were speaking of images in the Astral Light and H. P. B. said: "Well, you know that it moves as other things in Kosmos do, and that the time comes when it floats off, as it were, letting another mass of the same 'light' take its place."

It was with a feeling of some regret that we left this delightful place where such quiet reigned and where H. P. B. was able to work amid the beauty and the stillness of nature. It cannot be blotted from the memory, because there our friend and teacher was untroubled by the presence of curiosity seekers, and thus was free to present to us who believed in her a side of her many-sided nature which pleased, instructed and elevated us all.

One incident remains to be told for which we must depend on others. I took away with me a book which could not be finished there, and just before leaving France went out to Enghien to return it. There I met the Countess d'Adhémar, who said that the peculiar and unmistakable perfume of which I spoke above had come in the house after we had

all left. It was one evening about two days after H. P. B.'s departure
and the d'Adhémars had some friends to dinner. After dinner they all
went into the drawing room and soon noticed the perfume. It came, as
they said to me, in rushes, and at once they began to hunt it out in the
room, coming at last to the marble slab described, where, from one spot
in the stone, they found the perfume rushing out in volumes. Such was
the quantity of it that, as the Countess said to me, they were compelled
to open the windows, since the odour was overpowering in large masses.
In returning to Paris I told H. P. B. of this and she only said: "It
sometimes happens."

William Q. Judge, F.T.S.

On the Future: A Few Reflections

[*Lucifer*, Vol. X, March, 1892, pp. 20-23].

Although I am an American citizen, the place of my birth was in
Ireland, and in what I am about to say I cannot be accused of Colum-
biamania, for no matter how long might be my life I could never be
an American. For that perhaps it is right, since it is compulsory, to wait
for some distant incarnation.

Now, either H. P. B. was right or she was wrong in what she says in
the *Secret Doctrine* about the future of America. If wrong, then all this
may be dismissed as idle speculation. But, if right, then all thoughtful
Theosophists must take heed, weigh well, mentally appropriate and
always remember what are her words as well as the conclusions to
which they lead.

In the first pages of the second volume she speaks of five great Continents. *First,* the Imperishable Sacred Land [this is at the North Pole,
W. Q. J.]; *second,* the Hyperborean, now part of it is in Northern
Asia; *third,* Lemuria, sunk long ago, but leaving some remains, islands,
the points of high mountain ranges; *fourth,* Atlantis, presumably in
the Atlantic Ocean, now below the level of the water, but with perhaps
Teneriffe and Atlas as reminders; and *fifth,* "was America."

From a survey of the book, digging in notes and culling from the
text here and there, the conclusion is irresistible that, although the
present America is not the actual Continent as *it is to be,* it is a portion of it; and certainly is now the nursery for the race that will in the
future occupy the *sixth* Continent, which for the sixth Great Root-Race

will emerge from the waters. Where? Perhaps when the present America has been split up by tremendous cataclysms, leaving here and there large pieces of its western side, it is in the Pacific Ocean that the great mass of the new one will come up from the long sleep below the sea. Rightly then will the great far western ocean have been named *Pacific*, for that Race will not be given to contest nor hear of wars or rumours of war, since it will be too near the seventh, whose mission it must be to attain to the consummation, to seize and hold the Holy Grail.

Turn to page 444 and onward of the second volume. Read there that the Americans have become in only three hundred years a primary race *pro tem.*, in short, the germs of the sixth sub-race, to blossom in a few more centuries into the pioneers of that one which must succeed to the present European fifth sub-race in all its characteristics. Then after about 25,000 years, which you will note is meant for a great sidereal cycle of a little over that length of time, this new race will prepare for the seventh sub-race. Cataclysms will then fall upon you; lands and nations will be swept away, first of all being the European, including the British Isles—if not gone before—and then parts of both North and South America. And how puny, mongrel, indeed, will be the remains of the scientists of today, great masters of microbes now, but then to be looked upon as strange remains of the Nineteenth Century, when, as the people will tell each other then, so many, with Truth before them, laughed at it and stoned its apostles, dancing a fantastic dance meanwhile around the altar of invisible matter.

It seems as if some power, deliberately planning, had selected North and South America for the place where a new primary root-race should be begun. These two continents were evidently the seats of ancient races and not the habitat of wild undeveloped men. The red man of the Northern one has all the appearance and beliefs of a once great race. He believes in one God, a Devachan of happy hunting after death. Some tribes have diagrams of how the world was formed and peopled, that strangely resemble the Hindû cosmogony, and their folklore bears deep marks of having come down from an older and better time. Following the course of exploration southwards, we find accumulating evidences all the way of a prior civilization now gone with the cyclic wave which brought it up. Central America is crowded with remains in stone and brick; and so on south still we discover similar proofs. In course of time these continents became what might be called arable land, lying waiting, recuperating, until the European streams of men began to pour upon it. The Spanish overflowed South America and settled California and Mexico; the English, French, and Spanish took the North, and later all nations came, so that now in both continents nearly every race is mixed and still mixing. Chinese even have married women of European blood;

Hindûs are also here; the ancient Parsî race has its representatives; the Spanish mixed with the aborigines, and the slaveholders with the Africans. I doubt not but that some one from every race known to us has been here and has left, within the last two hundred years, some impression through mixture of blood.

But the last remnants of the fifth Continent, America, will not disappear until the new race has been some time born. Then a new Dwelling, the sixth Continent, will have appeared over the waters to receive the youth who will tower above us as we do above the pigmies of Africa. But no America as we now know it will exist. Yet these men must be the descendants of the race that is now rising here. Otherwise our philosophy is all wrong. So then, in America now is forming the new subrace, and in this land was founded the present Theosophical Society: two matters of great importance. It was to the United States, observe, that the messenger of the Masters came, although Europe was just as accessible for the enterprise set on foot. Later, this messenger went to India and then to Europe, settling down in the British Isles. All of this is of importance in our reflections. For why in America at first does she begin the movement, and why end her part of it in England? One might be led to ask why was not an effort made at all costs to give the last impulse outwardly in the land of promise where she began the work?

Do not imagine for one moment, O ye English brothers of mine, that London was selected for this because the beauties of your island called her, or for that she had decided at the finish that after all a mistake had been made in not going there first. It was all out of stern necessity, with a wisdom derived from many older heads, having in view the cycles as they sweep resistlessly forward. The point where the great energy is started, the center of force, is the more important, and not the place at which it is ended. And this remains true, no matter how essential the place of ending may be in the scheme. What, do you suppose India is not as important, and would not that land have offered seemingly a better spot than all for the beginning of the *magnum opus?* Adepts do not make mistakes like that.

America's discovery is ascribed to Christopher Columbus. Although it is doubted, yet no one doubts that the Spanish people did the most at first in peopling it, meanwhile working off some old and making some new Karma, by killing many of the aborigines. Thus it is that doomed people rush on to their doom, even as the troops of insects, animals and men were seen by Arjuna to rush into Krishna's flaming mouths. But later came the sturdy stock from England, who, in the greatest nation, the most enduring on this continent, have left their impress indelibly in the people, in its laws, in its constitution, its customs, its literature and language. Perhaps England and Ireland are the gateways for the Egos who incarnate here in the silent work of making a new race. Maybe there is some significance in the fact that more lines of steamships conveying human freight come to the United States from England, passing Ireland on the way as the last seen land of the old world, than from anywhere else. The deeds of men, the enterprises of merchants, and the wars of soldiers all follow implicitly a law that is fixed in the stars, and while they copy the past they ever symbolize the future.

Did H. P. B. only joke when she wrote in her book that Ireland is an ancient Atlantean remnant, and England a younger Isle, whose rising from the sea was watched by wise men from Erin's shore? Perhaps the people of that old land may have an important influence in the new race of America. It would appear from comparison that they might have had, and probably will in the future. Perhaps, politically, since many expect social disturbances in America. In such a case any student of character will admit that the Irish, ignorant or not, will stand for law and order—for her sons are not battling here with an ancient foe. Why, too, by strange freak of fate is the great stone of destiny in Westminster Abbey fixed under the coronation chair on which the Queen was crowned? Let us also be informed if there be any finger-shadow pointing in the future to the fact that England's Queen, crowned over that stone,[1] is Empress of India, from which we claim the Âryans came, and where their glorious long-forgotten knowledge is preserved? Her name is Victory. It is the victory for "the new order of Ages"; and that new order began in America, its advent noted and cut on the as yet unused obverse side of the present seal of the United States Government. A victory in the union of the Egos from East and West; for England stretches one hand over to the home of the new race, which she can never own, with the other governing India, and completes the circuit. It may be a fleeting picture, perhaps to be wiped out for a while in a stream of blood, but such is the way the cycles roll and how we may learn to read the future. For England's destiny is not complete, nor has the time struck. None of us hug foolish delusions too long, and even if Ireland were once a most sacred place, that is no reason why we should want to go there. For in America those whose Karma has led them there will work for the same end and brotherhood as others left in India and Europe. The dominant language and style of thought in America is English, albeit transforming itself every day. It is there that silently the work goes on; there European fathers and mothers have gone, establishing currents of attraction that will inevitably and unceasingly draw into reincarnation Egos similar to themselves. And

---

[1] It is an interesting fact that in India there is an important ceremony called "mounting the stone."

the great forward and backward rush is completed by the retarded Egos
as they die out of other nations, coming meanwhile into flesh again
among the older races left behind.

*　　*　　*　　*　　*　　*

At least such seemed the view while the clouds lifted—and then once
more there was silence.

William Q. Judge, F.T.S.

TWO LETTERS TO THE EDITOR OF THE *N. Y. TIMES*
(CONCERNING MR. FOULKE'S CLAIMS—(UNDATED)

[Lucifer, Vol. X, March, 1892, pp. 82-83]

Editor Times:

Will you permit me to correct the statement of Mr. J. R. Perry in
your issue of the 3rd that Madame Blavatsky appointed as her "successor" Mr. Henry R. Foulke, and "guaranteed" to him the "allegiance"
of the "higher spiritual intelligences and forces"? As one of Madame
Blavatsky's oldest and most intimate friends, connected with her most
closely in the foundation and work of the Theosophical Society, and
familiar with her teachings, purposes, ideas, forecasts, I am in a position to assure both Mr. Perry and the public that there is not an atom
of foundation for the statement quoted.

Madame Blavatsky has no "successor," could have none, never contemplated, selected, or notified one. Her work and her status were
unique. Whether or not her genuineness as a spiritual teacher be admitted matters not: she *believed* it to be so, and all who enjoyed her
confidence will unite with me in the assertion that she never even hinted
at "succession," "allegiance," or "guarantee." Even if a successor was
possible, Mr. Foulke could not be he. He is not a member of the Theosophical Society, does not accept its and her teachings, had a very
slight and brief acquaintance with her, and pretends to no interest in
her views, life, or mission. Of her actual estimate of him I have ample
knowledge.

But anyhow, no "guaranteeing of allegiance of spiritual forces" is
practicable by anyone. Knowledge of and control over the higher poten-
cies in Nature comes only by individual attainment through long
discipline and conquest. It can no more be transferred than can a
knowledge of Greek, of chemistry, psychology, or of medicine. If a per-

son moves on a lofty level, it is because he worked his way there. This is as true in spiritual things as in mental. When Mr. Foulke produces a work like *Isis Unveiled or The Secret Doctrine,* he may be cited as H. P. B.'s intellectual peer; when he imparts such impulsion as does *The Voice of the Silence,* he may be recognized as her spiritual equal; when he adds to these an utter consecration to the work of the T. S. as his life-long mission, he may participate in such "succession" as the case admits. But it will not be through alleged precipitated pictures and imagined astral shapes. The effect of these on Theosophy, whereof Mr. Perry inquires, may be stated in one word—nothing.

Yours truly,
William Q. Judge
Gen. Sec'y. American Sec.

Editor Times:

Will you allow a word—my last—respecting the Foulke claim to succeed Mme. Blavatsky, as I see Mr. Perry is perhaps laboring under a misapprehension as to the position assumed by me about this ludicrous affair.

First. If Mr. Foulke or Mr. Perry, or either, has precipitated pictures of Mme. Blavatsky produced since her demise, they are welcome to them, and, it being no concern of ours, Theosophists will hardly deny the assertions of these gentlemen in that regard. Precipitations are not uncommon, but are no evidence of anything whatever save the power to precipitate and the fact of precipitation. Spiritualists have always asserted that their mediums could procure these things. Chemists also can precipitate substances out of the air. So this point is wide of the Society and its work.

Second. As I said in my previous letter, when Mr. Foulke, or any one, indeed, proves by his work and attainments that he is as great as Mme. Blavatsky, every one will at once recognize that fact. But irresponsible mediumship, or what we call astral intoxication, will not prove those attainments nor constitute that work.

Third. Mme. Blavatsky was Corresponding Secretary of the Theosophical Society, and its Constitution years ago provided that that office, out of compliment to her, should become extinct upon her death. She has passed away from this sphere, and hence the office of Corresponding Secretary is extinct. The Society will hardly hurry to revive it for the sake of one who is not a member of the body and who has never thrown any particular glory upon it. Scarcely either because he is a medium—and not even a good one—who prates of receiving messages from beyond the grave assumed to be from Mme. Blavatsky. He may assert that he has baskets full of letters from Mme. Blavatsky written before her death, and we are not interested either to deny the assertion or to desire to see the documents.

Fourth. The Theosophical Society is a body governed by Rules embodied in its Constitution. Its officers are elected by votes, and not by the production of precipitated letters or pictures of any sort. It generally elects those who do its work, and not outsiders who masquerade as recipients of directions from the abode of departed souls. It is not likely to request proposed officers to produce documents, whether in ink, in oils, or in pastel, brought forth at mediumistic séances before the wondering eyes of untrained witnesses. And as it now has Branches in every country on this earth, Mr. Foulke, an ex-member wholly untrained in its executive work and out of sympathy with its true mission, will evince more effrontery than he ever has before if he shall present himself for the suffrages of the members of a Society in which he is not even enrolled.

Fifth. Mr. Foulke's possession of any number of letters written to him by Mme. Blavatsky prior to her demise, offering him "leadership" or "succession," might please and interest himself, but can have no other effect on the corporate body of the Society. Let him preserve them or otherwise as he may see fit; they are utterly without bearing or even authority, and if in existence would only serve to show that she in her lifetime may have given him a chance to do earnest sincere work for a Society she had at heart, and that he neglected the opportunity, passing his time in idle, fantastic day-dreams.

Yours truly,

WILLIAM Q. JUDGE
Gen. Sec'y. American Sec.

Mesmerism

[*Lucifer*, Vol. X, May, 1892, pp. 197-205]

This is the name given to an art, or the exhibition of a power to act upon others and the facility to be acted upon, which long antedate the days of Anton Mesmer. Another name for some of its phenomena is Hypnotism, and still another is Magnetism. The last title was given because sometimes the person operated on was seen to follow the hand of the operator, as if drawn like iron filings to a magnet. These are all used today by various operators, but by many different appellations it has been known; fascination is one, and psychologizing is another, but the number of them is so great it is useless to go over the list.

Anton Mesmer, who gave greater publicity in the Western world to the subject than any other person, and whose name is still attached to it, was born in 1734, and some few years before 1783, or about 1775, obtained great prominence in Europe in connection with his experiments and cures; but, as H. P. Blavatsky says in her *Theosophical Glossary*, he was only a rediscoverer. The whole subject had been explored long before his time—indeed many centuries anterior to the rise of civilization in Europe—and all the great fraternities of the East were always in full possession of secrets concerning its practice which remain still unknown. Mesmer came out with his discoveries as agent, in fact— though, perhaps, without disclosing those behind him—of certain brotherhoods to which he belonged. His promulgations were in the last quarter of the century, just as those of the Theosophical Society were begun in 1875, and what he did was all that could be done at that time.

But in 1639, one hundred years before Mesmer, a book was published in Europe upon the use of mesmerism in the cure of wounds, and bore the title, *The Sympathetical Powder of Edricius Mohynus of Eburo.* These cures, it was said, could be effected at a distance from the wound by reason of the *virtue* or *directive faculty* between that and the wound. This is exactly one of the phases of both hypnotism and mesmerism. And along the same line were the writings of a monk named Uldericus Balk, who said diseases could be similarly cured, in a book concerning the lamp of life in 1611. In these works, of course, there is much superstition, but they treat of mermerism underneath all the folly.

After the French Academy committee, including Benjamin Franklin, passed sentence on the subject, condemning it in substance, mesmerism fell into disrepute, but was revived in America by many persons who adopted different names for their work and wrote books on it. One of them named Dodds obtained a good deal of celebrity, and was invited during the life of Daniel Webster to lecture on it before a number of United States senators. He called his system "psychology," but it was mesmerism exactly, even to details regarding nerves and the like. And in England also a good deal of attention was given to it by numbers of people who were not of scientific repute. They gave it no better reputation than it had before, and the press and public generally looked on them as charlatans and upon mesmerism as a delusion. Such was the state of things until the researches into what is now known as hypnotism brought that phase of the subject once more forward, and subsequently to 1875 the popular mind gave more and more attention to the possibilities in the fields of clairvoyance, clairaudience, trance, apparitions, and the like. Even physicians and others, who previously scouted all such investigations, began to take them up for consideration, and are still engaged thereon. And it seems quite certain that, by whatever name designated, mesmerism is sure to have more and more attention paid to it. For it is impossible to proceed very far with hypnotic experiments without meeting mesmeric phenomena, and being compelled, as it were, to proceed with an enquiry into those as well.

The hypnotists unjustifiably claim the merit of discoveries, for even the uneducated so-called charlatans of the above-mentioned periods cited the very fact appropriated by hypnotists, that many persons were normally—for them—in a hypnotized state, or, as they called it, in a psychologized condition, or negative one, and so forth, according to the particular system employed.

In France Baron Du Potet astonished every one with his feats in mesmerism, bringing about as great changes in subjects as the hypnotizers do now. After a time and after reading old books, he adopted a number of queer symbols that he said had the most extraordinary effect on the subject, and refused to give these out to any except pledged persons. This rule was violated, and his instructions and figures were printed not many years ago for sale with a pretence of secrecy consisting in a lock to the book. I have read these and find they are of no moment at all, having their force simply from the will of the person who uses them. The Baron was a man of very strong natural mesmeric force, and made his subjects do things that few others could bring about. He died without causing the scientific world to pay much attention to the matter.

The great question mooted is whether there is or is not any actual fluid thrown off by the mesmerizer. Many deny it, and nearly all hypnotizers refuse to admit it. H. P. Blavatsky declares there is such a fluid, and those who can see into the plane to which it belongs assert its existence as a subtle form of matter. This is, I think, true, and is not at all inconsistent with the experiments in hypnotism, for the fluid can have its own existence at the same time that people may be self-hypnotized by merely inverting their eyes while looking at some bright object. This fluid is composed in part of the astral substance around every one, and in part of the physical atoms in a finely divided state. By some this astral substance is called the *aura*. But that word is indefinite as there are many sorts of aura and many degrees of its expression. These will not be known, even to Theosophists of the most willing mind, until the race as a whole has developed up to that point. So the word will remain in use for the present.

This aura, then, is thrown off by the mesmerizer upon his subject, and is received by the latter in a department of his inner constitution, never described by any Western experimenters, because they know nothing of it. It wakes up certain inner and non-physical divisions of the person operated on, causing a change of relation between the various and numerous sheaths surrounding the inner man, and making possible different degrees of intelligence and of clairvoyance and the like. It has no influence whatsoever on the Higher Self,[1] which it is impossible to reach by such means. Many persons are deluded into supposing that the Higher Self is the responder, or that some spirit or what not is present, but it is only one of the many inner persons, so to say, who is talking or rather causing the organs of speech to do their office. And it is just here that the Theosophist and the non-Theosophist are at fault, since the words spoken are sometimes far above the ordinary intelligence or power of the subject in waking state. I therefore propose to give in the rough the theory of what actually does take place, as has been known for ages to those who see with the inner eye, and as will one day be discovered and admitted by science.

When the hypnotic or mesmerized state is complete—and often when it is partial—there is an immediate paralyzing of the power of the body to throw its impressions, and thus modify the conceptions of the inner being. In ordinary waking life everyone, without being able to disentangle himself, is subject to the impressions from the whole organism; that is to say, every cell in the body, to the most minute, has its own series of impressions and recollections, all of which continue to impinge on the great register, the brain, until the impression remaining in the cell is fully exhausted. And that exhaustion takes a long time. Further, as we are adding continually to them, the period of disappearance of impression is indefinitely postponed. Thus the inner person is not able to make itself felt. But, in the right subject, those bodily impressions are by mesmerism neutralized for the time, and at once another effect

---

[1] Âtma, in its vehicle Buddhi. [ED.]

follows, which is equivalent to cutting the general off from his army and compelling him to seek other means of expression.

The brain—in cases where the subject talks—is left free sufficiently to permit it to obey the commands of the mesmerizer and compel the organs of speech to respond. So much in general.

We have now come to another part of the nature of man which is a land unknown to the Western world and its scientists. By mesmerism other organs are set to work disconnected from the body, but which in a normal state function with and through the latter. These are not admitted by the world, but they exist, and are as real as the body is—in fact some who know say they are more real and less subject to decay, for they remain almost unchanged from birth to death. These organs have their own currents, circulation if you will, and methods of receiving and storing impressions. They are those which in a second of time seize and keep the faintest trace of any object or word coming before the waking man. They not only keep them but very often give them out, and when the person is mesmerized their exit is untrammelled by the body.

They are divided into many classes and grades, and each one of them has a whole series of ideas and facts peculiar to itself, as well as centers in the ethereal body to which they relate. Instead now of the brain's dealing with the sensations of the body, it deals with something quite different, and reports what these inner organs see in any part of space to which they are directed. And in place of your having waked up the Higher Self, you have merely uncovered one of the many sets of impressions and experiences of which the inner man is composed, and who is himself a long distance from the Higher Self. These varied pictures, thus seized from every quarter, are normally overborne by the great roar of the physical life, which is the sum total of possible expression of a normal being on the physical plane whereon we move. They show themselves usually only by glimpses when we have sudden ideas or recollections, or in dreams when our sleeping may be crowded with fancies for which we cannot find a basis in daily life. Yet the basis exists, and is always some one or other of the million small impressions of the day passed unnoticed by the physical brain, but caught unerringly by means of other sensoriums belonging to our astral double. For this astral body, or double, permeates the physical one as color does the bowl of water. And although to the materialistic conceptions of the present day such a misty shadow is not admitted to have parts, powers, and organs, it nevertheless has all of these with a surprising power and grasp. Although perhaps a mist, it can exert under proper conditions a force equal to the viewless wind when it levels to earth the proud constructions of puny man.

In the astral body, then, is the place to look for the explanation of mesmerism and hypnotism. The Higher Self will explain the flights we seldom make into the realm of spirit, and is the God—the Father—within who guides His children up the long steep road to perfection. Let not the idea of it be degraded by chaining it to the low floor of mesmeric phenomena, which any healthy man or woman can bring about if they will only try. The grosser the operator the better, for thus there is more of the mesmeric force, and if it be the Higher Self that is affected, then the meaning of it would be that gross matter can with ease affect and deflect the high spirit—and this is against the testimony of the ages.

A Paramahansa of the Himâlayas has put in print the following words: "Theosophy is that branch of Masonry which shows the Universe in the form of an egg." Putting on one side the germinal spot in the egg, we have left five other main divisions: the fluid, the yolk, the skin of the yolk, the inner skin of the shell, and the hard shell. The shell and the inner skin may be taken as one. That leaves us four, corresponding to the old divisons of fire, air, earth, and water. Man, roughly speaking, is divided in the same manner, and from these main divisions spring all his manifold experiences on the outer and the introspective planes. The human structure has its skin, its blood, its earthy matter—called bones for the moment, its flesh, and lastly the great germ which is insulated somewhere in the brain by means of a complete coat of fatty matter.

The skin includes the mucous, all membranes in the body, the arterial coats, and so on. The flesh takes in the nerves, the animal cells so-called, and the muscles. The bones stand alone. The blood has its cells, the corpuscles, and the fluid they float in. The organs, such as the liver, the spleen, the lungs, include skin, blood, and mucous. Each of these divisions and all of their subdivisions have their own peculiar impressions and recollections, and all, together with the co-ordinator the brain, make up the man as he is on the visible plane.

These all have to do with the phenomena of mesmerism, although there are those who may think it not possible that mucous membrane or skin can give us any knowledge. But it is nevertheless the fact, for the sensations of every part of the body affect each cognition, and when the experiences of the skin cells, or any other, are most prominent before the brain of the subject, all his reports to the operator will be drawn from that, unknown to both, and put into language for the brain's use so long as the next condition is not reached. This is the Esoteric Doctrine, and will at last be found true. For man is made up of millions of lives, and from these, unable of themselves to act rationally or independently, he gains ideas, and as the master of all puts those ideas, together with others from higher planes, into thought, word, and act.

Hence at the very first step in mesmerism this factor has to be remembered, but nowadays people do not know it and cannot recognize its presence, but are carried away by the strangeness of the phenomena.

The very best of subjects are mixed in their reports, because the things they do see are varied and distorted by the several experiences of the parts of their nature I have mentioned, all of which are constantly clamouring for a hearing. And every operator is sure to be misled by them unless he is himself a trained seer.

The next step takes us into the region of the inner man, not the spiritual being, but the astral one who is the model on which the outer visible form is built. The inner person is the mediator between mind and matter. Hearing the commands of mind, he causes the physical nerves to act and thus the whole body. All the senses have their seat in this person, and every one of them is a thousand-fold more extensive in range than their outer representatives, for those outer eyes and ears, and sense of touch, taste, and smell, are only gross organs which the inner ones use, but which of themselves can do nothing.

This can be seen when we cut off the nerve connection, say from the eye, for then the inner eye cannot connect with physical nature and is unable to see an object placed before the retina, although feeling or hearing may in their way apprehend the object if those are not also cut off.

These inner senses can perceive under certain conditions to any distance regardless of position or obstacle. But they cannot see everything, nor are they always able to properly understand the nature of everything they do see. For sometimes that appears to them with which they are not familiar. And further, they will often report having seen what they are desired by the operator to see, when in fact they are giving unreliable information. For, as the astral senses of any person are the direct inheritance of his own prior incarnations, and are not the product of family heredity, they cannot transcend their own experience, and hence their cognitions are limited by it, no matter how wonderful their action appears to him who is using only the physical sense-organs. In the ordinary healthy person these astral senses are inextricably linked with the body and limited by the apparatus which it furnishes during the waking state. And only when one falls asleep, or into a mesmerized state, or trance, or under the most severe training, can they act in a somewhat independent manner. This they do in sleep, when they live another life than that compelled by the force and the necessities of the waking organism. And when there is a paralyzation of the body by the mesmeric fluid they can act, because the impressions from the physical cells are inhibited.

The mesmeric fluid brings this paralyzing about by flowing from the operator and creeping steadily over the whole body of the subject,

changing the polarity of the cells in every part and thus disconnecting
the outer from the inner man. As the whole system of physical nerves
is sympathetic in all its ramifications, when certain major sets of nerves
are affected, others by sympathy follow into the same condition. So it
often happens with mesmerized subjects that the arms or legs are suddenly paralyzed without being directly operated on, or, as frequently,
the sensation due to the fluid is felt first in the forearm, although the
head was the only place touched.

There are many secrets about this part of the process, but they will
not be given out, as it is easy enough for all proper purposes to mes-
merize a subject by following what is already publicly known. By means
of certain nerve points located near the skin the whole system of nerves
may be altered in an instant, even by a slight breath from the mouth
at a distance of eight feet from the subject. But modern books do not
point this out.

When the paralyzing and change of polarity of the cells are complete the astral man is almost disconnected from the body. Has he any
structure? What mesmerizer knows? How many probably will deny that
he has any structure at all? Is he only a mist, an idea? And yet, again,
how many subjects are trained so as to be able to analyze their own
astral anatomy?

But the structure of the inner astral man is definite and coherent. It
cannot be fully dealt with in a magazine article, but may be roughly set
forth, leaving readers to fill in the details.

Just as the outer body has a spine which is the column whereon
the being sustains itself with the brain at the top, so the astral body
has its spine and brain. It is material, for it is made of matter, however
finely divided, and is not of the nature of the spirit.

After the maturity of the child before birth this form is fixed, coherent, and lasting, undergoing but small alteration from that day until
death. And so also as to its brain; that remains unchanged until the
body is given up, and does not, like the outer brain, give up cells to be
replaced by others from hour to hour. These inner parts are thus more
permanent than the outer correspondents to them. Our material organs,
bones, and tissues are undergoing change each instant. They are suffering always what the ancients called "the constant momentary dissolution
of minor units of matter," and hence within each month there is a perceptible change by way of diminution or accretion. This is not the case
with the inner form. It alters only from life to life, being constructed at
the time of reincarnation to last for a whole period of existence. For it
is the model fixed by the present evolutionary proportions for the outer
body. It is the collector, as it were, of the visible atoms which make us
as we outwardly appear. So at birth it is potentially of a certain size,

and when that limit is reached it stops the further extension of the body, making possible what are known today as average weights and average sizes. At the same time the outer body is kept in shape by the inner one until the period of decay. And this decay, followed by death, is not due to bodily disintegration *per se,* but to the fact that the term of the astral body is reached, when it is no longer able to hold the outer frame intact. Its power to resist the impact and war of the material molecules being exhausted, the sleep of death supervenes.

Now, as in our physical form the brain and spine are the centers for nerves, so in the other there are the nerves which ramify from the inner brain and spine all over the structure. All of these are related to every organ in the outer visible body. They are more in the nature of currents than nerves, as we understand the word, and may be called *astro-nerves.* They move in relation to such great centers in the body outside, as the heart, the pit of the throat, umbilical center, spleen, and sacral plexus. And here, in passing, it may be asked of the Western mesmerizers what do they know of the use and power, if any, of the umbilical center? They will probably say it has no use in particular after the accomplishment of birth. But the true science of mesmerism says there is much yet to be learned even on that one point; and there is no scarcity, in the proper quarters, of records as to experiments on, and use of, this center.

The astro-spinal column has three great nerves of the same sort of matter. They may be called ways or channels, up and down which the forces play, that enable man inside and outside to stand erect, to move, to feel, and to act. In description they answer exactly to the magnetic fluids, that is, they are respectively positive, negative, and neutral, their regular balance being essential to sanity. When the astral spine reaches the inner brain the nerves alter and become more complex, having a final great outlet in the skull. Then, with these two great parts of the inner person are the other manifold sets of nerves of similar nature related to the various planes of sensation in the visible and invisible worlds. These all then constitute the personal actor within, and in these is the place to seek for the solution of the problems presented by mesmerism and hypnotism.

Disjoin this being from the outer body with which he is linked, and the divorce deprives him of freedom temporarily, making him the slave of the operator. But mesmerizers know very well that the subject can and does often escape from control, puzzling them often, and often giving them fright. This is testified to by all the best writers in the Western schools.

Now this inner man is not by any means omniscient. He has an understanding that is limited by his own experience, as said before. Therefore, error creeps in if we rely on what he says in the mesmeric trance as to anything that requires philosophical knowledge, except with rare cases that are so infrequent as not to need consideration now. For neither the limit of the subject's power to know, nor the effect of the operator on the inner sensoriums described above, is known to operators in general, and especially not by those who do not accept the ancient division of the inner nature of man. The effect of the operator is almost always to color the reports made by the subject.

Take an instance: A. was a mesmerizer of C., a very sensitive woman, who had never made philosophy a study. A. had his mind made up to a certain course of procedure concerning other persons and requiring argument. But before action he consulted the sensitive, having in his possession a letter from X., who is a very definite thinker and very positive; while A., on the other hand, was not definite in idea although a good physical mesmerizer. The result was that the sensitive, after falling into the trance and being asked on the question debated, gave the views of X., whom she had not known, and so strongly that A. changed his plan although not his conviction, not knowing that it was the influence of the ideas of X. then in his mind, that had deflected the understanding of the sensitive. The thoughts of X., being very sharply cut, were enough to entirely change any previous views the subject had. What reliance, then, can be placed on untrained seers? And all the mesmeric subjects we have are wholly untrained, in the sense that the word bears with the school of ancient mesmerism of which I have been speaking.

The processes used in mesmeric experiment need not be gone into here. There are many books declaring them, but after studying the matter for the past twenty-two years, I do not find that they do other than copy one another, and that the entire set of directions can, for all practical purposes, be written on a single sheet of paper. But there are many other methods of still greater efficiency taught, that may be left for another occasion.

William Q. Judge, F.T.S.

The Sheaths of the Soul

[*Lucifer*, Vol. X, June, 1892, pp. 323-26]

In my last article, "Mesmerism," I arrived at the point where we discover that the inner mortal man has several sheaths through which he obtains touch with Nature, feeling her motions and exhibiting in return his own powers and functions. It is a doctrine as old as any Esoteric School now alive, and far more ancient than the modern scientific academies; an understanding of it is absolutely needful if we are to gain an adequate comprehension of real Mesmerism.

Instead of looking at the human being as that which we see, it is to be regarded as a being altogether different, functioning and perceiving in a way quite peculiar to itself, and being compelled to translate every outward impression, as well as those coming from within, from one language into another, that is to say from pictures into words, signs and acts, or *vice versâ*. This statement is vague, I admit, yet nevertheless true. The vagueness arises from the difficulties of a language that has as yet dealt but slightly with these subjects, and the development of which has come on in a civilization wholly materialistic. Man is a Soul, and as such stands among material things. This Soul is not only on its way upward for itself, but is compelled at the same time to draw up, refine, purge and perfect the gross matter—so-called—in which it is compelled to live. For though we call the less fine stages of substance by the name "matter," it is, however, made up of lives which have in them the potentiality of becoming Souls in the enormously distant future; and the Soul being itself a life made up of smaller ones, it is under the brotherly necessity of waiting in the bonds of matter long enough to give the latter the right impetus along the path of perfection.

So, during the long ages that have passed since the present evolution began in this solar system, the Soul has constructed for its own use various sheaths, ranging from very fine ones, near to its own essential being, to those that are more remote, ending with the outer physical one, and that one the most illusionary of them all, although appearing from the outside to be the truly real. These sheaths are necessary if the Soul is to know or to act. For it cannot by itself understand Nature at all, but transforms instantly all sensations and ideas by means of the different sheaths, until in the process it has directed the body below, or obtained itself experience above. By this I mean that whatever Soul initiates, it has to pass along through the several sheaths, each reporting, as it were, to the one next below it; and in like manner they report from below upward in the case of sensations from natural phenomena and impressions on the outside. In the beginnings of evolution, during all its stages, this took appreciable amounts of solar time, but at this point of the system's march along the line of growth it takes such an infinitesimally short space that we are justified in calling it instantaneous in all cases of normal and well-balanced persons. There are, of course, instances where longer time is used in consequence of the slower action of some one of the sheaths.

The number of sharply defined sheaths of the Soul is seven, but the sub-differentiations of each raises the apparent number very much higher. Roughly speaking, each one divides itself into seven, and every one in each collection of seven partakes of the nature of its own class. There may, therefore, be said to exist forty-nine sheaths possible of classification.

Physical body may be recognized as one sheath, and the subdivisions in it are such as skin, blood, nerves, flesh, bones, mucous membrane and . . . .

Astral body is another, but not so easily recognized by the men of today. It has also its own sub-divisions answering in part to those of the physical body. But being one stage higher than the latter it includes in one of its own sub-divisions several of those in the body. For instance, the surface sensations of blood, skin, flesh and mucous membrane will be included in a single one of the astral sub-divisions.

And exactly at this point the Esoteric Schools diverge from and appear to contradict modern pathology and physiology. For the modern school admits only the actions of nerves along skin and mucous membrane and in flesh, as the receivers and transmitters of sensation. It would appear to be so, but the facts *on the inside* are different, or rather more numerous, leading to additional conclusions. Likewise too we clash with the nineteenth century in the matter of the blood. We say that the blood cells and the fluid they float in receive and transmit sensation.

Each sub-division among the physical sheaths performs not only the duty of receiving and transmitting sensations, but also has the power of retaining a memory of them which is registered in the appropriate ganglion of the body, and continually, from there, implanted in the corresponding center of sensation and action in the astral body. At the same time the physical brain has always the power, as is of course a common fact, of collecting all the physical sensations and impressions.

Having laid all this down—without stopping for argument which would end in nothing without physical demonstrations being added— the next step is this. The lower man who collects, so to say, for the Soul's use, all the experiences below it, can either at will when trained, or involuntarily when forced by processes or accident or abnormal birth, live in the sensations and impressions of one or many of the various sheaths of the physical or astral body.

If trained, then there will be no delusions, or any temporary delusion will be easily dispersed. If untrained, delusion walks arm in arm with the sensations. If diseased or forced, the outer acts may be correctly performed but the free intelligence is absent, and all the delusions and illusions of hypnotic and mesmeric states show themselves.

If the inner lower man be functioning among the sensations—or planes if you like—of some astral sense or center, then clairvoyance or clairaudience comes on, because he is conveying to the brain those impressions derived from similar planes of nature in any direction.

And when to this is added a partial touch of some minor physical sub-divisions of the sheaths, then delusion is made more complete, because the experience of a single set of cells is taken for the whole and reported, by means of the brain, in the language used by a normal being. Indeed so vast are the possible combinations in this department that I have only mentioned a few by way of illustration.

It is this possibility of the inner lower man being connected with one or more of the sheaths, and disconnected from all the rest, which has led one of the French schools of hypnotizers to conclude to the effect that every man is a collection of personalities, each complete in itself. The positions laid down above are not destroyed in the fact, as observed at Paris and Nancy, that the subject of hypnotic state No. 2 knows nothing about state No. 1, for each normal person, when acting normally, compounds all the various sets of sensations, experiences, and recollections into one whole, the sum total of all, and which is not recognizable as any one of them distinct from the rest.

It must also be remembered that each person has pursued in prior lives this or that course of action, which has trained and developed this or that Soul-sheath. And although at death many of them are dissolved as integral collections, the effect of such development formerly pursued is not lost to the reincarnating being. It is preserved through the mysterious laws that guide the atoms when they assemble for the birth of a new personal house to be occupied by the returning Soul. It is known that the atoms—physical and astral—have gone through every sort of training. When the Soul is reincarnating it attracts to itself those physical and astral atoms which are like unto its old experience as far as possible. It often gets back again some of the identical matter it used in its last life. And if the astral senses have received in the prior existence on earth great attention and development, then there will be born a medium or a real seer or sage. Which it will be depends upon the great balancing of forces from the prior life. For instance, one who in another incarnation attended wholly to psychic development without philosophy, or made other errors, will be born, maybe, as an irresponsible medium; another, again, of the same class, emerges as a wholly untrustworthy partial clairvoyant, and so on *ad infinitum.*

A birth in a family of wise devotees and real sages is declared from old time to be very difficult of attainment. This difficulty may be gradually overcome by philosophical study and unselfish effort for others, together with devotion to the Higher Self pursued through many lives. Any other sort of practice leads only to additional bewilderment.

WILLIAM Q. JUDGE, F.T.S.

Convention of the European Section

[*Lucifer*, Vol. X, August, 1892, pp. 509-10]

The Second Annual Convention of the European Section of the Theosophical Society was a most successful affair, and from beginning to end all went smoothly, as befits a Society taking Universal Brotherhood for its first object. Spain was first in the field with her delegate, Bro. José Xifré, a faithful friend and pupil of H. P. Blavatsky, who watched always with deep interest the work carried on upon Spanish soil by him and his brother-in-arms, Francisco Montoliu. Then came delegates from France, Bro. Coulomb, better known as Amaravella, with Bros. Tasset and Vescop. Next from Holland a group of five, Bros. Fricke and Meuleman, and Mesdames de Neufville, Meuleman and Windust. Germany sent Bros. Leiningen and Eckstein; Scotland, Bro. Brodie Innes; Ireland, Bros. Dick and Dunlop; England, Bros. Pattinson, Firth, Duncan, Thomas, Barron, Dr. King, Mrs. Londini, and many another, and so the numbers grew and grew till the St. John's Wood colony scarcely knew itself amid the Babel of foreign tongues. The President-Elect, William Q. Judge, was a prominent figure, now in one group, now in another, always welcomed warmly wherever he stopped to chat over the affairs of the Society he has served so long and so faithfully.

On Thursday morning the first meeting of the Convention was held; the General Secretary, G. R. S. Mead, calling it to order at 10:15 a.m. It met in the Blavatsky Hall at Avenue Road, and familiar faces— Countess Wachtmeister, William Kingsland, Mrs. Cooper Oakley, Miss Cooper, Herbert Burrows, R. Machell, Walter Old and others— were seen on every hand. W. Q. Judge was unanimously voted to the chair, when the roll-call of Lodges had been read, and G. R. S. Mead, W. R. Old, and J. Ablett were appointed Secretaries of the Convention. The minutes of the last Convention were taken as read, and then the Chairman delivered an earnest opening address, recalling the memory of H. P. B., and speaking of the work done by Colonel Olcott, the President-Founder, "work that no one else had done" and to be ever held in grateful remembrance in the Society. He also read a telegram from Colonel Olcott, wishing success to the Convention, and a letter of greeting from the American Section, as follows:

THE AMERICAN SECTION T.S. TO THE EUROPEAN SECTION T.S.

Dear Brothers and Sisters,

The American Section of our Society sends you through my hands its fraternal greetings. More now than ever does our Society, ramifying over the entire globe, need within its borders strong endeavour, high aspiration, solidarity, cooperation, brotherliness. This is not because strife and ambition are among us, but because we have now come to a point where our movement, led so long by our heroic H.P.B., commands the attention of the world, and it has ever been that whenever a society commands the gaze of the world it needs strength to push forward, aspiration to inspire, solidarity to resist, and brotherliness to give comfort to its members. This Section then once more assures you of its cooperation by hand and heart, of its loyalty to our cause, of its aim to so work that when the next messenger shall come from the great Brotherhood he or she shall find the materials ready, the ranks in order, the center on guard to preserve whatever small nucleus of brotherhood we shall be so fortunate as to have created.

At our Convention in April last we asked you to unite with us in a request to Colonel Olcott to revoke his resignation. This we did in candour and friendship, leaving it to you to decide your course. We recollected what was so often and so truly said by H. P. Blavatsky, that this organization, unique in the century, partook of the life of its parents. One of them is Colonel Olcott. It would be disloyal to our ideals to hurry in accepting his resignation even though we knew that we might get on without his presence at the head. And if he should hold to his determination our loving request would fill his remaining years with pleasing remembrances of his brothers without a trace of bitterness.

The three great continents of Asia, Europe and America hold the three children who compose our family, each different from the other, but none the less necessary to the work. Toleration will prevent dissension, leading surely to the hour when the West and East shall grasp hands with complete understanding. The Oriental may be dreamy, the European conservative, and the American crude and radical, but each can give the other what that other has not. Let us then strive toward the acquiring of the desire to have such toleration and cooperation as shall make certain the creation of the nucleus so necessary to success.

In America the work goes on steadily. The recent purchase of an establishment in New York City for headquarters was a necessity of the hour. Its uses and benefits are at once apparent, and that it will increase our usefulness cannot be doubted.This has left us in debt, but the donations received from all quarters will in time clear that off. It is owned by the Aryan T. S., which is an incorporated legal body, able to hold property and take bequests. It could not be the property of the Section by law, because every State in America is sovereign, and there is no provision in our federal statutes for a federal corporation. But none the less does the Aryan T.S. deem itself morally a trustee, although it has the legal title alone and also the sole management of the place.

Another thing accomplished by this Section, doubtless also something you will yet do, is the putting in the field with money subscribed by the Pacific Coast Branches of a regular lecturer, who travels over that coast visiting and helping Branches, and lecturing also to the public. This has already created much attention from the press, and has resulted in new activity. Other lecturers will in time cover the vast area of the United States. It is an important work and may be regarded as a sort of sending forth of apostles. But we should never allow it to degenerate into a race for money or for the establishment of creed.

Theosophy and the Society have at last made themselves universally, if even as yet superficially felt and recognized in our land, as also in yours. The future is in our hands and it ever grows out of, and is built upon, the present; shall that not be full of the energy in endeavor, which H. P. B. so long exemplified in Europe and India, and Colonel Olcott in the Orient?

Our best wishes, our fraternal sympathies are with you in your deliberations.

For the American Section T. S., The Executive Committee
WILLIAM Q. JUDGE, *General Secretary*

An Interesting Letter

[*Lucifer*, Vol. XII, April, 1893, pp. 101-104]

(*Written to an Indian Brother*)

144, MADISON AVENUE,
NEW YORK.

Dear Brother,—I have your last long and welcome letter. The fears you express of the T. S. leading to dogmatism or fanaticism seem to be groundless to me. If we had a creed there would be danger; if the Society declared any particular doctrine to be true, or to be the accepted view of the T.S., great danger would result. But we have no creed, and the T.S. has not declared for any doctrine. Its members have asserted certain beliefs, but that is their right. They do not force them on others. Their declaration of their own beliefs does not unfit them to be members. I have my own settled beliefs, but I do not say that another must accept these. The eternal duty of right thought, act, and speech, is not affected by my theories. Hence all I ask of another is, to do his own duty and let me do mine. Such, indeed, is the very genius of our Society, and that is the very same reason why it still lives and has an influence.

And when we come to examine the work and the foundation of the T. S. and its policy, I find it perfectly proper for me to assert, as I do, in accordance with my own knowledge and belief, that our true progress lies in fidelity to Masters as ideals and facts. Likewise it is perfectly proper for another to say that he does not know anything about the Masters—if such be his case—but is willing to work in and for the

T. S. But he has no right to go further and deny my privilege of asserting my belief in those Beings.

So also further; I have the right to say that I think a constant reliance on Masters as such ideals and facts—or either—will lead the T. S. on to greater work. And he has his right to say that he can work without that reliance. But neither has he nor have you any right to say that my belief in this, or any assertion of it, is wrong or in any way improper.

I belong to that class of persons in the T.S. who out of their own experience know that the Masters exist and actually help the T. S. You belong to a class which—as I read your letters and those of others who write similarly—express a doubt on this, that, or the other, seeming to question the expediency, propriety and wisdom of a man's boldly asserting confidence and belief in Beings who are unprovable for many, although you say (as in your present letter) that you believe in and revere the same Masters as I do. What, then, must I conclude? Am I not forced to the conclusion that inasmuch as you say you believe in these Beings, you think it unwise in me to assert publicly and boldly my belief? Well, then, if this is a correct statement of the case, why cannot you go on your way of belief and concealment of it, and let me proceed with my proclamations? I will take the Karma of my own beliefs. I force no man to accept my assertions.

But I am not acting impulsively in my many public statements as to the existence of Masters and help from Them. It is done upon an old order of Theirs and under a law of mind. The existence of Masters being a *fact*, the assertion of that fact made so often in America has opened up channels in men's minds which would have remained closed had silence been observed about the existence of those Beings. The giving out of *names* is another matter; that, I do not sanction nor practice. Experience has shown that a springing up of interest in Theosophy has followed declaration, and men's minds are more and more powerfully drawn away from the blank Materialism which is rooted in English, French, and German teaching. And the Masters have said: "It is easier to help in America than Europe because in the former our existence has been persistently declared by so many." You may, perhaps, call this a commonplace remark, as you do some others, but for me it has a deep significance and contains a high endorsement. A very truism when uttered by a Mahâtma has a deeper meaning for which the student must seek, but which he will lose if he stops to criticize and weigh the words in mere ordinary scales.

Now, I may as well say it out very plainly that the latter half of your letter in which you refer to a message printed in the *Path* in 1891 in August is the part you consider of most importance. To that part of your letter you gave the most attention, and to the same portion you wish for a reply more than to the preliminary pages. Now, on the contrary, I consider the preceding half of your letter the important half. This last bit, all about the printed message, is not important at all. Why? Because your basic facts are wrong.

(1) I never published such a letter, for I was not in America, although if I had been I should have consented. In August of that year I was in Europe, and did not get back to New York until after that month's *Path* was published. I had sailed for London May 13th, on hearing of H. P. B.'s death, and stayed there three months. Of course while away I had to leave all the publishing in the hands of Brother Fullerton and others. But I do approve their work.

(2) The next baseless fact is thus smashed: *I did not write* the article you quote. I am not Jasper Niemand. Hence I did not get the message he printed a *part of* in his article. Jasper Niemand is a real person[1] and not a title to conceal my person. If you wish to write him about the article, or any other, you can address care of me; I will forward; in time he will reply. This wrong notion about Jasper ought to be exposed. People choose now and then to assume that I am the gentleman. But several who have corresponded with him know that he is as distinct from me in person, place, and mind as you are yourself.

(3) Now, in July it was that Jasper Niemand got his message containing, I believe, things relative to himself, and also the words of general interest quoted by him. The general words he saw fit to use. Having had privilege to send his articles to *Path*, which accepts them without examination, his article was used at once without it being necessary for me to see it, for my orders were to print any he might send. Hence I saw neither the article nor proofs before publication. But I fully approve as I did when, in the next September, I read it.

It is true I had later the privilege of seeing his message, but only read the text, did not examine the signature, and do not remember if even it had a signature. The signature is not important. The means for identification are not located in signatures at all. If you have not the means yourself for proving and identifying such a message, then signature, seal, papers, watermark, what not, all are useless.

As to "Master's seal," about which you put me the question, I do not know. Whether He has a seal or uses one is something on which I am ignorant. In my experience I have had messages from the Master, but they bear no seal and I attach no significance to the point. A seal on other messages of His goes for nothing with me; the presence or absence of a seal is nothing to me; my means of proof and identification are within myself and everything else is trumpery. Can I be more definite? Anticipating—as a brother lawyer—your question, I

[1] See *Faces of Friends*, pp. 464-67.

say in reply that I have no recollection as to any signature or seal on this message to Jasper Niemand, because I read it but once.

Further, I think it a useful message. The qualities spoken of were more than ever needed at that crisis, and words of encouragement from Masters, however trite, were useful and stimulating. We do not— at least I do not—want Masters to utter veiled, mystical, or portentous phrases. The commonplace ones suit me best and are best understood. Perhaps if you were satisfied with simple words from Them you might have had them. Who knows? They have written much of high import, enough for fifty years of effort in the letters published by Mr. Sinnett in the *Occult World*, and attributed to K. H. Why should one desire private messages in addition? I do not. Some men would sell their lives for the most commonplace phrase from Masters.

But as Masters are still living in bodies, and that in your own country and not so far from you as I am, I consider you privileged in, so to say, breathing the same air with those exalted personages. Yet I know beyond doubt or cavil that we, so far away, are not exempt from Masters' care and help. Knowing this we are content to "wait, to work, and to hope."

Fraternally,

WILLIAM Q. JUDGE

P.S.—Perhaps I ought to say somewhat more fully that the message in *Path* from Master had, in my judgment, far more value than you attribute to it. There are in this Section many members who need precisely its assurance that no worker, however feeble or insignificant, is outside the range of Master's eye and help. My co-workers in New York were so impressed with the value to the Section of this particular message, that one of them paid the cost of printing it on slips and sending it to every member of the Section in good standing. Of course its worth and importance are better understood here than they can be by anyone not familiar with the Section, and I can see ample justification of the Master's wisdom in sending the words He did.

India

A TRUMPET CALL AT A CRISIS
[*Lucifer*, Vol. XII, April, 1893, pp. 143-47]

From the facts that I am now the General Secretary of the American Section of the T. S. and its Vice-President, and was one of those who participated at the very first meeting of the Society in 1875, and for many years was intimately acquainted with H. P. Blavatsky and also with Col. Olcott, what I have to say on the subject of this article should have a weight it could not have if I were a new member, or unacquainted with its history, its real aims, and the aims and purposes of those who, greater than I, were and are so long in the front of its ranks. I ask for these few remarks, therefore, a serious consideration by our members in all countries, and also by such persons in India, not members, who may read this article.

Is there a crisis, and if so what is it and what does it amount to? There is a crisis not noticeable on the top of our historical wave, and which will not be perceived by those among us who are much interested in the work in their own particular Section. In some places there is no cause for any alarm, as interest is great and work goes forward. But the T. S. is not a national body; it is international; it has an object that embraces the entire race; causes at work in any one part of it may react on all with force when the time comes. We must, for that reason, look over the whole field from time to time, and not confine our estimate to what goes on merely in our own Section or Branch.

The critical spot is in India, the land where at the present time the Masters live in person, and from where went out the real impulse for our foundation and work. If India is of no consequence in our movement, then discussion is useless, for to bother about a place of no importance would be waste of time. If Western members are so enamored of Western culture, civilization, and religion, as to look on Indian thought and philosophy as more or less fantastic, any consideration of the present would be out of place; to all such members I say, do not read this. But those who know that our forms of thought are really Indian, colored a little by our own short lives as nations; those who realize how important in the great family of nations the Indian race is; those who see that no part of the great human mind can be left out— all those will be able to appreciate the nature of the crisis, and then will act as discreetly as possible to the end that danger may be averted.

Centuries before the West had grown out of its savagery, the mighty

East had grappled with all the problems that vex the men of the Western world and the nineteenth century. The solutions of these were recorded and preserved among the people of the East. This preservation has been in many ways. In stone of monuments, in books of various materials, in the arrangement of cities, in customs of the people, and last, but not least, in the very beliefs of the common people, looked on by our great men—whom many follow like sheep—as superstition and folly, and often degrading. The monuments and temples need to be read in the light of symbolism; the books are cast in a mold not quite the same as the idioms of the West, and have to be read with that in view as well as holding in the mind the fact that those who wrote them knew more of the Occult machinery of the Kosmos than we now know; they are not to be thrown on one side as folly or phantasy, but should be studied with serious care and with the help of the Hindûs of today, who must naturally have some inkling of the hidden meaning. The philosophy in these books is the grandest known to man; the true religion there will be found, when the dust is cleared away, to be, as it says, the religion of Brahma, and hence the first. It will turn out to be the foundation for which the members of the T.S. are looking. But this does not mean to say that that true core and center is just what this, that, or the other school of Vedântins say it is, for it might turn out to be different. It is hence of the highest importance that our Society should not, at any time, needlessly bring into the minds of Brâhmans the idea or belief that the T. S. is engaged covertly or openly in bringing forward any other religion, or any particular religion or philosophy. And if by accident or fortuitous circumstance Brâhmans in general acquire such an idea or belief, then it is the duty of our members to show how that is a mistake and to induce the others to alter their attitude.

But some may say that it is not of much consequence what some or many Brâhmans who do not enter the T. S. may say or think on the matter. It is of consequence, for the reason that the Brâhman in India is the natural priest, the one who is supposed to preserve the truth as to religion and religious books; and as the whole country so far as Brâhmanism is concerned moves on by and through religion, a false attitude on the part of the Brâhmans is very serious, and should be done away with if possible, by all right means and arguments. If they in their own circle, having a false idea of our movement, preach against us, we shall find a silent, subtle, untouchable influence negativing all our work. On the other hand, these teachers of the Hindû can do much work if they have a mind, as they have shown in the past. As an illustration I may cite the Ârya Samâj, which rose up from the efforts of one Brâhman, but obtained the support of many more, and learned ones also, when it was seen that the object in view was necessary.

Now, then, the crisis is that the Brâhmans in general all over India are beginning to get the idea and belief that the T. S. is merely an engine for the propagation of Buddhism. They are therefore starting an opposition by means of their own power and influence, and the consequence may be that they will keep many worthy men there from coming into the T. S., or from giving it any encouragement whatever. They are not making a new society, but are privately arguing against the T. S., and that is more subtle than public effort, because no counter argument is possible.

It is true they are not supported by the real facts, but to some extent they have arguments from appearances. A famous book in our list is called *Esoteric Buddhism*, while, in fact, it is not Buddhism at all distinctively, but is distinctively Brâhmanical. Its entitlement was due perhaps to enthusiasm about the Guru of the writer. Col. Olcott has declared himself officially and privately to be a Buddhist duly admitted to the high priest, and has written a Buddhist Catechism, a great and useful work which has the approval of the same high priest. The Colonel also is now going about a strictly Buddhist work, which has not so much to do with religious or philosophical opinion as it has with mere questions relating to a theological foundation, a temple and its appurtenances in the heart of India. If these Brâhmans were able to gauge public opinion in America they would have more arguments from the outer look of things, because here everything in respect to Indian religion is called by the generic name of "Buddhism," as the people are too hurried to distinguish between that and Hindûism, and have been accustomed to the *Light of Asia* and other works bringing forward the name of the religion of the Buddha. So much is this the case that all newspaper matter on this subject is labeled with the one name, and very often people when speaking of a Hindû will say, "Of course he is a Buddhist."

Our crisis is, then, that all our efforts may be hindered in India, and we may be deprived of the very necessary help of the Brâhmans in the attempt to bring forward to the world the great truths of the Wisdom Religion. What then is the remedy? Is any one to blame?

No one is to blame. Col. Olcott's efforts are right and proper, as he could not be rightfully asked to give up one form of his general work just for the sake of one religion or system. We all know very well that he is not engaged in trying to make the T. S. an engine for the propagation of Buddhism. For many years he labored for Hindûism to almost the exclusion of the other system. Mr. Sinnett is not to be censured either, for his book really teaches Brâhmanism. Besides, all the work of Col. Olcott and of the book named must end in giving to the West a greater light on the subject of the Hindû religion, and in deepening the effect on the Western mind of ancient philosophy as found in the Wisdom Religion. In consequence of that, every day, more and more, the West will look for the treasures of the East, if these are not deliberately hidden away.

The remedy is for all the members who take the right view in this matter to persistently show to the Brâhman how he is mistaken, and how, in fact, the T. S. is the very best and strongest engine for the preservation of the truths of the Vedas. If the Brâhman non-member is convinced of this, he will then encourage the community to help the T. S., and the young men under his influence to enter its ranks; he will try to discover hidden manuscripts of value and give them to us. We should also show that in the course of progress and the cycles, the time has come now when the Brâhman can no more remain isolated and the sole possessor of valuable treatises, for the West is beginning to drag these from his hands, while at the same time it is doing much to spoil the ideals of the younger generations of India, by the mechanical and material glitter of our Western civilization. Waked up fully to this, he will see how necessary it is for him to seek the help of the only organization in the world broad and free enough to help him, and to give all that equal field without favor where the Truth must at last prevail.

We should all rise then at this call and do whatever we can at every opportunity to avert the danger by applying the remedy. The sincere Hindû members of the T. S., especially, should take note and act in accordance with this, and with the facts they know of their own observation, warrant, and demand.

William Q. Judge

Note

["Theosophy Generally Stated"—an article submitted by Mr. Judge to *Lucifer*, Vol. XIII, will not appear here, but later, in the section on the World's Parliament of Religions, where the talk upon which it is based was delivered in September of 1893.—*Compiler*.]

The Prayag Letter

[*Lucifer*, Vol. VI, July 1895, pp. 375-79][1]

Mr. Judge challenged me to give my opinion on this letter, but—acting within his right as Editor—excluded from the columns of the *Path* my answer to his challenge. Not only so, but he reverses my answer—and this is outside his right as Editor—by saying that I allege the message to be non-genuine, "and thus walks beside Col. Olcott in abuse of H. P. B." In my answer I said very distinctly: "I do not regard the letter as genuine, *but I have never attributed it to H.P.B.*" (italics in article), and I went on to give my reasons, drawn almost entirely from H.P.B.'s own writings, for not regarding the letter as authentic. I do not complain that Mr. Judge should suppress my answer, nor that he should convey to his readers' minds the opposite of my statement about H.P.B.; for I know that it is necessary to his position that I should be represented as attacking my dear friend and teacher, and that those who do not see my own words should be confirmed in their belief in this industriously-propagated delusion.

The publication of the letter, if it should be regarded as from H. P. B., may do some harm to the Theosophical Society in India, and will certainly injure her memory, as it is in flagrant contradiction with her definite and published teachings. The recipients of it wisely kept it to themselves, and thus little harm was done by it, beyond the shutting out of the Theosophical Society of a few men who would have been useful members. The gentleman who sent it to Mr. Judge is much distressed at the use that has been made of it, and the best that can now be done to repair the mischief is to publish Mr. Judge's own letters about it, which will show how anxious he was a short time ago that it should not be regarded as anti-Brâhmanical.

His second letter is an admirable one, and puts the matters in question in a very clear light. In the third, two points are interesting; one, that in January, 1894, Mr. Judge frankly stated that he was not in a position to ask as to the genuineness of the letter, and the second, his statement that the channel through which a message comes may distort the intended meaning of it—a view which, from the context,

---

1 [Important background and a facsimile of the original letter in H.P.B.'s handwriting is found in *Echoes of the Orient*, Vol. I, pp. 448-54.—*Compiler*]

was intended to depreciate this particular message, and which, taken in conjunction with Mr. Judge's present declaration that the message came through H. P. B., seems to put him in the position taken by Col. Olcott, and for which he so bitterly attacks the latter.

ANNIE BESANT

LETTER I.

LONDON
July 4th, 1893.

DEAR SIR, — I beg to thank you for writing to me and enclosing a copy of a message sent some years ago to the Hindu members of the Prayag Theosophical Society. On reading yours I at once felt a confidence that you were making me a correct report of the matter, but as important interests and probably events are involved, I deemed it my duty to examine the original, so that I might be able to say I had seen that with my own eyes. That examination I cannot make in time for the next mail, and have therefore to beg your indulgence and allowance of delay in replying directly to your questions. Being here in London to attend a convention of the Theosophical Society, yours was forwarded to me from New York.

I have read your letter with very great interest. But I do not retreat from my circular, nor do I think the letter you copy for me alters either the circular or the position of things. It was not because you or others were professors of orthodox Brahmanism that that letter spoke as it did; nor was it because Buddhism in its exoteric sense is the religion of the Masters. The letter distinctly speaks of esoteric Buddhism, and that must be the same as esoteric Brahmanism. I should be forced to conclude that the writer of that letter was neither an exoteric Buddhist nor Brahman. Further than the above, for many years I have known that the Masters are neither of above.

I would ask you to wait a little longer until I have seen the original here and formed my views a little more.

I am
Sincerely,
(*Signed*)   WILLIAM Q. JUDGE

LETTER II.

THEOSOPHICAL SOCIETY, AMERICAN SECTION,
GENERAL SECRETARY'S OFFICE
HEADQUARTER'S: 144, MADISON AVENUE
NEW YORK.
September 28th, 1893.

MY DEAR SIR,—This letter should have gone some weeks ago, but by a curious accident after having written it, it was rolled into the back of my desk, in a manner which prevented me from getting it, and thus I have had to re-write it as I had no time to take my desk apart. I promised in London to answer you more at length. I have read your letter very carefully, and beg to say:

(1st) Inasmuch as you have never published the message you copy, it cannot be possible that that message is the cause of any opposition from the Brahmanical community, however much effect it may have had on you.

(2nd) I think you are altogether mistaken in supposing that the letter quoted asks any one to become a *Nastika.* I do not think it does. If you construe esoteric

Buddhism to be the same as outside Buddhism, you might be right, but the whole of the letter speaks of inner Buddhism, which to my knowledge and from my investigation, is the contrary of *Nastikism*. The reference in the letter to Buddhism and Nastikism is, I think, meant for irony and nothing more.

(3rd) If you will look at the matter from an entirely outside point of view, not as an orthodox Brahmin but simply as a thinker, is it not quite true that there are thousands of "fakeers," Sannyinis, and Sadhus leading the most pure lives, and yet being as they, are in the path of error, never having had an opportunity to meet, see, or even hear of any of the Rishis? This is because these devotees follow a set of practices based upon some particular system of religion, and that clouds their minds from the real truth. It is the same with the Buddhist devotees who, sticking to a particular system of metaphysics, are clouded as to the truth. It must also be the same with many Brahmins. Is it not true that a sincere belief may be erroneous, and that its very sincerity will prevent the believer from seeing the highest truth? Furthermore, is it not a fact, that the Rishis, sages and Mahatmas are above all systems of Philosophy, Metaphysics and Religion? This is stated in the Vedas. It seems to me that in the letter quoted the intention was to show that many Brahmans who depended too much on orthodoxy could not get at the final truth, however sincere.

I believe most firmly in the Mahatmas, Masters of Wisdom, and that they are not confined to any particular race or time, and that they look down from the very height of truth, and see that in order to reach them the devotee must rise like them above all systems, and be able to see the truth under all. The Brahman has the greatest opportunity, because his religion is nearest the truth, but it is necessary for him to pierce through so-called orthodox teachings, and try to find the truth underneath, even though he continues as a Brahman to follow outwardly all the practices which custom enjoins.

The Brahmans have before them this fact, that centuries ago the Rishis were plainly visible and spoke with them, but nowadays they do not. What is the reason? There must be a reason, and the reason can doubtless be found by you in your own Shastras. I have not altered my opinion since reading your letter. I still think that the destiny of India is to give truth to the world, but that truth must be found underneath of all ceremonies and all practices. It is for the Hindus to find out how they should act, so as to bring back again the glorious supremacy in spiritual matters which India once held in fact.

I sincerely trust that you will not find it necessary to publish the letter, since it might lead to too much misunderstanding with men who are not as capable as yourself, and as the Bhagavad Gîtâ says, we should not confuse the mind of the ignorant. I beg to offer you the assurances of my fraternal regards.

Sincerely,

(*Signed*)   WILLIAM Q. JUDGE

LETTER III.

THEOSOPHICAL SOCIETY, AMERICAN SECTION,

GENERAL SECRETARY'S OFFICE,

HEADQUARTERS: 144, MADISON AVENUE,

NEW YORK

January 12th, 1894.

MY DEAR SIR,—I have your letter of the 27th of December, replying to my letters of respectively July 4th and 28th of September. I feel much honored that you have taken so much trouble to write me about this matter.

Respecting the letter in question, I was not able to see the original, as Mr. Sinnett was too busy to find it, and was not able to recollect all the details, and I could not wait in London long enough so as to secure his further attention.

I would like to put the case a little differently from yours, thus:

(*a*) I asked the Brahmans to cooperate with me in the Theosophical Society.

(b) I said that the Theosophical Society was not in favour of Buddhism as against every other religion, and that it could not be called a Buddhist Propagation Society. The question as to whether the Theosophical Society is, or is not, a danger to Brahmanism I do not think I raised in that way, for I am not sufficiently acquainted with the whole world to know whether the Society might or might not in some respect be a danger to that religion or any other. What I attempted to say was as stated above, and to that I still adhere. I know that Mrs. Besant, Mr. Fullerton, Mr. Mead, myself, and many others are sympathizers with Brahmanism, and not with Buddhism, and knowing this, I am qualified to state that the Society is not a Buddhist Society, and should not be looked at with prejudice by the Brahmans, because they thought it was Buddhist. I do not think that the message referred to is inconsistent with this opinion, for if you assume the message to be from one of those personages, it only gives the opinion of that personage. Hence I am not able to give any opinion yet on the question of the genuineness of the message, nor am I qualified to ask the direct question which you request me at the end to do. Supposing that such a question was asked, and the answer came that it was genuine, I do not see myself that it would make any difference in my position, as if such an answer was given I should not alter my beliefs nor my present attitude which personally is favourable to Brahminism, but as an official is neutral to all religions. I should think that this position which I have outlined now in my letter would be sustained as a mere matter of academic discussion by any of your friends with whom you are accustomed to discuss, and I would be very glad to have you discuss it with them if you see fit.

I knew that you did not mean ill to the Theosophical Society, although I am not well acquainted with you, and am very glad to have you state this to be the fact, *and also very glad to know that you are not in any hurry to publish the message.* I am also extremely delighted to have you as a Hindu, and as a Brahman, state that you believe that there are Mahatmas. You are, of course, quite justified in saying, if you so think, that the particular Mahatmas in question do not exist, or are of the sort which you believe in. But I do not regard even that as dependent upon that particular letter in question. I suppose you take the same view I do in regard to the question of letters and the messages from Mahatmas or sages, that it may often happen that the channel through which they come may distort the intended meaning, and that actual letters written by such personages are rare, because of the great forces which such an act on their part would engender; certainly if one of them actually wrote a letter with his own hands, no one except the most ignorant could fail to feel its force; and yet in such a case it might be quite possible that they, being above all religions, as the Vedas proclaim, might say in their wisdom something that would be contrary to the views of any religionist, whether he were Brahman or not.

I think the Theosophical Society is doing a great deal of good for the religion of India, and that it will be found in the years to come to do more and more, and certainly the present tour of Mrs. Annie Besant, who is a believer in Brahmanism, and not in any sense a Buddhist, is arousing a great deal of spiritual interest in your own country for which I am sure you will not be ungrateful. Please accept the assurances of my brotherly regard.

Yours truly,

(*Signed*) William Q. Judge

[The italics in above letters are in the original.]

"Blavatskianism" In and Out of Season

[*Lucifer*, Vol. XIII, December, 1893, pp. 303-08]

Theosophists! let us consult together. Let us survey the army, the field of battle, and the fighters. Let us examine our ways and our speech, so that we may know what we are doing in this great affray which may last for ages and in which every act has a future. What do we see? A Theosophical Society struggling as a whole against the world. A few devoted members struggling against the world and some opponents within its ranks. A Society grown to its eighteenth year, after the expenditure of much time and energy and fame by those who have been with it in infancy, those who have come in from time to time, those who worked and left it for this generation. It has its karma like any other body, for it is a living thing and not a mere paper organization; and with that karma is also woven the karma of the units composing it.

How does it live and grow? Not alone by study and work, but by propriety of method of work; by due attention paid by the members to thought and speech in their theosophic promulgations. Wise workers like wise generals, survey the field now and then to see if their methods are good or bad, even though fully convinced of the nobility and righteousness of their cause; they trust not only to the virtue of their aim and work, but attend to any defects now and then indicated by the assaults of the enemy; they listen to warnings of those who see or think they see errors of omission and commission. Let us all do this.

It happens to be the fact that most of those who work the hardest for the Society are at the same time devoted disciples, open or nonprofessed, of H. P. Blavatsky, but that leaves still a large number of members who, with the first-named, may be variously classified. First, there are those who do not rely at all on H. P. Blavatsky, while not distinctly opposed and none the less good members. Next are those who are openly opposed to her name and fame, who, while reading her works and profiting by them as well as by the work aroused by her in others, are averse from hearing her name, oppose the free assertion of devotion to her, would like now and then to have Theosophy stripped of her altogether, and opine that many good and true possible members are kept away from the T.S. by her personality's being bound up in it. The two last things of course are impossible to meet, because if it had not been for her the Theosophical Society with its literature would not have come into existence. Lastly are those in the world who do not belong to our ranks, composed of persons holding in respect to the T.S. the various positions of for, against and indifferent.

The active workers may be again divided as follows:

(*a*) Moderate ones, good thinkers who present their thoughts in words that show independent and original thought on theosophical subjects, thus not referring to authority, yet who are earnest, devoted and loyal.

(*b*) Those who are earnest, devoted and loyal, but present Theosophy more or less as quotations from H.P.B.'s writings, constantly naming and always referring their thoughts and conclusions to her, thus appearing to present Theosophy as solely based on her as an authority.

(*c*) The over-zealous who err like the former, and, in addition, too frequently and out of place and time, bring forward the name of H. P. Blavatsky; often relating what it was supposed she had done or not done, and what she said, attributing infallibility to her either directly or by indirection; thus arousing an opposition that is added to any impression or dogmatism or authority produced by other members.

(*d*) Believers in phenomena who give prominence to the wonders said to have been performed by H. P. Blavatsky; who accentuate the value of the whole field of occult phenomena, and sincerely supposing, however mistaken the notion, that occult and psychical phenomena will arrest attention, draw out interest, inspire confidence; when, in fact, the almost certain results are, to first arouse curiosity, then create distrust and disappointment; for nearly every one is a doubting Thomas who requires, while the desire cannot be satisfied, a duplicate of every phenomenon for himself. In *The Occult World*, the Adept writing on this very subject says that the demand for new phenomena would go on *crescendo* until at last one would be crushed by doubt, or the other and worse result of creating superstition and blind faith would come about. Every thoughtful person must surely see that such must be the consequence.

It is true that the movement has grown most in consequence of the effort of those who are devoted to an ideal, inspired by enthusiasm, filled with a lasting gratitude to H. P. Blavatsky. Their ideal is the service of Humanity, the ultimate potential perfectibility of man as exemplified by the Masters and Adepts of all ages, including the present. Their enthusiasm is born from the devotion which the ideal arouses, their gratitude is a noble quality engendered by the untiring zeal of the soul who brought to their attention the priceless gems of the wisdom religion. Ingratitude is the basest vice of which man can be guilty, and it will be base for them to receive the grand message and despise the messenger.

But does devotion, loyalty, or gratitude require that we should thrust our estimate of a person forward to the attention of the public in a way that is certain to bring on opposition? Should our work in a great movement, meant to include all men, intended to condense the truth from all religions, be impeded or imperiled by over-zealous personal loyalty? I think not. We should be wise as serpents. Wisdom does not consist in throwing the object of our heart's gratitude in the faces of those who have no similar feeling, for when we do that it may easily result that personal considerations will nullify our efforts for the good of those we address.

Now it is charged in several quarters that we are dogmatic as a Society. This is extremely easy of disproof as a fact, and some trouble has been taken to disprove it. But is there not a danger that we might go too far on this line, and by continuing the disproof too long increase the very belief which we say is baseless? "The more proof offered the less believed" is how often true. Our constitution is the supreme law. Its being non-dogmatic is proof enough. Years of notification on almost every document have prepared the proofs which every one can see. It would seem that enough has been said on the subject of our non-dogmatism.

But the charge then is altered, and "dogmatism" is supplanted by "Blavatskianism," and here the critics have a slight ground to stand on; here is where a danger may exist and where the generals, the captains, the whole army, should properly pay attention and be on their guard. In the words and methods of the various classes of members above mentioned is the case for the charge. I am not directing any remark to the question whether members "believe in Blavatsky or not," for the charge made is intended to imply that there is too much said about H. P. Blavatsky as authority, as source, as guide, too little original thinking, too much reliance on the words of a single person.

In the years that are gone, necessity existed for repelling mean personal attacks on H. P. Blavatsky's character. To take up arms in her behalf then was wise. Now her works remain. The necessity for constant repulse of attacks on her does not exist. Judgment can be used in doing so. Loyalty is not thrown to the winds when good judgment says there is no need to reply. One of the best replies is to carry on the work in the noble and altruistic spirit she always pointed out. Take, for instance, the almost senile attacks periodically made by the Society for Psychical Research. What good can be possibly accomplished by paying any attention to them? None at all, except what results to that body by inflating it with the idea that its shafts have hit a vulnerable spot. Ever since their *ex post facto* agent went to India to play at psychical investigation they have almost lived by their attacks, for by them, more than anything else, they gain some attention; her personality, even to this day, adds spice to their wide-of-the-mark dis-cussions. Even at the Chicago World's Congresses their discussions were mostly given up to re-hashing the same stories, as if they were proud that, even though they knew nothing of psychic law, they had at least discovered one human being whose nature they could not fathom, and desired to for ever parade her with the various labels their fancy suggested. But in districts or new publications, where a new attack is made, good judgment may suggest an answer bringing up the state-ment of charges and copiousness of former answers. Now our work goes on in meetings, in publications, in discussions, and here is where the old idea of repelling attack may run into an unnecessary parade of the person to whom in heart we are loyal, while at the same time the voluminousness of her writings is often an excuse for not investigating for oneself, and this leads to quoting her too frequently by name as authority.

She never claimed authority, but, contrariwise, disclaimed it. But few of the theories broached by her were new to our day, albeit those are the key-ideas. Yet these very key-ideas are not those on which the quotations and personal references to her are made so often. She neither invented, nor claimed as new, the doctrines of Karma, Re-incarnation, Devachan, Cycles, and the like. These are all exhaustively treated in various literatures—Buddhistic, Jain, Brâhmanical, Zoroas-trian. They are capable, like all theosophic doctrines, of independent examination, of philosophical, logical, and analogical proof. But, if we state them parrot-like, and then bring forward a quotation from H. P. Blavatsky to prove them, has not an opponent, has not any one, member or non-member, a right to say that the offending person is not doing independent thinking, is not holding a belief after due con-sideration, but is merely acting blindly on faith in matters where it is quite natural that a cry should be raised by some one of "Blavat-skianism."

If this were an age in the West when any respect or reverence ex-isted as a general thing in the people, the sayings of a sage could be quoted as authority. But it is not such an age. Reverence is para-lyzed for the time, and the words of a sage are of no moment as such. H. P. Blavatsky came in this irreverent time, holding herself only as a messenger and indicator, not as a sage pure and simple. Hence to merely quote her words out of due place will but arouse a needless irritation. It may indicate in oneself a failure to think out the problem independently, an absence of diligence in working out our own salva-tion in the way directed by Gautama Buddha. What, then, are the right times and places, and which are out of place and time?

When the assembly and the subject are both meant to deal with the life and works of H. P. Blavatsky, then it is right and proper and wise to speak of her and her works, her acts, and words. If one is dealing with an analysis or compilation of her writings on any subject, then must she and what she wrote be used, named, and quoted. But even at those times her words should not be quoted as and for authority, inasmuch as she said they were not. Those who consider them to be authority will quickly enough accept them. As she never put forward anything as original investigation of hers in the realm of science, in the line of experiments in hypnotism, in clairvoyance, mind-reading, or the like, we ought to be careful how and when we bring her statements forward to an unbelieving public.

But in an assembly of members coming together to discuss theosophical doctrines in general, say such as Karma, Reincarnation, the Septenary Constitution, and the like, it is certainly unwise to give quotation after quotation from H. P. Blavatsky's works on the matter in hand. This is not fair to the hearers, and it shows only a power of memory or compilation that argues nothing as to the comprehension of the subject on the reader's part. It is very easy to compile, to quote sentence after sentence, to weave a long series of extracts together, but it is not progress, nor independence, nor wisdom. On the other hand, it is a complete nullification of the life-work of the one who has directed us to the path; it is contrary to the spirit and genius of the Society. And if in such an assembly much time is given to recounting phenomena performed by H. P. B., or telling how she once said this and at another time did that, the time is out of joint with the remarks. Meetings of branches are meant for giving to the members and enquirers a knowledge of the theosophical doctrines by which alone true progress is to come to our movement. New and good members are constantly needed; they cannot be fished out of the sea of enquirers by such a process as the personal history of anyone, they cannot be retained by relations of matters that do not teach them the true aim and philosophy of life, they will be driven off if assailed with quotations.

If there is power in a grateful loyalty to H. P. Blavatsky, as for my part I fully believe, it does not have its effect by being put forward all the time, or so often as to be too noticeable, but from its depth, its true basis, its wise foundation, its effect on our work, our act, and thought. Hence to my mind there is no disloyalty in reserving the mention of her name and qualities for right and timely occasions. It is certain that as Theosophy brings forward no new system of ethics, but only enforces the ethics always preached, the claim, if made, that our ethics, our high endeavor, are to be found nowhere else described save in the works left by H. P. Blavatsky, is baseless, will lead to wrong conclusions, and bring up a reaction that no amount of argument can suppress. No greater illustration of an old and world-wide religion can be found than that provided by Buddhism, but what did Buddha say to his disciples when they brought up the question of the honors to be paid to his remains? He told them not to hinder themselves about it, not to dwell on it, but to work out their own salvation with diligence.[1]

That the views held by H. P. Blavatsky herself coincided with this can be seen by reading the pamphlet entitled *The Theosophical Society and H. P. B.*, being a reprint of articles that appeared in *Lucifer* of December, 1890. She requested the reprint, and some of her notes are appended to the articles. In those Bro. Patterson took somewhat the same ground as this article, and she commended it in most positive terms.   WILLIAM Q. JUDGE

THEOSOPHICAL CORRESPONDENCE CLASS
Preliminary Prospectus and Notice.

[*Lucifer*, Vol. XIII, December 1893, pp. 347-48]

GENERAL SECRETARY'S OFFICE,
AMERICAN SECTION T.S., N.Y.,

The increase of the purely routine work of the General Secretary's Office has made it impossible to fully reply to all the numerous questions put in letters, and enquirers have to be referred to books after the first usual correspondence has passed. But this does not do away with the needs of sincere enquirers, nor with the necessity for study and the obligation to help members to grasp the teachings of Theosophy so that they may be able to help others in their turn by presenting Theosophy and the aims of the T.S. in a reasonably clear manner to questioners. Many members also require help because of the hurry of our present life and from previous lack of training in metaphysical investigation. The different needs cannot be fully met by the issuance of Branch Papers and the *Forum*, as these are necessarily limited in area of influence.

Having been offered assistance by some competent members, I have decided to start a Correspondence Class as a part of the work of the American Section T. S., to enable those members desiring to avail themselves of it to pursue their studies in Theosophy more systematically, so that they may thereby gain a better understanding of the

---

[1] See the *Mahâparinibbâna Sûtta.*

philosophy of Theosophy and its application to daily life, thus making it more certain that the growth of the Society shall not merely be in numbers, but also in the Theosophical education of the units composing the whole body—at least in so far as concerns the American Section.

Method of Work

(1) All members in good standing of the American Section T. S. can join the correspondence class by applying in writing to the address given below.

(2) Every three months, or oftener if warranted, a subject will be selected for study and a list given of books and articles which are to be read. Discretion is reserved to include at any time more than one subject.

(3) Questions bringing out the most important points of the subject will be sent to members of the class. The number of questions will be decided on after some trial.

(4) Replies to these questions are to be sent to the office of the General Secretary, addressed as requested below, where they will be examined and returned to the senders with comments and suggestions in all particulars wherein they seem to require it or as enquiries made shall indicate.

(5) Members will be permitted to send *one* question with each set of replies. Such questions will be made use of in the general questions. Discretion is reserved as to dealing or not dealing with irrelevant questions.

(6) From time to time general notes and comments upon the replies, or a complete paper on the subject, will be sent out to all, either with the next set of questions issued or independently.

(7) Students will probably be divided into classes if such a method shall appear desirable. But this head may be altered as experience may indicate.

(8) Hints as to methods of study will be sent with the first set of questions.

(9) Members are not to reply to the questions until after the expiration of one month from receipt of the same, in order that they may have ample time to study and think over the subject, and also in order that the office may not be unduly burdened with work.

These regulations and methods are subject to alteration at the discretion of the Office.

It is hoped that no member of the Society will take up membership in this Correspondence Class unless with the determination to keep up the work. Some of the questions may appear to be very simple, but in that case the student should endeavour to make more complete answers and to throw fresh light upon the subject.

As there will necessarily be expenses of postages, paper, and some printing, members of the class are requested to help in this matter by sending stamps for the return of their papers, and also, if they can, by sending an *extra* two or five cent stamp. The class ought to be self-supporting, though as yet that is not demanded.

Preliminary Questions

All members joining the class are requested to answer the following questions for the information of the Office:

(1) How long have you been a member of the T. S.?

(2) What books have you studied and what merely read?

(3) Have you written any papers for any Branch Meetings or Magazines, or have you delivered any addresses or lectures?

(4) What topic, doctrine, or phase of Theosophy has struck you most forcibly or engaged your attention?

(5) What books do you possess, and have you access to a Theosophical Library?

All communications relating to the Correspondence Class are to be addressed to: Secretary T. S. Correspondence Class, 144 Madison Avenue, New York City, N.Y.

Correspondents are asked not to mix the business of this class in letters relating to any other matter: if this request is not complied with, all such letters will remain unanswered so far as concerns the Correspondence Class, as the various departments of work in the General Secretary's Office are distinct from each other.

Non-Responsibility of the Theosophical Society

The Theosophical Society is not responsible as an organization for any view or opinion to be expressed or intimated in any of the papers, documents, questions, or answers in this class; nor is the Society in any way bound thereby; nor are any such views or opinions authoritative or to be deemed as the views or opinions of the T. S.; they are only individual views and opinions of those who express them.

WILLIAM Q. JUDGE
General Secretary, American Section T. S.

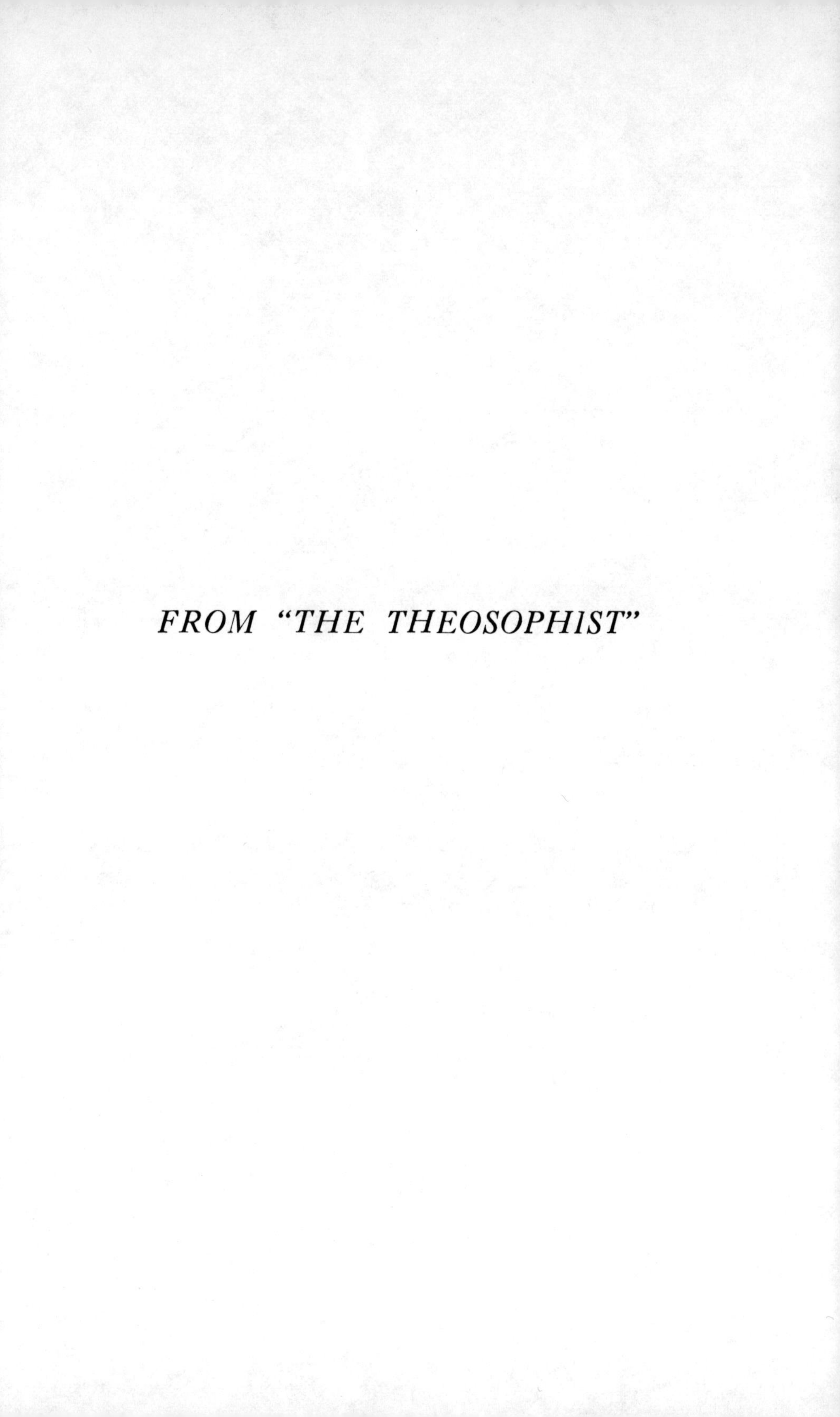

FROM "THE THEOSOPHIST"

The New York Theosophical Society

[*The Theosophist*, Supplement to Vol. II, September, 1881, p. 1]

Many of our members have pursued investigations in Spiritualism and kindred subjects with success and profit. In fact, one of the General Council, Mrs. M. J. Billing, is herself a medium for spiritual phenomena of a wonderful character, her familiars—if they may be so termed—exhibiting a knowledge of occult laws governing the universe which it would be well for the Spiritualistic fraternity to inquire into.

Others have given attention privately to the development of their own spirits, and this, it may be said, is the chief object of this Society, but they have refused as yet to divulge their experiences for publication, as they say such publication would retard their progress. And in this refusal they seem to be upheld by all the teachings of Jewish and Hindu Kabalism.

One, however, of our members has for a long time noticed a peculiar thing upon which he asks for opinions from other Branches. It is this: He sees, either in the air or in his spiritual eye, which he knows not, because it is always in the direction in which he may be looking, very frequently, a bright spot of light. The exact time is always noted, and is invariably found to be the hour when some one is thinking or speaking of him or about to call upon him. He would like some suggestions as to the law governing this appearance, and how to make more definite the information it is meant to convey.

Many applications from distant and various parts of the United States for permission to establish Branches have been received.

WILLIAM Q. JUDGE
Recording Secretary

19th July, 1881.

[Not only news items such as the above appeared in the oldest of our Theosophical journals, *The Theosophist*, but Mr. Judge contributed several articles as well. In the summer of 1884 he traveled in India and his lectures were summarized in the journal originated by H.P.B. in Bombay in 1879. *The Theosophist* also published his account, "Theosophy at the World's Fair" in Vol. XIV, pp. 588-92. That article will not be included in this section, but later as part of the section on The World's Parliament of Religions.—Comp.]

The Moral Law of Compensation

[*The Theosophist*, Vol. III, October, 1881, pp. 15-16]

"For thou shalt be in league with the stones of the field; and the beasts of the field shall be at peace with thee." Job v, 23.

As a Western Theosophist I would like to present to my Indian brethren a few thoughts upon what I conceive to be the operation of the Law of Compensation in part, or, to put it more clearly, upon the operation of one branch of this law.

It seems undeniable that this law is the most powerful, and the one having the most numerous and complicated ramifications of all the laws with which we have to deal. This it is that makes so difficult for a human spirit the upward progress after which we all are striving, and it is often forced upon me that it is this law which perpetuates the world, with its delusions, its sadness, its illusions, and that if we could but understand it so as to avoid its operation, the *Nirvâna* for the whole human family would be an accomplished fact.

In a former number a respected brother from Ceylon, speaking with authority, showed us how to answer the question so often asked: "Why do we see a good man eating the bread of poverty, and the wicked dwelling in riches, and why so often is a good man cast down from prosperity to despair, and a wicked man after a period of sorrow and hardship made to experience for the balance of his life nothing but success and prosperity?" He replied that our acts in any one period of existence were like the arrow shot from the bow, acting upon us in the next life and producing our rewards and punishments. So that to accept his explanation—as we must—it is, of course, necessary to believe in reincarnation. As far as he went, he was very satisfactory, but he did not go into the subject as thoroughly as his great knowledge would permit. It is to be hoped that he will favor us with further essays upon the same subject.

I have not yet seen anywhere stated the *rationale* of the operation of this law—how and why it acts in any particular case.

To say that the reviling of a righteous man will condemn one to a life of a beggar in the next existence is definite enough in statement, but it is put forward without a reason, and unless we accept these teachings blindly we cannot believe such consequences would follow. To appeal to our minds, there should be a reason given, which shall be at once plain and reasonable. There must be some law for this particular case; otherwise, the statement cannot be true. There must occur, from the force of the revilement, the infraction of some natural regulation, the production of some discord in the spiritual world which has for a consequence the punishment by beggary in the succedent existence of the reviler. The only other reason possible of statement is, that it is so ordered. But such a reason is not a reason at all, because no Theosophist will believe that any punishment, save that which man himself inflicts, is *ordered*. As this world is a world produced by law, moved by law, and governed by the natural operation of laws which need no one to operate them, but which invariably and unerringly operate themselves, it must follow that any punishment suffered in this way is not suffered through any order, but is suffered because the natural law operates itself. And further, we are compelled to accept this view, because to believe that it was *ordered*, would infer the existence of some particular person, mind, will, or intelligence to *order* it, which for one instant no one will believe, who knows that this world was produced, and is governed, by the operation of number, weight and measure, with harmony over and above all.

So then we should know in what manner the law operates, which condemns the reviler of a righteous man to beggary in his next existence. That knowledge once gained we may be able to find for ourselves the manner and power of placating as it were this terrible monster of compensation by performing some particular acts which shall in some way be a restoration of the harmony which we have broken, if perchance we have unconsciously or inadvertently committed the sin.

Let us now imagine a boy born of wealthy parents, but not given proper intelligence. He is, in fact, called an idiot. But instead of being a mild idiot, he possesses great malice which manifests itself in his tormenting insects and animals at every opportunity. He lives to be, say, nineteen and has spent his years in the malicious, although idiotic, torment of unintelligent, defenceless animal life. He has thus hindered many a spirit in its upward march and has beyond doubt inflicted pain and caused a moral discord. This fact of his idiocy is not a restoration of the discord. Every animal that he tortured had its own particular elemental spirit, and so had every flower that he broke in pieces. What did they know of his idiocy, and what did they feel after the torture but revenge. And had they a knowledge of his idiocy, being unreasoning beings, they could not see in it any excuse for his acts. He dies at nineteen, and after the lapse of years is reborn in another nation—perchance another age—into a body possessing more than average intelligence. He is no longer an idiot, but a sensible active man who now has a chance to regenerate the spirit given to every man, without the chains of idiocy about it. What is to be the result of the evil deeds of his previous existence? Are they to go unpunished? I think not. But how are they to be punished; and if the compensation comes, in what manner does the law operate upon him? To me there seems to be but one way, that is through the discord produced in the spirits of those unthinking beings which he had tortured during those ninteeen years. But how? In this way. In the agony of their torture these beings turned their eyes upon their torturer, and dying, his spiritual picture through the excess of their pain, together with that pain and the desire for revenge, were photographed, so to speak, upon their spirits—for in no other way could they have a memory of him—and when he became a disembodied spirit they clung to him until he was reincarnated when they were still with him like barnacles on a ship. They can now only see through his eyes, and their revenge consists in precipitating themselves down his glance on any matter he may engage in, thus attaching themselves to it for the purpose of dragging it down to disaster.

This leads to the query of what is meant by these elementals precipitating themselves down his glance. The ancients taught that the astral light—*Âkaśa*—is projected from the eyes, the thumbs and the palms of the hands. Now as the elementals exist in the astral light, they will be able to see only through those avenues of human organism which are used by the astral light in travelling from the person. The eyes are the most convenient. So when this person directs his glance on any thing or person, the astral light goes out in that glance and through it those elementals see that which he looks upon. And so also, if he should magnetize a person, the elementals will project themselves from his hands and eyes upon the subject magnetized and do it injury.

Well, then, our reincarnated idiot engages in a business which requires his constant surveillance. The elementals go with him and throwing themselves upon everything he directs, cause him continual disaster.

But one by one they are caught up again out of the orbit of necessity into the orbit of probation in this world, and at last all are gone, whereupon he finds success in all he does and has his chance again to reap eternal life. He finds the realization of the words of Job quoted at the head of this article: he is in "league with the stones of the field, and the beasts of the field are at peace with him." These words were penned ages ago by those ancient Egyptians who knew all things. Having walked in the secret paths of wisdom which no fowl knoweth and the vulture's eye hath not seen, they discovered those hidden laws, one within the other like the wheels of Ezekiel, which govern the universe. There is no other reasonable explanation of the passage quoted than the theory faintly outlined in the foregoing poor illustration. And I only offer it as a possible solution or answer to the question as to what is the *rationale* of the operation of the Moral Law of Compensation in that particular case, of which I go so far as to say that I think I know a living illustration. But it will not furnish an answer for the case of the punishment for reviling a righteous man.

I would earnestly ask the learned friends of the Editor of the THEOSOPHIST to give the explanation, and also hint to us how in this existence we may act so as to mitigate the horrors of our punishment and come as near as may be to a league with the stones and the beasts of the field.

BY AN EX-ASIATIC

Astrology Verified

[*The Theosophist*, Vol. III, April, 1882, pp. 172-73]

Writing in *The Theosophist* upon the subject of Astrology, C. C. Massey says that he thinks at present we are not fully acquainted with the science, and that, as now practiced, it is not always reliable.

His remarks as to its unreliability are justly applicable to that branch of it which relates to nativities alone, and so far I agree with him, because I have encountered numerous cases where judgments upon nativities have been most erroneous. That department of the science is very abstruse and beset with difficulties requiring constant years of study to master. Can we wonder then at the mistakes made by the professional astrologer? He cannot afford these years of patient toil, for even with but one foot upon the threshold of this hoary art he begins to dispense his judgments and prognostications.

The three first divisions of the science: *Genethliacal Astrology*, or telling what shall be the individual's fate; *Mundane Astrology*, or foretelling the circumstances of nations, the occurrence of wars and pestilence; and *Atmospherical Astrology*, or indicating the weather from certain aspects of the planets, are by no means easy to understand or practice, as they require not only a close application for several years, but a good education too. But there is another branch of the subject called *Horary Astrology*, or the answering of questions put to the Astrologer at any time upon any subject whatever, about which the questioner is anxious. This can be soon learned by close attention, and its practice will be found to reward the student with answers having in them as much of certainty as we can hope for in this illusionary world. Nor, need one wait for years before trusting himself to make replies to questions or to solve problems, excepting always *Elections*, or the determining of days and times for beginning or doing anything. This can be left untouched as it is not very useful.

Zadkiel, who was a well-educated man, an ex-officer of the English Navy, in writing on this subject, says that any one of average intelligence can soon learn by Horary Astrology, whom to do business with, what things to avoid, and what will be the result of any particular business engaged in or proposed. That Zadkiel was right I have had for some years abundant proof. And we have Lilly who preceded Zadkiel, saying the same as his follower. In Lilly's *Introduction to Astrology*[1] there are given hundreds of instances where Horary Astrology has furnished correct answers to questions then put. Lilly was the astrologer who predicted the great fire which in 1666 burnt down London, and also the plague that took off a vast number of her inhabitants. No matter how much the so-called scientific world may sneer at this, it remains a fact quite susceptible of proof.

In my experience with Horary Astrology I have found that some persons have not naturally the proper cast of mind for giving a correct reply to a question, which, by another reader of the figure, would be justly answered; and, again, that one who will always be correct in Horary questions may be quite unable to do well with a nativity.

It is permissible to name those professors who are dead, because then we cannot be accused of advertising them. In the city of New York there resided, up to within a short time ago, one Dr. Charles Winterburn who practiced medicine and incidentally Horary Astrology. I consulted him many times for which he would take no pay, and I cannot remember a case in which he made a wrong answer. His mind was peculiarly fitted to give a sound reply to any question astrologically put, and it was with a sincere sorrow that I heard of his death. From among the many questions answered by him I have taken a few, as well as some upon which judgments were given by other astrologers, by myself and some other amateurs.

Two years ago, at exactly 3 p.m., I signed a contract relating to the use of the electric light. The conditions were favorable, and every one interested thought much money would be made. I sent to Dr. Winterburn and three other astrologers—each being unaware that the others had the question and one living in a distant city—this question: "At 3 p.m. today I signed a contract; what will come of it?" No other data were given. With startling unanimity, they all replied that *nothing* would come of it, but that it would be abandoned. Dr. Winterburn said that I might get from it a small sum, but expenses would eat that up, and one of the others said that the opposite parties to the contract were disagreeing amongst themselves and had no funds. This I afterwards found to be true. Eleven weeks was the length of time given by astrol-

---

1 [Lilly, William, *Introduction to Astrology*, etc., London, Bell, 1907.—*Comp.*]

ogy for it to last. Within eleven weeks the whole matter was abandoned, and I made nothing whatever from it.

Subsequently, I entered into a matter having some connection with the Government and a certain manufactured article. For the sake of collecting evidence for, or against, Astrology, I obtained judgments on the affair, laying them away without paying enough attention to them to even read them. The business went forward with apparently good prospects, but at last it began to assume an unfavorable turn, and then I looked into the replies I had received. With one accord, as before, they declared I had better not go on; all stating that there appeared to be evidence of some money, but also of a greater amount of expense. Dr. Winterburn, in reply to a letter written on this point, said: "On the 20th of this month you will get some return from it, but then you should drop it. However, I see that you will give it up, and it will slip away from your neighborhood *in toto*." On the 20th I received the only money ever paid in the case, and from that day to this have had no more to do with it than if I had never heard of it.

In the year 1879, I contemplated a removal of my offices, and asked Dr. Winterburn for an astrological judgment. He replied: "Do not move yet, the place offered is not good, and you will have great annoyance and loss there: wait." Soon after a room, apparently no better in another building, was offered. Dr. Winterburn and others with the same unanimity said: "Move; the new offer is good, it will be pleasant in every way." As the new place was good and cheap I moved, and not because Astrology said so. But, singular as it may appear, in eight months afterwards the place against which they advised me—and the location and description of which they were perfectly unaware of—was invaded by masons and carpenters, the wall torn down in midwinter by order of the Municipal Government, and the whole place exposed for half a year to weather and dirt. Had I been there the expense would have been great, and the annoyance immeasurable. Let me say further that when the replies were given, neither the landlord nor the Government had these alterations in contemplation.

When President Garfield was shot, some friends and myself erected different astrological figures on the event and construing by the rules, we all said he would die. I placed his death about a week off. Our mistakes were of time and were not the mistakes of the art.

Previous to my father's death, Dr. Winterburn, having no acquaintance with him and never having seen him, said: "All the indications are bad; I think the direction I have named will be fatal. He will die in a few days, but his death will be easy and calm." He died in fifteen days as calmly and sweetly as a child would drop to sleep. The only datum given to the astrologer was the question: "My father is sick; what will come of it."

Such are a few of many instances I have had of the preciseness and truth of this ancient art. I could give hundreds.

These experiences lead me to the conclusion that Horary Astrology is a correct mode of divination. Those ancient men, who, with minds unfettered by the shackles of bigotry or theology, but having an over-flowing desire to benefit that "great orphan Humanity," were wont in part of India and Egypt to inquire into all of Nature's works, found that Nature is one vast machine whose wheels work one within the other. Calculate the motion and know the mode of motion of one, and you have a key for all. So they took the planets, with the heavenly road in which they travel, and erected a scheme based on experience and the universal reign of law, which enabled them and will enable us to guide the faltering steps of man through the dark and rugged valley of this life. Anxiety is one of man's greatest and most insidious foes. It fetters his energy and defeats his ends. If Astrology will relieve one at any crisis from anxiety, is it not well to foster its pursuit and spread its fame? It has relieved me often from anxiety which, without it, I would have felt for months. It will do the same for any one.

Let the light then shine from the East where Astrology began: let those whose forefathers gave to Claudius Ptolemy the materials for his Tetrabiblos, give to us what aid they can for the greater understanding and development of this most ancient art.

New York, January 28, 1882.

By WILLIAM Q. JUDGE, F.T.S.

The Adepts in America in 1776

[*The Theosophist*, Vol. V, October, 1883, pp. 16-17][1]

The following suggestions and statements are made entirely upon the personal responsibility of the writer, and without the knowledge or consent—as far as he knows—of the adepts who are in general terms therein referred to.

The reflecting mind is filled with astonishment upon reviewing the history of the rise of the United States of North America, when it perceives that dogmatic theology has no foundation in any part of the Declaration of Independence or Constitution for the structure which it

---

1 [For another view see H.P.B.'s article "Adepts and Politics" in *BCW*, Vol. VI, pp. 15-20.—*Comp.*]

fain would raise and has so often since tried to erect within and upon the government. We are astonished because those documents were formulated and that government established at a time when dogmatism of one kind or another had supreme sway. Although the Puritans and others had come to America for religious freedom, they were still very dogmatic and tenacious of their own peculiar theories and creed; so that if we found in this fundamental law much about religion and religious establishments, we would not be surprised. But in vain do we look for it, in vain did the supporters of the iron church attempt to lay the needed corner stone, and today America rejoices at it, and has thereby found it possible to grow with the marvelous growth that has been the wonder of Europe.

The nullification of those efforts made by bigotry in 1776 was due to the adepts who now look over and give the countenance of their great name to the Theosophical Society.

They oversaw the drafting of the Declaration and the drawing of the Constitution, and that is why no foothold is to be found for these blatant Christians who desire to inject God into the constitution.

In the declaration, from which freedom sprang, *"nature and nature's god"* are referred to. In the 2nd and 3rd paragraphs the *natural rights of man* are specified, such as *life, liberty and the pursuit of happiness.* The king is spoken of as being unworthy to be "the head of a *civilized* nation," nothing being said as to whether he was the head, or worthy to be, of a *Christian* one.

In appealing to their British brethren, the declaration says the appeal is "made to their *native* justice and magnanimity." All reference to religion and Christianity or God's commands are left out. This was for the very good reason that for 1700 years religion had battled against progress, against justice, against magnanimity, against the rights of man. And in the concluding sentence the signers mutually pledge each other to its support ignoring all appeals to God.

In the constitution of 1787 the preamble declares that the instrument was made for union, for justice, for tranquility and defence, the general good and liberty. Art. VI says no religious test as a qualification for office shall ever be required, and the 1st Amendment prohibits an establishment of religion or restraint of its free exercise.

The great Theosophical Adepts in looking around the world for a mind through which they could produce in America the reaction which was then needed, found in England, Thomas Paine. In 1774 they influenced him, through the help of that worthy Brother Benjamin Franklin, to come to America. He came here and was the main instigator of the separation of the Colonies from the British Crown. At the suggestion of Washington, Franklin, Jefferson and other Freemasons, whose minds through the teachings of the symbolic degrees of masonry were fitted to reason correctly, and to reject theological conservation, he wrote "Common Sense," which was the torch to the pile whose blaze burned away the bonds between England and America. For *"Common Sense"* he was often publicly thanked. George Washington wrote September 10th, 1783, to Paine: "I shall be exceedingly happy to see you. Your presence may remind Congress of your past services to this country, and if it is in my power to impress them, command my best exertion with freedom, as they will be rendered cheerfully by one who entertains a lively sense of the importance of your works." And again in June 1784, in a letter to Madison, Washington says: "Can nothing be done in our assembly for poor Paine? Must the merits and services of 'Common Sense' continue to glide down the stream of time unrewarded by this country? His writings certainly have had a powerful effect upon the public mind. Ought they not then to meet an adequate return?"[1]

In "The Age of Reason" which he wrote in Paris several years after, Paine says: "I saw, or at least I thought I saw, a *vast scene opening itself to the world* in the affairs of America; and it appeared to me that unless the Americans changed the plan they were then pursuing and declared themselves independent, they would not only involve themselves in a multiplicity of new difficulties, but shut out the prospect that was *then offering itself to mankind through their means.*" Further on he says: "There are two distinct classes of thoughts: those produced by reflection, and those *that bolt into the mind of their own accord.* I have always made it a rule to treat these voluntary visitors with civility, and it is *from them I have acquired all the knowledge that I have.*"

These "voluntary visitors" were injected into his brain by the Adepts, Theosophists. Seeing that a new order of ages was about to commence and that there was a new chance for freedom and the brotherhood of man, they laid before the eye of Thomas Paine—who they knew could be trusted to stand almost alone with the lamp of truth in his hand amidst others who in "times that tried men's souls" quaked with fear—a "vast scene opening itself to Mankind in the affairs of America." The result was the Declaration, the Constitution for America. And as if to give point to these words and to his declaration that he saw this vast scene opening itself, this new order of ages, the design of the reverse side of the U. S. great seal is a pyramid whose capstone is removed with the blazing eye in a triangle over it dazzling the sight; above it are the words "the heavens approve," while underneath appears the startling sentence "a new order of ages."

That he had in his mind's eye a new order of ages we cannot doubt

---

[1] *Writings of George Washington,* 1782-1785, Vol. 10, p. 393. Series edited by Jared Sparks, Boston, Little Brown & Co. 1853. See also Jared Sparks' *Correspondence of the American Revolution,* etc. . . . Vol. IV, pp. 71-73.

upon reading in his "Rights of Man," Part 2, [Introduction]: "No beginning could be made in Asia, Africa, or Europe, to reform the political condition of man . . . She (America) made a stand, not for herself alone, but for the world, and looked beyond the advantage she could receive." In Chap. 4, "The case and circumstances of America present themselves as in the beginning of a world . . . there is a morning of reason rising apon men in the subject of Government that has not appeared before."[2]

The design 'of the seal' was not an accident, but was actually in-tended to symbolize the building and firm founding of a new order of ages. It was putting into form the idea which by means of a "voluntary visitor" was presented to the mind of Thomas Paine of a vast scene opening itself, the beginning in America of "a new order of ages." That side of the seal has never been cut or used, and at this day the side in use has not the sanction of law. In the spring of 1841, when Daniel Webster was Secretary of State, a new seal was cut, and instead of the eagle holding in his sinister claw 13 arrows as intended, he holds only six. Not only was this change unauthorized, but the cause for it is unknown.[3] When the other side is cut and used, will not the new order of ages have actually been established?

More then is claimed for the Theosophical Adepts than the chang-ing of baser metal into gold, or the possession of such a merely ma-terial thing as the elixir of life. They watch the progress of man and help him on in his halting flight up the steep plane of progress. They hovered over Washington, Jefferson, and all the other brave free-masons who dared to found a free Government in the West, which could be pure from the dross of dogmatism; they cleared their minds, inspired their pens and left upon the great seal of this mighty nation the memorial of their presence.

NEW YORK,
June 25th, 1883.

AN EX-ASIATIC

---

[2][See Vol. II, pp. 401; 428-29 and 453 *The Writings of Thomas Paine,* collected and edited by Moncure Conway, New York, G. P. Putnam's Sons, 1894. —*Comp.*]

[3][See U.S. State Dept. archives.]

[LECTURES OF MR. JUDGE IN INDIA]

A Lecture at Bombay

"Theosophy and the Destiny of India," delivered on July 18, 1884.

[The Theosophist, Vol. V, Supplement to September,
1884, p. 128)]

Mr. Judge, the latest Theosophical arrival from America, gave his first public lecture in Bombay this evening before a crowded audience in the hall of the Framjee Cowasjee Institute. The subject chosen was, *"Theosophy and the Destiny of India."* Mr. Judge began by saying that, born of Christian parents, he very early saw that Christianity was inadequate to his moral aspirations and was unable to solve the many doubts and difficulties which perpetually rose before his mind. Led by an irresistible desire to find out the truth, he turned his thoughts to the religions of the East. And how were the labors of himself and his friends rewarded? The most superficial examination convinced them that their fables buried beneath the outward shell a code of morality far superior to any that the Bible has to offer, and that this inculcated a course of conduct based on *good thoughts, good words* and *good deeds.* It was to this desire to find elsewhere what the lecturer vainly sought in his own country, that the Theosophical Society owes its birth. The first public act of importance was the cremation, before the eyes, so to speak of America and Europe, of the body of Baron de Palm. Since then, Theosophy and the Theosophical Society have become known in America. In Europe, too, the ridicule which greeted its infant days, is fast dying out, if it has not ceased altogether, and at this moment the Society is exercising a considerable influence on the intellectual and scientific thought of the West. Men of mark in England, if they do not all belong to the Society, are yet in very active sympathy with its objects. Theosophical thought has moreover affected the current literature of Europe, as witness that wonderful book, *"The Occult World"* by Mr. Sinnett, *Esoteric Buddhism,* by the same author (both already within fourth and fifth editions and read with avidity by thousands) and *"Mr. Isaacs"* by F. Marion Crawford; which last Mr. Judge described as an essentially theosophical novel, being an attempt to put some prominent Theosophical truth in a popular form. Speaking of the Society's avowed objects, that which related to the so-called supernatural phenomena, the lecturer did not think it necessary or desirable to dwell upon at length. Not because he disbelieved in phenomena, but because it was impossible to convince every one of the genuineness by ocular demonstration. As regards the first object, universal brotherhood, he remarked that it was really the most important, and he hoped that the disarmament of the world, if still distant, was not, judging from the signs of the times, an impossible or improbable occurrence.

The West and What India Can Give It

[Summary of Mr. Judge's Lecture at Poona, July 23, 1884]

[*The Theosophist*, Vol. V, Supplement to September, 1884, pp. 128-29]

THE POONA THEOSOPHICAL SOCIETY

Mr. William Q. Judge (from America) arrived at Poona from Bombay on the evening of 20th July, when he was received at the station by several members of the Poona Branch. On the evening of the 23rd July, he gave a lecture at the Poona Town Hall on *"The West and what India can give it."* There were over 300 persons present in the Hall, and the lecture was heard with great attention and created an extremely favorable impression, as Mr. Judge is an excellent speaker. He gave a brief description of life in America, particularly with reference to the education and prospects of young men in that country, and pointed out how the West had progressed in material civilization—a part of which India would do well to follow, but other portions of Western civilization would prove injurious to this country where the intellectual part of the brain seemed to be more developed than the part referring to material progress. He said that this country had an immense store of learning in religion, philosophy and certain sciences called psychical, and that if those stores were unearthed and properly brought to light, they would be the means of giving to humanity the principles of that one true religion which is the highest science and the highest philosophy; that the destiny of India was to teach the people of the West spirituality, and that the learned sons of India ought to work in that direction to rehabilitate themselves in the eyes of the whole world, which would then look up towards India with the respect which it has the means to command.

Rao Bahadur Mahadev Govind Ranade, in thanking the lecturer for his eloquent, practical and instructive address, made a long speech, in the course of which he gave prominence to the energy of the Founders of the Theosophical Society, who, he said, had promoted the cause of the Society with marvellous rapidity and that that was the sort of energy which the sons of India ought to emulate. He said that he knew of no one amongst the Hindus of the present generation in the city of Poona that were worthy to sit by the side of these Founders who had so unselfishly worked to promote a good cause.

Mr. Mahadev Moreshvar Kunte, who occupied the chair, spoke some-what to the same effect, and said that the rising generation of scholars were ignorant of the beauties of the old literature of India, and that an effort should be made to enlighten the young men about the excellencies of their religion.

In the course of his remarks he said that he had translated some part of Patanjali's Yoga philosophy, and he wondered that Europeans from distant places had sent for it. He said that some copies were sent for from Corfu. Mr. Kunte ought to know that there is a Theosophical Society at Corfu, and some of the members there, owing to the light thrown upon such subjects by our Society, went to the trouble of ordering out his book; otherwise very few would have thought of his book in that distant place.

There have been by this time several lectures in connection with Theosophy in this place and the young men are always glad to hear these subjects discussed in an intelligent manner. Slowly and imper-ceptibly they are being imbued with correct ideas about their literature; and that is a positive gain.

Navroji D. Khandalavala,
Pres., Poona T.S.

"Theosophy and the Destiny of India,"

[Summary of Mr. Judge's Lecture at Secunderabad on July 29, 1884]

[*The Theosophist*, Vol. VI, Supplement to October,
1884, pp. 141-47]

Mr. W. Q. Judge arrived at Secunderabad on the 29th of July. He
delivered the same evening a lecture at the Mahboob College Hall,
the subject being "Theosophy and the Destiny of India." After he was
formally introduced to the audience by Mr. C. Sabapathy Iyer, B.A.,
B.L., he, in an eloquent manner, addressed the audience, numbering
more than 500 persons of all nationalities, castes and creeds, in words
to the following effect:—

He stated that he had come all the way from America, to help in the
work of the Theosophical Society. He said that, as the organization
of the Society in New York was made under the auspices of the ven-
erable Mahatmas, the Theosophical Society really had its rise in India,
or, as he called, "The Land of Mysteries." He gave a short and in-
interesting account of the circumstances under which it was organized,
and said he was one of the founders with Madame H. P. Blavatsky
and Colonel H. S. Olcott. While describing, in general terms, the
continent to which he belonged, and more particularly the country
where the Society was first organized, he said that *freedom of thought*
was one of the best privileges enjoyed by this place more than any
other, perhaps, England excepted—freedom brought about by the
people receiving *free education* up to a certain standard, so as to enable them to find employment congenial to their tastes. He impressed
upon the minds of the public the fact that *freedom of thought* led men
to practice Universal Brotherhood, to some extent, in the same way as
persons engaged in trading transactions, cultivate a kind of brotherhood with persons in foreign countries, forgetting the artificial differences imposed by caste, creed and color. He said that the country
always known as The Union, but now called The United States, is a
proof of the possibility of such a union: the Americans being free in
mind and in action, each one had his own mode of belief in speculative
affairs and consequently, though America is called a Christian country, the Americans having broken the shackles of the theological creed
of the country, embraced different faiths. He gave a brief account of

the rise and progress of Spiritualism and of the strength of its followers. He went on to say that he himself was one of those who believed in the facts of Spiritualism, or more properly spiritism, and was present at many of the spiritualistic *seances,* and further, that while he felt convinced of the truth of the astounding phenomena exhibited through the agency of the mediums, he disconnected himself from the institution, finding that there was something more in spiritism, which called for an investigation, and for which purpose he turned to the investigation of truths contained in Aryan literature which the Theosophical Society recommends every honest truth-seeker to study. Theosophy, he said, is "as old as the hills," but the Theosophical Society was of later growth. He made reference to the existence of Theosophists in England in more remote times and Rosicrucians and Kabalists all over Europe, all practicing Universal Brotherhood in the circles to which they severally belonged, and trying to discover the laws of the Universe. He gave the literal meaning of Theosophy as derived from two Greek words *Theos* (God), and *Sophia* (wisdom or knowledge), and he said that since God includes the Universe, the object of the Theosophical Society is to study the laws of the Universe, so that Pantheists, Deists and Theists could easily belong to the Society. One of those laws, he said, is Universal Brotherhood and in illustration of this fact, be pointed out that the laws of the Universe or the laws of Nature being just and unchangeable, the sun shines equally upon the just and the unjust, the selfish and the unselfish, the good and the wicked, the richest and the poorest, and in the same manner, the rain, instead of falling upon any particular person, falls equally upon all men, thus proving that the laws of Nature are impartial, though men, from king down to the beggar, may try their utmost to infringe such laws. On the strength of this, he asserted that the laws of Nature require Universal Brotherhood which the Theosophical Society declares to be its first and chief object.

He went on defining the second object of the Society and explained satisfactorily to the audience how "Modern" science has been found defective in treating questions on *Man, his origin* and *his destiny,* and how well the literature of the East offers a complete solution to those problems—problems which have always engrossed the attention of the intellectual classes in the different parts of the globe and on which speculations have been busy. While rejoicing in the fact that the Westerners have already begun to appreciate the literature, philosophies and sciences of the East, and that the persons who would have received the benefit of education in those branches in Eastern schools are actually engaged in translating them for the good of the public, he regretted to find that the translations are not always genuine, and that, for reasons which must appear quite plain to every Indian, the translators themselves could not help their being otherwise, since they did not receive a technical education in the different schools of philosophy and sciences, etc. He maintained that, for a person to translate works on subjects which are foreign to his land, it is necessary that he should, besides receiving a technical education, thoroughly understand the mental action and mode of expression of the people who produced them, so that, in translating them, he may not mistake the letter for the spirit, as is the case in the writings of Professor Max Müller and others. These translations, he explained, far from enlightening the readers on matters of doubt, serve only to increase confusion and to influence their minds with a belief that such philosophies are so very vague that they cannot be true. He further pointed out that, in all Eastern literature, each subject has two aspects, the exoteric or superficial, and esoteric or concealed, and that Professor Max Müller and others have tried to give only the exoteric significance of the subjects they had translated, forgetting that the ancients had left their writings in allegories, riddles and parables. He therefore hoped that the Indians knowing that they have the key to unravel the mysteries of their land, will set themselves to work, heart and soul, in the mine of truth without looking for any light from without.

He then formulated the third object of the Society. He commenced by saying that every man has psychical powers latent in him, in the same way as he has physical powers, and that such powers develop in proportion to the training which the several organs receive. He gave numerous illustrations in proof of the existence of these powers and said that *mesmerism* amply testifies to the same.

He said that, while persons who have made mesmerism their special subject of research, are spoken of in very high terms by all men in consequence of the powers which they have cultivated, it is nothing to be wondered at if the Mahatmas are accredited with extraordinary powers—powers which have been acquired after a process of training extending over years, which requires patience, perseverance, unselfishness and, above all, a strong will. He, in referring the hearers to the Eastern literature which teems with the works of Mahatmas and Rishis, etc., said, that if they would only cultivate their psychical powers, they could also, in course of time, become Mahatmas themselves, and was glad that the Society's third and last object was to promote enquiry in this direction and thereby to bring about this end.

He next proceeded to the second part of the lecture, *i. e.,* "The Destiny of India." He said that India, in spite of the frequent conquest by various nations, at different periods, had ever remained the same, preserving its literature, religions, laws and customs in their entirety. He referred to the vast amount of intellectual progress made by the Hindus, or rather the Indians, in very remote ages, and to the existing literature, sciences, philosophies, Vedas and Shastras, etc., which characterize such progress. He wished it to be understood that the existing works are only a few of those that had survived the fury of the conquerors and which had been carefully concealed from them at the time, at great sacrifice. He stated, and rightly too, that the mere fact that India, notwithstanding the frequent invasions she had been subjected to, had not changed materially her religions, laws, manners and customs, showed great moral strength and pointed to its destiny, which *always was* to preserve this great mine of truth and to give the West and the world the system of philosophy, religion and science that it very much needs. He detailed the progress which the Theosophical Society has made since its organization in almost all the places in India and, in fact, all over the world, with some exceptions; and said that most of the scientific men, far from discountenancing the objects which this movement has undertaken to propagate, have the more willingly joined, convinced as they are of the necessity for the formation of such a Society in the interests of humanity, and of the truths contained in Eastern literature.

The Chairman then said that the Theosophical Society has already done a world of good to India and to all places where its branches existed, and that it is making vigorous efforts to regenerate India in every sense of the word. He quoted some passages from the Vedas and the Upanishads and explained their exoteric and esoteric meanings. In doing so, he pointed out clearly how Hindu works on Theology and Religion have been entirely misunderstood and misrepresented by the Westerners, and how the idea of gods has always been laughed at. In proof of this, he stated that the events recorded in Mahabharata, Ramayana and several other works have, with the exception of a comparatively few, been mistaken by the people of the West for real facts, not knowing that they were written in allegories and that the several personages therein represented were so many forces in man which had been at war with the spiritual element in him. He referred to the incorrect translations by the Sanskrit professors of the West, and rejoiced that the Theosophical Society has undertaken to work in right earnest for the revival of Eastern literature, religions and sciences, etc., which have hitherto been entirely neglected by the enlightened Hindus so called. He, in conclusion, said that he perfectly sympathized with the Theosophical movement, knowing that it is for the good of India and of the world and hoped that all who call themselves Aryans, Hindus or Indians will heartily cooperate in the gigantic work which the Theosophical Society has undertaken to accomplish.

In the evening Mr. Judge made experiments in Psychometry with ostrich eggs and old Indian coins. The attention of the members was next directed to Crystal reading. Mr. A. took a fine Ceylon crystal belonging to Brother P. Iyaloo Naidu, and after gazing at it for about ten minutes, perceived a white cloud and then a large fierce tiger coming out of a jungle. The animal had such a fierce appearance and was so real to Mr. A. that he threw the crystal violently from him, suddenly exclaiming, "a tiger, a tiger." He had forgotten his surroundings and thought he actually saw the tiger. It was with great difficulty that he was persuaded to try again; but though he gazed at it for some time, he said he couldn't trace the tiger he had seen before, and that the fear which its appearance had occasioned made him unsteady and unfit to continue the experiment.

On the next evening Mr. Judge delivered another lecture at the Mahaboob College, Secunderbad, at 6 p.m., the subject being *"Is there a soul in man?"* Mr. N. M. Duraisami Pillai, B.A., who presided on the occasion, gave a very able speech by way of preamble and introduced Mr. Judge to the audience. Mr. Judge began by asking why such a question was needed, and said that although it was universally admitted that man has a soul, and although the burden of proof was not on him to prove it, yet, the address was needed, because many young untrained minds were being led away by the sophistry of persons who had only a superficial knowledge of what the West really believed, to think that there is no soul; supposing themselves thus to be imitators of Western progress. He regretted very much that the young Indians have become the disciples of Mr. Bradlaugh without studying deeply the literature, philosophies and sciences which their own ancestors had bequeathed to their children and without a due investigation of the truths therein contained. Science, he said, is a book of Nature, and is ever changing without a firm footing on which to stand. He gave several instances to show how people in all countries were at first slow to believe facts founded on sciences, and how, after lapse of time, the very facts which they once refused to believe, have afterwards been accepted as scientific facts. He also made allusions to the several persecutions which attended the authors of such discoveries. Western science, he stated, is yet on the road to progress and is consequently incomplete, there being several facts which cannot be explained away by science. In illustration of this statement, he said that the exact functions performed by the organ called the *spleen*, have not been fully defined by the faculties in medicine, beyond stating that it is an essential organ in a man's body. He asked whether Western science, in such an infantile state, is in a position to decide, once for all, the question of the existence or non-existence of the soul. Those who denied soul had to prove their position, because there was a vast mass of testimony and belief in it from remote ages and the disbelievers were in the minority.

He defined soul according to Hindu philosophy and esoteric doctrine, and read interesting passages from "The Theosophist" and Draper's *Conflict between Religion and Science* to illustrate the nature of the soul. He showed a vast and hoary tradition of the soul's existence in all times and places, and also that all the accepted authorities, Greeks, Romans and all else, including Christians, declared in favor of soul. He stated that Plato and Aristotle, the greatest philosophers who really founded Western Philosophy, and Cicero, the greatest orator, believed in soul. He read a passage from Draper's *Conflict between Religion and Science*, wherein Al Ghazâlî, the most learned among the Mohammedans, gives the nature of soul as understood by him and his co-religionists, and then showed that the investigation by means of Spiritualism, Mesmerism, Psychometry and kindred subjects, proved the existence of soul. He said that the science of soul had its own rules, and he could not expect to pursue the science by ordinary methods used with material objects.

He referred to the first object of the Theosophical Society, and invited all the persons who have the welfare of India at heart, and who wish to redeem India from her present morally degraded condition, to give their best assistance in promoting the same which, though it may appear a very difficult task, he said, can yet be accomplished by united efforts alone. He spoke at length about the Mahatmas, their powers and their modes of communicating to their *chelas,* and said that he was fully convinced of their existence and had heard several reliable accounts from persons who were the *chelas* of certain Mahatmas.

He concluded his lecture by refuting some malicious and ill-founded charges against the Society which were published and circulated in pamphlets by some *self-opinionated* and *narrow-minded* atheists and Christians, and showing how the Theosophical movement has been *wilfully* misrepresented, and how utterly ignorant the authors of those publications were of the declared objects of the Society and of the progress which it has, within the last five years, made in India. He said, with great emphasis, that, instead of the Society "going to a smash," as has been *kindly* represented by those *Truth-seekers,* it is growing stronger and stronger every day, forming branches all over the World, and that it is destined to be so *for ever and ever,* no matter whatever the opposition.

The Chairman next addressed the audience and seemed to fully endorse the views of Mr. Judge.

He received from the members of the branch the following Address:

Dear Brother, Mr. Judge,—It gives us the greatest pleasure to have to address you this evening, as the time for taking a farewell leave of us, has well nigh arrived.

It is no exaggeration if we say that we have been very much benefited by your advent to this station, and you have awakened in us a desire to further the interests of our Society in every possible way. We sincerely thank you for the most interesting instructions you have given us in Mesmerism and Psychometry, and hope that you will continue to aid us in this way, knowing that our Society is yet in its infant state and the members themselves in a state fit and ready to receive.

In conclusion, we again offer our sincere respects and obligations for the readiness with which you have condescended to pay this place a visit.

C. V. Loganada Moodr
Joint Secretary
Theosophical Society, Secunderabad
16th August 1884

[Mr. Judge's visit to Hyderabad was related by the secretary of the Hyderabad T. S., mentioning some experiments in psychometry. Included below with Mr. Naidu's account is a brief note on the American visitor's stopover at the Gooty Theosophical Branch.—*Comp.*]

MR. WILLIAM Q. JUDGE AT HYDERABAD

[*The Theosophist*, Vol. V, Supplement to September, 1884, p. 129.]

Mr. Wm. Q. Judge, Joint Recording Secretary of the Parent Theosophical Society, arrived at Hyderabad on July 25th. He was received by the members of the Society and escorted by the President Mr. Dorabjee to the lodging arranged for his stay, where he received many visitors and discussed philosophical questions with them.

On the 27th, Mr. Judge made some experiments in psychometry and gave some instructions to a few Theosophists who appeared capable of continuing the experiments and developing their powers. Among the experiments in psychometry were the following:

A small copper Indian coin was given to a member of the Secunderabad Branch, who held it to his head, and soon described a street, with palm trees, looking like Southern Indian scenery. The shops were shut and only a dog could be seen for some time, when a man appeared. This scene persisted before him for 20 minutes, disappearing when the coin was moved along the forehead, but always reappearing when it touched the sensitive spot. No one knew where the coin was from, until the Collector of Hyderabad said it was a Southern Indian coin.

Another member took the seal of a gentleman present, and holding it to his forehead began to describe the house of the owner with tank surroundings, etc., which he had never before seen or heard described. Many other interesting trials were made, and a record is to be kept in Hyderabad and Secunderabad of all such experiments for future publication.

In the evening of the 29th, Mr. Judge was conducted to the spacious hall of Mr. Shapoorji, a well-known Parsee gentleman here. The hall was filled with an audience representing all sects here. There were many well-informed European, Parsee, Mohammedan and other gentlemen present. Mr. Sabapathy Aiyah Garoo, a well-known member of the Madras Bar, was voted to the chair. He opened the meeting with a short and appropriate speech and introduced the American Brother to the audience.

Mr. Judge commenced his lecture by giving a short account of the conflict between Religion and Science; whence came man and whither he is to go? These momentous problems, he said, Western science is not yet able to solve satisfactorily. Spiritualistic phenomena, which then ushered themselves in the West, seemed at first to answer the purpose, but are now found to be not able to satisfy the spirit of enquiry which the modern science has kindled in the breast of man. He explained how the Theosophical Society came to be organized at New York under the prompting of the Mahatmas and why it was established in that country and why its Headquarters were subsequently transferred to India. He thus enlightened the audience for an hour, and then brought his interesting discourse to a close, by observing that the ancient books and wisdom of Aryans were able to sufficiently answer the many and various questions which man meets with, in his endeavors to find out his goal, and to ascertain whether there is a futurity or not for him after death. The audience gave a calm and attentive hearing to his beautiful speech.

The Chairman then thanked the speaker for his able exposition, and added that as Theosophy was not sectarian, no man could have any objection to join the Society whose object is one of enquiry.

After a vote of thanks to the Chairman and the speaker, the meeting was dissolved. Mr. Judge suggested and discussed plans for the future work of the Branch, and among those that were adopted are the following:

1. Captain Raghunath and Messrs. Bheemajee Rowjee and Hanoomuntha Row to continue their studies and experiments in Mesmerism.

2. Two or three others to take up the subjects of Psychometry and Crystal reading.

3. The Brothers Monlve Mansab Ali and Abdul Razack to assist those Mohammedan Brothers who do not know English, by translating into the Urdu language, some of the useful and instructive articles found in *The Theosophist*..

Mr. Judge's affability, patience, and self-denial have made great impression on our minds, and our Branch President found very great pleasure in accompanying him wherever he went and seemed to enjoy his company much.

P. IYALOO NAIDU,
Secretary.
HYDERABAD THEOSOPHICAL SOCIETY,
2nd August 1884.

———

THE GOOTY THEOSOPHICAL SOCIETY

Mr. William Q. Judge, our American brother, arrived here from Adoni on the evening of the 4th instant. That evening was spent in discussion upon the Eastern and Western social system and on hearing suggestions regarding work in the Branch . . .[1]

B. P. NARASIMMIAH, Sec'y.
7th August 1884.

———

Are the "Arabian Nights" all Fiction?

[*The Theosophist*, Vol. VI, October, 1884, pp. 8-9]

For many years it has been customary to regard that collection of interesting stories called "The Arabian Nights," as pure fiction arising out of Oriental brains at a time when every ruler had his story-teller to amuse him or to put him to sleep. But many a man who has down in his heart believed in the stories he heard in his youth about fairies and ghosts, has felt a revival of his young fancies upon perusing these tales of prodigies and magic. Others, however, have laughed at them as pure fables, and the entire scientific world does nothing but preserve contemptuous silence.

The question here to be answered by men of science is how did such ideas arise? Taking them on their own ground, one must believe that with so much smoke there must at one time have been some fire. Just as the prevalence of a myth—such as the Devil or Serpent myth—over large numbers of people or vast periods of time points to the fact that there must have been something, whatever it was, that gave rise to the idea.

---

[1] [The above summary mentioned the same lecture delivered in Bombay and Secunderabad.—*Comp.*]

In this enquiry our minds range over that portion of the world which is near the Red Sea, Arabia and Persia, and we are brought very close to places, now covered with water, that once formed part of ancient Lemuria. The name Red Sea may have arisen from the fact that it was believed really to cover hell: and its lower entrance at the island of Perim is called "Babel Mandeb," or "the Gate of Hell." This Red Sea plays a prominent part in the Arabian Nights tales and has some significance. We should also recollect that Arabia once had her men of science, the mark of whose minds has not yet been effaced from our own age. These men were many of them magicians, and they learned their lore either from the Lemurian adepts, or from the Black Magicians of the other famous land of Atlantis.

We may safely conclude that the Arabian Nights stories are not all pure fiction, but are the faint reverberations of a louder echo which reached their authors from the times of Lemuria and Atlantis.

Solomon is now and then mentioned in them, and Solomon, wherever he was, has always been reckoned as a great adept. The Jewish Cabala and Talmud speak of Solomon with great reverence. His power and the power of his seal—the interlaced triangles—constantly crop up among the other magical processes adverted to in these tales. And in nearly all cases where he is represented as dealing with wicked genii, he buried them in the Red Sea. Now if Solomon is a Jewish King far away in Palestine, how did he get down to the Red Sea, and where is there any mention made of his travelling at all? These genii were elemental spirits, and Solomon is merely a name standing for the vast knowledge of magic arts possessed by adepts at a time buried in the darkness of the past. In one tale, a fisherman hauls up a heavy load, which turns out to be a large *iron* pot, with a metal cover, on which was engraved Solomon's Seal. The unlucky man opened the pot, when at once a vapor rose out of it that spread itself over the whole heavens at first, then condensed again into a monstrous form who addressed the fisher saying that ages before he had been confined there by Solomon; that after two hundred years he swore he would make rich the man lucky enough to let him out; after five hundred years that he would reward his liberator with power; but after one thousand years of captivity he would kill the one who should free him. Then he ordered the man to prepare for death. The fisherman, however, said he doubted that the genii had really been in the pot as he was too large. To prove that he had been, the spirit immediately assumed the vaporous condition and slowly with spiral motion sank into the iron pot again, when at once the fisherman clapped on the cover and was about to cast him back into the sea. The djin then begged for mercy and agreed to serve the man and not to kill him, whereupon he was releasd.

Many persons will laugh at this story. But no one who has seen the wonders of spiritualism, or who knows that at this day there are many persons in India, as well as elsewhere who have dealings with elemental spirits that bring them objects instantaneously, etc., will laugh before reflecting on the circumstances.

Observe that the pot in which he was confined was made of metal, and that the talismanic seal was on the cover. The metal prevented him from making magnetic connection for the purpose of escaping, and the seal on the cover barred that way. There were no marks on the sides of the pot. His spreading himself into a vast vapor shows that he was one of the elementals of the airy kingdom—the most powerful and malignant: and his malignancy is shown in the mean, ungrateful oath he took to destroy whomsoever should be his liberator. His spreading into vapor, instead of at once springing out of the pot, refers to his invisibility, for we see that in order to enter it he was compelled to assume his vaporous state, in which he again put himself into the pot.

In another story we see a young man visiting an elemental of the nature of a Succubus, who permits him now and then to go out and perform wonders. But the entrance to her retreat is unseen and kept invisible to others. In India there are those who are foolish enough to make magnetic connection with elementals of this class, by means of processes which we will not detail here. The elemental will then at your wish instantaneously produce any article which the operator may have touched, no matter how far away it may be or how tightly locked up. The consequences of this uncanny partnership are very injurious to the human partner. The records of spiritualism in America will give other cases of almost like character, sufficient to show that a compact can be entered into between a human being and an intelligence or force outside of our sensuous perceptions.

In other stories various people have power over men and animals, and the forces of nature. They change men into animals and do other wonders. When they wish to cause the metamorphosis, they dash a handful of water into the unfortunate's face crying: "Quit that form of man and assume the form of a dog." The terrible Maugraphy is a Black Magician, such as can now be found in Bhutan, who had changed many persons, and the story of his destruction shows that his life and power as well as his death lay in the nasty practices of Black Magic. When the figure and the talisman were destroyed he was also. The white magician has no talisman but his Atman, and as that cannot be destroyed, he is beyond all fear.

But this paper is already too long. We are not forcing a conclusion when we say that these admirable and amusing tales are not *all* fiction.

There is much nonsense in them, but they have come to us from the very land—now bleak and desolate—where at one time the fourth race men held sway and dabbled in both White and Black Magic.

W. Q. J.

Thought Transference or Mind Reading

[*The Theosophist*, Vol. VI, Supplement to November, 1884. p. 147]

A writer in *The Saturday Review*, in 1882, said: "We had thought we had heard the last of thought reading."[1] It seems, however, that he was mistaken, albeit he was then expressing the current scientific opinion, as more definitely expressed by the senior physician of Westminster Hospital, who said he was amazed that any one with the slightest pretensions to scientific knowledge would have the hardihood to put forth any evidence in favor of thought reading.[2] The cycle moves on however, and dogmatic scientists are powerless to arrest it or to prevent its bringing to light what have been called "exploded fallacies." There are many ways of transferring thought and of reading minds. The clairvoyant can see and thus read your thoughts; but we cannot all be clairvoyants. The adept can read any one's thought, and with ease transfer what thought he desires to another brain; but "the adept is the efflorescence of his age." The mesmeriser can transfer a thought to his subject's mind, but just now we are not treating of mesmerism.

In 1882, Professor Barrett, of the Royal College of Science for Ireland, and others, presented to the Psychical Research Society, a report on this subject, from which we quote—"Is there or is there not any existing or attainable evidence, that can stand fair physiological criticism, to support a belief that a vivid impression or a distinct idea in one mind can be communicated to another mind, without the intervening help of the recognized organs of sensation [perception?].[3] And if such evidence be found, is the impression derived from a rare or partially developed and hitherto unrecognized sensory organ, or has the

---

1 [*The Saturday Review*, June 3, 1882, p. 697 of V. 53, London, 1882: "We hoped some time ago, . . . that we had heard the last of all the nonsense about what is called "Thought-Reading ."—*Comp.*]

2 *Nineteenth Century*, July, 1882. London. [In its early years (1877-1908) this journal was edited by James Knowles and eventually became: *Twentieth Century.—Comp.*]

3 *Proceedings of the Society for Psychical Research*, Vol. I, [1882], p. 13. London, Trübner & Co., 1883.

mental percept been evoked directly without any antecedent sense-percept?" There is plenty of such evidence as Professor Barret calls for. Thought reading and transference are as old as man. Even little children have a game in which one goes out of a room so that the others may select a word of which they are to think intently. The absent one returns, stands among the others, all of whom in silence are thinking hard of say, "trees." In a few minutes the experimenter suddenly thinks of *trees* and shouts it out. This is thought transference. The investigation of this subject may be made interesting. The researches of the Psychical Research Society are of great interest, and were pursued by the scientific men, who formed its committees, with pleasure as well as ardor. In 1875, one Dr. Corey made experiments in America, which were thus described in the *Detroit Medical Review*: "Bringing himself into direct physical contact with some person, Mr. Corey was enabled to discover objects which that person had secreted, and to select from a multitude of objects the one upon which the willer was intent. He usually placed the other person's hand upon his forehead."

The person who is to make the experiment ought to sit down quietly. Another person, who sits in front takes hold of the hands of the first, looks intently into the eyes and concentrates his thoughts upon an object or a place or a person: such as, upon "dog," "the palace," "the temple," a geological strata, a flower, or what not. In a few minutes then he asks the sitter, "What flower do I think of, or what place, or what person here, or what ornament or thing in this room, or which King of England or what geological strata," and so on. It will be found that in the majority of cases the answers will be correct, without fraud and without collusion.

Any company of persons can verify this, and if some of our members pursue this line of inquiry, which was not above the minds of some of the great scientific lights of England, reports of the experiments furnished to *The Theosophist* will be of great interest and value.

Another way is to blindfold the subject. Then take his hand, and draw yourself upon a piece of paper a simple figure or a face, no matter what. The subject then repeats with a pencil that which comes before his mind. Many experiments of this character have been made with great success, in some instances it was seen that the subject *reversed* the picture, or turned it topsy turvy.

Another mode is for the subject to remain seated and blindfolded while one of the party goes outside and draws a simple figure on a piece of paper, concentrating his mind upon it for a few minutes so as to get a vivid picture of it before his mental eye. Then he returns and concentrates himself upon the sitter who takes up pencil and paper and reproduces what he sees mentally. This is all done without contact. Many curious and startlingly accurate results may be obtained.

In making these drawings, it is best to use a soft pencil, drawing the lines very coarsely or boldly, so that you may produce upon your own mind a very strong impression of the form. In this way your thought, which is actually dynamic, will the more easily affect the sitter.

A third and easiest mode I will mention is to sit quietly with some-one who is to think steadily, while you rapidly relate what you find passing through your brain. It can be done either with or without contact. Contact with the other person of course will make it easier, but you will be surprised to find how often you report *exactly* what the other person is thinking of.

In drawing pictures, or setting down words to be guessed, it will be found much easier to concentrate the mind if a piece of paper or a blackboard be used as a background before which is placed the object to be guessed, as the contrast between the two causes a sharper image to be conveyed by the eye to the brain.

W. Q. J.

Chirognomy and Palmistry

[*The Theosophist*, Vol. VI, Supplement to December, 1884, pp. 159-60]

Chirognomy is the art of delineating character by means of the hand. One of the arts of the Gypsies of Europe is Palmistry, which is allied to Chirognomy. By means of the lines of the palm they pretend to tell the fate of the individual. Very often they make astonishing statements after having looked at your palm. Whether they do it by reasoning from the lines found therein, or by clairvoyant power, is a question. Being a strange and peculiar people living near to nature, it is very likely that clairvoyance aids them as much as anything else.

But there is no reason why from the hand the character cannot be determined; and many rules exist, easily verifiable, by which it is claimed the course of life of the man can be told.

In the West two Frenchmen, D'Arpentigny and Desbarroles, the latter still living, did much to give a certain respectability to this study.[1] In England, there are laws on the statute book, prohibiting under penalty any use of palmistry.

---

[1] *Proceedings of the Anthropological Society,* Paris, 1863, [Societé d' Anthropologie (1859) Paris.]

In that old Egyptian remnant, the *Book of Job,* which the Christians have purloined and put in their collection of sacred writings, it is said, in the Chaldean Version, Ch. 37, verse 7, "In the hands of all the sons of men God places marks that all men may know their own works." And as early as B. C. 428, the philosopher Anaxagoras taught the same views as the later Frenchmen.

If the anatomist can tell from a scale, or a single tooth or bone, just what the fish or animal looked like, the class to which it belongs, why should there be any doubt that, from the hand, the man's character can be known. Agassiz said that upon looking at a single scale he could at once see the whole fish.

In India palmistry is well known, and the memorandum is, it must be confessed, written in complete ignorance of the Hindu system. My only object is to incite inquiry, discussion, and comparison of results.

A natural division is into two parts, (*a*) the fingers, and (*b*) the palm.

The fingers are regarded as relating to intellectual life, and the palm to animal life. In the palm the blood accumulates more than in the fingers.

Smooth, pointed fingers indicate impressibility, spontaneity, love of pleasure, inspiration, want of practicability.

Knotty fingers show philosophical tendencies and practical abilities.

D'Arpentigny observed this by accident. He was a visitor at a house, where the husband delighting in science and mechanics, but whose wife did not, had a separate day for his own receptions. The wife liked art and music. D'Arpentigny went to the soirees of each and discovered that the visitors of the husband had knotty hands, while the hands of nearly all the wife's friends were smooth and pointed.

If the palm is thick and hard, animal instincts prevail; if thick and supple, egotism and sensuality are indicated. If it be hollow and firmly elastic, there is mental vigor. Of course different combinations of these peculiarities in the hand will denote differences of mixed character.

In the fingers, if the first, or end, joint is well pronounced, there is self-confidence, independence, and aptitude for the sciences; but this, in an otherwise feeble hand, shows pettiness, discontent and fault finding.

The tips of the fingers are divided into four classes, viz.: 1. spatulous or spread out; 2. square; 3. oval; 4. pointed.

In the same hand the fingers may present all these differences. One may be of one class and the others of another. If they are uniform, then the character will be an uniform one. No. 1 means activity, labor; No. 2, love of precedent and routine; Nos. 3 and 4, artistic ability, inspiration and laziness.

The thumb is a valuable index of the character. If small, then the man is irresolute and vacillating; if large, then the will is strong and the heart is governed by the reason. The palm, however, will modify this. Voltaire, whose will and reason were powerful, had enormous thumbs.

The first, or end, joint represents will; and the second, joining to the palm, reason or logic. The length or development of these are almost exactly proportional to the power of the qualities which they represent.

The root of the thumb, which constitutes a large part of the palm, indicates the presence or absence of sensual desires. If large and the joints of logic and will are also large, then the will and reason control the passions; but if those joints are small and the root large, the passions must rule. It is said that in the hands of debauchees and all lewd women, it will be found that the root is full and active, while the joints referred to are short, small and feeble.

Of course in making a judgment, one must keep in view the proportions of the whole hand and body,[2] for a small man may have joints in his thumb absolutely small but relatively large.

The 2nd finger is in general square, but if it be round, then vanity is indicated, and if the thumb be weak, frivolity. The root joint of this finger, if large, shows selfishness.

The 3rd relates to art. If it be round there is garrulity; if square, love of defined art and truth, while, if it be spatulous, there is love of action and of portrayals of art either in speech or gesture.

The little or 4th finger is related to abstract science and mathematics. This finger will be raised and disconnected from the others by those who are prone to exercise much artifice or address. In the days when great attention was paid to "deportment," it became the fashion to so raise and disconnect this finger; and it will be found in India that this pecularity is widespread.

The length of the fingers must be also taken into consideration. If they are short, the person is hasty, and one who comes to general conclusions. If they are long, then the owner is careful and attentive to detail. Des Barolles says: "Be on your guard against one who to long fingers joins the philosophical knot (or well defined first joint). He commences by a detailed investigation of your character, a knowledge of which he quickly obtains, more particularly if he possesses a thumb with a long second phalange (logic)."

---

2 [La Science de la Main by Casimir Stanislas de'Arpentigny, 2nd ed. Paris, E. Dentu, *Les Mystères de la Main* by Adrien D. Desbarrolles, 5th ed., Paris. —*Compiler.*]

Hard hands give action and strength; soft ones show love of ease. Both may be alike intellectually and yet differ essentially in habits.

Curiously enough small handed races with spatulous fingers seem to be those who produced works of colossal size. The mighty Egyptian civilization and buildings have been attributed to a small-handed people. In India this can also be seen.

The open hand shows joy, confidence and magnanimity, as well as want of secretiveness. The closed palm shows vexation, or doubt, or deceit and nearly always secretiveness. One who habitually walks with closed fingers over the thumb, will certainly be able to keep a secret and his own affairs to himself, as well as perhaps being a deceiver. It is certain that a deceitful or treacherous person will not show his palms.

As these notes are not intended to be exhaustive, and as the present publications in English are not wholly reliable in regard to the lines in the hand, by which it is said the destiny of the man may be told, I do not intend to go fully into this branch of the subject. A few references will suffice.

There are three principal lines in the palm. One runs completely around the thumb root and is called the "line of life." When strong, or double or unbroken, it indicates in general a good constitution and length of life. If there be also three lines running around the wrist, called the *Magic Bracelet*, then it is said the person will live to be nearly 100. If the line of life is broken, it indicates disease, if it occurs in one hand only; but if in both, it is said to mean early death.

The line of the heart begins at the root of the little finger, running across the palm part of the way. In Indian hands it very often runs completely into the space between the 1st and 2nd fingers, thus cutting off the 1st finger entirely.

The line of the head begins at the root of the 1st finger, joining generally the line of life with which it should form an acute angle. Its course is across the palm, seldom running farther than about 3 inches from the edge of the palm.

In many idiots there is but one line for these last two.

General rules may be laid down in the same way as regards reading the character. If the lines are strong, deep, broken, colored, lighter or interrupted, then a judgment in accordance with the modification can be given.

It is certain that there is a great deal of knowledge on this subject in India, and it is hoped it may be brought out by these suggestions, for as an index of character and consequently of fate in part, the hand of man is unequalled.

———

The Nadigranthams

[*The Theosophist*, Vol. VII, October, 1885, pp. 50-53]

The article by T. Subba Row Garu in the July *Theosophist* will be read with great interest by all Theosophists, not only because it is from his pen, but also because of the article previously written on the same subject by Col. Olcott, and called "Indian Sybilline Books." The difference between the two is, that Col. Olcott gave some extremely interesting details of a particular séance he had with a certain holder of nadigranthams. It is not stated whether the latter was the same person with whom Mr. Subba Row made his investigations in Black Town, Madras. [I have found the name of the visitor who was with our celebrated brother by the aid of a certain kind of nadi I myself possess.][1] The matters gone into in the July paper only relate to the investigation, and while they are clearly given, and seem to show conclusively that the Black Town gentleman is imposing on his public, yet they dispose only of that particular set of Nadis. It is by no means proved that no nadi is trustworthy and that at no time could they be relied on. I insist that the only conclusion to be drawn from Brother Subba Row's paper is that the Mint Street Operator has been effectually disposed of.

Now if we have any confidence in Col. Olcott, as certainly we have, then we know that in the instance given by him in the "Sybilline Books" he got hold of a genuine nadi. But even if he had in fact been imposed upon by one who previous to the appointment procured all needed facts, even that does not go any further than that particular instance. It still remains to be proved that the thing which the man in Black Town pretended to do could never be done.

Can, then, books or leaves be made or procured which may be used in the way pretended? I say that they can, and that there are two or more modes of doing it.

In the first place when Col. Olcott saw his man, if the latter had the faculty of prevision or the proper amount of clairvoyance, he could have given all the details related quite easily with the aid of a few figures, letters, or verses.

But, far better still, it is possible to cast up certain astrological

---

[1] I give here, not to be printed, the name of his friend. It was ....The Editor will say if I am correct at foot of this note. (J.) [Our correspondent has given the name correctly.—EDITOR, *The Theosophist.*]

figures to be used in certain days and hours, and for certain classes of questions from which a large number of replies and predictions can be given, that would startle the average hearer, and be true not only to the past but also to the future. And it is not an art that is so very difficult that it would take a man a very long time to learn it in order to be able to answer questions.

A large number of leaves could be prepared which would enable one to make replies to any kind of questions at once. Of course by saying *at once,* I mean at that particular sitting when the question was asked. They might be made ready for one week, or a month, or a year, or even a series of years; and it is very easy to understand why after say five years they must be changed, and also why after a whole precession of the equinoxes they would require further change— or become altogether useless.

The mode of preparing them, even if I could speak authoritatively upon it, is altogether too long to be gone into here, further than to say that it would be in accordance with certain astrological methods. Certain "houses of the heavens" must be arranged and filled in the proper way, and any one who has studied astrology will know that at the end of a solar year another set of prepared leaves would have to be used. It would be merely the using of well-known astrological rules, and instead of waiting for each question to be asked, to have ready set the houses of the heavens for a great number of hours in the day. If I had fixed upon the hour of 5 a.m. for rising, and knew my breakfast hour and the hour on which I commenced to hear questions, it would be easy enough to have ready all the astrological figures needed.

That by means of these figures predictions can be made there is no doubt. I can prove it by hundreds of instances. I will take two of a recent date.

When I was in Adyar in 1884, the question arose whether Mr. Damodar would go away at a certain time stated. Some thought he would and others that he would not. A figure for this question was erected and showed that he would not go at the time supposed, and for a certain reason. As for the reason we must leave that to him. But the fact was, that he did not go away for months after the time which had been fixed by some for his departure.

The other instance was in Paris in 1884, when a figure upon similar rules was set up regarding some letters just received from the now notorious Coulomb family. Plainly the figure said that there was a conspiracy going on in that charming circle; that it would all be *suddenly discovered,* and that it *would come to nothing.* Everything came out as predicted, notwithstanding that several Theosophists will differ from me on the latter point.

In the use of nadigranthams each sitting begins at a certain moment in time and continues a certain number of hours. Were I the reader, or nadigrantham maker, I should make say one set for the year 1885 to be used only at particular hours. Of course, then, I would never give an audience except near those hours. But if I thought it likely that I would want a greater quantity, or if I wished to be ready more quickly, then I would prepare sets fit to be used every fifteen minutes. Or, in other words, I would have ready set for use the horary astrological figures for every change of the celestial houses.

If in addition to this I knew certain mantrams, those could also be used, and thus I should have a complete and fairly reliable set of nadis.

Now then, and further, I maintain that anciently Indian astrologers had a vast quantity of astrological books and charts, and could predict the future and detail the past much better than we can. Why is it so strange that they might have devoted some time to the preparation of sets of nadigranthams on a far more elaborate and scientific plan than has been outlined?

In this utilitarian age the question is always asked, "what is the use" of anything that does not increase our wealth or add to the material comfort of the race? But considerations such as these do not, and never should, deter a philosopher from using no matter how much time in the pursuit of what seems to be a portion of truth. The ancient Indians did not hesitate because the preparation of elaborate systems apparently was not of much use or consumed much time. And I maintain, believing there are many who will support me, that the astrologers of those times knew far more than we do about these subjects, and could predict the events of a certain day or number of days with certainty. If this could be done for one day, there exists no reason why it should not be done for days to come in periods of time centuries in the future.

As to the use of the nadigranthams prepared by such astrologers only in and for certain definite districts, there can be found a perfect consonance with rules. It is well settled that parallels of latitude are subject each to different influences, and a nadigrantham set up for the city of Calcutta would not do for the city of Madras. In that case therefore there is nothing superstitious in the statement that such and such nadis must only be used in certain districts and in no others.

I cannot find in all this any strain upon faith or reason, and I maintain that real nadigranthams exist in India, and perhaps in other parts of the world. Quite likely some spurious ones are used by charlatans, who trust to luck and knowledge of human nature to enable them to earn their fees. But who has the custody of the real ones?

WILLIAM Q. JUDGE.

Theosophical Theories of the Microcosm
[*The Theosophist*, Vol. VIII, August, 1887, pp. 712-14]

The greatest schisms often come about through the supporters of one cause disputing over mere terminology. Mr. Subba Row, in his able addresses on Bhagavad Gîtâ, condemned "the sevenfold classification" which has come to be very largely accepted among Theosophists all over the world, and declared, that as that particular classification seemed to him unscientific and misleading, he preferred to adopt another. This brought out a reply which was published in *The Path*, and one which H. P. Blavatsky wrote for *The Theosophist*. As editor of the first named magazine I saw no occasion to enter into any part of the small contest, although at the time the first reply was not really on its face an argument newly propounded for the theory, but rather one pointing out possible inconsistencies in Mr. Subba Row's position. In the May *Theosophist* Mr. Subba Row goes at more length into the matter, and it seems that if his two articles are taken together a way out of the difficulty may be found.

As his articles appeal to my eyes and mind, the real difficulty seems to be, not with *any* and *all sevenfold* classifications, but with the *particular sevenfold classification* found in *Esoteric Buddhism* and other theosophical works. He has in many places given in his adherence to the number *seven* as a perfect number, but that does not necessarily bind him to the sevenfold division of *Esoteric Buddhism*. And although I have been an adherent of the Theosophical Society longer than our brother Subba Row, as well as an admirer and supporter of H. P. Blavatsky for many years and am still, yet I cannot adopt the manner in which the terms in the equation of man have been allotted by the author of *Esoteric Buddhism*. I have all along thought that that allotment was more or less tentative, but still have always believed that man—taken as a whole—could be called a sevenfold composition. While the changes of position given to the various "principles" have been going on, I have preferred to stick to the threefold division of *Body, Soul* and *Spirit*, leaving it open to me to say whether or not I would adopt a fourth—that is, the whole three together.

On page 506, May *Theosophist*, I find Mr. Subba Row saying:—
"I am yet to be convinced that the sevenfold classification we have adopted was the *real sevenfold classification of this ancient school of occultism*." (The italics are mine.) From this we must conclude that he

believes the ancient school did have a sevenfold classification, but that ours is not the same. In this—if it be his position—I agree with him. But we should never quarrel over mere words or numbers. If one should say "I believe in duality, and not in the septenary," he would be right so long as he admits that one of two making up the duad was not perfectly known to him in all its parts; for in the duality could be found every one of the seven or the nine, or the twenty-five principles into which some other philosopher chose to divide the human subject. So for the present, I say I believe in the *ternary* division, that being one more easily comprehended by the minds of this Kali-Yuga.

This brings us to the question: "Is it possible for the mind of this Yuga or perhaps of this part of it to thoroughly comprehend a psychological enumeration which includes seven numbers?" We can grasp seven easily enough in lower things, such as mathematics, the days of the week, and so on, but I doubt if the undeveloped man can, with his unregenerated mind, grasp *seven* when applied to the unknown quantities of the higher nature. The more especially is this difficult when one considers the poverty of the English language in psychological things.

It is a language that has come up out of piracy, brigandage and war. Very true that it has taken over words from almost all languages, but for what purposes? To suit the uses of nations bound on the path of self-aggrandisement, of mere money, getting, of individualism. How could European minds understand the statement that there may be an astral body and an astral shape also, each distinct from the other, when they have always known that *body* is a thing due to accretions from beef and beer? And if one were to tell them that upon approaching the hall of Brahman a point is reached where the flavor of Brahman is perceived, while at another point the glory of Brahman becomes apparent they would understand the flavor as something due to seasoning or sauce, and the glory to be a mere effulgence or wide extended fame. But it was necessary to direct their minds to the fact that there is more of man than mere body, and therefore such books as *Esoteric Buddhism, Zanoni* and others came before them. And in Mr. Sinnett's book some division had to be adopted that Western minds could grasp until they were able to go higher. But for my part I have never understood that his book was gospel truth. The great basis of our Society would be undermined by any such doctrine, just as much as his own progress would be retarded did he fancy that the views expressed by him were his own invention. In his work he has been careful to show that his teachers hold that a comprehension of numbers is coincident with a development of certain inner senses or principles in man; and as he says that our "fifth principle" is only in germ, it must follow under the law of correspondences,—that it is impossible for the present man to grasp an equation, relating to these higher states, which includes more than five terms. The result then is that when we deal with these matters we will have to use the unknown quantity x, and leave every one who deals intellectually with the problem to his own manner of placing the different terms. Those who investigate the subject, however, by means of the inner guide, will discover upon attempting to convey their experiences to their intellect-using fellows, that it is not possible to put their hearers into complete possession of the information gained in that way. But even if both of these classes in the West are left to their own devices, many decades will pass away, and many false as well as ridiculous systems will arise, grow up and disappear, before the whole truth will be known. But if that object of our Society which calls for a demonstration of the value of the ancient Aryan philosophy and psychology is sedulously pursued, we may hope for an earlier dawn of a better day. Who then are to be foremost in this? Our brothers who now possess Hindu bodies! They are within reach of the material, they are now in bodies that have grown on Indian soil, they are charged with a debt to the great sages of the past. Let them faithfully translate those books into English, explaining the terms as nearly as possible in every case, and not go on with mere transliterations of words that do not exist for the West. Thus the power and energy of the West will be wedded to the metaphysics and spiritual inheritance of the East, while both will be saved from a greater darkness. If this is not done, the day will come when the Hindu of today will find that he has failed to help his Western brothers who were in reality once themselves Hindus. Mr. Subba Row can very easily— owing to his mastery of English—enlighten us all by giving us better translations, or if his time will not allow that, by inducing many Brahmans in India by whom he is held in high esteem, to act upon suggestion of his in that direction.

William Q. Judge

Jacob Boehme and The Secret Doctrine

[*The Theosophist*, Vol. VII, April, 1886, pp. 417-21]

Jacob Boehme (or as some say Behmen) was a German mystic [1575-1624] and spiritualist who began to write in the 17th century. In his work he inserted a picture of an angel blowing a trumpet, from which issued these words: "To all Christians, Jews, Turks and Heathens, to all the nations of the earth this Trumpet sounds for the last time." In truth it was a curious emblem, but he, the author, was a mystic, and as all experience shows, the path of the mystic is a strange one. It is, as Job V, 28:7 says, a path which the "vulture knoweth not." Even as a bird cleaves the eternal ether, so the mystic advances on a path not ordinarily manifest, a way which must be followed with care, because like the Great Light, which flashes forth and leaves only traces when it returns again to its center, only indications are left for those who come after seeking the same spiritual wisdom. Yet by these "traces," for such they are called in the Kabbala, the way can be discerned, and the truth discovered.

Boehme was poor, of common birth, and totally devoid of ordinary education. He was only a shoemaker. Yet from the mind and out of the mouth of this unlettered man came mighty truths.

It would be idle to enquire into the complications of Karma which condemned him to such a life as his appeared to be. It must have been extremely curious, because though he had grasped the truth and was able to appreciate it, yet at the same time he could not give it out in its perfect form. But he performed his work, and there can be no manner of doubt about his succeeding incarnation. As Krishna says in the *Bhagavad Gîtâ*, he has been already or will shortly be "born into a family of wise devotees"; and thence "he will attain the highest walk."

His life and writings furnish another proof that the great wisdom-religion—the Secret Doctrine—has never been left without a witness. Born a Christian he nevertheless saw the esoteric truth lying under the moss and crust of centuries, and from the Christian Bible extracted for his purblind fellows those pearls which they refused to accept. But he did not get his knowledge from the Christian Scriptures only. Before his internal eye the panorama of real knowledge passed. His interior vision being open he could see the things he had learned in a former life, and at first not knowing what they were was stimulated by them to construe his only spiritual books in the esoteric fashion.

His brain took cognizance of the Book before him, but his spirit, aided by his past, and perchance by the living guardians of the shining lamp of truth, could not but read them aright.

His work was called "The Dawning of the Eternal Day."[1] In this he endeavours to outline the great philosophy. He narrates the circumstances and reasons for the angelic creation, the fall of its chief three hierarchies, and the awful effects which thereupon fell upon Eternal Nature. Mark this, not upon man—for he was not yet—but upon the eternal Nature, that is BRAHM. Then he says that these effects came about by reason of the *unbalancing of the seven equipoised powers* or forces of the Eternal Nature or Brahm. That is to say, that so long as the seven principles of Brahm were in perfect poise, there was no corporeal or manifested universe. So in the *Bhagavad-Gîtâ* we find that Krishna tells Arjuna that "after the lapse of a thousand ages (or Night of Brahmâ) all objects of developed matter come forth from the non-developed principle. At the approach of that day they emanate spontaneously." (*Bhagavad-Gîtâ*, Chap. 8.) Such is the teaching of the Secret Doctrine.

And again Boehme shows the duality of the Supreme Soul. For he says in his work *Psychologia Vera cum Supplemento* that these two eternal principles of positive and negative, the *yea* and the *nay* of the outspeaking *Supreme One*, together constitute eternal nature,—not the dark world alone, which is termed the "root of nature"—the two being as it were combined in *perfect indissoluble union.*

This is nothing else but Purush and Prakriti, or taken together, what is referred to in *The Bhagavad-Gîtâ* where it is said: "But there is another invisible eternal existence, superior to this visible one, which does not perish when all things perish. It is called invisible and indivisible. This is my Supreme Abode."

---

1 [The above title, translated by John Sparrow as *The Aurora*, (London, Watkins, 1960) was preceded by three other translations by Sparrow of Boehme texts mentioned in this article. They are:
Concerning the Three Principles of the Divine Essence, etc. London, Watkins, 1910.
High and Deep Searching out of the Threefold Life of Man Through the Three Principles. 1620 ed. Tr. by J. Sparrow. Reissued by C.J.B., London, Watkins, 1909.
Forty Questions of the Soul and the Clavis, tr. by John Sparrow and reissued by C.J.B. London, Watkins, 1911. This is based on *Psychologia vera, oder, Viertzig fragen von der seeken . . . vergasset von d. Balthasar.* Walthern . . . n.p. 1730. (bound with *De Triplici Vita Hominis,* in V. 4 in the series: *Theosophia Revelata*)
Judge also refers to *De Electione Gratiae and Quaestiones Theosophicae* which later was translated by John Rolleston Earle; London, Constable, 1930, and has a biographical sketch included.—*Comp.*]

Clearly the *Supreme Abode* could never be in Purush alone, nor in Prakriti alone, but in both when *indissolubly united.*

This scheme is adhered to all through this great philosopher's works, no matter whether he is speaking of the great Universe or macrocosm, or of its antitype in man or microcosm. In *De Tribus Principiis* he treats of the three principles or worlds of Nature, describing its eternal birth, its seven properties, and the *two* co-eternal principles; and furthermore in *De Triplici Vita Hominis,* he gives the threefold life of man from which the *seven* is again deduced.

In *De Electione Gratiâ* he goes into a subject that often proves a stumbling block to many, and that is the *inevitableness of evil* as well as of good. From this it is easy to pass to a contemplation of one of the difficult points in occultism as shown in the Secret Doctrine, that nothing is evil, and that even if we admit evil or wickedness in man, it is the nature of the quality or guna, which in the *Bhagavad-Gîtâ* is denominated रज: or rajas, foulness or bad action. Even this is better than the indifferent action that only leads to death. Even from wickedness may and does come forth spiritual life, but from indifferent action comes only darkness, and finally death.

Krishna says in *The Bhagavad-Gîtâ,* Chap. XIV: "There are three kinds of action; first, that which is of the nature of *Sattva,* or true action; second, that which is of the nature of *Râjas,* or bad action; third, that which is the nature of *Tamas,* or indifferent action." He then says: "Although thou wert the greatest of all offenders, thou shalt be able to cross the gulf of sin in the bark of spiritual wisdom"; and a little farther on "The ignorant and the man without faith, whose spirit is full of doubt, is lost and cannot enjoy either world." And in another chapter in describing Himself, he says that he is not only the Buddha, but also is the most evil of mankind or the Asura.

This is one of the most mystical parts of the whole Secret Doctrine. While Boehme has touched on it sufficiently to show that he had a memory of it, he did not go into the most occult details. It has to be remembered that *The Bhagavad-Gîtâ,* and many other books treating on the Secret Doctrine, must be regarded from seven points of view; and that imperfect man is not able to look at it from the center, which would give the whole seven points at once.

Boehme wrote about thirty different treatises, all of them devoted to great subjects, portions of the Secret Doctrine.

Curiously enough the first treated of the *"Dawn of the Eternal Day,"* and the second was devoted to an elucidation of *"The Three Principles of Man."* In the latter is really to be found a sevenfold classification similar to that which Mr. Sinnett propounded in *Esoteric Buddhism.*

He held that the greatest obstacle in the path of man is the astral or elementary power, which engenders and sustains this world.

Then he talks of "tinctures," which we may call principles. According to him there are two principal ones, the watery, and the igneous. These ought to be united in Man; and they ardently seek each other continually, in order to be identified with Sophia or Divine Wisdom. Many Theosophists will see in this a clue not only to the two principles —or tinctures—which ought to be united in man, but also to a law which obtains in many of the phenomena of magic. But even if I were able, I should not speak on this more clearly.

For many inquirers the greatest interest in these works will be found in his hypothesis as to the birth of the material Universe. On the evolution of man from spirit into matter he has much more than I could hope to glance at. In nearly all of it he was outlining and illustrating the Secret Doctrine. The books indicated are well worthy of study not only by Western but also by Eastern metaphysicians. Let us add a few sentences to support this hypothesis from Count Saint-Martin, who was a devoted student of these works.

"Jacob Boehme took for granted the existence of an Universal Principle; he was persuaded that everything is connected in the immense chain of truths, and that the Eternal Nature reposed on seven principles or bases, which he sometimes calls powers, forms, spiritual wheels, sources, and fountains, and that those seven bases exist also in this disordered material nature, under constraint. His nomenclature, adopted for these fundamental relations, ran thus: The first *astringency*, the second *gall* or bitterness, the third *anguish*, the fourth *fire*, the fifth *light*, the sixth *sound*, and the seventh he called BEING or the *thing itself*."

The reader may have begun to think the author did not rightly comprehend the first six but his definition of the seventh shows he was right throughout, and we may conclude the real meanings are concealed under these names.

"The third principle, *anguish*, attenuates the *astringent* one, turns it into *water*, and allows a passage to *fire*, which was shut up in the astringent principle."

There are in this many suggestions and a pursuit of them will repay the student.

"Now the Divine Sophia caused a new order to take birth in the center of our system, and there burned our sun; from that do come forth all kinds of qualities, forms and powers. This center is the separator." It is well known that from the sun was taken by the ancients all kinds of power; and if we mistake not, the Hindus claim that when the Fathers enter into Para-Nirvana, their accumulated goodness pours itself out on the world through the "*Door of the Sun*."

The Bhagavad-Gîtâ says, that the Lord of all dwells in the region of the heart, and again that this Lord is also the Sun of the world.

"The earth is a condensation of the seven primordial principles, and by the withdrawal of eternal light this became a dark valley." It is taught in the East, that this world is a valley and that we are in it, our bodies reaching to the moon, being condensed to hardness at the point where we are on the earth, thus becoming visible to the eye of man. There is a mystery in this statement, but not such an one as cannot be unravelled.

Boehme proceeds: "When the light mastered the fire at the place of the sun, the terrible shock of the battle engendered an igneous eruption by which there shot forth from the sun a stormy and frightful flash of fire—Mars. Taken captive by light it assumed a place, and there it struggles furiously, a pricking goad, whose office is to agitate all nature, producing reaction. It is the gall of nature. The gracious, amiable Light, having enchained unerupted Mars, proceeded by its own power to the bottom or end of the rigidity of Nature, whence unable to proceed further it stopped, and became corporeal; remaining there it warms that place, and although a valet in nature, it is the source of sweetness and the moderator of Mars.

"Saturn does not originate from the sun, but was produced from the severe astringent anguish of the whole body of this Universe. Above Jupiter the sun could not mitigate the horror, and out of that arose Saturn, who is the opposite of meekness, and who produces whatever of rigidity there is in the creatures, including bones, and what in normal nature corresponds thereto." (This is all the highest astrology, from one who had no knowledge of it). "As in the Sun is *the heart of life*, so by Saturn commenceth all corporeal nature. Thus in these two resides the power of the whole universal body, and without their power there could be no creation nor any corporificatiion.

"Venus originates in *effluvia* from the Sun. She lights the unctuosity of the water of the Universe, penetrates hardness, and enkindles love.

"Mercury is the chief worker in the planetary wheel; he is *sound*, and wakes up the germs in everything. His origin, the triumph of Light over Astringency (in which sound was shut up silent), set free the sound by the attentuation of the astringent power."

It is certain that if this peculiar statement regarding Mercury is understood, the student will have gained a high point of knowledge. A seductive bait is here held out to those striving disciples who so earnestly desire to hold converse with the elemental world. But there is no danger, for all the avenues are very secret and only the pure can prevail in the preliminary steps.

Boehme says again: "The Mercury is impregnated and fed continually by the solar substance; that in it is found the knowledge of what was in the order above, before Light had penetrated to the solar center."

As to the Moon, it is curious to note that he says: "She was produced from the sun itself, at the time of his becoming material, and that the moon is his spouse." Students of the story of Adam being made to sleep after his creation and before coats of skin were given, when Eve was produced from his side, will find in this a strong hint.

The above is not by any means a complete statement of Boehme's system. In order to do justice to it, a full analysis of all his works should be undertaken. However, it is sufficient if thoughtful minds who have not read Boehme, shall turn to him after reading this, or if but one earnest reader of his works, or seeker after wisdom, shall receive even a hint that may lead to a clearing up of doubts, or to the acquisition of one new idea. Louis Claude de Saint-Martin continually read him: and the merest glance at the *Theosophic Correspondence or, Man—His Nature*, etc. of de Saint-Martin, will show that from that study he learned much. How much more then will the Western mind be aided by the light shed on both by the lamp of Theosophical teachings.

"Let the desire of the pious be fulfilled."

WILLIAM Q. JUDGE

India and Her Theosophists

[*The Theosophist*, Vol. XIV, September, 1893, pp. 723-25][1]

I am moved to say a word, not by way of fomenting controversy, but merely to express my own view about a thing which needs discussion. I distinctly disclaim the right or the desire to criticize the life or manners of the Hindu nation; nor have I any proposals to make for sweeping reforms in their life and manners. What I would direct myself to is the Theosophical movement there in relation to the national character of the Hindu, and to matters connected therewith.

I cannot agree with the statement that the Hindus and Hindu Theosophists are not intellectually active. They are, and always have been too active intellectually altogether and at the expense of some other activities more important. That the peculiar characteristic of the educated Hindu is intellectual activity can hardly be doubted. It is exhibited on all occasions; in hair-splitting dialogues; in endless commentaries; in fine controversies over distinctions; in long explanations;

---

[1] The publication of the following article was inadvertently delayed—*H.S.O.*

in fact, in every possible place and manner. This is the real difficulty: it was the cause of India's decadence as it has become the obstacle against her rising to her proper place among nations. Too much intellectual activity in a nation like this, living in the tropics, with religion as a heritage and the guide for every act, is sure to lead in any age, to spiritual pride; and spiritual pride in them then brings on stagnation. That stagnation will last until gradually there arise men of the same nation who, without fear of caste, or favor, or loss, or ostracism, or any other punishment or pain, will boldly bring about the reaction that shall result in the death of spiritual pride and the acquirement of the counterbalancing wheel to pure activity.

Intellectualism represents the letter of the law, and the letter killeth, while the spirit maketh alive. For seventeen years we have had constant and complete evidence that the above views are correct. *The Theosophist*, full of the articles by Hindus, always intellectual; *Lucifer* printing similar ones by Hindus; *The Path* now and then doing the same; articles on mighty themes of abstract scope by Brahmins who yet belong to one of the eighty-four castes of Brahmins. But if the spiritual activity prevailed we would have seen articles, heard orations, known of efforts, to show that a sub-division of the highest of the four castes into eighty-four is not sanctioned by the *Vedas*, but is diametrically against them and ought to be instantly abandoned. I should not suggest the destruction of the four castes, as those are national divisions which exist everywhere. The Hindu, however, has the tradition, and the family lines, and the power to restore this disturbed state of things to equilibrium. And until it is restored the day of Aryavarta's restoration is delayed. The disturbance began in the Brahmanical caste and there it must be harmonized first. Spiritual pride caused it and that pride must be killed out.

Here then is the real opportunity for Indian Theosophists. It is the same sort of call that the Christians' Jesus made on the young man whom he told to take up the cross and follow him. No foreigner could do this; no European Secretary could hope to succeed at it unless he were an incarnation of Vishnu. It means loss, trouble, fight, patience, steadiness, altruism, sacrifice. Where then are the Indian Theosophists —most of whom are in the Brahmanical caste—who will preach all over India to the Brahmins to give up their eighty-four divisions and coalesce into one, so that they, as the natural teachers and priests, may then reform the other castes? This is the real need and also the opportunity. All the castes will follow the highest. Just now they all, even to the outcastes, divide and sub-divide themselves infinitely, in accordance with the example set.

Have those Indian Theosophists who believed that the Mahâtmas are behind the Theosophical movement ever asked themselves why those Masters saw fit to start the Society in America and not in India, the home of the Adepts? It was not for political reasons, nor religious, but simply and solely because of the purely "intellectual activity" and spiritual pride of the Hindu.[1] For the West is every bit as selfish as the East. Those in Europe and America who know of Karma think selfishly on it; those who do not know, live for self. There is no difference in this respect.

In the West there is as much to be fought and reformed as in India, but the problem is differently conditioned. Each hemisphere must work upon itself. But the Western Theosophist finds himself in a very uncomfortable corner when, as the champion of Eastern doctrine and metaphysic, he is required to describe the actual present state of India and her Theosophists. He begins to tell of such a show of Branches, of Headquarters buildings, of collecting manuscripts, of translation into English, of rendering into vernaculars, of learned pundits in the ranks, of wonderful Yogis, of the gigantic works of long dead Hindus, and then he stops, hoping his interlocutor has been dazzled, amazed, silenced. But pitilessly his examiner pushes, and inquires if it be true that every one of the four castes is sub-divided into nearly hundreds, if women are educated, if educated Hindu women are active in the Society, if the Hindu Theosophists are actively and ever as martyrs working to reform within itself, to remove superstition; if he is showing by the act of personal sacrifice—the only one that will ever bring on a real reform—that he is determined to restore India to her real place? No reply is possible that does not involve his confusion. For his merciless questioner asks if it be true that one of the Mahâtmas behind the Society had written to Mr. Sinnett that he had ventured down into the cities of his native land and had to fly almost immediately from the vile and heavy atmosphere produced by the psychical condition

-----

[1] I dissent from this theory as being unsound. Admitting H. P. B. to have been the agent of the Masters, would not that imply that she and they were unable to foresee and prevent the ignominious collapse of the Cairo attempt of 1871 at founding an Occult Society; although she did her best to make it succeed, and fortified her influence with psychical phenomena quite as strange as those we saw, four years later at New York? But for that *fiasco,* a T. S. would have been formed by French, Russians, Arabs and Copts, in one of the moral pest-holes of the world. And, furthermore, although it was actually started at New York, it had fallen almost into the article of death by the close of 1878, when the two Founders sailed for India; and it was not until its dry bones were electrified by the smouldering spiritual life of India that it sprang with resistless rush along the path of its Karmic mission. When Mr. Judge becomes my successor and comes to live in India, he will know more about the Hindus and what is possible and impossible for their would-be reformers. He writes now, in all kindness and good intent, in the strain of an Arya Samajist, and as H. P. B. and I did before and just after coming to India and replacing theory with actual knowledge of the Indian situation of affairs.—*H.S.O.*

of his people?[1] The reply is in the affirmative. No Rishi, however great, can alter a people; they must alter themselves. The "minor currents" that the Adepts can deflect have to be sought in other nations, so as to, if possible, affect all by general reaction. This is truth, or else the Mahâtmas lie. I believe them; I have seen the evidence to support their statement.

So there is no question of comparison of nations. The Indian Section *must work out its own problem.* The West is bad enough, the heavens know, but out of badness—the *râjasika* quality—there is a rising up to truth; from *tamogunam* comes only death. If there are men in India with the diamond hearts possessed by the martyrs of the ages, I call upon them from across these oceans that roll between us to rise and tell their fellow Theosophists and their country what they ought to know. If such men are there they will, of themselves, know what words to use, for the Spirit will, in that day and hour, give the words and the influence. Those who ask for particularity of advice are not yet grown to the stature of the hero who, being all, dareth all; who having fought many a fight in other lives rejoices in his strength, and fears neither life nor death, neither sorrow nor abuse, and wisheth no ease for himself while others suffer.

William Q. Judge

---

[1] Mr. Judge should not convey the false impression that the Mahatmas find the spiritual aura of India *worse* than those of Europe and America, for everybody knows that H. P. B. reiterated continually the assertion that the spiritual state of the West was unbearable, and she yearned for our transfer to India. What Mahâtma K.H. wrote Mr. Sinnett (*vide Occult World,* p. 120, 2nd edition) was that he had seen drunken Sikhs at the Golden Temple, at Amritsar, and heard an educated Hindu vakil declaring Yoga a delusion and the alleged *Siddhis* impossible; and that he could not endure even for a few days the stifling magnetism "even of his own countrymen"; *i.e.* that it was as stifling as those of other races. What he found the magnetism of London and New York [to be] has often been described by H. P. B. to a host of witnesses. Mr. Judge has forgotten that every true Yogi of our day finds the same state of things and flies to the jungle to escape it. It is the evil effect of modern education devoid of spiritual stimulus which has made the whole world spiritually leprous as it is—*H.S.O.*

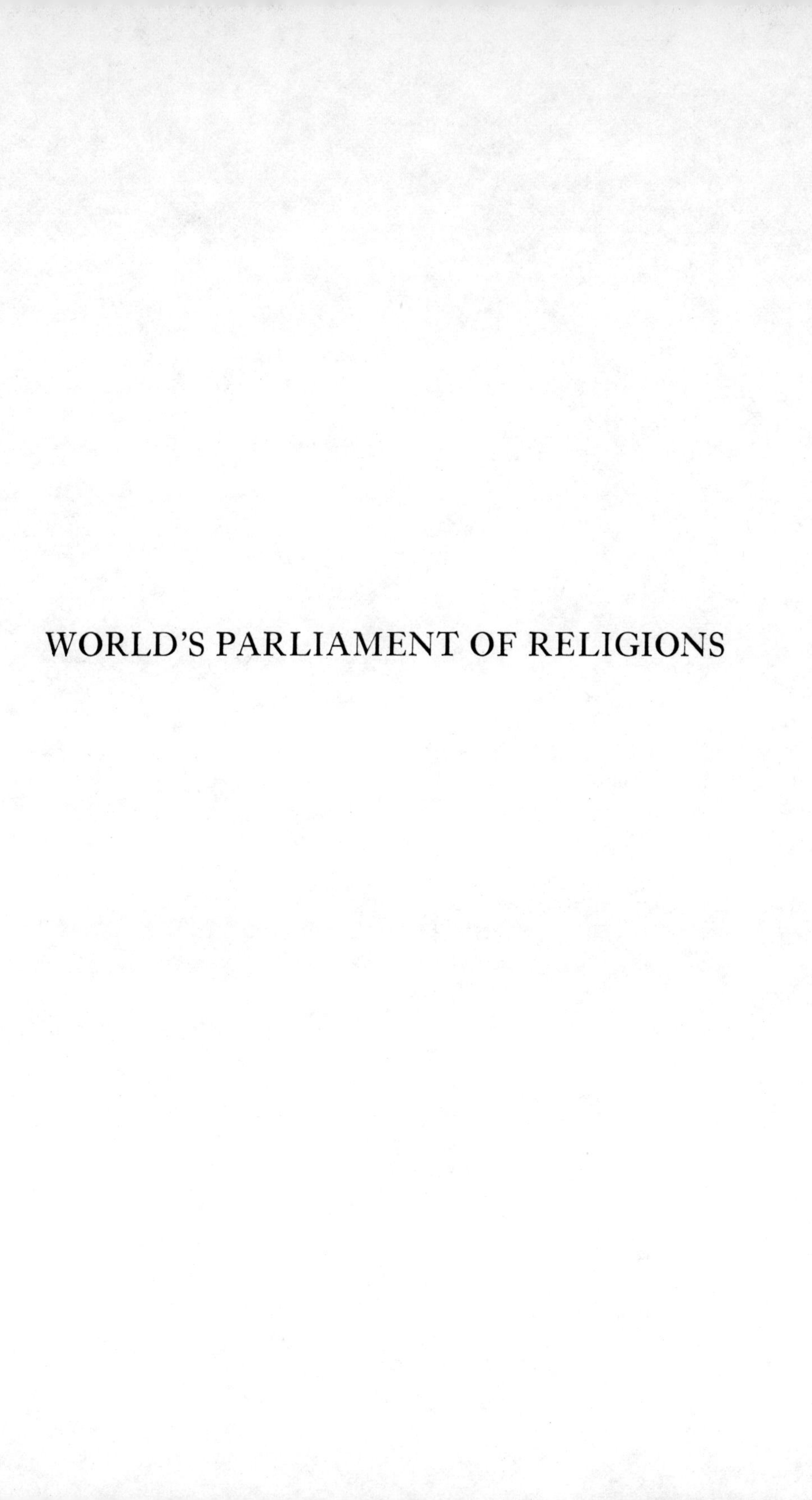
WORLD'S PARLIAMENT OF RELIGIONS

World's Parliament of Religions

[Aside from the publication of *Isis Unveiled* in 1877, no single event advanced the Theosophical Society in America more than the World's Parliament of Religions. It was held in connection with the *Columbian Exposition of 1893*, known as The World's Fair at Chicago. The articles in the section to follow show that once the Theosophists were accepted amidst the many religious sects, their Congress drew crowds by the thousands.

At the close of the festivities, a two-volume book was published by the Rev. John Henry Barrows, D.D., with the salient speeches and episodes. Entitled *The World's Parliament of Religions, An Illustrated and Popular Story of the World's First Parliament of Religions*, etc.,[1] a major address by William Q. Judge was included in Vol. II. Although Mr. Judge's talk appeared on pp. 1517-22 of that volume, we use here instead his own revised text published in *Lucifer* under the title: "Theosophy Generally Stated." The appended photograph of key participants is from the Rev. Barrow's book.—*Comp.*]

---

[1] Chicago: The Parliament Publishing Company, 1893.

Dr. Jirah D. Buck

Mrs. Annie Besant   Mercie M. Thirds

Gyanenda N. Chakravarti

William Quan Judge   Dr. Jerome A. Anderson

George E. Wright

[Appearing in *The Theosophist*, Vol. XV, October 1893, on pages 58-60, was an "Unofficial Bulletin" prefaced with the announcement that Mr. Judge would represent the Theosophical Society during the World's Parliament of Religions:]

AMERICA

The great event during the past month among American Theosophists has, of course, been the preparation for and holding of the Congress at the World's Parliament of Religions. In connection with this, Mr. Judge, who is acting for the President, as Chairman of the Advisory Council, has issued the following Unofficial Bulletin:—

THE WORLD'S CONGRESS AUXILIARY
Of the World's Columbian Exposition.
DEPARTMENT OF RELIGION.
THE THEOSOPHICAL SOCIETY'S CONGRESS.
September 15 and 16, 1893.
UNOFFICIAL BULLETIN.

COL. H. S. OLCOTT, the President, has written that he will send a message to the Congress, and it is also probable that he will send an official statement of the work in Asia . . .

It is possible that other arrangements may be arrived at, but the above is a general statement of the assignments now made. Mrs. Besant will lecture at one or two places before getting to Chicago, and it is also purposed to have her give a general free lecture to the public just after the Congress. If possible, arrangements will be made to have Bro. Chakravarti speak at the Chicago T.S. and those Branches which, in the time at his disposal, may be easily reached, but as to that nothing precise can be said until his arrival here and after consultation.

I can also report that the fund for the expenses of the Congress has grown much faster than the present commercial crisis would have led anyone to hope, and if any surplus shall remain at the close of the Congress it is proposed then to print for general distribution throughout the T.S. a full report of the proceedings and speeches. Bro. A. S. Brolley of Albany has volunteered to take stenographic reports of the proceedings.

It is well also to remind members that the President of the T.S. would have been Chairman of the Advisory Council were it not that he is so far away in India, and such being the circumstances he has extended his official sanction as President to me in the premises, delegating to me such of his powers as are necessary to carry this Congress to a successful conclusion. And I must also add that no success could attend these efforts were it not for the earnest and brotherly aid extended by individual members, to whom the thanks of the Society are due.   William Q. Judge

Vice.-Pres. T.S. and Chair. Advis. Council

[*The Eclectic Theosophist*, No. 42, September 1977, has the following description of this document.]

"The Library of Point Loma Publications has received from Mrs. Marguerite Barton of Porterville, California, items of historic and artistic interest from the estates of her late mother, Emily Lemke-Neresheimer, and of her earlier deceased stepfather, E. August Neresheimer. Of special interest is a hand-illuminatd document headed *ANANDAMAYA KOSA*: 'A Theosophical gathering on September 4, 1893,' inscribed with Sanskrit characters at the top and Sinhalese in the margins, and signed by the following thirteen representatives of different countries: Gyanendra N. Chakravarti (Allahabad, India), H. Dhamapala (Ceylon), Annie Besant (Ireland), William Q. Judge (Ireland), Henrietta Müller (Chile), Claude W. Wright (Ωγυγία) [Ogygia], E. Aug. Neresheimer (Germany), Alexander Fullerton (U.S.A.), H. T. Patterson (U.S.A.), Ella J. M. Judge (U.S.A.), Minnie Neresheimer (U.S.A.), C. T. Strauss (Switzerland), Maud Ralston (U.S.A.). As the first four signatories are known to have represented respectively Hinduism, Buddhism, and Theosophy (Annie Besant and W. Q. Judge) at the World's Parliament of Religions in Chicago in 1893, it is reasonable to assume by the date of the document that it was composed and signed on that occasion."

ANANDAMAYA — KOSA

सत्यान् नास्ति परो धर्मः !!!

A THEOSOPHICAL GATHERING

ON SEPTEMBER 4ᵀᴴ 1893

DAY OF ☉ ☽

	Ghaurindra N. Chakravarti	Allahabad. India
	H Dharmapala	Ceylon
Annie Besant		Ireland
William Q Judge		Ireland
J. Henrietta Müller		Chile
Claude F. Wright		N'yúzia
Guy Neresheimer		Germany
Alexander Fullerton		U.S.A.
H. T. Patterson		U.S.A.
Ella M. Judge		U.S.A.
Minnie Neresheimer		U.S.A.
C. T. Strauss		Switzerland
Maude Ralston		U.S.A.

[Announcement found inserted in *The Thesosophical Forum*.]

IMPORTANT

Theosophists have everywhere greatly desired the presence at the Parliament of Religions, World's Fair, Chicago, September 15th and 16th, of a high-caste Brahmin as a representative of Brahmanism. Arrangements have been made whereby Mr. Ganendra Nath Chakravarti, Professor of Mathematics, a man of fine presence, high education, and fluent command of English, and an earnest Theosophist, will accompany Mrs. Besant to Chicago, and in his address to the Parliament correct current misconceptions of Brahmanism, Theosophy, and the T.S.

As the expense of Prof. Chakravarti's visit must be met by Theosophists in Europe and America, I earnestly invite our members to send to me whatever they can spare for this object. Such great advantages to better knowledge of Eastern philosophy, and, in particular, to the status and welfare of the Theosophical Society and Cause, are ensured by this step that I think the occasion well meriting the participation of all brethren.

As it was necessary to borrow a part of the needed money in order that Prof. Chakravarti might sail in time, I am anxious for speedy response that this may be repaid and the remainder ensured. Friends will kindly send their gifts to me as below.

WILLIAM Q. JUDGE,
General Secretary.

144 Madison Avenue,
   New York City.

The Theosophical Congress
WORLD'S FAIR — 1893

[The following selections are extracted from a report by the American Section of the T. S., published in 1893 and entitled: *The Theosophical Congress held by the Theosophical Society at the Parliament of Religions, World's Fair* of 1893, at Chicago, Illinois, September 15, 16, 17. Included below are only those portions of the proceedings which were documented or participated in by Mr. Judge.

The first selection from this book appeared also in a modified form under the title: *Theosophy at the World's Fair*, as an article in the July 1893 issue of *The Theosophist* (see Vol. XIV, pp. 588-92.— *Comp.*]

[*The Theosophical Congress*, pp. 4-8]

CHICAGO, *April 18th, 1893.*

MR. GEORGE E. WRIGHT,

Pres. Chicago Branch Theosophical Society.

My Dear Sir: In reply to your favor of the 7th inst., I take pleasure in saying that I am advised that the Rev. John Henry Barrows, Chairman of the General Committee of the World's Congress Auxiliary on Religious Congresses, and Rev. Augusta J. Chapin, Chairman of the Woman's Committee of the World's Congress Auxiliary on this subject, have recommended that the Theosophical Society be given an opportunity in the World's Congress of 1893 to set forth the Religious and Ethical aspects and relations of Theosophy, and an assignment of a proper time and place for such presentation will accordingly be made. I understand that Dr. Barrows has suggested that he may be able to arrange for your presentation on Friday and Saturday, the 15th and 16th days of September, and upon that point I will refer you to him.

The matter of what is known as Psychical Research and Phenomena having been withdrawn from your application, it is understood that the presentation to be made in the Department of Religion will be confined to Theosophy as a Religion and a system of Ethics. I am advised that some of the most distinguished members of the Theosophical Society have already accepted other engagements in the Department of Religion, and will also take part in your own presentation.

On your return from the meeting soon to be held in New York City,

I will appoint the Committee of Organization, of which you will be Chairman. Please bring with you a list of your Advisory Council and a draft of the Preliminary Address for your Congress. As the entire matter of what are known as "Occult Phenomena" has been committed to the Psychical Research Congress, I trust you will take the pains to exclude that subject from your address and make it quite clear that the object of your demonstration is to give the Religious and Ethical world better information than they now possess of the Religious and Ethical principles of your order. This regulation I am quite sure will prove wholly advantageous to the demonstration you desire to make.

Awaiting the further action you are to take, I am

Very respectfully yours,
CHARLES C. BONNEY,
President World's Congress Auxiliary.

At the Convention of the T. S. above mentioned Brother George E. Wright made report in the matter, and what follows is abstracted from his report for dissemination among members by order of the Convention.

The World's Fair at Chicago has two sides or aspects; the first the Commercial one, the second its literary, philosophical, and intellectual side. The second phase is technically known as the World's Congress Auxiliary. It takes in a great many subjects, not the least being the PARLIAMENT OF RELIGIONS. Beginning in May the different Congresses are: Woman's Progress, Public Press, Medicine and Surgery, Temperance, Moral and Social Reform, Commerce and Finance, Music, Literature, Education, Engineering, Art, Architecture, Government, Law, Political Science, Science and Philosophy; in September: Labor, Religion, Missions and Church Societies, Sunday Rest; October: Public Health and Agriculture.

The World's Congress Auxiliary is officially constituted as follows:

1. A central organization authorized by the Directory of the World's Columbian Exposition, and recognized by the Government of the United States as the proper agency to conduct a series of World's Congresses in connection with the Exposition.

2. A local Committee of Arrangements for each Congress. The Committee constitutes the means of communication and action between the Auxiliary and persons and organizations that will participate in a given Congress. This Committee of Arrangements consists of a comparatively small number of persons who reside in or near the place where the Congresses are to be held.

3. Each Committee has adjoined to it and constituting its non-resident but active branch, an Advisory Council, composed of persons

eminent in the work involved, and selected from many parts of the world. The members of such Councils cooperate with the proper Committees by individual correspondence.

A further interesting and commendable feature of the organization is the recognition of Woman as entitled to equal rights and privileges in the management. There is a Woman's Branch of the World's Congress Auxiliary, and it is expressly provided that in each Congress there shall be two Committees, one of Men, reporting to President Bonney, and one of Women, reporting to Mrs. Potter Palmer, President of the Woman's Branch, the number of each being alike.

The Parliament of Religions begins on Monday, September 11th, and continues seventeen days. Following is a condensed statement of the program:

September 11th. Addresses of welcome and responses by representatives from Great Britain, Continental Europe, India, China, Japan, Australia, Canada, Africa, and South America.

September 12th. Origin and Universality of Belief in God. Primitive form of Theism as witnessed by the oldest Sacred Writings. God in History and in the light of Modern Science.

September 13th. Man, his nature, his dignity, his imperfection. The nature of Life. Various beliefs regarding the Future Life. Human Brotherhood as taught by the different historic religions.

September 14th. Religion essentially characteristic of Humanity. Expression of the relations between God and Man. What constitutes a Religious as distinguished from a Moral Life. Spiritual Forces in Human Progress.

September 15th. Importance of a serious study of all Systems of Religion. The Dead Religions, what they have bequeathed to the Living. To what degree has each Religion justified the God of all the Earth in the historic evolution of the Race?

September 16th. The study of the Sacred Books in Literature. Religion as interpreted by the World's poets. What the Jewish, Christian, and other Sacred Literatures have wrought for Mankind.

September 17th. Religion and the Family. The Marriage Bond. The Domestic Education of Children.

September 18th. The Religious Leaders of Mankind. Incarnation claimed by different Religions. Their Historicity and Worth. The Sympathy of Religions.

September 19th. Religion in its relation to Natural Sciences and to Arts and Letters. Can the knowledge of Religion be scientific? Has the Science of Religion given aid to the other Sciences?

September 20th. Religion in its relation to Morals. Essential Oneness of Ethical Ideas among Men. Agnostic notions of Conscience, Duty, and Right. Ethical Systems and Ethical Types produced by various historic faiths. Different Schemes for the Restoration of Fallen Man.

September 21st. Religion and Social Problems. Religion and Wealth. Religion and Poverty. Religion and Temperance. Comparative benefits conferred upon Woman by the different Religions.

September 22nd. Religion and Civil Society. Love of Country. Observance of Law. Perils of Great Cities. Is Present-day Religion adequate to meet the Requirements and Dangers of Modern Life?

September 23rd. Religion and the Love of Mankind. The Fraternity of Peoples. Duties of European and American Nations toward China. International Justice and Amity. Arbitration instead of War.

September 24th. The Present Religious Condition of Christendom. What Religion has wrought for America.

September 25th. Religious Reunion of Christendom.

September 26th. The Religious Union of the Whole Human Family. The World's Religious Debt to Asia, Europe, and America. What are the points of contact and contrast between the different Religions as disclosed by the preceding Conferences?

September 27th. Elements of perfect Religion as recognized and set forth in the different Historic faiths and characteristics of Ultimate Religion. What is the Center of the Coming Religious Unity of Mankind?

I have necessarily condensed the official program, endeavoring in the above to convey only its must salient features. But I desire now to ask all my listeners if they have noticed how perfectly Theosophical is the list of subjects presented. There is throughout no begging of the question, or assertion of dogma. Everything is placed upon the most liberal basis. In fact, the whole program sounds as if it might have been taken from a syllabus of one of the Theosophical Branches. We ought to remember also that these ideas are to be discussed not by one set of individuals or by representatives of a single creed, but they will be taken up by the most distinguished exponents of all the world's great religions. The plan of holding a Parliament of Religions, at which the representatives of the great historic faiths shall sit together in frank and friendly conference over the great things of our common spiritual and moral life, is no longer a dream. The religious world in its great branches will be represented in this truly ecumenical conference. There will be Buddhist scholars, both from Japan and India, and probably also from Siam. Our own beloved brother and Fellow-Theosophist,

H. Dharmapala, Secretary of the Maha Bodhi Society, has been commissioned to represent the Southern Buddhist Church. It is expected by the Auxiliary managers that he will be one of the greatest attractions in the Parliament of Religions, and every courtesy will be extended to him by them during his stay in Chicago. The Local Committee on the Theosophical Congress hopes to secure his services also during our sessions. But leaving that aside for the present and returning to the general Parliament, I may say that at least one of the high priests of Shintoism is expected to be present. Two Moslem scholars, eminent in India, have accepted invitations. The eloquent Mozoomdar will speak for progressive Hinduism. Arrangements are being made to secure papers from orthodox Brahmans. The Chinese Government has commissioned a scholar to represent Confucianism. It is expected that Parsees from Bombay will speak of their ancient faith. Jewish rabbis of Europe and American are in earnest sympathy with this movement. The interest in the Exposition and in the approaching Congress will draw to Chicago numerous representatives of the historic religions. The Catholic Archbishops of America at their meeting in New York in November, 1892, took action approving the participation of the Catholic Church in the Parliament of Religions. To name over the list of Protestant Churches which have arranged to take part in it would be but to make a schedule of the whole of orthodoxy.

Early last winter Brother William Q. Judge wrote to me as President of the Chicago T. S., suggesting that as I was on the spot it might be well to take steps looking toward our being represented at the Fair, and to see what could be done on behalf of the Theosophical Society. I thereupon visited the World's Fair headquarters, and subsequently in conjunction with Brother Judge as Vice-President of the T. S. and our General Secretary entered a formal application in writing for representation. When Mrs. Besant was in Chicago in December we visited together the officials of the World's Congress, and on the following day the Rev. Augusta J. Chapin, Chairman of the Woman's Committee on Religions, called upon Mrs. Besant at my house. It was then practically decided that we were to secure representation, but a question that arose later caused considerable delay. That question was, where, at just what point in the Congress, ought we to be located. There never was any question as to our right to be represented. Large bodies naturally move slowly, and there was a great pressure of business upon the Auxiliary, owing to the vast amount of correspondence and negotiations rendered necessary in giving all the various religions and other organizations their appropriate places. But all was finally brought to a satisfactory issue, so far as our application was concerned.

Our assignment of dates is in every respect of a most satisfactory nature. In the first place we are granted a separate and distinct Congress of our own, which will be duly and officially advertised as the Theosophical Congress. We are not lumped in, as many societies are, among several others under some general head, thus losing much of our individuality and no little of the publicity which is sought in such an affair. On the contrary, every effort will be made by the World's Congress Auxiliary to attract attention to our Congress and to give it the most favorable auspices. In my final interview with President Bonney last Wednesday, he said:

"You [meaning the Theosophical Society] are now a part of the World's Congress, and we are as much interested in making it a success as you are."

And this is in fact the case. Every facility will be extended to our people to make the best possible showing.

Then, as to the dates of our sessions, could anything be better? The Parliament of Religions formally opens on Monday, September 11th, and we are assigned to the following Friday and Saturday, September 15 and 16, 1893. The Unitarian and Universalist Societies meet at the same time, and certainly we can make a showing that will compare favorably with these organizations. As a matter of fact, there is no reason why Theosophy should not make a pronounced success of this occasion. We have our philosophy which has stood the test of untold ages. All of the really great philosophers of the past have taught it. Many of the most advanced thinkers of the present day, materialistic as it is, have embraced it. The Theosophical Society includes some of the most brilliant intellects in all lands. Our orators are eloquent, our writers convincing. Where can they find a better opportunity to spread the Theosophic idea than right here in this wonderful Parliament of Religions, the meeting-place of the best minds in Europe and America, the intellectual center towards which in this year of 1893 all the culture of the world will turn, whose proceedings are officially sanctioned by the Government of the United States, whose every act will be fully and faithfully recorded in the daily press, whose official records will be preserved in durable form, and, finally, whose sessions will form a grand historical event, marking the change from the old dispensation of darkness and dogmatism to the new era of light, liberty of thought, and religious expression, and, above all, the spirit of universal fraternity with which the Theosophical Society is animated, and of which it is indeed the standard-bearer?

All sessions will be held in the new Art Palace on the Lake Front, and during some of the time several Congresses will be in progress simultaneously. There are in the building two enormous halls capable of holding 3,000 to 4,000 people each, and besides these there are a dozen smaller halls accommodating from 300 up to 1,500 each. The Art Palace is erected in a park just in front of the Auditorium Hotel, near the center of Chicago. The Fair proper is held at Jackson Park, some distance towards the outer limits of Chicago.

In accordance with the rules of the managers of the Auxiliary, the Local Committee of the Theosophical Congress is named from citizens in or near Chicago. They are as follows: George E. Wright, Chairman; Prof. Frederic G. Gleason, Alpheus M. Smith, Mrs. E. H. Pratt, Dr. Elizabeth Chidester, Mrs. M. M. Thirds, Judge R. Wes McBride, Judge Edward O'Rourke, Mrs. Gen. M. M. Trumbull, Mrs. Anna Byford Leonard.

The Advisory Council is given in the Bulletin which will be officially issued by the Fair managers. The Chairman of that Council is William Q. Judge, as Vice-President of the Theosophical Society. The necessity of having representatives in Chicago is the reason for Brother Wright's being Chairman of the Local Committee; the need of having a general representative in America caused Brother Judge to be selected as Chairman of the Advisory Council; otherwise of course Col. H. S. Olcott would have been its Chairman as President of the Theosophical Society.

On the 26th of April a cable of information was sent to Col. H. S. Olcott to Madras, India, asking for his approval of the plans so far matured and the general appointments made, and under date of April 29th he replied by cable from there that he approved if we thought the matter judicious, he being too far away to know all the facts. He thus approves, as there can be no question of the propriety of our having our days in the Religious Parliament.

The General Secretary of the Indian Section being present at the Convention April 23rd gave a written approval of these plans and pledged the endorsement and cooperation of the Indian Section. A cable was at the same time sent to the European Section, and its officials replied giving their hearty approval also, and Mrs. Annie Besant telegraphed that the dates assigned were suitable for her and that she would be at the Congress and address it under one of the heads provided. Efforts are being made to have the best speakers in the T.S. attend the Congress, and it may be possible to have Brothers Mead, Keightley, Burrows, and others from England, and perhaps others from the Indian Section. Precise information cannot be given on these points now, as correspondence must first be had. In the United States we can of course obtain several good speakers.

While the Fair pays for the printing of the necessary Bulletins issued by us, it furnishes no money for such matters as the present nor for other incidental expenses. Therefore, under the resolution passed by the last Convention of April, I beg to ask all members who can afford it to send to me contributions for those expenses, no matter how small or large such remittances may be, and to specify in the letter accompanying any that they are for this object.

WILLIAM Q. JUDGE
Gen. Sec. American Sec. T. S.

144 Madison Ave., New York, May, 1893.

[*The Theosophical Congress*, pp. 16-17]

[Claude Falls Wright speaking:]

. . . Each paper to be presented has been prepared with the greatest pains, and every word that could be deemed superfluous has been left out. Indeed, so wide is the scope of the topics involved that only with the greatest difficulty could the entire program be condensed into the five sessions allowed for our Congress. But on Saturday evening, in the Hall of Washington, will be given what might be termed a general review of the topics treated of exhaustively in the Congress, and the speakers whom I have named will prove that Theosophy is not necessarily a dry system of metaphysics, but has in it all elements requisite for the most interesting narrative and the most thrilling eloquence.

I now have the pleasure of introducing the permanent chairman of the Congress, one who is known the world over as an indefatigable worker in the cause of Theosophy, a lover of truth and a hater of religious shams, the friend and coadjutor of the founders of the Theosophical Society, and, I may add, the leading organizer of the Society, William Q. Judge.

Brother William Q. Judge took the chair, and addressed the meeting as follows:

BROTHERS AND SISTERS—It is a very high honor to me to be allowed to preside over this Congress. It is a triumph for the Theosophical Society to be permitted to hold this Congress after eighteen years of violent abuse and ridicule continued up to the last moment; and we may consider that the Theosophical Society, after all these years of persistent work, has at last got a footing in the West. It always has had it in the East, but now at last we have it here. And I think the best thing to do today is to proceed at once to business. More is done and accomplished by work than by compliments and speeches one to another. We are all supposed to be brothers and sisters together and not to need flattery, or at least we ought not to need it; we ought not to ask it. I only have to say that I am very glad personally to be able to preside over you, but I should be just as well pleased if any of you were selected to have this position.

Mr. Wright has given you an outline of this Congress. Perhaps it may seem to some singular that the Theosophical Society should be in a religious parliament, because we have no creed and have always said that we were not a religious body. But we hold that religion and science and human life cannot be separated from each other, and for that reason when the Parliament of all the Religions of the World comes together it is very proper that the Society, the only one in the world which represents the union of science and religion, should be represented in it, and we were very fortunate in being allowed to be represented on that basis and on no other.

This Congress has been sanctioned by the President of the Theosophical Society. That sanction was necessary because we should not go into a Parliament of Religions without the sanction of our own President, who has deputed Mrs. Annie Besant to represent him as special delegate. He has deputed me to represent the Theosophical Society throughout the world, as he himself, being so far away, could not come here. The other delegates whom we have here, as already mentioned, are Brother Chakravarti, from Allahabad, India, who is in a peculiar position in this Congress. His position is that he is a delegate from the Theosophical Society, not particularly from India; he comes from India, requested and brought here by the whole Society to represent his form of Theosophy before us, but he is the delegate of the entire Society. Mrs. Annie Besant is the delegate of the European Section, together with Miss F. Henrietta Müller and Mrs. Isabel Cooper-Oakley of London. These ladies were appointed delegates by the European Section at the last Congress, which was held there in July. Mrs. Cooper-Oakley, who is one of our leading members and who has been traveling all over the world in behalf of the Theosophical Society, has also been especially delegated by the Australian Branches. In addition to these particular delegates we will have as speakers a member of the Chicago Branch, Mrs. Thirds; a member of the Cincinnati Branch, Dr. Buck; a member of the San Francisco Branch on the Pacific Coast, Dr. Anderson; and a member who has come from London, Mr. Claude F. Wright. Thus we have representatives and speakers from almost every part of the world to take part in this Congress. I have asked my Brother Claude Wright to relieve my voice by acting as my secretary at this meeting, and after Mrs. Besant shall have read to you a message, he will read to you some credentials which we have and Colonel Olcott's executive order, so as to make this meeting perfectly regular. I now ask you to give your attention to Mrs. Annie Besant, who will read a message sent to us by Colonel Olcott, President of the Society, from Adyar, Madras, India.

Mrs. Besant—I have in my hands from Colonel Henry S. Olcott, the President-Founder of the Society, a message of greeting to all assembled here and of congratulation upon our gathering, which has been received by cable in code form. Being translated, it is:

PRESIDENT T. S. TO CONGRESS

To William Q. Judge, Vice Pres. T.S.:

Across seas and continents your Asiatic brethren salute you; mingling their congratulations with yours for this auspicious opportunity to tell the representatives of many nations and of the world's great faiths the fraternal message of Theosophy. From ancient temples and rock-cut fanes the voices of the ancient Teachers once more utter the words of wisdom that showed our ancestors the true path to happiness, liberation, and spiritual peace. May the blessing of the Sages be with you all, and may the truth prevail.

H. S. Olcott, P. T. S.
Headquarters T. S., Adyar, Madras, September 5, 1893.

Theosophy Generally Stated

[*Lucifer*, Vol. XIII, December, 1893, pp. 273-77]

[From the Official Report, World's Parliament of Religions.]

The claim is made that an impartial study of history, religion and literature will show the existence from ancient times of a great body of philosophical, scientific and ethical doctrine forming the basis and origin of all similar thought in modern systems. It is at once religious and scientific, asserting that religion and science should never be separated. It puts forward sublime religious and ideal teachings, but at the same time shows that all of it can be demonstrated to reason, and that authority other than that has no place, thus preventing the hypocrisy which arises from asserting dogmas on authority which no one can show as resting on reason. This ancient body of doctrine is known as the "Wisdom Religion" and was always taught by adepts or initiates therein who preserve it through all time. Hence, and from other doctrines demonstrated, it is shown that man, being spirit and immortal, is able to perpetuate his real life and consciousness, and has done so during all time in the persons of those higher flowers of the human race who are members of an ancient and high brotherhood who concern themselves with the soul development of man, held by them to include every process of evolution on all planes. The initiates, being bound by the law of evolution, must work with humanity as its development permits. Therefore from time to time they give out again and again the same doctrine which from time to time grows obscured in various nations and places. This is the wisdom religion and they are the keepers of it. At times they come to nations as great teachers and "saviors," who only re-promulgate the old truths and system of ethics. This therefore holds that humanity is capable of infinite perfection both in time and quality, the saviors and adepts being held up as examples of that possibility.

From this living and presently acting body of perfected men H. P. Blavatsky declared she received the impulse to once more bring forward the old ideas, and from them also received several keys to ancient and modern doctrines that had been lost during modern struggles toward civilization, and also that she was furnished by them with some doctrines really ancient but entirely new to the present day in any exoteric shape. These she wrote among the other keys furnished by her to her fellow members and the world at large. Added, then, to the testimony through all time found in records of all nations, we have this modern explicit assertion that the ancient learned and humanitarian body of adepts still exists on this earth and takes an interest in the development of the race.

Theosophy postulates an eternal principle called the Unknown, which can never be cognized except through its manifestations. This eternal principle is in and is every thing and being; it periodically and eternally manifests itself and recedes again from manifestation. In this ebb and flow evolution proceeds and itself is the progress of the manifestation. The perceived universe is the manifestation of this Unknown, including Spirit and Matter, for Theosophy holds that those are but the two opposite poles of the one unknown principle. They co-exist, are not separate nor separable from each other, or, as the Hindu scriptures say, there is no particle of matter without spirit, and no particle of spirit without matter. In manifesting itself the spirit-matter differentiates on seven planes, each more dense on the way down to the plane of our senses than its predecessor, the substance in all being the same, only differing in degree. Therefore from this view the whole universe is alive, not one atom of it being in any sense dead. It is also conscious and intelligent, its consciousness and intelligence being present on all planes though obscured on this one. On this plane of ours the spirit focalizes itself in all human beings who choose to permit it to do so, and the refusal to permit it is the cause of ignorance, of sin, of all sorrow and suffering. In all ages some have come to this high state, have grown to be as gods, are partakers actively in the work of nature, and go on from century to century widening their consciousness and increasing the scope of their government in nature. This is the destiny of all beings, and hence at the outset Theosophy postulates this perfectibility of the race, removes the idea of innate unregenerable wickedness, and offers a purpose and an aim for life which is consonant with the longings of the soul and with its real nature, tending at the same time to destroy pessimism with its companion, despair.

In Theosophy the world is held to be the product of the evolution of the principle spoken of, from the very lowest first forms of life, guided as it proceeded by intelligent perfected beings from other and older evolutions, and compounded also of the egos or individual spirits for and by whom it emanates. Hence man as we know him is held to be a conscious spirit, the flower of evolution, with other and lower classes of egos below him in the lower kingdoms, all however coming up and destined one day to be on the same human stage as we now are, we then being higher still. Man's consciousness being thus more perfect is able to pass from one to another of the planes of differentiation mentioned. If he mistakes any one of them for the reality that he is in his essence, he is deluded; the object of evolution then is to give him complete self-consciousness so that he may go on to higher stages in the progress of the universe. His evolution after coming on the human stage is for the getting of experience, and in order to so raise up and purify the various planes of matter with which he has to do, that the voice of the spirit may be fully heard and comprehended.

He is a religious being because he is a spirit encased in matter, which is in turn itself spiritual in essence. Being a spirit he requires vehicles with which to come in touch with all the planes of nature included in evolution, and it is these vehicles that make of him an intricate, composite being, liable to error, but at the same time able to rise above all delusions and conquer the highest place. He is in miniature the universe, for he is as spirit, manifesting himself to himself by means of seven differentiations. Therefore is he known in Theosophy as a sevenfold being. The Christian division of body, soul, and spirit is accurate so far as it goes, but will not answer to the problems of life and nature, unless, as is not the case, those three divisions are each held to be composed of others, which would raise the possible total to seven. The spirit stands alone at the top, next comes the spiritual soul or Buddhi as it is called in Sanskrit. This partakes more of the spirit than any below it, and is connected with Manas or mind, these three being the real trinity of man, the imperishable part, the real thinking entity living on the earth in the other and denser vehicles by its evolution. Below in order of quality is the plane of the desires and passions shared with the animal kingdom, unintelligent, and the producer of ignorance flowing from delusion. It is distinct from the will and judgment, and must therefore be given its own place. On this plane is gross life, manifesting, not as spirit from which it derives its essence, but as energy and motion on this plane. It being common to the whole objective plane and being everywhere, is also to be classed by itself, the portion used by man being given up at the death of the body. Then last, before the objective body, is the model or double of the outer physical case. This double is the astral body belonging to the astral plane or matter, not so dense as physical molecules, but more tenuous and much stronger, as well as lasting. It is the original of the body permitting the physical molecules to arrange and show themselves thereon, allowing them to go and come from day to day as they are known to do, yet ever retaining the fixed shape and contour given by the astral double within. These lower four principles or sheaths are the transitory perishable part of man, not himself, but in every sense the instrument he uses, given up at the hour of death like an old garment, and rebuilt out of the general reservoir at every new birth. The trinity is the real man, the thinker, the individuality that passes from house to house, gaining experience at each rebirth, while it suffers and enjoys according to its deeds—it is the one central man, the living spirit-soul.

Now this spiritual man, having always existed, being intimately concerned in evolution, dominated by the law of cause and effect, because in himself he is that very law, showing moreover on this plane varieties of force of character, capacity, and opportunity, his very presence must be explained, while the differences noted have to be accounted for. The doctrine of reincarnation does all this. It means that man as a thinker, composed of soul, mind and spirit, occupies body after body in life after life on the earth which is the scene of his evolution, and where he must, under the very laws of his being, complete that evolution once it has been begun. In any one life he is known to others as a personality, but in the whole stretch of eternity he is one individual, feeling in himself an identity not dependent on name, form, or recollection.

This doctrine is the very base of Theosophy, for it explains life and nature. It is one aspect of evolution, for as it is re-embodiment in meaning, and as evolution could not go on without re-embodiment, it is evolution itself, as applied to the human soul. But it is also a doctrine believed in at the time given to Jesus and taught in the early ages of Christianity, being now as much necessary to that religion as it is to any other to explain texts, to reconcile the justice of God with the rough and merciless aspect of nature and life to most mortals, and to throw a light perceptible by reason on all the problems that vex us in our journey through this world. The vast, and under any other doctrine unjust, difference between the savage and the civilized man as to both capacity, character, and opportunity can be understood only through this doctrine, and coming to our own stratum the differences of the same kind may only thus be explained. It vindicates Nature and God, and removes from religion the blot thrown by men who have postulated creeds which paint the creator as a demon. Each man's life and character are the outcome of his previous lives and thoughts. Each is his own judge, his own executioner, for it is his own hand that forges the weapon which works for his punishment, and each by his own life reaches reward, rises to heights of knowledge and power for the good of all who may be left behind him. Nothing is left to chance, favor, or partiality, but all is under the governance of law. Man is a thinker, and by his thoughts he makes the causes for woe or bliss; for his thoughts produce his acts. He is the center for any disturbance of the universal harmony, and to him as the center, the disturbance must return so as to bring about equilibrium, for nature always works towards harmony. Man is always carrying on a series of thoughts, which extend back to the remote past, continually making action and reaction. He is thus responsible for all his thoughts and acts, and in that his complete responsibility is established; his own spirit is the essence of this law and provides for every compensation, for every disturbance, and adjustment for all effects. This is the law of Karma or justice, sometimes called the ethical law of causation. It is not foreign to the Christian scriptures, for both Jesus and St. Paul clearly enunciated it. Jesus said we should be judged as we gave judgment and should receive the measure meted to others. St. Paul said: "Brethren, be not deceived, God is not mocked, for whatsoever a man soweth that also shall he reap." And that sowing and reaping can only be possible under the doctrines of Karma and reincarnation.

But what of death and after? Is heaven a place or is it not? Theosophy teaches, as may be found in all sacred books, that after death the soul reaps a rest. This is from its own nature. It is a thinker, and cannot during life fulfill and carry out all nor even a small part of the myriads of thoughts entertained. Hence when at death it casts off the body and the astral body, and is released from the passions and desires, its natural forces have immediate sway and it thinks its thoughts out on the soul plane, clothed in a finer body suitable to that existence. This is called Devachan. It is the very state that has brought about the descriptions of heaven common to all religions, but this doctrine is very clearly put in the Buddhist and Hindu religions. It is a time of rest, because the physical body being absent the consciousness is not in the completer touch with visible nature which is possible on the material plane. But it is a real existence, and no more illusionary than earth life; it is where the essence of the thoughts of life that were as high as character permitted, expands and is garnered by the soul and mind. When the force of these thoughts is fully exhausted the soul is drawn back once more to earth, to that environment which is sufficiently like unto itself to give it the proper further evolution. This alternation from state to state goes on until the being rises from repeated experiences above ignorance, and realizes in itself the actual unity of all spiritual beings. Then it passes on to higher and greater steps on the evolutionary road.

No new ethics are presented by Theosophy, as it is held that right ethics are for ever the same. But in the doctrines of Theosophy are to be found the philosophical and reasonable basis for ethics and the natural enforcement of them in practice. Universal brotherhood is that which will result in doing unto others as you would have them do unto you, and in your loving your neighbor as yourself—declared as right by all teachers in the great religions of the world.

William Q. Judge

"Theosophy in the Christian Bible"

[*The Theosophical Congress*, pp. 33-35]

. . . Mr. William Q. Judge—I have been asked to say a few more words on the subject of Theosophy in the Christian Bible; that is, I have been asked to show what Theosophical doctrines can be found in the Christian books.

One of the Theosophical doctrines is the doctrine of Karma; that is, exact justice ruling in the spiritual as well as in the physical; the exact carrying out of effect from cause in the spiritual nature of man, the moral nature as well as in the physical world. That is, that every man is ruled in his life, not by a vengeful and partial God, but by justice. This life is just; whether one is miserable or happy, whether he is poor or rich, it is just. Where is this doctrine found in the Christian Bible, this doctrine that as ye have sown so shall ye reap? That is, having lived before in this world you have made causes which bring about today the life you lead now, which have made the characteristics that you have, which made you what you are now, and have plunged you into a living hell or into a happy heaven today. We say this doctrine has not of late been taught in Christianity; but it is in the books of the Christians and it ought to have been taught, it would have been profitable had it been expounded. Now, where can it be found?

Does not Jesus say, among other things, you should not judge others? Why? Because if you do you will be judged yourself. What you mete out to others will be meted out to you. That is, what men do to others will be done to themselves. Where and when is this to be done? When is the measure to be meted out if not in this life or some other? St. Paul says: "Brethren, be not deceived, God is not mocked, for whatsoever a man soweth that shall he also reap." Do not these quotations prove that in St. Paul and in the words of Jesus can be found this doctrine of Karma: that as you sow so shall you reap? That your circumstances now are the result of your own acts? This is the doctrine which is the most prominent in the Theosophical field. I call it Theosophical, not because the members teach it, nor from its presence in our literature, but because it is found in the religion of every nation; that is why it is Theosophical. But you have been taught that you must be good or you will be punished. In the West you are told you will be rewarded and punished in this life and in the next. But men are not punished in this life. Today thousands of men live lives of luxury, strife, and crime, but they are not punished here, and, according to the teachings of Christianity, they stand a pretty good chance of escaping punishment hereafter if they only believe. We see that many are not rewarded who are good, but are often born into misery.

The doctrine of reincarnation is taught in the Christian Bible, that is, that you will be born over and over again in this world according to your destiny, to follow the effects of causes you yourself have put in motion in whatever life. Where is that found? In the mouth of Jesus; and certainly if Jesus, the founder of Christianity, has stated this, has any man or any body of men, has any person any right to say that it is not true? I deny their right, and I say that Christianity has been deprived by theologians of a doctrine which Jesus himself declared, when reincarnation is taken away from it. We say that the doctrine is in the Gospels. One day they brought to Jesus a man who was born blind and asked him why was this man born blind; was it for some sin he had committed or those his parents committed? Now, how could a man be born blind for a sin he had himself committed unless he had lived before that time to commit it? This was a doctrine believed in at that day. The Jews believed it and Jesus was a Jew. He did not deny the doctrine on that occasion. He only said, "Not for that reason." If the doctrine were wrong, certainly Jesus, as the Son of God, would not only have denied it, but he would have said, "The doctrine you enunciate is false." He said nothing of the kind. At another time he himself declared the doctrine, and he asked his disciples, "Whom do men think that I am?", meaning and referring to what was believed at that time, that great sages were born over and over again for the enlightenment of mankind. They call them Avatars in the East. They had an idea great sages and prophets would come back. Will you tell me how such men then could be reborn at all unless under natural law and unless such law governs every man? So Jesus, referring to this idea, said to his disciples: "Whom do men think that I am?" And they said: "Some men think that you are Elias, who was for to come." St. John had been killed just then by the ruler of Judea, and Jesus said to them that Elias had already come back in the person of John and the rulers had killed him, not knowing he was a reincarnation of Elias. So in one case he did not deny and in the other he explicitly asserted the doctrine. And if we take this view we know what he meant when he said to Nicodemus that a man must be born again. He meant not only the regeneration of the soul, but reborn into the body again; that is, that man is a soul who comes into a house to live life after life, and he must go from house to house until he has learned the whole architecture of human life and is able to build a perfect house. In Revelations, the last word of all the books, we find the great speaker writing that he heard the voice of God saying to him that him who overcometh the flesh and the devil, the world and sin, "I shall make a pillar in the house of my Father and he shall go out no more." Does not that mean he had gone out before? The old Fathers in the early ages of Christianity taught that if we triumphed over the flesh and the devil, the world and sin, God would make each one a pillar in the house of his father and he would not have to go out again. That is the doctrine of reincarnation.

Then if you will look at the history of the Christian Church you find that the doctrine was taught for five hundred years and not until the Council of Constantinople was it rejected. At that time it was turned out by ignorant monks, and since then it has not been taught by the teachers, but it is in the Christian books, and to these Christian books we appeal. I say these very doctrines are in many other places found there. Another doctrine is that man is not merely a body, but is a composite being of many divisions. St. Paul taught we have a spiritual body as well as a material body, that we are a spiritual body and a physical body and spirit. That will bring in every one of the seven principles of the Theosophical category. So we say, all through the Christian books, in the Old Testament and in the New, we may find the great doctrines of Theosophy, by which I mean the great universal ideas of unity, of universal brotherhood, of strict justice and no favoritism, of reincarnation, and of the composite nature of man, which permeate every religion as well as the books of the Christians, both old and new.

Adjourned until 3 p.m.

FRIDAY AFTERNOON, SEPTEMBER 16TH.

MR. JUDGE—I inadvertently this morning forgot to state that Mrs. Cooper-Oakley is one of the delegates from the European Section. She is a resident of London, and has been appointed by the Australian Branches also, because she has just come from there. The next session after this will be this evening in this hall, unless we shall be able to secure a larger one, as a great many persons have gone away because this one is so full. This evening we shall have addresses from Mrs. Besant and others on various important doctrines of Theosophy. I understand that many persons who are not fully acquainted with Theosophy and suppose that in one short meeting we could describe it all, go away with the impression that Theosophy is too high a philosophy for the common people. Theosophy is exactly the reverse. It is not for the parlor merely, and it has never done much good through the parlor. The parlor does not like it. It is an everyday religion, and if those who had any other idea will remain for all our sessions, they may be able to find out how Theosophy may be of use in daily life. The next session after this evening will be tomorrow, when we meet again here or in some other hall. The evening session on Saturday will be in the Hall of Washington, which is a larger hall, and which has been given to us for the purpose of enabling three or four of us— Mrs. Besant, Professor Chakravarti, probably Mrs. Oakley and myself—to make a general presentation of Theosophy to the Parliament. Of course that means you, because you constitute the Parliament. I wish also to state that there is also an overflowing meeting in the next hall, which, if it grows to sufficient size, will be addressed by Bro. Claude F. Wright on some Theosophical subject. You will now please give your attention to Dr. Buck of Cincinnati.

Universal Brotherhood a Fact of Nature
[*The Theosophical Congress*, pp. 70-74]

I have been requested to speak on the subject of Universal Brotherhood as a fact in nature; not as a theory, not as a Utopian dream
which can never be realized; not as a fact in society, not as a fact
in government, but as a fact in nature. That is, that Universal Brotherhood is an actual thing, whether it is recognized or whether it is not.
Christian priests have claimed for some years, without right, that
Christianity introduced the idea of Universal Brotherhood. The reason
the claim was made, I suppose, was because those who made it did
not know that other religions at other times had the same doctrine.
It is found in the Buddhist scriptures, it is found in the Chinese books,
it is found in the Parsee books, it is found everywhere in the history
of the world, long before the first year of the Christian Era began.
So it is not a special idea from the Christian scriptures. Every nation, then, every civilization has brought forward this doctrine, and
the facts of history show us that, more than at any other time, the
last eighteen hundred years have seen this doctrine violated in society,
in government, and in nations. So that at last men have come to say,
"Universal Brotherhood is very beautiful; it is something that we all
desire, but it is impossible to realize." With one word they declare the
noble doctrine, and with the other they deny the possibility of its ever
being realized.

Why is this the case? Why is it that although Christianity and other
religions have brought forward this doctrine, it has been violated?
We cannot deny that it has been. The history of even the last few years
proves it. The history of the last forty years in America, without going
any farther back, proves that this doctrine has been violated in the
West. How could it have been a doctrine that the Americans believed
in when they had slavery in their midst? How could it have been believed in by the French when they stretched out their hand and demanded of Siam, a weak and powerless nation, that it must give up
to them its own property? How could it have been believed in by the
Germans and French when they constructed engines of war and went
into battle and destroyed each other by the thousands? Does not the
American War of the Rebellion and the vast amount of treasure wasted
and the thousands slain in that civil war prove conclusively that Uni-

versal Brotherhood has not been practiced? It has been professed but not practiced. Now, go further back, go back in the history of the nations in Europe, without going to any other country, and what do you find? Do you not find sectarian prejudice? Their view of Universal Brotherhood has for years prevented the progress of science. Is it not true that only since science became materialized—a most remarkable thing, but it is true—I insist that since then only science has made progress. If Universal Brotherhood had been a belief of this nation, then we would not have had the burning of witches in America; nor in other countries would we have had the burning of Catholics by Protestants, nor the burning of Protestants by Catholics; we would not have had the persecutions that have stained the pages of history; and yet we have always claimed that we have had Universal Brotherhood. We have had the theory but not the practice. Now, then, has there not been something wanting? It is a beautiful doctrine. It is the only doctrine of the Theosophical Society, the only thing that any man is asked by us to subscribe to. What, then, is the matter with it? Why so many men who say that it is beautiful, but it is impossible, simply impossible? There are even some branches of the Christian church which say, "There is Jesus; why, the altruistic, noble teachings of Christ are beautiful; but no State could live three months under such doctrine." The reason that it has not prevailed in practice is that it has been denied in the heart.

The Theosophist who knows anything about life insists that Universal Brotherhood is not a mere theory. It is a fact, a living ever present fact, from which no nation can hope to escape; no man can escape from it, and every man who violates it violates a law, violates the greatest law of nature, which will react upon him and make him suffer. And that is why we have had suffering; that is why you have in Chicago, in London, in New York, in Berlin, in all the great cities of the world, masses of people who are claiming with violence what they call their rights and saying they must have them, and that another class is oppressing them; and danger lurks in every corner because men are insisting on Universal Brotherhood. This noble doctrine has already become a danger. The reason of all these things is that men have denied the fact. Now, we propose to show you, if we can, that it is a fact.

If you will notice you will find that when it rains over a certain area vast numbers of men are affected similarly. The rain has to fall on the fields in order that the harvest may grow, so that afterwards it may be gathered, and all the farmers are affected together by the rain. If you examine society you will find that at the same hour every day almost all the people are doing exactly the same thing. At a certain hour in the morning thousands of your citizens are going down that railway or rush all together to catch the train, and at another few moments afterwards they are rushing out of the train to get to business, all doing the same thing, one common thought inspiring them. That is one of the proofs—a small one—in social and business life that they are affected together, they are all united. Then in the evening they will come home at the same hour, and if you could see, at the same hour you would see them all eating together and digesting together, and then later on they are all lying down together at the same hours. Are they not united even in their social life? Brothers even in that? And what do we see here in business? Lately I have felt it; every man has felt it, and many women; doubtless all have felt it; lately we have had a financial crisis, perhaps have it yet, in which dollars have been scarce, during which men have discovered that there are only just so many dollars and half dollars to each person in the country, and we have altogether been suffering from that panic all over this vast country. Suffering, why? Because commercially we are united and cannot get out of it. China even is affected by it, and Japan. India, they say, was the cause of it. Some men say the reason for this panic is that India put the price of rupees down, and we who produce so much silver began to feel it. I do not know that that is the reason. But I think there is another cause. I think the American nation is so fond of luxury, so fond of fine clothes, so fond of having a heap of money, that it has gone too far and there was bound to come a reaction, because it is all united together with the whole world, and when it spread itself out too far the slightest touch broke the fabric. That is the reason, and that is another proof of Universal Brotherhood. We are all united, not only with each other here, but with the entire world.

Now, then, go further still materially and you find that all men are alike. We have the same sort of bodies, a little different perhaps in height, weight, and extension, but as human beings we are all alike, all the same color in one country, all the same shape in any country, so that as mere bodies of flesh they are united, they are the same. We know every man and woman has exuding from him or her what is called perspiration. The doctors will tell you there is a finer perspiration you cannot see, the invisible perspiration which goes out a short distance around about us; we know it comes out from every person, and the emanations of each person are affecting every other person, being interchanged always. All those in this room are being affected by these emanations and also by the ideas of each other, and the ideas of the speakers speaking to you. So it is in every direction; wherever you go, wherever you look, we are united; in whatever plane, the plane of mind as well as the plane of the body; the plane of the emotions, of the spirit, what not, we are all united, and it is a fact from which we cannot escape. Now, then, further: science is beginning to admit what the old Theosophists have always said, that there is going on every minute in every person a death, a dissolution, a disappearance. It used to be taught and thought in the West that we could see matter, that this table is made of matter. It is admitted today by your best scientific men in every part of Western civilization that you do not see matter at all; it is only the phenomena of matter we see; and it is my senses which enable me to perceive these phenomena. It is not matter at all, and so we do not see matter. Now admitting that, they go further and say there is a constant change in matter so-called; that is, this table is in motion. This is not a purely Theosophical theory. Go to any Doctor of Physics and he will admit to you as I have stated it. This table is in motion; every molecule is separate from every other, and there is space between them, and they are moving. So it is with every man; he is made of atoms and they are in motion. Then how is it we remain the same size and weight nearly always from the moment of maturity until death? We eat tons of meat and vegetables but remain the same. It is not because of the things you have eaten. In addition to that the atoms are alive, constantly moving, coming and going from one person to another; and this is the modern doctrine today as well as it was the doctrine of ancient India. They call it the momentary dissolution of atoms; that is to say, to put it in another way, I am losing, all of you in this room are losing, a certain number of atoms, but they are being replaced by other atoms. Now, where do these other atoms come from? Do they not come from the people in this room? These atoms help to rebuild your body as well as does the food you eat. And we are exuding atoms from our minds, and we are receiving into ourselves the atoms other men have used. For, remember, science teaches you, and Theosophy has always insisted, that matter is invisible before it is turned into this combination of the life cycle, which makes it visible, makes it tangible to us. So these atoms leave us in a stream and rush into other people. And therefore the atoms of good men go into bad men, the atoms impressed by bad men go into good men, and *vice versa*. In that way as well as others we are affecting everybody in this world; and the people in Chicago who are living mean, selfish lives are impressing these invisible atoms with mean and selfish characters, and these mean and selfish atoms will be distributed by other men, and by you again to your and their detriment. That is another phase of Universal Brotherhood. It teaches us to be careful to see that we use and keep the atoms in our charge in such a condition that they shall benefit others to whom they shall go.   (Applause.)

There is another view of Universal Brotherhood, and I don't pretend to exhaust the argument on this point, for I have not the time nor force to state all that is put forward in the Theosophical books and literature and thought. That is, that there is in this world an actual Universal Brotherhood of men and women, of souls, a brotherhood of beings who practice Universal Brotherhood by always trying to influence the souls of men for their good. I bring to you the message of these men; I bring to you the words of that brotherhood. Why will you longer call yourselves miserable men and women who are willing to go to a Heaven where you will do nothing? Do you not like to be gods? Do you not want to be gods? I hear some men say, "What, a god! Impossible!" Perhaps they do not like the responsibility. Why, when you get to that position you will understand the responsibility. This actual Brotherhood of living men says, Why, men of the West, why will you so long refuse to believe you are gods? We are your brothers and we are gods with you. Be then as gods! Believe that you are gods, and then, after experience and attainment, you will have a place consciously in the great Brotherhood which governs the entire world, but cannot go against the law. This great Brotherhood of living men, living souls, would, if they could, alter the face of civilization; they would, if they could, come down and make saints of every one of you; but evolution is the law and they cannot violate it; they must wait for you. And why will you so long be satisfied to believe that you are born in original sin and cannot escape? I do not believe in any such doctrine as that. I do not believe I was born in original sin. I believe that I am pretty bad, but that potentially I am a god, and I propose to take the inheritance if it is possible. For what purpose? So that I may help all the rest to do the same thing, for that is the law of Universal Brotherhood; and the Theosophical Society wishes to enforce it on the West, to make it see this great truth, that we are as gods, and are only prevented from being so in fact by our own insanity, ignorance, and fear to take the position.

So, then, we insist that Universal Brotherhood is a fact in nature. It is a fact for the lowest part of nature; for the animal kingdom, for the vegetable kingdom, and the mineral kingdom. We are all atoms, obeying the law together. Our denying it does not disprove it. It simply puts off the day of reward and keeps us miserable, poor, and selfish. Why, just think of it! if all in Chicago, in the United States, would act as Jesus has said, as Buddha has said, as Confucius said, as all the great ethical teachers of the world have said, "Do unto others as you would have them do unto you," would there be any necessity for legal measures and policemen with clubs in this park as you had them the other day? (Applause.) No, I think there would be no necessity, and that is what one of this great Brotherhood has said. He said all the troubles of the world would disappear in a moment if men would only do one-quarter of what they could and what they ought. It is not God who is to damn you to death, to misery. It is yourself. And the Theosophical Society desires above all things, not that you should understand spiritualism, not that wonderful occult works should be performed, but to understand the constitution of matter and of Life as they are, which we can never understand but by practicing right ethics. Live with each other as brothers; for the misery and the trouble of the world are of more importance than all the scientific progress that may be imagined. I conclude by calling upon you by all that humanity holds dear to remember what I say, and whether Christians, Atheists, Jews, Pagans, Heathen, or Theosophists, try to practice Universal Brotherhood, which is the universal duty of all men.

WILLIAM Q. JUDGE

[INVOCATIONS]

[The Theosophical Congress, pp. 80-81]

SESSION OF SATURDAY MORNING, SEPTEMBER 16TH, 10 A.M.

MR. JUDGE—One or two persons have said since our sessions began that they noticed that other Congresses began either with the Lord's Prayer or with some religious Christian hymn, and ended with the doxology or some other religious function, and they wondered why the Theosophical Congresses were opened in a business manner and closed in the same way. What is the reason for this? The reason is not very far to seek; it is found in the words of Jesus; and if we were in India we could give reasons from their scriptures, but here the words of Jesus are quite enough. Jesus told the Pharisees, who existed in that time as they do now in ours, that they should not make prayers in the streets nor shout prayers, but to retire to their closets and pray to the Father who seeth in secret, and he would reward them openly.[1] So we do not begin with prayer, nor end with the doxology. Every individual can pray himself or herself to the God who seeth in secret, and we prefer to follow the words of Jesus and not to make long prayers in the streets nor to be seen of men at our secret devotions, but go at once to our business, which is to endeavor to give men and women a philosophy of life so they will be able to pray sincerely to the Father who seeth in secret.

---

[1] [*Matt.* vi:5-9.]

The Organized Life of the Theosophical Society

[*The Theosophical Congress*, pp. 96-102][1]

[THE SOCIETY ABSOLUTELY UNSECTARIAN, WITHOUT A CREED, AND OPEN TO PERSONS OF ALL FAITHS. ACCEPTANCE OF DOCTRINES LARGELY TAUGHT IN THEOSOPHICAL LITERATURE NOT INCUMBENT, ITS RELATION TO CIVIC AFFAIRS AND EDUCATION.]

BROTHERS AND SISTERS—

It is now my duty to attempt to deal further with the subject of the Organized Life of the Theosophical Society. Brother Wright has taken up some points which I would have taken up in other circumstances; Brother Chakravarti has outlined to you as a Brahman, as a member of the Indian Section, what he thinks is the mission of the Theosophical Society and what its mission there so far has resulted in. You have had from Brother Wright a great deal of fact. He must have conveyed to you the impression that the Theosophical Society has accomplished a good deal of work, or else that we have been telling a lie, one or the other. I think that you will believe him, that we have accomplished an enormous amount of work in eighteen years against most strenuous and bitter opposition. And it is the custom in America, and especially in the West, and most especially in Chicago, to measure results by money. How could we have accomplished all this, how could we have printed all those books without printing presses, without paper, without salaries, without people to do the work, and that you think takes money? Perhaps you think we have a secret fund from which we have drawn some millions, laid away amongst the buried treasures of India, which one or two of us can draw from now and then, so as to enable us to do work which other bodies can accomplish only by the use of money. But it is not so. We have little money and never had much. We do not want it, do not expect it, and the day when we shall have a large fund and be able to collect $5,000,000 in imitation of Western missionary bodies will be the day when the Theosophical Society will die. It is not money that has done this. It is the energy of the human heart. These people who are here with me are only representatives of many, many persons all over the world who are willing to give their life, their energy, their time to a movement which they think will benefit man. They get

---

1 Entered here under original title, headed by a summary of the talk.

nothing for it; they get no preference. What is it of honor to preside at a meeting like this? What is it for any person to be a member of a Branch? What is it to be the President of the Theosophical Society? Nothing at all. There is no honor in it whatever. There are no places, no salaries, nothing at all but work.

Brother Chakravarti gave you an idea of our future. It has been said against us that this movement of ours was an invention of the East, but he must have made you suspect that perhaps this movement is unique, that it came neither from the East nor the West. The East has solidified, crystallized, stood still; it would never have commenced such a movement. The West did not know about such things; it did not want them. We are wrapped up in material progress; it never would have started such a movement. Where, then, was the movement really started? It was started in the spiritual world above, both East and West, by living men. Not by spirits of dead men, but by living spirits, living spirits like yourselves, who have risen above creeds and nations and castes and peoples, and are simply human beings. They started this movement by giving the impulse and the message; that is why we who have been in it so long have the confidence born of knowledge, knowledge that it will succeed. And as Claude Wright told you, we began at the time under direction, when we knew that materialism was spreading, not only over the West, but was spreading insidiously all over the East. As Brother Chakravarti told you, it was turning the mind of the East, not to Christianity—never could that be done—but into the grossest forms of materialism. That is to say, that the West itself with its missionaries was corrupting a vast mass of men and turning them into men who believed in nothing but annihilation after this life. If you could have succeeded in converting them to Christianity, it would have been well enough, for then they could rise up higher out of that into another spiritual life. But instead of succeeding with them in that, as I know from facts, from having been there, you were simply flinging them from their own beliefs into materialism, and the Theosophical Society was started to prevent that, and to prevent it in the West also. It has done something towards it. It has not been the one cause, but it has been the little lever, the little point in the center, around which we are all working with all effectual means for the good of humanity. It is trying to offer the key to all these Congresses and to show all men where the truth is.

Now, when the Theosophical Society was founded in 1875, if you could have heard what I did, you would have heard a huge laugh pass over the country by means of the newspapers. There was nothing else but laughter and jokes. The Society was an immense joke, they said; a new kind of spiritualism; something of that sort to tickle men's fancies, and we have had that to contend with all the time. But we have succeeded always in remaining at the post and saying just what we meant to say all the time for all the laughter. We took no salaries, but we had belief in the human heart.

The objects of the Theosophical Society having been explained to you by Brother Wright, you know the Society has but one doctrine, that of Universal Brotherhood. You cannot belong to it unless you believe in that; you won't want to belong to it unless you believe in that. But you are not required to believe anything else. You are not required to believe in Brother Chakravarti; you are not required to believe what, as the newspapers say, are the doctrines of "that woman Besant"; you are not required to believe in Madame Blavatsky, who was a woman, a human being, just the same as the rest of us; you are not required to believe in those great beings of whom Brother Chakravarti has been speaking. It has been supposed by some that in order to be a Theosophist you must believe in Mahatmas, that you must believe in H. P. Blavatsky, in reincarnation, in Karma; but you do not have to believe in any of those things at all. But, I take it, you must believe in Universal Brotherhood. And the reason why people have been a little confused is this: they have seen the Theosophical Society absolutely without a creed, absolutely without any dogma, and as inside of it they know of a large number of people who believe in those ideas and doctrines, they think that is what the Theosophist must believe. But it is not. For, don't you see, if we started a Universal Brotherhood, and started a Society to find out the truth, and then fixed a dogma, that moment we would be telling a lie and forfeiting the whole object we started to accomplish. We can never have a creed. We do know what the truth is. It may be that we are wrong; it may be we will find out more. It is true we will never go back to those old dogmas and creeds, although there are still many members on the books of the powerful churches. We can never go back there, but we may go further on, and we are quite willing to. We are promulgating our philosophies which we talk about as individuals and on our own account. As Vice-President of the Society I have no right to say that any particular thing is true, and I never do say so. But I have the right to say, as I myself emphatically do, that I as an individual believe certain things are true, and I would be a poor sort of man if, believing certain things to be true, I did not try to show that they are. But at the same time I have no right to say, as man or official, you must believe it because I do. I simply present it to you for your consideration, and it is for you to decide, not for me. I am not going to stop saying that I believe so and so because a few other persons cannot believe it. They can go on with me and we will agree to disagree, and we will only forward the cause of Universal Brotherhood. Because beliefs in particular creeds have nothing to do with how you treat another man. What creed is there in the statement republished by Jesus, promulgated by him, to do to others as you would have them do unto you? No creed about that; no paving of hell with the skulls of infants about that; no belief in a particular sort of transmission of the spiritual life from St. Peter or Paul in that; nothing at all to abridge the treatment of man and woman by man and woman in the way they should treat them. We have no creed, then, and we should have none.

But the question is often asked: What have you as an organization to do with labor, with legal questions, labor-saving forces, with education, with society? We have nothing to do with them. Is it not true that man, if he has a knowledge as to how he ought to live, needs no law whatever? Was not St. Paul right when he spoke of that and said: you would become your own law; knowing the truth, you need no law? What, then, has the Theosophical Society to do with law? If there are to be laws, let them be passed and execute them, but the Theosophical Society has nothing to do with it as such. But every brother in the Theosophical Society must obey the law of the land in which he lives, for he would be a poor Theosophist if he did not. And the Theosophical Society has nothing to do with education. But its members may have as much to do with it as they please. But they have no right to say what is the Theosophical Society's idea of education. They can only say "That is my idea of it." And always they must and shall preserve these distinctions. We have been asked, what about this labor struggle? We have been asked why we do not join the Bellamyites[1] and other cooperative societies? If you want to go in, go in. The Theosophical Society, as such, has nothing to do with it. I am perfectly satisfied to live where I am and do my duty where I stand, without any new law of property, or with it, whichever you please. And the religion of the West which logically ought to support all the various socialists and anarchists and nihilists is the Christian religion, because in the beginning it was a community. Jesus' system was a community in which everything was common property, and the early Christians threw all their money and property into one common box. Why, then, should not the Christian religion logically carry out all the plans of the socialists, anarchists, nihilists, and all the other 'ists who want to change the face of the earth by legislation? But the Theosophist knows that legislation changes nothing whatever. There are laws now on every statute book in every State in the United States, laws enough if men would only execute them and live up to them. But a law that socialists shall share in this, or that there shall be no Trust in that, is passed; and then there are the lawyers to get around the law, as they always can. So what is the use of passing

---

1 [See *Edward Bellamy* by Arthur E. Morgan, Columbia University Press, N.Y., 1944, pp. 260-75. Excerpt of a Judge letter to Bellamy is on p. 262—*Comp.*]

the law at all? There is no use whatever. Hence the Theosophical Society, as such, has nothing to do with such trumpery and democratic things as legislation. Let the men engaged in legislation go on legislating. If a Theosophist and he is born to be a legislator, or is born to be a judge, let him legislate as a citizen and not as a Theosophist, or let him be a judge and skilled lawyer. If they will know that philosophy which shows them what human life is, they will have begun to follow the law without knowing what the law is. America is the only land of all countries where the law is followed without the people knowing much of it. In America the people are orderly; they understand life a little better than other people in the world, but they don't know so much about the masses of laws they have on their books. I believe personally that the day is coming when America is to be the country where the new race will be born that will know all about the true laws and what is right, and will be able to perform it. So, then, the Theosophical Society is not prepared to give out promulgations as to this or that particular item of legislation or education or civic affairs that people would have taught.

They ask also about marriage. Why, you understand about marriage. You know how it is accomplished. We have nothing to do with it as a Society. We know there are many kinds of marriage, sometimes merely by tying a string, sometimes by walking around the fire. As a body we have nothing to do with these forms nor interfere in them, And as to prayer, if you want to pray, pray. But if you pray, and if you say you have a certain belief, live up to it. If you do not do so you are no Theosophist, nor a man, nor a proper living person. You are only a hypocrite.

Now, the Theosophical Society is an unsectarian body. It does not have a creed. It never will have one if those persons in it now can possibly prevent it. It does not need a creed. It is open to everybody, of all sects and faiths, and for that reason it has been possible to bring into it men of all religions, men from India, China, Japan, Brahmans, as you have seen and as you have already before your eyes, which could not have been accomplished by any sect, Christian, or Buddhist, or Brahman. If the Buddhists started in India a Buddhist society, the Brahmans would not accept it. And if the Brahmans started a Brahman propagandist society, the Buddhists would say they did not want it. So it is with the various Christian denominations: the Baptists, the Catholics, the Methodists, the Presbyterians. If any one of them, as a society, asked others to come in, none of the other different stripes or classes of Christians would come in. Each says it teaches the truth; still the others do not come in. But Theosophy comes forward boldly and says: "All religions have underneath one single truth. None of the religions are perfectly true. It is impossible that they should be, because man is prone to err. Come into the Society in which as brothers helping each other we will examine all these faiths so that we may find out the truth under all. For we believe that in the beginning of human evolution great teachers gave the truth out, one single truth before the mingling of tongues on the tower of Babel, to man." That single truth was variously accepted and variously perceived, and out of these different perceptions they built up different creeds, and so they made a great many different sorts of faiths. But suppose you look into all of them. You find the Christians teaching for many years that man has a soul. Do you think that the Christians are the only ones who taught about the soul? The Hindus have been teaching about the soul for ages. They have said always that man has a soul. The Japanese do the same thing. So do other races and religions. So in that one point they have always together been teaching the same thing. The Christians have been teaching about heaven and hell; about a sort of heaven which is very material, I admit, with pearly gates and golden streets and angels with robes such as no one ever saw and crowns upon their heads; and hell full of fire and brimstone, with devils throwing people around with forks into the fire. The Buddhists have been teaching the same thing for ages. I can read to you out of their books about a copper vessel full of boiling oil into which they say fate puts a man. In this he goes down and down for thousands and thousands of years until he gets to the bottom; then he begins to rise again to the top, rising for ages again, and when he gets to the top and thinks he is going to be let out, he begins to sink again, and that goes on for ages more. Is not that as bad and as material as the Christian hell? And then the Eastern teaching of heaven, of an inimitable and incomprehensible place, yet just as material but better than the Christian heaven.

The Abbé Huc went to Tartary many years ago. He was a Catholic priest. There he found ministers, monks, nuns, similar ceremonies to the Romish, the ministers using the different vestments and draperies of the Catholics, the taper, bell, candle, the book, the rosary, what not, everything. He brought back the tale to Europe and he published it. The explanation of the priests—of course they would not say so now— was that it was the invention of the Devil, who, knowing that Christianity was going to be abroad, went ahead of it and founded that imitation in the East so that Christian people would be confused. Well now, that is not the way to explain it. The proper way is, that man has these things as a universal property and always makes some mistakes. And so it is in Buddhism and every other religion. In Tibet they have a pope who is the great successor of the original founder of the thing, just the same as the Catholic pope. I don't care what sort of Western religion you bring forward; the religions in the East are the older religions and the fountain, but there is a single stream of truth underneath all, and

that single stream is what the Theosophical Society digs for and implores these religious men to find out. We ask them not to go before
each other and say their own religion is the true one. But they ask if we
can give mercy to a man's soul, wash away the blood from his hand,
and take away his sin? We say, "Come, we will wash away your sin."
How? By giving men reasons to make them do differently.

The history of the past shows that belief does not make men better.
We think there is a philosophy which will compel them from within to
do right, and that is what this search will reveal. It will reveal underneath all these religions this one diamond which shows its light through
them all; then all men can perceive it, then there will no longer be any
necessity for the Theosophical Society, or for either creed or church;
it will simply be truth and the people will know. Look fairly and
squarely at Christianity. I am simply asking you to consider facts. Here
we have Jesus saying: Worship in secret. The Christians do not do it.
Then there are all the different contradictory statements made by the
same religion. How can churches have the enormous cathedrals, the
immense wealth, the cannons and soldiers in their possession, if they
are the representatives of Christ? How can that be possible unless men
are running after creeds and not truth? Even in the words of Jesus is
to be found everything we want. I simply repeat to you that old truth
taught by him long ago, for to find out the truth in respect to ethics is
the chief object of the Theosophical Society, and to establish by Universal Brotherhood a basis from which that ethic may be preached,
practiced, and followed without any mistake. Therefore, then, we ask
you this: You have seen us here and you have seen our heathen; some
of them are now on the platform. We would like to know what you think
of our heathen, and what you think of this heathen Society that has
been so much abused? Is it a Society for spiritualism, for wonders,or for
folly? It is here to talk common sense and not merely to talk about H. P.
Blavatsky, a woman who is dead, but who was the grandest woman or
man that I ever knew. It is not for that. It is to bring back the truth
about the soul, which truth these heathens represent as well as we, and
they themselves are just as much in error as we. They do not know
much more about it than we do. But these poor heathen have in their
philosophy a little better statement of the truth than we have been able
to invent. So I would ask you to wipe out of your mind that hymn
which has done so much harm to Christian men and women which
reads:

What though the spicy breezes
Blow soft o'er Ceylon's isle,
Where every prospect pleases,
And only man is vile.

Wipe that idea completely out with a sponge, and then you will see
that we are all brothers and that by tolerating each other, by looking
into each other's beliefs, not setting up creeds and dogmas, we shall at
last realize that great ideal germ of perfection, human brotherhood,
which object has equally engaged the attention of the great Initiates
of all the human race.

W. Q. JUDGE

[On "Common Doctrines"]

[*The Theosophical Congress*, pp. 148-54]

WILLIAM Q. JUDGE—Mr. Chairman; brothers and sisters; men and
women; members of the Parliament of Religions: The Theosophical
Society has been presenting to you but one-half of its work, but one-
half of that which it has to present to the world. This is the Parliament of Religions. This is a Parliament of the Religions of the day.
Theosophy is not only a religion; it is also a science; it is religious
science and scientific religion, and at a Parliament of Religions it
would not be possible, indeed it would not be proper, to present the
science of Theosophy, which relates to so many matters outside of the
ordinary domain of the religions of today. The time will come when
religion will also be a science. Today it is not. The object of Theosophy
is to make of religion also a science, and to make science a religion,
so we have been presenting only one-half of the subject which we deal
with, and I would like you to remember that. We could not go into
the other part; it would be beyond the scope of this meeting.

Now, we have discovered during the last week, as many have discovered before by reading, by experience, and by travel, that the religions of the world are nearly all alike. We have discovered that
Christianity is not alone in claiming a Savior. If you will go over to
Japan you will find that the Buddhists of Japan have a doctrine which
declares that any one who relies upon and repeats three times a day
the name "Amita Buddha," will be saved. That is one Savior of the
Buddhists, who had the doctrine before Christianity was started. If
you will go among the Buddhists elsewhere you will find that they also
have a Savior; that by reliance upon the Lord Buddha, they claim
they will be saved. If you will go to the Brahmans and the other religions of India, you will find they also have a Savior. In some parts
of that mysterious land they say: "Repeat the name of Rama"—God—

"and he will save you." The Brahmans themselves have in their doctrines a doctrine which is called the "Bridge Doctrine": that which has God for its aim, has God himself as the means of salvation; is itself God. And so wherever you go throughout this wide world, examining the various religions, you find they all have this common doctrine. Why should we then say that the latest of these religions is the inventor of the doctrine? It is not. It is common property of the whole human race, and we find on further inquiry that these religions all teach, and the Christian religion also, that this Savior is within the heart of every man, and is not outside of him.

We have discovered further by examining all these religions and comparing them with the Christian religion, which is the one belonging to the foremost nation of today, that in these other religions and in Christianity are found certain doctrines which constitute the key that will unlock this vast lock made up of the different religions. These doctrines are not absent from Christianity any more than they are absent from Buddhism or from Brahmanism, and now the time has come when the world must know that these doctrines are common property, when it is too late for any people West or East to claim that they have a special property in any doctrine whatever.

The two principles which unlock this great lock which bars men sometimes from getting on, are called Karma and Reincarnation. The latter doctrine bears a more difficult Sanscrit name.

The doctrine of Karma put into our language is simply and solely Justice. What is justice? Is it something that condemns alone? I say, No. Justice is also mercy. For mercy may not be dissociated from justice, and the word justice itself includes mercy within it. Not the justice of man, which is false and erring, but the justice of Nature. That is also mercy. For if she punishes you, it is in order that she may do a merciful act and show you the truth at last by discipline. That is the doctrine of Karma, and it is also called the ethical law of causation. It means that effect follows cause uniformly; not alone in mere objective nature, where if you put your hand in the fire it will surely be burned, but in your moral nature, throughout your whole spiritual and intellectual evolution. It has been too much the custom to withdraw from use this law of cause and effect the moment we look at man as a spiritual being; and the religions and philosophies of the past and the present have the proof within them that this law of cause and effect obtains on the spiritual, the moral, and the intellectual planes just as much as it does on the physical and objective. It is our object to once more bring back this law of justice to the minds of men and show them that justice belongs to God, and that he is not a God who favors people, but who is just because he is merciful.

The doctrine of reincarnation is the next one. Reincarnation, you say, what is that? Do you mean that I was here before? Yes, un-undoubtedly so. Do you mean to tell me that this is a Christian, a Buddhist, a Brahmanical, a Japanese doctrine, and a Chinese one? Yes, and I can prove it; and if you will examine your own records with an unprejudiced and fearless mind, afraid of no man, you will prove it also. If you go back in the records of Christianity to the first year of it, you will find that for many centuries this doctrine was taught. Surely the men who lived near Jesus knew what the doctrine was. It was admitted by Jesus himself. He said on one occasion that Elias had already come back in the person of John, but had been destroyed by the ruler. How could Elias come back and be born again as John unless the law of nature permitted it? We find on examining the writers, the early Christian fathers who made the theology of the Christian churches, admitting, by the greatest of them, Origen, that this doctrine was true. He, the greatest of them all, who wrote so much men could not read all his books, believed in it. It is said in the Christian scripture that Jesus also said so much they could not record it, and if they had, the volumes could not be counted. If these teachings were not recorded, we can imagine from what he spoke and from what his early followers believed, that this doctrine was taught distinctly by him in words. (Applause.)

It is the doctrine of which the Reverend Mr. Beecher, brother of the famous Henry Ward Beecher, in a book called *The Conflict of Religions*, said, "It is an absolute necessity to Christianity; without it Christianity is illogical. With it it is logical." And a great writer, the Rev. William Alger, whose book, *A Critical History of the Doctrine of a Future Life*, is used in the religious educational institutions of all denominations with perhaps one exception, has written twice in two editions and said that after fifteen years' study of the subject he had come to the conclusion that the doctrine was true and necessary.

Furthermore, we find that in these countries where Christianity arose—for Christianity is not a Western product—reincarnation has always been believed. You ask for human evidence. You believe, in this city, not only in this city but everywhere, in a court of law, if many witnesses testify to a fact it is proved. Well, millions upon millions of men in the East testify that they not only believe in reincarnation, but that they know it is true, that they remember that they were born before, and that they were here before, and hundreds and thousands of men in the West have said the same thing. That they not only believe it, but that they know it. Poets have written of it all through English literature. It is a doctrine that almost everybody believes in their hearts. The little child coming straight from the other shore, coming without any defects straight from the heavenly Father, believes that it has always lived.

If the doctrine of immortality which is taught by every religion is true, how can you split it in halves and say, you began to be immortal when you were born and you were never immortal before? How is it possible you did not live before if there is any justice in this universe? Is it not true that what happens is the result of your conduct? If you live a life of sin and wickedness, will you not suffer? If you steal, and rob, and lie, and put in operation causes for punishment, will you not be punished? Why should not that law be applied to the human being when born, to explain his state and capacity? We find children are born blind, deformed, halt, without capacity; where is the prior conduct which justifies such a thing, if they have just been born for the first time? They must have lived before. The disciples asked Jesus "Why was this man born blind; was it for some sin he had committed?" When committed? When did he commit it if he had never been born before? Why ask Jesus, their master, this question, unless, as we think, it is the true one and one then prevalent?

This doctrine of reincarnation, then, we claim is the lost chord of any religion that does not promulgate it. We say it is found in the Christian religion; it is found in every religion, and it offers to us a means whereby our evolution may be carried on, it offers an explanation to the question, Why are men born with different characters? We find one man born generous, and he will always be generous; we find another born selfish, and selfish he will be to the end of his life. We find one man born with great capacity, a great mind that can cover many subjects at once; or a special mind and capacity like that of Mozart. Why was he born so? Where did he get it if not from the character he had in the past? You may say that heredity explains it all. Then please explain how Blind Tom, born of Negro parents who never knew anything about a piano, who never knew anything about music, was able to play upon a mechanically scaled instrument like the piano? It is not a natural thing. Where did he get the capacity? Heredity does not explain that. We explain it by reincarnation. Just so with Mozart, who at four years of age was able to write an orchestral score. Do you know what that means? It means the writing down the parts for the many instruments, and not only that, but writing it in a forced scale, which is a mechanical thing. How will that be explained by heredity? If you say that among his ancestors there must have been musicians, then why not before or after him? See Bach! If Bach could look back from the grave he would have seen his musical genius fading and fading out of his family until at last it disappeared.

Heredity will not explain these great differences in character and genius, but reincarnation will. It is the means of evolution of the human soul; it is the means of evolution for every animate and inanimate thing in this world. It applies to everything. All nature is constantly being re-embodied, which is reincarnation. Go back with science. It shows you that this world was first a mass of fiery vapor; come down the years and you see this mass re-embodied in a more solid form; later still it is re-embodied as the mineral kingdom, a great ball in the sky, without life; later still animal life begins evolving until now it has all that we know of life, which is a re-embodiment over and over again, or reincarnation. It means, then, that just as you move periodically from house to house in the city, you are limited by every house you move into, so the human being, who never dies, is not subject to death, moves periodically from house to house, and takes up a mortal body life after life, and is simply limited a little more or a little less, just as the case may be, by the particular body he may inhabit.

I could not go through all this subject to answer all the objections, but Theosophy will answer them all. The differences in people are explained by the fact that the character of the individual attracts him to the family that is just like himself, and not to any other family, and through heredity he receives his discipline, punishment, and reward.

The objections to reincarnation are generally based upon the question, why we do not remember. In the West that objection arises from the fact that we have been materialists so long, we have been deceived so long, that we have forgotten; we are not able to remember anything but what makes a violent impression on our senses. In the East and in some places in the West the people remember, and the time will come when the people in the West will remember also. And I warrant you that the children of the West know this, but it is rubbed out of their minds by their fathers and mothers. They say to the child, "Don't bother me with such questions; you are only imagining things." As if a child could imagine that it had been here before if it had not been. They never could imagine a thing which has not some existence in fact or that is not built up from impressions received. As you watch the newborn child you will see it throw its arms out to support itself. Why should the child throw out its arms to support itself? You say, instinct. What is instinct? Instinct is recollection imprinted upon the soul, imprinted upon the character within a child just born, and it knows enough to remember that it must throw out its arms to save itself from being hurt. Any physician will tell you this fact is true. Whether they explain it in the same way as I do or not, I don't know. We cannot remember our past lives simply because the brain which we now have was not concerned with these past lives. You say you cannot remember a past life, and therefore you don't believe it is true. Well if we grant that kind of argument, apply it to the fact that you cannot remember the facts of your present existence here; you cannot remember what dinner you ate three weeks ago; you cannot remember one-quarter of what has happened to you. Do you mean to say that all these things did not happen because you cannot remember? You cannot remember what happens to you now, so how do you expect to remember what happened to you in another life? But the time will come when man not so immersed in materiality will form his soul to such an extent that its qualities will be impressed upon the newborn child body and he will be able to remember and to know all his past, and then he will see himself an evolving being who has come up through all the ages as one of the creators of the world, as one of those who have aided in building this world. Man, we say, is the top, the crown of evolution; not merely as one who has been out there through favor, but as one who worked himself up through nature, unconsciously sometimes to himself, but under law, the very top and key of the whole system, and the time will come when he will remember it.

Now, this being the system of evolution which we gather from all religions, we say it is necessary to show that cause and effect act on man's whole being. We say that this law of cause and effect, or Karma, explains every circumstance in life and will show the poor men in Chicago who are born without means to live, who sometimes are hunted by the upper class and live in misery, why they are born so. It will explain why a man is born rich, with opportunity which he neglects; and another man born rich, with opportunity which he does not neglect. It will explain how Carnegie, the great iron founder in America, was a poor telegraph boy before he was raised to be a great millionaire. It will explain how one is born with small brain power, and another born with great brain power. It is because we have never died; we have always been living, in this world or in some other, and we are always meeting causes and character for the next life as well as for this.

Do you not know that your real life is in your mind, in your thoughts? Do you not know a great deal is due to your own mind, and under every act is a thought, and the thoughts make the man, and those thoughts act upon the forces of nature? Inasmuch as all these beings come back and live together over and over again, they bring back the thoughts, the impressions of those they have met and which others have made upon them there. When you persecute and hurt a man now, you are not punished afterwards because of the act you did to him, but because of the thought under your act and the thought under his feelings when he received your act. Having made these thoughts, they remain forever with you and him, and when you come again you will receive back to yourselves that which you gave to another. And is not that Christianity as well as Brahmanism and

Buddhism? You say, No. I say, Yes; read it in the words of Jesus, and I would have you to show you are right if you say, No. St. Paul I suppose is authority for you, and St. Paul says "Brethren, be not deceived; God is not mocked; for whatsoever a man soweth, that shall he also reap." I ask you where and when shall he reap that which he has sown? He must reap it where he sowed it, or there is no justice. He must come back here and help to cure that evil which he caused; he must come back here if he did cause any evil and continue to do all the good he can, so he may help to evolve the whole human race, which is waiting for him also. Jesus said: "Judge not, that ye be not judged; for with what measure ye mete, so shall it be measured out to you again." When? If you go to heaven after this life and escape all you have done, certainly not then, and you make Jesus to have said that which is not true, and make St. Paul say that which is not true.

But I believe that St. Paul and Jesus knew what they were talking about and meant what they said. (Applause.) So, then, we must come again here in order that God shall not be mocked and each man shall reap that which he has sowed.

It is just the absence of this explanation that has made men deny religion; for they have said: "Why, these men did not get what they sowed. Here are rich, wicked men who die in their beds, happy, with a shrive at the end of it. They have not reaped." But we know, just as Jesus and St. Paul have said, they will reap it surely, and we say according to philosophy, according to logic, according to justice, they will reap it right here where they sowed it, and not somewhere else. It would be unjust to send them anywhere else to reap it but where they did it. That has been taught in every religion ever since the world began, and it is the mission of the Theosophical Society to bring back the key to all the creeds, to show them that they are really at the bottom in these essential doctrines alike, and that men have a soul in a body, a soul that is ever living, immortal and can never die, cannot be withered up, cannot be cut in two, cannot be destroyed, is never annihilated, but lives forever and forever, climbing forever and forever up the ladder of evolution, nearer and nearer, yet never reaching the full stature of the Godhead. That is what Theosophy wishes men to believe; not to believe that any particular creed is true. Jesus had no creed and formulated none. He declared the law to be, "Do unto others what you would have them do unto you." That was the law and the prophets. That is enough for any one. Love your neighbor as yourself. No more. Why, then, any creeds whatever? His words are enough, and his words and our ethical basis are the same. That is why we have no form of religion. We are not advocating religion; we are simply pointing out to men that the truth is there to pick up and prize it. Religion relates to the conduct of men; nature will take care of the results; nature will see what they will come to; but if we follow these teachings which we find everywhere, and the spirit of the philosophy which we find in all these old books, then men will know why they must do right, not because of the law, not because of fear; not because of favor, but because they must do right for right's own sake. (Applause.)

"CYCLES AND CYCLIC LAW"

[The Theosophical Congress, pp. 164-68]

EXTRA SESSION, SUNDAY EVENING AT 8 O'CLOCK, IN HALL OF WASHINGTON

The Hall was crowded long before the hour for opening the session, and on the platform with the speakers were many members of the Society. Dr. J. D. Buck had the chair, and said:

This evening the session has been divided between several speakers who will each make short addresses upon subjects that are of interest to students of Theosophy. It was thought that this method would be more profitable and prove more satisfactory than any other.

I now beg to introduce to you again Brother William Q. Judge, who will speak on the subject of Cycles and Cyclic Law.

MR. JUDGE—Ladies and gentlemen: This is our last meeting; it is the last impulse of the Cycle which we began when we opened our sessions at this Parliament. All the other bodies which have met in this building have been also starting cycles just as we have been. Now, a great many people know what the word "cycle" means, and a great many do not. There are no doubt in Chicago many men who think that a cycle is a machine to be ridden; but the word that I am dealing with is not that. I am dealing with a word which means a return, a ring. It is a very old term, used in the far past. In our civilization it is applied to a doctrine which is not very well understood, but which is accepted by a great many scientific men, a great many religious men, and by a great many thinking men. The theory is, as held by the ancient Egyptians, that there is a cycle, a law of cycles which governs humanity, governs the earth, governs all that is in the universe. You may have heard Brother Chakravarti say the Hindus are still teaching that there is a great cycle which begins when the Unknown breathes forth the whole universe, and ends when it is turned in again into itself. That is the great cycle.

In the Egyptian monuments, papyri, and other records the cycles are spoken of. They held, and the ancient Chinese also held, that a great cycle governs the earth, called the sidereal cycle because it related to the stars. The work was so large that it had to be measured by the stars, and that cycle is 25,800 and odd years long. They claim to have measured this enormous cycle. The Egyptians gave evidence they had measured it also and had measured many others, so that in these ancient records, looking at the question of cycles, we have a hint that man has been living on the earth, has been civilized and uncivilized for more years than we have been taught to believe. The ancient Theosophists have always held that civilization with humanity went around the earth in cycles, in rings, returning again and again upon itself, but that at each turn of the cycle, on the point of return it was higher than before. This law of cycles is held in Theosophical doctrine to be the most important of all, because it is at the bottom of all. It is a part of the law of that unknown being who is the universe, that there shall be a periodical coming from and a periodical returning again upon itself.

Now, that the law of cycles does prevail in the world must be very evident if you will reflect for a few moments. The first cycle I would draw your attention to is the daily cycle, when the sun rises in the morning and sets at night, returning again next morning, you following the sun, rising in the morning and at night going to sleep again, at night almost appearing dead, but the next morning awaking to life once more. That is the first cycle. You can see at once that there are therefore in a man's life just as many cycles of that kind as there are days in his life. The next is the monthly cycle, when the moon, changing every 28 days, marks the month. We have months running to more days, but that is only for convenience, to avoid change in the year. The moon gives the month and marks the monthly cycle.

The next is the yearly cycle. The great luminary, the great mover of all, returns again to a point from whence he started. The next great cycle to which I would draw your attention, now we have come to the sun—it is held by science and is provable I think by other arguments —the next cycle is that the sun, while stationary to us, is in fact moving through space in an enormous orbit which we can not measure.[1] As he moves he draws the earth and the planets as they wheel about

---

1 [It may be of interest to readers to note that today's science has computed the sun's orbit as a distance of about 200,000 light years, which takes about 230,000,000 years for one revolution around the center of our galaxy. See *Planets, Stars, and Galaxies* by Stuart J. Inglis. John Wile, & Sons Toronto, 1976—Comp.]

him. We may say, then, this is another great cycle. It appears reasonable that, as the sun is moving through that great cycle, he must draw the earth into spaces and places and points in space where the earth has never been before, and that it must happen that the earth shall come now and then into some place where the conditions are different and that it may be changed in a moment, as it were, for to the eye of the soul a thousand years are but a moment, when everything will be different. That is one aspect of cyclic doctrine, that the sun is drawing the earth in a great orbit of his own and is causing the earth to be changed in its nature by reason of the new atomic spaces into which it is taken.

We also hold that the earth is governed by cyclic law throughout the century as in a moment. The beings upon it are never in the same way and moved by the same law. This law of cycles is the law of reincarnation that we were speaking of today: that is, that a man comes into the world and lives a day, his life is as a day; he dies out of it and goes to sleep, elsewhere waking; then he sleeps there to wake again the next great day; after a period of rest, he again enters life; that is his cycle. We hold in Theosophical philosophy it has been proven by the Adepts by experiment that men in general awake from this period of rest after 1,500 years. So we point in history to an historical cycle of 1,500 years, after which old ideas return. And if you will go back in the history of the world you will find civilization repeating itself every 1,500 years, more or less like what it was before. That is to say go back 1,500 years from now and you will find coming out here now the Theosophists, the philosophers, the various thinkers, the inventors of 1,500 years ago. And going further back still, we hold that those ancient Egyptians who made such enormous pyramids and who had a civilization we cannot understand, at that dim period when they burst on the horizon of humanity to fall again, have had their cycle of rest and are reincarnating again even in America. So we think, some of us, that the American people of the new generation are a reincarnation of the ancient Egyptians, who are coming back and bringing forth in this civilization all the wonderful ideas which the Egyptians held. And that is one reason why this country is destined to be a great one, because the ancients are coming back, they are here, and you are very foolish if you refuse to consider yourselves so great. We are willing you should consider yourselves so great, and not think you are born mean, miserable creatures.

The next cycle I would draw your attention to is that of civilizations. We know that civilizations have been here, and they are gone. There is no bridge between many of these. If heredity, as some people claim, explains everything, how is it not explained why the Egyptians left no string to connect them with the present? There is nothing left of them but the Copts, who are poor miserable slaves. The Egyptians, as a material race, are wiped out, and it is so because it is according to the law of cycles and according to the law of nature that the physical embodiment of the Egyptians had to be wiped out. But their souls could not go out of existence, and so we find their civilization and other civilizations disappearing, civilizations such as the ancient civilization of Babylon, and all those old civilizations in that part of the East which were just as strange and wonderful as any other. And this civilization of ours has come up instead of going down; but it is simply repeating the experience of the past on a higher level. It is better in potentiality than that which has been before. Under the cyclic law it will rise higher and higher, and when its time comes it will die out like the rest.

Also religions have had their cycles. The Christian religion has had its cycle. It began in the first year of the Christian era and was a very different thing then from what it is now. If you examine the records of Christianity itself you will see that the early fathers and teachers taught differently in the beginning from that which the priests of to-day are teaching now. Similarly you will find that Brahmanism has had its cycle. Every religion rises and falls with the progress of human thought, because cyclic law governs every man, and thus every religion which man has.

So it is also with diseases. Is it not true that fevers are governed by a law of recurrence in time; some have three days, some four days, nine days, fifteen days, three years and so on? No physician can say why it is so; they only know that it is a fact. So in every direction the law of cycles is found to govern. It is all according to the great inherent law of the periodical ebb and flow, the Great Day and Night of Nature. The tides in Ocean rise and fall; similarly in the great Ocean of Nature there is a constant ebb and flow, a mightier tide which carries all with it. The only thing that remains unshaken, immovable, never turning is the Spirit itself. That, as St. James said—and he doubtless was himself a wise Theosophist—is without variableness and hath no shadow of turning.

Now, this great law of periodical return pertains also to every individual man in his daily life and thought. Every idea that you have, every thought, affects your brain and mind by its impression. That begins the cycle. It may seem to leave your mind, apparently it goes out, but it returns again under the same cyclic law in some form either better or worse, and wakes up once more the old impression. Even the very feelings that you have of sorrow or gladness will return in time, more or less according to your disposition, but inevitably in their cycle. This is a law it would do good for every one to remember, especially those who have variations of joy and sorrow, of exaltation and depression. If when depressed you would recollect the law and act upon it by voluntarily creating another cycle of exaltation, on its returning again with the companion cycle of lower feeling it would in no long time destroy the depressing cycle and raise you to higher places of happiness and peace. It applies again in matters of study where we use the intellectual organs only. When a person begins the study of the difficult subject or one more grave than usual, there is a difficulty in keeping the mind upon it; the mind wanders; it is disturbed by other and older ideas and impressions. But by persistency a new cycle is established, which, being kept rolling, at last obtains the mastery.

We hold further—and I can only go over this briefly—that in evolution itself, considered as a vast inclusive whole, there are cycles, and that unless there were these turnings and returnings no evolution would be possible, for evolution is but another word for cyclic law. Reincarnation, or re-embodiment over and over again, is an expression of this great law and a necessary part of evolution.

Evolution means a coming forth from something. From out of what does the evolving universe come? It comes out from what we call the unknown, and we call it "unknown" simply because we do not know what it is. The unknown does not mean the non-existent; it simply means that which we do not perceive in its essence or fulness. It goes forth again and again, always higher and better; but while it is rolling around at its lower arc it seems to those down there that it is lower than ever; but it is bound to come up again. And that is the answer we give to those who ask, What of all those civilizations that have disappeared, what of all the years that I have forgotten? What have I been in other lives, I have forgotten them? We simply say: You are going through your cycle. Some day all these years and experiences will return to your recollection as so much gained. And all the nations of the earth should know this law, remember it and act upon it, knowing that they will come back and that others also will come back. Thus they should leave behind something that will raise the cycle higher and higher, thus they should ever work toward the perfection which mankind as a whole is striving in fact to procure for itself. (Applause.)

The Theosophical Congress

AND THE PARLIAMENT OF RELIGIONS

[*The Path*, Vol. VIII, November, 1893, pp. 247-49]

[Judge's *Path* magazine carried, in addition to several preliminary announcements, a summary of the events at *The World Parliament of Religions*, printed below.—*Comp.*]

The Congress of the Theosophical Society in September as a part of the Great Parliament of Religions was a significant as well as successful event. In another article the Chicago Chairman shows how we had but little hope at first of having any place whatever in either the merely intellectual or the religious side of the World's Fair; how we found the old yet senseless opposition to Theosophy obstructing the path for so long as to cause us to cease efforts; and how suddenly the scene changed and the managers of the Parliament of Religions became our friends and helpers. This change will never be explained by those who do not know the forces working behind the acts and thoughts of men. It not only took us into the Parliament, but gave us the best date of all sittings and made our Congress the real Parliament itself.

Not at any time but now during eighteen centuries could such a meeting have been possible, and it was distinctly a Theosophical step because, being an effort to get on one platform representatives of all religions, it was just what our Society has been accomplishing steadily during the past eighteen years, and what our objects and constitution have always expressed.

It marked a cycle in the development of religious thought. For centuries until the American Republic was founded men's minds in western civilizations were chained to bigotry and dogma. Then, as expressed on the seal of the United States, "a new order of ages" began. Steadily creeds and churches, religious ideas and religious interpretations altered, the freedom of America making it a possibility that men should here think more boldly and act upon their thoughts, should not be afraid of their opinions but be more willing to proclaim them unchecked by state interference until at last among the hosts of the dissenters from Roman Catholicism the idea of a Religious Parliament was born. And that the presiding officer of the Parliament should be a Presbyterian was still more significant, as that cult is surely the fatalistic iron-bound one of all the different stripes of Christianity. The cycle being almost complete, its ending and the beginning of another were fitly marked by the calling of the gathering at Chicago. In ending his opening speech, Dr. Barrows, the president, said the whole world is bound by chains of gold about the feet of God.

Our part in the Parliament was not merely to prove that the Society had grown strong enough and sufficiently respectable to compel a place therein, but chiefly to show, as an integral portion of the whole body, that the true attitude for all religious bodies to take is to seek for and disclose the truths in each, and not confine themselves merely to their own pet theories. And as we exemplified this in truth, the other bodies confining themselves to explications of particular creeds or views of salvation—and one, the Roman Catholic, declaring that only in that sort of Christianity were truth, ethics, and salvation—it follows that the Theosophical Congress was in actuality, though not in form, *the* Parliament of Religions.

The occasion enabled us to present a great object-lesson illustrating what we had been saying for years, that the Oriental is no heathen, that he should not be treated as such, and that an examination of his religions will show them to be the real source of those professed by the Occident. And when all those Greeks, Chinamen, Japanese, Buddhists, Shintos, Hindus, and Confucians appeared on the platform, beyond doubt the Brahman we brought towered above them all by virtue of the ancient system he represented as prime source of all religions. Our Buddhist, Dharmapala, with Annie Besant an old agnostic, combined with all others, proved that the Theosophical movement, though small by comparison with the world's great set systems of religion, voices the great underlying note of the mental, moral, and religious evolution of the human race. This note is changed, distorted, and colored by any and every form of religion, but in Theosophy it sounds forth without fault. No one religion gives it clearly, no single system will present it to the perception; only by the combination and from the examination of all can it be discovered for the delight and benefit of humanity.

And that the minds of Western people are beginning to hear the first faint vibrations of this great sound was evident at our Congress. All our meetings were crowded to overflowing, every shade of opinion was on our platform as well as in our audiences, and, recognizing the effect produced by such an epoch-making Congress as ours, the newspapers of the city, which only attend to that which forces itself to the surface, gave us in their reports the greatest prominence, saying one day, "The Theosophical Congress is a competitor of the whole Parliament."

But remembering the words of our old Teacher, the Master's Messenger—H. P. B., that it may be dangerous for the T. S. to grow too fast, out of proportion to its strength, let us one and all try to make ourselves centers for Theosophical influence, so as to constitute a body of power from the power of each element duly fostered and educed. This we shall do only by personal effort, by attention and by service to others; and thus, and in no other way, we may reap for the Theosophical Society all the benefits that such a congress and such success should justly lead us to expect.

[Letters concerning the funding and the success of the *World's Fair* often appeared in *The Theosophist*. The introduction to the report by Mr. Judge below reflects the enthusiasm felt by T. S. members. It appeared in *The Theosophist*, Vol. XV, November 1893, pp. 125-26. —*Comp.*]

In addition to Mr. Judge's advanced brief report of the result of the Theosophical Congress at the Chicago World's Parliament of Religions, we have received private letters affirming the entire success of the gathering; in fact, the tone of one and all is most enthusiastic. The crowds which attended the several sessions of the Congress, the hushed attention with which they listened to the several speakers, and the fervency of their applause at the utterance of our tolerant and altruistic views, give one more convincing proof of the widespread interest and sympathy which is felt by the public in our movement. The demonstrations at Chicago give a dignity to the diploma of every member of our Society, and show how strong and firm is the foundation upon which our movement stands. This wave of popular enthusiasm sweeps away like chaff the sorrows and mortifications of past years, and should thrill every true heart among us with bright hope for the future. Our ship is now sailing on sunnier seas and keeping well to her course. For this great success we are indebted to the wise planning and tireless labor of Mr. Judge, Mr. G. E. Wright of the Chicago Branch, and other American Theosophists who have given the money for expenses or had a share in the preliminary arrangements. All honor to them!

All honor and loving gratitude, too, to Mrs. Besant, whose name was one of the potent attractions which drew the multitudes to the Parliament building and made it necessary for us to move from one hall to another, the largest, to accommodate the crowds in attendance. An American paper reports that some 4,000 persons listened to her grand oratory. The local papers speak very highly also of the addresses of our Indian delegates, Gyanendranath Chakravarti and H. Dharmapala. It seems that so much enthusiasm was aroused that people rushed forward to the platform to grasp their hands and even to embrace them in our Eastern fashion. It will be a lifelong consolation to these gifted young men to think that they were able to speak so boldly and effectively for their two national religions, Brahmanism and Buddhism, in the hearing of such multitudes of people of many races and creeds. Without my saying it, it must have suggested itself to every Theosophist who reads this report, that we have lived to see the brotherhood plank of the platform of our Society adopted by the most eminent representative of all the world's great faiths. For the first time in history our Society set the pattern by gathering into our Convention at Bombay in 1880, delegates of the Parsi, Jewish, Mussulman,[1] Christian, Buddhist, S'aivite,[2] and Vaishnava[3] religions, and now Dr. Barrows has bettered this by collecting High Priests, Rabbis, Pandits, Mobeds, Archbishops, Catholic Bishops and Priests, and clergymen of the chief dissenting sects of the whole world into one soul-expanding brotherly alliance, to clasp hands and utter vows of devotion to mankind. What a pity that H. P. B. did not live to see this day!

Following is Mr. Judge's report:

New York, 21st September, 1893.
Col. H. S. Olcott,
   President, T. S., Adyar, Madras, India.

Dear Sir and Brother:—

The Theosophical Congress having finished its work, I have to report briefly to you, hoping that you may be able to find this of some use in advance of the printed report which will be soon gotten out here when we have the transcript from the shorthand writers.

The foreign delegates were Mrs. Besant, Prof. Chakravarti, H. Dharmapala, Miss Müller, and Mrs. Cooper-Oakley. In addition to being one of the European Delegates, Mrs. Cooper-Oakley was also delegated by the Australian Branches. Brother Dharmapala had a delegation from the Ceylon Branches.

Summing up the Congress briefly in advance, I can assure you that it was an entire and extraordinary success. Public interest was roused to an enormous extent; every meeting was crammed with people, hundreds being turned away; the newspapers of the city gave us the first place in their headlines, and, as one of them said, the Theosophical Congress was a competitor of the entire Parliament of Religions. This is absolutely true inasmuch as the newspapers do not like the Theosophical Society and made the admission against their own desires. I am satisfied that if the entire building had been given up to us we

---

1 Moslem.
2 Shivaite (followers of Shiva).
3 Followers of Vishṇu [Vaishṇavism]

should have filled every corner of it at each session. No recriminations were indulged in, and no attacks were made on any system of religion in our Congress.

The first day opened with all the delegates present, and the first in order was the reading of your Executive Order sanctioning the Congress; this was followed by the reading of your message by Annie Besant, and next the credentials were read. We then proceeded with three sessions a day, and were compelled to have two overflow meetings in extra halls assigned to us in the building. In accordance with my custom for many years at all such meetings, as well as in print, the fact was made quite prominent that the Society had no creed and spoke for no dogma whatever and claimed no authority. It is of course needless in view of my well known views on this point and constant publication thereof to state this, but I do so because it is an important point and the one thing on which the T. S. always insists. The Sessions continued for two days and public interest was so great that the managers of the Fair assigned us an extra meeting on Sunday night, the 17th, in the largest hall in the building. This meeting was held and was filled with 3,500 people, who stayed until half-past ten at night. And this closed the proceedings. A full report will be in *The Path*, and later on a *verbatim* report will be sent out throughout the world, if our fund is sufficient, which I think will be the case.

At the opening of the Parliament as an entirety on the 11th we were also represented, as the managers invited Prof. Chakravarti and me to be present. We were on the platform and he replied to a welcome and stated publicly that he was there for the T. S. Brother Dharmapala also replied, but of course having been brought over by the Parliament itself, he did not mention the Society at that meeting. Mrs. Besant was also invited but, being engaged in lecturing in another town, was not present until our own Congress. Your educational and literary statistics were read by Brother Claude F. Wright after the conclusion of his own paper. The shorthand reports were taken by two devoted Theosophists, Brothers Brolley and Solomons, who gave their services gratuitously. Uniform courtesy and appreciative interest were extended to us by the managers of the Parliament, and at the conclusion of our Congress I took occasion with Brother G .E. Wright, the local Chairman, to send a letter of thanks to them on behalf of the Society.

I think you might very well insert the foregoing in the magazine as an advance information.

Fraternally yours,
William Q. Judge
Vice-President, T. S.

[Again enthusiasm is reflected in the following from *The Theosophist,* vol. XV. December 1893, p. 198.—*Comp.*]

AMERICA

Mr. W. Q. Judge writes to us with reference to the report of the Theosophical Congress:—

"I desire to give notice that two earnest members of the American Section having given their services as stenographers freely at the Congress, I have thus been able to secure a *verbatim* report of the proceedings and speeches from beginning to end. As the event seems to justify the expense, I will issue, as soon as possible, a printed complete report of the Congress. The transcripts of the notes have been received and are now in the printers' hands; the number of copies to be printed is 2,500.

"One copy will be sent to each T. S. Branch in the world, several copies to each donor who gave $25 or over, one copy to each of the other donors, and several copies to the different headquarters.

"When the reports are all done and distributed I shall be able to issue a full statement of the fund and how it was disposed of.

"A later letter informs us that 'So generous has been the response of brethren to my appeal that there will be a surplus left over after all expenses, which will be sufficient to enable me to publish all the Theosophical addresses in full, and the pamphlet is now under way'."

[Although dated in December of 1893, the next item actually was printed in a Supplement to *The Theosophist,* March 1894 on p. xx.— *Comp.*]

THE THEOSOPHICAL CONGRESS

NEW YORK, *December 18th,* 1893.

To Col. H. S. Olcott, P. T. S.

The principal matters connected with the Theosophical Congress having been concluded, I hereby send you the supplemental account in respect to the fund and its disposition, which shows a surplus on hand of $71.82. In this item there is a difference of 11 cents between the actual surplus found on hand and the surplus shown by account; but I have no time to find out where the 11 cents error is. This may be called the conclusion of this account as all subsequent moneys will result from sales of the copies left on hand of the Report and those sales will be added to the $71.82. When the whole number of Reports is sold I will then ask your opinion, and the opinion of the three Sections as to whether the sum should be put in the Headquarters' treasury in India, which is the place I think it ought to go to, unless it amounts to a very large sum, which is hardly possible. I make this report to you as President of the Society inasmuch as I acted on your behalf at the Congress and there is no one else to report to. The matter of auditing the account can very properly be attended to at our Convention as they will have the books here. The excess of $45.50 for printing was because the estimate was upon 175 pages, whereas the Report actually took a good many more. You will do me a favor if you will either publish this account in the *Theosophist* as received by you or publish a summary of it. The $2.59 accredited to the Indian Section in this account is a small sum received subsequent to the former account.

William Q. Judge
Vice-President, T. S.

SELECTIONS FROM "THE PATH"

[This section contains items of interest, including several literary reviews not printed along with articles from *The Path*, published in Volume I of *Echoes of the Orient*. Chronological sequence is retained except where tied in by a common theme or serially arranged.—*Compiler*.]

Notice To Inquirers

[*The Path*, Vol. II, October, 1887, p. 220]

Within the mind and heart of every thoughtful individual there exists some vital question unanswered. Some subject is uppermost, and asserts itself obtrusively with greater persistency because he is obliged to deal with it without a visible prospect of a solution of the problem. As the center in a circle so is every individual with regard to his environment. At times it seems impossible for him to pass beyond the circle owing to one unanswered question. In obeying the command to do good we learn that by the interchange of different thoughts, these questions are often solved, sometimes by an unintentional word or phrase, which opens up a new view and starts one thinking in another direction, or in other ways. This interchange of question and answer is not only valuable to the questioner but also for the questioned, and brings both into a closer union of mutual interest. In consequence of this view we express a wish that all who desire will ask their questions, to which an answer will be given. Perhaps not just such an answer as they look for, but it will be a sincere one from the standpoint of the questioned. The answers will be from one who seeks "the small old path"—a student like other mortals, and will be given as such, and not as autocratic or infallible. It is not intended to limit in any way, and all will be responded to, be they Jew, Gentile, Theosophist, Spiritualist, Pagan or Christian. Where permissible a certain portion will be published in THE PATH. The remainder will be answered by letter direct. All communications should be addressed, with return postage, to ZADOK, P.O. Box 2659, N.Y.

ZADOK

Contemporary
Literature and Theosophy

[*The Path*, Vol. III, June, 1888, pp. 92-94]

There is growing every day among contemporary writers a strong disposition to take up theosophic doctrine, and especially in those light stories that always flow from ideas that are "in the air." This will grow as time goes on, for every one with any means of judging knows that the doctrines of Karma and Reincarnation are gaining a hold, slowly perhaps, but surely, on the public mind. Both of these offer a wide field for novelists and magazine writers.

In a recent number of the *Century*, Mr. Stevenson, who writes such charming stories, and also weird ones like *Dr. Jekyll and Mr. Hyde*, gave an account—in some sense a confession—of how his best stories and plots came to him. He said that all his life, in dreams and waking visions, his "little Brownies" showed him scenes, incidents, and plots that he wove into his writings, and that the main situations in *Dr. Jekyll and Mr. Hyde* were obtained in that manner.

The field is extended enough. None of the possibilities of black or white Magic have been touched on except by such writers as Mabel Collins, one of the Editors of *Lucifer*, but as that comes to be better understood—or misunderstood, which is the same thing for those who write for their daily bread—we shall be flooded with a series of tales and sketches based on these ideas. This suggestion is not copyrighted, so that aspiring authors can use it as they will, to their heart's content.

The rising tide is shown when such a staid, and anciently somewhat bigoted, magazine as *Harper's Monthly* treats of these matters. In *Harper's* for May last, Mr. Charles Dudley Warner, in the "Editor's Drawer," takes up the subject of Heredity so as to use it for the bringing in of Karma and Reincarnation, together with some light remarks about the theosophists of India, Boston, and Ohio. He considers Heredity to be a puzzle, mourning a little that the progress made in questions of the effect of breeding and descent was to some extent impeded by these notions. But he also gives a fair resumé of Karma, clearly showing that responsibility for deeds done in the body must rest upon the individual, and cannot be shifted to his ancestors. We have to thank him for his words, since he reaches clearly the gist of the matter in saying: "The notion is that all human beings in this world undergo successive incarnations, preserving unconsciously the personal identity

Mr. Judge at Work   (From an unknown source.)

in all the changes of condition. Therefore, every human being is the result of all the influences in all his previous conditions. . . . . The form in which he shall reappear in the world is not determined by his visible ancestors, but by his conduct in his former lives . . . . But whatever he was, now in this present incarnation he suffers the penalty of all his misdeeds in all former states of being, or he enjoys the reward of good conduct in any of them. And it behooves him now to live the higher life—perhaps of expiation—in order that he may rise into a still higher life in the next unknown incarnation, and not sink into a lower. Therefore no effort is thrown away, and no act is without its infinite personal consequences. The law of Karma, it is explained, is the law of the conservation of energy on the moral and spiritual planes of nature . . . . The Drawer, of course, has nothing to do with an investigation of this theory of life; it simply notes it in reference to the prevalent study of the doctrine of heredity."

This is just the doctrine the people need, and it can easily be understood. When they come to believe that there is no way of escape, either through priest or mere lip-acceptance of a dogma, they will begin so to live, if only for selfish reasons, as that the "next unknown incarnation" will not find them in suffering and misery. While the motive at first may not be of the highest character, it will lead to a wide belief in the doctrines, so that, as the spirit of the age is changed, those who are sincere and unselfish will not have such a hard fight to wage against subtle and dangerous influences. In fine, it will prepare the conditions for the dawn of the day when human brotherhood shall be admitted and lived. Men will then see that legislation and strikes and outward temporary reforms can cure no evil. The evil lies within, in other lives, in this one. In a sense, we are our own ancestors; we are building now the houses we are to live in during our coming lives. For our ignorance of this, nature recks not; she holds us fast in an iron-grasp, and will compel us at last through pain to believe in the true doctrine, and to live our lives and think our thoughts in submission to the Higher Law that no human assemblies can revoke.

Editorial Note

[A brief editorial notice appeared on page 260 of *The Path*, Vol. III, November 1888, several months prior to the article immediately following it here. Both the editorial and the article concern slanders leveled at H. P. Blavatsky and the Society in *The Religio-Philosophical Journal.—Comp.*]

BROS. BRIDGE and STEARNS of the Boston T.S., have two articles in the *Religio-Philosophical Journal* of Chicago in reply to those in which W. E. Coleman attacked Mme. Blavatsky. The two Boston writers argue that the life and work of H. P. Blavatsky outweigh all the alleged charges of smoking, swearing, and profanity. In this we fully agree, and as we personally know that Mr. Coleman knows nothing about his subject, although he pretends to a great deal, we are glad to have the life and work of H. P. Blavatsky, so intimately connected as they are with the Society, written about in the Spiritualistic papers. Such writers as Coleman do no good to the cause they espouse, and no harm to those they attack. But we forgive his bitterness, as we know the dreary life he leads in the government military Post in San Francisco— although we do not know whether his diatribes are written at the Post or in a room at home after the day's work is done. Theosophists can gauge the power of his attacks when they know that he began his vile articles as long ago as 1881.

"Peace with Honor"
or "A Scientific Frontier"

[*The Path*, Vol. IV, July, 1889, pp. 115-16]

The PATH has never been a controversial magazine, and does not intend to be. But it cannot in justice to its readers fail to notice the recent exposures, in the *Religio-Philosophical Journal,* of self-confessed lying, jealousy, and violation of confidential relations. These are shown forth in the letters of Mabel Collins and Dr. Coues about *Light on the Path,* and later by the extremely vulgar Chicagoan wit of an article giving the confidential papers of the Esoteric Section of the T.S. "Peace with honor" has become impossible, and the lines that demark the frontier between true theosophists and those who are in the Society for gain or glory must be drawn.

The course of the *Religio-Philosophical* matters not. Its editor is a Chicagoan who will fight when his property is in any way attacked, and having shot off the missiles furnished by two recreant theosophists, will probably not soon indulge in similar work. But the others must continue if they are not exceptions to the rules that govern in similar cases. Dr. Coues, a president of a T.S. Branch, chairman at one General Convention, Mabel Collins, late joint editor of *Lucifer* with H. P. Blavatsky, are now, quite evidently, embarked on a campaign designed to bully and injure an old and dying woman. Both, actuated by similar motives of jealousy, present a sad spectacle. Dr. Coues, after losing the management of the old Board of Control, begs and implores Mme. Blavatsky for two years to make him President of the Society which he had ever injured by his presence; failing in this struggle, he casts about him for means of injuring her who had no power to raise to the head of our Society a man who had done nothing to deserve it. The heavy guns hurt none but the conspirators, for the explosion serves but to tear off the masks they held between theosophists and themselves, revealing them as moved solely by disappointed vanity and jealousy, while *Light on the Path* remains a gem as before and the Esoteric Section proceeds with its work.

The issue raised by the *Religio-Philosophical Journal* is a false one. It is, that H. P. Blavatsky has attempted to coerce the press. It also thinks that an Esoteric Section of the T.S. is wrong and unjustifiable. Inasmuch as the editor of that Journal joined the T.S. in 1885, and the upper and other Sections of the T.S. have always been in existence embracing many members, it is rather late for him to propose an amendment,[1] and it was improper to remain in the T.S. and attack its organization.

As long ago as 1881 the *R. P. Journal* printed articles by W. E. Coleman attacking the personal character of H. P. Blavatsky and the T.S. in general. To these the editor of THE PATH replied, but the reply was not printed; and the *Journal* has ever since been admitting similar scurrilous articles to Coleman's first. Without orders or suggestions all fair men, let alone theosophists, should have hastened to reply. Doubtless silence made the Editor think the attacks were justified The press must have lately acquired the right to dictate to bodies of men and women that they shall not follow a common policy of rebuking

---

[1] In the Supplement to the June *Theosophist,* 1881, the other sections are mentioned.

caluminators and denouncing slanders: but we have yet to hear that the press has any such prerogative.

This whole trouble started in the *Religio* is but a tempest in a teapot. What if such a circular as he prints *was* sent in the Esoteric Section, or if a pledge was signed? Every one has a right to join such a body and to sign a pledge; and the *Religio,* or any other paper, has no right to object. Many of these journalists who object to these things are Knights Templar who take most binding oaths; perhaps the Editor of the *Religio* is one; we should like to ask, if he does not object; and if the published oath of that body is the correct one, perhaps he can explain how his present attitude is consistent with that oath, or maybe American civilization permits some fine distinctions not admitted by us.

"A scientific frontier" must be drawn. Theosophists who supinely sit down inactive while fellow theosophists are slandered and the cause itself dragged through the mud by scoffers, are only paper and straw theosophists: the mildew of self will destroy the paper, and the straw will be blown away by the wind, and those others who, while in the T.S., try to exalt themselves and misrepresent the Society are much less theosophists.

Yet all these things will do the Society good, and will tend to separate the wheat from the chaff in readiness for the closing cycle.

To Theosophists Willing to Work

[*The Path,* Vol. IV, November, 1889, pp. 256-57]

For some 18 months past, private zeal has carried out a system by which a single copy of one of the tracts expounding popularly some Theosophic topic has been mailed to names gathered from newspapers published in smaller towns through the United States. In this simple way the seed of much Theosophic truth has been scattered broadcast, and many minds have thus for the first time received word of that Wisdom which is in time to reform humanity. To take part in such sowing is a privilege to all who love their fellow-men, and, while it is impossible to learn the results achieved, we may be sure that no such effort *can* be wholly without fruit. The present time is peculiarly ripe therefore. Ample evidence demonstrates that "Theosophy is in the air," and every judicious publication of its doctrines hastens the day when its motives too shall become operative and its reforms be realized.

The system referred to above appears the only way by which a knowledge of Theosophy can be carried direct to every town, village, and hamlet in the land. In a smaller form it was recommended to Theosophists in a brief article on page 154 of *The Path* for August, 1889. Through responses to this, and otherwise, the General Secretary has been enabled to thoroughly organize a scheme by which a proffer of help from any Theosophist willing to devote from $1.00 up and some time may be utilized, while all danger of duplicating addresses is avoided. To each one thus proffering, the General Secretary will supply a printed circular of instructions and assign a definite field. It is only needful to inform the General Secretary of the amount of money the offerer feels prepared to expend, and thereupon he will be furnished with the circular and the field, as well as with printed blanks for convenience in ordering the copies of the newspapers indicated.

Every Theosophist desirous to aid the Society, to promulgate its teachings, and to serve the highest interests of man is invited to communicate with the General Secretary briefly and to the point. No name is divulged. A few score of earnest, active, generous Brethren can thus in time sow seed over this whole continent, and prepare the harvest which is sure to come, but which will come the sooner if we fail not in our labor.

WILLIAM Q. JUDGE, General Secretary
P.O. Box 2659, New York City

The New "Department of Branch Work"

[*The Path*, Vol. V, June, 1890, pp. 102-03]

The following circular addressed to Branches will explain itself. It is proper, however, to state that the original plan, dictated by the need for economy, contemplated a division of the country into three Sections, the production upon a type-writer, by the multiple process, of three copies of a selected paper, and the transmission of a copy from Branch to Branch through each Section. But this was open to grave objections. There would always be danger of loss in the transmission, in which case all succeeding Branches would have no paper; complaints of dilatoriness in preceding Branches would be incessant; Branches would necessarily have to read the paper at their next meeting or forward it unread; and the last Branch in one Section would not receive the paper until four months after its issue. Besides, the General Secretary could not supply new Branches with back papers, and the Branches could not retain papers for future study or reference. Upon conference with several active Theosophists in New York, he was proffered aid towards printing the papers, and so the consent of the Executive Committee was obtained to the use of the General Fund. By the present arrangement a Branch retains its papers and can bind them in a volume from time to time, as well as circulate them among members absent from the meetings where they were read, and the General Secretary will be able to supply new Branches with complete sets from the beginning.

Every Branch is invited to forward for examination any paper which has been read before it and found pleasing. But it is well to state in advance that it is useless to forward papers which are common place or incorrectly spelled. There are some hints on this subject in *The Path* for Sept. 1889, page 192.

Into what this new Department may ultimately develop, cannot be now foreseen. But at present no papers can be furnished to individuals, nor at any time can unaccepted papers be returned unless postage shall have been enclosed.

To the President of the......................*T.S.*
  Dear Sir and Brother:

I had not expected so soon to encounter the need to avail myself of the authority granted by the Convention to appeal to the Branches for a renewal of their subscriptions towards the expenses of the General Secretary's office; but a proffer of mechanical help towards one of several important schemes I have had much at heart has determined me to ask your aid thus early in the year. If the Branches respond at all liberally, I may be able to effectuate the others. The one now pressing upon me is expounded below, and will be known as the

DEPARTMENT OF BRANCH WORK

The General Secretary has long been conscious of that deplorable waste by which valuable and interesting papers, once read at a Branch meeting, are unused again, and has desired some arrangement making possible their circulation among other Branches, particularly among those weak in membership or in capacity for originating discussion. It is needless to enumerate the various difficulties, but a leading one has been the expense. He believes that the result of an organized and regular system of circulation will be threefold; 1st, to greatly extend the range of the best and newest Theosophical thought; 2d, to supply weak Branches with interesting matter for instruction and debate; 3d, to promote that attractiveness in Branch meetings which will make them sought by intelligent outsiders, thus giving the Branches a status in their communities, and tending to increase both their growth and influence.

Having secured the consent of the Executive Committee to the plan, he now purposes to print from time to time on the Aryan Press a selected paper, and mail a copy to each Branch. The number of papers issued will depend upon the amount of attention he and his aids can spare from the constantly increasing work of the office, and also upon the funds placed at his disposal by the Branches and individuals. While no certain periodicity can be pledged, it is thought that a bi-weekly issue will prove practicable.

If the plan commends itself to your Branch, I invite you to apprise me what contribution, if any, it can make towards the expenses of the General Secretary's office during the present fiscal year. It must be distinctly understood that any Branch desiring the papers will be supplied with them, whether contributing financially or not, it being not doubted that the stronger Branches will feel it their privilege to assist the more liberally because there are weak Branches really unable to give at all. As the summer season is that wherein most time can be found for effectuating much of the work involved, I shall be glad of as early a reply as you can make.

Very truly and fraternally yours,
WILLIAM Q. JUDGE,
General Secretary

Libel by Dr. Coues and the "New York Sun"

[*The Path*, Vol. V, August, 1890, p. 153. Background on Dr. Elliott Coues may be consulted on p. xli of Vol. I, *Echoes of the Orient* in the Biographical Section about Judge.—*Comp.*]

In the *New York Sun* of Sunday, July 20th, appeared an article by Dr. Elliott Coues of Washington, D.C., purporting to be an interview with a reporter, and consisting of voluminous and minute attacks upon the Theosophical Society, Col. Olcott, Madame Blavatsky, and myself. The language is coarse and violent, and the animus of the writer is so plainly disclosed that it might well serve as an ample answer to the attack. Inasmuch, however, as certain moral charges cannot be permitted utterance with impunity, I have brought suit for libel against both Dr. Coues and the "Sun," and am awaiting instructions from Madame Blavatsky as to her own course.[1] In the meantime it is proper to recall to members of the Theosophical Society, and not less so to others interested, the following facts:—

1st. That Dr. Coues repeatedly threatened me in time past that, unless made President of the American Section of the T.S., he would withdraw his own followers from the Section and break it up.

2nd. That in letters to Madame Blavatsky of Dec. 25, 1888, April 16th, 1889, and April 17th, 1889, he assures her of his devotion and friendship, but in that of April 16th repeats the threat that, unless made President, he will withdraw his followers and break up the Society.

3rd. That until June 22nd, 1889, Dr. Coues continued as a member of the Theosophical Society and as Acting-President of the local Branch in Washington.

4th. That on that date he was, by a unanimous vote of the Executive Committee of the American Section, expelled from the Theosophical Society for defamation of character and untheosophical conduct.

His correspondence with Madame Blavatsky, together with other letters of like kind, was printed in a pamphlet on June 14th, 1889, and a copy of this pamphlet will now be sent to any one enclosing a stamp to my address.

William Q. Judge,
P.O. Box 2659,
New York

---

1 [A statement of facts by Mr. Judge, and correspondence involving M.C., H.P.B. and Dr. Coues about this libel suit, as well as one against *The Religio-Philosophical Journal* appears in two pamphlets now in the Archives of the T.S. The first, *Light on the Path and Mabel Collins,* contains a reference by Mr. Judge to an 1887 *Path* magazine statement by M.C. claiming well before the Coues accusations that indeed she had been inspired by adepts in the world-famous devotional book. The second pamphlet, under the heading: *Dr. Elliott Coues in his letters,* closes with factual points by Judge attributing the true underlying reasons for the Coues attack as follows:

"Dr. Coues' hostility to Madame Blavatsky and the Theosophical Society springs from his failure to be made President of the American Section and from his ignominious expulsion from the Society itself." (Dated July 28, 1890)

The above pamphlets were originally printed by the Aryan Press, New York, 1890. They are in the Archives of The Theosophical Society.—*Comp.*]

The Oriental Department

[The Oriental Department papers were started by Mr. Judge in January of 1891. The Indian Section of the Theosophical Society furnished material for the first number. In spite of financial delays the serial continued to print Vedic hymns, sutras and shastras, as well as verses from the *Upanishads* and mystical treatises, until March 1897, well after the passing of Judge.—*Comp.*]

[*The Path*, Vol. V, February, 1891, p. 359; Vol. VI, September, 1891, pp. 199-200; Vol. VIII, July, 1893, p. 126.]

The year 1891 is to mark an era in the Theosophical Society. The General Secretary desires to announce that with the consent of the Executive Committee he will begin this month the work of the ORIENTAL DEPARTMENT in order to carry out more effectually than ever before the second object of the Society—*the investigation of Aryan and other religions, sciences, and literature.* It is purposed to procure articles or translations relating to eastern religions, philosophies, literature, folklore, social customs and observances from competent Hindus, Parsees, and other Asiatic members and persons. These will be issued in pamphlet form monthly or oftener as funds allow, and will be distributed free to all Branches and members-at-large in good standing.

An extension of this scheme includes the employment of pandits—scholars—in India and elsewhere as soon as the funds come to hand. It is obvious to anyone who will inspect the cash book that our funds will not now permit of the enlargement of this scheme, but it could be put into extensive operation at once if members would give more than the small fee required by the Constitution. Through this Department the General Secretary hopes to be able to furnish a fund of valuable and interesting information such as cannot be otherwise obtained except at great expense for books and other means of study. It is certain that what little has been said to our people by interested missionaries and travellers has been very wide of truth in respect to the people of Asia, their manners, customs, literature, and social life. Indeed, but little can be got from Asiatics by such agents, and it is believed that only through our Society the real truth may be reached. Such a general and correct knowledge of distant people, all brothers of the human family, will do much to enlarge the boundaries of our thoughts, to abate race prejudice, and in all ways tend to strengthen the feeling of brotherhood which it is the aim of the Theosophical Society to arouse. Nor is there any reason why the T.S. should not be a great Asiatic investigating Society.

Any one desiring to aid the Society in this work can do so by making donations to the General Treasury, as the Executive Committee has passed an order that the general fund may be used for this purpose in addition to the items of rent, clerk hire, *Forum* and Branch paper printing to which it is now devoted.

William Q. Judge,
General Secretary

This Department of our work was set on foot in the U.S. with the object of bringing about a closer union between East and West by giving our American members a more complete knowledge of India than they could otherwise obtain. The example has been followed in Europe, where the new European Section has started a similar activity.

In order to make the work more uniform, the European Convention directed its Secretary to endeavor to have the American Oriental Department act in concurrence with the European, and this will no doubt be done. As the General Secretary here has been enabled to secure the services of a pundit in India, it will be easy to transmit to Europe paper matrices of the matter set up here, and the Blavatsky Press can cast metal stereos so that the two issues may correspond.

As the Adyar Oriental Library is gradually growing in importance, that may also be regarded as a part of our Oriental work, and it is purposed to utilize it as much as possible. Indeed, if circumstances had permitted it, the pundit secured for us would have resided there so that it might be made the central office for this branch of the Society's activity. But all this will come in time. With such great distances between us it is difficult to perfect our system quickly, and racial differences of method have also delayed us slightly in the beginning. As time goes on, all defects will be corrected and greater efficiency acquired.

Nor should our members judge the Oriental Department by the issues already published, for they have been necessarily hurried and somewhat imperfect in form. Indeed, there are so many difficulties to overcome that some time must elapse before everything will be running smoothly. Our funds as yet will not permit the employment of an American with the ability and time to thoroughly examine each issue so as to find and correct every error in style, fact, or transliteration and translation of words. As the General Secretary's entire time is already engrossed, as well as that of his staff, mistakes will creep in because of the ease with which words in a foreign language, carelessly edited, may be misunderstood. But as we have not yet claimed to be Orientalists, any slurs cast upon the Department can be easily passed aside. Time, which proves all things, will prove this enterprise to be of use and value, or will show the necessity of giving it up. The latter contingency is not regarded as possible. W. Q. J.

The issues of this department were, in the American Section, suspended temporarily in June, 1891, with No. 12, which completed a year. Lack of funds and also lack of the time required for such work compelled suspension. But as the European Section had then begun its Oriental Department, the work projected was really carried on elsewhere. The second year begins with an issue, in this June, of sixteen pages under a new style as to size of printed page. No obligation having been taken to issue monthly, it is contemplated to have the papers appear less often than during the first year, and, if possible, to devote more space for the present to studies in Oriental religions and thought. "The Game of Knowledge" given in No. 13 is extremely interesting, illustrating as it does the fact that the social life of India is moulded almost entirely on the religion of the country. We believe this is the first time this game has been described in a publication in our language. In subsequent issues I hope to be able to present studies of different Oriental religions in the form of compilations from the best authorities, as our funds will not yet allow the continuance of a salaried pundit in Hindustan.

WILLIAM Q. JUDGE,
General Secretary,
American Section, T.S.

"The Brotherhood of the New Life"

[*The Path*, Vol. VI, February, 1892, pp. 346-47]

This is one of the many enterprises gotten up to catch the unwary who seek after spiritual things, and the words of the Bible are good to remember hereupon:—"By their fruits ye shall know them". It is an alleged community run by Thos. Lake Harris out under the mild skies of California, and a continuation of the same work of Harris wherein he entangled the late lamented and gifted Oliphant. Harris reigns supreme, and never to die, imposes upon and hypnotises all the weak ones whom he can catch. It has the usual broad hint of sexual affinities and such disgusting doctrines. With it the Theosophical Society has nothing in common, and all Theosophists should beware of it. This is the day for the arising of false prophets. We had Butler and the Esoteric, Burgoyne and the Hermetic Brotherhood of L., and the Bath (England) set, Teed in Chicago as Jesus Christ reincarnated, and so to the end of an uncompleted list. Harris has steadily maintained his hold on some, as he is a man of strong will and good worldly judgment. His power over Oliphant was very great, for M. de Blowitz has written not long ago that Oliphant came to be correspondent of the *Times*, at Paris during the siege, by Harris' order. Beware, Theosophists, you cannot gather figs from thistles. Better read Mrs. Oliphant's book about it.

The New York *Tribune* of Dec. 13 printed a special dispatch from San Francisco stating that Miss Chevallier had just returned from a six months' sojourn in Mr. Harris' community, and briefly gave her account of what goes on there. *The Chronicle* of San Francisco subsequently printed the entire account given by Miss Chevallier, in which she declares her intention of attempting to break up the community. These facts should be well known, because there is a tendency on the part of such people as this "prophet" to assume now and then a theosophical guise. Our Society must be kept as free as possible from being mixed up with these enterprises. For now that theosophy is becoming better known through the years of effort made by devoted members of the Society, the cranks and false prophets in all directions are attempting to trade for their own advantage on the public interest so aroused.

The Light of Egypt

[*The Path*, Vol. VII, April, 1892, pp. 22-23]

In several quarters there has been of late a persistent attempt to push the sale of this book, particularly among Theosophists, and this attempt, combined with the inquiries reaching *The Path* respecting its character, make important a recalling to F. T. S. of the facts given in *The Path* of July and August, 1889. In the former the book was reviewed and its inadequacy—outside of plagiarisms—shown, as also its denial of Karma and Reincarnation as applicable to this earth! At that time the author was understood to be Mrs. E. H. Britten, but proof as to the real authorship was immediately sent *The Path*, and in the following number correction was made, the right name given, and the history of the publication disclosed. The author was Mr. T. H. Burgoyne.

Briefly, these are the facts. A spurious Occult Society, known as the "H. B. of L.", was started about 1884, and pretended to give to its members occult teaching *free*. In August, 1887, Mr. Burgoyne, styling himself "Private Secretary," issued to the members a secret circular, the essence of which was that he had studied Chaldean Astrology for eighteen years, but could not communicate the "lessons" in it and Occultism without a payment to him of $60; that his teachings had the full approval of the Masters; and that the $60 subscription was a necessity to Initiation. A synopsis of the course accompanied the circular. When *The Light of Egypt* was published, a subscriber placed in the hands of the Editor of *The Path* the instructions, "lithographs of the original produced by the Autocopyist," and examination showed that the book was mostly a reprint at $3.00 of "secret teachings" for which $60 had been exacted!

The present edition of the book states it to be by an "Initiate." Even without H.P.B.'s assertions as to the "H. B. of L." and her statement (in *Lucifer*) as to the author, no instructed Theosophist should need assurance that Initiates do not proclaim themselves such; that they do not deny doctrines which are pivotal to the whole Theosophic scheme; that they do not *sell* Esoteric teachings—much less in books at a fraction of the rate charged privately till the latter demand ceased; and that no man can enjoy instruction from or approval of Masters whose life and character would exclude him from Their presence and far more from Their endorsement. Hence they should perceive that *The Light of Egypt* is an impudent fraud.

The Ashes of H.P.B.

[*The Path*, Vol. VII, August, 1892, p. 168; Vol. VII, January
1893, pp. 306-08; Vol. VIII, May, 1893, p. 64]

THE ASHES OF MADAME BLAVATSKY

A permanent Headquarters building for the American Section being
now actually possessed, the General Secretary, pursuant to the arrangement made by Col. Olcott at the London Convention last year,
will bring with him on his return to America that portion of Madame
Blavatsky's ashes which was assigned to the guardianship of the American Section. It is to repose in the Headquarters. The purchase of a
suitable urn and the preparation of a secure mural receptacle will involve some expense—one, however, to which her pupils in Theosophy
may well feel contribution a privilege. As the work should be undertaken immediately upon the General Secretary's return, American Theosophists are invited to forward their kind offerings to me before August 15th if possible. Acknowledgment under initials will be made in
September *Path*, and a full description of the plan adopted will be
published promptly.

WILLIAM Q. JUDGE,
144 *Madison Ave., New York.*

The little cut below is a picture of the bronze urn in which reposes
that portion of the ashes of H.P.B. which was given to the English
Headquarters, at 19 Avenue Road, London. When Col. Olcott arrived
at London from Australia, the body of H.P.B. had been already in-
cinerated and all of the ashes were at the English Headquarters awaiting his arrival. Our English brethren of course felt a certain amount
of delicacy, for there has as yet grown up no accepted method of dis-
posing of the ashes of the cremated dead in Western lands. To bury
them seems often not the proper way because they never are large in
quantity, and to scatter them to the winds of heaven might hurt the
feelings of the survivors, so there is a sort of custom of preserving
such ashes in a receptacle like a jar or a niche. Indeed, the creeping
on of this latter custom is evidenced by the proposals of Cremation

Bronze Urn Designed for H.P.B.'s Ashes

societies to provide niches for the purpose. So came naturally to Western minds the idea of preservation. Probably for those reasons and in the absence of a better way Col. Olcott resolved to have them preserved. Then arose the question of whether there should be any division, and the President himself arrived at the conclusion to divide the whole quantity into three parts, one for India, one for Europe, and one for America, because in England, at any rate, there was a certain shade of desire to have, in the place where H.P.B. had spent the last years of her life, some portion of her ashes, and naturally if one place had any of them the other should also. The President spoke of this when he felicitously said that "If we consider the Theosophical career of H.P.B. we shall find it divided into three stages, *viz.* New York, India, and London—its cradle, altar, and tomb." This is how the division came to be made.[1]

At the same time an agreement was made by the three sections through their officers that in the event of the European or American Headquarters being discontinued, the portion of the ashes intrusted to that section should go at once to India. Col. Olcott carried the quantity reserved for India with him across the ocean to America, across America to Japan, and thence to Madras, and thus once again after H.P.B. had passed away her ashes made the circuit of the globe. The General Secretary of the American Section next carried his portion across the ocean to New York where they now remain.

At the time the above took place at London a celebrated Swedish artist in bronze hand-work offered through the Countess Wachtmeister to make for the ashes in London a bronze urn. The kind offer was accepted, and at the Convention there in 1892 the completed urn was presented to the Section. The artist is Herr Bengtsson, who is so well known and whose work is so highly valued that rulers in Europe come to him for his work, and he will refuse to do anything for anyone unless his heart moves him. So in this case his voluntary offer is a compliment. The urn is just about two feet high, two wide, and two deep. It rests on a bronze platform of three steps, and locks upon this

---

1 [The portion of her ashes which Col. Olcott brought with him to India in 1891 was buried under H.P.B.'s Statue in the Headquarters Hall at Adyar. That portion of the ashes which was for a while in London, was kept in the casket designed by Reginald Willoughby Machell (1845-1927), and executed by Sven Bengtsson (1843-1916) a renowned carver of Lund, Sweden. Mr. Machell was a personal pupil of H.P.B., noted both as a painter and wood-carver. The London portion was later carried to India by Annie Besant when the Headquarters at 19 Avenue Road were given up. At Benares (Varanasi) these remaining ashes were dropped into the Ganges, as was a portion of Col. Olcott's, in 1907. The urn of Machell's creation is now at Adyar. It should be added that the other third of H.P.B.'s ashes was for some years at the New York T.S. Headquarters, and later for many years at Point Loma, and is now in the Archives of the Theosophical Society International at Pasadena, California.—*Comp.*]

by an ingenious arrangement. All around it are emblems and also the motto of the Society, as well as the three important dates in the life of H.P.B., her birth, her going to India, her death. The design was made by Brother Machell of the Blavatsky Lodge, London, and the whole shows the influence of loving hearts and grateful recollection. Its top is crowned with a fiery heart resting in a silver lotus. Within and under the dome is a smaller Indian vase in which are the ashes, and with these is a document signed by witnesses and executed at London on the day the ashes were put within and the whole presented to the Convention. The signed declaration is to show that the contents are the ashes of H.P.B., and when and by whom they were placed inside.

In America the sum of about two hundred dollars has been given for the purpose of having a suitable receptacle here, but it is not enough to allow us to as yet construct according to the design made by the General Secretary. Hence up to this date the ashes are under private lock and key. The design is of an Egyptian character, two pillars supporting an Egyptian roof with the flying globe at the top, and on the space between the pillars the name of H.P.B. and the great dates of her life, as also the complete symbol of the T.S. It is impressive as well as beautiful, but would cost over seven hundred dollars, and it is likely that some modification will have to be made if we are to retain the ashes here. Great pressure of important work has prevented any new designs being considered, but there is hope that soon we shall have a proper receptacle for what has been entrusted to our care.

On Saturday, the 22nd of April, the General Secretary had succeeded in having the receptacle in the Headquarters Room finished to receive the ashes of H.P.B., and the same was inspected by the delegates to the Convention during the recesses. It consists of a portion of the design adopted, being the central marble slab and the receptacle combined. On the slab are the seal of the Society, the word "Om", Madame Blavatsky's full name, and the prominent dates of her life, 1831, 1875, 1879, 1891. The slab is of Sienna marble. The receptacle is a bronze box faced with plate glass, and inside is the casket made of pure onyx, resting on four crystal balls, and in which rests the portion of H.P.B.'s ashes given to the American Section. When funds are in hand the remainder of the design adopted will be added. A full description of the receptacle and the casket, both as now erected and as to be finished, will be published in a subsequent issue of the Path.

Impossibilities Demanded

[*The Path*, Vol. VII, September, 1892, pp. 173-75]

Many impossibilities have been at all times demanded by members of the Society from those who have by the misfortunes of Karma been put in the front row like ninepins to be knocked down by self-appointed critics. Very often H. P. Blavatsky, Col. Olcott, and others in official position have been requested to state why every member other than the questioner—or as well, perhaps—is not a saint; why it is that the enrollment of a person in our ranks did not at once alter the human nature which eighteen hundred years of un-civilization have produced; why the possession of our diploma does not immediately admit to the presence of those glorious Adepts who have occupied incarnations in striving to become real and active altruists; and so on with an immense number of other things as difficult and as presently impossible. In a former issue *The Path* related the experience of the office with the demands of ordinary correspondents, when an order for a book from India or a magazine from London was required to be filled in a week although the mail to and from India usually takes thirty days each way for transit. But the unattainable and impossible are required most assuredly, and the opposite to fact is stated in a note of which the following are the words:

Our organization [a local one] must first establish its own center, even though the existence of any such center *is persistently ignored* by *The Path* and Mr. Judge. Mr. Judge sees only New York and Europe and India (later), but notwithstanding *this visual incapacity* there *is* a center in—And much Theosophical activity that *never gets mentioned* goes on.

Quite so; "the visual incapacity" to see what is going on at a distance of a thousand miles from *The Path* office is not confined to the editor of that unfortunate magazine, especially when the members of that "center" never say one word to the editor of *The Path* about what *is* going on. No doubt they work, and that very energetically, but unless they inform the editor, or unless he obtains the capital to permit the employment of a regular and intelligent reporter at every such center, it is quite unlikely that the pages of this magazine will be able to record and to encourage their admirable activity. It is an impossibility that is asked and implied in the statement of our "visual incapacity" and "persistent ignoring" of that about which we never have information.

But it is very wide of the fact to say that we see only New York, India, and Europe. Our history shows our Conventions held year after year in Illinois, and the enormous correspondence of the office with every State in the Union indicates in some degree, we presume, an interest in all our work here. The Indian correspondence is very small, and the European the same; the news we print from England is generally obtained from sources outside the members; and nearly all that about the U.S. is culled from stray letters. California is an exception, as from there the members send the facts. But the above complaint is not the only one of the same kind, and these words are meant for every Branch.

If you wish *The Path* to give accounts of the various activities of Branches, you must send them to the office, or else wait the far distant day when our individual purse will allow us to pay for the news we desire. But please do not accuse us of ignoring your work if we never know what you are doing, for as yet we have none of us in *The Path* office developed the power to read thoughts and see actions across hundreds of miles of our country; we are still compelled to rely very much upon the mail-bag and the telegraph-wire.

But since this matter has come upon the carpet, we may remind complaining members that *The Path* has from the beginning sustained its course through the help of the pockets of its editor and a few friends. There are enough members to thoroughly sustain it if they only chose to subscribe, but as a cold matter of fact the majority of its subscribers are to be found outside the ranks of our own fellows. This is probably due in part to general poverty; and yet we doubt not that even many of those poor ones frequently belong to clubs, to benefit societies, and spend many a dollar on amusements and ice-cream. We do not complain; there are other worlds and other *man·vantaras* in prospect, and perhaps the day may come when filthy lucre will not be indispensable to work in the world.

Two Theosophical Events

[*The Path*, Vol. VII, November, 1892, pp. 248-50]

A Libel Retracted—Col. Olcott still President

September, 1892, will stand as a red letter month in our history. Two events of importance occurred, the one removing a cloud, the other reassuring the Society that its President-Founder would remain in office.

In July, 1890, *The Sun*, a daily newspaper of great influence in the city of New York, published a news article in which gross charges were made against the character of H. P. Blavatsky, the Founder of the Theosophical Society, and charging also Col. Olcott, William Q. Judge, and many others with assisting her in fraud and with living upon the Society. It was intended to be a general sweeping attack on all who were in the Society, and, having been written by an enemy who once was counted in the ranks of our members, it was carefully sent by him to as many people as he could think of who would be hurt by it in feelings or warned off from the work of the T.S. Two suits for libel were then begun by Mme. Blavatsky and Mr. Judge against the *Sun* and Dr. E. Coues of Washington.

Some members thought then that we ought not to have gone to law, but as we do not profess to live by the code of Jesus but felt that the honor and the peace of mind of the members at large were involved, we took the only course given by the laws of the land. The suits went on the calendar of the courts of New York, and there were delayed by the immense mass of cases ahead of them. Meanwhile the author of the libel and certain Spiritualistic friends in another city kept up the attack and asserted that nothing would ever be heard of the suits again. In 1891 H.P.B. died, and, as her action was for a personal injury to character, her demise worked a determination of the suit begun in her name, and by that fact the paper that put out the libel was at once released from any fear from that action. This should be noted in view of what follows. On the 26th of Sept., 1892, the *Sun* published the following in its editorial columns:

We print on another page an article in which Mr. William Q. Judge deals with the romantic and extraordinary career of the late Madame Helena P. Blavatsky, the Theosophist.[1] We take occasion to observe that on July 20, 1890,

---

1 [This article, "The Esoteric She . . . ," will be reprinted with other miscellaneous articles in a future volume of this series.—*Comp.*]

we were misled into admitting to the *Sun's* columns an article by Dr. E. F.
Coues of Washington, in which allegations were made against Madame Blavatsky's character, and also against her followers, which appear to have been without
solid foundation. Mr. Judge's article disposes of all questions relating to Madame Blavatsky as presented by Dr. Coues, and we desire to say that his allegations respecting the Theosophical Society and Mr. Judge personally are not sustained by evidence, and should not have been printed.

The news columns of that issue contained a sketch of Madame Blavatsky by Mr. Judge, which although having some errors as printed, is
in the main correct. The retraction is small in respect to the area of the paper covered, but it is a general one, and at a single blow sweeps away all
that our enemies had thought was accomplished by the libel. As many
newspaper men since have said, it is as complete as anything of the
kind that was ever published. And in view of the fact that no suit by
H.P.B. was then pending, it reflects credit on the paper in this age
when newspapers in general never retract except when forced by law
or loss of money. Thus ends this libel. The suits against the *Sun* have
been discontinued, and the only one pending is that by Mr. Judge
against Dr. Coues.

When Col. Olcott resigned the office of President before our Convention of April last, the universal desire in this country was that he
should remain in office even if he did no great amount of work in
consequence of bad health, and the Convention asked him to reconsider his decision. India had expressed the same thought before. Replying to the cable sent him from the Convention meeting in Chicago,
he said he was willing to do what was right, and later announced that
the important matter of the legacy left to the Society in Australia
was not settled so as to be secure to the organization, and also that
the property owned in India had not been transferred to trustees so as
to put the title in a shape to prevent loss or trouble. These delayed
his going out of office. Just before the July Convention in Europe he
published a notice rather ambiguously worded, but which was meant
to read that very likely he would revoke his resignation. This possibility of two constructions led the European Convention to assume
that he had declared definitely he would not revoke, and it therefore
saw no need of taking any action on the question as had been done
in America.

But in August Col. Olcott came to the conclusion that as his health
had been fully restored he could not do better than revoke the resignation, and so telegraphed to the Vice-President, and the official circular
to that effect went out last month. He is thus still our President, and

surely no one there is but hopes he may so remain until the day of his death.

Some words by H.P.B. on the matter, written years ago, may be of interest. She says, speaking of Col. Olcott:

As long as I live I shall never go against one who for ten years was my best friend, my staunchest, dearest, most loyal defender and brother, and one, moreover, whom the Master wants to stand firm at his post till his death-day.

To another:

It may be that you and others and even myself do not always agree with Olcott, and find faults in him, but it is Master's wish that he shall be president until his death or that time which is equivalent to it. There is a quality in him that not many have, and that is the power and disposition to stand for his cause against all and every obstacle.

These serve to show that it is better, wiser, and safer for him to remain, and that it is not time, nor right, nor just, nor wise that he should go out either corporeally or officially. But let us hope that with the month in which the American Section heard of his action, and of the retraction of the libel on H.P.B. and all Theosophists, a new era began for the movement.

Theosophical Correspondence Class

SOME WORK OF THE CLASS

[*The Path*, Vol. VIII, January, 1894, pp. 320-22]

This Class was started in the American Section for the purpose of helping the members in the course of study and in all matters pertaining to the Society. Very soon after the first notice was given members began to come in, and at this date, December, one hundred and forty-six persons have joined, coming from all parts of the Section. No authority is claimed, and members are helped by comments made on answers and by references to books and articles. At the same time it is likely that a large index or reference book may result from the work, referring to all sorts of articles and subjects in the whole field of T.S. literature. This in itself will be a valuable thing to have, and if means and energy warrant it might finally be gotten out in book form.

In the first list of questions the following among others was put:

What is the basis, genius, and spirit of the T.S. constitution?

Its object was to direct the mind to the organization itself, and to give an opportunity to personally with each one point out certain matters which ought to be better understood than they are, as the replies demonstrate. Some sample replies are here given without names.

39. I have been a member of the T.S. for eight years, and have never seen its constitution *nor ever heard of any.*

42. The basis of Theosophy is the revelation by letters and speech from Mahâtmas; its genius and spirit, the teachings of eternal truths of nature and universe.

62. Its basis is the establishment of a Universal Brotherhood. Its genius is to awaken the sleeping soul of man to a knowledge of its true powers, its true work, its true destiny. To arouse and stimulate to action the untried, undeveloped forces of the soul. To lift man out of the illusions of matter that he may make a more steady and rapid progress toward his spiritual development and perfection. To teach him to estimate correctly between material and spiritual progress, just how much one is worth in comparison with the other and just *what* ends are *to be obtained with one or the other.*
Its spirit is to eliminate selfishness, to inspire in the individual a beneficent, universal love of humanity in preference to a selfish, personal love. To persist in an increasing endeavor to purify the soul, lift the aspirations, ennoble the thoughts, not so much for the sanctification of self, as for the sake of purity and righteousness as principles of the Divine Will and for the maintenance of the Divine Harmony. And also for the psychical influences unconsciously engendered by holy thought and holy living. To eradicate error, false conceptions, mistaken interpretations. To annihilate prejudice and all systems of hasty conclusions. To follow out the golden rule "Do unto others as you would be done by." To incite to an exact uprightness *in all things.* To cultivate tolerance, patience, gentleness, sweetness, humility, and devotion in the cause of others.

41. The basis, genius, and spirit of the Theosophical Society is unselfishness, or the Fatherhood of God and the Brotherhood of Man.

69. The basis of the T.S. is a belief in the unity of all life, spiritual and physical; its genius that this unity of all life brings us into such relations directly or indirectly with other races, nations, and brother men as to cause any injury done by one to another to mutually affect other races, nations, and men upon the earth. Its spirit is that of compassionate sympathy for, and mutual helpfulness to, all beings.

90. The basis, genius, and spirit of the T.S. Constitution are expressed in the first object and in its motto, "There is no Religion higher than Truth". It would unite men of all creeds and races in a bond of brotherhood and mutual toleration upon the common ground of Truth, which is the nucleus about which all creeds and dogmas have crystallized.

58. Sincere and earnest belief in the Masters of Wisdom seems to me to be the basis of the Theosophic Constitution.

9. The basis of the T.S. is the Brotherhood of Man; its spirit is entirely unsectarian and has no creed or dogma to promulgate; respectful tolerance is shown to all religions, creeds, and races of men; the genius of the T.S. is the desire to uplift humanity to a higher level.

33. Oneness, development, charity.

The above are fairly representative of all, and of the general spirit of this Section. They show that all have missed the gist of the question, which was directed to the organic law under which we work, but at the same time demonstrate that the true idea of the movement as a human development is pretty well understood. If the question had been as to the movement apart from the Constitution of the Society, all the replies would have been very good. Number thirty-nine apparently saw the precise point from the reply that he or she had not even heard there was a Constitution. But that also illustrates another thing, that it is possible to proceed vigorously with such a work as ours even if the members do not think there is any organic law. Of course it would not do for officials to be ignorant of the Constitution, but it appears that if men are working as so many in the T.S. do work the law need not be known, inasmuch as they become in themselves the right law. However, the way to have replied properly to the question as put is something like the following:

"The Basis: (*a*) Equality of members irrespective of caste, sex, color, race, or creed; (*b*) Autonomy or self government of all Branches and Sections; (*c*) Federation, in which, though each Branch and Section governs itself, all must act in conformity to the general Constitution; thus the Branches of a Section are under the jurisdiction of the federated Section and governed by its general law, which in turn must conform to the law of the whole T.S.

In addition to the foregoing, the basis, genius, and spirit of the organic law or Constitution are autonomy, equality, non-sectarianism, non-dogmatism, absence of creed, and tolerance of opinion. The objects of the Society *are the aim* to which the Constitution is directed.

The Theosophical movement as distinguished from its Constitution is based on fraternity and unity, its genius is the pursuit of truth and tolerance, its spirit is unselfishness leading it to spread the truth with tolerance and to work for the uplifting of the race.

From all the above a branch might exist as one of the T.S. and be composed wholly of members who had a specific belief, provided they did not force it on others nor claim for the belief the endorsement of the organized Society."

Of Funds and Property

[*The Path*, Vol. VIII, February, 1894, pp. 354-57]

It was thought by some at one time in the history of the Theosophical Society that a society fund was an indispensable prerequisite to the growth of the movement. This was a natural idea to a Western man because most of the achievements of the West are the result of the use of money, but if one has a good knowledge of human nature and remembers what has happened in other organizations it must be evident that, while money is necessary in order to get bread to eat, it is not entirely necessary for the work of the Theosophical Society. The Roman Catholic Church is probably the most powerful religious body, controlling vast sums of money and owning the best property everywhere, but its great achievements have been in the line of fostering dogmatism and chaining the minds of men; its latest one a few months ago consisting in compelling St. George Mivart, who is a Roman Catholic, to recant what he said in a prominent review tending to show that eternal damnation is impossible. The Methodist and other Churches of the dissenting side of Christianity sustain large missionary enterprises for which they get millions of dollars from their adherents, and the result is that they pay the salaries of many missionaries, enabling their secretaries at home to accumulate money, produce but few converts abroad, and keep up the breach in brotherhood between the East and West by fostering the idea that the heathen are unregenerate and damned. If the Theosophical Society as an organization had always possessed a fund and property, there would always be those who, moved by selfish motives, would struggle to gain possession of the money and the use of the property for their own benefit. But without a fund belonging to the treasury, the Society has steadily grown in influence and numbers. This is because instead of money to fight for we have had an inspiring ideal, and instead of corporate funds to work with we have had devotion which causes the members to use in the work of the organization their own private means untrammelled by the treasury rules. Thus the Society is poor, and it is sincerely to be hoped that it will always remain without a fund as a temptation to the cupidity of man.

The Headquarters in America, situated in New York City, is a piece of property the title of which is vested in the local Branch, which is a corporation formed for the purpose of holding the property. It does not belong to the Theosophical Society, but it is devoted, under the same spirit of devotion as has moved all true Theosophical workers, to the uses and the benefit of the T.S. The Headquarters in London belongs also to a body of persons, not to the Theosophical Society. Exceptionally, the Headquarters in Adyar belongs as a center to the Theosophical organization as a whole. It has been said by some that all donations, all legacies, all bequests of property, all general acquisitions of all property for the T.S. work should be to and for the Theosophical Society as legal beneficiary, but with this view I for one cannot agree. The funds that are used in the work, outside of the necessary funds belonging to the various Sections and spent during the year, should remain the property of private persons who devote them to the uses of the Society freely and in whatever direction their conscience permits. If we accumulate a large corporate fund we will also accumulate around it those human beings who unconsciously as well as deliberately conceal their motives, who ask to be allowed to work so that they may be paid, and who as members of the whole body owning the fund have a right to demand its division. May Heaven defend us from such a state of things! If persons have money which they desire to devote in large sums to the Society's work, they should either use it themselves in the line of that activity or deliver it over to such devoted workers as have shown that their guide in life is self-sacrifice for the whole.

Take a few concrete examples. In the American Section, for instance, salaries are not paid, unless you call board and lodging a salary to certain persons who are without means. There are workers in the official departments of that Section who spend their entire time from early morning till night, and all the money they can spare over their actual necessities, in toiling for the Theosophical Society without a salary and at the same time giving out of their means to the needs of the work. In England it is the same. There Mrs. Besant and others work unceasingly for the Society, she supporting herself and contributing all that remains of her earnings to the needs of the Society. H. P. Blavatsky did the same. Col. Olcott did also and is still doing it. Thus in every direction the real lasting and beneficial activities of the Society are carried on by those who, willing to work for it, do not ask a salary; and those of them who possess means do not wish to be trammelled by rules and regulations relating to a general fund which will always be source of annoyance and a temptation to the wicked. In our history of many years we have had this proved in the case of a treasurer in India who, having the small general funds under his control, stole all that he could lay his hands upon. He was but a mortal thrown into the midst of temptation. If the money were his own and he were working in the Society with it, he would not steal it for he could not.

We ought not to encourage large donations to the treasury, but should spread abroad the principle that private means should be liberally given to the tried ones for use in their discretion when the giver does not know how or has not the opportunity to use it himself. Let them do as has been done; just as one man gave H. P. Blavatsky $5000 for the Girls' Club at Bow, London, for which it was judiciously used by Mrs. Besant as agent; or as another gave a large sum to help start a headquarters; or like another in giving the money to print quantities of tracts and pamphlets; or as another who paid over from time to time to an official enough to sustain a well-tried, devoted, but penniless worker in further hard travelling and speaking for the Cause. In this way devotion becomes more valuable than millions of money; those who are capable of speaking and writing but have no means will be enabled to go on by others who, favored by material fate, have a surplus. But make a large treasury fund, and then no barnacle or drone could be shaken off once it had fastened on the old ship, because he would have a voice in the management of means. Again, those captious, suspicious persons who always know the date of a penny or the number of a bill woud harass those who had the spending.

Again, our poverty and lack of earthly applause and reward have saved us from cranks and sectarians who subliminally attracted by wealth, would prate of doctrine and duty while they stood guard over the cash-box. In the strength of our ideal and devotion is our power, and that work which is done without reward or the hope of it and without the blighting influence of a debit and credit account goes further and lasts longer than any which is given as return for a money consideration.

The Theosophical Society

Inside facts as to its organization.—A *de facto* body— the real
T.S. in New York—the president still a delegate to
foreign lands, and holding over in office.

[*The Path*, Vol. X, May, 1895, pp. 55-60]

These facts are extracted from a paper prepared for the Convention
at Boston in April, 1895. The historical documents and records used
in the preparation of the matter are: the original minutes of the T.S.;
the original constitution; the records published in India, Europe and
America from time to time; *Old Diary Leaves*—not considered however as wholly reliable—original documents drawn up and signed as
far back as between 1875 and 1878.

STATEMENT OF FACTS

1.   At a meeting held in the rooms of H. P. Blavatsky, 46 Irving
Place, New York City, September 7, 1875, it was agreed to form a
Society for the purpose of Occult Study. Upon motion of William Q.
Judge, Henry S. Olcott was elected Chairman of this meeting, and
upon motion of H. S. Olcott, William Q. Judge was elected Secretary
of the same. Adjourned to September 8, 1875. This is asserted as the
facts by those who were present.

2.   Pursuant to adjournment, a meeting was held at the same place
September 8, 1875. It is with this meeting that the minute book begins. Upon motion of William Q. Judge it was voted that H. S. Olcott
take the Chair, and upon motion it was voted that William Q. Judge
act as secretary. Upon request of the Chair, sixteen persons handed
their names to the Secretary, as agreeing to found and belong to such
a society. A committee of four, including the Chairman, was appointed
"to draft a constitution and by-laws and to report the same at the next
meeting". Adjourned to Monday, September 13, 1875, at the same
place.

3.   Pursuant to adjournment, a meeting was held September 13,
1875. H. S. Olcott acted as Chairman and C. Sotheran as Secretary.
The Committee on "Preamble and By-laws" reported progress. It was
resolved that the name of the Society be "The Theosophical Society".

The Chair appointed a committee to select meeting rooms. "Several new members were nominated and upon motion those persons were added to the list of Founders." The meeting adjourned subject to the call of the Chair.

4. Pursuant to a notice dated at New York, October 13, 1875, signed Henry S. Olcott, President *pro tem.*, a meeting was held at 206 West 38th Street, October 16, 1875, "to organize and elect officers". Eighteen persons were present. The report of the Committee on "Preamble and By-laws" was laid on the table and ordered printed. The meeting adjourned to October 30, 1875, at the same place. H. S. Olcott was Chairman, and J. S. Cobb, Secretary.

5. October 30, 1875, the Society met pursuant to adjournment. Mott Memorial Hall, 64 Madison Avenue, New York City, was selected as the Society's meeting place. By-laws were adopted, but with the proviso that the "Preamble" should be revised by a committee and then published as the "Preamble of the Society". Officers were elected as follows: President, Henry S. Olcott; Vice-Presidents, Dr. S. Pancoast and G. H. Felt; Corresponding Secretary, Mme. H. P. Blavatsky; Recording Secretary, John Storer Cobb; Treasurer, Henry J. Newton; Librarian, Charles Sotheran; Councillors, Rev. J. H. Wiggin, R. B. Westbrook, LL.D. Mrs. Emma Hardinge Britten, C. E. Simmons, M.D. and Herbert D. Monachesi; Counsel to the Society, William Q. Judge. Adjourned to November 17, 1875.

6. The Society met in Mott Memorial Hall, November 17, 1875, pursuant to adjournment. The President read an address and after the transaction of business, adjourned to December 15, 1875.

7. It is probable that Col. Olcott selected this as the date of organization, because of his inaugural address, but it is not correct, and he had no authority to do so. About this time members fell away and there was no quorum.

8. A few odd meetings were held until 1878. The minute book was mislaid. Resolutions were made by two or three persons writing them out and declaring them passed.

9. In the year 1878 H. P. Blavatsky and H. S. Olcott were appointed a "Committee of the Theosophical Society" to visit foreign countries and report. The *Theosophist* for October, 1879, Vol. I, No. 1, p. 1, first item, says: "For the convenience of future reference, it may as well be stated here that the Committee, sent to India by the Theosophical Society, sailed from New York December 17, 1878, and landed at Bombay, February 16, 1879, having passed two weeks in London

on the way." In *The Theosophist* for January, 1880, Vol. I, p. 85, Col. Olcott says he "came to India with two English colleagues and their learned Corresponding Secretary, Madame Blavatsky. They came only expecting to study Eastern Religion and Yoga Vidyâ and report their discoveries to the Western Theosophists," which were the Society in New York, consisting of over forty members at this time.

10.   Before the departure of their Committee to foreign countries, the Theosophical Society elected General A. Doubleday as President *pro tem.*, to serve during the absence of the President. This election of President *pro tem.* was never revoked; nor was the appointment of this Committee. On arrival in India H. S. Olcott had their pictures taken and sent to America endorsed by him "The Delegation to India".

11.   Meetings of the Theosophical Society were held at New York for some years after the departure of the Committee, and were presided over by General Doubleday and William Q. Judge.

12.   From October 30, 1875, to December, 1878, all alterations of the By-laws were made in regular and formal manner by the Society at New York.

13.   These By-laws provided that new members could not be elected until after thirty days' consideration of their application.

14.   The original organization was kept up at New York certainly until after January 1, 1882.

15.   What purported to be "Revised Rules of the Theosophical Society" were adopted at Bombay in October, 1879, by a body which called itself the "General Council of the Theosophical Society", but had no legal existence whatever. There was published in the *Theosophist* for April, 1880, (Vol. I, p. 179): "The Theosophical Society or Universal Brotherhood. Principles, Rules, and By-laws as revised in General Council, at the meeting held at the palace of H. H. the Maharajah of Vizianagram, Benares, 17th December, 1879." To this was subjoined the statement: "Revised and ratified by the Society, at Bombay, February the 26th and 28th, 1880.—Attest: Kharsedji N. Seervai, Joint Recording Secretary". This meeting at Benares was merely one held by H. S. Olcott without notice and was irregular. It was here that Col. Olcott worked out the resolution that declared him President for life. The original Constitution fixed his term at one year and was never amended. The so-called ratification at Bombay was irregular and amounted to nothing.

16.   None of the admissions to membership nor any alterations of the By-laws adopted at the instigation of the Committee sent to foreign

lands were in accordance with the By-laws of the Theosophical Society in New York and could only be changed by a like vote. None of these alterations of the By-laws were ever submitted to the Society in New York and that Society never voted on any of them.

17.   From December, 1878, down to the present time, various sets of "Rules", "By-laws", and "Constitutions" have been promulgated by alleged "General Councils", but none of them have ever been adopted in accordance with the only By-laws of any validity.

18.   No lapse of time, no passive assent, and no active assent given in ignorance of the legal status of the case, would confer any validity upon the otherwise illegal acts of the President of the Committee to foreign lands or those claiming to act through or under them, or either of them.

19.   Up to 1880 members were admitted to the Society in New York in accordance with the By-laws.

20.   Before H. S. Olcott and H. P. Blavatsky went to India the name of the Society was altered in New York, in the manner which prevailed after members had dropped off, to "The Theosophical Society of the Arya Samaj of Arya Vart". This made it a Branch of the Arya Samaj, over which Dyanand presided. Diplomas were printed thus and issued as late as September, 1878, with Dyanand's name and seal printed on them.

21.   In India, again, Col. Olcott, in the same manner as before, altered the name of the Society back to the old style by striking off "of the Arya Samaj of Arya Vart". If the Society properly voted to change in New York to the Arya Samaj, it certainly never voted to reconsider.

22.   Before the departure to India in 1878 the Recording Secretary was sent to London to form the British Theosophical Society. He did this and Dr. Wyld presided over that for a time. This body finally became, it is asserted, the "London Lodge", now controlled by Mr. Sinnett.

23.   The London Lodge has always claimed to be autonomous, has continued its work, always claiming to be perfectly independent of the President, the parent Society, the Section in which it is, the Constitution, and all and every person and body whatever. This anomalous position has been always recognized and permitted by the President, and also by the European Section in which that Lodge is. This is finally exhibited in the letter from the Lodge, found in the Proceedings of that Section for 1894.

24. When H.P.B. for the last time settled in Europe, she autonomously, independently, and at the request of the Europeans (except the London Lodge), founded "The Theosophical Society in Europe," of which she was President. After she had made her declarations, Col. Olcott issued a paper so as to seem to approve of what had been done. On these was built up the present European Section.

25. An examination of the records from the beginning to the end of 1893 shows that there is no record whatever of the election of William Q. Judge as Vice-President of the T.S. In July, 1894, at London, Col. Olcott and the Indian General Secretary upon William Q. Judge's raising the point, decided that they would assert that the record was defective and could be cured by stating the fact that such Vice-President had been elected in India many years before, and it was so ordered in Council. But as the meeting at which said election took place—if it ever did—was not one participated in by those who could bind the whole Society, and as the real T.S. existed in New York, if anywhere, it follows that William Q. Judge was not regularly elected Vice-President.

The following by Col. H. S. Olcott occurs in a letter from him to W. Q. Judge, dated May 17th, 1893: "If you want separate T.S. Societies made out of the Sections, have them by all means: I offered this years ago to H.P.B., and even to A. P. S[innett]".

In July, 1894, at London, he enunciated the same idea and plan to W. Q. Judge and Dr. Buck, after the dismissal of the Committee.

26. From a consideration of the above statement of facts it follows that:

(a) The present existing so-called "General Council of the Theosophical Society" has merely a *de facto* status and not a legal one, as it has grown out of and upon wholly illegal proceedings.

(b) The By-laws adopted October 30th, 1875, and such amendments thereto as were made according to the terms of those By-laws, are the only legal ones at present in force and the only ones having any validity whatever.

(c) The Theosophical Society formed at New York in 1875, never had any legal existence outside of the United States and cannot have except upon amendment of the By-laws.

(d) The Theosophical Society was founded at New York, September 8, 1875, by some eighteen persons, and there was no such society founded November 17, 1875, that being simply the date upon which the President delivered his inaugural address.

(*e*) The present existing so-called "Theosophical Society and Universal Brotherhood", with its officers and "General Council", has no legal connection with "The Theosophical Society" founded at New York, September 8, 1875.

(*f*) The authority of the so-called "General Council of the Theosophical Society and Universal Brotherhood" over members, Branches, and Sections, who have submitted to it in ignorance of the real facts in the case, exists only so long as its authority is not called in question, but when so called in question it ceases to have any lawful authority whatever.

Note. A diploma made and issued in due form in 1883 to a member in St. Louis, was signed by Gen. Doubleday as President *pro tem.*, and William Q. Judge as Recording Secretary. This shows the Society as then active in New York. We will print next month a reproduction of this diploma.

A Parent T.S. Diploma

[*The Path*, Vol. X, June, 1895, p. 92 & facs.]

On the opposite page will be found a photographed copy of a diploma made and issued in due form in Jan. 1883. This is the diploma we referred to in an article in May issue under the title "The Theosophical Society." It is of course only one of many, but is introduced here to substantiate the statement in that article that the parent T.S. was active in New York as late as 1883, Abner Doubleday being then its President *pro tem* in the absence of Col. Olcott, the delegate to India.

The Theosophical Society

OF NEW-YORK

admits **Elliott B. Sage**, to the number of its Fellows.

In Witness it has issued to him the present Diploma signed by the President pro tem. and Recording Secretary at New-York, on the nineteenth day of December, in the year 1882.

Abner Doubleday
pro tem. President

William Q Judge
Recording Secretary.

Parent T.S. Diploma

H. S. Olcott versus H.P.B.

[*The Path*, Vol. X, June, 1895, pp. 81-83]

In the April *Theosophist* Col. Olcott makes public what we have long known to be his private opinion—a private opinion hinted at through the pages of *Old Diary Leaves*,—that H.P.B. was a fraud, a medium, and a forger of bogus messages from the Masters. This final ingrate's blow is delivered in a Postscript to the magazine for which the presses were stopped. The hurry was so great that he could not wait another month before hurling the last handful of mud at his spiritual and material benefactor, our departed H.P.B. The next prominent person for whom we wait to make a similar public statement, has long made it privately.

Col. Olcott "stops the press" and rushes off the Postscript, "for the honor of the Masters". He wishes to defend those Masters, who sent H.P.B. as their messenger, by declaring that she "cooked up", forged, and humbugged with, a long and important message to Brahmans at Allahabad in 1881.[1] The Colonel is H.P.B.'s first Western disciple, ignorant to this day of practical occultism and not able to propound a question to the Masters; never heard of Masters except through H.P.B. He now preserves the honor of Masters by blackening the character of their messenger. Splendid defence, this, of the Masters!

How does he explain the long silence of the Masters since 1881 on the subject? And another very pertinent question is this: How does this "defender of the Masters" explain his own silence in 1881 and since? He was present when the message was sent and knew of it. If he knew then that it was bogus why did he not divulge? If he did not know then, was it because he was unable to tell? If he has since been told by one of the Masters—*á la* Besant in the Judge case—will he kindly let us know which of the Masters told him, and when?

All these questions ought to be answered, and many proofs given by him showing the least occult ability to decide on false or genuine messages, because he has attempted to classify H.P.B. with frauds, forgers and mediums. Hence the Masters who sent her are put by him in similar categories. Observe that the forgery now alleged by him was at the very time H.P.B. was giving out from the Masters the series of messages which have become known to all. If we believe him, then

---

1 [See *Echoes* Vol. I, pp. 448-54; also 403-404.—*Comp.*]

the delivery by this irresponsible medium of one false message must throw doubt on every message. Certainly Col. Olcott is no occultist whose decision we will accept. Each of us will be left to decide for this, that, or the other message according to fancy. Olcott does not like the one in question because he lives in India, and it is too gallingly true. Perhaps others may like it, and not be willing to accept other messages that contradict their partisan view of the London Lodge papers or metaphysics and science. For my part, the message in question testifies to its genuineness by its text, except for those who are hit by it, or those who have the Indian craze and think themselves Brahmans, or those whose self-interest and comfort are against it.

The message condemns bigotry. The persons to whom it was sent were then of the most theologically bigoted families. They were wondering, like Pharisees, how it was possible that the Mahâtmas could communicate with a beef-eating, wine-drinking Sinnett and not with them, who took no such things and never shook hands. To these very points, to their superstitions, to their upholding idolatry, to the horrors of caste, the letter adverts. The whole letter rings true and strong. Were one at all disposed to join Olcott in his absurd explanations by mediumship, this letter is the one that would be selected as true.

If for a moment we accept this view of H.P.B. put forward by Olcott then there is, as she published herself, no certainty about any message. Who is to decide? If she hoodwinked with one message, all may be the same—bogus—and the great force and strength derived from a firm belief in Masters will be swept away, because she, their first messenger to us, is made out a fraud. All this is precisely what Olcott *et al* wish to do. He cannot tolerate the idea that H.P.B. was greater than himself, so he throws around her memory the dirty cloak of tricky and irresponsible mediumship. That done, anything can be explained and anything accounted for.

Well, for my part, I will not accept such nonsense, Col. Olcott being incompetent to decide on Mahâtmic messages on occult lines, and being a disciple of H.P.B. is certainly much below her. His present utterance settles nothing about her character, about her mediumship or about the message; but it does serve to brand him as an ingrate and to place him plainly in view as one who calls that great teacher a fraud and a medium.

Now let the next and the next come on, so that we may have the lines clearly drawn and the hypocrisies unveiled.

MRS. A. BESANT vs. H.P.B.

Mrs. Besant has sent an advance copy of an article to appear in *Lucifer* entitled "East and West". It is a very long article devoted chiefly to William Q. Judge, but in it she takes up the message from the Master to the Allahabad Brahmans, which Col. Olcott deals with in his April Postscript. *She says the message is not genuine*, and thus walks beside Col. Olcott in abuse of H.P.B., for everyone with correct information knows that the message came through H.P.B.

WILLIAM Q. JUDGE

The Work Since May

[*The Path*, Vol. X, December, 1895, pp. 265-67]

This month ends the year and gives us, for examination and review, seven months of experience in theosophical work. Last April, after the Boston Convention, there were some who had fears that great difficulty, perhaps disaster, was soon to come upon the work. It was a sort of superstition for which they could hardly account—a superstition connected solely with the mere framework of an organization. In the general mental development of the world there could be found no basis for the notion that Theosophy was decaying. So the superstition was connected with forms as a ghost is with a house. But there were others who had no fears and no sort of superstition. They perceived the truth of the idea thrown out by others wiser than we that the unity of the movement depends on singleness of purpose and aspiration and not on a world-wide single organization. By this time the fears of the first must be allayed and the hopes of the second justified.

The echoes of the Convention had not died away when active, widespread work went on as before, without a halt. We reported to the meeting, and before any voting on the Constitution, that there were 102 branches in the jurisdiction. This was true as to the record, but some of those were even then so inactive as to be subjects of grave consideration. Today—when this is penned—notwithstanding losses and prophecies and croakings, domestic and foreign, we have ninety branches. These ninety have among them several new ones formed since April, out of new material and not resulting from a split. This part of the seven months history is in itself enough to show the wisdom of our course, and to give to everyone the greatest encouragement.

The very first result of the vote at Boston was to infuse into all "loyal" branches new energy and determination to increase the activity while trying to make brotherhood practical. All the new branches are made up of good working material. In those cases where—as in some cities—the new body was formed by half of the old, the branch was doubly determined to be of still more use than was the old. So now the entire body of branches may be regarded as strong, active, inspired for action and trying to work for brotherhood.

Official activities began the day after Convention. The *Forum* was made of greater value by changing its plan and shape. Reports from everywhere commend it and show that its usefulness has increased. The other official papers were continued as before. Almost immediately a new, active, and actual working Committee was formed for propaganda in the Central States—a vast territory. Another was formed in New England. While the Central Committee was being formed, Mr. Burcham Harding worked in the New England district, lecturing in public and visiting branches. When everything was ready he started work in the State of Indiana, and succeeded in spreading Theosophy in nearly every town, and by means of the reports given by newspapers, must have reached nearly every inhabitant. The best sort of people came to hear him. When, as did happen, bigoted ministers publicly denounced him, the people came to his rescue and snubbed the priest. Everybody seemed to want to know about Theosophy, and papers would give columns to his lectures. This may be taken as an indication of the liveliness of Theosophy and as proof that more people desire this philosophy than members seemed to think. The case of Indiana I select out of many because it furnishes a condensed example. At the same time the New England, the Atlantic and the Californian work went on unabated. The San Francisco members had for some time been holding Sunday theosophical services for the convicts in the prison there. This is continued. And there, also, every Sunday a free public lecture is given, to which very good audiences come. The old Pacific Coast Committee did not stop work a day and its lecturers went up and down among the people as usual, finding as much interest as ever in Theosophy. In New York an additional series of popular lectures was started at Chickering Hall by Mr. Claude Falls Wright with the aid of the Aryan T.S. These seem to be likely to attract large audiences very shortly. All this time the correspondence with enquirers went on and new members came in as before and in greater numbers.

I have brought forward these facts—and they are not all that might be selected—to show in a measure what the seven months' work has been since the eventful last Convention. It proves once more that "the Theosophical Movement is greater than any Theosophical Society." It ought to show that the Theosophical Society in America is a strong, active, intelligent body, not depending on personalities but upon hard, common-sense work. And behind that hard work there are forces and a spirit which will keep it alive for more than a century if members always look for the spirit and not for the letter. No member has now the right to be gloomy or afraid. If seven months can show such facts, where is there cause for fear? There is none. The future grows from the present, and nothing but a cataclysm can stop our progress.

W. Q. J.

HIDDEN HINTS IN THE
SECRET DOCTRINE

Hidden Hints In The Secret Doctrine

[*The Path*, Vol. V, January, February, March, 1891; Vol. VI,
May, June, September, October, 1891; January, February, 1892.]
(*The Secret Doctrine*, Vol. I, from p. 1 to p. 67)

A PROPHECY. In the 20th century—1900—the scholars of our era
will begin to recognize that *The Secret Doctrine* has neither been invented nor exaggerated, but simply outlined (I, xxxvii). In other
places the author hints at surprises in store in the way of manuscripts, etc. It would seem that by 1900 some "discoveries" will
be made by scholars that will support our author. "Once the door is
permitted to be kept a little ajar, it will be opened wider with every
new century. The times are ripe for a more serious knowledge than
hitherto permitted . . ." (I, xxxviii, footnote). "We have not long to
wait, and many of us will witness the Dawn of the New Cycle, at the
end of which not a few accounts will be settled and squared between
the races." (I, xliv.)

AN ARCHAIC MANUSCRIPT. Some of the doctrines given out are
found by her in a collection of palm-leaves made impervious to the
elements by some unknown process (I, 1). It is well known that some
of the most ancient eastern manuscripts are on palm-leaves which are
cut in oblong, narrow form and tied with a string. How is this seen
by her? Either in the astral light or objectively, being brought to her
table. By whom or what?

CONTINUITY OF PLAN FROM ONE MANVANTARA TO ANOTHER. In this
old MS. it is said that during the pralaya the plan for the next manvantara slumbers until the dawn of the next evolution, when its potential power goes forth to action. There is, therefore, a continuity
from manvantara through pralaya to succeeding manvantara (I, 4
and 5).

THE BASIS OF AFFINITY, hence for all correlations of force. It is
stated that Leucippus taught an occult law when he declared, 500 B.C.,
that the *lateral motion of atoms* is the root for affinity and correla-
tion of force (I, 2).

EACH PERIOD OF EVOLUTION is *sui generis*. ". . . yet at each new
Manvantara, its organization [speaking of the Kosmos] may be re-

garded as the first and the last of its kind, as it evolutes every time on a higher plane." (I, 3).

A NEW ELEMENT AT THE END OF OUR 4TH ROUND. ". . . Occult Science recognizes *Seven* Cosmical Elements—four entirely physical, and the fifth (Ether) semi-material, *as it will become visible in the air* towards the end of our Fourth Round, to reign supreme over the others during the whole of the Fifth." (I, 12.)

ÂKÂŚA AND MANAS CORRESPOND (see I, 13, footnote). ". . . Âkâśa . . . the fifth universal Cosmic Principle (to which corresponds and from which proceeds human Manas) is, cosmically, a radiant, cool, dia-thermanous plastic matter, creative in its physical nature, correlative in its grossest aspects and portions, immutable in its higher principles." It must therefore follow, under the law of correspondences, that *manas* in the sevenfold division is creative, correlative, and immutable in the same way and portions as stated for Âkâsa.

MANAS IN THE 5TH ROUND. By following out the correspondence we find that as Ether, the lower form of Âkâśa now semi-material, will become visible in the air at the end of this Round—the 4th—so *manas*, now only semi-developed in this race, will be further evolved in the 5th Round at the same time with the parent source, and as the form of Ether spoken of will then be the superior element in nature, so at the same time the superior principle reigning in the septenary constitution of man will be *manas*. The full development of *manas* imposes full re-sponsibility on the race, and thus we see how the turning point is reached and what it may mean, and also what is the meaning of the "moment of Choice." With full responsibility the choice must be made by the race which thus has perfect *manas*. It is for and towards that period that the Masters of Wisdom are now working so as to prepare the present Egos for the momentous days when the choice of the good or evil path must be intelligently made.

And as in many places in *The Secret Doctrine* the author says that we are the same egos who were in the Atlantean bodies, and that they had a very weighty karma, we may perceive why it is that we are those who will be compelled to make the great choice for good or evil destiny in the next Round.

DIFFERENCE BETWEEN EFFECT OF GREAT AND MINOR PRALAYA. The question, "What happens to the planets during a minor pralaya or dissolution?" is answered in I, 18, footnote. They are dead, as it were, but not dissolved, for, as she says, they "remain intact, though dead, as a huge animal, caught and embedded in the polar ice, remains the same for ages." After the great Pralaya no planets remain in *corporibus*, but all are dissolved, their âkâśic "photographs" alone remaining. This must be taken metaphorically, or else we will again make objective that which is subjective. But in a minor pralaya the "dead planets" are objective in space, but with all their active life and energy gone.

Dhyâni-Chohans not the only Term for the Highest Beings. ". . . each of the various groups has its own designation in the Secret Doctrine." (I, 22.) Nor are they "personifications" of the powers of nature (I, 38).

Each Round has its special class of Dhyânis to watch over it. The same for races (I, 42). The present Round is watched especially by the Fourth Class of Dhyânis.

The Absolute not understood by the Dhyâni-Chohans (I, 51). And yet some theosophists ask to have definitions or explanations of the Absolute. We heard of one who claimed to have "communed with the Absolute."

The Breath of Brahma. This may be said to be the same as "The Eternal Breath" spoken of in *The Secret Doctrine*. It is motion, and proceeds through space ceaselessly. It does not stop during the pralayas (I, 55).

Ideals and Types in the Astral Light. The prototype is present in an ideal form in the Astral Light from dawn to night during the manvantaric period—everything "from man down to mite, from giant trees down to the tiniest blade of grass." (I, 63) There is a clear correspondence here with the formation of the astral man, which is the copy, plan, or prototype on which the corporeal man is formed.

The Primordial Form of every manifested thing is like that of an egg (I, 65). A *Paramahansa* once wrote for *The Theosophist* an article in which he said that Theosophy was that Branch of Masonry which showed the universe in the form of an egg.

The Verbum, or Word, and its Force. All religions speak of "the Word." The Jews, from whom the Christians get their religion, say that the all-powerful name of God if pronounced will shake the Universe; the Freemasons speak of the lost word; the Hindus tell of the great word; it is the Greek *Logos*. The question is often raised: "Supposing there be such a word, wherein is its force?" H.P.B. says it is in *motion* and not in number (I, 67, footnote). The Hebrew Kabala leans more to *number*, as being the force or power of this word.

Matter during Pralaya. It is in a state of great tenuity seen only by Bodhisattvas. When evolution begins again it appears like curds in space (I, 69).

ELECTRICITY AN ENTITY (I, 76). It is an emanation from an entity of power (I, 111, footnote); and is coexistent with the ONE life (I, 81); it is primordial matter of a special nature (I, 82).

PULSATION OF THE HEART AND THE TIDES. Probably due to the universal expanding and contracting of the atoms, which in turn are caused by the expansion and contraction of matter of space (I, 84). " 'There is heat internal and heat external in every atom'." (*ibid.*)

TWO SORTS OF FIRE OR HEAT. One in the central Sun and the other in the manifested universe and solar system (I, 84 & 87).

MAGICAL POTENCY OF WORDS is in the vowel sounds and not in the numbers (I, 94).

THE TERM "HUMAN" IS NOT TO BE CONFINED TO THIS GLOBE. It must be applied to all entities who have reached the fourth stage of development on any planet in space in its fourth round in any chain of planets (I, 106, 2nd para.).

BUDDHI AS COMPARED WITH SPIRIT is material, although for us and the highest conceptions we can form it is wholly beyond materiality (I, 119).

THE HUMAN MONAD is the union of the ray from the Absolute with the soul (I, 119, para 1).

SYMBOLISM AND NUMBERS. They are intimately connected with the hosts of the Dhyâni-Chohans. The basic numbers refer each to distinct groups of ideas which vary according to the group of Dhyâni-Chohans referred to. In other places the author says that, as the Dhyânis are connected with evolution in all its intricacies and mysteries, it follows that symbolism is of the highest importance (I, 119).

THE ONE FUNDAMENTAL LAW OF OCCULT SCIENCE is "The radical unity of the ultimate essence of each constituent part of compounds in Nature— from Star to mineral Atom, from the highest Dhyâni-Chohan to the smallest infusoria," (I, 120). And this is to be applied spiritually, intellectually, and physically.

KARMA NEEDS MATERIAL AGENCIES to carry out its decrees (I, 123). The material agents spoken of here are not merely those that we class as such, but many others which are generally conceived of by us as spiritual. For as said above, even Buddhi is material when compared with Âtman of which it is the vehicle. The clue here given is in regard to the operations of Karma through the atoms that are used by the egos in their various incarnations. But in following this out it must not be forgotten that there is no particle or point of materiality which is not at the same time mixed with or in company with another particle—if the word may be used for this purpose—of spirit or the one life.

THE THREE GROUPS OF BUILDERS. These are as follows: The first is the group which constructs the entire system as a whole and which includes more than this globe system; the second is the group of builders who come in when the system as a great whole is ready and form the planetary chain of this earth; and the third is that group which builds or projects Humanity, as they are the great type of the microcosm—man (I, 127-28).

THE LIPIKAS AS COMPARED WITH THE BUILDERS are the great Spirits of the universe as a whole, the builders being of a special nature. The Lipikas, like the others, are divided into three groups, but it is asserted that only the lowest of these three groups has to do with this system of ours and that the other two cannot be known, and also that those two are so high that it is doubtful if even the highest of the Adepts know about them. It may therefore be supposed that for the Adepts the Lipikas of the higher degrees are as great a mystery as the Mahâtmas are for us, and that this ascending scale of greatness ever gives to the soul something still higher, no matter how far it may progress, to which to look and aspire (I, see whole of page 128).

But as each of the three groups is divided into seven others (I, 127), it may be the 21st sub-group which has to do with this globe; and it is said that as to the highest of the groups it is directly connected with our Karma (I, 128 *last line*). Now as Karma rules the entire universe, it must follow, in order to make and keep harmony, that the "highest grade of Lipikas" referred to on page 128 is not the highest of the last series of 21 sub-groups, but the highest of the whole three great groups.

NOTE WELL: Whenever an "entity" is spoken of among the various "hosts" it is to be known as composed of many entities, just as man himself is similarly constituted, his total consciousness being that of the whole mass of beings who go to make up his intricate life.

NIRMÂNAKÂYAS. First reference to these is on page 132 (footnote), where they are called "the surviving spiritual principles of men," and in the text they are those who *reincarnate for the good of the world* if they choose.

ELECTRICITY AGAIN is mentioned as *Life* (I, 137 and 139); also a form of "Fohat" (I, 145).

Ether only partially manifested, and not to be fully so until the 5th round (I, 140).

That Entities are constituted of many units, each an entity. Thus that "Fohat," elsewhere called "an Entity," is not one undivided entity but is made up of others; and that there are as many Fohats as there are worlds (I, 143, footnote, and 145).

Elixir of Life. A hint thereupon (I, 144, footnote).

Elementals Concerned in all forces, *e.g.* that electricity, magnetism, cohesion, and the like are made up of elementals. These of course, are not all of one class, but of several (I, 146). Near the end of this page it is inferentially stated that elementals are generated in millions by other beings. This must be, in fact, a transforming process in the atoms. By referring to p. 143, a broad hint will be found as to this in the remarks upon the "fate of an atom" once caught into any world sphere, and the means of getting out through "a current of efflux." Is this *efflux* through the transforming being?

The Moon. In what sense dead? Only as to her inner principles. Her physical principles are not dead, but have a certain activity (I, 149, footnote). And her spiritual principles have been transferred to this earth (I, 155, footnote, and I, 156.)

Disappearance of the Moon will have occurred before this earth has passed through her 7th human round (I, 155, footnote).

Archetypal Man on Globe A (I, 159, last para.). Here is a most interesting hint not often referred to and opening up a vista of thought. In the first round of the monads in this chain of planets, the monads from the preceding chain of worlds—say the moon's chain—*become human beings* on Globe A. But in the 2nd round the process alters, and it is in the 4th round that man appears on this earth, the 4th Globe. To quote: "It is only during the 1st round that (heavenly) man becomes a human being on Globe A; (rebecomes) a mineral, a plant, an animal, on Globe B and C, etc. The process changes entirely from the second round; but . . ." (I, 159-60). This abruptness is to give the hint to intuitional investigators, and opens up as great a problem as the 8th sphere seemed once to be and still perhaps is. But we may ask if on Globe A—unseen by us the archetypal process does not obtain?

Mars and Mercury bear an occult relation to the earth which will not be explained (I, 163). This is not because no explanation exists, but because, as said (I, 164, footnote), these explanations belong to high grades of initiation.

Figures and Numbers are the key to the whole system (I, 164). This has often been stated. Among the Jewish Kabalists it is said that the Universe is built by number, weight, and measure, and that harmony is the law reigning over all. Now if the hint given be true, that figures and numbers *will not* be given for the above reasons, then it is useless for students to bother their minds about the occult meaning of numbers, as so many now do; for this occult meaning cannot be found without assistance.

Venus in her 7th Round. See italicised para. on p. 165, where it is said that that planet is in her last round. This must be her 7th. Hence the men there are as gods to us, and, if the argument from analogy is to be relied on, some of her great light must emanate from those beings and not all be from the sun.

Mars with two moons not his own (See p. 165, ital. para.). This is taken from the letter by a Master who, replying to the query as to why Mercury and Venus have no satellites, says: "It is because Mars has two to which he has no right and—for other reasons." That is, we infer that Mars absorbed these moons or dragged them off into his orbit at some time enormously distant and still keeps them. They cannot therefore stand to him in the same relation as our moon does to us. One of the "other reasons" may be that, Venus being in her 7th round, all vestiges of old moons have been sublimated and absorbed into her atmosphere.

Esoteric Metaphysics must be understood (I, 169). This rule is laid down by the Adepts and is therefore of greater weight than if formulated by a student. It is useless to attempt to master the system on the lines of modern research, which at best are empirical, very faulty, and leading almost always to a materialization of the whole scheme. Metaphysics deal with the real because the ideal, and physical science with the phenomenal and therefore illusory and changeable.

Evolution of the Monad a basic principle (I, 171). This is laid down with extreme clearness and should not be forgotten. It is not expanded so that inattentive minds may get it through much repetition, but it is postulated once for all. It is still altogether too customary for students to separate the Monads, first from the globes and then from the beings thereon. They cannot be thus divided off. All the globes and their objects are and ever will be monads in stages of evolution, just as we who now study the question are monads ourselves in other stages. The false notion should at once be discarded that there was a time when there were no monads on the globe but that there was here in waiting this ball of earth coming from no one knows where, and that later on monads arrived to occupy it.

If we carry out the principle laid down, then the globe is the creation of the monad; and when the globe is evolved, at once monads needing that experience enter into its corporeality to continue its existence. These later monads are those far behind in the race who will, in some succeeding period of evolution, be in a position to evolve on their own account some new globe in ages yet far distant, for the carrying on of the same process eternally. For, as a material object cannot spring out of nothing, neither can education or knowledge or ability to plan arise out of nothing, but must be based upon and flow from some prior experience or education. So it must be that even now there are monads encased in the mineral, vegetable, and animal kingdoms which have never been farther than that, and will during the remainder of the race evolution continue their education in those lower kingdoms until their time shall come when, the door opening for their exit, they will pass out and higher to make room for others.

LIMIT TO NUMBER OF MONADS.   Although there can be no such thing as a metaphysical limit to the monads, yet practically, for the purposes of any one manvantara, there must be a limited number of monads included within its evolutionary sweep. Since a manvantara, however vast and inconceivable by us, is wholly a finite period, it sets its own limit—within the illimitable Absolute—for the monads attracted to it. This of necessity must be, since the natural world which makes experience possible, being finite because material, sets the limit by reason of its capacity being bounded (I, 171).

THE FATE OF THE ANTHROPOID APES.   This interesting question is raised first on pp. 173 and 175, and not disposed of. There, in describing the course of the evolution of the monad, it is said that the laggards will not be men at all in this cycle *save one exception*. On p. 184, it seems to be answered: "In this Round . . . the anthropoids destined to die out in this our race, when their monads will be liberated and pass into the astral human forms (or the highest [human] elementals) of the Sixth and the Seventh Races, and then into lowest human forms in the Fifth Round." . . . These descendants of men through union with animals will thus be karmically rewarded in the next round after this, instead of having to wait until another manvantara.

THE IMPULSE OF EVOLUTION is found in the force of the spiritual breath. It is not to be supposed because "human monads" cease to come into this chain of globes that therefore there is no impulse. The term "human monad" means that *monad which having been through all lower experiences is fitted to inform the so-far perfected human body.*

Man first in the 4th Round (I, 187). The flow of human monads is at an end, except that those still incarcerated in the anthropoids have yet to come in. Full blown [monads]—or rather those that have been through all lower experiences—must proceed in their order through the strictly human evolution. The necessities of evolution demand this, and the turning point is reached in the fourth round which represents the square figure or number, and all monads in the lower kingdoms have to go on with the work of evolution in those until the next manvantara. At that time the monads now in human forms will have progressed beyond, thus leaving room for those below to come up higher.

Our Natures from what (I, 189). In the note it is distinctly pointed out that the quotation from Shakespeare about our *natures* being marvelously mixed, refers to the part which the Hierarchies of progressed souls throughout the system to which this globe belongs play in giving us our different combinations.

Correspondence of Human Evolution with the nebular evolution and condensation is to be found on these last lines of p. 191: "As the solid Earth began by being a ball of liquid fire, of fiery dust and its protoplasmic phantom, so did man."

Origin of White and Black Magic. See note on p. 192, where it is stated that at the highest point of development of the Atlantean Race— the fourth—the separation into right and left-hand magic, or consciously good and evil thoughts, took place. Under the action of Karmic law and by the reincarnation over and over again of those engaged in these thoughts, the thoughts were preserved in the realm of mind in the double form of mental deposits and astral impressions. The mental deposits were brought back again and again to earth life, and the astral impressions affected all others who came under their influence. In this way not only were seeds sown in individual minds through their own thoughts, but a vast reservoir of good and bad impressions or pictures has been created in the ethereal medium about us by which sensitive persons are impelled to good and bad acts. And all repetitions of evil thoughts have added to the stock of evil thus remaining to affect and afflict mankind. But as the good also remains, the earnest friends of mankind are able to produce good effects and impressions which in their turn are added up to the sum of good. There need be no feeling of injustice on the ground that sensitive persons are affected by evil pictures in the astral light, because such possibility of being thus impressed could not have arisen except through sympathetic attractions for them set up in former lives.

The Astral Light is not in its nature truth revealing or "good"

(I, 197, footnote). It "stands in the same relation to Âkâśa and *Anima Mundi,* as Satan stands to the Deity. They are one and the same thing *seen from two aspects.*" It may be said that the astral light is the next step above material concerns. It is the first field into which the seer steps in his progress, but it is dangerous because misleading, and misleading because it reverses all things, as well as being the chief reservoir for the bad or material deeds and thoughts of men. Because it is strange, new, and extraordinary, it influences those who see in it, since it presents images of a weird character, and just from its newness and vividness those who see in it are not to consider it to be of consequence. It is to be studied but not depended upon. Somewhat as the brain has to accustom itself to the reversed image on the retina—turning it straight by effort—so the inner senses have to become accustomed to the reversals made by the Astral Light.

The Fall into Generation is explained from page 192 to page 198 (Vol. I, Stanza VI). Necessarily this raises the question: "Why any fall whatever?" The author says: "It was the Fall of Spirit into generation, not the Fall of mortal man" (I, 192). Hence, if this be true, man has not fallen, but is, for this period of evolution, on the way upward. Spirit in order to become self-conscious "must pass through every cycle of being, culminating in its highest point on earth in Man. Spirit *per se* is an unconscious negative ABSTRACTION. Its purity is inherent, not acquired by merit; hence . . . to become the highest Dhyâni-Chohan it is necessary for each Ego to attain to full self-consciousness as a human, *i.e.,* conscious Being, which is synthesized for us in Man" (I, 192-93). So the question, why any fall if it was pure originally, is based on the assumption that to remain in a state of unconscious abstraction is better. This cannot however be so. When a period of evolution begins, with spirit at one end of the pole and matter at the other, it is absolutely necessary for spirit to proceed through experience in matter in order that self-consciousness may be acquired. It is a "fall" into matter so far as the fact is concerned, but so far as the result and the object in view it is neither fall nor rise, but the carrying out of the immutable law of the nature of spirit and matter. We ignorantly call it a fall or a curse, because our lower consciousness does not see the great sweep of the cycles nor apprehend the mighty purpose entertained. Following the lines of the philosophy elsewhere laid down, we see that at the close of each grand period of evolution some Egos will have failed to attain the goal, and thus some spirit—if we may say—is left over to be again at a new period differentiated into Egos who shall, helped by Egos of the past now become Dhyâni-Chohans, once more struggle upward. Such is the immense and unending struggle.

States and Planes of Consciousness in Kosmos and Man (I, 199). It is here stated that of the seven planes of consciousness three are above the entire chain of globes to which the earth belongs, and that the earth is in the lowest of the lower four. But in man, as said here, there are seven *states* of consciousness which correspond to these seven cosmical *planes*. He is to "attune the three higher states in himself to the three higher planes in Kosmos." Necessarily he must have in him centers or seats of energy correspondingly, and, as the author points out, he must awaken those seats to activity, to life, before he can attune them to the higher planes. They are dormant, asleep as it were.

First and Seventh Globes of the chain are in the Archetypal plane (I, 200, note to diagram). That is, that in the first globe of the chain—A—the whole model of the succeeding globes is made or laid down, and upon that evolution proceeds up to the 7th, where, all having reached the highest stage of perfection after seven rounds, the complete model is fully realized. This is distinctly hinted at in the note, for she says: "not the world as it existed *in the Mind* of the Deity; but in that of a world made as a first model, to be followed and improved upon by the worlds which succeed it physically——though deteriorating in purity." The reader will remember that in another place it is plainly said that on Globe A man appears, but that in the second round the process changes. If we assume, as we must, conscious Beings at work in the scheme of evolution, they have to create the mental model, as it were, of the whole planetary chain, and this has to be done at the time of the first globe. The plan is impressed on all the atoms or particles which are to take part in the evolution, and is preserved intact in that plane. The seventh globe is the receiver of the entire result of evolution in each round, and transfers it once more to Globe A, where it proceeds as before, and again the whole mass of evoluting beings is impressed with the original plan. This is repeated for every round.

The Three Higher Planes of Consciousness spoken of in the *second note to diagram on page* 200 as being inaccessible to human consciousness as yet, does not involve a contradiction. For the attuning of our three higher *states* of consciousness to the three higher *planes* is possible, although attainment of those planes is impossible for ordinary human consciousness. The attempt has to be made so as to come into harmony in ourselves with those planes, so that the potentialities may be made active and development of new faculties made possible.

Function of Comets. Comets are the wanderers which, in the great struggle and rush of matter in any place where a system of worlds is to come into existence, act as aggregators or collectors of the cosmic matter until at last sufficient collections are made to cause the beginning of globes (I, 201).

Cycles. There is always much discussion respecting this vast and interesting subject, not only in theosophical circles but outside as well. Indeed, the discussion was begun ages before our T.S. was formed. It will hardly be finished in our life. The dispute or difficulty has not been as to whether there are cycles governing men and affairs, for the most materialistic are wont to talk of the cycles of recurrence of diseases, wars, and the like, but about when any cycle begins, and especially the larger ones. One of the Moon's cycles is known, and that of the great sidereal vault is approximated, but when we come to such as the latter there is considerable vagueness as to what was the state of things 25,000 years ago. On page 202 of Vol. I, the hint is given that the fundamental basis controlling number and ground-work of the cycles is laid in the very beginning of the cosmic struggle anterior to the aggregation of matter into globes and suns. For this is the basic and fundamental stone of the secret cycles. "The assertion that all the worlds (stars and planets, etc.)— as soon as a nucleus of primordial substance in the *laya* (undifferentiated) state is informed by the freed principles of a just *deceased* sidereal body—become first comets, and then Suns to cool down to inhabitable worlds, is a teaching as old as the Ṛishis."

Now in each system to "struggle" is different from every other, a different proportion arises, and, the percentage of loss or remainder being variable, the cyclic bases in each system differ from others. It is very plain, then, that our present-day scientists can know nothing of these original differences and must remain ignorant of the true cycles. Only the eagle eye of the high Adept can see these numbers as they are written upon the great screen of time, and in the whispers that reach us from the ancient mysteries can be found the information we are seeking. Who shall hear aright?

The Very Beginning. Definitely as to the very beginning of manifestation—not of this little system of ours, but of the one vast whole— it is not possible nor permissible to speak. But a hint of seductive nature is thrown out on p. 203, 3d para., where, taking us back to the first act in the great drama of which our puny play is but a short sentence, H. P. B. says that the secret science declares that when the one great All has been thrown out into manifestation, seven special differentiations of It appear, and from those seven all the countless fires, suns, planets, and stars are lighted and go forth. So that, although in various systems of worlds the cycles and the numbers and bases may differ and be any whole number or fractional number, the great and perfect number is still *seven*. But no man now among us can understand that great *seven* when it includes all numbers the mind may reach by chance or by calculation.

From p. 212 to 221 the reader can for himself find all that the author of *The Secret Doctrine* desired to give out in those pages.

WHAT ARE ELEMENTALS? In describing the groups of the Hierarchies, the 6th and 7th groups are touched on at page 221, where it is said that elementals are a part of the numberless side groups "shot out like the boughs of a tree from the first central group of the four." And they are all subject to Karma (I, 221), which they have to work out during every cycle. As it is said, lower on the page, "A Dhyâni-Chohan has to become" such, it must follow that even a Dhyâni-Chohan was once at work in the planes of being where elementals are, and from that rose up to the higher place; this must be under the laws of evolution, of Karma, of Reincarnation.

MAN'S GREAT DESTINY. Following the argument hinted at about elementals, on p. 221, it is said that the celestial Hierarchy of this Manvantara will be transferred in the next cycle of life to higher, superior worlds, in order to make room for a new hierarchy, of the same order, which will be composed of the elect ones of our own human race. Such is our destiny, and such the path up which we climb; and when that point is reached, we must work still on for the benefit of those below us. This is the basis of altruism, and without altruism the consummation cannot be reached.

THAT HIGH SPIRITS WORK ON EARTH in bodies of men, while those spirits are still in the highest spheres (see I, 233-34, 235 and footnotes). On p. 233 it is clearly explained that the author does not mean that which is called among the spiritualists "control" of mediums by a spirit, but the actual continuance of the status and functions of the incarnated spirit in the supersensuous regions, while actually using as its own and working in a mortal envelope on earth. So that, according to her, there are certain persons on this earth, living and working as ordinary human beings and members of society, whose informing divine part is so immeasurably high in development that they as such high beings have a definite status and function in the "supersensuous regions." We should say—assuming the correctness of the author's statement—that she herself was such a case, and that "H. P. B.," whether hourly in the day or at night when all around was still, had a "status and function" in other spheres where she consciously carried on the work of that high station, whatever it was. There were many events in her daily life known to those who were intimate with her that this hint may unravel, or at least shed much light upon. And in one of her letters this sentence appears—

in substance—"The difference between you and me is that you are not conscious except at day, while I am conscious day and night, and have much to do and to endure in both of these existences from which you, being thus half-conscious, are happily saved."

In the Hindu books and teachings there is a reference to this when they speak of high jñânis—that is, persons full of knowledge and spiritual power—being attracted to this earth by certain acts and at certain times in the history of nation, race, or city.

Loss of the Soul. The possibility of the abandonment of the body by the soul is outlined on p. 234 of Vol. I thus: "The soul could free itself from and quit the tabernacle [of the body] for various reasons—such as insanity, spiritual and physical depravity, etc." And at the end of the note on p. 235 it is hinted broadly that such freeing of the soul from the body, leaving the latter to run out its course, is not confined to the case of those who are insane or depraved, but may occur with those who make great advance in knowledge and such consequent alteration in the constitution of the soul, is it were, that they no longer can dwell on earth, using the old body. It does not appear, however, that this subject is carried any further than this hint, found, as is so usual with H. P. B., in a note. In this the words are: "For the occurrence is found to take place in wicked materialists *as well as in persons 'who advance in holiness and never turn back'.*" [Italics added.] From my knowledge of her methods I regard this note as a deliberate reverse of sentence, in which the object of it is found in the words which are used in the underlined part.

The Necessity for Individual Effort. This is very emphatically put, and in precisely the style of H. P. B., in the third paragraph on page 244, in the parallelisms, where *Âtman* is spoken of. Here she shows that *Âtman* is not subject to change or improvement, but is the "ray of light eternal which shines upon and through the darkness of matter—*when the latter is willing.*" [Italics are mine.] If matter, in the human being, the personal self, the body, and the astral body, with passions and desires, is not willing to be fully informed by the Spirit, then *Âtman* will not shine through it because it cannot, inasmuch as matter then does not submit itself to the Divine behests. The willingness can only be shown by individual effort toward goodness and purification. It would seem that this ought to do away with that negation and supineness indulged in by even theosophists who talk of "not interfering with Karma."

Only Three Dimensions of Matter. The "fourth dimension" is combatted on pages 251-252 et seq.: "So long as there are foot-rules within the resources of Kosmos, to apply to matter, so long will they be able to measure it in three ways and no more." (p. 252).

Order of the Elements Esoterically is *Fire, air, water, earth.* (I, 252). Counting up from the earth, the order for the elementals, or the nature-spirits in the elements, is: earth elementals, water elementals, air elementals, fire elementals. And it has always been said that those of the fire are the wisest and most distant so far as cognition of or by us is concerned, that the airy ones are also wise, and those of the water dangerous. Those of the earth have been described by seers in the form of gnomes sometimes seen by clairvoyant miners in the depths under us, and of this class also are those that have given rise to the superstition among the Irish respecting the fairies.

Fire in the Preceding Rounds. She says (I, 253): "For all we know, fire may have been *pure âkâsa,* the first Matter of the *Magnum Opus* of the Creators and 'Builders,' . . ." The phrase "For all we know" is sometimes to be translated "Thus it was."

The Fifth Element in the Fifth Round. This, as said before in these Notes, will be "*Ether*—the gross body of Âkâsa," and, "by becoming a familiar fact of Nature to all men, as air is familiar to us now, [will] cease to be as at present hypothetical" (I, 257-58).

What is the Sixth Sense to be? In the first paragraph of page 258 she says that at first there will be a partial familiarity with a characteristic of matter to be known then as permeability, which will be perceived when certain new senses have been developed, and after that this singular characteristic will be fully known, as it will be developed concurrently with the sixth sense. We may therefore argue that she means to describe the sixth sense as one which will (among other things) give to us the power to permeate matter with ourselves. Let some one else now carry this idea further, as it is no doubt correct. It would seem that both the matter-characteristic and the power in man are being here and there exhibited, or else some of the phenomena seen at spiritualistic séances could never have happened; but alas, we need not look for aid there so long as the beloved "spirits from the summer-land" continue to hold sway over their votaries.

The Earth in its Early Periods. Some students have thought that [on] this globe in its early times, when, following the statements in *Esoteric Buddhism,* the human life-wave and so on had not come, there was no life on it, supposing in a vague way that there was, say in the fire-mist time, a mass of something devoid of life.* This is contradicted and explained on page 258 in the second paragraph: "Thus Occultism disposes of the [so-called] Azoic age of Science, for it shows that there never was a time when the Earth was without life upon it." This is asserted for no matter what form or sort of matter thus: "Wherever there is an atom of matter, a particle or a molecule even in its most gaseous state, there is life in it, however latent or unconscious."

Of Spirit and Matter. In the commentary on page 258, the author plainly writes: "*Spirit is the first differentiation of (and in) SPACE; and Matter is the first differentiation of Spirit.*" This is a clear statement of what she desired to teach respecting spirit and matter, and as in other places it is said that spirit and matter are the opposite poles of the One—the Absolute—an agreement has to be made between the two. There is no real disagreement, since it is evident that differentiation must proceed in a definite order, from which it results that there must be always one state, plane, place, power, and idea in nature that is above and different from and beyond all others. And when we go beyond spirit, the highest we may speak of is the Absolute, which is the container of the next two—spirit and matter, the latter following the first in order of differentiation. These are said to be coeternal, and, indeed, are so, as far as our minds are concerned, for the reason that we cannot grasp either the first or the second differentiation of the Absolute. But because this doctrine of the coeternalness of spirit and matter has been taught, there never being the one without the other also present, some students have fallen into a materialistic view, probably because matter is that which being near to us is most apparent, and others, remaining somewhat vague, do not define the doctrine at all. Spirit and matter are coeternal because they exist together in the Absolute, and when the first differentiation spoken of above takes place, so does the second immediately. Hence, except when we are dealing with metaphysics, they must be regarded as the two poles of the one Absolute. And the *Bhagavad-Gîtâ* does not support the contrary, for it only says there is no spirit without also matter, as it is dealing through the words of Krishna with things as they are *after* the differentiation has taken place.

There is another class of theosophists who speaks of the "super-personal god," asserting at the same time that they do not mean "a personal God," and they are opposed by still another class who point to the well-known denial by H. P. B. of the existence of a personal god. It is

---

[*To paraphrase: Some students have thought that this globe had no life on it in its early times, when, following the statements in *Esoteric Buddhism,* the human life-wave and so on had not yet come; supposing in a vague way that there was (say in the fire-mist time) a mass of something devoid of life.—*Comp.*]

in the sentence quoted that both of these may come to an agreement, for the believers in the super-personal deity can without doubt find support in the lines on p. 258. For if spirit is the first, then matter is a grade below it, however fine and imperceptible that distinction may be.

If further we say, as many of us do, that the great inherent ideas of man were given to him by the first great teachers whose descendants and pupils the Adepts are, then we here also see how it is that there is such a wide and universal belief in a God. It must also be the origin of that universal optimism which may be found also in the ranks of the theosophists, who while for present days are pessimistic, must be called the greatest optimists on the face of the earth. There are many other matters in this sentence. Many a student has puzzled his head very often in trying to discover from where come the impulse and the plan as well as the idea of perfection, for it must as a first thing reside somewhere, whether abstractly or concretely. Perhaps it is here; those students can look here at any rate.

A Mysterious Principle Mentioned. After going for a little space into the formation of this globe by the first builders, she speaks (page 259) of a certain *Âkâsic* principle to which no name is given but left in hiatus. But in the note on that page we see, and I am violating nothing in referring to it, that very clearly it is pointed out that the primordial substance of which she then writes *"is the body of those Spirits themselves, and their very essence."* Now in many places in her writings, and also in those of other knowing ones through all time, this primordial substance is said to be one that, once controlled, gives him who has power over it the most transcendent abilities—sway alike over mind and matter.

She and all of us are quite safe in speaking of it, since there are but few indeed who will see anything in it at all. Yet the few can have the hint if they never got it before. This, however, should always remain as a hint, and there ought to be no attempt to make it clear to science, for nothing will be gained except ridicule and maybe worse.

"The Vahan"

"THE VAHAN"

[Issued under the auspices of the European Section of the T. S., *The Vahan* (Skt. for vehicle) was distributed free of charge by the General Secretary and editor of the magazine, G. R. S. Mead.[1] In its first number of August 1, 1891, second series, Mr. Mead stated:

> "We propose to make *The Vahan* as useful and as practical as possible. We therefore especially request our contributors to avoid the use of technical terms *as far as possible* . . . and to reserve all distinctly metaphysical questions and disquisitions for the pages of *Lucifer* . . . Moreover our "Vehicle" is meant for the benefit of the public generally and not simply for the members of the Society."

[We see here a distinct task delegated to this periodical, and can well understand why Mr. Judge's valuable every-day-life approach was welcomed in its columns.—*Compiler.*]

The Enquirer

[*The Vahan*, No. 1, August 1891]

Q. *Is it well to talk about Occultism to the ordinary enquirer into Theosophy?*

W.Q.J.—It is better not to do so. Ordinary enquirers may be attracted to Theosophy because of its mysterious appearance, but that is no reason for giving them just what they demand. For surely later on they will find that the pursuit of the mysteries and the occult is hedged about with many difficulties and that it demands an acquaintance with every other philosophy that ought to have been offered to them when they first enquired. Furthermore it is not the many who are fitted for Occultism, but rather the few, and those few will soon find their way into the path no matter how they may have approached it. Enquirers will then be directed to this philosophy and the ethics of the Theosophical system, as true Occultism springs from philosophy, and its practice is alone safely possible for those who have a right system of ethics.

[*The Vahan*, Second Series, August, 1891, #1 pp. 1-6]

QUESTION I

W. P.—*I am very much interested in Theosophy and should like to help the Society. What work can I do?*

---

1 [See biographical sketch of Mead in final section: "Faces of Friends."—*Comp.*]

W. Q. J.—This is a Theosophical business question. Service is rendered in many different ways: by work in the Branches, by spreading literature, by explaining the doctrines and doing away with misconceptions, by contributing money to be used in the work, by constituting oneself a loyal unit if ability and time be lacking; and chiefly, always by acquiring a knowledge of Theosophical doctrines so as to be able to give a clear answer to inquiry. One could also procure some inquiring correspondent and by means of letters answer questions as to Theosophical literature and doctrines. These are all general answers, while the question requires almost a personal examination. Any work that is sincerely done in the Society with good motive and to the best of one's ability is good Theosophical work.

Question III

If another by altruistic service benefits one, is not such action vicarious and inconsistent with Karma?

W. Q. J.—A common error, which arises from incompletely viewing the doctrine of Karma, is the idea that we interfere with Karma when we benefit another. The question is equally applicable to the doing of any injury to another. It cuts both ways; so we might as well ask if it is not inconsistent with the law and vicarious for one to do any evil act which results harmfully to a fellow creature. In neither case is there vicarious atonement or interference. If we can do good to our fellows, that is their good Karma and ours also; if we have the opportunity to thus confer benefits and refuse to do so, then that is our bad Karma in that we neglected a chance to help another. The Masters once wrote that we should not be thinking on our good or bad Karma, but should do our duty on every hand and at every opportunity, unmindful of what may result to us. It is only a curious kind of conceit, which seems to be the product of nineteenth century civilization, that causes us to falsely imagine that we, weak and ignorant human beings, can interfere with Karma or be vicarious atoners for others. We are all bound up together in one coil of Karma and should ever strive by good acts, good thoughts and high aspirations, to lift a little of the world's heavy Karma, of which our own is a part. Indeed, no man has any Karma of his own unshared by others; we share each one in the common Karma, and the sooner we perceive this and act accordingly the better it will be for us and for the world.

Question IV

What place have mercy and forgiveness in Theosophy, and are they consistent with Karma?

W. Q. J.—Mercy and forgiveness should have the highest place in that branch of Theosophy which treats of ethics as applied to our conduct. And were it not for the perfect mercifulness of Karma—which is merciful because it is just—we ought long ago to have been wiped out of existence. The very fact that the oppressor, the unjust, the wicked, live out their lives is proof of mercy in the great heart of Nature. They are thus given chance after chance to retrieve their errors and climb, if even on the ladder of pain, to the height of perfection. It is true that Karma is just, because it exacts payment to the last farthing, but on the other hand it is eternally merciful, since it unerringly pays out its compensations. Nor is the shielding from necessary pain true mercy, but is indeed the opposite, for sometimes it is only through pain that the soul acquires the precise knowledge and strength it requires. In my view, mercy and justice go hand in hand when Karma issues its decrees, because that law is accurate, faithful, powerful, and not subject to the weakness, the failure in judgment, the ignorance that always accompany the workings of the ordinary human judgment and action.

QUESTION V

G. E. L.—*I am a married man, without children, and my wife, who takes no interest in Theosophy, complains that I am neglecting her to attend Theosophical meetings or lectures in the evenings. Should I give up the lectures?*

W. Q. J.—Justice to ourselves and those dependent on us would seem to answer that no wife has the right to demand the whole of a man's time. If she cannot attend a lecture or meeting once a week, she ought to be willing that her husband may. But if she considers herself the "legal owner" of the man she married to the extent that she wishes to eat up his entire attention, then of course dissatisfaction will supervene, unjustly founded and wholly inexcusable. If her complaint of neglect is based upon one night in a week devoted to a Theosophical meeting which she has no taste for, the man who submits is his own taskmaster, who ought not to ask other Theosophists to lay down his duty in daily life. Questions between man and wife ought to be settled in the family forum, and not dragged into the field of Theosophical discussion, where they are utterly out of place.

[*The Vahan*, Vol. I, January, 1892, #6, p. 1]

QUESTION XXXIIa

-R.M.—*In both Europe and America I have met a good many Theosophists who enquire into and appear to dabble in practical applications of the directions found in some of our literature, in the "Upanishads," and in a little book of one Sabapathi Swamy, respecting psychic development, by means of postures, regulating the breath and the like. What can be said upon this?*

W. Q. J.—These attempts at practical Yoga—as it is called—are most dangerous, and in addition presumptuous and foolish. It is well understood in the right circles in India, that the directions found in many of the *Upanishads* should never be practiced except under the following conditions: (*a*) a complete knowledge of all, and of the consequences, with a knowledge of correctives to be applied when changes take place; and (*b*) the possession of a thoroughly competent guide to point out errors, to restrain endeavor and to indicate danger, as well as to cure troubles that ensue. Yet in the face of all this, and of repeated warnings, there are those who will foolhardily begin the practices in complete ignorance. They do not even pursue the ethical regulations that accompany all the others, such as the doing away with all vices, bad habits, uncharitable thoughts and so on; but go in for the practices, merely in the hope of procuring psychic powers. It is time it were stopped, and time that those who give out this literature looked into what they give out to a grasping and stiff-necked generation. That damage has been wrought both to the Society and some of its members cannot be contested, in face of actual experience in all parts of both countries. It is well known that these postures, even when ignorantly used, bring on physiological changes in the body, with great nervous derangements. Further than that the enquiring public is frightened off from our movement by the ill-balanced view of Theosophy and of the Society which these dabblers promulgate. Let us halt before it is too late. Let us give out the ethical and philosophical doctrines for the promulgation of which the Theosophical Society was founded. Thus alone can we accomplish our mission, which is to the world at large and not for the benefit of a few cranky investigators in a field that can only be safely trodden by the thoroughly prepared, the fully armed and the deeply experienced man who has a sound mind and high pure aspirations, joined to a sound body.

Question LIII

P. C. W.—If animals do not reincarnate, how do they receive a just reparation for the life of suffering which some have to endure?

W. Q. J.—The answer is easy. They do reincarnate, but that which from them goes forth to reincarnation is not similar to the reincarnating principle of the human being. Were we to suppose that the monads now going through the present animal life were reincarnating in a haphazard way, then surely law disappears, our philosophy tumbles to the ground, and a reign of terror in the scheme of evolution ensues.

Question LIV

F.J.D.—What is the difference between forms seen in dreams or vision on an astral plane and those seen on a Kâma-Mânasic plane? And which of the two are considered as having the greater objective reality? If Kâma-Mânasic forms accompany Devachanic consciousness, how is this connected with the Higher Ego?

W.Q.J.—Forms seen in dreams and visions are almost always pictures; those on the Kâma-Mânasic are more often actual forms of that sort of matter. The difference—when existing—is that which there is between a photograph of a form and the form itself. The "forms" of Devachanic consciousness are not objective to us, but are to the being in the Devachanic state of consciousness. As the entity is not free—hence in Devachan—the mind creates for itself all its surroundings in every detail, and also thereby cultivates departments of the nature which could not be cultivated to the same extent elsewhere. The connection with the Higher Ego, as to which F. J. D.'s ideas are vague, is the same connection as in earth-life, only operating by a different channel.

QUESTION LV

A.J.W.—From the occult standpoint is it good to keep vitality in an old person by the use of brandy and other stimulants?

W.Q.J.—Great heavens! Whence such queries? Is the "occult standpoint" next to be inquired into on the question of what sort of paint is best to be used on the front door? But, if the physician thinks the stimulants are wise and their use does not lead to drunkenness of the old person, then they may be used, one would suppose, uncondemned by occultism or the divulged sciences.

QUESTION LVII

F. G. B.—How am I to reconcile these two statements?—(a) The Seven planes of Cosmic Consciousness correspond to the Seven States of consciousness in man. (S.D. I, p 199.) (b) The Seven States of consciousness in man pertain to quite another question (than the planes of Cosmic Consciousness). (S.D. I, p. 200.)

W. Q. J.—Quotation (b) does not conflict with (a), as attempted to be shown in the question. On p. 199 the seven planes are said to correspond to the seven states of consciousness in man; the third note on p. 200 says that the reference in the diagram to the fourth plane and above includes—or refers to—the four lower planes of *cosmic* consciousness—which is a totally different thing from *human* consciousness—and that the three higher planes of *cosmic* consciousness are inaccessible to present human intellect; and that the seven states of *human* consciousness pertain to another question. Quite so, and quite plain. The querent left out the word "human" in quotation (b), thus making "a totally different question" of the matter, for there is a great difference between saying "human consciousness" and "consciousness in man." The entire seven planes of cosmic consciousness must correspond with, and may yet not be the same as the seven states of our present human consciousness, for there is a radical dissimilarity between a *plane* and a *state*, for you may be in a certain state of consciousness and yet function on a plane quite different; as when the drunken man has all his consciousness in a *Kâmic* state and functions with it on the earthly plane. Further, the seven states of human consciousness may perfectly well be our possession and not be developed for the race beyond the first four states of cosmic consciousness, its sevenfold character being potential with its own upper four divisions based on those of the cosmic. The confusion lies in the words *plane* and *state*.

[*The Vahan*, Second Series, Vol. I, May 1892, No. 10 pp. 1-6]

Question L

E. W. B.—Is it correct for Theosophists to postulate that 'a phase of Idolatry is necessary for the poor in mind?' I made and still make a very strong objection to any phase of Idolatry being necessary.

W. Q. J.—Common-sense, truth, discrimination and right rules of life all seem to declare that idolatry is not necessary for the Western world; that we cannot judge the mind of the East any more than we can understand why a Western hero-worshipper should indulge in such a practice.

Question LII

G. W. R.—The Ego passes through a series of incarnations, in some of which it may inform the body of a man, in others of a woman. Is sex of the vehicle chosen consciously by the spiritual Ego to perfect knowledge, or does it depend upon the Karma engendered in a preceding life? Can any principle be said to preponderate in one sex more than in another?

W. Q. J.—If masculine quality is the predominate characteristic, the Ego probably will be next in a male body; if not, the other sex. But the whole question is answered by that doctrine of Visishadwaitism which says that "Good Karma is that which is pleasing to Îsvara (the Ego) and bad Karma that which is displeasing to it."

[*The Vahan*, Vol. I, Second Series, June 1, 1892, No. 11 p. 3-4]

Question LIX

M.R.—Is not the Brahmanical faith the antipodes of universal brotherhood, in that no one who is not born a Brâhman can ever be received into their religion?

W. Q. J. That faith is not such antipodes, for the Brahmanical faith is not the same as the Brahmanical law of caste, now only a perversion of the actual and eternal divisions among men. Rightly understood and practiced, the real, the pure Brahmanical faith increases universal brotherhood and furnishes for Egos the right stream of heredity for future true progress. But nowadays it is corrupted and hence fulfils not its objects.

[*The Vahan*, Vol. II, August, 1892, #1, pp. 5-6]

Question LXXIII

S. C.—Can anyone explain the following sentence, quoted from H. P. B. in the Path *for June: 'Those who fall off from our living human Māhatmas to fall into the Saptarîshis—the Star Rîshis—are no Theosophists?*

WILLIAM Q. JUDGE—This is explained by the fact that there are two classes of beings able to influence mankind at large; the one being the "living human Mahâtmas," and the other the non-human beings, who, though not strictly in our stream of evolution, can and sometimes do affect certain human beings. For the purposes of this answer— but not at all as a full description—the Saptarishis as meant by H.P.B., are in a very advanced class of elementals, able sometimes to communicate with man, and by their apparent knowledge to make him suppose them to be high spiritual beings regularly evolved from the human stage, but, in fact, they are not human spirits, but of the same character as some of the Devas of the Hindûs, and only by accident, as it were, work to the real benefit of the race. That is to say, by communicating with them one is deflected from the normal line of human development. In some cases they have influenced certain mediums, who, being deluded, or rather dazzled, by the extraordinary experiences passed through, do not lean to the human side of spiritual evolution. On the other hand, the "living human Mahâtmas" form the direct link with the human spirits of all degrees, who have charge of human spiritual evolution.

THE THEOSOPHICAL FORUM

THE THEOSOPHICAL FORUM

[This magazine was distributed free of charge to members-at-large of the Theosophical Society in America, who were invited to "send questions, answers to questions, opinions and notes upon Theosophical subjects." Sometimes they were handled by Mr. Alexander Fullerton, who shared the editorship with Mr. Judge. Though some of the unsigned answers (attributed to the editors) were probably by Judge, we include only those contributed under his own initials or pen-names. —*Comp.*]

The Theosophical Forum

[April 1889 through April 1895, Questions 2 through 345, in Numbers One to Seventy, First Series.]

QUESTION 2

What are the meaning and scope of the term "Universal Brotherhood"?[1]

Eusebio Urban—I have heard of "Righteous anger," of a "proper withdrawal of sympathy," and of "punishment for evil doers," but these seem to me untheosophic and opposed to Universal Brotherhood. The teachings of Jesus and of Buddha insist upon forgiveness and eternal sympathy. Hence it appears to me that, although the selfish

---

[1] [Seven answers are given to this question, of which the following by *Eub. U.* (Eusebio Urban, a *nom de plume* of W. Q. Judge) appears as the 6th and has special reference to the 5th immediately preceding Mr. Judge's answer, a statement by "B.F.D." which reads: *B.F.D.*—I sometimes think that zealous Theosophists, in a creditable anxiety to promote general charity, go a little too far in their assertion of fraternal duty. They speak as if anything is pardonable because done by another man, who, because a man, is a brother. Yet it would seem that the basis of Brotherhood is equal rights and mutual affection, and to these I have the same claim as any other man. He is no more privileged to violate my rights than I to violate his, and I am therefore entitled to the same protection as is he. Hence it cannot be the fact that I am any more bound to look leniently on unfraternal aggressions by him upon me, than I should be upon like acts by me upon him. In other words, it is as much my duty to restrain him from outrage upon myself, as myself from outrage upon him. Theosophy cannot, and does not, teach that all protective appliances are to be thrown down, and that the way is to be freed for every attack by the greedy or the selfish. We must be careful, in our zeal for charity, to remember that justice is the antithesis, not to charity, but to injustice.—*Comp.*]

may infringe upon my rights, I should at once forgive the offense, extending to them my sympathy for their spiritual loss and degradation. In insisting upon the opposite course, theosophists ignore the law of nature well known to occultists, that mental positions have effects in every direction, causing disturbances or creating harmony. Each punitive attitude assumed by me acts both on my brother and myself, producing in him a tendency to repeat the act condemned, and increasing in me whatever seeds of evil I may have. While, by my "righteous anger," what I call my rights are for the moment protected and declared, the real and interior effect is bad, and the results in this incarnation as in a succeeding life are painful. Each time I thus pass judgment upon and enforce sentence against my fellow man, I attract to myself from him certain well known and powerful influences that abide in that part of his nature which caused his fault, and thus my own faults and evil tendencies are strengthened. Buddha said, "Hate never ceases by hate." These "rights" we care so much about protecting are merely self-declared, and we own no rights but those which our Karma may accord to us.

QUESTION 4

What are the three books referred to in Forum No. I, as dictated or inspired by Higher powers?

W.Q.J.—These books[2] should be judged upon their intrinsic merits regardless of the authorship or inspiration. As to *Light on the Path,* the author, Mabel Collins, has just lately asserted in print that she knowingly perpetrated a fraud in saying that any adept inspired that work, and that she alone is the author. For those who know her and the limit of her ability, this assertion will go for nothing inasmuch as neither by nature nor by study is she capable of writing the book, which contains statements of basic principles in occultism that were wholly unknown to her when she wrote. The too plain inference from the statement that she committed a fraud at the request of a prominent theosophist need not be drawn here.[3] The fact, as I believe it to be, is that a learned Adept inspired and dictated the work from beginning to end, just as Mabel Collins said, and the sole effect of her present declaration ought to be wholly to disentangle her name and personality from a book which is a gem in itself and can stand by its own strength.

---

2 [*Light on the Path, Isis Unveiled* and *The Secret Doctrine.—Comp.*]

3 [See an important clarification about this assertion in *Blavatsky Collected Writings,* Vol. VIII, p. 428.—Comp.]

QUESTION 6

If every one starts from and returns into "that" (spirit), what is the object of existence in matter? Is this the only way to fulfil the soul's desire?

W.Q.J.—The questioner should enquire a little further as to the meaning of "matter," for if thereby mere mortal material life is meant, the truth about matter has not been grasped. The worlds of heaven, of the "devas" or "angels," are worlds of matter, and such worlds are sought after by those who ask the question under consideration.

Furthermore the occultists hold that *spirit* has not as yet incarnated fully in the existing race, but will do so in future ages; then men can say that they have a spirit. At present the men who are incarnated spirits are Adepts or Mahâtmas. Toward the moment of this grand incarnation we are hastening, and the experience now being undergone is to settle the question whether we will become fit for such a tremendous event or whether we will fail. Assuredly all are called to this grand work, but just as certainly some will not be chosen.

QUESTION 11

How can a "Black Magician" be known? How should he be treated —as a part of the Universal Brotherhood?

W.Q.J.—This question comes from America. It is premature, and very much in the nature of "crossing a bridge before you reach it." It also seems to indicate either a loose use of the term "black magician" or a total ignorance of what such a being is, as well as a forgetfulness of what has often been stated—that a black magician is the efflorescence of an age.

Such a being as this is one who has acquired knowledge of recondite laws of nature such as those known to the White Adepts, and who uses that knowledge for purely selfish purposes. He is the triumph of selfishness, not in that degree which we so easily recognize about us every day in the lives of men of strong will used for selfish ends, but in a degree and to an extent that raise the black adept to a pinnacle of knowledge and power far above the pigmies of this century. He can perform marvels, read thoughts, and do all the wonderful feats usually attributed alone to White Magicians.

How many of such, then, are there to be found now, either among those who study occultism, or in the ranks of the money-loving or fame-pursuing multitude? I have never heard of one. Why, then, need to enquire how one should treat a black magician? If the questioner shall ever be so unfortunate as to meet one of those as yet fabled monsters, he will quite likely have opportunity to reflect that the magician knew more than he did.

It is wiser to turn aside from the aspect of the matter brought up by the question, to the reflection that we all have within us potential black magicians lying in the lower and stronger part of our nature, and that it is important to see that we shall not furnish the opportunity for that potentiality to manifest itself in future lives through the giving way now to selfishness in any of its forms. The black magician, therefore, we are really concerned with is in ourselves. This talk of meeting or dealing with black magicians in the flesh, with powers developed, is purest nonsense.

But it will probably be said, "If there are White Adepts now working in the world, why are there not black ones as well?" The answer is easy. It is this. Although the full-fledged White and Black Adepts are both the efflorescence of an age, there is a great difference between them. There is as great disparity between them as between day and night, for those who follow the White Law represent spirit, unity, love, while the others represent nothing but self and disruption. Hence, although the Black Magician—in those days when they shall be abroad on the earth—may prolong his life for an enormous period, he is surely silently attacked by nature herself, and at last, when the great day of dissolution, the end of a period of manifestation, arrives, all those black ones left will be swallowed up and annihilated. But at that day all the White Adepts, those called by the Hindus "Jîvanmukta," although absorbed into Brahmâ are still in possession of consciousness, and will come out at the new day just as powerful as when the night came on. Hence, as the day of Brahmâ is divided into the four Ages—of which Kali Yuga is the last, the White Adepts alone are known or in existence in the ages preceding Kali Yuga, and in that age the Karma fitted to bring forth Black Adepts begins to act, and the seeds sown long ago sprout up more and more as the years of Kali Yuga roll on. Now as that dark age has 432,000 years, and only 5,000 of those have passed by, there has not yet been time to evolve the real black magician. But this civilization pre-eminently shows the seeds are sprouting, and nowhere with greater power than in America. Here the national characteristic is individualism, and that existing as a tendency of the nature will differentiate some day into individualism concentrated into some few men. Imagine this concentration as occurring in a future century when wonderful advances will have been made in knowledge of great forces of nature, and you can easily see without any need of prescience the future black magician.

QUESTION 12

In 1888 in "Lucifer" a contributor used "F. T. S. 2°" in signing an article. Can we have any information relative to the degrees in the Theosophical Society, if there are any?

W.Q.J.—The article printed in *Lucifer* was not a contribution to that journal, but was a reprint of an article published in a Chicago journal and hence the signature had to be copied. As yet there is no F. T. S. 2° who will thus sign, for the reason that that degree has not been given. The writer of the article referred to was no doubt deluded by one who, knowing that there had always been three lower degrees in the T. S., had pretended he could confer it. These three degrees were spoken of in the early years of the Society, and can be found mentioned in the earlier diplomas as having an existence. The higher degrees are held only by adepts and certain of their disciples. The whole Society in general is in the first (or rather 3rd) or lowest degree, and it was very early found that as yet but few were competent to enter the next higher one, for that must be won and cannot be secured by either boasting, money, or favor. And some of the few who have entered the second are not aware of that fact, since they are made to pass through a time of probation which is long or short according to their own efforts *and* merits. And the efforts and merits of some years of probation may be reduced to a beginning *de novo* by a month of folly or of doubt. Were the real leaders of the T.S. in want of mere followers by number instead of quality, they might long ago have taken in hundreds of anxious members. But They are not; and They can wait.

QUESTION 13

Does the cyclic law bring about its intended result without the conscious intervention of races and individuals? Or is it part of the working of that law that races and individuals shall consciously interfere in behalf of their own progress or retrogression?

If either or both, will not things be what they will be and should be, in spite of any or all of our efforts?

W.Q.J.—The cyclic law has no "intended result," since it is a blind force. The cyclic law ruled in the days of the early races just as it now does, and before there were any races at all who could act consciously or unconsciously. The power of choice for the human race as a whole does not come until the turning point in evolution is reached—when *four* is turned into *five*—and, of course, until that time comes, "conscious intervention" by a race is impossible.

Individuals—meaning individual monads—may and do help on the progress of a race or a nation or oppose a contrary effect, but even that is under the cyclic law. In *The Occult World* by Mr. Sinnett, we have the words of a Master on this point, as follows, speaking of the Adepts:

"There never was a time within or before the so-called historical period when our predecessors were not molding events and 'making history,' the facts of which were subsequently and invariably distorted by historians to suit contemporary prejudices. . . . We never pretended to be able to draw nations in the mass to this or that crisis in spite of the general drift of the world's cosmic relations. *The cycles must run their rounds.* . . . The major and minor yugas must be accomplished *according to the established order of things.* And we, borne along on the mighty tide, can only modify and direct some of its minor currents. . . .[1]

"Sometimes it has happened that no human power, not even the fury and force of the loftiest patriotism, has been able to *bend an iron destiny aside from its fixed course,* and nations have gone out like torches dropped into the water, in the engulfing blackness of ruin."[2]

But this does not lead to negation or apathy. "Things will not be what they will be or should be, in spite of our efforts," but rather— "things will be as they should be, in spite of the apathy of those who see no use in action that is for the good of Humanity."[3] Those who believe that the final good will in any case be accomplished are those who, sunk in the dark pit of selfish indifference, are forever an obstruction in the road of the aspiring souls who work for man's welfare.

In considering the subject we should not lose sight of the fact that other souls are reincarnating every day, bringing back with them the experience and Karma of distant past ages. That must show itself in them as they mature in this life, and they will furnish new impulses, new ideas, new inventions, new pieces of knowledge to the general sum, thus affecting the progress of the races, but all under cyclic law. And if we, by supinely sitting down, do not create for them, as they may have in the other days done for us, the right material, the right vehicle of civilization, the end of the cycle may be reached with *their* task unfinished—through our fault. The Karma of that will then be ours, and inexorable justice will bring us upon the scene in other cycles which eternally proceed out of the womb of time, to finish with heavy hearts the task we shirked. No theosophist, therefore, should ever begin to think that he need not offer any help because all will come right anyhow.

In our small way we should imitate the Great Brotherhood in its constant efforts to help Humanity. They know the cycles, and, using that knowledge, can see when the impulse of a new cycle is beginning. Taking advantage of this prescience, new ideas are projected among men and all good reforms are fostered. Why should we, merely because we are ignorant of the cycles, do nothing to help these great bene-

---

1 [*The Occult World,* A. P. Sinnett, 1885, Houghton, Mifflin, Boston, pp. 134-35]
2 [*Op. cit.* p. 120.]
3 [*Op. cit.*]

factors of the races? They offer to all men the truths of the Wisdom-Religion, making no selections but leaving results to the law. Is it for us to assume in our theosophical work that we, poor, weak, ignorant tyros, are able to select from the mass of our fellows the one or the many who may be fit to receive theosophy? Such a position of judge is vain, ridiculous, and untheosophic. Our plain duty is to present the truths of theosophy to all men, leaving it to them to accept or reject.

QUESTION 18

Is it possible by a strong desire before sleep to receive from the Higher Self in dream an answer to questions respecting right thought and conduct?

W.Q.J.—This question is one of deep importance to those who are in earnest. My answer to it would be "yes." Bulwer Lytton says in *A Strange Story*, that man's first initiation comes in dreams. In the *Book of Job* it is written (iv, 12. 13): "Now a thing was secretly brought to me, and mine ear received a little thereof. In thoughts from the visions of the night, when *deep* sleep falleth on men." And (xxxiii, 14): "For God speaketh once, yea twice, *yet man* perceiveth it not. In a dream, in a vision of the night, *when deep sleep falleth upon men*, in slumberings upon the bed." The state spoken of in Job is the same as that called *Sushupti* by the Hindus. Man has three principal states or conditions—waking, dreaming, and dreamless or deep slumber. In the last it is held that communion is enjoyed with the Spirit, and that the inner man returning or changing from that condition goes into a dream, short or long, from which he changes into the waking state. The influences of *Sushupti* are highly spiritual. They are common to all men. The greatest villain on the earth, as well as the most virtuous man, goes into *Sushupti* and receives benefit from it. If it were not so, wickedness would triumph in the earth through the overpowering influence of the body and its constant downward tendency. Now, if this is believed and the reality of the Higher Self admitted, it follows from what is called *the mysterious power of meditation* that a sincerely devoted man who earnestly calls upon the Higher Self for aid in right conduct will receive in the dream state that succeeds the condition of *Sushupti* the aid asked for. In other words, one can make the dream impressions received out of the highest—or *Sushupti*—state more clear and valuable than is usual with those who think nothing about it. But the questions asked and impressions desired must be high and altruistic, because the Higher Self has no concern with material things nor with any temporal affairs. This power will of course vary with each man according to his nature and the various combinations between his physical, astral, and psychical planes.

QUESTION 21

It is authoritatively stated in Esoteric Buddhism *that the Hindu Race is the most spiritually developed now existing—as the Anglo-Saxon is the most highly developed intellectually. Are we, then, to understand that the Hindu Race has in the past experienced an intellectual state analogous to that of the present state of the Anglo-Saxon, and with it a similar material prosperity, and that the present Hindu civilization, including caste, as the fruit of a higher development—the spiritual, is, upon the whole, preferable to that of the Anglo-Saxon?*

*Ananda.—W.Q.J.—*1: *Esoteric Buddhism is no more "authoritative"* than any other book. The statements in it are not binding on any one but the author.

2. The conclusion at the end of the question, about caste system does not follow from the premises if their affirmative were granted.

3. According to the general law of racial development we are to assume that the Hindu nation, ages ago, passed through an era similar to our own present one. Further than this, historical and archeological *facts* show this to be so, for the ruins alone in India point to an enormous extent of material progress in her past, and all through the Indian literature is proof tending to the same end.

4. But the present degraded form of caste is not due to the "spirituality" of the Hindu. Caste today is not the caste of the ages when prosperity reigned; and there is as much "caste" now in Europe and America as there is in India, although not given that name. The true castes will always exist. They are four: the teacher (*Brahman*); the warrior (*Kshatriya*); the merchant (*Vaiśya*); and the servant (*Śûdra*). In the ancient days the people changed caste when they actually changed their nature; but now the divisions are fixed by custom— not by spiritual law—and are innumerable.

5. As Indian civilization is now in its decadence, it certainly is not preferable to that of the Anglo-Saxon, since the latter has the elements of improvement in it. But if the present Western civilization is fixed and not to change, then, in my opinion annihilation were preferable. The Hindu nation being very ancient it must have distinct traces of its old-time glory; the Anglo-Saxon is in comparison quite new, and the greater part of its past is crude and brutal. Hence it is natural that the Hindu has more potential metaphysical and spiritual power in its corporeal frame than the Anglo-Saxon. What the actual psychic endowments of either are can only be told by an Adept, for the science and statistics of the day do not deal with or record anything but the physical inheritance. The questioner should never forget that each

nation, like each man, has its own particular psychical inheritance, which may or may not be the same as the physical one.

QUESTION 22

Do the Masters know one's earnest desires and thoughts? I desire to become a chela in my next incarnation. What effect will it have upon my condition and environment in that life? Is my desire forgotten or lost, or is there record made of it?

W.Q.J.—The effect of a desire to become a chela in the next incarnation will be to place one where the desire may be probably realized. Its effect on the next condition and environment depends on so many things that no definite reply could be given. If the desire be held determinedly and unceasingly, the goal is brought nearer, but that also brings up *all* the karma of the past, thus precipitating an immense conflict on the individual: a conflict which when once begun has only two ways of ending, one, total defeat, the other, success; there is no half-way. As Dante wrote, "Who enters here leaves hope behind". Therefore, in general, the next life, or rather the life of a chela, while full of noble possibilities, is a constant battle from beginning to end. As to times and periods, it is said in the East that when the probationary chela steps on the path he will reach a goal in seven births thereafter.

QUESTION 27

In the PATH *it is stated that "a dream is the going out of a part of our principles into the Astral Light." This raises a desire for information relative to the inspiration—so called—of poets, artists, inventors, and others.*

W.Q.J.—The definition of dream referred to is not to my mind adequate, for there are many sorts of dreams all due to different causes. Believing, as I do, that in the Astral Light are the pictures of all that man has ever done or made, and that at this stage of evolution it is not possible to bring forth anything really new, the so-called inspirations may often be due to the fact that the organism of those "inspired" more easily permits the influx of the pictures in the Astral Light, and then their production in verse, paintings, inventions, or what not. In an article entitled "Genius" by H. P. Blavatsky in *Lucifer* for November, 1889, the idea is advanced that the great geniuses, of whatever kind, are examples of the Ego, which is all-knowing, shining through and informing the physical body inhabited. It is not necessary to dream in order to be inspired, for the sudden inrush of poetical ideas and of new inventions may be due wholly to the pervious state of the organism. While we often hear of such ideas arising in dream, yet from what is known of the poets, painters, and others, we are forced to the conclusion that the greater number of inspirations are during the waking state, and this supports the view put forward by H. P. Blavatsky in the article upon "Genius."

E.U.—The question about dreams leads to the reflection that the dreams we have are nearly always absurd. Clear dreams or those prophetic come rarely. When they reach us we remember them for years. Those of us who often dream know that nonsense is their characteristic and overfeeding often their cause. But as some rare and valuable ones are known of, we must admit a power to dream connectedly and with sense. Is it not, then, true that such a prevalence of foolish dreams shows that there is something wrong with our waking state that reflects itself into sleep? If we regulated ourselves every moment during the day, would not our dreams become coherent? And how many of us could mark any one day with a white stone showing that it had been free from folly, anger, or desire? Not one.

Z.—If the dreamers of dreams and these wise explainers of them knew what dreams really meant, they might say less and dream more. There is in the dreaming condition a faculty exercised and which may be called, for the want of a better word, "'exaggeration of circumstance," and another that we can call "reversion of images." Then there is "symbolical diminution," as well as diminution due to absence of all power to relate. Add to these the fact that, until you have your senses about you, even in a dream, so as to be able to know what the physical brain is doing, none of these disturbing and producing causes can be observed and allowed for.

QUESTION 28

In what manner does entrance on the path of occultism cause the special evil latent in the individual to express itself in his life and acts? Is it because early steps in occult knowledge destroy the force of the conventional ideas of morality and abrogate the laws which society and formal religion have adopted for their security; and that, therefore, for a time, until the principles of ALTRUISM *assume definite sway over his mind and motives, the individual is without practical and efficient restraints upon his* LOWER SELF? *Or is it, on the other hand, the operation of a* KARMIC LAW *upon the character of the individual, making use of his* PERSONAL VANITY *as a fulcrum for forcing the special weakness of his Lower Self into a reckless expression of itself?*

W.Q.J.—While the questioner answers his question himself, it only gives half of the subject. The real study—on the path—of occultism, not only brings out latent evil but also latent good. The right way to express it is, "the study of true occultism, or the walking on its path, brings up the entire latent character of the person." Hence while some in this case suddenly seem to grow worse and worse, others suddenly grow better, deeper, broader, and finer. It is customary to look at the shadow in these matters. While it is true that the majority of men are inherently bad, there are examples of the opposite. The study of occultism does not destroy rules of right and wrong, but the student, having opened up the fires below the surface, may be easily carried away in the sudden heat engendered. The dweller of the threshold in *Zanoni* is no fiction. It is ever with each student, for it is the baser part of humanity that he begins in real earnest as never before to fight. At the same time, the brightly shining Adonai is also there to help and save if we will let that be done. Karma that might not operate except after years or lives is called upon and falls, as H.P.B. has so clearly stated, in one mass upon the head of him who has called upon immutable law. "Fools rush in where angels fear to tread," and, rushing in before they have the slightest idea of their own character even on its surface, they are often destroyed. But the practice of altruism is not by itself occultism, and it saves from danger and prepares one for another incarnation in some body and age when everything will favor us. We have yet left some few hundred thousand of mortal years, and, ought not to be too precipitate.

QUESTION 30

What relation does Mr. Sinnett's "Esoteric Buddhism" bear to Theosophy and the Theosophical Society?

Z.—As this work was the first definite presentation to the West of the old doctrines about man and nature, it certainly has an important relation to the present Theosophical movement, and when one remembers the efforts made to convince the author of the truth of the doctrines propounded, and sees the wide acceptation of the book in both Europe and America, the wisdom of the effort made and the importance of the result are apparent. Furthermore, it is well known that *Esoteric Buddhism* is made up almost wholly of selections from letters alleged to have been written to Mr. Sinnett by the Mahâtma. This gives it importance. And while some few errors have crept into it, as was inevitable and as H. P. Blavatsky has shown in *The Secret Doctrine*, yet it is certainly correct in the main. But no one should conclude from its title that the doctrines contained in it are those of the Buddhists, any more than they are peculiar to the Brahmins. They were first published in *The Theosophist*,[1] while Mr. Sinnett was in India, under the title "Fragments of Occult Truth," and later on cast into the present form with copious additions: for this we have the

---

[1] [*The Theosophist,* Vol. III, October, 1881 and serially for many months.]

author's word in the preface to the first edition. Every student of Theosophy should not merely read this book, but ought to study it with care, and all the more so if the ideas are unfamiliar; but at the same time the corrections made in *The Secret Doctrine* should be used to clear up points that otherwise would not perhaps be perfectly plain. *Esoteric Buddhism* in my opinion, therefore, will always rank as one of our best works, not only because of the clearness of the author's style, but also because it is the first concrete presentation of Theosophical doctrines to the West in this Theosophical cycle.

QUESTION 37

Does the termination of the 19th century of the Christian era coincide with any of the great cycles referred to in "The Secret Doctrine"? And if so, does not that fact strongly corroborate the actual existence and the divine mission of the man Christ Jesus?

W.Q.J.—The first part of this question could not be answered to the satisfaction of the questioner, for the reason that the true cycles, their commencement and termination, are not given out by the Adepts, as that is a sacred matter pertaining to high initiations. But I should like to ask the questioner how he can, by any fair logic or argument, take the views of the writer of *The Secret Doctrine* in regard to the subject of cycles—about which she is fully informed and he knows nothing—and then base upon them an argument for the "actual existence and divine mission of the man Christ Jesus." And, as she says that there was no Christ Jesus as a man with a divine mission, no such conclusion as is drawn by the questioner could result from an affirmative answer to the first question.

But suppose we admit that the termination of the 19th century A.D. coincides with some of the great cycles referred to in *The Secret Doctrine*, nothing would be proved respecting the "actual existence and divine mission of the man Christ Jesus," for the reason that there are many other eras, in other nations and religions, running at the present time, and doubtless it would be found that the termination of the century of some of them would more nearly coincide with some of the great eras than the Christian 19th century. In such a case, the founders of those religions or eras would have proof in the coincidence of the cycles—in case that constitutes any proof at all. There are the Christian era, the Mohammedan era, the Hindu era, the Buddhist era, the Jain era, the Persian era, the Chinese era, and others. Now as some of the centuries in these various eras must coincide with some of the great cycles, it should follow from the questioner's position, that there is corroboration for the "actual existence and divine mission" of the various great personages alleged by the various peoples and followers of the several faiths to be appearances of God upon earth, and the ones from whose births their respective eras may be reckoned. However, in my opinion, all these coincidences prove nothing for any great religion or any Savior, in any time or nation.

QUESTION 40

A teacher of Theosophy says that no more than one in ten thousand is immortal. Is the statement correct? If so, what is the use of reincarnation, and for what are Theosophists working?

W.Q.J.—The second of the questions would not have been asked if more attention had been paid to the acquirement of an accurate understanding of the Theosophical philosophy. It has never been a secret doctrine that "but few among mortals strive for perfection and out of those only one in ten thousand reaches the end desired." These words are to be found in the *Bhagavad-Gîtâ*, which was printed first in English 100 years ago. But even if we did not have the direct statement in the *Bhagavad-Gîtâ*[1] the fundamental Theosophical doctrines compel us to the conclusion that many will fail to reach immortality. Since, however, the same doctrines teach us to analyze and determine as to what "many" or "us" means, we find that the theory under discussion applies solely to the lower or strictly human ego and not to Spirit. The object, therefore, of reincarnation is that all the possible egos may have the chance to become immortal by uniting themselves with Spirit. If they do not, they lose. But further yet, it is laid down that the periods of evolution succeed each other in endless succession, and all who are "left over" unsaved at the end of any one of such periods are taken up again, in the succeeding evolution, for the purpose of working up to perfection. Thus in every Manvantara numbers of egos reach perfection, for that period is very long as mortals count years. I say "numbers" because in fact the number is very large, although, if compared to the entire whole, they may not seem to be many. This is what Theosophists are working for—not only to reach perfection themselves but to help all other men to do so likewise. And they should remember that whether they like it or not the laws of life will bring them upon earth again and again until they believe in the doctrine, and acquire aspiration, and turn both into action.

But who is the "teacher of Theosophy" spoken of by the questioner?

QUESTION 43

The "Guardians of the Gods" opposite to the entrances to the temples in India are represented as having one foot on the head of a cobra; is this typical of the triumph of the Hindu religion over the worship of the serpent—or not?

---

1 [See *Bhagavad-Gîtâ, Chapter VII, śloka 3.*—Comp.]

W.Q.J.—I should say it is not. The serpent has many meanings, and to stand with the foot on its head might mean that you have obtained complete mastery over the lower nature, for the snake then stands for nature and its powers. And as the Hindu religion has a good deal in it about the serpent, the figures spoken of cannot mean the triumph of that religion over serpent worship.

QUESTION 44

Was the "fall into generation" on the physical plane a normal feature of human evolution, as stated in some Theosophical books; or was it abnormal and not intended by nature, as said in other Theosophical books?

W.Q.J.—It would be well if everyone were to quote when they say, "as said in some Theosophical books," giving name of writer and of book, for it is very unfair to the Forum and any writer in it to be compelled to answer to the purport merely of a statement in some volume. The context of such statement might put the whole matter in a different light, or we might find that there was a misquotation.

It cannot be said by a well informed Theosophist that nature has any "intentions," nor should any man have the temerity to claim an acquaintance with those if they existed. If in the writings of some Theosophist a reference can be found to "nature's intentions," the context will certainly show that the words were used figuratively in describing apparently settled natural laws.

It seems to me that the "fall into generation," when explained Theosophically, is not abnormal. Since things are as they are under Karmic Law, according to law and not by chance, there can be no step in it that is abnormal. Besides this, the word "abnormal" is one that is used by us to designate that which appears to be out of the usual course solely because we do not know all the facts and factors. As in the case of the eccentric movements of certain planets, which led to the discovery of another one which had caused the eccentricity. Before the last one was found the movements of the others were certainly abnormal, but ceased to be so considered when the discovery was made. Hence "abnormal" is a word that describes a thing only relatively and not absolutely.

But H. P. Blavatsky, who is, we suppose, a good Theosophical authority, speaks clearly enough upon our question. In *The Secret Doctrine*, Vol. II, p. 62, line 19, she says: "Moreover there are two 'Falls' in Theology: the rebellion of the Archangels and their 'Fall,' and the 'Fall' of Adam and Eve. Thus the lower as well as the higher Hierarchies are charged with a supposed crime. The word 'supposed' is the true and correct term, for in both cases it is founded *on a misconception.*

Both are considered in Occultism as Karmic effects, and *both belong to the law of Evolution*: intellectual and spiritual on the one hand, physical and psychic on the other. The 'Fall' is a universal allegory." And on p. 228 of the same book she gives a more detailed view of the fall of certain of the Dhyanis, "whose turn it was to incarnate as the *Egos* of the immortal, but, *on this plane, senseless,* monads," stating in the second paragraph on the same page: "the 'fall of *man* was no fall, *for he was irresponsible.*"

Then as if to furnish forth the answer for the question as to the "intentions" of nature, the same author heads her explanation of Stanza II (in the 2nd Vol., p. 52) "Nature unaided fails," and on p. 56, second paragraph, she says: "Thus physical nature, when left to herself in the creation of animal and man, is shown to have failed." If the second volume of *The Secret Doctrine* proves anything about "intentions" in the matter of evolution, it is that nature had none whatever, and, if she had, failure would follow attempt at realization. This subject is interesting and, studied with the help of Madame Blavatsky's book, will be of benefit to the student.

QUESTION 47

In answer of "F.L.M." to question No. 3 in the FORUM *in regard to "Meditation," the writer several times refers to the control of the "vital electric currents or agents of unconscious mind."*

By the latter term, I understand, is implied the inner consciousness or the Will force distinguished from mental effort, and also that the writer is able not only to recognize the physical expression of this force but also to control it.

We are conscious of mental effort, but usually the impulse of the Will produces no physical sensation of itself.

Many of us now groping in a boundless void could at least feel our way in the darkness, could we thus ascertain that our inner consciousness was indeed impressed and working in the direction of our convictions.

Let us have some elementary elucidation of this subject.

Can such consciousness be cultivated, and, if so, what are the initial steps?

W.Q.J.—The answer referred to was made by a student who had discovered that, as far as he was concerned, the vital currents could be centered upon desired parts of the body, and that in his case, if they were centered in the head, he would be engaged more in mental works than bodily, and *vice versa.* Proceeding with this, he found that some ailments could be thus driven away by centering his vital force upon the place where they existed. It is a form of will power, which to be used requires a well cultivated and balanced imagination. Much abused word as "imagination" is, it is the only one that will express the necessities of the case. If your imagination cannot make a *picture* of the spot and of the force, you can never — except by accident — cause the forces to flow there. Hence the initial step is to cultivate the interior image-making power. Unless this is done, the will in these planes can hardly be directed to its end, for with no image the forces have no place to focus upon; and it is a huge error to suppose that scientists are right in saying that imagination is a useless, although perhaps pleasant, power. As each human being is *sui generis*, has his own methods interiorly, peculiar to him and to no other, one should not look for hard and fast rules for all, but go to work upon himself, find himself out of whom he is most ignorant, and proceed upon the lines thereby indicated. All methods should be tried, and one's own processes of thought and feeling carefully observed. Without such inspection, rules and discussions are useless; by it—if truly pursued—anything can be discovered.

QUESTION 49

"Five Years of Theosophy" states there are 36 Tattvas.[1] *As Shiva Sanhita says, "From ether came air; from ether and air, fire; from ether, air, and fire, water; and from ether, air, fire, and water was produced the earth, all of them forming the Universe." Now, I cannot arrange the combination of these 5 tattvas so as to make 36. I make 5 primal tattvas. 10 double, 10 triple, 4 quadruple, 1 quintuple, or 30 in all. Can you supply the deficiency?*

W.Q.J.—It has been generally understood that the study of the tattvas by beginners, including all men of every sort who are still in the world, is discouraged by the Masters of Occultism, since it may lead to abuses. Furthermore the subject is so mixed up as far as any treatises on it are concerned, that it is well protected from enquiring minds. And as several Hindu writers will differ as to the number of *tattvas*, none of the writers at the same time being able to use any of them, or tell how to do so, one may be justified in leaving the matter untouched for the present. For my part I am willing to confess ignorance of any more than 4 of these forces, to wit, those of fire, air, earth, and water, and to assume but slight knowledge of those. Just here it is well to read on page 290, of *The Secret Doctrine*, Vol. I, "So there are seven forces in man and in all nature."

---

1 P. 111 ff. [Subtitle reads "Mystical, Philosophical, Theosophical, Historical and Scientific Essays, Selected from 'The Theosophist';" London, Reeves & Turner, 1885.—*Compiler.*]

QUESTION 51

Can we find the God in ourselves before we have realized the Divine Life outside of us?

W.Q.J.—But I would like to add, that as there is no such possibility as *divine life outside of us*, for all, heaven, earth, hell and God, are within, the question cannot be answered by either Yes or No.

QUESTION 54

Is it right or safe for one who has discovered a lead to a mine by one of his psychic senses to search for the mine, even if for a noble purpose? If he does find it, is he not liable to come to grief?

W.Q.J.—It is not the province of Theosophy to furnish pointers regarding mines or stocks, but since the question has arisen it does not seem wrong for one to find a mine by means of psychic sense. The number of successes in that line are very, very few, as psychics generally grossly overestimate the discovery, and often suppose there is a deposit worth going after, when in fact there is only a mere speck of metal. Nor have I ever heard that trouble is likely to result to one who finds a mine or anything else in that way. But at the same time the search for treasure by using the psychic senses is an ignoble pursuit. Yet if accidentally any sense of that sort revealed to me a mine and I felt sure of it, I might seek it. Disappointment, however, generally is the consequence.

QUESTION 61

Is there a wide difference between Karma and destiny?

W. Brehon.—Destiny is the English word applied to a Karma so strong and overpowering that its action cannot be counteracted by other Karma; but in the sense that all happenings are under Karma, then all things are destined as they occur. Men have always found that some events were so inevitable that, for want of knowledge of the law of Karma, they have said, "These things were destined." But when we grasp the meaning of Karma, we see that *destiny* is only the working out in action of causes so powerful that no act of ours and no other sort of Karma could by any possibility either avert or modify the result. This view does not conflict with what some call the "immutable decrees of Karma," because those decrees are the resultant of numerous Karmic factors, the absence, nullification, or postponement of any one of which would change the supposable result. If, however, we imagine that our life today is only that due to past Karma from a previous incarnation, we make the error leading to a belief in destiny or fate. But as we are experiencing the effects of Karma from this life as well as from many previous ones, it follows that the events in a man's life are due to the *balancing* of Karmic causes.

QUESTION 63

If while in the present incarnation we are able to arrive at the "free" spiritual condition, the great reality, as designated in the tract "Spirituality," when during the long interval between reincarnations, while the spirit is not chained to the body, but experiences that unreal state "sleep, a sleep of dreams"—as stated in "Lucifer," what progress is made?

W.Q.J.—There is much confusion in this question, and hence I infer a similar state in the mind of the questioner as to the matter propounded. Two states or kinds of development are mixed together, one the free or liberated state of a *Jivanmukta* and the other that of a being who is obliged to reincarnate. Only those are free who are *Jivanmuktas;* having reached that state they are no more confined to mortal birth, but may take up a body or not as they see fit. A *Jivanmukta* participates in the souls of all creatures and works for the good of the human family. To take a known case, it should be remembered that the Adept who is helping the T.S. is a *Jivanmukta,* but is all the time engaged in the great work of assisting the great orphan, Humanity. And it is thought by some that he is waiting for the time to come when the races have reached a higher state of development, and he can reincarnate as some great personage to carry on the work now begun.

It could not therefore be possible that, having reached the liberated or free state referred to, there should be any "long interval between reincarnations," or any interval at all; and thus the question "What progress is made?" is a *non sequitur* which needs no other specific reply.

If by "that unreal state sleep, a sleep of dreams," is meant the state of devachan, the answer is that he who is liberated does not experience devachan, since that is a state possible only while one is still subject to delusion.

But on examining the tract on Spirituality I do not find the statement made which the questioner quotes. I must infer, then, that some lesser, lower view of "free" and "spiritual" states was in the mind of the person, some idea that one might in this present incarnation reach to the state of *Jivanmukta,* and that one who is free could still be obliged to reincarnate. From having referred to an intermediate state of sleep and dream, such might be inferred to be the case. But a study of the philosophical basis of all these Theosophical ideas would prevent such confusion as I have attempted to point out and to cure. Indeed, on the third page of the very tract spoken of, on lines 19 *et seq.*, I find a direct claim that we are really only aspiring to the state referred to, and that we can begin now that training which shall lead us up to the heights on which the liberated stand. No reference at all is made to "long intermediate periods of reincarnation."

QUESTION 64

If all our sufferings in this life are caused by the misdeeds of a former life, how can any combination of sidereal influences at birth affect our fate?

W.Q.J.—A thorough acquaintance with the doctrine of Karma and with what is actually claimed for Astrology by those qualified to speak, would result in an answer to this question. Astrology is not soothsaying nor card-reading; reading omens is soothsaying; reading cards is a form of divination: Astrology is neither of these. All that is claimed for it is that the whole assemblage of stars indicate, as being a vast machine or clockwork, just exactly what is the state or condition of any one spot in the whole mass. Is this any more absurd than to say that a watchmaker can tell from the movements of a watch just where the hands will be at any particular moment, and likewise from the hands alone where the different cogs and other parts are within? If common minds, and ignorant as well as venal practitioners of Astrology, make a stock of their imitations, wrong conceptions, and base uses of it, that is no reason why the FORUM should sweepingly denounce Astrology. As well denounce real Christianity because of the base coinage labelled with its name. Taking now the oft-made assertion that "Karma governs all worlds up to that of Brahma," we reply to the question that our Karma and the stars are inextricably linked together, for if we had no Karma there would be for us no stars. It is just because the Karma of any being at birth is fixed from his prior one that the great clockwork of the skies shows unerringly to the sage—but not to the dabbler nor to the modern abusers of Astrology—the Karma or present fate of the being. But if, as so often done by even the best of Theosophists, we separate any part of our universe from any other portion, putting one under the influence of Karma and another not, then of course such questions as this one cannot be answered. The doctrines of the Wisdom-Religion are naught if not all-embracing, are useless and misleading if not applicable to the greatest as well as the very least of circumstances or worlds; and so we answer that not only do sidereal positions *indicate* our Karma, but even the very clouds, the wind, and the hour of the day or night in which we may be born, do the same.

QUESTION 66

Is the seventh principle, the Âtma, ever incarnated, or are our bodies simply projections of that principle and formed by it, as was the statue Galatea by Pygmalion? From some Theosophical books I gather that the seven principles are all incarnated from the beginning, and that each principle is evolved in turn. From others it would seem that the higher principles are never incarnated.

W.Q.J.—The fiction of the formation of Galatea by Pygmalion is such a faint and inadequate symbol or illustration that there is nothing to be gained by its use, as it will surely mislead. The evolution of the bodily form came about in the same way as that of all other forms; as said in the *Bhagavad-Gîtâ*. "All is due to the mystic power of self-ideation, the eternal thought in the eternal mind,"[1] and only in the sense that all forms are projections from the eternal can we say that "our bodies are projections of that principle" (*Âtma*). The second sentence of the question shows that here is another case in which the very materialistic view of the sevenfold constitution of man given in *Esoteric Buddhism* and used by so many thereafter has resulted in inducing the notion that there is a separation between the so-called "principles." This idea of seven distinct things, entities, or principles in man ought to be abandoned, and is due almost wholly to erroneous nomenclature, as was strongly urged in several papers published in *The Path*. There can only be one principle, and all the rest are but aspects of it, or *vehicles* for it to work and manifest through. Therefore but the one principle is involved in generation, when it takes to itself six sheaths or vehicles, or shows itself under six aspects. But as it is Theosophic doctrine that this *one* principle—call it *Âtma*—is in essence the Supreme, then its involution in matter is but partial. In order to understand nature and to reach self-consciousness, it is necessary that the six vehicles be found to work through, and what is meant in some Theosophical books by the statement that each "principle evolves in turn" is that from the beginning of a Manvantarà the six material vehicles have to be evolved one after the other in due order and in correspondence with the rest of nature, none lagging behind and none ahead. For instance, at that period in evolution when we might assume that but one vehicle had been fully evolved, then man (so-called) would not be man as we know him. So we see in *The Secret Doctrine* that man, strictly as such, is not spoken of until several races or vehicles had been first fully evolved in due order and proportion.

---

1 [*Bhagavad-Gîtâ, Chapter IV,* śloka 6.—Comp.]

From these considerations the old Hindu idea that what we see of
man is but the inner (or outer) hard core—the material body—and
that he, in fact, in his whole nature reaches even to the moon, would
seem to gain some support. And I should incline to the opinion that
Âtma is never incarnated, but overshadows and shines into the being
called man whom it has chosen to connect itself with.

QUESTION 71

*Is it intended to be conveyed, in answer to Question 68, that true
Occultists and sincere Theosophists would countenance or practice any
lawful arts of White Magic for pay?*

W.Q.J.—My reply to this would be that the taking of pay for any
act of "White Magic" is untheosophical and injurious to the taker.
The example of all great men known to history or Scripture is against
the taking of pay in such cases. Jesus would not take it, nor Apollonius,
nor Buddha, although, if persons insisted, they were allowed to donate
food or for food. Buddha depended on voluntary contributions of
food, and accepted the gift of a garden or park from a rich man for
the use of the disciples, but not for himself. A "right means of liveli-
hood" does not permit the practice of powers belonging to another
plane than this for pay. If we have to starve unless we take pay for
what the querist calls "arts of White Magic," then I say, starve, and
you will be the better off.

The accepting of pay at once takes away the character of White
Magic from the act and makes it Black, for there is a selfish purpose
in receiving the pay which no amount of argument or self-cheating
can remove. There are many degrees of "Black Magic," running all
the way from effort to get money for food up to deliberate, conscious
work for self alone. If one has the natural gift of healing and then takes
pay for its use, he is cheating. This is wide apart from the practice
of medicine, which you have to give effort, time, and money to acquire.

But if a natural healer or a "spiritual healer"—to use a most absurd term now in vogue in America—practices healing, and takes of
alms only enough for sustenance, there is no Black Magic. But all such
healers can ask themselves if they have made money, saved money,
bought property, lived in luxury on the proceeds of their art or practice—or whatever they call it—and, if they have, then certainly they
have "robbed the gods," who gave freely a power and compelled no
pay. The "gods" see these things, and have a time and place when and
where the stolen property has to be accounted for.

QUESTION 73

(1.) *Is there not a confusion involved in portions of the answers to Question 66 and 69 with respect to Âtma?*

(2.) *In what sense is the word "correspond" used in Theosophical writings and the works of Swedenborg? In the sense of "cause and effect," and that things never "correspond" unless this relation exists between them?*

W.Q.J.—(1.) There is no reference to *Âtma* in Question 69, and hence no confusion. A re-examination of answer to Question 66 shows none. It is clearly stated there that there is but one principle—call it *Âtma*— which incarnates, so to say, through its six vehicles and at the end of the answer a private opinion is given that *Âtma* does not incarnate except in the sense that it overshadows and illumines.

(2.) I presume the questioner refers to the use of the words "it corresponds," "there is a correspondence." This does not refer to cause and effect, but rather to similarity or likeness, as: "Good *corresponds* to light, and evil to darkness;" "Selfishness *corresponds* to frigidity and iciness, and generosity to heat." There is no relation of cause and effect between these, for generosity is not the effect of heat nor its cause, nor is the light the effect or cause of goodness. You are therefore essentially wrong in supposing the word "correspondence" is used to express cause and effect. An examination of a good dictionary discloses the meaning to be "fitness, agreement, proportion," hence "similarity." The questioner should study this word and obtain a clear understanding of its meaning and use, for if the conception of it remains so confused as the question indicates, many other errors will result. A more or less complete knowledge of *correspondences* gives the power to gain knowledge gradually from one plane to another.

QUESTION 74

In view of the condition of Astral Man stated by W. C. T. in Forum *No. 9, Question 32, what was the effect of our civil war on the astral plane, and reflexively on ourselves?*

W.Q.J.—To answer this question aright would require the powers of an Adept who could see into the astral light and measure the exact results. But sudden deaths in war are not the same in effect as the killing of a murderer or a wicked man who has violated the law. The men destroyed in battle are engaged in the moving of troops, the arrangement of batteries, firing of volleys, and using the sword. Their attention is almost wholly thus occupied, and when they are suddenly killed it is with this idea of present attack and defence fixed in their nature. If we suppose them as lingering in the astral plane, then they will there continue the same actions which occupied them at the time of death. But the criminal, who has led a criminal life, who is full of evil passions, and who steps off into the other world with a heart full of passion and revenge, will linger on the other plane full of those unsatisfied desires, and not overmastered, as is the warrior, by a single strong idea. The astral warrior confines himself to the repetition of attack and defence, while the criminal seeks to satisfy his revenge and bad instincts in general. These considerations seem to me to point out a difference. I do not pretend to answer the whole question, however, as to the effect of war acting from other planes.

QUESTION 76

To be a good Theosophist, is it necessary to believe actively in Occultism? I mean: If a man feels the ennobling influence of the philosophy of Theosophy and endeavors to live by it, is it absolutely necessary for his profit and development to do more than believe that certain occult facts are facts, while he personally dislikes Occultism and avoids it in any form, finding Theosophic teachings sufficient to him without it?

W.Q.J.—The questioner has either heard from others or read that a good Theosophist *must* believe that Occultism is our highest goal as members of the T.S. Such is not the truth. At present "the T.S. is not," as an Adept once wrote to Mr. Sinnett, "a hall for teaching Occultism," although that is pursued by some. It is a Society meant for the giving of true views of life and of Nature to a suffering race which otherwise would sink into a spiritual death brought on by the joint efforts of materialists and theologians. Hence, at present, the true Theosophist is the true Altruist who sinks his personal desires for progress in a secret and fascinating art, so that he may give this true view of life, of death, and of immortality to as many of his fellowmen as he can reach. Many members of our Society, dazzled by the wonders of Occultism, have hastily taken up its study without realizing that it is something that demands not only will but wide intellect and unflinching memory; and many have failed as many others will.

QUESTION 77

Fellows of the T.S. using tobacco defend the habit as having certain qualities very protective in studying Occultism. Is this true; and, if so, why is it incompatible with one of the five precepts taught by the Lord

Buddha, viz: "Shun drugs and drinks that work the wit abuse; Clear minds, clean bodies need no soma juice!"[1] *And is it not possible to educate the will, the spiritual will, to resist effectually everything which this deleterious weed tends to annul, if it does annul?*

W.Q.J.—I should like very much to know who is that F.T.S. who "defends the use of tobacco as a protective in studying Occultism," for he or she cannot know what protection means or Occultism either. The Editor of the FORUM has well answered the question, since the sentence I refer to, being only narrative, is not a question. Yet it is important as pointing to error of a vital sort. There are hundreds of Hindu occultists who never have indulged in tobacco; but they have not interdicted it to others. They protect themselves by means that can only be used in the plane where such protection is needful, and that is the plane where neither tobacco nor sentiment on that or any other subject has place. Tobacco may protect the carcass from germs of disease, but that security to safety is needed by all men, whether they are studying Occultism or not. The whole question of tobacco or no tobacco is purely material. It has been discovered that it does not degrade except by abuse, but at the same time it was found and declared that other narcotics and stimulants, such as hemp, opium, and spirits, do dynamically obstruct and spiritually degrade. Hence these tears—and tobacco.

QUESTION 78

Mr. Sinnett says:"It is not the goody-good or devoutly aspiring man that attains to the highest development." What is the highest development, and how best attained?

W.Q.J.—I should like to add that Mr. Sinnett had in view the doctrine found in many books old and new that wisdom as well as virtue is needed in him who aspires to the "highest development." Virtue leads only to heaven, wisdom leads to union with the whole. But wisdom must at last have virtue as companion. Virtue pursued and practiced through many lives will lead at last to wisdom, yet wisdom first attained makes the cultivation of virtue easier. The highest development cannot be attained in any single incarnation. The teachers say that we must seek the company of those who are pure and wise, who lead holy lives, and that we must look for knowledge with persistency, humbleness, and faith, and that thus setting our feet upon the path the goal will loom in sight after many weary struggles.

---

[1] [*Light of Asia*, Book VIII.]

QUESTION 80

Has any Theosophical theory been advanced in regard to the atmospheric and electrical disturbances so prevalent in this country during the last few years?

W.Q.J.—Some theories have been advanced by theosophists respecting the great atmospheric and electrical disturbances, but they are not specially confined to that; they include other great changes, and reach over into the realm of thought and the minor changes in the race. Atmospheric and electrical changes occur at all times, and are intensified at certain periods. The changes of the great cycles—from one to another make all sorts of upheavals possible. The sun moving slowly in his great orbit carries the small earth's path out into new fields of space where entirely new cosmic conditions are met with, and the sun also goes through alterations of place and state. These latter must affect our atmosphere and electrical condition, for it is held by some theosophists that the sun is our great source of electricity. Science has lately admitted the possibility of there being an actual connection between spots on the sun and our great electric storms; the old Hindu astrologers always asserted this, for they claimed that, as the sun altered, so did the condition of the earth. But it would be premature to definitely state either that the sun causes the changes alone, or that they are due to a different situation of the earth in her great path through space.

QUESTION 88

In The Path for Aug. 1889, under the heading "Some of the Evil Consequences of Mediumship,"[1] we are told that the calling back of suicides and those who have met with accidental deaths is "productive of untold evils for the Ego that will be reborn under its nefarious shadow," and, further on, that "it is now cursing many men who find themselves forever in a mental hell, at war with themselves and with their best thoughts, they know not why." Are we to understand from the first quotation that some of us are born with this vampire fastened upon us? If so, then in the interest of those of us who seem to be in the condition described in the last quotation, how can we rid ourselves of this old man of the sea?

W.Q.J.—The FORUM's title presupposes free expression of views, and of that I take advantage. All the conclusions of the Editor do not meet my approval, and many seem to be contrary to some accepted Theosophical premises. The septenary scheme of man's constitution and the

---

1 [pp. 134-36.]

conclusions as to how the separation of the so-called principles takes place, as well as their "fate" after death of the body, seem to be against the assumption that it is superstition to suppose that evil results from suicides and those dead by accident being drawn to *séance* rooms. It is well known that after violent death of the body the principles above the material do not separate as in other cases, do not go to Devachan, do not dissipate. In a case of natural ordinary demise the astral body dissipates, so does Kâma-rûpa; with the other cases it is not so. The man who kills himself is not really dead. Only his body is dead; he remains a living man in the astral spheres close to us, minus a body. If left alone he comes to his end in due course, but a long way off, generally measured by the length of years he would have lived if he had not raised hand against himself. But if he is drawn into a medium, he is given a new attraction which ties him to earth and makes him drunk, as it were, with the fumes of life. This retards him and causes him to live long, long years in Kâma-Loka, and curses too the one who draws him thus further down. How does "the orderly working of Karma" go against this? It is his Karma that made him a suicide, that put it in the power of mediums to disturb him. It is exactly the case of a man who drinks to excess, and who thus puts himself where he may be harmed by other evil influences. Also in the case of accidental death. Karma made by the same person decrees that he shall so punish himself and so lay himself open to all the consequences that may follow. That is no reason why we should ignore the law and pay a dollar to gratify our whims and at the same time hurt a fellow-being. Hypnotism is an admitted fact. We know that people may be hypnotized and against their will made to make fools of themselves by ridiculous gestures and antics. Some people pay to see it done. In that case we may see the harm with our eyes. It is all improper. But is it therefore superstition to believe it and to declare what are its evils? I hardly think so. I may add that the "private letter" was by a high chela, and was endorsed by several high occultists as true.

QUESTION 89

Is the use of hypnotism for intended good, as in the case of surgical operations, looked upon with disfavor by Theosophists? What relation have the investigation and practice of hypnotism, when only good is intended, to the 3rd object of the Theosophical Society?

W.Q.J.—Replying in part to this question, one can only give a personal opinion, and mine is that hypnotism should be prohibited by law. No one but some very few high-minded and learned physicians should be allowed to practice it. I would as quickly prohibit the general mass of physicians from using it as the general mass of the public, for I regard it as a dangerous and injurious power. The great Charcot who has popularized it says he would have only competent physicians use it. In the present age of black selfishness I would vote for its total seclusion from use for the present.

QUESTION 91

Is Kâma-Loka definitely stated to be a state of suffering merely (therein somewhat analogous to the R. C. Purgatory), characterized solely by dissolution, or a violent wrenching apart of the four higher elements? If this be so, how comes it that after the separation of Kâma-Rûpa and lower Manas from Manas proper the surviving entity carries with it to Devachan the recollections of the earthly personality?

W.Q.J.—I am unable to decide whether T. E. K. infers that suffering in Kâma-Loka destroys memory, or that the separation of the "principles" takes it away. But if the question turns on "suffering," then I should say that that does not deprive of memory. This leaves for discussion the other query: How does the surviving entity carry with it into Devachan the recollections of the earthly personality? *The Key to Theosophy* in Section IX describes the process in general to which the question refers. There it appears that at death the body, life-force, and astral body are lost, and the middle principle (Kâma-rûpa), together with Manas, Buddhi, and Âtma, is in Kâma-Loka, which is a state or condition and not a place. Then the separation between Kâma-rûpa and the higher triad begins, after the completion of which Manas-Buddhi-Âtma fall into the Devachanic state. Turning to page 92 of the same book, we find in the column "explanatory" that if the Manas naturally gravitates to Buddhi and away from Kâma-rûpa, the "Ego goes into Devachanic bliss." This gives the process. It cannot be said to be suffering or painful. The only point left, then, is as to memory. T. E. K. rightly says "recollections." Section VIII of *The Key* makes this clear. *"Memory"* is the physical brain-memory; *reminiscence* is the "memory of the soul." Each new brain makes a new physical memory used by Manas in each life, but Manas itself is the seat of memory proper, called by H. P. Blavatsky "reminiscence." It is not meant that Manas takes into Devachan the remembrance of every circumstance in life, but only the efflorescence of its life, the reminiscence of its best hours, leaving the painful and evil portions to the dying brain and to Kâma-rûpa. If the questioner desires, as a help, an objective illustration of what happens to Manas through the separation from Kâma-rûpa, this may do: Imagine Manas as attached on its lower side to Kâma--rûpa just as a photograph may be attached to a glass plate. When dry, the paper can be taken from the plate, leaving on it the film of the picture. Thus when Manas is separated, its lower film may be left attached to Kâma-rûpa, its higher portion going into Devachan. And it is in Higher Manas that real memory is.

QUESTION 93

Is it a fact that we have no right to condemn men, and should only condemn their conduct?

W.Q.J.—While I agree with much of the editor's answer to the above question I disagree from its spirit and certain inevitable conclusions flowing from it.

First, I fail to see that in order to train the moral sense one has to practice condemnation of others. *Second,* The necessity for condemnation will never pass away if we occupy ourselves in such practice while waiting for the world to grow so good that there will be no one to condemn. *Third,* It appears to me to be a new and untheosophical doctrine that our moral sense is to be or can be properly cultivated by engaging in condemnation of others.

The maxim cited in the Question was never intended by the writer or writers as one for application in the State, but solely for earnest disciples who endeavor to follow the very highest rules of conduct. We are so prone to condemn others and let our own faults go by that sincere disciples are taught, as a discipline, to cultivate their moral sense by inspecting their own faults, and let others do the same for themselves, but when the occasion demands condemnation, that it shall be of the wrong act. This cannot apply to a judge, or any other proper inquisitor, teacher, or guide. It is meant solely for those who, believing that our span of life is so short that there will be no time left if we busy ourselves with faults of others, prefer to improve their opportunity by purging themselves, by cleaning their own doorway, by taking the beam out of their own eye. For all sages and occult practitioners declare that among the necessary facts to be known, as the editor of the Forum observes, though not admitted in his conclusions, is the fact that each time a man indulges in condemnation of another he is himself prevented by his own act from seeing his own faults, and that sooner or later his faults increase. If a sincere student thinks this be true he will hesitate about others and occupy himself with self-examination and self-conquest. This will take all of his time. We are not born as universal reformers of all people's faults and abuses, and theosophists can not waste their energies in criticizing others. Furthermore I strongly doubt if anyone was ever improved by the fault-finding of his acquaintances. It is natural discipline that makes the improvement, and that only. Indeed, I have observed in much experience with those who constantly criticize others that nothing results in 99 cases out of 100 but a smirking self-satisfaction in the breast of the critic, and anger or contempt in the heart of the victim of the fault-finding. One illustration will do for all, and it is this: One evening I was leaving the elevated railroad car with a friend who hardly misses a chance for pointing out omission or commission by others. As he went out first, a roughly-dressed man blocked the way, appearing as if attempting to enter. My friend, being strong, caught him by the shoulders, shoved him back, and said: "The rule is that passengers are let out first." Result: as he walked off feeling that he had properly corrected a fault, the man cursed him loudly, and audibly asked for an opportunity to kick him. Thus naught resulted but anger and malice in one heart— perhaps in the heart of a man born in adversity—and in the critic a self-satisfaction which is known to be the handmaid of delusion.

QUESTION 94

In [Ques. 78] *it says: "Virtue leads only to heaven. Wisdom leads to union with the whole." What is here meant by virtue?*

W.Q.J.—According to the dictionaries the radical meaning of virtue is *strength*. Other meanings are bravery, efficacy, valor, moral goodness, the abstaining from vice, or conforming to the moral law. In this last sense the word is used. There is nothing synonymous between *virtue* and *wisdom*. In the Christian scheme fear of God is the beginning of wisdom. There is the mere wisdom of erudition, but properly *wisdom* means *having knowledge* or *to know;* or skilled in arts, science, or philosophy, or in magic and divination. (2 *Samuel* XIV.) In homely language, then, to be virtuous is to be good; to be wise is to possess knowledge. If the kingdom of God is the perfectness of evolution, then knowledge is what leads to it sooner than virtue. Of course these terms are used with the theosophical scheme of man and nature in view, and in that light it appears that in addition to virtue we must have knowledge, for a life of virtue leads to pleasures of devachan, with good karma for next life and thus through many lives; but knowledge added to virtue shows how to use virtue and its results in finding and treading the path leading to the Supreme which is *all*.

QUESTION 97

Is it right to restrain the impulse to benefit another, either by teaching or by furnishing necessities for physical use, for fear of interfering with Karma?

W.Q.J.—A little more ought to be said upon this question. It has been raised in several places, and is due to a slight misconception of what karma is, and also as to our position as men in the whole natural scheme, whether as judges or as executors. If karma were something about each man which we could plainly see, as for instance, if each one of us had written upon him what was his karma and what punishments or rewards should or should not be meted out to him, then it would be easy for one to say in any particular case what one should do in the premises. But such a state of things does not prevail. No one of us knows the karma that is coming to another or to himself, and it is only when events have arrived that we know. For each event small and great is karma, and the result of it as well as the maker of new, since this great law is action and the results of action. Hence, even if we knew the coming karma or that which was due and should then decide, "I will help this person although I know it will interfere with karma," acting accordingly, we could not interfere in the least, because it would still be karma. This is an absurdity, but it is just the absurdity of those who talk of interfering with karma. We cannot interfere with it for it is beyond our power, and we are, indeed, the very instruments it uses to carry out the decrees we have ourselves been the means of passing. The idea of possible interference has arisen out of the statement now and then made that Adepts have not done this or that because it would interfere with karma; but this has not been understood. What was really meant by such words was that Adepts themselves are karma just as we are, only they see what we do not, and, as some of us asked for a reason, they said they would not interfere, or, in other words, the law is strong and no being, god or devil or man, can interfere with it. Any attempt to "interfere" is merely new karma carrying out that seed of karma already sown, no matter how many ages or years ago. But, still further, it seems to me that if we assume to decide what we shall do out of fear that our brother may not be sufficiently punished, we not only lay up wrath against ourselves, but at the same time set the germs in our own character which will sprout in selfishness and pain. We need not fear that karma will not do justice. It often does it by offering to us a chance to help another, and, if we stand aside, it will at another day give us the punishment for our selfishness and arrogance.

QUESTION 99

As Karma punishes all sins, is it right or desirable that human laws should punish crime by death or imprisonment?

W.Q.J.—My individual opinion upon the death penalty is that it is neither right nor desirable that human laws should punish crime by death, but this answer presupposes in the race such a knowledge of proper conduct and a constant practice of the same that every human being is a perfect law unto himself and for all, and that no laws are needed because all know and keep the laws of morality and nature. As, however, men as yet are very imperfect and are struggling to find the right rule of conduct, laws are necessary for evil-doers. Here, then, arises the question whether society is benefited by law imposing the death penalty, and as to that many able writers speak on one side and many on the other. To my mind it appears that the crime of murder has not diminished because of capital punishment, nor do I think any law will ever stamp out that offense. Indeed, I know that the majority of Theosophists regard capital punishment as a greater evil than that which it is directed against. But as Theosophists we have not much to do with such a question, since it lies in the domain of government. Our duty is to teach those ethics and that philosophy which alone will remedy the evil by raising men above the possibility of committing crime or becoming amenable to law. If we waste our energies in attempting reforms on the surface, either in law or in politics, a great opportunity will slip away before we know it. The remaining query is upon the subject of punitive law in general, and on that my view is that the question put flies wild of any point, because even these very laws enacted for the punishment of evil-doers are themselves the product of Karma. The state of the race which evinces crime is due to its Karma, hence the present system, the criminals who fill our jails, the judiciary and the executive departments administering the laws, are all products of Karma. It therefore follows that where, through man-made laws, offenders are fined or imprisoned, such punishments are those of Karma. It thus appears to me that the question is wholly one relating to reform in a mere social or political institution.

QUESTION 102

Is it honest for a sincere Theosophist to celebrate in any way, whether by present-giving or by entertainments, the festivals of Christendom, such as Christmas and Easter? What is the practice of Occultists and the leaders of the Theosophical Society in this regard?

W.Q.J.—Theosophical sincerity is not a strange moral product of a new reform, but is exactly sincerity as always defined by philosophers and moralists in every age. The word *sincere* is derived from a Latin word which is in its turn supposed to be from *sine* "without" and *cera* "wax," that is, *pure honey.* The wax is prejudice, and he who harbors that, be he an F.T.S. or not, may consider his practice right in preventing him from viewing broadly all customs of all men, but one who accumulates the pure honey of sincerity may just as well join in Christmas festivities in Christendom as he would in those of Buddha's birthday in Ceylon.

QUESTION 105

As to there being seven earths: to me analogy would suggest that there are not seven earths; rather that our fellow globes are the more ethereal principles of that of which this earth is but its lowest aspect. "As above, so below."

W.Q.J.—I do not understand what sort of analogy the questioner uses, but the point raised is evidently in respect to the statement in *The Secret Doctrine* that as there are seven moons, so there are seven earths and seven principles or divisions in man. The *seven earths* referred to are not the seven globes of the earth-chain—the only one of which has been called "earth" is this one, but are the seven principles of this globe, the most gross of which is that seen by us. No other word could be used for these except "earth," since as yet we are not well enough acquainted with them to give them distinct names. Were we to name them we should say (1) earth's physical shell, (2) earth's *jîva* principle, (3) earth's *linga-śarîra* or astral body, and so on through the whole seven. This applies equally to all the globes of the earth-chain, and the other six of those cannot be called "earths" and were never intended to be, because they are composed of matter which is not perceptible to our eyes. So, when the questioner says that "there are not seven earths" there is a confounding together of two subjects, for the seven earths referred to are this earth and its principles, whereas the "fellow-globes" are the other globes in our chain and not our earth's higher principles. Each of the globes in the chain is septenary, (see *The Secret Doctrine*, Vol. I, p. 167) and hence if we count these globe principles we have seven times seven, equals forty-nine, instead of only seven for the whole, as would follow from the questioner's position.

QUESTION 107

What is the Theosophical view of "Obsession?" Are the New Testament accounts of "casting out devils" to be regarded as literally true? If so, is it a retribution coming under the law of Karma, as with persons under seven years of age? There are cases where the so-called obsessing power seems so far superior in force of will as to be wholly irresistible by the victim: where is the remedy?

W.Q.J.—The T.S. has no "view" about obsession. All on such subjects must be the expression of individual opinion. The editor appears to intimate that there are really no cases of obsession, and if that is the intention of the answer, it must result from the fact that he has never met a case. It is true that as superstition abates instances of obsession do also, but that does not prove the phenomena to be the product wholly of belief in their possibility. Nor do the writings of men like Lecky prove much to my mind on these topics, since he thinks from a standpoint entirely at variance with mine. Since I have, in common with many other members of the Society, known of clear cases of obsession, no amount of argument by one who had never encountered such would be of any avail; and it is quite likely that those who do not believe in the possibility of these abnormal occurrences will never meet one, because the mind is not directed in that direction. There are obsessions, then, as we think from observation, but the classes of obsession given in the first answer, two in number only, are not adequate. We have to include in obsession that most mysterious thing— insanity. Physicians do not understand this affliction. They cannot explain how a man suddenly loses his identity and becomes a raving maniac. Or in milder cases, where a man periodically becomes for months at a time some other person with no memory of the former state, and so relapses from one to the other. I know of such a case in which a boy first showed this form of insanity, and has gone on for years with the alternation of personality until now he is of age. His trouble would long ago have brought him to the insane asylum if it were not that he was born in a rich and fortunate family. What is to be said of such cases? Are they voluntary or not? They do not come under either of the heads in the answer by the editor. As they are wholly involuntary, is free-will invaded or justice dethroned? I think not. Karma rules in this as in all else, and it is only when one limits his view of karma to this one life that he can be confused. Acts in a former life set up such tendencies in the ocean of life that when the ego came back again it was sure to one day become insane, which only means that a disarrangement of astral and physical forces was brought about resulting in a total inability to correlate the soul and body, and this is called insanity. It was free will that laid down the causes, and free will has no power to alter the effects. But, as in the case I cited, there may be ameliorations brought about by karma in the same way. For in that one we see—as is often not the case with others— that the poor insane person is protected by reason of the effect of another kind of karma, and is in this long insane or obsessed life cared for and made as happy as is possible. Remember, the mind of each is connected with the body in a certain definite manner and not merely in an imaginary way. This definite method is by certain channels and filaments or nerves; among the most difficult to explain are the magnetic and electric ties for the mind. Now our hold upon the body we have been born into may be so weak that we are not able to keep possession of these channels, and stronger forces may even unconsciously go in where we have tried to stay. This is not caprice any more than it is caprice that water will leak from a tank if there

be any cracks. So there may come a time that the building called
the body, which we hoped to occupy for a long time, becomes so
imperfect that our mental tenancy is no longer possible and we drift
off altogether, leaving it to the use of other forces or intelligences
good or bad; or, as is often the case, we are now driven out for a time
and then again get complete posession for a short term, until in that
process the cords of magnetism and the electric channels are clogged
up or destroyed so far as we are concerned, when we leave altogether.
All this of course may happen by what is called the man's own will or
act, as where one suffers from paresis brought about by gross dissipa-
tion, but all the cases are not of this kind, nor are they all due to
spiritualistic *séances*. As to remedies, those suggested by the editor
are good, but there are others possible by the use of strong magnetism
used by one who knows all these laws in every detail and can intelligently apply the remedy.

QUESTION 121

*Are there well-authenticated cases on record of clairvoyance in per-
sons born blind, where correct descriptions of things have been given
as they appear to the organ of sight?*

W.Q.J.—I have heard of one or two such cases, but as now they
cannot be produced they are not of present value. But it is well known
that blind people have ideas as to objects and localities which they
have never perceived as those who do have perfect sight. In these cases
they must have concepts, probably the same as those arising in others
from good sight. This, however, is not clairvoyance. It is, however,
certain that cases such as the question calls for must be very rare,
inasmuch as blind people would not be usually credited with clairvoyance, but would, in telling of places, naturally be thought to describe scenes of the imagination. Furthermore, it is extremely doubtful
if a clairvoyant blind from birth could have possession of terms to
use in describing objects so as to be understood by others not blind.

QUESTION 132

*If it is wrong to cure disease by mesmerism or magnetism,—at
least, if thereby the patient is controlled to any extent, how did Col.
Olcott heal so many in India by such means?*

W.Q.J.—There seems to be no necessary connection between the
premise on this question and the query put. Even if it were "wrong
to cure disease by mesmerism or magnetism," it would not therefore
follow that one could not heal people thereby. But I have never heard
from any source of weight that it is wrong to so cure people of their
ailments. To relieve distress must be right in general. There is much

dispute as to magnetism, but Col. Olcott seems to be of opinion that its cures are effected by actual virtue in magnetic fluid, and not by "control" of any patient. But in many of his cures there was a lack of permanence, due probably to lack of continuance of treatment, as he was constantly on the move. Questions of this sort ought to refer to some fact or publication in support of the assumption put in the question, as otherwise it is not possible to answer intelligently or adequately.

QUESTION 161

Has a mother a right to use her will power in throwing off disease and the painful result of accidents from herself and children? Please draw the line clearly between white and black magic in such work, occult work?

W.Q.J.—It is not clear from the question whether the querent means to ask about the use of the will pure and simple or about the practice of mind-cure, as it is called, or spiritual healing. In respect to the use of the will considered alone, the editor of *Forum* has replied sufficiently, I think, especially pointing out that the use of that power is not well understood; and it would seem that the questioner does not understand it.

There is a remarkable absence of treatment of the question of the will in such books as the Yoga Aphorisms and the like, the very books where one would expect to see something about it if it is a thing that can be treated of separately. But we may see the reason for this when we remember the old saying of the Kabalists, that "behind will stands desire." And by considering men as we see them, this saying appears to be a true one, for in everyday life and in every act we perceive that the prime mover is desire, and that the question of weak will or strong will depends on that in nearly every case. The wicked are of strong will because they have strong desires, and the weak person will be found to act with the most powerful will when the desire is strong. Their appearance of being weak arises from the fact that they are pulled about every moment by contrary wishes, not being concentrated enough to have definite wishes of their own. And it is here that the distinction between White and Black Magic can be easily found, for if the desired object be a selfish one or against the general good, then the act performed will be of the nature of Black Magic. The will is only used as an agent to carry out the desire. So in the case of an actual adept of either school, will is at his disposition no matter what be his object.

Now if the question put is in view of the practices of the so-called metaphysical healing schools, then a very different set of questions arises of mixed nature, some including moral aspects and some not, but every one raising a doubt about the claims made of curative power, as also about the way in which any cures that do take place have been accomplished.

The editor has pointed out that a well-balanced and centered mind will conduce to health, as has been held for ages; even savages know this and act accordingly. And if one finds from actual experience that the fact of his or her being of a cheerful, happy, contented, charitable, loving, faithful, sunny disposition will always have the effect of giving health to those about in the family or elsewhere, then there can surely be nothing wrong or inexpedient in such a state. And that, in my opinion, is the right limit for the practice of metaphysical healing. For if one goes beyond that, and, following the rules of these schools, proceeds to send his thoughts out to another with the object of taking hold of that other's mind, then there is the greatest danger and also Black Magic. For no one has the right to take the mind of another, for any purpose, into his possession. If such be done, then the other ceases to be a free agent. And this is true as much in the case of one's child as in that of any other person. Moral wrong attaches here because one is acting on another. But in the event of acting on oneself there can only be a question of expediency, and that is a very wide and important one, since momentous consequences may flow to us and to others from the tendencies we set up in ourselves.

Bodily ailments may be roughly divided for the purpose of the present into two classes, one being those that are acute or due to the imagination or the reaction of the imagination on the processes in the bodily economy; the other being those due to strong physical karma showing out in diseases in the mortal envelope, and being entirely beyond the reach of the imagination and not due to reactions from the mind of the sufferer. These last are of the greater number; we see them in small children as well as in adults, and also in savages and the semi-savages of our own civilization who compose what some people call a lower element in the social body.

In the first class the physical troubles from reaction will of course disappear so soon as the person trains himself to look at life cheerfully and to grow into a more independent frame of mind. The cures are not due to the causes assumed in the schools we refer to. They come about as a natural result of the new state of mind withdrawing from the nerves and fluids of the body the old strain and oppression. When those are removed the actual state of health at the bottom comes to the surface. And the result would be the same in the instance of the most degraded savage who might be induced by accident or by the words of his medicine man to fix his mind in another direction. Obviously there it would not be due to a system of philosophy. And additional proof of this is to be had in the very schools we speak of. In those we see widely different systems; one requires faith in the Bible and in Jesus, and the other does not, and yet each makes equal claim to success. H. P. Blavatsky says: "This is all the secret. Half, if not two-thirds of our ailings and diseases are the fruit of our imagination and fears. Destroy the latter and *give another bent to the former, and nature will do the rest.*"*

In the second class of diseases it is quite true, as has been often said by the metaphysical healer, that the disease comes from thought, but the error is in supposing it to be present thought had in this body. The thoughts are those of a past life, and have passed altogether from the mind plane into the realm of causes for dynamic disturbance, or of tendency, that are quite beyond the reach of the present imagining power, but sure to result in the course of time in visible difficulty suddenly appearing, or resulting from our going into situations that bring to us the germs of disease. For Karma acts on us not only in inherited troubles but also in accord with the tendencies we have set up in ourselves in a previous life. Those latter impel us to go to places or to mix with such people as that the inevitable result will be to cause effects on our mind or body that otherwise would not be felt. As in the case of one who set up in a previous life a tendency to consort with good and cultured people; this will come out and lead to a similar line of action with very different results from the case of one whose tendencies were in the opposite direction.

These causes for disease then being in the mind plane from the last life, and having become mechanical causes in this, are now *on their way out* of the system in the proper channel, and that channel is a physical, mechanical one. They are leaving us by the way of the body, are on the way down, and should not be stopped and sent back to the mind plane again. They should be treated by the ordinary methods of hygiene, of medicine, of surgery, of food. Hygiene and food furnish the right conditions for adjustment, and make no new present cause for trouble; medicine helps nature in her mechanical acts of purging and alteration; and surgery replaces dislocations, removes dead tissues, or puts bones that are broken into position for proper joining. No one would be so foolish as to say that thinking will remove from the brain the pressure of a fractured bone that is making the patient mad, or that imagination will set a dislocated shoulder. And if rotting food in the stomach is affecting the head and the whole system, it is certainly wiser to get rid of the offending substance as quickly as possible, supplying the body with good food in its place, than to let the evil stay to be absorbed as evil into the tissues while one busies himself by call-

---

1 ["Hypnotism," *Lucifer,* London, Vol. VII, Dec. 1890, p. 301. See *BCW,* Vol. XII.]

ing on the higher powers of mind to make him think he is not disturbed while nature is going on with her cure. In many cases this latter is all that happens, for any strong-minded person can resolve to
endure great pain during the process of rectification of internal trouble
by ordinary change of tissue and of fluids. So a disciple of the schools
in question may be so full of the notion that mind, or God, or Christ
is curing him that he endures until the *vis medicatrix naturae* has done
its work.

Granting that these causes are on their way down and out, the effect
of calling with a powerful will on the same plane of power is that the
cause may be sent back to the inner mind and disappear from the
body. But this is no cure: it is something like one's cutting off his hair
because the flies walk in it, it is planting once more in our deathless
body disease that will surely come out again in another life as disease,
or as madness in that one or presently in this. And in the life of many a
practitioner nowadays this has happened. For wherever one is very
sensitive the practices enjoined create abnormal states that have resulted in dementia.

But a still more pressing danger lies in the half-truth of the practices. They are, divested of all pretention to systematic and right philosophy, partially correct yoga practices.

As soon as they are begun they set up in the astral currents in the
practitioner definite changes that at once begin to react on the humors
and fluids in the body and are strong enough to bring about definite
alteration in the physical envelope. This has been known for ages and
has been treated of by the older Hindus. But they have always been
careful to say that they ought not to be gone on with in the absence
of a guide who is competent to know every symptom, to note every
effect, and to give the right corrective.

These correctives were not purely mental either, for many of them
have to be physical, since the rapidity of the changes and the effects
of the practices far outrun any application of mental correction in
many instances. And this knowledge did not mean a mere following of
a definite rule, but included an ability to see the peculiarities of each
person as he proceeded. For as each is under a different set of laws
peculiar to himself, the strict following of a general rule would lead
to the greatest danger.

But what do the "metaphysical healers" know of this?

Nothing but the vague rule of the doctors that one must watch the
patient and know, if possible, something of his medical record. Outside of that they are at sea with no pilot. They are inviting the explosion of forces they know nothing about, and when the difficulty
arises they are powerless. From actual experiment I know the facts
to be as stated. The pulse may be lowered or increased, or the first

symptoms of paralysis produced, or fainting brought on, singing in the ears and mist before the eyes made to show themselves; but where is the corrective? Unknown, for the simple reason that when we are dealing with such forces as these we are out of the realm of general rules for correction and must be able to at once see the exact inner state of the person and to select unerringly out of the vast range of possible cures the right one so that it shall work without any mistake.

What, then, shall the querent do for herself and her children, as she asks? Use her best judgment, follow the best rules for the cure of diseases, train her children to be self-reliant and careful so that they shall have few accidents, teach them to avoid evil and danger and keep their minds and bodies in right condition, and karma, and will take care of the rest. And if they are hurt or really sick, then send for a good physician.

QUESTION 161a

Is it unwise or wrong to say mentally to a person "You are well," or "You are virtuous, Your higher nature can control your lower?" Is that kind of mental treatment a wrong use of power if the motive is pure and unselfish?

W.Q.J.—Buddha and Jesus—two great teachers—performed cures. Not by assertion and denial but by scientific use of power. To the wicked whom they cured they said "sin no more." Both taught that the cause of sorrow was evil thought leading to evil act, but neither said that that existed not which was plain before one's eyes. They recognized the existence of fact, of law, of reason. In some cases they could not cure. Why? Because the causes working on the sufferer were too strong for them. Mere optimism which says all is good is of a kind that grows out of sentiment unsupportable by reason. We ought to do all the good we can, but that does not mean we should blind our minds to the reality which is necessary for cognition.

QUESTION 162

Do persons remain in Devachan for a time proportioned to their previous life on earth? For example: does one dying at 100 remain in Devachan ten times as long as one dying at ten?

W.Q.J.—On this the ancient writers say: "And when the reward is exhausted the being sinks back again into mortal life."

QUESTION 165

In the Jan. "Forum" H.P.B. is quoted as saying, "This is all the secret. Half, if not two thirds, of all our ailings and diseases are the fruit of our imagination and fears." In the same number W.Q.J. says,

*"The greater number are due to strong physical Karma," and "are en·
tirely beyond the reach of imagination." Will the* FORUM *point out the
reconciliation?*

W.Q.J.—It is quite true that I said in reply to Question 161 that
the greater number of diseases are those which are due to physical
Karma and beyond the reach of the imagination rather than to the
reaction of the imagination upon the body, and that H.P.B. in *Lucifer*
said that "half if not two-thirds of our ailings and diseases are the fruit
of our imagination," but there seems to be no great contradiction since
both statements were general, and in the last *Forum* mine was declared to be in respect to a rough classification and not to a specific
accurate one. H.P.B.'s expression *"half if not two-thirds"* is well known
to be an idiom which means much or little. It is one of those constantly used when one is not speaking of exact quantities. Hence it
need not be set over against mine. But if any think it important, then
let them consider that I did not say what I did as to the proportions.
However, there are no statistics obtainable as to the two classes of
causes for disease, and it is very evident that H.P.B. had no thought
of being mathematically exact, nor was there need for her to be. Her
remark was not to point out proportions but to show how strong imagination may be and how, just as I sought to point out that when the
direction of the mind is altered the strain is taken off from the body
and nature makes a further change, instead of our minds bringing
about a state of health. A careful glance at the substantial point aimed
at in the reply criticized would have revealed nothing of the nature
of contradiction between writer and H.P.B.

QUESTION 166

*In a recent discussion upon Karma a prominent Theosophist con-
tended that at death a regular balance-sheet of good and bad Karma
was, as it were, automatically made, and the resultant, always bad
Karma, was what guided the next incarnation. That the product was
always bad Karma, he stated, was proven by the fact that the particular Ego incarnated at all; incarnation being considered a misfortune and necessarily resulting from evil Karma. The other side of the
controversy maintained that there was no such process as could be
analogued to a balance-sheet; that both good and bad Karma held
over; that good Karma as well as bad necessitates reincarnation; and
that the future condition of the Ego is the resultant modifications of
some or all of both kinds of Karma. The point was unsettled. Will not
the* FORUM *illuminate us?*

W.Q.J.—Sorry to disagree from the EDITOR, but I must on the distinct
assertion that "Karma is not the cause of incarnation." The word

Karma means "action." Each incarnation of a being is action; each manifestation of a system of worlds is action on the part of the entities that manifest. It is our Karma that brings us into whatever sort of body, in no matter what sort of environment, with whatever character, good or bad, high or low, broad or narrow. Karma in respect to things about us produces circumstances of environment, of change, for reward, for punishment, for pleasure or for pain. As to ourselves considered as moral beings, it produces from life to life a *tendency* for good, virtuous, wise actions and thoughts, or the reverse. Thus we see one man of lofty character environed by circumstances of the most painful nature, while another of a bestial or vicious character is placed where all circumstances appear to be pleasant. Which is good or bad Karma here? And what is the formula to determine whether Karma is good or bad? In the case of the good man surrounded by adversity it may well be good Karma, if so be that it strengthens him and broadens his sympathies; while with the other it may be wholly bad, since he only wallows in the mud of sensuality, thus redeepening his evil tendencies. "Good Karma—or action—is that which is pleasing, and bad that which is displeasing, to the Higher Self."

So too the balance-sheet illustration is good, for it is by balancing of our Karma that we arrive here at such and such a place, with such and such a character, to experience differences of environment. That Karma which works on circumstances may be ordinarily unpleasant and thus by some called bad, but our character, acquired by other Karma, may be such as to enable us to triumph over adversity and now glean help and strength from the field badly sown in other lives by error or by mischance. So to me the discussion seems to have proceeded on wrong lines, while each of the disputants was right in his way but made wrong application. Karma is a doctrine too vast and complicated to be disposed of by set rules applied like balance-sheets to commercial enterprises; but one thing is certain—Karma is action viewed from every side and on each occasion.

QUESTION 167

What is meant in the Proem of The Secret Doctrine (Vol. I, page 14) by the term "bare subjectivity" as contrasted with "Unconditioned Consciousness," for the latter would seem to be "bare subjectivity" itself? It is entirely comprehensible how the Absolute "Be-ness" may be symbolized, on the one hand, by abstract Space, and, on the other, by abstract Motion, but not so readily perceived how Space may be defined as "bare subjectivity" when Motion is contrasted with it as the pure noumenon of Thought.

W.Q.J.—In the *Proem* cited the author distinctly says under (*a*) that "speculation is impossible" about the omnipresent Principle, and

then to give one way of symbolizing it—which is certainly not definition—proceeds to state that the Infinite Principle is the same as the
"unconscious" and "unknowable" of European philosophy, in which,
indeed, the FORUM editor takes delight. She then says it is symbolized
in *The Secret Doctrine* as absolute abstract space, which one must
conceive of as *space* distinct from all things existing therein; we cannot
exclude this, nor at the same time really conceive of it. And in the
same way, when we come to regard this omnipresent Principle from the
point of view of the root of consciousness, we postulate it as being—in
this aspect—*absolute abstract motion,* because consciousness has the
quality of motion in it and not the quality of space in which to move.
So then, having thus vaguely symbolized space, which is not consciousness, we have to say that, on the other hand, considering it as apart
from consciousness, it may be said to be "bare subjectivity," although
we have to use our consciousness in order to deal with it at all. The
editor's question, "Can any one conceive of abstract color?", seems
peculiar, since it is not foreign to all the schools of Western thought,
where many assert—as, indeed, it would appear they must—that apart
from any particular motion or color we can conceive of motion and
color in the abstract apart from particularization.

QUESTION 173

*Is it possible that our lower nature is composed of groups of elemen-
tary beings (sub-human) which under the higher tutelage can be
welded into a force for good, rather than something evil that has to be
cast off? If so, ought not the Higher Ego to be considered a trainer
and teacher of the Lower Manas rather than as a foe, even as a parent
restrains his children from wrong-doing, and would not this view make
the conflict between the animal and spiritual nature easier to most
people?*

W. Q. J.—The editor is right in saying the lower nature cannot be
cast off, but must be subjugated. We might as well say we can annihilate universal mind as to say we can "cast off" anything that is a part
of nature and going to make us what we are. The lower nature must
be discovered in all its ramifications and carefully subdued, as thus
it is transformed and not cast off. But I cannot agree with him in
respect to "sub-human elementals" composing us and which he calls
"fanciful." They are not fanciful, even though the questioner views
them in the wrong light and the editor in no light at all. If there is any
point strongly made in occultism it is that we are a compound of lives,
that every part of us is so made, and hence it follows that our lower
nature is made of these lives. There is no vacuum in the universe
void of a life. But while this is so, these lives, in so far as they go to

make up man, are not to be considered as separate beings from himself whom he can "educate," as inferred in the question, from a position as man which is apart from them. They exist in him, and as he lives and thinks so he impresses on them his thoughts and acts, and as they are leaving him every moment of time it follows that a stream of these lives of many grades and sorts is continually being projected from him into space and forming his own karma. For they are unintelligent and only act in their own way, just as water acts when it runs downhill. If we regard them as beings that we are educating we will fall into super-stition, but if, on the other hand, we say they do not exist and have no place in us, as the editor infers, we will never come to right knowledge of the universe as it is.

They are matter, in fact, and a certain quantity of it comes into the charge, so to say, of every man, and everyone is therefore responsible for the impressions he gives to the atoms that make him up, and if he does not live aright he will have to suffer the consequences sooner or later. For these very elementals are the means whereby karma operates, for without them—considering atoms as points of sensitiveness—there would be a break and no way for karma to have effect. If they do not exist, then there is no way to make the connection between matter and mind and thought and circumstance.

The conflict between the higher and the lower can be made easy only by the old rule "to look on all parts of the universe as containing spiritual beings, the same in kind and only differing from each other in degree."

QUESTION 179

Is there any statement in the writings of Madame Blavatsky or of any one else who might be supposed to know, to the effect that the Ego incarnates alternately in the different sexes, or at all in the opposite sex?

W. Q. J.—I do not remember reading anywhere in the writings of H. P. B. a statement to the effect referred to, nor in the written remarks on various subjects by the Adepts who sent her into the world can there be found, as far as my recollection goes, a declaration to the effect that the Ego incarnates alternately in male and female bodies. There may be found the doctrine that by this time in our evolution the egos now in human bodies have been through every sort of experience and both sexes, but that does not support the inference that such incarna-tion as to sex is alternated regularly—nor does it refute. It simply has nothing exactly to do with the question.

The question, it seems, is interesting to many, but I must confess an entire lack of interest in it. If my next birth shall be in the body-female, it is a matter of indifference. It is of record that an ego did very well in the body called Helena P. Blavatsky; and contrariwise, another did well in the body-male called Sankarâchârya. It is said that one Maji—a woman—in India is a great Yogi also. So, as I am perfectly indifferent, my remarks may be concluded to be uncolored by the partisanship of sex, so clear to some and so often productive of clouds over vision.

Well, then, I do not adhere to the alternating theory. It is too cut-and-dried at the very first impression. Further it appears to violate, with the appearance of a personal director behind it, the natural conclusions to be drawn from human life and character,—our only guide in such matters. If we assume an anthropomorphic God, who made it a law that every ego should now have male and next female form for living in, no matter how the laws of tendency of attraction and repulsion work in other directions, there might be some probability of sustaining the position that regular alternation of sex is the rule. But the universe is governed by law, not by caprice. Let us, then, look a moment at one or two points.

Karma—from other lives—determines where, how, and when we shall be born. But in the matter under debate, one of the ramifications of the law of Karma which must have most to do with this is *tendency*. In other words, the tendency set up in a prior life will determine the tendency toward a particular family next birth. And we must look also at the question of male and female character essentially, and not as a mere question of appearance or function. If we discover what is the essential distinguishing characteristic of the female character as opposed for comparison to the male, then we can perhaps arrive at a probable conclusion—though, as I above remarked, a very uninteresting and useless one in any event.

Now to my limited vision the female character is *per se* concrete; that is, its tendency in thought, speech, and act is toward the concrete; while the male character seems to me to be *per se* the opposite. The Kabalists and the ancients of all lands may not stand as authority for my readers, but they support this view. And the existence of exceptions in both sexes does not contradict the opinion, but rather goes to sustain it, forasmuch as we so easily recognize a woman who has a man's character or a man who has a woman's. The difference was not invented by tyrannical men, but seems actually to exist in the race. For no matter where you go, or how civilized or barbarous, modern or ancient, your examples are, they ever show the same differences and characteristics.

And whether you admit or deny the particular description by *concreteness* and *abstractness,* it still remains true that the essential female character—whatever be the distinguishing mark—is totally different from the essentially male one.

Now, then, if Ego (A) has evolved with infinite pain and many lives the female character, is it likely that that *tendency* will exhaust itself at once? Or if it has been set up by one life, is it likely to exhaust at death so as to permit the next incarnation to be in the opposite sex? I think not. It might be that the Ego could, as man in prior life, incarnate next as woman, but that would mean that he had set up a tendency to whatever is the essential character of the female,—in my opinion, concreteness of thought in the depths of his nature—or for other of many reasons. It is not wise to set down such fixed and iron rules. Nature does not thus work. She is always about to break some rule we have foolishly thought to be of eternal duration. So I conclude on this that the Ego will go on as woman or man just so long as its deeper nature is of the same cut, fashion, and tendency as the particular sex in general in which it incarnates. For my poor judgment, the regular alternation theory is wholly without foundation. But, after all, it is a question none of us can decide. The Christian Apostles decided female incarnation to be lower in scale than male when they said women are saved only by marriage, but even some Christian Theosophists may reject the Apostles on this.

QUESTION 180

What is Imagination, and what are its limits? Often I see mental pictures of myself and others, acting, talking, etc. Sometimes these pictures are realized, sometimes not. Where is one to draw the line?

W.Q.J.—In my opinion *imagination* is exactly what it imports on its face, that is, the *image-making power* possessed surely by man, and inferred in brute creation. It was so defined by the ancient occultists and by the hermetic philosophers. But nowadays it is given a low place generally, yet has been raised to slightly greater eminence by the Metaphysical Healers who have stumbled unknowingly on a great law. That which is often called *imagination* is, in fact, only fancy, or the idle creation of images whose tenure of life is short. But conscious exercise of this power raised to its highest degree is one of the necessities of occult art, for no occult feat can be performed without it. Experiments in mesmerism for a century, and lately those in hypnotism, show that each person has the power to create an image about himself which is perfectly objective to the inner senses of the seer. This creation is done by the use of imagination solely. If the image be indefinite, owing to the imagination not working strongly, the seer or subject will only see indefiniteness, because the subjective picture was badly constructed. But the constructor, poor or good, was the imagination. The Indian fakir makes you see the snake or other object—though you have all your senses—because through centuries of heredity and years of training his imagination has been put into such order that it sees before it the form so vividly that you perceive, as you suppose, an objective reality when none in fact exists. And turning to the letters from Adepts to Mr. Sinnett, we find them saying that in order to precipitate a note they must see (in imagination) each and every letter complete and unwavering before they can precipitate the material elements through that matrix upon the paper. So not only have we the testimony of all the mystics, but also that of those Adepts who in later days have shown those things to some.

As to drawing the line for the questioner. That can hardly be done. For if he is a clairvoyant partial or wholly, then he sometimes sees the pictures of what we improperly call the future. For there is no future; it is all now. In such seeing he does not use imagination. But where vain day-dreams interpose, then he is either using his fancy, or is bringing forgotten combinations of thought, or is being influenced for the moment by the fleeting thoughts of another. Johann Georg Gichtel once saw come out from heaven the hand of a widow who desired to marry him, and then a voice saying, "You must have her." He knew then that his stray thought and imagination had momentarily thrown a picture before his inner sense. That had but little to do with his imagination.

QUESTION 185

The Key to Theosophy, page 306, speaking of the attempt made by by Masters during the last quarter of every century to help on the spiritual progress of humanity, says, "Some one or more persons have appeared in the world as their agents, and a greater or less amount of occult knowledge and teaching has been given out. If you care to do so, you can trace these movements back, century by century, so far as our detailed historical records extend." Have these movements ever been so traced out, century by century, and if so, can the Forum *give such as have been tabulated?*

W. Q. J.—No one, to my knowledge, has so far taken the trouble to tabulate these movements. One was in Anton Mesmer's time. He founded a Society of Harmony with objects like ours. In Europe there were Theosophical Societies. In Dr. Buck's library I have read an old book, of about two hundred years ago, called *Theosophical Transactions.*[1] Without doubt very careful research would give a complete record all through the centuries even to the time of Ammonius Saccas. The name adopted, however, would not necessarily be "Theosophical" in each case. In Germany there were many attempts, and Baron de Liebistorf

---

[1] [Published by the Philadelphian Society, London. Nos. 1-5, March-November, 1697.]

and Louis Claude de Saint-Martin were engaged in one of those. Although the Encyclopedias call Cagliostro an impostor, he was engaged in such an attempt and was no impostor. Count de Saint-Germain is another of the messengers.

QUESTION 188

Does the Ego enter the body at or before birth?

W. Q. J.—The Ego does not enter the body at any time. The body is a grossly material instrument which is overshadowed or informed by the Ego. We are accustomed to saying that our souls are caught *in* our bodies because the ancients so spoke. But when they used that phrase there was an additional explanation current about *body*, and it was believed that the latter was more than merely physical, visible carcass. The body and its entanglements extend much further than is visible to our eyes. In fact, what we see of our bodies is only the hard or visible part; each person carries around at the same time the more intangible parts of body, which, however, are very powerful in their action. Visible body is the material nucleus, and the rest is the less material fringe or emanation. So when the ancients spoke of the soul entangled in body, they included in the word "body" the above enlarged meaning. At the time of conception the astral body—or model form—is made, and the potentiality of an Ego being enmeshed by the person is created; the connection of the Ego with the body—by means of the principle *Manas*—is made, in general, at seven years of age, and from then on the Ego is involved or entangled in body. But before such material entanglement it was first caught and involved in the passions and desires—or in the principle *kâma*—which is always the efficient or producing cause for the embodiment of the Ego. This *kâma* is known to form a part of the *skandhas* or aggregates, of which material body is one.

I cannot see the force of the objection to reincarnation that it conflicts with the power of the mother to influence the child. It does not, for she gives it the body with all the tendencies thereof, and she gives it milk, thus increasing those tendencies. She certainly cannot directly touch the Ego, and it is fortunate she cannot, because then she might actually thwart its development. It is the karma of the past that brings the child to that mother, and that karma may be to have a good or a bad birth, to be influenced for benefit or for injury by the mother.

QUESTION 190

If the soul passes into Devachan during sleep, why are not all dreams agreeable?

W. Q. J.—It is not strictly accurate to say the soul passes into Devachan in sleep, because Devachan is a word applied to a state after the death of the body and the abandonment of the latter. The word to designate dreaming is in the Sanskrit *Swapna*, and that state may be pleasant or unpleasant because the body and *Kâma* still affect the soul, whereas in *Devachan* all is blissful and pleasant. The Soul does not pass into *Devachan* during sleep, but sometimes in dreaming or *Swapna* state dreams are pleasant and often not. This being the fact, it is a sufficient reply to the question as put. With this explanation the Editor's above reply gives an answer to the question "Why are not all dreams agreeable?"

QUESTION 191

If the victims of accidental death, like suicides, do not enter Devachan till the time when they would have died naturally, they must remain in the earth-sphere as a whole and with all their faculties. Why, then, should they not be able to communicate with the living, whether through mediums or otherwise? Is not their case an exception to the usual law?

W. Q. J.—As I understand our philosophy, victims of accidental death and suicides do remain out of Devachan until the time they would have died naturally shall have come. Kâma-Loka, where these and all others go, has its grades in the same way as human living states. The first statements of these doctrines were naturally general, but elaborations have also appeared in which specific points have been dealt with. Not all suicides are alike. Certainly a thoroughly insane person who kills himself is not like one who, while sane and cowardly, does the deed, nor is this last the same as he who from a foolish philosophy or the want of it cuts off his life. They all differ one from another, and hence their stay in Kâma-Loka will vary. But in those general cases where the person stays in Kâma-Loka, the personality, consisting of astral body with the passions and desires, can and does communicate with the living, whether a medium or not. This is exactly the danger of mediumship, of suicide, and of legal murder or execution of criminals. The last is a very great danger—one of the unseen but powerful curses of the times. An executed criminal's death is the same as that of one who is accidentally killed in effect, only that it is deliberately done, and in most cases the elements of hate, revenge, and anger in the criminal are added. His fierce and angry personality—compound of astral body and Kâma—is thrust suddenly out of life; his higher principles wait in upper Kâma-Loka in a benumbed or torpid state; but his personal life flits about the abodes of men, attempting to get revenge or to do other wicked things, and every day injects into the sensitive human natures it meets all its mass of vile and unappeasable thoughts. It thus creates picture after picture of murder and hate. Mediums are not the only ones affected by these astral personages; indeed, they are often too closely associated with other sorts of shells, and the personality of the criminal has definite attractions towards other persons. Is it any wonder, then, that the Theosophist who has worked out our doctrines of man's nature to their proper conclusions should deplore the custom of executing criminals? He knows that one legal execution may and nearly always does lead to many another sudden murder or suicide. And as the astral personalities of suicides and executed criminals are in closer touch with us than any other sort of spook, it follows that they also are more likely to come first to any Spiritualistic *séance*. All those who respect the suggestions of H. P. B. will be interested to know that the above was her own view, often given to me, and further certified as reasonable by Adepts who can see the facts behind the scenes.

QUESTION 193

In "The Secret Doctrine," Vol. I, among the remarks upon sentiency of matter and force, I find this statement—"This consciousness has no relation to our consciousness." Now as all knowledge is the result of comparison, and our "consciousness" being at one and the same time the cause and instrument of knowledge, as acts the process of obtainment and knowledge itself, why does "The Secret Doctrine" make affirmations, the data of thought or knowledge being absent?

W. Q. J.—The statement made by H. P. B. as above is a copy of that made by her teachers called "Masters" by her. These are supposed to know the facts they give. Whether the claim be true or not, it is evident that insects have a consciousness which is different from ours, as we seem to add the element which makes ours "self-consciousness." And when H. P. B. spoke of our consciousness it is very plain she meant the ordinary sort and not the extraordinary. If the questioner will reflect that she has no comprehension of the consciousness of elemental spirits—which yet do actually exist and function in their own sphere —she may see that there may be varieties of consciousness not ours as yet.

QUESTION 194

In Forum No. 37 [Ques. 180] Mr. Judge asserts that "Metaphysical Healers have stumbled unknowingly on a great law." Now as I have been, and am still, possessed with the idea that each individual is herself alone conscious of her conscious efforts to obtain knowledge of principles and laws, I shall esteem it a favor if Mr. Judge will explain the principle by which he determines the fact that others, knowingly or unknowingly, find truth.

W.Q.J.—I do not claim that there is some "principle by which I determine that others knowingly or unknowingly find truth." I merely state the fact that in my opinion the healers spoken of have stumbled on *a* law. I did not nor do I now state what that law is. If they know what law I mean, then they need no information from me. But I do not agree that the questioner is right in saying that "each individual alone is conscious of her (why *her* and not *his* also) conscious efforts," since I have for many years known that other individuals may also at the same time be fully aware of these "conscious efforts" by others. I know —in a way I am not obliged to detail—that the members of our Great Lodge have full information, unknown to those outside the Lodge, of the "conscious efforts to obtain knowledge of principles and laws" on the part of good men and women, and in this search that help is frequently extended but is not seen nor recognized, although it is felt and has results. But I am wholly at a loss to see any sequence whatever between the premise of the question and the question itself. The healers have hit upon a law, but they fail as yet to know it fully, and I for one should be sorry that they knew it all until they show to my limited understanding that they are philosophically fitted to have complete possession of a very dangerous force. However, if the march of cyclic evolution decrees that people should find edged tools to play with and cut themselves withal, I am too puny to be able to prevent it. But each day more proof is offered that H. P. B. was right when she wrote to the American Section that powers were surely coming forth in this people, and that efforts must be made to provide a new soil for them to grow in instead of our present selfish, greedy, and individualized but uncivilized human nature, from which of course I claim no exemption.

QUESTION 196

Do earthly friends recognize one another during their passage through Kâma-Loka? If so, who or what is the recognizer.

W. Q. J.—Kâma-Loka being a state and not a place, there is no passage through it. No doubt in some cases, if two beings are in the Kâma-Loka state at the same time, and for similar reasons, and with the same magnetic currents, they may recognize each other. But as Kâma-Loka is the state in which the Soul is freeing itself from the astral body and the passions and desires, it cannot with ease be concerned with any other process than that one; and hence, in the sense of the question as put, there is no recognition, although the being has what it may suppose to be a recognition of friends and enemies. In Kâma-Loka all its old thoughts take shape, and torment the soul if the life has been evil, or merely temporarily detain it if the opposite has been the case.

QUESTION 197

How can a soul be lost?

W. Q. J.—A great deal depends here upon the emphasis to be put on these words. If upon the word "how," then the process of loss is desired to be explained; if upon the word "can," or the rest of the question, then there is an implied doubt as to the possibility of loss of soul. I do not know which question this is intended to be.

If we consider the matter from the Buddhist side, we may briefly sum it up. The soul is a composite thing (or entity) and therefore not necessarily permanent. Hence it may be destroyed. It is that which has in it the potentiality of immortality. To put it another way: There are body, soul, spirit. Of these three, spirit alone is immortal. Body we know is quickly proved to be impermanent and destructible. Soul is that which lying between body and spirit is the connecting bond. If the course of our many lives be persistently wicked, then at last the soul no longer can remain as such but is resolved into its original elements, becomes a part of unconscious nature, to coin a phrase, and no longer acts as the connecting bond. Now the very question raised implies that it is really spirit which causes it to be asked,[1] for it cannot be body that loses soul nor soul that loses itself. This is approaching a great mystery which I am not capable of dealing with. All one can say is that the Monad—spirit—for its own purposes selects this connecting bond called soul, giving it thereby the chance to become consciously joined with spirit. If soul refuses to so join, there occurs what is called "loss of soul."

This soul so selected by spirit—I omit the article "the," since Spirit is one and not multiple—has a so-called immortality, so considered because its term of life as such is said to last through a whole manvantara, which is a period so inconceivably long that for our mind it is eternal. But it has an end in fact, and if by the close of that immense period the soul has not effected union with spirit, then the loss or destruction of soul as such takes place. Meanwhile during the manvantara the soul migrates from body to body and world to world in the eternal struggle to reach reunion with the divine. But such union may be attained long ages before the end of the manvantara by dispassion, discipline, and effort unremittingly continued.

QUESTION 198

In his reply to Question 180 Mr. Judge affirms the sole requisite for occult feats to be the exercise of imagination raised to high intensity by cultivation, and refers to the Indian fakir who makes one see snakes, etc. because through centuries of heredity and years of training his

---

[1] [Lost?]

*imagination sees the form so vividly that the bystander supposes him-
self to see an objective reality, though none exists. Now if occult feats
consist in immediate formation in gross matter, and not only the means
of these feats but the processes by which these means are obtained are
in all instances the same, how is it possible for the fakir to fail in producing objective reality, while the feat of the Adept is a successful materialization? For since the function of a knife is to cut, it will perform
that function irrespective of the hand which holds it.*

W.Q.J.—I certainly never intended to say "the sole requisite for occult feats to be the exercise of the imagination raised to high intensity
by high cultivation," and a careful reference to my reply to Question
180 ought to show that I stated the above to be but *one* of the requisites.
It is one of the absolutely necessary requisites to the performance of
those feats I had in mind, and they include the greater number. But
while it is an absolute prerequisite, there are other things and requisites
to be taken into account if one is to perform certain feats. Any hypnotic experiment or effect needs only this *image-making power* joined
with strong will to concentrate the image. But where more difficult
performances are to be accomplished, such as apportation of solid objects, precipitation upon paper, condensation of image so as to make
it actually tangible, or controlling elementals, then there has to be
added a knowledge of chemical, electrical, and magnetic substances
and laws, together with will and high mathematics. For if the imagining
power is weak, there is no possibility of forming the currents to work
upon nor a matrix for certain occult chemical work. Having, then, thus
declared other "requisites for occult feats," it seems that the rest of
the question must fall to the ground or be considered from other points.
A "knife with a cutting function" will not cut unless some hand not
only holds but also wields it. Nor do I see how a good trained, wonder-
working fakir should fail to produce an objective reality if he so desired and carried his occult operation far enough for the purpose. And
as, indeed, I have seen fakirs do this very thing, I cannot deny what
I know has been accomplished.

QUESTION 203

*The more I think of it, the greater mystery this appears to me. If we
are reincarnated either for better development or for punishment for
sins committed in a former incarnation, why should there be so many
infants who only live a few days or weeks? They go out of the body
again without being advanced any, nor do they suffer a great deal.*

W.Q.J.—Mysteries will deepen for the questioner if he lays down
definitely that any one statement of a part of a Theosophical doctrine
is necessarily the whole doctrine. In the question it is assumed we are

incarnated only *for better development or for punishment,* whereas this is but a partial view of the matter. We are reincarnated as a *result of causes set in motion.* Thus we may be here for reward, or punishment, or by choice, or merely to work again, or for pleasure, or for punishment of others or their discipline, or for our own discipline, and so on for a thousand purposes. The race evolution compels us to reincarnate, and we do so according to law. The first answer fully explains most of this, but still another view is possible. Looked at from the side of the parents, the birth and early death of the infant are at once a pleasure, a discipline, and a punishment. If the loss is properly accepted, then discipline results; if rebelled against, then only punishment is felt; the pleasure and reward came with the child's birth, and though soon the cause of that pleasure disappeared, its possible effect on father and mother was not destroyed. Then, again, the Ego that attempted to begin life in that family only to quickly fall out of it may have either made a short step toward better environments than it had before, or escaped from a family where nothing save obstacles and evils would have surrounded. By such reflections as these the "mysteries" will be made plain.

QUESTION 205

Did Swedenborg's visions extend to the Devachanic loka, or were they entirely confined to the astral plane defined as Kâma-Loka?

W.Q.J.—Without doubt his visions often touched the Devachanic state of other egos, and also too he went into a Devachanic state almost completely for himself while living. But it is not a proper use of "loka" to apply it to Devachan, as here the latter describes a more metaphysical state, while Kâma-Loka is still quite physical. Swedenborg had visions in Kâma-Loka, as can be easily seen in his books; but he also saw facts of earth life. His heavens were the different Devachanic states—of himself and others—into which he went. Many mediums, seers, and clairvoyants have done the same and are doing it every day. In some cases Swedenborg partook of the Devachanic thoughts of highly developed Egos, but as Devachan is as much a delusion as are Kâma-Loka and Earth life, his visions are not of the highest value.

QUESTION 206

It is the duty of every one to help in represssing criminals, or is the bringing to light of unknown crimes a cause of inducing avoidable Karma on the head of the revealer? In other words, when a man knows of a crime or a criminal, is it his duty to give warning to humanity; or, from the point of view of Karma, is it better to treat the thing with

mercy and act on the principle "Qu'il aille se faire pendre ailleurs."[1]
trusting to the criminal's own Karma to warn society?

W.Q.J.—In a proper social organization the King or Ruler should be the final protection against all troubles from criminals within or assaults from without. But such an organization does not exist with us. The citizen should therefore act up to his duty without thinking of *his* Karma, because he cannot have a Karma which his fellow citizens do not share with him. So, if he knows of a crime to be committed, he should warn. A crime past he may have some connection with compelling denunciation, but with others he may not. The man who expends energy to denounce criminals when his particular duty does not require it wastes and scatters nature's forces and does no good. And general rules do not settle these particular cases. The hunting and catching of criminals is the duty of the final protector, and not that of the single citizen.

QUESTION 208

Are misfortune, accident, physical deformity, etc., due to Karmic causes?

W.Q.J.—And to add, the indissoluble unity of the race demands that we should consider every man's troubles as partly due to ourselves, because we have been always units in the race and helped to make the conditions which cause suffering.

QUESTION 209

As I understand it, the astral body is first formed, and around it is built the physical body, its vehicle. The astral changes but slightly during life. The physical body is constantly changing, and is renewed about once in seven years. Why do we grow old physically?

W.Q.J.—The premises laid down answer the question exactly. For that which is made up of component parts must come to an end: the combination must wear out; such is experience; that which changes cannot endure. All bodies, in whatever sphere, change and disappear. "Growing old " is only a term which describes the ossification of tissue, the wearing out of the physical cohesive force. For a reality the body does not grow old, since it is made of matter up to its last moment, and after death it changes into still live matter, young again and divided into elements. But when the inner forces reach their limit the body can work no longer, and hence men invented the expression "old."

---

1 ["Let him go elsewhere to get himself hanged."—*Comp.*]

QUESTION 210

Theosophy holds God to be One and eternal—Absoluteness itself. The Bible says that man was made in the image of God. Man we understand to be composed of seven principles—a union of the three higher, the immortal, principles with the four lower, those which disintegrate and go back to the dust. Are not all these principles, or parts, which are found in man, found also in God? I ask because some teach "Nothing is but Spirit." Matter seems to me to be one aspect of Spirit. It comes from something and goes back to its place, and there is no place outside of God.

W.Q.J.—I have not the hardihood, as the Editor has, to affirm in one breath that we must not speculate on the Infinite, and in the next to give attributes to the Infinite, such as immanency in all things, separability from us, and the like, and, taking his advice to confine ourselves to common-sense and what we can know, I waive the discussion on the question of the Absolute or an infinite God. It is hopeless. The quotation in the question proceeds in use therein upon the assumption of a God who can be understood and described either directly or by analogy or contrast. This is wholly beyond me. But I am quite willing to repeat that the Teachers whom I follow say that the Absolute exists and cannot be discovered nor known; that at the dawning of what is commonly called creation and evolution Spirit and Matter appear in space. This I accept, for it fits in with the logic of the rest of the doctrine. They call this the first differentiation. The assertion—made chiefly by the schools of mind-cure—assumes that spirit only is, but cannot explain nor justify the assumption, which is only, indeed, for the purpose of founding other assertions regarding mere bodily ills of no great consequence except to the weak or those devoted to material enjoyments. It is further taught and seemingly with reason that, in all, seven cosmic differentiations take place, and from these the sevenfold constitution of man is derived. His gross body stands for the whole of gross matter, his astral body for another differentiation, his passions for the energy of the heterogeneous cosmos, his life copies another of the seven, and so on until all are complete. But if you postulate a God, you must put man either in him or outside; and if the latter then your God is not infinite, but has in his universe something that is not himself—for the Infinite must be all. It is much safer to construe these Bible verses in the old Theosophical way, which would in the present instance show that man is made in the image of his God, who is his Higher Self. If the other position is adopted, that of postulating a God and giving him any attributes whatever, then your mind can have no possibility of reaching a conclusion save by the arguments and distinctions made by the schoolmen of Europe and the disputing theologians of India—and that conclusion may temporarily, say for one life, satisfy you, but it will remain false. It belongs to the great number of the illusions of matter which are ever deluding the mind of man.

QUESTION 211

Since the time spent in physical life is the time of actual progress and the time spent in Devachan is merely a time of rest, or, at most, digestion, why should the law of evolution require such a vast disproportion of time to be wasted in Devachan—a disproportion of something like eight thousand years of rest to less than one hundred years of work?

W.Q.J.—The general proportion as I have always known of it between earth life and Devachan is that between 70 years of life and 1500 years in Devachan. Further it is known that many persons emerge from the Devachanic state very soon after entering it. A reflection on the fact that the years of our life are full of thoughts attached in vast numbers to every single act will show why Devachan is so much longer than earth-life. The disproportion between the act done and the thoughts intimately belonging to it is enormous, and, compared with Devachan as related to earth-life, it is vast. In Devachan these thoughts, which could never find but the very smallest fraction of expression in this life, must exhaust and can be exhausted nowhere else. This is what is required, not by evolution, but by thought itself. And those who have but little aspiration here, who indulge in act more than thought, lay but little basis for Devachan, and hence emerge from it sooner than others.

QUESTION 213

Can an Adept who has never studied music, but who has the wonderful powers (to us, omnipotent) ascribed to him by Theosophical books, go to a piano for the first time and play one of Beethoven's symphonies? There has been a debate upon this point with unsatisfactory conclusions.

W.Q.J.—The question discloses in its concluding words that some persons, presumably Theosophists, have wasted valuable time in a debate upon a point wholly trivial just now. What possible use to the Society or to Humanity would this debate upon pianos and Adepts have or even lead to? None that I can see. It is like wasting time and energy in destroying Nature's works. And I would like to ask if the debaters on this matter have such a knowledge of the doctrines of Karma, Reincarnation, and the Sevenfold Constitution as to be able to impart them to anxious inquirers. If not, then the debate on the pianos and Adepts was time worse than wasted.

The piano is a false instrument with an entirely false scale, as all musicians know. It is therefore perfectly mechanical. Yet we see that

Blind Tom from birth almost can use this mechanical false instrument. Therefore the playing of it by him brings up the question of the power of co-ordination between an ordinary brain and body and mind. If the querents know something of those questions first and foremost, then they will be qualified to see how an Adept might play a piano although never in this life having learned to do so. This enters deeply into the nature of man's sevenfold constitution. For if uneducated Blind Tom could do it, why not an Adept? And if this be so, how can an Adept do so? I affirm my thorough belief that an Adept—of the degree evidently in view in the question—can do all and more than the question asks. For by the aid of elemental forces he could play on the piano in this century even if he had never, in any incarnation, seen or heard of one. But having replied in the affirmative, what good does the reply do unless it is in a discussion regularly and intelligently pursued upon those doctrines, the truth of which must be shown before one passes to a discussion of trivialities?

QUESTION 216

Is the sinful nature of man located in the reincarnating Ego or in the perishable personality? If in the former, what becomes of the teaching that nothing but what is good enters Devachan? If in the latter, how is it just to punish one perishable personality for the faults which another perished personality committed centuries ago?

W.Q.J.—The Ego is deluded by ignorance, and hence incarnates and reincarnates in various states; that is, it obtains a vehicle for every state into which ignorance puts it. So it obtains an earthly vehicle (body and personality) which is delusive and binding on the Ego so long as ignorance of the truth continues. It leaves the earthly vehicle and goes to another state—Devachan—where it has a vehicle appropriate to that sphere, and is there deluded and retained by the ignorance which is related wholly to pure, noble, and pleasant thoughts. From that it comes again to the earthly sphere, and so on until the hour when ignorance is destroyed. The so-called "sinful nature" is in the earthly vehicle, but as that is a part of the whole which includes the Ego, the latter is responsible for permitting the lower to rule it, and therefore suffers. For the body and astral body do not suffer nor know nor feel; they are merely blind instruments for the Ego who knows and feels through them, and are also the weights and clogs which keep the Ego down so long as ignorance prevails. Hence the continual revolving from one sphere to another, and in this is the reply to the question.

QUESTION 217

In the "Seven Principles of Man" by Mrs. Besant, on pages 1 and 14, she says, "Many of the movements of objects that occur at such séances and at other times, without visible contact, are due to the action of the Linga-Śarîra [the etheric double] and the student can learn how to produce such phenomena at will. They are trivial enough: the mere putting out of the astral [etheric] hand is no more important than the putting out of the dense counterpart and neither more nor less miraculous."[1] Now I want to know how an astral hand can lift a physical book, for instance. Not that I doubt the fact, but I want the philosophical explanation.

W. Q. J.—It may be added to the foregoing very good reply that by considering weight and gravity to be in fact the working of negative and positive poles, to be really the result of attraction and repulsion, we may see how an astral hand can move a book. The book has no real weight of its own for if taken to the top of a very high mountain it will not weigh the same as at the bottom. Alter the polarity of the book, and at once it may become as light as a feather. Alter the relation between the largest or the smallest object and the earth immediately under it, and it may be either greatly increased in weight or deprived of all weight. It is under this law that the lightning often carries heavy bodies great distances,—yet that fluid is imponderable. Now in the case in point the book might be depolarized as one way of taking it from its place. If this process were not used, then the astral hand has to be made dense and compact enough to lift it, but always when the astral hand approaches any object that object is immediately depolarized to a great extent because the astral hand has the natural power to effect this result; hence a very great density of the astral member is not required. But when Mrs. Besant called this trivial, she meant that it is not an important matter, although it may not be trivial as an act or occurrence.

QUESTION 219

I often read the assertion that we come back to earth with our former friends and companions, and that this is a reason for having only agreeable relations with all we meet, because otherwise they might retaliate and harm us. Do all people who are on earth at one time come back together?

W. Q. J.—In answering this question every department of Occultism as well as all fundamental theosophical doctrines have to be kept in view; how, then, clearly and succinctly reply in these short papers? To the Adepts we must turn, because science and records are dumb, with the question about the number of times the Monads now in human

---

1 [Revised and corrected edition of 1902, Theosophical Publishing Society, London.—*Compiler.*]

bodies have reincarnated and since when have new Monads ceased arriving into the human stage? For if there is a definite number to the Monads and if Monads in our human stage have ceased coming in or arriving at that stage some ages since, then the question is not so easily disposed of as would appear, by references to the resemblance between cold coffee and Karma. Karma is subtle, ceaseless, relentless, and not subject to cooling; cold coffee is something so entirely different that even for illustration it is of no utility. Quoting the Adepts, H. P. B. writes in *The Secret Doctrine*[1]—just as anyone might expect from the use of reason—that the number of Monads is definite in this system of worlds, and, secondly, that the door to the human kingdom has been closed for many thousands of years, that is, at the middle of the Fourth Round. Hence the reincarnating human Egos have all met now over and over again with the certainty with every century of all meeting each other more and still more times. There is no escape. The door being closed and the human Egos having been numbered since the middle of the Fourth Round, they meet with increasing frequency because no new acquaintances can come forward from either lower kingdoms or other spheres. This therefore establishes the probability of encountering at almost every turn Egos whom we have been with before in lives on earth.

The Editor assumes that time will use up the Karmic effects of our acts. Time has no such effect *per se* (as it has on cold coffee); the Karma will not act until the time comes when the Egos connected with it meet in life; until then it is inactive. For this reason the man you abused 10,000 years ago will react upon you when you and he meet, and this meeting will happen, for action and reaction will draw you into reincarnation together. Nor can I understand why the Editor also assumes the likelihood of enmities not being carried over while he thinks likes and affections are. There seems no difference to me between these two—likes and dislikes—as to the carrying over. It is true he used his words in respect to "coming back together"; but any person whom we meet, intimately or casually, in family or out of it, has "come back" to reincarnation with us. And from my knowledge of human nature the conclusion is forced on me that enmity has the stronger hold on man, and the presumption is enormous when we observe such an enmity as that described—exceptionally strong—that its roots lie in another life.

There is no safe ground in calculations about Devachan and rebirth based upon the times when people die after or before one another, because each rebirth has power to so immensely alter the forces that A, who died 200 years before B, a friend of two lives back, may emerge into rebirth exactly with B, in time, because of the effects and causes

---

[1] [Vol. I, pp. 171-73.]

produced and generated by B in the intervening lives. And so on indefinitely. They may swing off again and be separated for many, many lives. If it were all an iron-bound rule and dependent on man's free will and mental action, it would be easy to calculate. But as it depends on his mental action, and as each rebirth throws the Ego into the line of probability of meeting one who will alter his course of thought, no one can safely say when they will meet again any Ego they have ever met before.

Every inimical and uncharitable thought makes for disunion, and every opposite one for harmony. The skandhas are full of all the impressions we received; those skandhas wait and are ours again when we emerge from Devachan. If we meet those Egos who are related to our good or evil, charitable or uncharitable thoughts, the force acts at once—not before—and unless the man we injured, condemned, or filled with anger meets us in next life or the one after, or whenever, we have to await his return with us (and that does not mean in family, it means wherever he can act on us) before we can tell whether he will repay in kind. If he has not become a saint meanwhile, he will at once be the cause of our hurt for hurt received, of benefit for benefit. These laws act through us with automatic regularity until we know them and bring up counteractions. And the value of it all is, that we know if we treat all men now with unfailing charity and love we are wiping off old scores clean and making no new sorrows; but if we will condemn, punish, resent, in short, consider ourselves Karmic agents without knowing the meaning of that term, we are sowing dragons' teeth, we only are planting cause for future sorrow.

QUESTION 220

On page 175, Vol. I, of "The Secret Doctrine" there are the words " . . . from the 'mineral' monad up to the time when that monad blossoms forth by evolution into the DIVINE MONAD," while on page 178 it is said that "It would be very misleading to imagine a Monad as a separate Entity trailing its slow way in a distinct path through the lower Kingdoms, and, after an incalculable series of transformations, flowering into a human being." These passages seem a flat contradiction.

W. Q. J.—The passages quoted are not a contradiction. In reading this book, just as in reading any serious book, all the passages must be taken together and construed together and not separately. Now H. P. B. definitely explains that in using the terms "Mineral monad, vegetable monad, and animal monad," and so on, the same monad is always meant, the qualifying word simply designating the particular kingdom in which the monad is at work. And if you will reflect a moment, the word "monad" precludes any other construction—since monad means one. The very quotation at page 178 which you give agrees with what I say, because she is there stating that it would be misleading to suppose that a monad is a separate entity which makes its way through the lower kingdoms and then instantly becomes a human being. No such thing as this is a fact, nor is it stated, although if you read these pages hurriedly or carelessly you may think that the statement is made. For when the monad reaches the human stage it is the same monad which was once in the mineral stage, meaning that the monad is necessary to each kingdom, and what we call the human monad is simply the unchangeable monad now functioning in bodies called human which are of a higher capacity for experience and cognition than the bodies of the lower kingdoms. A mineral is as much a body as a human body is. And as Dr. Archibald Keightley says today, the second passage you quote explains the first, and in many parts of *The Secret Doctrine* it is shown that the monad manifested in any department of nature has to be designated by some name which indicates the particular kingdom in which it is manifesting; but this does not alter its character. All men are "men," but we are in the habit of saying "Englishmen," "Chinamen," "Fiji men," "African men." Are these all human beings or are they not? The particular qualifying title given to each simply designates the variety of man, and the particular qualifying title given to the monad simply designates the particular department of nature in which the monad is incarnating and at work. I think these will show you the necessity for very careful reading and thinking while you read on subjects such as these, since they are new to our thought.

QUESTION 221

What would be the correct name for that "thing" which can be conscious of the physical body, feeling hunger, thirst, the pain of a cut or blow, then go to the state of Kâma and feel passion and emotion, or enter into a state of mentality and act on the plane of thought?

W. Q. J.—Read the chapter of the *Bhagavad-Gîtâ** which treats of Kshetra and Kshetrajña, or the Knower and the Known, as also those which describe the three qualities, their action and function. Your question deals with consciousness, and no one has yet been able to finish its definition. The Self, who is made up of *Manas-Buddhi-Âtman*, three in one, is the knower and the perceiver. If there were no Self present, all that you have described would be merely motions in *Prâna* or the movement of the three qualities, for it is the Self who enables us to give names, derived from sensation, to these effects. And any name given to the Self, in any language, will be but the attempt of the man to name that which is nameless. In your own remarks under the question you

---

*[Cf. Ch. XIII.]

have skipped from one subject to another, for you began with what relates to the perception of the knower while dwelling in the body, and ended with the essential nature of the monad, an entirely different matter. This confusion of topics will only create confusion in your own mind. There is no benefit from increasing words on the self-perceptive cognition, for all that you can say of it is that you possess the *I am I* consciousness. Hence all that you have said can be resolved by the statement that the consciousness functions in many different planes of experience, and in each one uses the means or instruments appropriate thereto. And in order to so pass from one plane to another, holding intelligence in each, the presence of *Manas* is necessary as one of the integral parts or powers of the Self, for without *Manas* we are only of the brute or lower kingdoms. For one moment consider the brutes who, moving and dwelling in the mental plane with man, know nothing of our mânasic sensations. It is because *Manas* is dormant in them; but in you it has begun to awake, thus enabling you as man to note the effects upon yourself of the motions of the qualities of nature.

QUESTION 222

On page 29 of "What is Theosophy?"[1] Mr. [Walter R.] Old accounts for the existence in arctic regions of the remains of tropical mammalia and vegetation on the theory that the earth's axis was once in the plane of its orbit. Given this position of the axis, it follows that while for half the year the regions mentioned would be in perpetual sunlight, during the other half they would be turned from the sun. Such terrestrial refrigeration would then take place as would destroy every vestige of animal and vegetable life that had not already been burned up in the fiery heat of a nightless tropic. How can the claim of Theosophy that life flourished on the planet under such conditions be supported scientifically?

W. Q. J.—Nearly the whole page of Mr. Old's book quoted from is devoted to showing that the record of the rocks and the discoveries of the men of science prove the claim advanced by Theosophical students. His remarks do not seem to sustain the implication in the question nor to justly provoke it. The facts stated by him—following many who are older than he—that fossil mammalia and tropical vegetation are found in regions now arctic are indisputable. Today you can see in a Russian museum the bones and skin of a gigantic hairy elephant 25 feet high which was cut out of the ice. An imitation of it belongs to the city of San Francisco. He distinctly asks how tropical vegetation and mammalia—such, for instance, as the elephant described by me—could be

---

1 [Published in London by Hay, Nisbet & Co., 1892, 128 pp.]

there in fossilized condition unless the equator at one time was at or near that spot. Theosophy never having made any claim that life in bodies like those of today flourished under impossible conditions, there is really no question left to answer. It is not the province nor duty of the FORUM to go into scientific speculation as to what would happen if the pole of the earth altered so as to be on the equator. Opinions differ, but all agree with the theosophical writers that such an alteration would at once bring on great seismic convulsions. On such changes accruing, life would have to proceed in bodies suitable to such a state of affairs; and that is about all Theosophy has to say on the matter. But as to life itself it points to water, air, and earth to show that anyone who asserts that he knows under what conditions living beings may or may not exist is rash in the extreme. Were we condemned to function in perpetual fire, nature no doubt would provide that sort of covering or body which would be in every way convenient for use in the fiery element but not serviceable in water or ice, and so on for every changed condition or environment, be those physical, astral, or otherwise.

QUESTION 223

Devachan, I understand, is a state and not a locality; but evidently there must be some sort of locality in which the Devachanic state can take place. Is there any information as to the whereabouts of this particular locality?

W. Q. J.—Inasmuch as the doctrine of Devachan is postulated and declared only in respect to the inhabitants of our world, it must follow that those of us who go into that state must keep within the attractive limits of the earth's chain of planets. This would give the "place" in space in which the Ego undergoes Devachanic experience, but as the earth and its "companion globes" are always moving through space, it is evident that this *loka* is moveable. Imagine a huge hollow ball containing the earth and rolling through space. The hollow ball may stand for the attractive limits of the Ego who belongs for the time to the race, and within those limits—fixed in themselves but ever moving in space —the being goes into and remains in the devachanic state. And as there the weight of the physical is not felt nor its density perceived, the Devachanic state may as well be on the earth as anywhere else outside up to the limits of attraction spoken of.

QUESTION 224

Do the physical atoms reincarnate? Personally, I think they do, and I think that an article by H. P. B. in "Five Years of Theosophy" en·

titled "The Transmigration of the Life-atom"[1] furnishes authority for the belief. It would seem that the law of reincarnation acts upon every plane, and that the Ego carries the same atoms through its evolution. But I have found so few to agree with me that I desire the opinion of other Theosophists.

W. Q. J.—The analysis and explanation by the Editor of the word "reincarnation" are undoubtedly correct. The word is often loosely used, indeed sometimes quite unavoidably, because the English has as yet no word to express the recombination of the same atoms on the physical plane. And it is quite possible to imagine a certain number of atoms—this word being also loosely used—being combined in one mass, going out of it and recombining once more. For instance, a mass of quicksilver may be volatilized by heat and thrown into the invisible state, and being kept in the limits of a receiver may be recombined into quicksilver again. While they are vaporized who can say that they are quicksilver, inasmuch as that is the name for a definite thing? Similarly with a mass of water changed into steam and vapor and back to water and then to ice. So, while the Editor is right as to the proper use of the term "reincarnation," the real question put is not solved.

It relates to the greater combinations, permutations, and probabilities of the cosmos, upon which mere argument sheds no light unless it proceeds from the actual facts in respect to atoms or molecules and their method, power, and time of combination. The Adepts know about this, but have only given hints, as we are not yet ready to know. Now *first*, there must be a definite amount of matter in use in our solar system; and *second*, it is definitely stated—and is metaphysically necessary— that there is a definite number of Egos using that quantity of matter. To me there seems to be no improbability and no materialism in supposing that a time may come when any one Ego shall recombine into a body in which it incarnates the exact atoms it once before used, which of course have also been used by other Egos. But when such a cycle of recombination is, I do not know. The Egyptians made it 3000 and 5000 years. It is an idea not of any great use at present, but very interesting, and I find it illustrating for me the idea of universal brotherhood. For if we have all, as Egos, used over and over again the atoms physical which all other Egos have used, we lose all individual property in the atoms and each is common owner of all. I believe, but am unable to prove, that we use over again the atoms we once used in a body, but how many times the great wheel of the solar system allows this permutation and recombination to happen is beyond me and my generation.

---

1 [See BCW, 1883, Vol. V, pp. 109-17; or *"Five Years of Theosophy"* pp. 531-39; London, 1885 ed. It was originally printed in *The Theosophist*, Vol. IV, No. 11 (47) August, 1883, pp. 286-88.—*Compiler.*]

QUESTION 225

Do Theosophists know of the previous incarnation of H. P. B. and can they identify her with any historical personage?

W. Q. J.—Speculation on such personal matters was always very distasteful to H. P. B., and from my own knowledge, backed by that of several men who have advanced far on the path of knowledge, I can say that the soul known to us as H. P. B. was and is so far in front of this race that it is mere idle talk for us to connect her real self with an aunt in her family or with a Hindu or other woman. Furthermore I know from her own lips that she cared not whether she was in male or female body, but took that body (regardless of sex) which would enable her to do the most work; and also she said that, given the power to control a female incarnation and all that that implies, more could now be done in such than in the male form, but such control and ability were impossible for the general run of people, and solely for the latter reason would she—if unable to control—prefer a male incarnation. I know also that she often smiled at the petty personality and feeble notions that lead us weak mortals to desire either male or female bodies for our next rebirth. She had other matters on hand, and was too great inside to be understood by those who have claimed to know her so well, and from this I except no one, not even Col Olcott who knew her so many years.

QUESTION 227

In reading "Esoteric Buddhism" I was much struck with what was said in the chapter entitled "The Progress of Humanity"[1] about the sort of Rubicon in the middle of the 5th Round, beyond which point no entity can go unless he has previously reached a certain definite degree of spiritual development, all not reaching this degree of evolution becoming unconscious until the next Planetary Manvantara. I remember nothing in H. P. B.'s writings to confirm this statement, yet it is very positive and clear. Is it one of the points, like the "Eighth Sphere," where Mr. Sinnett drew upon his imagination, making wrong deductions from true but insufficient premises?

W. Q. J.—This is not one of the points in which Mr. Sinnett erred. All through *The Secret Doctrine* this is taught, though not perhaps so definitely. The race as yet has not fully evolved *Manas*—the 5th principle—and will not until the next round. For that reason it cannot, as a race, make a fully intelligent choice. But each man's life now is important, inasmuch as in it he is either sowing seeds or weeds or wheat. If weeds, they may grow so as to choke all the rest; if wheat, then

---

1 [pp. 188-208, Boston & N.Y., 1884 ed.]

when the time for the great reaping comes he will be able to choose right. Those who deliberately in the 5th round make a choice for evil will be annihilated as far as their souls are concerned; those who drift along and never choose right or wrong, but are whirled off to the indifferent side, will go into that state Mr. Sinnett describes until the next Manvantara, while the consciously wicked who deliberately choose wrong will have no place whatever. In a smaller degree it is the same for each man in every life or series of lives; for we are setting up tendencies in one direction or the other, and thus in the end compel ourselves to make very disagreeable choices for next life. And man's little life is a copy in miniature of the greater life included under the word *Manvantara*. If the system in respect to the human Ego is understood the cosmic system can be grasped, as it is the same, only enlarged.

QUESTION 229

The most authoritative books on Theosophy teach that the monad passes up through the lower kingdoms to the animal and then to the human, and yet also teach that man appeared before the animals. If the latter is true, how can the former be?

W. Q. J.—If after the word "animal" we insert the words "in this round," then both statements will be correct and there will be no confusion. On this matter we have to accept or to reject the teachings of those Adepts who gave the system out through H. P. Blavatsky, for modern science knows nothing about the matter and believes still less. Now if anything is plainly taught and reiterated over and over again in *The Secret Doctrine*, it is that the time of the appearing here of the human form alters after the second round of the life-wave in the earth's chain.

The teaching that the monad passes through the lower kingdoms from metals up to man is right as a general statement, for it is alleged to be the fact and is also in accord with reasoning from the other premises of Theosophical doctrine. But on this chain of globes the stream of monads of all stages begins in the first two rounds—the whole number of rounds being seven—by going steadily through the lower orders up to man as the last form and stage for those rounds. In the third round the plan alters, because the first class of monads has obtained in prior rounds enough knowledge to be able to emerge into the form of man ahead of the lower classes who are yet at that time in the lower kingdoms of nature. And in the fourth round, which is the one we are in now, Man as we know him appears before the others just because the monads of that class of progress have the power, and in this round all the lower kingdoms in respect to their outer coating of materiality get all that coating from what man casts off. This is also clearly taught and not an inference of mine.

The first rounds had in them the potentiality of the rest, and as it was the fate or the law that materiality should prevail in this round, it was prepared for by the most advanced class of monads. All this does not negative the standing and general rule that the monad must (at some point in its career) go through all the kingdoms in regular order from the lowest to the highest, and must follow that line for whatever is the necessary period from the lowest first and not skip any; but when the class of monads which came into this evolution first has obtained the right knowledge and power, it will then alter its rule and come in with the fourth round as first of all. In our own life on earth as individuals we do the same thing, for some of us are able to skip over in some life that which others have to painfully acquire; and this is because reincarnation and previous experience enable us to do it. The same rule holds in the greater scheme, and there by reason of reincarnation and experience in the first two rounds the monads of that class are first as human beings, and not last in the fourth round. Meanwhile the general rule governs other and lower classes of monads, who are even now slowly creeping through lower kingdoms of nature and have been unable to emerge with man in this round ahead of the other forms. But in future rounds and manvantaras they also will come in ahead of the lower orders of nature. Let those of us who accept the statements of the Masters remember that they have certified in writing that *The Secret Doctrine* is the triple production of those two great beings and H. P. Blavatsky. Such a certificate they have given of no other book. Their certificate will not be accepted by outsiders nor by that small class of Theosophists who loudly proclaim they will accept nothing that does not accord with their reason; but one is puzzled to know how their reason can work in respect to matters such as these about which the Adepts alone know the truth. As for myself, I find the teaching quite consistent with the whole of the philosophy and explanatory of natural facts; for the rest I am willing to believe the parts I cannot yet verify and to wait a little longer.

QUESTION 230

In "The Secret Doctrine," Vol. I, p. 15, H.P.B. says: "This Infinite and Eternal Cause . . . is the rootless root of 'all that was, is, or ever shall be.' It is of course devoid of all attributes and is essentially without any relation to manifested, finite being." H.P.B. repeats the state·ment in other places in her works, and it has been a constant puzzle, for I cannot understand how It can be without relation to manifested being and at the same time be the root, however rootless, of all that was, is, or ever shall be. To my mind the essential idea of "root" is relation, and, as the word is used in the text, the ultimate of all relativity is reached.

W.Q.J.—I may use the laconic style of the Editor and reply: You are wrong. Not wrong in being puzzled, for that is evident, just as it is a fact that the quotation you make is *not* on page 15 of *The Secret Doctrine*, Vol. I, but is found on p. 14. A little matter you think this error. Yes, but in high metaphysics little errors assume immense proportion, and the mistake as to the page will show liability to the other mistake of not looking into the whole subject. Only a few lines above the words quoted, H.P.B., defining a highly abstruse metaphysical position, lays down the proposition that there is "an Omnipresent, Eternal, Boundless, and Immutable PRINCIPLE on which all speculation is impossible." This is the "Rootless Root" spoken of. Its nature cannot be speculated on, although we may say IT IS, for we have to start from that. Necessarily it is out of relation to manifested things, since relativity begins only upon manifestation. You can perhaps say that this Rootless Root is potential of all things, but not that it is related. The "Rootless Root" is only a means of stating in convenient form what is said in the larger sentence I have quoted, and not to permit disputes as to relativity because of the meaning of "root." That such is H.P.B.'s meaning—in which she agrees with many old philosophers as well as some modern ones—is very clear indeed, for but four lines above the place where you culled your quotation she asks you to remember that this Principle "antecedes all manifested conditioned being." But long and wordy speculations avail nothing, and unless you take the time to saturate your mind with metaphysics and the relative terminology which every philosophy is compelled to use—especially English—in speaking of things and ideas not relative, and become familiar with time and place for seeing a new meaning in words so materialistic as ours, you will always be puzzled. The word "spirit" is used in English in reference to God, to Man's Soul, to Man's nervous currents, to elementals, to astral shells, to mere alcohol, and to describe simply a quality of an act, all these running up and down the gamut from most gross to highest spirit. Is it to be wondered at that you and the Editor found a difficulty in the question? In Sanskrit you would find no such difficulty.

QUESTION 232

I have seen (I think in "The Path") that Buddha orders his disciples not to have anything to do with music nor to live by it, though in many works on Theosophy music is represented as having a civilizing effect. Can you say why Buddha condemned music and those who practiced it? Is it because it is time wasted and prevents meditation?

W.Q.J.—It would be well to consult references before stating premises on which questions are put. I do not remember any statement in *The Path* of that kind quoted. Secondly, it is quite important to know what sort of music Buddha referred to when he prohibited it—if he did so. It is more than probable that good organs were not then in use. Can we say that he would have prohibited those? Again, we do not know to what school of music he adverted. Was it sensuous, or sensual, or trifling, or what? All this is important, for supposing the music of that day was of a highly sensuous or sensual style, he would have been perfectly right in ordering his disciples to give it no attention. So first I conclude that there is no way of answering the question properly until we have exact knowledge of the styles and schools of music of Buddha's time, as well as of the kinds of instruments in use. So far as my recollection extends, Buddha did not condemn those who practiced music.

But having looked at the purely instrumental and objective side of the matter, we come to the real question on which Buddha, like all other great teachers, laid stress. It is found not only in his words but in the older Brahmanical religion. It is the direction to the student— not to the man of the world—to leave off sight and sound, meaning that unless *sensation* is overcome the mind will be bound to rebirth. This will include music and all sounds. It covers a large subject relating to how and by what the soul is attached to the miseries of rebirth, but it has very little to do with the music to which the questioner refers.

QUESTION 234

What in Theosophy is regarded as having been the original cause of the "obscuration of the effulgence of the mysterious Being of Tathâgata"?

W.Q.J.—The Being of Tathâgata is the Being of Buddha. It is a mystical statement made by Orientals of the doctrine that the Divine Man, the Higher-Self of the Universe, has been obscured by its "descent into matter." For they hold that all Buddhas throughout eternity are the same, and that the Highest nature of Man is the same as the Buddha. Hence this sentence is only a statement that the original effulgence or glory radiated by the Highest Self becomes temporarily obscured by dwelling in matter during evolution; but that effulgence will be restored and shine again at the end of the seventh Round because then matter will have been altered and refined by the indwelling effulgent Buddha. But such quotations as that in the question should never be given without the context in which they occur.

QUESTION 244

Does an individual when acting as an agent for Karma entail any Karmic consequences upon himself because of the acts thus committed?

W.Q.J.—A great many of the things said by the Editor in the foregoing are very good, but I am compelled to differ from him on the main point. And I may say that while the articles "Topics in Karma" are very well written, they do not by any means dispose of the question raised here. In the first place, the questioner assumes in the first ten words of the question that a human being sometimes is not an agent of Karma. According to my studies, and as I think inevitable according to the law of Karma, there is no time when a human being is not an agent of Karma, for in every act and thought we are carrying out Karma, making new Karma, suffering old Karma, or producing effects on other people, or all these together. This is clearly stated by the Editor in the first paragraph of his answer. So I take it that the questioner means to ask whether one is justified in attempting, of his own motion, to administer as judge, jury, and executioner, to another the effects of Karma. This is involved in the question, as well as whether any consequences are entailed upon a person so acting. Now the first paragraph of the Editor's answer stating clearly the law, it must follow that consequences are entailed upon some one in this supposed case of a person making himself a direct Karmic agent. Certainly both the actor in the case and the person to whom the punishment or reward is administered must have consequences entailed upon them, because the "Karmic agent" is the center from which the action flows, and upon whom it must react, and the other person is the person who receives the present consequences. Merely to say to yourself that you are enforcing a right or administering what you conclude is punishment or reward does not absolve you from the consequences, whatever those may be. And those consequences will come to you in two ways. First, through your own attitude, and second, from what you set up in the other person. Involved in the first is a seemingly third possibility, which is, a possible violation by you through ignorance of a law of nature. For instance, if you assume to administer punishment, considering yourself a Karmic agent, it is more than possible that you are simply gratifying some old spite or ill-feeling, under the guise of a judicial enforcement of right or punishment for wrong. We see this possibility every day in those cases where a person, declaring himself to be impartial and judicial, administers on the one hand to persons whom he does not particularly like punishment which he considers their just due, and withholds similar punishment from another person for whom he has such a regard that he fails to administer punishment, but exercises instead forgiveness and charity. This being a common human experience, does it not indicate that inasmuch as a person is through old Karmic likes and affinities led to be kind and charitable through what is called partiality, he may on the other hand, through old dislikes and antipathies, be led by a repulsion to administer punishment, when he might as well have exercised forgiveness? Each man, I think, can be left to himself to decide what is his duty in redressing wrong done to another, which redressing involves perhaps the punishment of a third. But in my opinion no one is wise who considers himself a Karmic agent for any purpose. Further, and overlooked by the Editor and apparently by the questioner, the term "Karmic agent" has a technical significance under which only certain persons are so considered; that is, the larger class of men are not Karmic agents, except in the mere sense that they are in the very act of life making or experiencing Karma in the mass. A few persons are what is known as "Karmic agents," that is, human beings who by a certain course of training and previous life have become concentrated agents for the bringing about of certain definite effects which are well foreseen by the trained and initiated seer. This is one of the declarations of the Initiates who are supposed to know about these matters, and therefore any person assuming to be a Karmic agent may possibly be assuming too much altogether, and be bringing himself within the range of laws which will operate upon him with ten-fold force in future lives. It is therefore more charitable, more wise, more kind, more theosophic to follow the words of Jesus, Buddha, and hosts of other Teachers which direct us to forgive our brother seventy times seven times, which tell us that charity covers a multitude of sins, and which warn us against the self-righteousness that might induce us to presume we have been raised up from the foundation of the world to correct abuses in other men's actions rather than to attend to our own duty.

QUESTION 246

Mr. Mead says on page 26 of September "Lucifer":—"There are two paths which lead to Nirvâna, the selfish and the unselfish, the 'open' and the 'secret'."[1] A man can attain to the knowledge and bliss of the Nirvânic state by keeping the former for his own selfish advantage, and he can gain the latter bliss at the expense of his fellows. I had previously supposed that a life of altruism was absolutely necessary to the attainment of that state. If it can be gained without laboring and suffering for others, and especially if they occupy a higher place, the "Buddhas of Compassion" being "lower in rank," then it would seem that the majority would prefer "their own selfish ad-

---

[1] [Vol. IX. London, September 15, 1891, No. 49. G. R. S. Mead, *The Great Renunciation* pp. 21-26—*Comp.*]

vantage" and act accordingly. We are taught here and now that the more we do for others the more rapidly we advance ourselves. Is this law changed or reversed when one has reached a certain plane of unfoldment?

W.Q.J.—It seems certainly correct for Mr. Mead to say that there are two methods of attaining Nirvâna, one selfish and the other unselfish, but the word selfish here would designate really unselfishness among us. It refers to the refinement of selfishness in that a person is working by unselfish acts to obtain that which, in the end of all analysis, is selfish, because it is for the benefit of the person involved. But it never was taught that a man could obtain Nirvâna by working for his own selfish advantage as his motive, and he does not gain it at the expense of any one; therefore his selfishness in obtaining Nirvâna, being at no one's expense, is of a very different quality from what we ordinarily call selfishness. As a matter of fact it is stated that at a certain point of development the highly spiritualized person may in a moment pass into Nirvâna through an instantaneous personal desire to gain that state.

QUESTION 250

What evidence is there of the existence of any such exalted beings as the Masters or Mahâtmas?

W.Q.J.—Evidence is of several different kinds, and the inquirer should not confine himself to one single department of evidence or testimony. I assume that in using the word "evidence" the questioner means to include testimony as well. There is testimony of very extensive nature of the existence of Masters or Mahâtmas in history and tradition, and these two again divide themselves into many sorts. There is profane as well as religious history, tradition depending on recollection solely, and also tradition which has been turned into an historical account of tradition. In religious history and tradition there are many accounts of such beings, reaching from the earliest known religious book down to the very latest date. And in the history of nations, aside from religion, there are numerous accounts of Adepts, magicians, Masters, and others of like character. In almost every country on the globe the traditions of the people are full of statements of the existence and powers and appearances of master minds, magicians, great men, who knew the secrets of nature. United States history of course is very young and need not be called upon for an answer, but the history of Europe as well as its traditions confirms the statements I have made. Going to Asia we have an immense mass of tradition and history telling the same story, while China and all her dependencies relate similar tales of such beings. In the East everywhere there is a universal belief that they exist, have existed, and will appear again. All this cannot be set aside as folly or useless or insufficient, unless one determines to believe nothing but what he himself has seen. If that position be assumed, then no one living today can say that they know or believe that the historical characters of the past, known to every nation, had any existence. Turning now to later testimony, we have that of H.P.B., A. P. Sinnett, H. S. Olcott, Mrs. Besant, hundreds of Hindus, many Europeans, some Americans, all telling the same story that they know that the Adepts, Masters, Mahâtmas exist and have communicated with or to them. The fact that the inquirer may not have communicated with the Adepts does not dispose of them, nor does it invalidate the testimony of other persons.

Turning from this department of proof we have that which depends upon argument, illustration, deduction. Here everything is as strongly in favor of the existence of the exalted beings spoken of as in the other department; for evolution demands that such beings shall exist. To this conclusion even such a doubter as Prof. Huxley has come, and in his last essays declares for the existence of beings of superior intelligence who are as much beyond us as we are beyond the black beetle, and this is more than any Theosophist has ever yet said for the Adepts. If the questioner proceeds along these lines he will come to the same conclusion as many another inquirer has come to.

QUESTION 251

Will not the force which tips tables, causes flowers to be produced, etc. do more astonishing things if properly directed? How do you explain the phenomena?

W.Q.J.—There is not the slightest doubt that the force referred to in the question will do more astonishing things, and it looks as if the person asking the question had not read of the most extraordinary and astonishing things which have been done by that force, both when it was properly and improperly directed. The limits of the FORUM would not permit of the explanation of the phenomena asked about, but full explanations have been given in *The Path,* in *Lucifer,* by Éliphas Lévi, in *The Key to Theosophy,* and elsewhere.

QUESTION 252

If Masters really exist, why do they not make themselves known to earnest seekers after truth, and especially to such as are working for the good of mankind? And why do they not effectuate peace on earth and right education of the young?

W.Q.J.—This question has been very frequently answered, and even by the Masters themselves. As to the last part, they said in *The Occult World* that if it were possible to alter the state of things and to make a peaceful earth and a right humanity without following the law of evolution, they would willingly do it, but mankind can only be altered step by step. They have also stated that they do not make themselves objectively known to believers in them except in those cases where those believers are ready in all parts of their nature, are definitely pledged to them, with the full understanding of the meaning of the pledge. But they have also stated that they help all earnest seekers after truth, and that it is not necessary for those seekers to know from where the help comes so long as it is received. In *The Path* this subject was discussed in its other bearings. Personally I know that the Masters do help powerfully, though unseen, all those who earnestly work and sincerely trust in their higher nature, while they follow the voice of conscience without doubt or cavil.

QUESTION 253

Is sympathy a quality of Kâma? If not, of what principle is it a part? Should it be indulged to the extent of having one's enjoyment of a pleasure almost destroyed because so many who would like to enjoy it cannot from want of money?

W.Q.J.—Sympathy comes from *kâma* sometimes, and sometimes is derived from other parts of our constitution. It is often a disease with unintelligent persons, or in those who have not disciplined their minds and do not use their judgment or whose judgment is deficient. But sympathy in its highest aspect must flow from the spiritual part of our nature. However, I think that in its ordinary exhibition it is derived from the principle of desire acting with the mind, the memory, and the sensations. Very often it is false; but true sympathy can never be false, and no matter what principle in our nature it arises from, being a noble and healthful thing, it should be exercised, always however with judgment.

It would certainly be folly to allow our sympathies to carry us so away that we are plunged ourselves into needless sorrow, for in such case we will lose power to judge how to be able to act for the benefit of others. The mere fact that others have no money is not in itself a proper cause for arousing sympathy. The want of money is not the cause of trouble, but the desire for money is. We may sympathize with others who have no money, but not because they are deficient in that means; it should be on account of their failure to see that within themselves is the realization of happiness, and that in fact they should not depend upon anything outside for true enjoyment.

QUESTION 254

Does the Devachanic or incarnating Ego possess qualities or propensities which draw it back to incarnation here?

W.Q.J.—A careful study of the philosophy will show that it is held that the Ego in Devachan, consisting of Âtma, Buddhi, and Manas, must contain within it the seeds, qualities, or propensities which will draw it back to life on earth again. If this is not so, then there would never be any reincarnation whatever. If this be so, as I believe it is, then all the rest of the discussion seems to be merely discussion in a circle about nothing, but that which will lead to mental confusion. The last part of the discussion is settled by reflecting that if the Ego using Manas in Devachan keeps itself in a state or condition which is connected with earth life, it will inevitably return to earth-life because of the attraction which it retains for that state of existence.

QUESTION 256

The "Secret Doctrine," in its theory of sequential relations between the astral and the gross physical body, adduces spiriutalistic phenomena as evidence of the truth or validity of said theory, Vol. I, pages 276 and 297, Vol. II, pages 86, 149 and p. 737. In Vol. I, page 258, is found the statement "Like must produce like," which admission, taken in connection with the other statements, amounts to a negation of the usual "shell" explanation of spiritualistic materializations, unless it can be shown that these phenomena are realistic (having an intelligent basis) when they support certain theories, and are seemings upon all other occasions.

W.Q.J.—It does not appear to me that the statement in *The Secret Doctrine,* "Like produces like" — which is a very old Hermetic maxim—taken in connection with the other matters brought forward in *The Secret Doctrine,* is a negation of the Theosophic theory that many, if not all, Spiritualistic materializations are brought about by the agency of astral shells of once-living persons. Nor is the connection at all apparent between this assumed negation and the necessity for showing that those phenomena are "realistic," the questioner appearing to have some new meaning for the word "realistic," as she adds after that word the words "having an intelligent basis." The Theosophical theory about Spiritualistic phenomena has been given over and over again in *Isis,* in *The Secret Doctrine,* in *Lucifer,* in *The Path, The Theosophist,* and elsewhere.* It has always been claimed that materializations had an intelligent actor or actors behind them. That intelligence is the intelligence of the living medium, of the living sitters

---

* [See *Echoes of the Orient,* Vol. I, pp. 183-86.]

of the *séance,* or the automatic or natural intelligence of elemental spirits. H. P. Blavatsky and those who think as she does have always used the phenomena occurring in *séance* rooms as proof of the theories about the astral world and the astral body, as well as also other established facts such as the facts of hypnotism and the like. The sentence "Like must produce like" does not mean nor support the idea that because the transitory materialized thing seen at a *séance* and which exactly resembles a deceased or living person is the same person; in such a case it would mean that the astral form existing on the astral plane enables us to produce its similar on the physical plane, and by the use of that Hermetic sentence in H.P.B.'s book or in any other the astral shell explanation for materialization is not negatived. It is very plain that the questioner does not fully understand H.P.B.'s explanation about materializations and other Spiritualistic phenomena.

QUESTION 257

Man having free-will, is it not probable that some individuals suffer or enjoy that to which their individual Karma does not entitle them, by reason of the acts of others? If so, is not this temporary surplus suffering or enjoyment balanced by the merit or demerit of succeeding incarnations?

W.Q.J.—It seems to me impossible that any person suffers or enjoys anything whatever except through Karma; whether we are in families, nations, or races, and thus suffer and enjoy through general causes, it is still because of our own Karma leading us to that place. In succeeding incarnations we are rewarded or punished according to the merit or demerit of preceding lives, and wherever it is stated in Theosophic books by competent writers that people are "rewarded for unmerited suffering" it always refers to the fact that a person does not himself perceive any connection between the suffering or reward and his own act. Consequently in Devachan he makes for himself what he considers a complete reward for any supposed unmerited suffering, but in his life upon earth he receives only that which he exactly merits, whether it be happiness or the opposite. This is a brief statement of the doctrine, but I think it can be sustained by argument. It seems to me the whole philosophy would fall to the ground if for a moment we admitted that any suffering or reward was not that to which the individual was exactly entitled, for the largeness of the reward which the Ego makes for itself in Devachan is something that he is entitled to, inasmuch as it balances the mental attitude he assumed while living and satisfies his individual needs without disturbing anyone else.

QUESTION 258

Are the majority of people, those who are neither very wicked nor very spiritual, conscious in Kâma-Loka that they are dead; and are they able to see the Kâmic sights with which it is said to be filled? I have read Stanton's "Dreams of the Dead,"[1] and although I cannot accept all he says, the information gained from other sources has been too meager to permit of my discriminating accurately between what is true and what is false.

W.Q.J.—Precisely as physicians know that every human body has its own physical idiosyncrasies, which are well known in their effects upon and relations with medicine, so in the state after death the idiosyncrasy of the person has an effect upon the state there. There is no positive or definite rule which applies invariably to every being after death. Consequently there are many different kinds of states in "Kâma-Loka." Some people are aware that they left the earth, others are unaware of it; some are able to see those they have left behind, others not; and certainly everybody in Kâma-Loka is able to see all that pertains to the particular division of that state in which he may be at the time. Mr. Stanton's book is excellent in many respects, but cannot be exhaustive. What he describes is beyond doubt what happens to some persons in Kâma-Loka, but he by no means describes all the possible cases or facts of that state. But one thing may be asserted as positively so, or else the whole system is at fault, and that is that the being in Kâma-Loka sees whatever pertains to the state in which he is, as it is all a question of state.

QUESTION 259

If H.P.B. was taught of Masters for years in Tibet as stated, previous to giving out Their teaching to the Western world in 1875, why was the doctrine of Reincarnation disavowed by her in her early writings? The Masters could not have spoken then, any more than later, in an uncertain tone on this great tenet of Theosophy, which is so interwoven with all Their teaching as to be inseparable from it. Yet in "Isis Unveiled" it is emphatically stated that "Reincarnation is the exception, not the rule, for the race at large."

W.Q.J.—*First*, there is no evidence published that "H.P.B. was taught of Masters for years in Tibet." I should like to know where such a fact is alleged by any competent witness. *Second*, the doctrine of reincarnation was not disavowed in her early writings. *Third*, the quo-

---

[1] [Stanton, Edward, *Dreams of the Dead*, Boston, Lee and Shepard, 1892.]

tation from *Isis* at the end of the question is incorrect.[1] Reincarnation is not denied; but *reincarnation of the astral monad* is denied as the rule. The words omitted from the quotation are the hinge on which this question and reply must turn. Inquirers and members should be careful in making references, as well as in getting the real import of what is read.

Turn to *The Theosophist*, pp. 288-9 of August, 1882, and you will find the question answered and the remark in *Isis* explained. Turn to *Path*, Vol. I, p. 232, November, 1886, and you will find the article *Theories about Reincarnation and Spirits* dealing with the same matter and by H. P. B. She wrote that article at my request because of a similar question arising from a like misunderstanding. Furthermore I assert as a witness that from 1875 to 1879 H. P. B. taught and explained Reincarnation, and in my case in respect to a relative of mine who died during that period. But when *Isis* was written, the full scheme of man's real constitution had not yet been given out, though hinted at broadly. Attention was then paid to the Kardec school of Reincarnationists with the object of overthrowing their theory, and H. P. B. then, as later, denied *personal reincarnation*. The re-embodiment of the personal astral—called "astral monad" in *Isis*—never was taught and is not taught by the school from which *The Secret Doctrine* emanates. Hence her denial of it as the rule in 1877 still holds good and is reasserted in the articles I have pointed out. There is therefore no inconsistency, though it must be admitted that her English in 1877—by one who had never written for publication—was not as clear as these abstruse subjects demand. For this we must allow, and we ought not to hold all her words to the strict rule we follow in dealing with an English philosopher, but should construe all together.

Reincarnation of the "astral monad"—that is, the personal being and the astral body—is *not* the rule but is the exception; but reincarnation of the Individual or "spiritual monad" is the rule and the doctrine; and it is taught in *Isis*, to which readers are referred. Wherever H.P.B. seems to deny reincarnation in *Isis*, she is referring to personal reincarnation, using the word "man" or "person" in that sense. By consulting the various paragraphs it is seen that the doctrine of successive rebirths is taught plainly, and when she speaks of reincarnation—a new word for her then—she refers to the idea of personal reincarnation. Some of her paragraphs go with detail into the causes for rebirths, but then she is referring to the reincarnation of the "thread-soul," which is not the astral soul. It should also be remembered that terms have

---

1 [See *Isis Unveiled*, Vol. I, p. 351, as well as a later comment on this passage by H.P.B. herself, quoted on pp. 47-48 of the "Introductory" to the 1972 ed. —*Compiler.*]

been better defined and more often used since 1875 than they were then when all was new, even though such mediums as Cora Richmond had before that taught now and then reincarnation as a law without defining it. It is of course to be regretted that Col. Olcott tries with labor to show H. P. B. ignorant of the law in 1875, but that only convicts him of not then knowing the doctrine himself and as not having referred to her full explanations of 1882 and 1886. It does not prove anything against her save bad English. Yet with all her unfamiliarity with our tongue, the very sentence around which these discussions arise—and the sole important sentence that can be found—contains in itself in the words "astral monad" the solution of the difficulty. She began by saying "reincarnation of the individual," the words *personality* and *individuality* then and worse than now being doubtful and interchangeable, but immediately qualifies the description by adding "or rather of his astral monad." If she were to construct the sentence now, the same idea would be there, but expressed in words intelligible to Theosophical students. But even up to this day our words are inadequate, for the terms *personality* and *individuality, soul* and *spirit,* are causes of confusion to different minds.

[Citing various quotations, K. E. Turnbull further challenged Judge concerning H.P.B.'s obscure references to her training in a Himâlayan retreat. However, Mr. Judge counters with the following reply:]

W. Q. J.—The Countess Wachtmeister in *Reminiscences of H. P. Blavatsky, etc.,* published since the last FORUM, quotes (page 57) H.P.B.'s statement to her that the Master forewarned her that she would have to spend three years in Tibet, which is certainly authoritative.

QUESTION 262

There seems to be a glaring inconsistency not only between the two answers to the question [No. 257] in FORUM 51 about unmerited suffering and its reward, but between what W.Q.J. says now and what he said when answering a question in relation to the unmerited Karma of some of the people who perished in the Johnstown flood. In his old answer he took for granted the existence of some unmerited suffering, but now he says there is no such thing.

W.Q.J.—Quite possibly the reply made by me in FORUM 51 may not agree with the Editor's, but that is only because my view and his are not the same, and in the T. S. each man is entitled to his own opinion. But I find no inconsistency between my answer and what I said respecting the Johnstown sufferers; however, as the question does not say where the Johnstown matter is printed, it may be left on one side.

I do not think any suffering or any enjoyment is unmerited. Whatever we have comes by law and justly. But as this is a world governed by cause and effect, the mental attitude of those who suffer or enjoy must be considered; it has its force and effect; it must be provided for. Men in their ignorance do not always see why they suffer, as no connection is visible between the punitive circumstances and the prior cause, which, indeed, had arisen in some long-gone life. Hence, while suffering, the person feels deeply that he does not merit it. This is what is meant by "unmerited suffering." In the mind is lodged the thought that pain has been suffered which was not merited. Devachan provides for this just as it provides for many another supposed ill or injustice. There the person—due to the thought I have spoken of—finds for himself the reward for "unmerited suffering." If he were fully enlightened, of course he would see that all that had happened was just, and no unmerited suffering would exist in that case.

Modern minds are always dwelling on objective modes of thought which constantly ignore the truth that the mind is the source alike of pain and pleasure, of punishment and reward. The Universe is a vast ideation alone, and everywhere we must remember that the mind rules. Until the mind is free, illusion exists on every plane. In Devachan and in Earth-life the illusions are equally great. Inasmuch as the mind is the ruler, the guide, and the standard, it must happen that we will often suppose we have been unjustly treated. Now the mere fact that we were not does not prevent the feeling of unmerited suffering unless the person is fully aware of the fact and accepts it. And as most of us are not fully enlightened, we are constantly subjected to what seems unjust. Criminals often think they have been victims of injustice. This must be taken into account in nature, for their minds and thoughts are as much a part of it as any other mind. Hence a large sum of suffering must exist that is classed as unmerited. This is provided for in Devachan. But in Earth-life exact objective as well as mental results follow. If this "unmerited suffering" is not to be so classed, we will have to find some other word. At present we would have to use a long sentence to express the idea, thus: "In Devachan the person finds compensation for those sufferings which in earth-life were supposed by the sufferer to be unmerited, in consequence of prior causes not being known."

But most certainly every circumstance, all suffering, all pleasure, each reward and every punishment, are the due and exact result of causes set up by the person who is the experiencer. And the richness or the barrenness of Devachan itself is in each case also an exact result of causes set up in the preceding Earth-life, which in turn are the outcome —due to evolved character—of all previous lives.

QUESTION 263

How is one to learn the nature of and how to practice the specific course of training, physical, intellectual, and spiritual, spoken of in the "Epitome of Theosophy"?

W. Q. J.—The specific course of training spoken of in the tract referred to in the question is found in many Hindu, European, and other writings. It was practiced in part by the Christian mystics just as much as by others, but it is specially given and explained in Patañjali's *Yoga Sûtras.* If one follows all the directions of that book he will reach the highest result of spiritual cultivation, but the difficulty is that many Theosophists, after reading that book, attempt to practice portions of it without attending to the high moral precept therein, and naturally they create disturbance within themselves without any very beneficial result.

QUESTION 264

In Forum *No. 43, Question 216, the doctrine of the Antinomians is denounced. How are we to understand in "Tea Table" of "Path" for January, 1892, "For desire ceases to attract us when we no longer identify it with ourself"?*

W.Q.J.—I see no connection whatever between the doctrine of the Antinomians and the passage quoted from *The Path.* The Antinomians, doubtless arguing upon St. Paul's statement that certain persons become a law unto themselves, held that they were not subject to any law and could satisfy or work their desires in any direction. The statement in the "Tea Table" is intended to convey the idea that when we have gotten beyond desire it ceases to attract us, which is an entirely different matter from the Antinomian question. The Theosophic philosophy teaches that by overcoming desire, by ceasing to desire, by controlling the appetites, by turning away from the objects which attract the appetites, desire ceases to attract us, all of which seems to me to be almost the statement of a truism.

QUESTION 266

What is the process whereby the Kamic elements of man become embodied after death in the entity known as the Kâma-Rûpa? How can intangible subjective desires, passions, and the like become "rûpa," or whence comes the body or rûpa?

W.Q.J.—If the process were given it would not be understood, since it is one for which our language has no words. It is for this reason that descriptions given by clairvoyants of various occult things seem pure twaddle and vague mutterings to those who for themselves cannot clairvoyantly see the same thing. How could it be possible to describe the operations of the occult Cosmos in the terms of materialistic science and philosophy? That hidden Cosmos is ideal in its fineness, and the very attempt to fully describe the process enquired of would convey only doubt and certainly result in confusion. But it is no more hidden than is the process by which the body builds itself up every day; nor than that by which a thought will affect the entire nervous system. A simple thought will bring a hot flush or a cold shiver. How? No one knows. Certainly no scientific terms exist to describe the mode and means whereby the thought connects itself with the human physiological machine. And if this be so on this plane, is it likely that an Adept's description of the coalescence of Kâma with an astral body after death would be comprehended save in the most general way? This general way may be gotten at by considering the action of the magnet. It attracts, but no scientific man can look behind that fact; it even can attract an electric flame, but there too the process is occult. In the same way there is an attraction between the mass of desires called Kâma and the astral form which causes them to come together just as a similar attractive force brought Ego and body together.

But desires and passions are not intangible and subjective in the sense given by the question. They are in their sphere—though not in this—quite tangible and objective, and those two words must be altered when we pass beyond the consideration of this plane. If the questioner insists that on every plane desires and passions are intangible and subjective, that will dispose of the question, because in such a case they certainly could never attract anything. But it will first have to be explained how such "intangible and subjective" things as passion and desire can and do have an objective effect even on this plane. As on their own plane they are full of force and tangibility, they attract to themselves the necessary quantum of astral matter, invisible to us but still there, to form a sheath of covering. Having their center in the thinker they radiate from that and cause their effects until cut off from their center, when they begin to dissipate unless linked with some other center from which they might get activity. But the whole difficulty grows, it seems to me, out of the prevalent habit of regarding this so-called objective world as real, and forgetting that the mental and spiritual realms are the only real ones, this being simply the phenomenal expression of those. I therefore disagree from the editor when he says that such and such desires "are not existences apart from the mind and capable of assuming an objective form," for I think they are just such existences and have the capacity to take on an objective form. He is simply stating modern conceptions, which are wholly erroneous and springing from a system of philosophy which does not know that the mind is an entity, and while his illustrations are all good for the school to which they belong, they are completely negatived by the facts of Occultism. For instance, if a practitioner of magic—and not a very high one either—were to fix in his mind the image of an object, it would soon become objective to our physical senses, just as it was first in fact objective to our inner senses. This could not be possible if the objective and subjective of one plane are forever on every plane subjective and objective. That which we now from this plane call "abstract qualities" change on another plane into "objective things." So I regard it an error to call the desire and passions abstract qualities, unless we say at the same time that we mean it relatively.

QUESTION 268

If the cause of rebirth is in unsatisfied desire to live (Tanhâ), why should they be reborn who are weary of life and have no desire to continue or repeat it?

W.Q.J.—There is slight but important inaccuracy in the doctrinal statement of the question, and the question also leaves out of account the desires of life counting from the cradle as well as those desires of other and past lives which were never satisfied.

The inaccuracy is, that it is *not* the doctrine that *unsatisfied* desire leads to rebirth, but that desire is the cause of rebirth, and this makes a great difference in the matter. The want of satisfaction of desire only adds another element leading to rebirth. Desire of any sort, satisfied or not, deludes the Ego, and it is thereby drawn into the magnetic attractions (from which through ignorance it cannot escape) which must and will operate in time to cause rebirth. The desire operates the instant it is entertained, and, sinking into the inner recesses of being, is a cause for rebirth. The mere fact that it is forgotten or that all earthly life in time becomes distasteful does not do away with its force in those parts of our nature which while we are ignorant remain hidden from us. For with each desire—and there are millions of them—there is a thought, and it is these thoughts which make the bonds which draw us back to earth. And with each person this goes on for many years, for but few children are wise enough to control desires. This immense mass of desires and thoughts is to be taken into account. The question appears to ignore them altogether. If in mature years one begins to see the futility and uselessness of desire for life or any other desire, it means that experience has been gained, but not by any means that the forces engendered during preceding years have been exhausted.

Furthermore, there is behind each one the whole sum of other lives with all their desires, much of which must be yet unexhausted. These are each a cause for rebirth.

And it is not merely the desire to live which causes rebirth. That is a prime cause, and one that being seated in general human nature is more subtle and powerful than any other, for it relates to life itself, no matter where. And I take it that if the person who says life here seems worthless were offered life on some other planet in most harmonious, beautiful, and gratifying circumstances, he would find the deeply seated *wish for life* suddenly blazing up, causing him to immediately accept the offer.

QUESTION 269

My own experience, and the statements of candid and observing men like Mr. Sinnett, convince me that intelligent beings "on the other side" sometimes — perhaps frequently — communicate with mortals through sight and sound, sometimes voluntarily, at other times by solicitation, both by night and in strong light, natural and artificial. I should much like to know what and who these beings are, that is, "with what body do they come" and of what grade of intelligence. I ask because, 1st, I have myself seen, known, and felt such beings at different times through their manipulation of the finer elements of matter about us; 2nd, I am sure Theosophy is able to enlighten me, and, since they have taken the initiation of intercourse, the question seems proper.

W.Q.J.—Without claiming any authority on this matter, it seems to me that the "intelligent beings" are in most cases elementals, of which there are some of very high grade but all of which are below the human as to soul and conscience. They do not in the end lead to good, but most frequently to the opposite. The door once open to them, others of any sort may just as well come in. But every case of the sort experienced by the questioner is not necessarily the coming of any other intelligence than one of the many interior selfs we are made up of; many of them may be the production of the power of the person's own astral body which has had some education retained in itself in some other life and now only kept back by Karma and environment. Such is the case with many mediums who do strange things, using their own astral senses and members without at the time knowing that such is the method, just as a man may walk quite well in his sleep. And as it is taught in all good books on this, the elemental world, acting with the inner principles of living men and with the strong shells of gross persons and the astral bodies of those in the astral world who are not wholly dead but live in the passions and astral bodies, is able to "mold matter" in many strange ways and to bring about phenomena of a remarkable character. A simple thought evolved in a definite manner and with a certain intensity will, acting automatically with an elemental, produce a rap of great or small force, and may also bring about sensation, such as sight and feeling and hearing. If, however, a seemingly higher order of intelligence had taken the initiative, one should then exercise the very greatest care, as it is certain such intercourse cannot yet be carried on without a disturbance in the system that is for this age out of the normal. But what exactly each experience is or may be would have to be decided on its own merits and by one who could look behind the veil.

QUESTION 270

Are Plane and Principle ever interchangeable terms? Can a Principle be said to be a Plane of the working of the next higher Plane, i.e., as Buddhi is the vehicle of Âtma, or the ethereal double necessary as the bridge for Prâna to cross over to the physical body? May they be said to be analogous to Spirit and Matter, opposite poles of the same thing?

W.Q.J.—It does not seem to be right to try to interchange these two words, for it will result in mixing up the ideas. A plane is, like a plane surface, quite different from a principle, just as gas is different from the place in which it may exist and be felt. Plane of consciousness is used to designate the stage or metaphysical place the consciousness has reached or may be on or in. But to say that a principle of this plane is a plane for some higher state is very mixed, for it would result that thereby our individuality would be lost and all be reduced to annihilation. Whereas each individual retains his identity and thus must preserve the identity of his principles, whatever those are, it must follow that his principles are not planes but remain as before principles. However, it must be remembered that the word "principle" is used loosely, and sometimes that which is not such is so called. It is easy and definite to retain the actual meaning of "plane" and not try to mix it with some other word. I cannot see any analogy between these two words and "spirit and matter," inasmuch as *plane* means a place for operation or use, and *principle* is that which uses or operates on a plane.

QUESTION 271

Does not the law of Karma set men an example to be retaliative, since the workings of that law are essentially retaliative in retribution, apparently enforcing "an eye for an eye and a tooth for a tooth"? Or should we not look upon the law as retaliative or retributive at all, only our short-sighted conception of justice making it appear so?

W.Q.J.—I do not understand how any one could imagine that the law of Karma, rightly understood, could lead one to retaliation. Certainly a law such as this cannot "set an example," for that infers the action of a being such as a God, or other being. The law of Karma should not be regarded as a law of retaliation, because retaliation again infers the action of a being and not the working of law. Karma is the working out of effect from cause, as well as the creation of cause from which an effect must follow. Hence Karma is completely merciful, because justice and mercy in their highest aspect are one. The exact result must follow the cause, and from every act will flow many effects, both good and bad. Those who wish to have an excuse for retaliation can of course warp any law to their own ends, and the way to warp the law of Karma so as to support retaliation is to talk of it as setting an example, or doing some other thing which can only be performed by an individual with conscience, intelligence, and responsibility.

QUESTION 271A

I am not able to see that the law of Karma as expounded by most Theosophists is not retaliative in both its retributive and its beneficent aspect. "W.Q.J." says: "The law of Karma should not be regarded as a law of retaliation, because retaliation infers the action of a being and not the working of a law." But how can a law work without the action of some being or beings; and even if it did so work, a law can have a retaliative character as well as a being. And since a law expresses the will of some being or beings, this will may express retaliation through its laws just as many human laws do. Such a law could emanate only from an anthropomorphic being, and furnishes a selfish motive for right doing or abstention from evil doing. If wrong doing is the cause of suffering, and if right doing is invariably rewarded, we should find these effects always following these causes, but such is not the fact. Right doing is very often the cause of suffering, and wrong doing the cause of pleasure. If there is any such law that rewards us for doing right and punishes for doing wrong, it should be inoperative among beings which had no sense of right and wrong, such as animals; yet we find that animals have suffering and sorrows, pleasures and joy. Is it not nobler and more spiritual to do right because it is our duty and from love of the right and of our fellow-creatures? Such has been the motive of all great souls. The law of Karma is the law of cause and effect, or of evolution, and as such of course includes all causes of suffering or pleasure, but when it is stated that the ethical character of the cause determines what the effect shall be, we state what cannot be substantiated by fact.

W.Q.J.—This question has been referred to me because, I suppose, my name is mentioned. It seems to deal chiefly with the meaning of words. As I understand good and bad Karma, they mean respectively action which is pleasing and that which is displeasing to the Higher Self. Hence seemingly retaliative Karma may be for the good and benefit of the soul experiencing it, while pleasure may be the opposite. The word "retaliation" carries with it in my mind the notion of a person who retaliates, and I would not apply it to a law or to a natural result. As, for instance, burning will follow on placing the hand in the fire, for the reason that it is the law or nature of fire to burn, but how can it be other than vague and confusing to say that the fire retaliates on the hand? If such a use of words were common we would have to make gods and deities of all natural forces and operations. Karma as a cosmic law metes out the exact result for act, but this is cause and effect, and not retaliation. The man, however, who hits back because he is hit retaliates on the hitter. The effect in such a case is that in the mind of each is set a seed or cause which must sooner or later make an effect. If a blind and helpless man accidentally hits another in the eye, causing hurt, it is usual for the hurt person to excuse the act and to feel no resentment, and hence to bear within no seed for future hate; but the same sort of act done on purpose generally rouses hate or resentment. Imagine now the resentful person dying at once. He carries the seed of hate in his mind, and in some other life it will come out when the time is ripe under the law. But the act in both cases was the same, while the ethics and the mental states in both were not the same.

QUESTION 272

What is the source of Conscience? From what plane does it come? Why does the savage delight in cruelty to his enemy, and the so-called enlightened man in sharp practices which the really enlightened know to be wrong? In other words, is Conscience a matter of education?

W.Q.J.—Conscience seems to be a faculty which may be stilled or made active. In my opinion its source is in the Higher Self, and as it comes down through plane after plane it loses its force or retains power according to the life and education of the being on earth. The conscience of the savage is limited by his education just as were the consciences of the New Englander and the European religionists who destroyed men for the sake of God and Christ. We cannot assert that the men who indulged in religious persecution were not going according to what they called their conscience. By this I do not mean that conscience is a matter of education, but that the power of its utterances will be limited by our education, and consequently if we have a bigoted religion or a non-philosophical system we are likely to prevent ourselves from hearing from our conscience. And in those cases where men are doing wrong according to what they call their conscience, it must be true that they have so warped their intuition as not to understand the voice of the inward monitor.

QUESTION 273

Is it a fact, as sometimes asserted in print, that everything in Nature is dual, and that nothing can exist or even be conceivable without its opposite? I don't see the necessity for this.

W.Q.J.—The editor's easy disposal of the question is also pure assertion, it seems to me. I can think of no proposition so easy of proof, and of which there is so much evidence in the material, mental, and psychic realms, as the one that duality rules universally in Nature. The Sun is the day ruler, the Moon the night ruler; the first giving direct light, the other reflected beams,—in both cases dual. The day is one side, the night the other; and thus light and dark are a duality. In the earth's travel it brings two opposites—heat and cold. Man and animals are male and female—dualities in sex. The word "male" would not connote its present meaning unless there were its opposite. The magnet—a mundane universality—has two opposite poles, one attracting, the other repelling; they are opposite in position as well as in effect. Indeed, it would be tedious to prolong a list that could be extended over the whole range of nature from the little to the great. In the argument used by the Editor that "Intelligence would be intelligence just as truly if there were no such thing as" its opposite, and in other like arguments and illustrations, there is pure assumption. The word "intelligence" describes a quality found among men, but "stupidity" is also to be found there, and one is hardly justified in assuming that a time will come when stupidity will be gone from the cosmos, leaving only intelligence, unless it also assumed that the complete and exclusive prevalence of intelligence is the known object and end to which the universe is tending. Of course optimistic thought may make this assumption, but pessimism is as much entitled to construct an opposite one and say that stupidity and chaos are the final end and aim. In order to apply the editor's illustration we must grant the possibility underlying his words "if", but no one knows that intelligence is the quality that shall finally prevail above all, and it is allowable to reunite his sentence thus: "Stupidity would be stupidity just as truly if there were no such thing as intelligence."

We are dealing with Nature wherein there is the duality referred to. Every illustration used by the Editor is in itself a duality and understood only through the existence of duality. To assume the destruction of duality is to reduce into a state of nothingness both as to consciousness and the thing cognized. If we take his illustration of evil disappearing and good prevailing, then there must be assumed for the event a cognizer to perceive the good and to feel its effect, which at once makes the final all-embracing duality of a cognizer and the thing cognized, felt, or perceived. If no cognizer is present, but the Universe is simply goodness and naught else, then we have nothingness once more, since there is no mind or consciousness to note it. But as this is not so, we have to conclude that in the final analysis, whether objects be one or many, there must be a perceiver and that which is perceived.

QUESTION 276

Do we begin a new round of embodiments after Pralaya? If the past does not suffice to end the "descent into matter," can we expect the future to do so?

W.Q.J.—One of the cardinal principles of Theosophy is that evolution by means of manifestation is periodical, one *manvantara* succeeding the preceding one as its logical and natural successor. Hence the present one is the legitimate successor of that which preceded it, is its resultant in every way, but necessarily higher since there can be no going back. It is postulated in *The Secret Doctrine* that the descent into matter changes into the reascent to spirit in this present round. Those of the race who shall not succeed before Pralaya comes on in attaining to truth will necessarily have to go through whatever re-embodiment is needed in the succeeding *manvantara*. This is natural, just, and reasonable. Those who attain in the vast stretch of centuries yet before us to the height of power, wisdom, and perfection will not have to go through reembodiment unless they wish to do so; it is quite likely that a great many of them will, out of love for the new and struggling ones of that future *manvantara,* descend into matter for the help and benefit of those below them. Perhaps by that time, so many millions of years hence, the questioner will have developed so much through struggle and effort as to be quite undismayed by the prospect of another fight with matter then. But certainly now it is looking a long way ahead, seeking for a fanciful idea to dwell on this future possibility in a *manvantara* which is for us inconceivable in time as well as in quality.

QUESTION 277

Are those who predict that the United States are to be the theater of Black Magic in time to come able to foresee what will be the catastrophe? Will our race be left to itself until it shall work out its own destruction by a cataclysm, like the Atlanteans; or will an Avatâr appear at the crisis, as Kṛishṇa did in the days of Kansa? Is there any record or tradition of an Avatâra's having appeared among the Atlanteans previous to their final extinction?

W.Q.J.—If the Adepts have predicted that the United States will be the scene for a catastrophe of Black Magic, they certainly are able to know what that catastrophe will be. The question does not seem to me profitable, but rather one of those arising more from curiosity, quite natural but still not valuable. It is doubtless true that at important epochs in the World's history under the law of cycles and Karma great beings appear for the confusion of the wicked and the re-establishment of virtue. We have no information as to the appearance of such beings amongst the Atlanteans, as nearly all we have heard about that race is in *The Secret Doctrine*, and there it merely says that such beings have appeared periodically; hence they must have come to the Atlanteans.

QUESTION 279

What finally becomes of thoughts, both good and bad, sent out by human beings?

W.Q.J.—So far as the remarks of the editor go they are very just, but a wider field appears to have been overlooked. It has been said that "thoughts are things," an assertion with which I am prepared to agree entirely; and I also firmly believe that the time is not far off when their substantiality will be recognized and understood by science more fully than at present.

A thought implies many things besides pure force exerted. If force is exerted, then there must be that which exercises it. What is this, and what is the effect of the exercise? When we think, it is known that there is a disturbance or disintegration of the grey matter of the brain. But next we must observe that there is at the same time physiological disturbance, change, or alteration, in the whole frame. For instance; a thought of shame or disaster or punishment may bring all over the body a hot flush or a cold shiver; the thought of a great danger just escaped has made men dizzy and women faint. Is there nothing in this? Further, each thought makes a picture, save perhaps a purely metaphysical syllogism, but even there it is difficult to escape the formulating by the mind of some concrete illustration as the syllogism proceeds; and even in pure mathematics it will be impossible for the thinker to prevent the rising up of a picture of the figures used in the operation, because from youth the numerals were impressed on his memory. Going on with this, we see that clairvoyants report that each thought makes a flash or picture objective to the inner sense, and from all the experiments in hypnotism we find that the old claim of occultism that each thought makes a definite picture must be true. Every clear seer will confirm this from personal experience. Still further, the astral light being a preserver of these pictures like a photographic plate, it follows that every thought has its picture preserved, and by that means what has been done or is being done may be known unerringly. Therefore thoughts, while they may be fugitive so far as concerns the thinker, are not so otherwise, but persist as seeds for good or evil in the whole race.

But, still more, every thought leaves a seed in the mind or manas of the thinker, no matter how fugitive the thought was. The whole sum of such small seeds will go to make up a larger seed for thought, and thus constitute a man of this, that, or the other general character. Thoughts, then, are highly important, for, as the Buddha said, we are made up of thought and built of thought; as we think, so we act and will act, and as we act and think so will we suffer or rejoice, and the whole world with us.

QUESTION 286

Are the statements in the 9th chapter of "Esoteric Buddhism"[1] regarding the later incarnations of Buddha as Sankarâchârya (sixty years after Buddha's death) and Tsong-ka-pa (born in the 14th century) correct? I do not remember anything by H.P.B. which confirms these very interesting statements.

W.Q.J.—The statement in *Esoteric Buddhism* referred to is not the first time that such a view has been given out, as for many, many years the assertion has been made in India and other Oriental countries that Buddha reincarnated in Sankarâchârya for the purpose of making a reform in Hindu philosophy. From reading Mr. Sinnett's words it would seem that he is using the terms of the letters from the Adepts on which the book is founded, but that cannot be said certainly until he admits it or the letters themselves are published. I do not remember now any passage in which H.P.B. said anything about it, but other students may be able to find such. The same may be said as to Tsong-ka-pa. The doctrine of reincarnations of an Avatâra is clearly put in *The Bhagavad-Gîtâ* in the fourth chapter,[2] thus: "And thus I incarnate from age to age for the preservation of the just, the destruction of the wicked, and the establishment of virtue"; and so also is it given in many other of the old scriptures. As Buddha came to those who were outside the Vedic law, so it was natural at that time, a little later, he or someone else should come to make a reform in Hindu Vedic philosophy. Whether both were the same souls is not very important, but it is quite evident that the soul of each was in every sense a "mahâ-âtma," for the influence of Sankara is as much felt to this day in the Vedic philosophical schools as is that of Buddha outside of them. The coming and going of such highly advanced egos is always "by a secret path," as is the phrase, and generally curiosity is what brings out references on the point of identification, for did we know who any particular person was in another birth nothing much of value would be gained. Supposing it to be certain that Buddha and Sankara were one and the same soul, we gain nothing but some confusion, since much that one said will not harmonize on the surface with that said

---

[1] [*Op. cit.* See also *BCW*, Vol. IV, pp. 8-19.—*Comp.*]
[2] [Verse 8]

by the other, inasmuch as we know nothing of their secret reasons, and the systems given by each have many radical differences.

QUESTION 288

Why did the Egyptians, whose priests were many of them advanced Adepts, teach the necessity of carefully preserving the bodies of the dead, while the advanced Theosophists of the present day advocate the rapid destruction of the body by means of cremation?

W.Q.J.—In asking a question why the Egyptians did this or another thing you expect too much of us. We really cannot know. And no matter why they did what they did with mummies, it would be no reason for or against what now is advanced by Theosophists and others. But cremation is not a thing the Theosophists proposed; it was proposed long before the T.S. was founded, and but little is said of it by Theosophists. But at the same time it is not known what was the real origin of making mummies, as the examples we have belong to very recent periods of the Egyptians, who must have existed many thousands of years before the times we can know of their history. It has been suggested very justly that the practice began with their Adept kings for reasons of their own, and that it came to be imitated afterwards. If this is so, then it would be natural for the kings to permit it among the people so as to create a greater security for their own mummies; for if there be mummies for all, no one will bother to look for any particular mummy for some special reason, whereas if only kings were known to be mummied, then later people might want to exhume and inspect them, for the early kings were thought by the people to be Adepts, as is evident from the records. But on all this we are as yet but making assumptions.

QUESTION 289

How can we discern whether it is the divine conscience animating us and directing us in a certain direction, or the animal soul seeking release from seemingly unfavorable environments?

W.Q.J.—The divine conscience acts in all struggles for betterment, but clouded more or less in each by reason of education and habit of thought; hence it varies in brightness. It is not possible to make a hard-and-fast fixed rule for finding out what is the animating motive. If we are trying to get into a better state, it is for us to decide if that be simply and wholly selfish. All actions are surrounded by desire as the rust is round the polished metal or the smoke round the fire, but we must try. So if we fix for ourselves the rule that we will try to do the very best we can for others, we will generally be led right. If we rely on the higher self and aspire to be guided by it, we will be led to the right even if the road goes through pain, for sorrow and pain are necessary for purification of the soul. But if we wish to run away from an environment because we do not like it and without trying to live in it while not of it, we are not altering ourselves but simply altering the circumstances, and may not always thereby gain anything.

QUESTION 290

What is the real meaning of that phrase so often seen in Theosophical papers, "the great orphan, Humanity"?

W.Q.J.—This phrase has a deep significance for me. An orphan may also be one who had no parents, as the state of orphanage is that of being without father or mother. If we imagine a child appearing on the earth without a parent, we would have to call it an orphan. Humanity is the "great orphan" because it is without parents in the sense that it has produced itself and hence from itself has to procure the guidance it needs. And as it wanders in the dark valley of the shadow of death, it is more in need of help and counsel than the mere body of a child which is the ordinary orphan. The soul is parentless, existing of itself from all eternity, and considered as soul, mankind is hence an orphan. Plunged into matter, surrounded on every side by the vast number of intricate illusions and temptations that belong to earthly life, it stands every day and hour in need of protection as well as guidance.

If the idea of a loving parent be applied to the notion that a definite God has produced mankind, then we find that this supposed parent has at the same time invented the most diversified and ingenious series of bedevilments and torments to beguile, hurt, harass, and finally destroy the child. For if a certain one God is the maker or parent of man, then He also is the one who made nature. Nature is cruel, cold, and implacable. It stops for no man, it never relents, it destroys without mercy. When inhabitants of earth multiply, Nature manages to destroy millions of people in a night or two, as has now and then happened in China; the very elect of the earth are swept off the earth in a moment; slowly and painfully the infant races creep up the ladder of time, leaving as they go vast heaps of slain at the foot. The whole of life presents, indeed, to man more frowns than smiles. It is this fact that has made so many who are told of a loving father and at the same time of an illogical scheme of salvation revolt altogether from the idea of any meaning to life but despair.

I cannot see how the phrase "great orphan" carries with it the notion of being without guide or helper. The orphan is everywhere; but among the units composing it are some who have risen through trial to the state where they can help the lower ones. Orphans themselves, they live to benefit mankind of which they are a part. They are the head of the body of which the lower members are the less developed units or atoms. Enthusiasm for the "orphan" is that which will lead to devotion and sacrifice; and that enthusiasm must be developed not only in the Theosophist, but in all the men of earth. Having it they will help all on their own plane, and each stratum of men rising in development will help all below until all belonging to the globe have risen to to the perfect height. Then they can proceed to other spots in cosmos where are also wandering vast masses of souls, also units in the "orphan," who require and can then receive the same help that we had extended to us. If this is not the destiny of man during the time when all things are manifesting, then the remark of Spencer to the effect that altruism is useless because when universal there is no one to benefit, must be accepted. However, the phrase in the question is one of those rhetorical ones that must not be read in its strict letter and ordinary meaning.

QUESTION 291

In a recent lecture by an F.T.S. the grand possibilities open to a multi-millionaire for the accumulation of an enormous wealth of Karma by the altruistic expenditure of riches were dwelt upon so rapturously, while the Karma born of the "Widow's Mite" was mentioned with such marked decrease of consideration (perhaps not intentionally or even consciously) that the following queries suggested themselves:

(1.) Is it not inconsistent to suppose that good Karma can be accumulated in larger quantities by the altruistic expenditure of a millionaire's wealth than by the giving of the "Widow's Mite," since a man can only be judged generous by what he has left after the gift?

(2.) Can Karma be acquired, or deposited like money in a bank to be drawn upon for future needs; and is not the contemplation of it as a thing to be stored up illogical, illusory, and a direct incentive to self-seeking?

(3.) Is any Karma good " per se," or in fact good at all, except in so far as it compensates and atones for past transgression; and is it operative any more after all misdeeds have been expiated, i.e., can a man have Karma to his credit?

(4.) Does not Nirvâna follow the full satisfaction of Karmic law, and, if so, how can there be any more place for Karma of any kind?

W.Q.J.—As to (1) the altruistic expenditure by a millionaire of his wealth in large quantities must accumulate to him more "karmic credit" than if he had but little. Mere expenditure of money is nothing, but the really altruistic, unselfish use of it is much. Every time such a person thus expends for the good of others he thereby excites in all who are benefited a sympathy and a portion, small or large, of love. This cannot be wiped out, any more than an evil act, until it is exhausted by a corresponding action on the part of the person who thus gets benefit. Hence such a millionaire necessarily makes to himself friends who will one day in some life benefit him. If this is not so, then all the doctrines of karma and cause and effect are of no value.

(2) Karma may not be acquired like money in a bank; it cannot be deposited; but a store of merit may be laid up to the account of any one who acts so as to lay it up. If the law is looked at from the selfish side as something that one may lay up for himself, of course it will tend to self-seeking; but it is hardly possible for one to believe in and act under the law and fail at the same time to see that if he does so selfishly he limits his store and sometime will nullify all its effects. It is not good karma to act selfishly; hence he makes bad karma by so acting from a self-seeking of benefit under the law.

(3) Good karma is that act and thought which is pleasing to the Higher Self. Hence sorrow and pain and discipline may be good karma. Bad karma is that act and thought which displeases the Higher Self. Hence all self-seeking acts, no matter how high and outwardly virtuous they are, are bad karma, since the Higher Self desires no such acts for its sake.

(4) Nirvâna comes to those who have risen up over all delusions and have realized the supreme unity of all; then it may be taken; but if it is then taken for oneself, leaving others in the mire of life unhelped, it becomes an enormous selfishness which later on must result in the being having to do penance in some other manvantara.

QUESTION 292

Somewhere in Theosophy we are told that the Egos now on the planet are largely the reappearance of the Atlanteans. But I notice more resemblance to the Romans and Greeks. Our style of architecture, our ideas of pastime, such as prize-fights, foot-ball, wrestling, and rough or unrefined amusements, are all in line with the classice ones. Even the Greek type of feminine beauty is apparent once more, and women affect Greek ideas in dress and fixings. How does this consist with the statement in question?

W.Q.J.—The questioner seems to have misunderstood the matter. As the Atlanteans preceded the Romans and the Greeks by many millions of years, the Romans and Greeks themselves may have been and likely were an appearance of the Atlanteans. It was said by H.P.B. that all the present Race are Atlanteans. This must be so if the first parts of her anthropological scheme are correct, for the reason that that old form of race preceded all the later, the latter being simply the various reincarnations of the former. If, then, the sports of the present or any other form of life led by us seem like the Roman or the Greek, that is only because we do not know what were the forms in which the Atlanteans in their time indulged. Similarly as we have no knowledge of what was the Atlantean type of beauty or of intellectual achievement, there is nothing in what the questioner says which in any way militates against the Atlantean theory. When we shall have discovered fully all about the Atlantean civilization and the physical form as well as mental caliber of that race, we can then say what subsequent smaller race most resembles it. It must also be remembered that we as souls are quite likely to be the same souls that inhabited the bodies of the Atlantean man, because that race existed so very long ago as to be *sui generis*.

QUESTION 293

In killing out desire, do you not also kill out worldly ambition? When a man has done this, is he fit to fight the battle of life, or to be the head of a family?

W.Q.J.—In killing out desire we do not kill out right action, though we may kill ambition. It is likely you have a wrong meaning for the word "ambition," as it is wrongly used by many. It is used out of its way to mean energy and action, whereas it does not mean that. It means the desire to get gain and power and glory and wealth for oneself, and that is selfishness of the worst, and hence ambition may be rightly killed and no true progress is made till it is put under. But by following the rules given, that is, to do your duty, you cannot neglect your great and small duties, hence you will care for your family. But if you give the word "ambition" the meaning of the opposite of "apathy" and say that he who kills ambition becomes apathetic, then all would be folly. Fitness to fight the battle of life is not from worldly ambition at all, but from a right and strong sense of duty, from a determination to do it, and from a true sense of your duty to your neighbor.

QUESTION 294

What entities, besides Kâma-Rûpa, communicate with man from the astral plane, and what vehicles for manifestation are used besides the Rûpa and astral body of the medium? Which of the communicating entities are friendly and which hostile and what are the means of distinguishing between them? Have in mind the evocation of Apollonius of Tyana.

W.Q.J.—Hundreds of classes of beings communicate from the astral plane with the living through mediums and otherwise. Of this subject the West does not know. Hence you will have to take on faith if you believe at all what I reply. Many degrees of elementals communicate. These are all of no use to us, but harmful. Many of them are used by black magicians who live in the astral world in their kâma-rûpas. They use the elementals, they live thus on the living by absorption, and this is the great danger of all such things. Some of them may be friendly, but unless you have the means and sight of your own to tell which, no direction would be of any use. Even while friendly they are injurious, for they must use a part of you or some one for the work, and they thus set up the likelihood of another not friendly using you the same way. Apollonius was an adept and cannot be safely imitated by any less person. If you are too strong to be influenced and get another person as the means for it, then you will be wrongly exposing the other to a danger you are yourself exempt from.

QUESTION 303

In the Ocean of Theosophy, *on page 46, is made the statement that it is desire and passion which caused us to be born, and will bring us to birth again and again in this body or in some other. How could we again inhabit this body? Please explain.*

W.Q.J.—The statement on p. 46 of *Ocean of Theosophy* was a slip of the pen. The intent was to say that desire and passion make rebirth in some body, and should have said "in some body on this earth or another globe." I do not believe we come back to this body. I also think it is from the context reasonably clear. The *"Ocean"* was written in a very few days, and hence some slips have occurred in it; this is one, and will be corrected in another edition.

QUESTION 307

In regard to the third object of the T.S., what, if anything, is being done in the way of investigating the "psychic powers latent in man"?

Ans.[1]—This is a very interesting question, one which is not infrequently met in private and official letters, and which should be answered with some fulness. *Nothing* is really being done by the T.S. to investigate man's psychic powers, although that investigation is avowedly one of its three objects. It may even be said that such investigation is discouraged by the highest officials and most influential members of the Society, strange as this seems. Why?

The history of the Theosophical Society shows that it has undergone

---

1 [We include Alexander Fullerton's editorial reply because of the historical setting it supplies.—*Comp.*]

a process of evolution steadily to higher planes, a process paralleled by that in many individual members. It was avowedly formed for investigation of psychic phenomena, several of its original members were active spiritualists, and one of its first acts was to effect an arrangement with Mr. Felt for explaining his (asserted) experiments upon Elementals. This phase was very soon passed through, and was followed by a stage of philosophic elucidation by H.P.B., notably in the publication of *Isis Unveiled*. After this preparatory work and the removal of the Founders to India, the larger field of direct Theosophic exposition was entered, fuller help from Masters was given, and Mr. Sinnett's great works, *The Occult World* and *Esoteric Buddhism*, sounded through the West the first promulgation of the Wisdom Religion. The Society had now taken a bolder stand as the nucleus of a Universal Brotherhood, and had invited all searchers after Truth to its membership. It exerted itself to supply a growing demand for philosophic and religious knowledge, particularly drawing upon Eastern treasures, and *The Theosophist* and *The Path* were successively established. Then came a movement to popularize Theosophic doctrine, leaflets, pamphlets, and elementary books appearing, and arrangements being made to spread them as far as possible. Into the purely intellectual or didactic purpose soon became perceptible a moral and spiritual aim, and the practical bearing of Theosophy was made more impressive. Meantime phenomena dropped into the rear, the philosophic explanation of spiritualism discontented spiritualists and caused them to hold aloof, emphasis was placed on true spiritual development rather than on any form of psychism. As the Society grew, to its members was pointed out the importance of knowledge, interior discipline, and exterior work for the Society's aim of bettering mankind through right perception of Karma and Reincarnation as the great motor to reform. H.P.B.'s settlement in Europe, the establishment of *Lucifer* and the London Headquarters, the publication of *The Secret Doctrine*, the organization of the European Section, all meant more ample instruction, propaganda, and T.S. work. *Light on the Path*, the first work for distinctly devotional purposes, was followed by *The Voice of the Silence*. And for years the main labor of the now thoroughly aroused Society has been to prepare and disseminate literature of all grades and for every want, to perfect its system of interior instruction and exterior enlightenment, to consolidate its membership in effort to gain and to give truth,—in short, to make the T.S. a grand agency for teaching and uplifting its own Fellows and all the race.

One may sum up this evolutionary career in saying that the Theosophical Society started with phenomenalism, and progressed through intellectualism and spiritual devotion to the stage of uniting intellect and devotion in a persistent attempt to elevate humanity.

As has been said, this organic evolution is paralleled by individual. Many a man has been aroused from materialism or apathy by spiritualism, then has craved a philosophy not found in spiritualism, experienced interest in Theosophic doctrine, undergone a soul-awakening in connection therewith, and gained full satisfaction in that union of truth and duty which constitutes a real Theosophist. It is a progressive course most natural in an age conditioned as is this, and officials of the T.S. see it exemplified repeatedly.

In the unfoldment of fact effected by expanding literature, particularly that from H.P.B. herself and from her immediate pupils, great light has been cast upon psychic matters in two respects; *first,* their actual nature and laws, *second,* their relative inferiority to spiritual interests. It has been shown, for instance, that psychism is deceptive, illusory, unprofitable, often injurious and never safe, that it cannot be properly pursued without such a trained guide as does not exist in this longitude, that its acquirements, not being in character, do not pass over into later incarnations, and that time spent on it is really unremunerative. And also it has been shown that the true aim for man is the union of his Manas principle with his Buddhi principle, *i.e.,* the flooding of his human nature with his Divine Nature; after which the psychic realm is of right his to enter, understand, and rule. As the teachers put it, that realm is to be entered from above, not from below. Hence it follows that one is unwise to expend upon inferior pursuits strength and time which can so much more profitably be expended upon superior; and also that it is but right to follow that order of attainment which "Those who Know" both by experience and acquisition testify to be just, consecutive, satisfactory, true, and safe.

Furthermore, it is matter of observation that interest in psychic pursuits declines as interest in spiritual growth augments. Men who are more and more intent on higher themes are less and less intent on lower. The greater displace the smaller. This is from the nature of the respective topics, but also from the satisfaction in the former which, when once truly felt cannot be given up for the latter. And so there has been noted by Theosophic leaders the fact that students who follow the course recommended care less for phenomena as they sense better the spiritual philosophy.

As the evolutionary process continually drew the T.S. more directly to its real work as we now know it, and as enlarging perceptions enabled its leaders the better to conduct it, the subject of phenomena dropped to the rear. Phenomena had their value for certain evidential purposes, and for these they were fittingly quoted and expounded, but H.P.B. discarded them when that end was accomplished, and the Society did likewise. Its strength was given to the aims heretofore spoken of. The greater import of its first and second declared "Objects" obscured the third, just as in individual cases. And so when an inquirer asked of its officials how he should develop psychic gifts, or what advice was offered to aspirants after "powers", or whether it was well to cultivate incipient ability for clairvoyance, clairaudience, going out in the astral, and the like, he was told that there was something far more important than these things, something to which they might well be postponed, something of enduring and surpassing value. The advice might be summed up in the Scripture passage, "Seek first the kingdom of God and His righteousness, and all these things shall be added unto you". In other words, Make yourself fit for powers and the powers will in due time come; but you will not become fit by seeking the powers.

In an indirect way the T.S. is really, however, contributing to right treatment of psychic problems. For through its exposition of the septenary nature of man and of *post mortem* states it is making possible to Western psychologists a systematic study, with adequate data, of hypnotism, mesmerism, dreams, clairvoyance, and kindred phenomena. Probably it can effect more for general enlightenment by furnishing scientists with indispensable tools now lacking and by thus letting secular science do preparatory work, than by doing that work itself. At first it had to do it, but now that science has advanced to the point where these tools can be handed over to it and the T.S. spend its strength more advantageously, that is the right policy.

So, then, to epitomize the answer to the Question: the T.S. has overpassed the stage wherein direct pursuit of its third object was fitting; it has entered evolutionally into a region more important, more beneficial, more largely philanthropic: it has provided from its Eastern acquisitions facts needful to Western psychologists for studies which they can now prosecute in certain departments better than can it; in its specific field and for its specific work it devotes itself to teachings and trainings more distinctively religio-philosophic; and it applies its as yet limited resources to a function (propagandic) as to which it stands alone and for which every resource will long be needed. If it does nothing directly for psychic study, it is doing much for the establishment of principles which will make psychic study more efficient for investigators outside its membership, and which will tend to discourage that study within only until the date when it can be undertaken at the true stage, with the right preparation, and with beneficent effects.

W.Q.J.—There are two ways to understand the word "investigate". Either it means an actual physical and experimental investigation, or another sort, the other being investigation of the philosophy and the laws underlying the phenomena. The former has not been done by the

T.S. for the reason that the philosophy as given out by writers like H.P.B. indicates a danger to the experimenter; and experience sustains the views promulgated by her and those who follow her lead. It is said that a profitable investigation of the psychic realm is only possible when we have first the instruments and next the character—in the line of purity and virtue—without which no right investigation in a practical way is possible. There are no mechanical tools or instruments that are of use; the realm is full of delusion and darkness; mediums, seers, and psychics are all alike (until we get those who really know) unaware of the source of the phenomena or the meaning of them when they come; they give different explanations for the same thing, and they contradict each other as often as not. Unsensitive experimenters, equally with the seers and psychics, are ignorant of the realm they deal with in almost all cases, and in many they deny obvious explanations known to be true by those who have studied the philosophy. And as far as the T.S. is concerned, it has not from the beginning paid attention to this so-called practical investigation. The phenomena of H.P.B.'s production were her own and not the Society's, and no one has since been like her. Evidently she had, as she said, a distinct purpose and reason for the doing of her phenomena. It was to draw attention and to leave a record of a different sort from the long and sad one of mediumship. Experience in that has amply sustained her views. We know that the medium's record is sad and full of instances going to prove the grave dangers incurred by those who attempt to deal before they are inwardly ready with forces belonging to other planes of being. All through the ages the wise have said that the mere wish of the practical man of the day for phenomena and for the production of them is not a good reason for complying with the request. H.P.B., a later teacher, said that the moral and ethical philosophical ground must be fully and precedently prepared for the new growth that is to come in the line of psychic powers, for if they are permitted to develop in such a selfish and sordid soil as is now afforded in our civilization they will come to be a menace and terror in place of being a blessing. This is why I for one would be sorry to see any of the T.S. Branches engaged in such practical investigation.

But of the other sort of investigation we have had and still have a good deal. Our philosophy explains the facts already at hand, and shows distinctly how the virtues and excellences of character must be developed and realized before we are at all ready for practically touching the psychic forces. At the same time, by giving a sufficient analysis of man's composite nature it tends to prevent and do away with all superstition in respect to the many psychic phenomena that daily have place. This latter method of investigation is the right one in my opinion, and the one to be retained rather than the other.

QUESTION 308

What effect, if any, does the cremation of the body have on the remaining material principles?

W.Q.J.—Cremation has no direct effect on any of the sheaths or vehicles, but it must have the indirect effect of freeing the astral form from the influence of the material body and thus give the astral a chance to more quickly dissipate. It has much less effect on *kâma* and the others above, and none on *prâna,* for the latter is ever present, and in the case of death is simply at work somewhere else. Material fire can have no effect directly on any sort of matter that is not on its own plane, and hence has no effect at all on *manas* or those above that. From a sanitary point of view cremation is of high importance, as it does away with injurious matter or matter in such a state as to be injurious to the living.

QUESTION 311

Are our human souls born as infants or as adults into the Devachanic state? I am of opinion that a soul may or may not enter that state as an infant, according to the knowledge acquired by the person while living.

W.Q.J.—It seems to me to be a mistake to consider questions relating to the soul from the materialistic point of view of "infant" or "adult." The soul is not born, nor does it die; it cannot be called an infant or an adult; those terms should only be used as more or less metaphorical, to show, as the editor points out, a difference in character. The soul assumes in the astral or ethereal realms of being that shape or form which most resembles its real character: it may seem to be what we would call infant or adult irrespective of the age of the body it had just quitted, or it might take the form of a beast or maybe a deformed, misshapen human body if its real life could be but fitly thus represented. This was well known to Swedenborg and many other seers, who saw souls wandering in such shapes which the very law of their being compelled them to assume. And it does not require physical death to bring this about, for in life many a person presents to the clairvoyant the actual picture of the inner character, no matter how horrible that may be. Form, shape, or lineament has then in the life of the soul to do with essential character. It is reported that one of the Adepts writing of Devachan spoke of our growing old there and then dying out of it. But this means, as was also then explained, only the uprush of force, its continuance in activity, and then at last its gradual decline to extinction or birth into another life. Adhering strictly to the words of the question, I do not think infants—and those are mere babes—have any Devachan, but that they pass on at once to another human birth as soon as the body of the baby is dead. They have accumulated no force for Devachan; they have but in them the impulse for birth, and that having been thwarted by death, it is continued by an immediate search for another body, to be continued until a body is found with sufficient vitality in it to allow the soul to go on with its pilgrimage among men. It is true that mediums and clairvoyants often report this, that, or the other infant as present from the so-called "world of spirits," but I think that all such cases are only occupations by elementals of the images or shapes of infants who have died out of earth-life, and hence prove nothing at all but the infinite power of delusion possessed by the astral world.

QUESTION 317

If our Higher Self was primarily an emanation from the Divine, why the necessity for this pilgrimage of successive incarnations? What advantage does the Ego derive from its association with the mass of matter we call our personality? If it is said that it is for the sake of gaining knowledge and experience in relation to every aspect or manifestation of the universe and on every plane of consciousnss, why the necessity of such to what was divine from the beginning, and must from its very nature possess a consciousness of all existence and be in itself the source of all knowledge?

W.Q.J.—It seems to me very difficult if not impossible to answer this question. It is one of those which the great sages and teachers of the world have refused to answer, on the ground that it was profitless to attempt it when we are unable to understand much simpler matters of consciousness, and, were one able to cognize spirit, the question would not be brought forward. Hence they were accustomed to make enquirers wait until they got more interior light. It would seem as if all one could do would be to give probable reasons why no full answer can be made.

If we say that God is not the universe but is an entity apart, then placing the spirit of man as a third separate entity, it will be seen, I should think, that for it to descend into the material universe would be a great degradation from our point of view. But it does not follow that our view is correct; we know that our knowledge of material nature is so limited that we often think that degraded which in fact is not, as is perceived by other minds more comprehensive. Even in the case supposed the spirit might of itself make up its mind to sacrifice and for its own reasons descend into matter. Similarly in life we know there are instances where pure, good, and happy persons take up with relatively degraded conditions for sacrifice or for charity combined with sacrifice. This would be sufficient answer to the question under the assumptions made, unless we think that our individual opinion of what is and what is not the best thing to do must govern.

But I view God and Man and Universe as one whole. As an un-manifested whole I can only name it the Absolute; when it manifests it becomes what is called Spirit and Matter, still of the whole. Without such manifestation there would be nothing: it would abide in itself as what we should have to call "nothing," because then there would be neither cognizer nor cognized. Since it is evident that it has mani-fested, it must follow that it has done so for its own purposes, said by us to be for obtaining consciousness and experience. If so, any "descent into matter" will not be a fall nor a degradation at all, since those are relative terms altogether, and since spirit and matter acting together do so for the one purpose. Man's present state is described by man to be a fallen one, but that is because living in a world of relative things he has to use terms to describe his present state. It does not follow that he will always deal in such words. When evolution shall have car-ried the whole race to a point of immense progress, knowledge, and wisdom, the mind of man will see more of truth, and doubtless be well satisfied with all the work and discipline gone through, leading up to the new and better state.

I think questions of this nature arise unconsciously from a sort of dissatisfaction with present environment in the world, and evolution from a desire of personal satisfaction and betterment, according to a standard made up from and in a civilization that is based on a funda-mental idea of separateness. For if we think we are separate from God and his universe, then alterations of state and condition will be na-turally thought of as needful, and the question will arise, "Why did we fall if we were once divine?" I do not admit that "we were once divine and have fallen"; but say that we are divine and always were, and that the falling is but apparent and due to the personal conscious-ness which calls that soul which is not and that not which is. We are God, and working out in various personalities and environments the great plan in view, and that plan is well known to the dweller in the body who calmly waits for all the material elements to come to a realization of their oneness with God.

QUESTION 319

I should like light on some contradicting points in the fifteenth chap-ter in "The Ocean of Theosophy."

(1) Man did not come from any tribe or family of monkey.

(2) No more Egos from the lower kingdoms will come into the hu-man kingdom until the next Manvantara.

*(3) The Egos in the lower kingdoms could not finish their evolu-
tion in the preceding globe-chain before its dissolution, and coming to
this they go forward age after age, gradually approaching nearer the
man stage. One day they too will become men and act as the advance-
guard and guide for other kingdoms of this and other globes.*

To my understanding this is two different teachings.

W.Q.J.—Beyond question *The Ocean of Theosophy* must have faults.

But I cannot see a contradiction between No. 1 and any of the other
paragraphs in the question. The statement that "man did not come
from monkeys" is one that relates wholly to his physical evolution. It
does not relate to the Ego. The inrush of new Egos ceased at a period
long passed. What can be drawn from this is that Egos and Monads
now involved in the earth's evolution are restricted from this on to
the end of this Manvantara from coming into the human stage of
evolution, with the exception of those confined in the true anthropoid
ape family. What this has to do with contradictions I fail to perceive.
The statement in No. 3, if correctly quoted (and no page is given),
is general and not specific. The Egos in lower kingdoms will become
men—but not in this Manvantara—and then will have to begin the
next Manvantara to help those below them. No assertion being made
that the Egos thus lower now will be men in this Manvantara, there
is no contradiction. In order to make a contradiction one has to import into the sentence that which is not in it nor strictly inferable,
and this is not an allowed rule of construction. Especially so when
the whole of the book is construed together. There are, therefore, not
two different sorts of systems or evolutions present, but at most a
slight want of clearness due to great condensation of a good deal into
a small book. A better writer than I am would undoubtedly have prevented the slightest confusion in the reader. But in reading a book
the best rule of construction is that which harmonizes the whole rather
than one which finds errors by isolating sentences.

QUESTION 322

*If the Ego does not ensoul the body of a child until seven years of
age, how is the suffering under that age to be justified? Of what benefit can it be to the Ego?*

W.Q.J.—Certainly no child could suffer unless such were its Karma.
And as some children do not suffer, the question may be put, why is
it that such a child has only joy? The answer must be that such is
its Karma. In the same way as to suffering: that is the Karma of the
soul. It must be, too, that the Ego perceives the suffering and knows
what it is for. The child may not, but even in one's life it often is
seen in mature years why and for what certain sufferings were under-

gone. Take the case of a youth who has many hardships and priva-
tions from the very earliest moment, and who thereby has developed
in him fortitude and other good qualities, but who might if always
in easy circumstances in youth have become much less strong and not
so good; the suffering here was of value. Again, take the cases of children of savages, who are subjected to what a civilized child would call
suffering. In those there is no suffering at all unless we say there is
an absolute definition of what suffering is. But while it is said the
soul does not gain full possession of the body until seven as a general
rule, it is Karma alone that leads the soul to that body, and hence all
the suffering or the joy is exactly the property of that soul through
the molecules of the body, as we should always remember that the
whole man, body and soul, is united as one, and the mass of molecules
per se is as much the Karma of the incoming soul as any other circumstance, environment, or quality. The question is not to be determined solely on the ground of "benefit to the Ego," but from the point
of view of cause and effect, of relation and of Karma.

QUESTION 324

*Does Theosophy teach that this earth is the hell of this planetary
system? And, if so, does each solar system have its own hell?*

W.Q.J.—Very many writers affirm it to be their opinion that the
real hell is this earth, but it is not clear that such is the view "of
Theosophy," meaning thereby the exact truth. It was taught, apparently,
by Buddha that there is a hell after death of the body, and some of
the conditions of Kâma-Loka are a hell most surely; it is also taught
in Hinduism that there is a hell apart from earth-life. Some Kabalists
seem to lean to the view that earth is hell, and when we consider the
troubles of the soul therein it would appear to be so. For what could
be more dreadful than to be living on the earth with a full knowledge that your acts will lead to a worse state after death and may
finally blot out the soul? But in my opinion the question of hell, like
that of heaven, is to be decided on a consideration of a man as a
thinker who thinks always and who is because he is a thinker. Hence
his life at any time or place must be the result of his thoughts, must be
founded on his thoughts, and have its color and effect from his thoughts.
So if after the death of the body his thoughts before that naturally
lead to the weaving of a beautiful, heavenly web, he will reside in
those thoughts until they are exhausted, and then coming back to
earth again his only hell will be this life. But if, enjoying himself or
not here, he indulges in those thoughts that inevitably lead to the
bitterness of a black life in Kâma-Loka, then his hell must be a stage
or condition of that state of the very worst description, to which earth-
life is heaven in comparison; in his case the return to life here would

be heaven and the other life hell. This leads me to the conclusion that the very lowest and worst hell must be a condition of the mind, and that it must have place out of a body and hence be a stage or degree of Kâma-Loka. This would explain the various statements as to hells, because the awful condition that some souls must be in after the limitations of the body are shaken off, would be of just the sort described, and their particular locus should be in the vicinity of the earth, as that is the representative of the grossest form of matter.

If the law of analogy is to rule, then other worlds must have their own hells of this sort; but the solar system seems to be quite a large enough subject for us to be content with for the present. But it seems to me that all the theories of hell, no matter of what awful variety, are founded on the life of the mind and the soul, and to be drawn from descriptions of that life according to natural results. A dream of oppressive character will give some idea of what a hell may be, for there the mind devoid of body is suffering that which the body afterwards knows to be wholly of thought.

QUESTION 325

Is the sixth principle (Buddhi), in union with the fifth principle (Manas) acting as spiritual consciousness, identical with what has been called "the voice of conscience"?

W.Q.J.—The voice of conscience may be said to be Manas guided by Buddhi, but at the same time the Âtman must also be concerned or there would be no real spiritual basis and no true certainty nor justice in the moving influence of conscience. Call the voice of conscience the voice of the Higher Self and you will be nearer right, and certainly safer from falling into a mere intellectual conception of the Soundless Sound that is very difficult to hear.

QUESTION 326

Two inferences may be drawn from Theosophical writings with regard to the Ego of man: one, that the Ego is a direct incarnation of a god descended from a higher plane to take up its abode in the human form evolved for its use by Nature; the other, that the Ego is latent until the body is sufficiently evolved, when the Ego gradually awakens to activity. While aware that there is only an apparent contradiction, I should be glad to see the two conceptions reconciled.

W.Q.J.—Unless the questioner has some special and peculiar meaning for "direct incarnation," there does not appear to be any actual or apparent contradiction between the two inferences stated. What the special meaning is I do not know. Assume that the Ego is a "god on a higher plane," and there is no impossibility in supposing that, coming to this plane, it is so surrounded by the clouds of matter as to become latent or hidden until the time when the form suitable for this plane is evolved. This is the only sort of latency which can be alleged of the Ego. This also is what Theosophical writings say to me, and among those writings I place *The Bhagavad-Gîtâ*. In that, Krishna, the Supreme Being, identifies himself with *Îśvara*, who is the Ego "seated in the hearts of all beings." Patañjali also says the same, naming that Ego, who is the Spectator of all things, by the name *Om* or Lord of Glory. *The Secret Doctrine* continues the same view. The Christian view and Theosophy must also agree, since Jesus, in exhorting his disciples to be as perfect as the Father in heaven, must have had in view the doctrine that the Father dwelt in and is Man: otherwise we could not become perfect as he is. I therefore do not see the need for reconciling contradictions which do not exist.

The Ego—meaning thereby the Self, Îśvara, Krishna, the Supreme— is unborn, changeless, all-knowing. It knows evolving Nature, the instrument, but the latter comes but slowly to a knowledge of the Self. It is therefore latent only in the sense that there are periods when the instrument, the false personality, recognizes it not. Such a period is the present, when although the body has been evolved by Nature— with the aid of the Ego—we do not know the Ego. Why not, then, if the inferences of the question are right, apply them to the present time? If thus applied, then, under the position thus taken, the Ego is still latent and will be until *Manas* is fully developed in a succeeding round.

To assume that the Ego is latent until Nature has had time to evolve the suitable form is to give to Nature power and consciousness which we withhold from the Ego. Why, then, not call Nature the Ego and do away altogether with the latter? Or you would have to assume a God beyond and above both Nature and Ego. The universe is either self-existent or it was projected into existence by some being whom we will call God. The Ego either was created by this God or is this God in itself. If the universe was not projected but is self-existent, then it and the Ego are one—God. Hence Nature in "evolving a body" which the Ego chooses to use is only showing forth the action of one of the powers of that Ego. But we can never solve the question of why the Universe or the Ego chooses to have two sides or ends, the negative and positive. All we know is that it must be so. The negative is— Nature, qualities, false personality, matter; the positive is—God, Ego, Spirit, Life.

QUESTION 332

In what way and through whom have the special efforts been made by the Masters the last quarter of each century to bring about the results now attempted through the TS.?

W.Q.J.—On the belief held by so many that the Masters have acted through the T.S. and have done so before in other centuries, many names might be mentioned as possibly those who at other times have been made or induced to act to the same end. Jacob Boehme seems to be one. He was acted on thus and wrote much in the same line, though with a Christian and anthropomorphic tendency and bias. He was followed by many, and to this day has influence through his books. He was very ignorant as the world goes, but showed great interior learning. He was a poor shoemaker. He was once interviewed by a total stranger who told him he was destined to wield such an influence, and never saw the person again. De Saint-Martin in France was another, and Count de Saint-Germain, both having, as would appear from their writings, a knowledge of the source of their inspiration absent from Boehme. De Saint-Martin was learned and had much correspondence with other lands on these very matters, but of course not so specific in detail. Cagliostro was another, and from all the records left of him, much of which was used by the novelist Dumas, he was an active agent of similar influences and spoke the same words and dealt in similar matters. He was not a charlatan, but was a man of great power. At the same time was Swedenborg, who was an unconscious instrument, but one who wielded a very great influence in all directions even down to the present day. His theories were in advance of the time.

As to the manner of setting the work going, it differs with each place and time, and according to the time assumes a different phase. Boehme, for instance, was moved from within, and Swedenborg the same, for if an Adept has the powers credited to him it is easy for him to inject the right thought and aspiration at the right time to bring on the desired effect. In the case of H. P. Blavatsky we have one who evidently was fully aware of the work and who and what was at work. Hence her greater and wider power. This was exactly in accordance with the times she lived in, for now thought and religion are free; and hence, as she said, the time was come to make it more plain and definite. Doubtless at the next messenger's coming it will be plainer still, as it is not likely the world will go back to barbarism.

QUESTION 338

Is it an advantage or otherwise for a child to be psychic? If an adult is mediumistic, is it to be regarded as an evil, or, properly trained, is it a help on the Path? If sometimes a person suddenly feels impelled—the words tumbling out of one's mouth, as it were—to foretell future events, which more often than not come true, is that mediumship and to be avoided? There is no seeing or hearing, only an impelling force: is that to be struggled against? These questions have come up in our Branch.

W.Q.J.—If a child is born as a psychic in a family where the true philosophy of life is understood, so that right training is given to faculties so much misunderstood and abused, then such psychic inheritance might become a boon. When the opposite is the case—as will generally be in these days—then the difficulties and dangers may be many. However, the question seems profitless to me, because birth, like death, is inevitable for all who are born—it is a fact, and so will the possession of psychic powers be a fact. To be born in a wise family is fortunate, to come into a wicked one may be the reverse.

Mediumship, in general, is not a blessing, but often the opposite. Preliminary inquiry should be made to see if proper training can be had, if right knowledge of philosophy is possessed by the person. But as mediumship means—as now used—being under the control of some other power or consciousness than one's own, then it ought to be avoided. Inspiration from or by one's Higher Ego is not mediumship; it is illumination. It cannot be secured save by discipline, altruism, charity, deep love, and highest aspiration.

The editor has excellently answered the query referring to prophetic and other utterances. If those come naturally they ought to be allowed. No selfish use should be made of the power, and if the utterer remains pure in motive, thought, and act, sufficient protection will be afforded by the power of those virtues. Lastly, I should think that questions like these are not profitable for Branches. They relate wholly to phenomena which cannot be understood nor explained until one has thoroughly and accurately grasped the philosophy of man's nature. They are matters more for personal and individual attention and investigation than for the serious consideration of a Branch.

QUESTION 345

If we follow out the Law of Analogy, would we not naturally suppose that other worlds, in this or any other chain, would have similar forms if in the same state of development? Would not those inhabiting them, if endowed with reason and Manas, naturally have forms similar to ours? Would not the chemical conditions be similar to our own? I ask because there seems to be a difference of opinion. The great ocean of nebular matter from which worlds are formed must have been of one and the same matter, operated on by the same force, moved by the same Spirit.

W.Q.J.—I do not think the law of analogy will show that in other worlds, save those that go through the same sort of evolution, the human being will have the same form as ourselves. The law of analogy as to plan and general matters may apply, but form is something that is infinite in variety not only here but probably everywhere. If here we find, as we do, an almost endless difference as to form, then why should we suppose that in other worlds the same form for man obtains? I do not think it does. Nor do I think that the form we now have is the one we will have for our bodies in the distant future, nor that it was the first form man had on this globe. He began, in my opinion, quite differently, and will end for this earth as different as he began. Of course as to this we have definite statements from H.P.B. alone, but hers seem to me to agree with general laws and with the course of evolution.

Take, for instance, what she says as to the pineal gland, its former use and future possibilities. She shows quite strongly that at one time it was on the outside of the frame and had its use as an eye, and asserts that in the far future it will again be in use with the other two, thus making three. This will be a substantial variation. Similarly as to the spinal column: she says later there will be two, and this would add another variety. And so on, could we go through many other departments. For if, as she says, the Fifth Race will witness the coming out in the air of a new and now unknown element that will correspond to fully-developed Manas, that must also produce greater difference and variety. So if we find now so much difference here as to form and think there may be still more for the future, what ground is there for supposing that on other worlds men will have or do have our form?

But there is another reason for the negative answer. It is in the septenary necessities of nature. Each of the companion globes has its place, use, and evolution for the race which goes around the whole chain of seven, and on each a different form might be the one appropriate, for there all will be quite different and just as real then as what we have here is real to us. And if similar great laws prevail elsewhere, as we are bound to think, then the differences as to form must be entirely beyond comprehension now.

While it is held to be true that one law and one spirit are in and under the whole, it is also held that that great whole has in itself, as we can see from a view of nature, infinite possibilities for change of form, function, power, environment, or anything else. So I am not able to see how a difference of opinion can rightly arise on the point raised, since to hold the contention that the forms must be similar is to say in effect that nature does not and will not change and has not, and did not present to our eyes and perception the most wonderful variety of form. The facts seem to throw the burden upon those who think the form must be the same, for all the facts as far back as we can go are against that view.

The Theosophical Forum

NEW SERIES

[May 1895, through February 1896]

QUESTION 1

If we admit the truth of theosophical doctrines regarding the inner constitution of man and his fate after death, what would be the Forum's *view as to capital punishment?*

W.Q.J.—My view is that capital punishment is both useless and injurious. It is as great an injustice to the world of beings left unexecuted as to the one so violently sent out of life. They used to kill men in England for stealing a ten-penny nail or a loaf of bread, but thieves and thieving did not lessen. Murders have not decreased. In the country districts executions are means for brutalizing the people, who make a hanging an occasion for a gala gathering in order to see a man legally killed. But theosophically it is far worse. The fact that the sudden killing is legal makes no difference with the laws of nature. The man is suddenly cut off from his body, and, just like a suicide, is condemned to be a 'spook'. He is dead so far as the body is concerned, but is astrally alive. Worse than a suicide he is filled with hate and revenge which he must wreak on some one. At first he is not able to do much, but soon he finds that there are sensitive persons on the earth who can be filled with his vicious and raging passions. These poor souls are then influenced to commit crimes; being filled mentally— from the inner planes—with the ideas and passions of the criminal, they are at last moved to do what their mind is filled with. The executed criminal does not have to know what is going on, for his raging passions, untouched by the executioner, excite and influence of themselves whoever is sensitive to them. This is why many a crime is suddenly committed by weak persons who appear to be carried away by an outside force. It seems hardly possible that anyone could believe in theosophical and occult doctrines and at the same time commend capital punishment.

QUESTION 2

According to Theosophical teaching, intuition is the sixth sense of man. Can it be cultivated, and, if so, how? If it is a sense like hearing, seeing, and smelling, why cannot it be trained as they are?

W.Q.J.—I do not know that it is "according to theosophical teaching that intuition is the sixth sense." It would be well to have citation of chapter or article where this statement is made. The question of the sixth sense is speculative as yet, nothing being decided. Like the fourth dimension, it is involved in doubt. Hence it should not be assumed that the assertion in the question is correct. Many persons hold that intuition is not the sixth sense, because it may very well be that a species of very rapid reasoning enters into intuitional acts, making them so rapid in conclusion as to appear devoid of reasoning as a means to find the conclusion arrived at. For myself I do not believe that intuition is the sixth sense nor any sense at all. But whatever intuition is, it can only be cultivated by having the right mental poise, the right philosophy and the right ethics; and by giving the intuition scope, or chance, so that by many mistakes we at last arrive at a knowledge of how to use it.

QUESTION 3

What is precisely meant by Soul *in Theosophical literature? We say the "Soul of man," the "Soul of the world," the "Soul of things."*

W.Q.J.—Theosophical literature has not as yet come to a *precise* meaning for "soul," nor can it until the English language has been so altered as to remove the confusion now existing among such terms as "soul" and "spirit," and in the uses to which both are put. So long as we have in fact but two terms, *soul* and *spirit*, to designate so many beings, kinds of beings and powers as those are used for, just so long will there be confusion.

QUESTION 4

If it is true that to ascertain the truth of the doctrines put forward by Theosophy many lives will be required after one has started on the Path, how and where am I to find that Path and to know it when I do?

W.Q.J.—Do not look at this matter as if you had never been on the path before. It is more than likely in every case where an inquirer asks this question, either mentally or of some other person, that he has trod the path in another life. Some hold that all Theosophists were on this path hitherto. Each life is a step on the path, and even though we may make many and huge mistakes, we can still be on the way. One should not be anxious to know if he is on the path by reason of a constant conformity to some set rules or regulations about a path. That anxiety is mechanical. Nature and the path of true wisdom are not mechanical, but for each soul there is a way and means suitable to it and to none other. By watching these mechanical ways mistakes are made. For instance, one becomes a vegetarian from a secret desire to get nearer the astral world thereby, and not because it is deemed a sin to take life. The rule will not be violated. Great inconvenience is undergone and much watching indulged in so as to keep the rule, and much attention and energy is given to it which is taken from some other duty. All this is a mistake, for the kingdom of heaven is not gained by eating meat or by refraining from it. This mistake is due to too much desire to be sure one is on the path.

But it is not necessary one should know that he is on the path. If he uses his best reason, best intuition, and best effort to find out his duty and do it, then one may be sure the path is there without stopping to look for it. And the path for one person may be the carting of packages, while for another it may lie in deep study or contemplation. On this the *Bhagavad-Gîtâ* says that the duty of another is full of danger, and it is better to die in the performance of one's own duty than to perform most wonderfully the duty of another.

QUESTION 9

If India is the birthplace of the Theosophical philosophy, and if the Hindus have more natural capacities for occult knowledge than we, should we not accept those of them who come here and offer themselves as our teachers rather than waste time at Branch meetings in discussing questions concerning which we really know but little?

W.Q.J.—Doubtless India is now the most ancient storehouse of Âryan philosophy which may be called theosophical—but no one is able to say that it is the birthplace. Egypt with its tremendous civilization, its philosophy and magic, is silent, and there is no one to put forward its claim. Beyond question also, the Hindus of today have more metaphysical acumen than we have. But the West is creeping up. And intellectual, metaphysical gifts are not spiritual gifts. We have all the intellect we need, active and latent. The Hindu of today is a talker, a hair-splitter, and when he has not been altered by contact with Western culture he is superstitious. Such we do not want as teachers. We will hail them as brothers and co-workers but not as our Magisters. But those Hindus who come here are not teachers. They have come here for some personal purpose and they teach no more nor better than is found in our own theosophical literature: their yoga is but half or quarter yoga, because if they knew it they would not teach a barbarian Westerner. What little yoga they teach is to be read at large in our books and translations.

The craze for present-day India is an eminently foolish one. If one will calmly examine the facts he will find the nation as a whole superstitious to the last degree; the few theosophists and Englishized ones being but as a drop in the ocean. It is not a united nation and cannot itself help the West. For centuries it has helped no one outside itself. As a whole—there are grand exceptions—the Brahmans keep up the superstition and proud isolation. We have the words of Master

K.H.—an Indian[1]—that India is spiritually degraded. Fakirs and wonder-workers and hypnotizers do not prove spirituality. It is the destiny of India to hold as a storehouse good things to come out later; the West, as newest, youngest, and hence least degraded spiritually, has to work and learn so as to help the East.

And the questioner speaking only of India seems to forget great Tibet and all Buddhist countries. What of those? What of their ignorance and superstition? Is India to be talked of alone, and all these others left out? It is time to call a halt, and for theosophists to broaden their conception of what and where the East is, and to stop talking as if the sun in the morning shone only on India.

QUESTION 14

What mental obstructions are in the way of meditation and most frequently present?

W.Q.J.—The greatest foe and that most frequently present is memory, or recollection. This was at one time called *phantasy*. The moment the mind is restrained in concentration for the purpose of meditation, that moment the images, the impressions, the sensations of the past begin to troop through the brain and tend to instantly and constantly disturb the concentration. Hence the need for less selfishness, less personality, less dwelling on objects and desiring them—or sensation. If the mind be full of impressions, there is also a self-reproductive power in it which takes hold of these seeds of thought and enlivens them. Recollection is the collecting together of impressions, and so it constitutes the first and the greatest obstruction to meditation.

QUESTION 16

Are theosophical doctrines for the cultured classes? Should we pay most attention, in propaganda, to the cultured and "respectable," or to those in a lower stratum?

W.Q.J.—If theosophical doctrines are to be of any benefit to the race, then they must be for all classes, poor and rich, cultured and uncultured, young and old. Some people think that these doctrines are really only comprehensible by the educated and cultured; that most attention should be paid to these classes, to learned scientific persons, and to those who possess a worldly and powerful reputation. For, they argue, if we can get hold of such, then we may the more quickly affect the others.

But what has experience shown? Merely that the cultivated and respectable and scientific have laughed at Theosophy, and never would

---

[1] [A Kashmiri.]

have paid it any attention if not forced to. A very prominent scientist, Prof. Crookes, early became a member of the London Lodge, but nothing has resulted therefrom to the distinct benefit of the movement. Many attempts have been made in the parlors of the rich, with hardly any result; certainly not enough to justify the outlay of strength and time. The theosophical propaganda has gone forward in the face of considerable opposition and coldness from the so-called better classes. Very true it is that the working, laboring classes have not pushed it, nor do they, as a whole, know a very great deal about it; yet that indefinite section of the working classes sometimes called the "middle class" has been its great propagator and supporter.

As to understanding the doctrines, it is my opinion that this is as easy for the uneducated as for the educated. Indeed, in some cases, over-education has been a bar, and deep intellectual study of Theosophy has led to a want of comprehension of the principle of Brotherhood and to a violation of it. The purpose and aim of Theosophy in the world is not the advancement of a few in the intellectual plane, but the amelioration of all human affairs through the practice of Brotherhood. The theosophical doctrines show what Brotherhood is and how it is to be practiced, and if we cannot succeed in the practice of it then we are *failures*. Brotherhood is more likely to arise in the ranks below than to spring from those above, for it cannot be declared that present conditions—even in governments abroad—are largely due to the better, the upper, the educated class.

However—and here lies the duty of those Theosophists who have education—it is necessary to clearly explain the doctrines to the uneducated classes before these can grasp them. But when so explained, it will be found that in practice alone the doctrines are understood. We must not forget, in all this, that in America the proportion of illiteracy is not large, and hence in this land it is easier to propagate Theosophy among the masses. And history, the facts of today, amply prove this.

QUESTION 23

Believing in reincarnation as many Theosophists do, and considering the fact that our ten preceding births may have been in ten different nations or races, how can the sentiment of patriotism be defended?

W.Q.J.—Patriotism is love for the land in which your body was born, and it would seem on reflection that whether ten preceding births were in other nations and races or not has nothing to do with the patriotism felt in this. In each birth the same feeling would be felt for each country. All this has no connection with a defence of patriotism. Inasmuch as the sentiment has been always recognized as noble and good its defence seems unnecessary. Why should Theosophists, I may ask, raise a question of doubt as to such a high sentiment as this? It needs no defence at all. At first the man may love only himself; then he enlarges his love and extends it to his family; then a little more and he takes in his town or county; until at last he still further enlarges his love so as to embrace his country. Patriotism then is a love that is larger than the personal and hence a nearer approach to that feeling which would make all men brothers. A person cannot die for his country unless his love has gone beyond the confines of his family. Patriotism is in fact the best example humanity can furnish of an attempt at the universality of love that belongs to the Self within.

QUESTION 30

In what respect does a Master differ from an Adept, an Initiate, or a Mahâtma? These terms seem to be used rather loosely and as if interchangeable; strictly speaking, how would they rank, and what qualifications and powers are the adjunct of one who has earned the name Master?

W.Q.J.—It is not possible to clear up these difficulties of language. They are all—except *Mahâtma*—interchangeable. That term of course stands alone, but when it is put into English as "Great Soul," then those two words begin the confusion again, because *Soul* is not definite. A Master is an Adept and an Adept is a Master, and both are Initiates. For my part I see no way of settling the question, and personally I do not want it settled yet; I want no strict limitations in terms until the English language has become scientific.

QUESTION 33

In several writings I have noticed belief in lost souls. If such belief be correct how can that passage of Arnold's in The Light of Asia,[1] *which ends with this, be true: "All* will reach the sunlit snow"; *and also the thought of Nirvâna?*

W.Q.J.—The two statements can be true. The quotation is simply from Mr. Arnold's words, and he is not a religious authority at all. Again "all will reach" is not defined. All what? Is it all souls, or all atoms, or all monads? And in what way, or as what, will "all reach the thought of Nirvâna" did Buddha teach? They could all reach it even were some of them lost to individual consciousness by being absorbed into some of the others. Arnold's work does not decide such questions; it is popular. If you will read discussions of the priests of Buddha almost immediately after his death you will find many things

---

[1] [Book VIII.]

to contradict present views of what was taught by Buddha. There is one long discussion, a report of which is in the Royal Asiatic Society's archives, upon Individuality, in which the priests who knew Buddha or his friends decided that there is no Individuality. Hence it is not very important to decide about Mr. Arnold's verses. The subject of lost souls is treated in theosophical literature slightly and is held by many to be true. But one must then be careful and accurate in the use of terms and be sure to decide what is called soul. The "several writings" referred to should be quoted as has been asked in the FORUM notice.

QUESTION 35

In the Theosophical Siftings,[1] *Vol. I., "Epitome of Theosophical Teachings," Page 15, it says: "When the Adept has reached a certain very high point in his evolution he may, by a mere wish, become what the Hindus call, a 'Deva'—or lesser god. If he does this, then although he will enjoy the bliss and power of that state for a vast length of time, he will not at the next Pralaya partake of the conscious life 'in the bosom of the Father,' but has to pass down into matter at the next new 'creation,' performing certain functions that could not be now made clear, and has to come up again through the elemental world; but this fate is not like that of the Black Magician who falls into Avîchi." Now in what form does he pass into the next new creation and what is the work he has to do?*

W.Q.J.—As I wrote the passage cited, I may properly reply. The very quotation shows that "the work he has to do" cannot be told, for, as I said he would perform "certain functions that could not now be made clear." The whole matter is a reference to a very obscure doctrine, but little known, that if the Adept voluntarily takes the delights, pleasures and powers referred to, he is compelled, after millions of years of enjoyment, to re-enter objective nature at the elemental stage. That is plainly related. So it is quite clear that the quotation as made answers the question put. This the questioner will see himself if he will rewrite, after his question at the foot, the whole of the statement quoted in the beginning.

QUESTION 36

Please explain the following passage from The Bhagavad-Gîtâ, Chapter II, [verse 31], Judge's edition, page 14: "A Soldier of the Kshatriya tribe has no duty superior to lawful war," and especially show why the answer to Question I, New Series, is not inconsistent with the passage.

---

[1] [London, *Theosophical Pub. House,* 1888-89 etc.]

W.Q.J.—It is a phrase meaning that the duty one is born to, or has, is the one to be performed and that no other assumed duty is superior. From the Hindu point of view it refers to caste and that a member of the warrior caste is born for fighting which for him is, according to his religion, a duty. As Arjuna was a Kshatriya, Krishna naturally referred to his caste duty. Had he been a Sûdra, or servant, then the verse would read that a "slave of the Sûdra tribe has no duty superior to performing service as required." The Vedic religion, unlike the Buddhist, permits a certain caste to fight and kill, *lawfully* and in defense of the country. But the Brahman and the merchant are not permitted to thus kill. Hence each in his caste performs the duty of that caste into which he was born. Looking at the verse from an American and non-caste standpoint, then it is simply an assertion that present duty, when known, is superior to any assumed or unknown duty.

I fail to see what Question I has to do with this. That question was upon capital punishment. If one is of the Vedic religion he will allow of lawful war for defense of country, if he is a Buddhist he will be against all killing; and both may be against capital punishment; the answers to Question I, did not declare anything as to what particular religion was followed. Capital punishment for crime is a very different matter from sudden death in lawful war.

QUESTION 37

What theosophical reasons are there for preferring cremation to earth burial?

W. Q. J.—I find in the answer to this question which appeared in September, some statements regarding the Egyptians to which I would like to take exception on the ground that they cannot possibly be proved. It is said that because the Egyptians thought the soul could not gain its freedom until the body disintegrated, they therefore embalmed the body in order to chain the soul to it. I cannot agree to this at all. And all that we read of the aspirations for freedom and desire to be with the Gods which the Egyptians indulged in, would tend to show that if they knew how to allow the soul to gain its freedom they would not try to prevent it by making it stay in a mummy.

The answer then goes on to say that the soul being thus cut off from physical life and pent up in the body with its desires, it there had to fight its own nature, and if it did not succeed it had to fight again; this, the answer said, enabled the soul to have immense power upon its return to earth where it might achieve union (with the highest) without difficulty. It seems therefore from this that for a time at least it would be better to be a mummy than a man. I do not agree with the propositions made, they cannot be proved, and I do not think they can be shown to be anything more than fanciful; at present I do not know of any book or record in which there is any account or hint of this doctrine.

QUESTION 38

The effect of alcohol being degrading, why is it that a person under its influence will sometimes give expression to lofty sentiments and high moral teachings? A friend of mine knows a case of this kind. The person when in a drunken fit quotes many fine passages from the Bible and other sources.

W.Q.J.—The assertion in the question is too sweeping. Some of the effects of alcohol are degrading, and some are not. It has many good uses. The abuse of it is what is degrading. There is no necessary sequence between the degrading effect and the utterance of lofty sentiments in every case, and yet in many cases there is. It is well known that—just as happens in hypnotism—the effect of alcohol may sometimes be to dull the outer brain and release the recollection of the teaching in early life of religious or lofty sentiments. This is like a phonograph which, as a machine, may repeat any good thing; the drunkard has become a maudlin machine. But the inner memory cannot be made drunk, and it is that memory which brings out the expression of lofty sentiments. In the same way morphine, more degrading in effect than alcohol, causes the taker sometimes to utter high sentiment and write magnificent literary matter.

QUESTION 40

Was Jesus the only Avatâra who asserted that thought and intent was as culpable as actual deed? A friend states that to be the case and therefore holds Jesus to have gone further in ethics than any other reformer.

W.Q.J.—The friend who states that Jesus was the only teacher who asserted "that thought was as culpable as deed," should be compelled before being allowed to make a conclusion, to bring forward his or her authority. It would be found that there is no authority for such a statement but that history is directly opposed to it; Buddha always taught that the thoughts were the most important and were the actual deeds, the things in themselves, and that the outer deed was but the expression of a thought, and that only by good thoughts could we attain to perfection. In many ways this can be found in the Buddhist and Indian teachings and indeed in the teachings of all great reformers before Jesus. Buddha and his disciples taught that although a man might do a very charitable act, yet if he did not think charitably and if he was doing the act for the sake of gain or glory, it was his thoughts that determined the result for him. Therefore the thought which was not charitable was to be blamed. This shows how important they held the thought to be. Jesus having been educated in the schools of the Essenes and probably all the other mystics, all of whom dwelt upon the importance of thought, simply gave out what he had been taught.

QUESTION 41

On page 10 of May FORUM, *in answer to Question 5, appears the following: "Those actions which in the moment are like nectar, are, in the long run like poison;—and those actions which in the moment are like poison, are, in the long run like nectar." (The Bhagavad Gîtâ)*[1] *This sentence seems to indicate that one should always do that which is disagreeable; that that I would do, I should not do, and that that I would not do, I should do. We are all seeking the truth from a strong desire to know of the truth;—should we curb that desire and seek falsehood? For one, I would like to see every man reap the full rewards of his labor;—should I curb that desire and despoil him (or assist) of those rewards? No man, however base, loves to be deceived, and there are some who do not like to practice deception;—should I curb that desire and practice deception? Shall or should we learn to sip poison from nectar, and then nectar from poison? If so we must learn to love both; evidently there is something lacking in the sentence quoted.*

W.Q.J.—The confusion produced as shown in this question is due to the fact that *C.F.W.* did not quote the words of the chapter in question, and that the questioner did not consult the *Gîtâ* for himself. It refers solely to pleasure or benefit or enjoyment and not to actions specifically. It mentions three kinds of pleasures. The first is due to a purified understanding and will appear in the beginning to the man who has lived in the senses to be *as* poison, that is, objectionable, but the end will be "as the waters of life," because it arises from *sattva* or truth. This does not mean we are to seek for poisonous or disagreeable things. The second sort of pleasure is derived from our senses, seems sweet at first, but in the end will be as poison, being derived from passion or *rajas*. The third includes all those so-called pleasures which in beginning and end are bad in themselves. Looked at in this way and having read the chapter the questioner will not ask the question; he ought to read the poem.

QUESTION 43

Do monsters of depravity ever seek rebirth through any but mothers of like character?

---

[1] [In Mr. Judge's own rendition, Chapter 19, p. 127, he translates the term nectar as the "water of life." *Bhagavad-Gîtâ* 18, p. 98, ślokas 37, 38.]

W.Q.J.—I would like to answer this question so as to satisfy the questioner, but it being a question of statistics it is not possible to be exact from want of data. The question seems to bear the inference that the questioner thinks monsters of depravity seek mothers of like character. But is this so? Do we not know that all through time very bad men and women have been born of virtuous, righteous mothers? It was the mother's Karma to be so unfortunate. In Indian history there was a monster named Kansa born of a good mother; doubtless the mothers of Nero or other wicked Roman emperors were good women. All this being the case, we are at liberty to assume that sometimes monsters of depravity obtain birth through mothers of opposite character. If we were to insist on the opposite, then we must say, in the case of great sages and Avatâras, such as Buddha, that they only seek birth through mothers who are great as they; but this is known not to be the case.

QUESTION 50

The fundamental question, "What is the criterion of Theosophy?" calls for an answer. Has Theosophy the power of growth, progress and advancement in line with all new expositions of truth? In the minds of many the writings of H.P.B. are regarded as the infallible oracles of Theosophy. But in time criticism is sure to do its work. Consequently it is necessary soon to give out a definition of it much broader, simpler, and more unequivocal than any heretofore offered.

W.Q.J.—This is in fact a request to formulate and promulgate a dogmatic statement of Theosophy as we understand it. That is, to go completely back on the genius of the Theosophical movement, which is for the destruction of dogmatism. The strength of Theosophy lies in the fact that it is not to be defined. It is the wisdom of the gods, or of nature. This means that evolution, slowly progressing, will bring out new truths and new aspects of old truths, thus absolutely preventing any dogmas or "unequivocal definitions." Were we to make and declare a definition of Theosophy it would be only the words of those who participated in drawing it up, and not acceptable to all. And were it possible that all would accept, then would be sounded the doom of the movement. Hence the reply to the question, "What is the criterion of Theosophy?" is that it is found in each man's perception of the Truth: therefore there is no single criterion.

If any persons regard H.P.B.'s writings as the infallible oracles of Theosophy, they go directly against her own words and the works themselves; they must be people who do not indulge in original thinking and cannot make much impression on the times.

As for the Theosophical Society, the moment it makes a hard and fast definition of Theosophy it will mark the first hour of its decay.

Inasmuch as Theosophy is the whole body of truth about man and nature, either known now or hereafter to be discovered, it has the "power of growth, progress and advancement," since every new truth makes it clearer. But among the truths will not be reckoned at any time the definitions, dogmas, creeds or beliefs laid down by man.

QUESTION 51

I should like to have explained what is meant by "all experience" in The Secret Doctrine, *Vol. I, page 17, where it is stated that it is necessary to pass through "all experience" in this manvantara before the Divine Spark can be individualized. Does this mean that one must in the human kingdom have experience of each phase of civilization? Must one be a plumber, carpenter, painter, minister, lawyer, physician, etc., before he can reach full consciousness? I am aware that all experience cannot be attained in any way but by repeated re-embodiments, but the stumbling-block in my mind is what is meant by all experience. Further, is it necessary to go through the whole school of crime in order to develop strength to progress?*

W.Q.J.—First, experience, under evolution, in and through all nature's kingdoms is a necessity for all egos because they constitute the spirit, spring and impulse of evolution; without them there would be no evolution. Hence all of that general experience is necessary because inevitable; and only by that great experience is individuality attainable. That is so because such is the law of our being.

Now, take any one of such progresses or kingdoms. It was full of variety. Such variations were inevitable and necessary. Curious shapes of animals were evolved in the evolutionary struggle, all necessary in such a struggle to make perfect. But they were only details in a grand whole, like steps on a journey. Does it trouble us, does the question about "all" arise here? If not, why should it arise about mere details of changing human life, not yet perfect, still struggling to attain, to alter, to polish? Plumbers, painters and carpenters are mechanics, as are those in many other more desirable occupations, but all are for mechanical experience due to our, or any, form of civilization. And the ego cannot get intuition of mechanics if it never is put through that sort of experience. "All experience," being thus found in a statement relative to great outlines and objects of evolution, must be considered thus and not as a mere detail. All possible experiences can be put under a few heads and it is those general types of experience we have to pass through. How would an ego know of motherhood and fatherhood if it never had the experience? Telling about them would not suffice. How would it know of governing if it had never governed, nor of submission if it had never been in bonds? There should be no stumbling-block in the word "all."

QUESTION 52

I understand Devachan to be a state in which the highest ideal of the late personality is attained. H.P.B. says, "He who has placed himself beyond the veil of mâyâ or illusion can have no Devachan."[1] Is it then to be understood that the farther advanced the Ego in the knowledge of Truth, and the closer it has come into communion with the one Great Truth, the less need it has for that dreamlike state, Devachan?

W.Q.J.—I never heard that in Devachan the "highest ideal of the late personality is attained." Were that so the question would answer itself. I have therefore to drop the first statement when considering the question. Attainment of "highest ideals" is only possible when one is above all illusions; certainly Devachan furnishes no such condition. There the soul pursues its highest ideals spiritually, and, seeming to carry those all out to highest perfection, it is benefitted, enlarged and strengthened. Devachan is for rest and recuperation and not for action. Not alone do evil and mediocre people go to Devachan, but pre-eminently those who have high and deep—though unfulfilled—aspirations. These are artists, musicians, dreamers, religious enthusiasts. And they, having impetuous thoughts, stay there longer than others.

But those who have been through all those experiences here and in Devachan, and who have triumphed over illusion through self-conquest, do not need Devachan because they have grown to their full strength and cannot against their wish be thrust into it by natural force. So they do not become subject to it. But that is the Adept. And he can enter into the Devachanic state of another so as to help and benefit the other. We are not such as yet, but may perhaps some day, in the distant future, be able to do such great and altruistic work.

QUESTION 55

How far should branches go in permitting the discussions at their meetings to be led into questions concerning topics not directly bearing on the theosophical philosophy or in permitting members or outsiders to detail their views on socialism, spiritualism, single tax, or the like, unless they have a direct bearing on Universal Brotherhood?

W.Q.J.—While branches have the right to have any sort of discussion they please, it has been found that those which import into the meetings

---

1 [*The Key to Theosophy,* p. 148.]

subjects not such as we call theosophical, have a quarrelsome and precarious existence. Special topics, such as Socialism or Single Tax, always lead to friction and away from Theosophy, because they create partisan strife. And again, members should not attempt to make special applications of Theosophy to such topics unless they know both so well as to be able to instruct their hearers. And do members in general know Theosophy, even, so well as to be qualified to apply it to anything but daily life and conduct? I do not think so. If a Socialist or Single Taxer, or rabid Spiritualist is asked to speak on any one of those subjects, he will be found to be a partisan or extremist, and most likely, if well up in his particular topic, he will not be versed in Theosophy.

Theosophy is so new, and its adherents so few, and all reformatory questions (as specialties) are so changeable and evanescent, it is far wiser for a branch to go on studying Theosophy and propagating it together with the idea of Universal Brotherhood than to offer particular explanations on empirical topics. Were Theosophy understood and practiced, everything needing reform would be at once reformed.

I think the time to settle this question is later, because as yet the mass of members in general are not versed in Theosophy. They are unwilling to go to school though they need schooling in Theosophy. When they can thoroughly and at the word explain the doctrines we promulgate they will then be competent to touch other matters.

QUESTION 56

It has been said that all sounds are still in existence, and that if we could rise high enough we would be able to hear every sound that has ever been produced. If this be true, would not the intermingling of so many sounds only produce a roar as of thunder?

W.Q.J.—This is not a profitable Theosophical query. The Forum is not for scientific replies, but for theosophical discussion. This question relates solely to natural physical laws. Science deals with it and says the resultant sound would be a harmonious tone. Questioner should read books on vibrations of air; music; sound-waves; and consult practical scientific men on this question. Suppose the Forum replied "No," or "Yes," to the question, what would be the effect on theosophical doctrines? Nothing at all, and no advance made either way.

QUESTION 57

When great teachers like St. Paul, St. John, Socrates and others incarnate, do they commence with the degree of development with which they closed the preceding incarnation? If so, why are there so few great souls in the world teaching and living the proper life?

W.Q.J.—Let us take the last part of your question first, and ask you how do you know there are "so few great souls in the world"? It would not be right to judge all other men by yourself nor by a limited number of persons you may have known, hence it is likely you do not so judge, but have merely assumed that there are very few souls in the world like unto those you mention. Such an assumption does not seem to be a correct one. There very probably are among us now many great souls of the past. Nothing in philosophy or the doctrine of reincarnation is against such a view. We being actors on the present stage are not able to judge whether some others of whom we know are great men or not, who may be regarded by posterity as great personages like to St. Paul and your other examples. It is more than likely St. Paul was not highly regarded in his time; now, in the distance, he shines out. Certainly we know that Socrates had such poor regard from his contemporaries as to be poisoned because he was thought not to be a good man; now we, so far off, look at him differently. In the same way will it be respecting our own present times after the lapse of centuries.

As to where any Ego will begin in any life is determined by karma and the needs of development. The whole front, or mass, of our nature is so enormous that one life or one sort of development is only a small part of it: there is no possibility of at once exhibiting it all. So the former life of St. Paul may be now certainly hidden for future use while he is undergoing another necessary development which had formerly been neglected. If we look at his life we find he was a persecutor once. That was not at all atoned for by his subsequent conduct—unless of course you admit vicarious salvation—which I do not. He must atone for all that hurt done to others, and his reincarnation in some obscure place and body for several lives would quite accord with the needs of the case. So you can reason out the whole matter, recollecting that karma goes by cause and effect, and that the whole vast nature of man must be considered, and that you and I do not know the whole nature of those people you refer to. Hence we must conclude that the present age and the karma of past sages do not coincide in such a way as to produce many living before us. And if we ask what is the use, we must conclude that in such a selfish, superficial time as this they would be useless and out of place.

QUESTION 59

It is said that at the time of death everyone reviews all the actions of his past life and even knows the object for which he took upon him the now fading personality. Is this knowledge or vision possible at any other time during life?

W.Q.J.—It is said to be possible for one who knows all the secret laws of nature and of his own being. Certainly it would appear that no other sort of person could possibly do it. And such individuals must be almost as rare as the horns upon a hare.

QUESTION 61

What is the opinion of the leaders of the T. S. in regard to vegetarianism?

W.Q.J.—Physicians and those who have tried vegetarianism are those who should speak on this. The opinions of "leaders," as such, are of no consequence. I tried it for nine years, and found it injurious. This is because the western man has no heredity of vegetarianism behind him, and also because his dishes as a vegetarian are poor. They should be confined to rice, barley, wheat, oats, some nuts and a little fruit; but westerners don't like such a meager variety. The stomach does not digest vegetables, it is for meat; the teeth are for tearing and grinding meat. Most of those vegetarians I know eat a whole lot of things injurious to them and are not benefited. Had we an ancestry going back thousands of years, vegetarians always, the case might be different. I know that most of the experienced physicians we have in the Society— and I know a great many—agree with my view, and some of them insist that vegetarianism is wrong under any conditions. With the latter view I do not agree. There ought to come a time in our evolution when new methods of food production will be known, and when the necessity for killing any highly organized creature will have disappeared.

The other branch of the subject is that regarding spiritual development and vegetarianism. It has been so often dealt with it is sufficient to say that such development has nothing to do with either meat-eating or the diet of vegetables. He who gives up meat-eating but does not alter his nature and thoughts, thinking to gain in spirituality, may flatter himself and perhaps make a fetish of his denial, but will certainly thereby make no spiritual progress.

QUESTION 62

"Lower manas" and "kâma-manas" are terms in frequent use in Theosophical literature and conversation, and from the fashion in which they are used they seem to mean many things to many minds, while not infrequently they are used as though their meanings were synonymous. Will the FORUM *kindly give a clear-cut definition and so clear up this haze?*

W.Q.J.—It is not the FORUM's place nor is it possible, to give these definite replies and informations. Lower manas is English and Sanskrit, kâma-manas is all Sanskrit, and *lower* may mean *kâma* to many. Each one is entitled to what he likes. Only after lapse of much time can the "haze" be cleared.

QUESTION 63

Sometimes a hypnotist makes his subject blind to some of the objects before him while he is able to see others. How is this phenomenon explained?

W.Q.J.—Doubts have been raised as to whether this was ever done. But taking it for granted, man is a *thinker* only and sees nothing but ideas. Hence if the idea of any object is inhibited, as in mesmerism, he will not see the idea of the subject being disjointed, the operator imposes his own mind and inhibits ideas.

QUESTION 64

Ages of blind, usurious laws have brought the world to ruin. Our struggle for physical existence prevents the full study of Divine Wisdom. Would it not be wise for Theosophists to unitedly advocate improved conditions, say through the Labor Exchange system or some such method? One may ask, why should we strive for that which would place us on the higher planes of thought or feeling when conditions are so unfavorable?

W.Q.J.—I cannot admit the two first assertions of the question. The world is not yet in ruins; the struggle for existence does not prevent the full study of Divine Wisdom. The study of self, the attempt to carry out the old direction, "Man, know thyself," does not depend on human laws, nor upon conditions. The body may be in prison, or engaged in incessant labor, but the soul and mind cannot be bound by environment unless we ourselves allow it. The soldier does not seem to be in a business or conditions favorable to self-development, but even while in his sentry box he can still think on the matter and thus study it—for study does not mean mere reading of books and writing of compositions. People fail in their efforts to study truth just because they start out by formulating a need for different conditions, or by insisting on having surrounding objects in just such a position and of such a quality before they will begin the work. They are wrong.

Inasmuch as Divine Wisdom and the nature of the Self are not material, physical things or objects, they are not to be confounded with mere physical surroundings. Hence material environments should not be permitted to confuse or throw back the man who desires to study that Divine Wisdom.

Again, as all things down to the most gross from the most ethereal are a part of Divine Wisdom, it is a mistake to try and destroy or put away because one does not presently like them, the very conditions in which under Karma one is obliged to study Divine Wisdom.

The second part of the question contains a proposition for the T.S., or Theosophists as a body, to advocate some one or other of the many proposed reforms. This should never be done. The T.S. is free and independent of all such reforms, while it applauds all good results. But it does not follow that the reformatory measures are the best. Nor has the last word been spoken on those subjects. It is very wise and right to alter if we can the oppressive conditions about the poor or others. But so long as the philosophy, the religion, and the view of life held by the people are wrong, just so long all reforms will be temporary. The people must be altered in thought and heart, and then conditions will right themselves. I therefore strongly oppose any propositions looking toward binding the T.S. down to any system of reform or of legislation. Individual members can do as they please about it so long as they do not involve the Society.

QUESTIONS FROM "THE PATH"

Questions from "The Path"

[Although the newly started serial, *The Theosophical Forum*, was first circulated in April, 1889, curiously there is no mention of it in *The Path* issue for that month. *The Path* continued to print its own dialogues under various titles such as "Answers to Questioners," or "The Stream of Thought and Queries." We continue with them here.— *Comp.*]

[*The Path*, Vol. II, November, 1887, pp. 249-51]

The notice published last month, that questions might be asked, addressed to "Zadok," has elicited several queries, from which we select the following. Hereafter "Zadok" will continue his answers, but they will be given through *The Path's* columns, except where their private nature may call for personal correspondence.
From C.

1st. *Is celibacy necessary to the highest spiritual life and attainment? Is this your ideal of true occultism?*

Answer—By no single way is the highest spiritual life attained. The highest Adept and the true occult student, have at some time been wedded to woman. The highest attainment is never reached until a man has passed through this experience. Under certain conditions and at a certain time celibacy is a great aid, but if the student is wedded then it is his *duty* to continue in that condition, and instead of proving a barrier it will be an assistance to his progress if he rightly comprehends its significance. All the lessons which are taught the true occult student are given in daily life and through nature's laws. The celibate loses some of these lessons—lessons which he must inevitably learn—because he violates a great law of nature.

The result of celibacy is that the student works by intellect alone. It is necessary for true occult work that the heart be used also. One of the greater of the "mysteries" can never be learned by the celibate, for he never stands as hand in hand with God: a controller of a creative force.

2nd.—*Is a purely vegetable diet indispensable to a high and serene spiritual life?*

Answer—One might eat grass, grain and turnips, a million years, but that *of itself* would not produce a high or serene spiritual life. All these things are aids, not necessities.

If the physical condition is such that animal food can be dispensed with, or without disturbing other people or neglecting the labor given, then it is wise to do away with it. The physical is thereby purified, making it less gross, material and animal like. But "one man's meat is another's poison." Use that which seems the wisest to you. "It is not that which goeth into the mouth but that which cometh out that defileth a man." The right thought, the proper motive, the true Will have more to do with true Occultism than any exterior acts or practices.

Fraternally,

ZADOK

From T.

1st.—Am I the result of a series of existences or a series of co-existences?

Answer—That which is known as you is the result of one continuous existence of an entity. Your present body and your soul (or the personality) are the results of a series of existences. Your Karma is a result of co-existence. The individuality, or spirit, is the cause of the soul and personality, or what is called "you". You are the manifestation of an entity and are the result of many appearances of that entity upon this stage of action in various personalities.

2nd.—May one walk for any distance along the Path without being able to see into the Astral Light, or without recognizing anything extraordinary?

Answer—One may journey an entire lifetime on "The Path" and not see into the Astral Light *consciously*. All men see into it, for all who dream are looking there, the body being asleep and not receptive.

One may journey a long distance and not see, for all do not work in the same manner. Some may hear "ages before they see," or may feel a long time before either seeing or hearing. The tool most efficient at a certain period is the one used.

We may journey the entire way without recognizing anything extraordinary or encountering phenomena. The most extraordinary things are found in the most ordinary, and are overlooked because of their seeming familiarity. When the understanding is directed to the natural, one finds the supra-natural or supra-human things.

All questions are vital so long as they remain unsolved but all will be answered. It requires patience in yourselves, for many times the answers do not come until years after the question has been propounded. If I can be of further use to you please consider me at your service.

ZADOK

From J. V.

"There are two ways to ascend and descend, the direct and indirect."
Tea Table, *Oct. Path,* [1887, p. 220]

1st. What are these ways?

Answer—The thistledown is blown hither and thither with every breath of wind: The arrow speeds straight to the mark from the powerful bow.

The indirect way is that of the thistle down; the Astral going out when the body is asleep, does so in a diffused condition—a passive state—with no adequate force to control it or master unseen forces. It floats at the mercy of every current in the Astral, gleaning here and there as a butterfly but taking the good and bad indiscriminately. It may reach high spheres, but is more likely to remain in those nearest to the physical. This way is traveled by all when asleep, and there dreams are made. It is the passive state where desire is the ruler, and is sometimes traveled in the waking conscious state, but is uncontrollable and unreliable.

The direct way is that of the arrow from the bow. The Astral speeds directly to the sphere which holds the knowledge it is to receive. It does so in obedience to an irresistible force—the Will: Will in accordance with divine law. It is concrete going and returning in obedience to this force, bringing little with it from intermediate spheres other than that for which it is seeking. This occurs in dreamless slumber and knowledge acquired is not communicated in a dream. This way is travelled in the conscious state for it is the way of the student of the Occult. Unless the man's thought and motive are pure, he is incapable of using the true will, and his Astral goes where other wills or forces drive it. It pauses when other forces interfere—learns from the place it happens to be in, and brings back a horrible jumble sometimes.

2nd. Where do these ways lead?

One way leads to Theosophia—Illumination—when travelled awake or asleep.

The other to consideration of self—ordinary living with its erroneous conceptions—as an Occult way, to love of phenomena and spiritism.

They lead to spheres within the astral, for the astral body passes not beyond astral limits. Only when the soul is freed from the astral and material bodies does it pass to higher spheres. These ways also lead to planets, stars and other worlds, for all these may be within the astral of this globe.

Zadok

[*The Path,* Vol. II, December 1887, pp. 278-81]

From C. H. V.

Apollonius is said to have worn a mantle of wool to aid in insulating himself from the astral currents. Has wool in itself any such property as is seemingly ascribed to it? The question has this value, perhaps, whether the occult laws which govern the merely physical regulation of the toiler toward adept-ship, may not be of great value from a sanitary point of view and form, if properly understood, a useful medical creed.

Answer—Wool in itself has no especial occult power. It is a nonabsorbent to the exhalations of the human body; is lighter, cooler in hot and warmer in cold weather than any other fabric. The late discoveries of a German scientist prove it the best of all materials from a sanitary point of view. It is a conductor for electricity and other unseen forces. Apollonius, as well as other occult students, knew its value and uses. Being a student of nature's laws he was well aware of nature's requirements. Upon the knowledge gained by occult students touching the human body are founded all the schools of medicine. Bathing is essential; a woolen dress where permissible; as little animal food as possible; a sparing diet at best—a high ideal—an exalted motive and strong will, a total forgetting of self otherwise, and neither elementals nor human beings will oppress one.

From J. C. V.

What is the true Will?

Is it a faculty of the soul?

How is it one with the Divine Will and how may we make our will at one with the Divine? Is it something which now we know not, or may we perceive its germ in our own Will, or is it an instinctive movement of the soul?

Answer—The will as known to man is that force which he exerts for the accomplishment of his aims—he uses it blindly and ignorantly— and self is always the one for which he uses it. It is used as a brute force. As ordinarily used it has little tendency to lift the personality farther than the attainment of material results. It has for its source, the lower elements of the soul. The true will is a concentrated force working steadily yet gently, dominating both soul and person, having its source in the spirit and highest elements of the soul. It is never used for the gratification of self, is inspired by the highest of motives, is never interposed to violate a law, but works in harmony with the unseen as well as the seen. It is manifested through the human will for things visible.

(2.) It is more than a faculty of the soul, for it is the soul at work. The spirit is unmanifest except through the soul. The soul manifesting the spirit is the true will. The human will is the lowest form of this manifestation.

(3.) As the true will is the manifestation of the spirit through the soul, it must be at one with the divine, inasmuch as the spirit is the divine in man. It is the God in man, a portion of the all-pervading. Asserting itself through the soul, the true will is brought forth and in truth we say, "It is the will of God." We may make our finite wills at one with the divine by elevating our aim, using it for good or in the search for God, in striving to find how to use it in harmony with the laws of God. By proper use in the right direction the human will becomes purified, elevated, and being exerted only in conformity with our highest ideal, eventually becomes at one with the highest in man.

In our ordinary material state we know only the human will. Through the human will we reach the divine will. We become aware of the true will through the ordinary will just as we become aware of the soul through the body. It is not instinctive of the soul. The soul is father of the human will—the spirit is father of the true will.

From E. L. T .

"A great deal depends on purity of thought and motive," (*Oct.* Path, 1887, *p.* 220.)

Please explain what should be the actuating motive in developing psychic capacities.

Answer—The desire to find God, the desire to know one's self, our possibilities and capabilities, that we may be of true use to the world, these are the motives. The thought should be unselfish, undisturbed by material affairs — free from wonder-seeking curiosity, concentrated, and in entire accord with the motive, the search for God.

Is Sinnett's explanation of the origin and extinction of "Intermediate Forms," accepted as being clear and satisfactory by the majority of students who are beginning the study of Buddhism?

Answer—By the majority who are *beginning* yes—but not by those who are advanced.

Sinnett claims that Kâma-Loka is (like earth) a condition of unsatisfied longings, progressive idealization. It might be the "ne plus ultra" at the time of entrance, but how after a period of years?

Answer—All these states may be entered into while in the body. The condition of unsatisfied longings does not cease except in Nirvâna. Beyond a certain point the intellect is useless. Up to and at that point the intellect is increased in its powers. It is never decayed or paralyzed. It is useless because a better tool is used.

Do advanced students contemplate "Rûpa-Loka" and "Arûpa-Loka" as at present desirable conditions? If desirable then in what sense: absolutely or comparatively as regards earth life? Is Sinnett's statement of the entire satisfaction of the soul's longings, to be regarded as "Ex Cathedra," or is it only Sinnett's personal conception?

Answer—All states and conditions above the ordinary material are desirable. In the absolute sense, any "conditioned" existence is undesirable. "Advanced students" try to be free from desires. "Rûpaloka" means *place of form;* "Arûpaloka," *place of no form.* There are many Lokas.

His statements are his personal interpretation of the teachings he has received. Read Nov. *Path.* [1887] p. 252.

Are we to understand that the 'medium' who provokes a representation of phenomena from departed spirits is thereby riveting the chains by which the said 'spirit' is held fast to low conditions?

Answer—Yes—as you use those words—but I do not call them spirits.

Is Sinnett's use of the word 'spirituality' to be used as synonymous with our word conscientiousness?

Answer—No.

Does he not rather use it in the sense of imaginative or intuitional capacity?

Answer—No.

How do Buddhists regard this faculty as compared with conscientiousness, self-sacrifice and integrity?

Answer—It is not a faculty. Conscientiousness, self-sacrifice, integrity, duty, are all portions of the whole, which is spirituality.

Do they not accord respect and honor to preponderance of intellect over purity of heart?

Answer—No, they honor intellect when governed by purity of heart.

How can I cultivate thought reading. The impressions received are involuntary?

Answer—By continual exercise of the power. By concentrated thought in obedience to the will. By purifying the thoughts as well as the body. But your aim must be higher than the mere acquirement of a wonder-working power, or you will fail. With all the power you possess concentrate your thought upon the object you desire, and receive that which is given by what is termed intuition.

From M. E. C.

What steps must I take to open the heart so as to exercise the Will for governing the Astral body?

Answer—There is but one way to open the heart. That is by living the life. It is a simple matter to govern the will, but this is not the true will. The governing of the Astral Body is the smallest of the tasks of the true will. The will should be used to obtain wisdom, and when so used it will control the Astral body without effort. We should exert psychic powers only to benefit others, never to free ourselves from the disagreeable. Let your aim be to find God; your motive, to know yourself for the sake of Theo Sophia and humanity: your desire, to help humanity, and the true Will will be developed, the heart opened and you will not only control the Astral body but all in the Astral. You must seek beyond the Astral for powers, but it is not wise to desire the acquisition of powers. Let your aim be beyond that, and the powers will grow of themselves. If the strong-willed or sick depress you, seek to aid each in some way, forget that you are depressed, *forget your self*, and they will not affect you. The life of the Occult student is full of sorrow, anguish and depressing influences. These go to make him a student in the Occult. A portion of his training is to become aware of these only in so far as they affect others. As to their affecting his own personality, he does not know they exist. If you desire to help humanity, then you possess the true motive. If you use your will in this cause, wisdom, peace and all the powers will be given.

ZADOK

[*The Path*, Vol. II, January, 1888, pp. 309-10]

From Walter B.

1st.—Is it well to cultivate the intellect at the expense of the heart? Do we not pay too much attention to intellectual progress, and in so doing allow the Heart-Mind to wander where it may?

Answer—It is not wise to cultivate either at the expense of the other. Each alone will end at the same place—The Threshold. Both are excellent means for the manifestation of that which is higher than either, when cultivated to their highest in unison. Both are useless after a certain point, except as tools for truth. Metaphysics, logic and emotion all end at a dead wall.

2nd.—Do not the words and teachings of Jesus, taken in their esoteric sense, point one (the) way to the Theosophic Path?

Answer—Taken in the sense he intended the people to take them, they lead to *the way*. Taken in the sense in which he desired his Disciples to receive them, they are teachings upon *the way*. Taken in their esoteric sense—as he knew them—they *are the way*. Were the wisdom of Egypt and India today blotted out from both the seen and unseen worlds—the true seeker would find in his teachings, *when rightly studied,* all the teachings of Isis and Buddha. As he received his instruction from Egypt, heired from India, it is more than probable that esoterically his teachings are identical with both.

ZADOK

From F. F.

Will the Devachanic period form an interruption to work for humanity in the case of one devoted to this during earth life? Is Devachan then a rejuvenating, strengthening period necessary for us while in the bonds of flesh, and is the Elixir of Life the only escape from this egoistic period? May an answer be given to this?

Answer—As the Devachanic period is a result of work for humanity —the true and pure Devachanic state being only thus obtained—it should form no interruption to such work. It only does become such when the soul is selfish enough to prefer Devachan to continuance of work for other men, and even then to a certain extent the soul continues its work. There is rest in Devachan, but not idleness. As this state is frequently entered and passed through while yet in the body, it should be an aid, not a hindrance, to true work. In truth it is a state of reward, but in that state no rewards are received. There is no state up to Nirvâna that can be an obstacle to work for humanity for those who are devoted to that work. The Elixir of Life is the only means by which we can pass beyond both Devachan and the thoughts of it; the Magnum Opus is the only thing that entitles us to it.

ZADOK

From M. E. S.

1st—Are the Astral and the lowest plane of mental life synonymous terms?

Answer—They are not. The impulses for all mental life originate beyond the Astral. The outer man with his mind interprets these as he conceives they should be. The lowest as well as the highest mental life may receive knowledge from the Astral, but it is not the Astral. All that all forms of mental life produce is indelibly impressed upon the Astral.

2nd—Is the "rising above the Astral" in effect rising above the stings and approbation of public opinion?

Answer—For us, there is no public opinion. We know neither sting nor approbation. Rising above public opinion is merely rising above the material. Until men forget the material, they can not rise above self. Until they forget self, they can not rise above the Astral: All things that please as well as those that distress men are in and through the Astral. Rise above both.

From M. J. G.

Whence come the visions seen just before dropping to sleep? They are uncontrollable—sometimes unpleasant, and have increased since childhood, and since beginning the study of Occultism?

Answer—When we enter that condition called sleep, we open wide the doors and windows of the body or this house we live in, and the soul goes forth as a bird freed from its cage. In partial unconsciousness or falling into sleep, the body has, to a great extent, ceased to act, but the brain is still sensitive or receptive to the pictures or impressions of the Astral. Of the lower principles the Astral is the last to cease action either in sleep or death. The brain is its instrument. In the partial somnolent condition, the pictures of the Astral are conveyed to the brain; through that the outer man realizes and beholds the visions. If he were fully asleep these visions would be dreams. Precisely, as dreams, they may be either pleasant or the reverse. Like dreams they are uncontrollable by the ordinary every day mortal. The Occultist being master of himself beholds only that which he desires, either in vision, or dream, or neither. As one makes himself more sensitive to impressions from the Astral when and after he begins the study of Occultism, visions and dreams will increase in frequency for a time.

ZADOK

[*The Path*, Vol. II, February 1888, pp. 344-46]

From Adelphi.

A most perplexed individual is writing to you. I have been for three years endeavoring to study Theosophy. I have heard lectures, have read an immense amount of literature devoted to that cult, from the sages of old down to the Sinnetts, Olcotts, and Blavatskys of the present day.

I have conned the Yoga Philosophy and I read The Path. *Light on the* Path *aids me not, nor does* Bhavagad-Gîtâ, *and why? Because I am yet without the first steps towards practice. (Surely Theosophy—like other sciences—must have something practical about it?) Guide me with your friendly hints. Imagine me alone in a room. How to commence? Show me the first step upon the practical ladder! All I have heard and read seemeth to me so elaborately unintelligible that I lay it aside and beg you to instruct me in my Theosophical A B C. Astral Light! Is it a figurative light, i.e. Revelation?Or is it a light, as electricity—the Heavens—coal—gives light? If abstraction (into insensibility) is necessary, can you instruct me upon Hypnotism (self mesmerism)? "A shining object' 'is advised to stare at! A mirror is a shining object, for instance. But of what avail to stare at a mirror and see reflected ugliness!*

Answer—You say that for three years you have been endeavoring to *study* Theosophy. Such being the case, you will meet with but little success. Divine Wisdom can not be a subject for *study*, but it may be an object of *search*. With the love for this same wisdom uppermost in our hearts, we ask you if it would not be wiser to lay aside the *study* of so-called Theosophy and study yourself. Knowing yourself you know all men, the worlds seen and occult, and find Theo Sophia. One cannot absorb Theosophy as a sponge does water, to be expelled at the slightest touch. Our conception of Theosophy is apt to be based upon the idea that it is an especial line of teaching—a larger, wider, and greater doctrine than others perhaps, but still a doctrine, and therefore limited. We must bear in mind that the true Theosophist belongs to no cult or sect, yet belongs to each and all; that he can find the true object of his search equally as well in the Hebrew bible as in the Yoga philosophy, in the *New Testament* equally as well as in the *Bhagavad-Gîtâ.*

You say you have "conned the Yoga philosophy." This is not enough; merely to "con" it is not to know it. It is in fact a most practical system (if you refer to that of Patañjali), and one that will meet all requirements you have in the way of difficulty; for it is one of the most difficult. It is not possible for you to judge its merits without practice: and it gives full directions. If for three years you study and practice it—aye for one year—you will find that you need no other. In these matters there is no child's play nor the usual English and American method of mere book-learning,—we must absorb and work into the practice and the theory laid down, for they are not written merely for the *intellect,* but for the whole spiritual nature. There must be within the man something which he already knows, that leaps up and out when he scans the books of wisdom; a thing already existing, which only takes an added life or confirmation from books. True Theosophy has all that is practical, but many forget this; there is no greater system of practice than that required by it.

Desire wisdom; love all men; do your duty; forget yourself; let each thought and act of your life have for its aim the finding of divine wisdom; strive to apply that wisdom for the good of other men. If you search in every direction, Light must come to you. Let the place in which you now are be the lonely room you speak of, and seek to find in everything the meaning. Strive to know what they are, and by what governed or caused. This is the first step. Live your life with this ever before you. Purify your thought as well as your body. Reason all you can, feel all with your heart you may, and when intellect and heart fail you, seek for something higher. This is the A. B. C.; it is enough for the present.

It is not Theosophy that is a science, but its application. It is not a "cult," for it covers and includes all.

The Astral Light is an actuality. It is not revelation, but a means through which that which causes revelation acts. Electricity, the heavens, all lower fires, are but the shadows of the Astral Light, just as the Astral Light is but the darkness of the Ineffable Light.

Abstraction into insensibility is not intended. If it had been so intended it would be unnecessary for us to be in these bodies. If you can forget yourself sufficiently—forget that you exist as a human body, you will not need to stare at a mirror; but so long as you realize, when staring into a glass, whether you be pretty or ugly, you can not reach Celestial sensibility or terrestrial insensibility.

Hypnotism is the controlling of other personalities. Under this you would be but a puppet for the thought of another. Your outer self had better become a puppet for your own thought.

We seek to make the body alive, not to kill it.

Zadok

[*The Path*, Vol. II, March, 1888, pp. 378-80]

To Zadok.

Suppose persons have reasons to believe they have found the beginning of the Way, and then find they do not care to investigate the mysteries of Occultism; that they are content to remain without knowledge on these subjects, though they found Truth through Theosophy, and that they are happy because they feel that whatever God orders in their lives must be right, whether it is pleasure or pain.

Suppose also that such persons, though having put themselves in a spiritually receptive condition, feel no weight of Karma, though will-

ing to suffer to whatever extent is needed from it. Do you not think such persons may be deceiving themselves in thinking they are Theosophists, when they have lived many weeks in this condition? Do you think it harder for women to attain spirituality than men, and if so, still should they not strive all the more to obtain it? I know we should not avoid anything merely because it is irksome or uninteresting.

Do not Theosophists allow themselves to feel happy if happiness comes to them without their desiring it? Also why do Theosophists wish to avoid feeling pain or pleasure, if God orders the circumstances which produce them, after we have subjected our will to His?

Please answer in your next issue of The Path.—L.

Answer—Men attach an erroneous meaning to Occultism. If one has found the beginning of *the Way* he has found some of the mysteries of Occultism, for none find *the Way* until they find something of the Unseen. It is impossible for one to put himself in a spiritually receptive condition without *"investigation"* of or being under the sway of Occultism or Occult conditions; and it is through these same conditions that he knows that pain and pleasure are one and all wise. Karma does not always manifest itself as suffering, by any means; it is quite as likely to produce joy as sorrow, and Karma is not always weighty. Such persons of whom you speak may be trying to become Theosophists, but are not Theosophists. A seeker for Divine wisdom seeks in all directions and refuses none.

2. It is as hard for man as for woman to enter the mysteries. Man works through the intellect, woman through the emotions or heart. Both are equally useless after a time, and of the two the heart is the better tool. But woman becomes engrossed or overwhelmed by her emotions, and passes no farther. The greatest Teachers have been those who have had most of the womanly in their natures. It is more difficult to master the body as a woman than as a man. This can be answered only partially in print.

3. The *True* Theosophist allows himself, or *is taught* to feel, both pain and pleasure, happiness and sorrow, for he knows them all to be wise. Men long for and desire; they fight for happiness and do not find it. We have given to us peace, which is far beyond happiness. Happiness is of this world and is a mockery of the True; yet as all other men we feel it, for we feel all things, for in all these things lie the lessons to be learned as men. I dare not speak for other men, but were I to wish to avoid either pleasure or pain, knowing them to be God's will, then would I utterly fail. Once having subjected *my* will—my human will—to His, then I avoid nothing that *is* His will.

To Zadok.

1. *Why, since the Deity chose of His own divine will to make the descent into matter, or—as some put it—by this process alone came to Him a realizing sense of His being, in the manifestation through and by matter, why should this be considered a "fall," or, indeed, an evil at all, since being the work and choice of the Deity, it must necessarily have been both wisdom and goodness which dictated the "descent;" and, as Theosophy teaches the inner Light and indwelling Emanuel (God with us) to be ever present in all forms of life, wherein consists the evil of this divine descent, and why must this experience be necessarily associated with evil at all?*

2. *I met an F.T.S. the other day who believes he has arrived at "Saintship" and cannot therefore err. He cannot bear the slightest contradiction, believing that he has arrived at such a state of "enlightenment" that he is infallible, whereas we less gifted mortals feel that he often makes grave mistakes. Of course this assumption is untenable in this case, but are sainthood and consequent infallibility likely to result from the humdrum every-day life of an ordinary nineteenth century man?*

Answer—For the Deity there is no fall. He cannot fall. In the so-called descent into matter, He must manifest *through* something. Never does the Ineffable stand unveiled before mortal man. When the All Wise deemed it good to manifest Himself as individualities, He did so through the soul. After creating the human man with the soul that all things possess, "He breathed into his nostrils and became a *living* soul," or the Deity manifested Himself through the soul in the man. Nothing below man is immortal. Man is not immortal; his soul is not immortal; but the breath of God, which is God's life or God himself, *is forever*. Man was to have lived as the angels, "for they also were made"; but, although by the grosser elements of matter or nature, by its lusts and desires, its seductive beauties and deceptive pleasures, realized most fully through the senses of the human body, the *soul* was drawn *down* instead of upward, into *ignorance* of *the true* instead of toward the wisdom of God, holding and binding thus the spirit in the meshes of the grossest part of nature, and so *fell*. God did not fall,— [i.e.] the spirit; nor did man as the human man; but the soul, being a free agent, did so, causing the spirit to be limited, and entailing pain and anguish upon the human man. Man with the Divine manifest in him was to know only the good, or wisdom; but not content, he must eat of the *tree of the* KNOWLEDGE of good and evil, or the misapplication of the good, and *fell* into ignorance. There can be no greater evil than losing the wisdom of a God for the ignorance of a man. Herein consists the only evil of the *fall* after the descent into matter.

2. How do you know that he makes grave mistakes? I may not say that anyone errs or makes mistakes, other than my own self. Neither you nor I may say another is saint or devil from our own standpoint of what makes either. Both you and I have been taught, however, that one who has arrived at the state of "Saintship" never lays claim to it or to "enlightenment."

Saintship and a certain measure of infallibility will result from hum-drum every-day life in the nineteenth century, and in no other way, if rightly comprehended. Otherwise one would not be here at all, or would have lived in some other time, before time was. To become a saint one must know what sinners are and what sin is. The best way to arrive at this knowledge is through the nineteenth century or the time in which we live, through life and all it tells us. Believing that one cannot err and in one's infallibility is, however, not a characteristic of saintship.

Zadok

[The Path, Vol. III, April 1888, pp. 21-23]

From G. M.

(1) *During sleep I have a feeling that I can fly by an intense act of will. I then do float in dream over the ground, my body seeming rigid. The force exhausts, then I have to descend. What is your explanation of this?*

Answer—It is part of the effort of your inner man to demonstrate to your outer self the existence and action of unrecognized and unfamiliar forces, which every man has in him the latent power to use. Dreamless slumber is better.

(2.) *In Theosophical books I find occult or magical phenomena referred to. I am disposed to reject these and consider their publication of a very questionable character in light of matter for the improvement of intelligent seekers after truth. Still I do not deny them, and hold myself open for conviction in any direction.*

Answer—Why then bother yourself with the phenomena of your dream state? The dream of flying is as much a phenomenon as any other that Theosophical literature contains. The proper attitude for true theosophists is not to be ready or anxious to bring conviction as to any phenomena to inquirers. Hence we cannot enter into proofs. We know personally that phenomena of a most extraordinary character have taken place, and are still occurring; we also agree with you that the constant publication of accounts of phenomena is unwise. Still it must sometimes be done, as some minds have to advance through the aid of these things.

We also know that the Masters who are behind the Theosophical Society have, in writing, condemned the thirst for phenomena made so often degrading, and stated that the Society ought to progress through its moral worth. One phenomenon can be seen by but a limited number of people, some of whom even will always doubt, and each one hearing of it afterwards will want a repetition for himself. Further than that, it would be certain to bring on a thirst for mere sight-seeing, resulting in a total forgetfulness of spirit. But, on the other hand, there are laws that cannot be guessed at without phenomena. And in each human being is a complete universe in which daily occur phenomena that should be studied. This is the proper realm for each student to investigate, for therein—and nowhere else—is placed the gate through which each one must advance.

Zadok

From G. B.

Why does the Baron in Mr. A. P. Sinnett's "Karma"[1] *advise Mrs. Lakesby not to communicate with the "astral spectres" she saw about the Professor?*

Answer—The answer to this will not yet be well understood. The English language has not acquired the needed words. The Baron's reply was that thereby the real ego of the deceased would be retarded in its advancement, and Mrs. Lakesby might lay herself open to influences from the astral world that would prey upon her unexpectedly.

This answer opens fire at once upon the whole "philosophy" of spiritualism, and contains a challenge of the ignorance of most seers and nearly every student of psychical laws. The ordinary spiritualist sees complete proof for the returning of deceased friends in the phenomena of the séance room, and nearly every seer is fascinated with his or her own pictures in the astral light and the absolute truth of what is seen.

Mrs. Lakesby did not see the spirit of any person, but only the *reliquiae*. The *spirit* is never seen, and the soul is engaged in experiencing a certain portion of its deserts in other states. These states are unnameable and incomprehensible to English speaking people. But for a period there is a magnetic connection between that soul and the

---

1 [*Karma,* a Novel, Chicago: Rand, McNally & Co., 1887.—*Comp.*]

reliquiae seen at séances and by seers. By means of that connection the soul is prevented—against its will, except when it is extremely wicked —from passing through its purification preparatory to entering into *devachan*. This purification, or preparatory state anterior to *devachan*, has not been explained by theosophical writers. It is, nevertheless a fact of the highest importance.

The second portion of the Baron's reply is also valuable. When a seer or medium perceives these shades of the departed and desires to communicate with them, a crowd of nature-spirits, of no moral character but solely moved by magnetic impulse, rush into the shade of the deceased and give it a temporary life. They too are then able, on their part, to see the seer or medium, and may and do often transfer themselves from the shade to the medium, whose lower, baser nature they occupy and vivify. By thus incorporating themselves with the *reliquiae* of dead persons, these elementals stop the process of disintegration of the atoms of matter composing the shade, which would have gone on to completion if left to nature. As soon as this disintegrating process is inhibited, the soul itself is held, so to say, in a vise which it is powerless to open, and unaware as well from whence comes the disturbance. Thus, then, these who run after their deceased friends' shades or reappearances are each day condemning their loved ones to a longer and more painful stay in a state that closely corresponds to the Christian hell.

I know my words will sweep unheeded over the forest in which our spiritualistic friends are wandering, but some sincere students will believe me.

Hadji

[The Path, Vol. III, June, 1888, pp. 96-97]

From M. C. D.

I am told that an Adept has said "that one can help or cure another if his Karma does not prevent it." Am I to understand that when suffering is before me I am not to relieve it if in my power to do so, on the ground that the suffering person's Karma has brought him there and I must not interfere? Some Theosophists have enunciated this rule.

Answer—If an Adept said this it is not incorrect. But no Adept ever drew the conclusion you give. Some Theosophists have, we are sorry to say, declared that they may not help for the reason stated. It is not theosophical to take such a position. The sufferer's Karma truly produced the suffering, but your Karma offers the opportunity for a kind deed that may relieve him; it may be his Karma to be relieved by you. It is your duty to do this kind act, of whatever nature it be. The meaning of the declaration attributed to the Adept is that you are to try to relieve suffering, which effort will have a beneficial effect unless the Karma of the sufferer prevents: but you know nothing of his Karma and must not judge it; your duty lies in the act presented to you for performance, and not with its result nor with the possible hindrances resulting from the Karma. The wrong view given by you in your question arises from the conceited attitude of persons who, having slight knowledge, presume to be the judges of others and of the great and hidden causes springing from Karma. Knowledge of these causes and of their operation in any particular case comes only to those who have reached Adeptship; for, in order to rightly judge how to rightly act, you must know absolutely the other's Karma, together with your own, in order not to fall into the awful error of deliberately sinning. It would be wiser for all students to seek to do their duty and to act as true brothers on every occasion than to run about endeavoring to imitate Sages and Adepts.

Moulvie

From B. J.

What can you tell me about the Mind Cure and Christian Science? Are they true, are they theosophical? Ought I to study them so as to be mens sana in corpore sano, *as it were?*

Answer—As we have not made a thorough study of these, we could not assume to tell you much about them, and hence cannot say if they are true or theosophical. Many earnest theosophists are believers and followers of both. We, however, have been trained in the Eastern theosophical school. Following the teaching of the latter, our advice is to have a healthy body by paying regard to rules for health, so that your mind whether it be healthy or not, may exhibit its workings untrammeled. And the teacher has ever said, as taught by the Sages of old, that the body must not be *the object* of the student's care. The same teacher also warned us that, as the body is a material thing, the proper remedies needed to counteract extreme discordant vibrations are also of a material nature. Our work lies not with your body, but with your mind and heart. See to it that the latter is right. The quantity and quality of mind that are yours may be little or poor, but even if great and good, the heart and soul are greater, and mind has its limits beyond which it passes not.

Moulvie

[*The Path*, Vol. III, November, 1888, pp. 250-52]

From M. X. D.

What is the right pronunciation of the word OM found at the beginning and end of The Path, *and which is the first letter of the Sanscrit alphabet and the Hindu sacred word?*

Answer—We have not spelled the word right in either instance. In order to give the sound as the Hindus make it, it is necessary to spell it OHM so as to represent the very long sound of "O." We have not used that mode because it is associated with electrical science as the measure of the power of the current.

From E. A. K.

*We are told that Spirit—a portion of the Absolute—becomes embodied in matter. Passing through numberless gradations in the ascending scale of being, it eventually returns whence it came and is absorbed in the Infinite. Now does it return exactly as it left the Infinite? If so, what is the use of the terrible ordeal and almost interminable experiences that it has undergone? * * * * If it is said that the Spirit returns to the Absolute enriched and improved, then we have to admit that the Infinite can be improved and added to, and such a conclusion is impossible.*

Answer—If the premises were right the conclusion would be also; but the first proposition is incorrect, and I have never heard that "we are told" anything of the kind. The spirit does not "become embodied in matter" except in the case of a perfected man or a Mahâtma. During the pilgrimage the spirit is *connected* with matter, and it is for us to win recognition or to lose the Spirit. Nor does it pass "through numberless gradations in the ascending scale of being." It is ever perfect, and has no ascension or declension.

The confusion has arisen because of the confused use of the term "spirit." I should like to have pointed out by the questioner in what book I may find it stated that the spirit becomes embodied in matter, &c. It is the same sort of confusion introduced by the use of the word "jîva" in Mr. Sinnett's books. This is the same word as is used to refer to what the present questioner calls spirit.

We are all said to be "Jîvas" on our way to the eternal and absolute reality, and we are also called "jîvâtma"—or soul spirit; and then again the jîva is also the mere life-principle in the body. But we may use English and say that the SPIRIT is not embodied and does not pass through matter in the way the question has it, but that at all times it knows all things and is the witness only of all these struggles spoken of; and it is necessary to get some grasp of the idea that all this material world is an illusion, and all the sufferings and interminable experiences are also illusions, and the long periods of time are seemingly long because we ourselves make them so. We would also advise a careful study of Patañjali's Yoga Philosophy.

But, after all, these questions are the same as that one asked of Buddha as to the first cause and why is all this universe here; to which he would make no reply.

KARMA

A. C. R. asks if a long definition of Karma given in the letter is in harmony with the Asiatic definition.

Answer—We do not think that the definition of A. C. R. is good, for the reason that it is not clear what is meant. One thing is certain, and that is that Karma is the governor of all our circumstances, and is also in part a cause of acts, and is again the act and the circumstance also. The Universe itself is the Karma of the Supreme. Karma means work or action, and, as action is performed in more ways than by the bodily organs, the field of Karma must not be limited to the body. As A. C. R. says, the most important thing to consider is how we think and what is the motive with which we do any act.

On the subject of Karma the sect of Visishtadwaitas of India say:

"Karma is the cause of connection of Jîvâtma—or the particular spirit—with matter in the shape of Kâranaśarîra, as well as the cause of misery or happiness. Karma is the producing cause of birth, death, rebirth, and every kind of body. Karma is the result of the conscious action of Jîvâtma, whether good or bad. Good Karma is that which results in pleasing, and bad Karma is that which results in displeasing, Îśvara, [He is held to be the particular spirit in each body—our Higher-Self]. The action of Jîva produces Karma through ignorance, and this ignorance is of two sorts: one the confounding of the attributes of one thing with those of another; and the second the confounding of one thing with another. Thus, the Jîvâtma first confounds the body with itself, and then such attributes as birth, death, and so on, with the attributes which really belong to Jîvâtma only; then certain actions are done, and they lead to other Karma composed of ignorance and of habit. Thus Karma works without any definite beginning, and the causes of Karma mentioned above remain latent during a pralaya or night of Brahmâ, and when a new evolution begins they again become active and produce results as before."

Karma even works in Svarga or heaven, for, as soon as the causes that take us there are exhausted, we are brought back to rebirth under the operation of Karma; thus it is seen to be stronger than the blissful state of Heaven. This going to and returning from Swarga goes on until salvation is obtained,—one who attains that state is called Jîvanmukta. This condition is defined as "an entire separation of Jîva from all connection with matter, and complete destruction of Karma, whether good or bad." The word *Moksha* literally means "release from bondage."

NARAYAN NILAKANT

[*The Path*, Vol. IV, May, 1889, pp. 55-56]

From Hadji:

What is the meaning of newspaper references to Mme. Blavatsky thus: "Theosophy, too, despite the exposure of Mme. Blavatsky's impudent impostures is still flourishing."?

Answer—In 1885 the London Society for Psychical Research took upon itself to investigate the alleged letters from Adepts received by Mr. Sinnett and others in India, and sent out a young man named Hodgson to inquire into facts that had happened months and years before. He reported that they were all frauds by Mme. Blavatsky, and that she had a tremendous combination of conspirators ramifying all over India. His report was published by the Society for Psychical Research. It is so preposterous, however, that no well-informed Theosophist believes it. The newspapers and superficial thinkers often refer to it. Mr. Hodgson, in addition to inventing the great conspiracy theory, was full of prejudice which he has since displayed in various cities of the United States by declaiming against H. P. Blavatsky, although he says she is not worth pursuing.

[EDITOR]

[*The Path*, Vol. IV, June, 1889, pp. 87-89]

From C. N.

1.—*Is there a "Parent" Theosophical Society?*

Answer—Strictly there is not. Such term would imply a separate parent body which gave out Charters or Diplomas. The Society is composed of its members who are, for administrative purposes, in Branches or unattached; the latter are called "members-at-large," but all are fellows of the T.S. The government is in the General Council, which now meets in India, in which all sections of the Society have a voice, and which issues charters and diplomas. But aside from Branch members and those at-large, there is no parent Society. The term "parent" should be abandoned, as it implies separation.

2.—Is there an Esoteric Section of the Society in America different from that governed by H. P. Blavatsky?

Answer—There is not, and there never was. In the first establishment of the T.S. other degrees than that of a mere diplomaed member were recognized, but no one save H. P. Blavatsky has had the authority to confer those degrees. She has now fully announced the first of those, although during all these 14 years they have existed and included certain members who were also fellows of the T.S.

Some misguided persons may have pretended to confer those degrees, but such a thing was improper on their part, and absolutely worthless to the recipient. These real degrees in occultism may not be trifled with, and yet they protect themselves because pretenders and triflers can make neither entry nor progress.

In 1875 H. P. Blavatsky directed a certain fellow of the Society to attend the needs of all the members of the T.S., who were then called "entered apprentices" by her, and her letter of that date is still extant in which the present Esoteric Section was plainly referred to.

3.—Why has H. P. Blavatsky waited until now to so publicly proclaim the Esoteric Section?

Answer—As a matter of fact she has not so waited. In 1875 and since, many knew of its existence and have been in it, and she has frequently spoken of it; but until now there have not been enough members interested in the realities of theosophy to justify her in a definitive statement and organization. These efforts have to proceed slowly; people must first be waked up and directed towards theosophical doctrines before it is wise to open up that which is plain to those who know how to use their intuition. But the Western mind, for all its boasted progressiveness, is generally unable to know what is behind a wall unless a hole is cut through it: others, however, can guess what is hidden when they perceive signs and sounds that are quite plain and made on purpose.

But for the first 14 years of a theosophical effort—periodically made in every century—the work of such persons as H. P. Blavatsky is always directed to preparing the ground, and then more open invitation is extended. It is so done in the last 25 years of each century.

Hadji

From R. L. R.

1.—*What is a Nirmânakâya?*

Answer—Such is one of the appellations given to an Adept who, in order to devote himself to mankind, has consciously given up his right to pass into Nirvâna. He has no material body, but possesses all the other principles; and for such an one space is no obstacle. There are many of them, and they perform various works; some take full possession of great reformers, or statesmen who carry on a beneficial policy; others over-shadow sometimes several persons, causing them to act, speak, and write in such a way as to produce needed changes in their fellow men. These Nirmânakâyas pass through the haunts of men unseen and unknown; only the effects of their influence and presence are perceived, and these results are attributed to the genius of the individual or to chance alone.

2.—*Has a Nirmânakâya any sex?*

Answer—No. The pronoun "He" has been used because it has a general application just as "man" or "men" has. In such a development as that of a Nirmânakâya the distinctions of sex have disappeared, because in the spiritual plane there is no sex.

MOULVIE

From T. D.

If there be any defect in the Mind Cure system, what would you say it is?

Answer—I should say the constant assertion that there is no evil or badness is that prime defect. For if one so asserts, he should also admit that there is no good. These two opposites stand or fall together; and they cannot disappear until all has passed to that plane which is above all good and all evil. Yet those who say that there is no evil are on the plane of consciousness where they perceive these two opposites. It appears to me that here in the Western world the old Hindu doctrine that all is illusion because impermanent is half-used. The illusionary quality is attributed only to so-called "evil," whereas the good is equally illusionary, since it as well as evil is so judged to be from some human standard. As in a community in which death is a blessing disease will be called "good," since it hastens death's advent; or, in another where insanity is supposed to be due to the presence of some god, such a condition is not esteemed to be evil.

NILAKANT

The Stream of Thought and Queries

Number I

[*The Path*, Vol. IV, August, 1889, pp. 139-42]

I have watched the stream of thought, the battalions of questions pouring along the channels that reach out from *The Path*, and am asked to put a few on these pages with some answers.

WHAT IS RESIGNATION?

In what way are we to understand this word, as it is used, for in-stance, on p. 35 of the May Path?[1] *If it is used in a special sense, that should be made clear.*

This word was not used in a special sense. Theosophists should strive not to strain or specially allot terms. The English language has quite enough words to meet most of our present wants. The intention was to give the deepest meaning possible to the term. *Resignation* was used in the sense of total mental resignation, not a mere appearance or pre-tence. We must do as commanded by Krishna, resign all interest in the event of things, and be able to say that any event whatever that comes to us is our just due. This is perfect resignation: it is difficult and yet easy to reach. We reach it by reflecting that the object of the soul is union with the Supreme Soul, and that all our desires grow out of our bodily nature alone. It is really the first step; as the author in the May *Path* said, it is the one seldom thought of by students.

IS KARMA ONLY PUNISHMENT?

Karma is action. The law of Karma operates to bring about rewards as well as punishment. The man who is now enjoying a life of ease and wealth has obtained it through Karma; the sage who has attained to great knowledge and power reached them through Karma; the disciple drinking the bitter drops from the cup of failure mixed the draught himself through Karma; Buddha's great disciple Moggallâna—greater than any other—was suddenly killed, apparently in the height of his usefulness, by robbers: it was Karma; the happy mother seeing all her children respected and virtuous dies the favorite of Karma, while her miserable sister living a life of shame in the same city curses God by her life because she knows not that it is Karma. The world itself rolls on in its orbit, carried further and further with the sun in his greater orbit, and grows old through the cycles, changes its appearance,

---

[1] [See *Letters That Have Helped Me*, Los Angeles, Theosophy Company, 1946, p. 18.—*Comp.*]

and comes under laws and states of matter undreamed of by us: it is the Karma of the world; soon or late, even while revolving in its orbit, it will slowly move its poles and carry the cold band of ice to where now are summer scenes—the Karma of the world and its inhabitants.

How then shall Karma be applied only to reward or punishment, when its sweep is so vast, its power so tremendous?

Pictures and Symbols in the Astral Light

I have seen pictures and symbols of wonderful beauty in the Astral Light. A beautiful face surrounded with light . . . a head with wings which soon seemed to sink into my brain. Were these seen through the action of manas and buddhi?

I do not think so. These beautiful things belong to a lower plane and are seen by several senses and departments of senses. Many different causes might have produced them. Today you might see the face of a woman or a child whom you will not meet for the next ten years and have never yet seen; or a long-forgotten and slightly-noticed object in the past of the present life may be suddenly opened to clairvoyant sight; again, there may be deeply laid in your nature mental deposits from long past lives, and these may tinge your visions. I cannot answer individual cases; such is the work of a vulgar fortune-teller. Each one must with patience study his own experience through many years, carefully noting and verifying and eliminating as time goes on. Each person who has clairvoyance has his or her own special phase—and there are millions of phases; hence five separate clairvoyants may see five different pictures or symbols, all produced by one and the same cause; or four of them may see four different pictures while the fifth sees the result of a combination of his own with the other four phases.

How did the Symbols get into the Astral Light?

The world is so old that man's acts and thoughts for many millions of years have stamped the Astral Light full of pictures. But the Astral Light itself has cycles, tides, and changes, so those must be allowed for; it is useless to try to explain this, but in the changing of the cycles the symbols sometimes are mixed and interblended. When a class of elementals is fully developed and ready to run its appointed course from the beginning of an Age, there is a symbol for it that can be used until the complete decadence or extinction of that class, but at the change of certain cycles the symbol ceases to have power because that to which it once applied has altered and we know not the new symbol. You ask to know more about these symbols? It is not useful or necessary.

About the Cycles

I have heard and read much about cycles and their changes. I believe in cyclic law, and in the greater and lesser cycles, although I know them not. But are the cycles definite in limit, or are they shadowy?

Much that has been said on this subject is vague except as regards the number of years included in certain cycles. The lunar cycle and some others are known, but it is well to clear up some of the shadows. Many persons think of one cycle beginning, say today, just as another has ended. This, however, is not correct, for the cycles overlap each other, and before one has really closed another has begun. The best way to understand it is to draw two circles intersecting each other thus.

Now No. 1 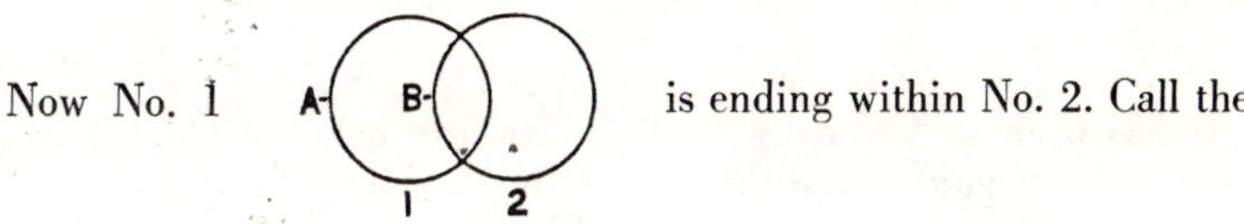 is ending within No. 2. Call the

beginning of No. 2 at B, and it is seen that it had its inception while No. 1 was finishing. The real point of ending for one and commencement for the other is probably at a point found by drawing a line through where the circles touch at top and bottom, and let the spaces on either side of that line be called the dawn and twilight.

Then, again, there are some important cycles which begin and end wholly within the limits of larger ones, and, in fact, it is these smaller cycles that we notice most, for they are more quickly felt. All of this relates to physical cycles; there are others of a higher and more spiritual nature very difficult to trace and comprehend. It may be partially understood by any one who has observed a man working for several years at some occupation in itself not particularly elevating, but who at the end of the period has altered his mental attitude in such a degree as to vastly change his entire life and development. In his case the occupation represented a cycle of debasement or expiation, and all the while another cycle of a higher character was running its course in his mental and moral nature quite unknown to anyone else and perhaps also to himself. There are also great cosmic cycles that proceed slowly to our comprehension because they cover such stupendous periods, but they powerfully affect mankind and can only be faintly imagined by students.

The ancient Egyptian civilization illustrates the power of one of the greater cycles long since run down. That brilliant civilization rolled on through a vast stretch of years with no appearance of diminishing glory, but gradually the change took place. We can imagine the hopeless and frantic efforts of her sages to counteract the decay. But they were powerless, and Egypt gradually sank to the place where we find her blazing in the records so far discovered and yet then in her decline; and at last all that remains are sand heaps and degraded ignorant Copts.

But the sweep of that mighty cycle merely moved on to other spheres, and when Earth again meets the same impulse the old civilization will return, the old force revive within a better body.

To me the cyclic laws are full of hope and eminently just.

About Black and White Magicians

How is one to recognize a black magician, and how to treat such an one?

It has been well said by H. P. Blavatsky that "each one has a potential black magician within." The black magician is the fruit and perfection of selfishness; selfishness is the triumph of the lower nature. The black magician is the opposite pole in human development to the white Adept, and the latter is the fruit and perfection of the highest qualities in man conjoined with entire communion with spirit; this is the triumph of all that is best in the human being; it is the conscious union with the divine. The black magician stands for self alone, and therefore for discord, separation, and destruction; the white one is the embodiment of union, harmony, and love. In the words of *The Bhagavad-Gîtâ* the white adept "is the perfection of spiritual cultivation," and it must follow that the black one is the perfection of material cultivation. In this question, "black" represents self and "white" the spiritual whole.

The query then arises, "Why are there now only white magicians and merely embryo black ones?" We think there are but few black adepts existing today, but of the white school there are many. The age and the cycle have not yet come to that point where the black magician has blossomed, and it is easy to understand why there are perfect white ones. The question is answered in *The Bhagavad-Gîtâ* [Chapter VIII] where it says, "At the night of Brahmâ the Jîvanmuktas are not absorbed nor destroyed, but all others are; and at the coming forth of the new creation those Jîvanmuktas (white adepts) come forth intact and conscious."[1] This means that at the preceding pralaya—or dissolution—all the black adepts were destroyed; and as now but the first 5,000

---

[1] A free translation.

years of Kali Yuga have elapsed, there has not yet been time to evolve enough full black magicians to make a sensible impression upon us. The first part of the question, therefore,—"How are we to treat a black magician"—is premature.

Each one of us may become a black magician if we let selfishness have its course, and hence we should ask ourselves, "How may we prevent the possibility of our becoming black magicians in some future age?"

As to the latter part of the question regarding the treatment to be accorded to these as yet mythical beings, it also is very far ahead of time. If such an adept were to appear to you now, he would laugh your threats to scorn. But the sole and sovereign protection against such things and persons is a pure heart and right motive.

HADJI ERINN

Number II

[The Path, Vol. IV, September, 1889, pp. 186-88]

PRACTICING FOR OCCULT DEVELOPMENT

Several questions have been received on the subject of the best method to be pursued by members of the Theosophical Society for the development of occult powers.

This desire for such development cannot be commended. Such a desire, standing by itself, while seeming to the questioners to be of great importance, is really of the very least consequence for beginners or to the present state of the theosophical movement. The Society was not organized for the purpose of teaching the practice of occult arts, and it has been distinctly stated in a letter from one of the Masters,[1] who are themselevs fully acquainted with all the laws of occultism, that our body was never intended to be a hall of occultism or for the training of aspirants to chelaship. But in the face of that declaration and in spite of all that has been said and written in the magazines of the Society, there are numbers of members still thinking that they will be helped in such sort of study and practice, and who have for some time used what leisure they had in endeavoring to cultivate their psychic powers to the exclusion of work upon the lines laid down by the founders of the Society.

Further than this, some of these devoted students have been reading such works upon practical yoga—or Hatha-Yoga—as they could pro-

____

1 [Letters from the Masters of the Wisdom, 1870-1900, First Series, p. 9; transcribed and compiled by C. Jinarâjadâsa, 4th ed., T.P.H., Adyar, 1948. —Comp.]

cure, and trying to follow the rules laid down, notwithstanding the distinct caution in all such books that the practices should not be pursued by the student unless he has a competent guide and teacher to help and protect him on the way. Now as there are no such such guides in the United States—but all here being alike mere tyros, students, or probationers—it is evident that the very first rules have been violated.

All these practices and studies, so long as they are pursued merely for the powers to be developed, will lead to trouble only and greater ignorance. This is not because there is no truth in practical yoga, but solely from the method adopted and the pure selfishness of the aim before the mind.

What, then, is a Sincere Theosophist to do? Shall he or not Practice Yoga?

We answer by saying that the sincere study of the philosophy and rules of Patanjali's Yoga System may be taken up by any theosophist— on one condition. That is that he shall, as a theosophist, try to carry out the fundamental object of the Society—Universal Brotherhood. In no other way can he receive assistance from any source. Altruism must be made the aim of life, or all practices are absolutely void of lasting effect. We do not speak from a mere theory but from experience; nor do we claim to have perfected altruism in ourselves, but only that, as far as possible, we are trying to make altruism the rule of life.

The Occidental Mind is not fitted for Yoga

This may be stoutly denied, but what matters it? The fact remains patent to all that among western people there are few persons masters of any part of occult practice. Partial concentration of mind, even—the first step for any practical use of the recondite laws of nature,—is conspicuously absent from our people. Altruism has been for so many centuries a dead letter, and individualism has been so much cultivated, that the soil has become almost barren. Western peoples are not even fitted to attain perfection in Black Magic, which is supposed to be easy to pursue, though in fact not so; but we are able to lay the seeds in this incarnation for further development upon the evil side of our nature in future lives. The practice of altruism as far as we can is the only way in which to avoid suffering in the future.

If Students believe that Adepts are behind the Society, they should follow Their Advice.

Those aspirants for whom these words are written have been laboring under a mistake. They have entered a society formed by Beings in whose existence they profess belief, and have not acted upon the instructions given, but have selected such portion of those as suited them. The Adepts have distinctly said that occult powers can be obtained, but They have also said that the Society, *which has Their protection and assistance,* is not for occult development, and that the latter cannot be forwarded by Them unless members will preach, teach, and practice Altruism. There is therefore no sort of obligation upon either the Adepts, or the disciples who do know, to help members whose chief aim is occult development. We must deserve before we can desire.

While we are endeavoring to understand and practice altruism, and while spreading broadcast the doctrines given out by the Adepts respecting man, his status, future fate, and right way of living, each theosophist can devote some of his time to daily meditation and concentration, and all of his time to extirpating his faults and vices; when he has made some progress in this, the good karma he may have acquired by working for the cause of Humanity, which is the same as Universal Brotherhood, will help him to get ready to begin occult practices.

What is the "Daily Initiation"?

It is supposed by some that initiation is always and in every case a set and solemn occasion for which the candidate is prepared and notified of in advance. While there are some initiations surrounded by such solemnities as these, the daily one, without success in which no aspirant will ever have the chance to try for those that are higher, comes to the disciple with almost each moment. It is met in our relations with our fellows, and in the effects upon us of all the circumstances of life. And if we fail in these, we never get to the point where greater ones are offered. If we cannot bear momentary defeat, or if a chance word that strikes our self-love finds us unprepared, or if we give way to the desire to harshly judge others, or if we remain in ignorance of some of our most apparent faults, we do not build up that knowledge and strength imperatively demanded from whoever is to be master of nature.

It is in the life of every one to have a moment of choice, but that moment is not set for any particular day. It is the sum total of all days; and it may be put off until the day of death, and then it is beyond our power, for the choice has then been fixed by all the acts and thoughts of the lifetime. We are self-doomed at that hour to just the sort of life, body, environment, and tendencies which will best carry out our karma. This is a thing solemn enough, and one that makes the "daily initiation" of the very greatest importance to each earnest student. But all of this has been said before, and it is a pity that students persist in ignoring the good advice they receive.

Do you think that if a Master accepted you He would put you to some strange test? No, He would not, but simply permitting the small events of your life to have their course, the result would determine your standing. *It may be a child's school, but it takes a man to go through it.*

HADJI ERINN

Are There New Souls? Why Reincarnation?

[*The Path*, Vol. V, April, 1890, p. 20]

M. E. A. asks: *We all know that the population of the earth is increasing yearly, and that in time this globe will not be able to support its population unless the future inhabitants can get along on air. Does Theosophy teach us that new souls are created? Each one of these future unfortunates must have a soul. Will* The Path *please explain?*

Answer. There are some assumptions in this inquiry about which no one has positive information. It is not settled that the population "is increasing yearly." For the apparent increase may be only a more accurate knowledge of the number of inhabitants, following a more accurate knowledge of the globe on which we live. For instance: we have only lately acquired information of vast quantities of people in Africa previously unheard of.

Nor does it follow that the earth will not be able to support its population in time. A great many well-informed persons think exactly the opposite. Not very long ago several millions of people were destroyed in China, Japan, and elsewhere in a single week; this would leave a good deal of room for a population—in the United States for instance—to expand. Hence the question is narrowed down to the single one—"Does Theosophy teach us that new souls are created?" Mme. Blavatsky answers this in *The Secret Doctrine* by stating that from now until the end of this period of manifestation there will be no new Monads (which will answer to the word "souls" of the questioner), but the old ones will be reincarnated on this globe. If her view is the correct one, then the reincarnations from now onwards will be incarnations of Monads who have been here many times before. That is to say, we will all be worked over many times. This opinion of Mme. Blavatsky's is held by many Theosophists.

"If we started as spirit and therefore perfect, why need we these reincarnations of suffering, only to finally attain what we started with?"

Answer. This is the old question, the old inquiry, "What has the Absolute in view, and why is there anything?" The question contains its own answer, for if we started as "spirit," and therefore "perfect," we must still be and so remain forever perfect. But in the *Upanishads* it is said that "These radiations from the Great All are like sparks from a central fire, which emanate from it and return again for its own purposes." Furthermore, there is nothing more distinctly and frequently taught in Theosophical literature than this, that it is the personal, the illusory, the lower "I," who asks such questions as these, and that the real person within, the spirit, sees no such thing as suffering but rejoices forever in immeasurable bliss. "We" did not start perfect, but imperfect, and "our" progress to union with spirit is the perfection of the lower "we" and "our."

[UNSIGNED EDITORIAL]

Transmigration of Souls

[*The Path*, Vol. V, March, 1891, pp. 383-84]

"Is there any foundation for the doctrine of transmigration of souls which was once believed in and is now held by some classes of Hindus?" is a question sent to *The Path*.

From a careful examination of the *Vedas* and *Upanishads* it will be found that the ancient Hindus did not believe in this doctrine, but held, as so many theosophists do, that "once a man, always a man"; but of course there is the exception of the case where men live bad lives persistently for ages. But it also seems very clear that the later Brahmins, for the purpose of having a priestly hold on the people or for other purposes, taught them the doctrine that they and their parents might go after death into the bodies of animals, but I doubt if the theory is held to such an extent as to make it a national doctrine. Some missionaries and travelers have hastily concluded that it is the belief because they saw the Hindu and the Jain alike acting very carefully as to animals and insects, avoiding them in the path, carefully brushing insects out of the way at a great loss of time, so as to not step on them. This, said the missionary, is because they think that in these forms their dead friends or relatives may be living.

The real reason for such care is that they think they have no right to destroy life which is not in their power to restore. While I have some views on the subject of transmigration of a certain sort that I am not now disposed to disclose, I may be allowed to give others on the question "How might such an idea arise out of the true doctrine?"

First, what is the fate of the astral body, and in what way and how much does that affect the next incarnation of the man? Second, what influence has man on the atoms, millions in number, which from year to year enter into the composition of his body, and how far is he—the soul—responsible for those effects and answerable for them in a subsequent life of joy or sorrow or opportunity or obscurity? These are important questions.

The student of the theosophic scheme admits that after death the astral soul either dies and dissipates at once, or remains wandering for a space in Kâma-Loka. If the man was spiritual, or what is sometimes called "very good", then his astral soul dissipates soon; if he was wicked and material, then the astral part of him, being too gross to easily disintegrate, is condemned, as it were, to flit about in Kâma-Loka, manifesting itself in spiritualistic *séance* rooms as the spirit of some deceased one, and doing damage to the mental furniture of mortals while it suffers other pains itself. Seers of modern times have declared that such eidolons or spooks assume the appearance of beasts or reptiles according to their dominant characteristic. The ancients sometimes taught that these gross astral forms, having a natural affinity for the lower types, such as the animal kingdom, gravitated gradually in that direction and were at last absorbed on the astral plane of animals, for which they furnish the sidereal particles needed by them as well as by man. But this in no sense meant that the man himself went into an animal, for before this result had eventuated the ego might have already re-entered life with a new physical and astral body. The common people, however, could not make these distinctions, and so very easily held the doctrine as meaning that the man became an animal. After a time the priests and seers took up this form of the tenet and taught it outright. It can be found in the *Desâtîr*,[1] where it is said that tigers and other ferocious animals are incarnations of wicked men, and so on. But it must be true that each man is responsible and accountable for the fate of his astral body left behind at death, since that fate results directly from the man's own acts and life.

Considering the question of the atoms in their march along the path of evolution, another cause for a belief wrongly held in transmigration

---

[1] [See pages 7-12 of *The Desatir*, or *Sacred Writings of the Ancient Persian Prophets*, translated by Mulla Firuz Bin Kaus, Bombay 1818. Reprinted by Wizards Bookshelf, San Diego, Calif., 1975—*Comp.*]

into lower forms can be found. The initiates could teach and thoroughly understand how it is that each ego is responsible for the use he makes of the atoms in space, and how each may and does imprint a definite character and direction upon all the atoms used throughout life, but the uninitiated just as easily would misinterpret this also and think it referred to transmigration. Each man has a duty not only to himself but also to the atoms in use. He is the great, the highest educator of them. Being each instant in possession of some, and likewise ever throwing them off, he should so live that they gain a fresh impulse to the higher life of man as compared with the brute. This impress and impulse given by us either confer an affinity for human bodies and brains, or for that which, corresponding to brutal lives and base passions, belong to the lower kingdoms. So the teachers inculcated this, and said that if the disciple lived a wicked life his atoms would be precipitated down instead of up in this relative scale. If he was dull and inattentive, the atoms similarly impressed travelled into sticks and stones. In each case they to some extent represent the man, just as our surroundings, furniture, and clothing generally represent us who collect and use them. So from both these true tenets the people might at last come to believe in transmigration as being a convenient and easy way of formulating the problem and of indicating a rule of conduct.

HADJI

Evolution

[*The Path,* Vol. VII, July, 1892, pp. 117-19]

A correspondent of *Path* says: *"I am unable to get a comprehensive view of evolution theosophically. Does a 'round' mean once around the seven planets which belong to the earth chain? If so, how is the moon our parent?"*

A round means a going once around the seven globes of the earth-chain. It was also called a "ring." Some have confused it with incarnating in the seven races on any one planet. The seven races have to go seven times around the seven globes of this chain, developing in each the characteristics of each, which cannot be obtained in any other way.

There are seven globes in the chain, of which the earth is one. The other six are not visible to us, as they are made of matter in a different state, and on a different plane from matter as we know it and see it. The first race began on Globe No. 1 and carried on evolution there, and then went to Globe No. 2, and so on all around the seven. This it did seven times. Race No. 2 proceeded similarly, having in its possession all that was gained by No. 1. We are now the Fifth Race engaged in going round the whole chain; hence we are called those of the Fourth Round, but are the Fifth Race. We must go round the whole chain of seven planets three times more before as a race we are perfected.

When the Seventh Round is finished, as well as the halt for rest that follows, we begin again as a Sixth Race and go through Seven Rounds as such. When that is concluded we begin as the Seventh Race and repeat the process of Seven Rounds through the chain, thus bringing the grand evolution for this chain to a perfect end. After that we pass on upon a higher plane, the possessors of all the knowledge and development acquired during that sevenfold progress. This is the outline of the grand scheme, and, as you see, includes the whole series of seven planets.[1]

But in every round of planets, on each one, and in each race as it begins and proceeds, there are many sub-races, root races, and offshoots, all necessary in the process of development for each race. For a race cannot spring up in a moment, out of nothing; it must grow forth from something. Therefore a new race is made by offshoots making sub-roots that finally grow slowly in the main race which will be. This is occurring in America, and hence here is afforded a present and perfect illustration. For here many examples of various root and sub and offshoot races coming together, by generation of children among themselves, are producing the sub-root for the new race. This process will go on for a long period, during which old, decayed branchlets and offshoot families and races will be absorbed into the new growing stem, and when the time is ready—a long way off—for a new race, all will have to migrate to the next planet.

It is now plain that *ring* and *round* do not mean the process of going through the race in its process of formation on any planet, as its beginnings come on and are finally replaced by its finished product, but that these words refer to the grand march around the whole chain of globes, of which this earth is the fourth.

The question about the moon ought now to be clear. It is evident that the moon is not one of the seven planets. By reading *The Secret Doctrine* we see that the moon is a *deserted planet* on the same plane as the earth—a fourth-round globe of a previous manvantara. It is the old fourth globe of an old chain, and is the parent of the earth, while

---

1 [Mr. Judge gives a clearer over-all picture regarding the Rounds and Races in Chapter III of his *Ocean of Theosophy.—Comp.*]

the other six globes of our chain have similar parents, visible only from those globes. It is our parent because we came from it when the hour struck, long ago, for the migration from it of the humanity that had thereon passed through its grand sevenfold pilgrimage. In like manner, some future day, this earth will become "a moon" to some newer planet not now born.

Question 2—If the prototype of all forms has always existed, how can new forms come through evolution of the physical or material?

New material forms may come, but they are not prototypes. The latter are not material, therefore no confusion between the two can exist. There is evolution of material forms, but prototypes remain unaffected. This is a question which requires the questioner to look up exact meanings of the words used by him. It is not substantial. Fix the true meanings and the confusion will vanish.

Question 3—If man made his first appearance as a material body, why does the embryo pass through all the changes, vegetable and animal, before birth?

It is the order of nature. All the atoms have to grow used to their work before they can do it well and quickly. At first as astral atoms only, they do it over and over again until all the atoms acquire the *habit* of doing it without fail. They then go on to other work. This having been the way for ages, the human body is now gestated in nine months, whereas at earlier periods such gestation took years, later on fewer years, and finally as now. In future times the process will be finished more quickly, and then the embryo will pass through all these old states almost instantaneously. The reason, therefore, is that the physical human molecules of this period of evolution have only acquired the ability to pass through the series in nine months, as a result of millions of years of prior slow work. For nature goes by steps, one at a time. The embryo exhibits these phases because there are still left in the matter used the old impressions, and racial evolution is gradually wiping them out by transforming them into new organs, by eliminating those not useful and by condemning others. When the work is fully understood by *every* atom so that it acts with unerring, machine-like precision, it will be possible to bring out a body in a very short space of time.

Rings, Rounds, and Obscuration

[*The Path*, Vol. VII, November, 1892, pp. 255-58]

A number of correspondents have propounded questions growing out of a recent article on "Evolution" and relating to the great progress round the chain of globes of which this earth is one. One of these is:

If we are transferred to the next planet of our chain, shall we be born there like a child on this one, or have we to evolve through minerals, plants, etc.?

No details, such as are requested in this enquiry, have been given out by the Adepts, all that has been said being general in its nature wherever the other planets of our chain were spoken of. In *The Secret Doctrine* H. P. Blavatsky distinctly says the teaching has to do with this earth particularly, and that when other planets are mentioned there are only hints, except in regard to the grand fact that the human life-wave passes from this to the next globe, and so on through the chain. The only other writer on this who quotes authority is Mr. Sinnett in *Esoteric Buddhism*, and in that he copies the letters sent him by H. P. B.'s Masters. He has information of detail regarding only this earth. Consequently, to hazard an answer to the question would be guessing. No one knows what exact function the other planets in the chain perform; all we know is that the human life-wave does pass into the next planet when the cycle is completed for this one. Whether we shall be born there as human children or into other forms we do not know. And doubtless it is not necessary we should be informed, inasmuch as ages must pass before we shall be released from this world. By that time we should have forgotten the facts.

These considerations apply to another question, whether only a part, or the whole, of the human family is at the same time on one globe. Of this we cannot speak with authority. But in *The Secret Doctrine* the author says the Adepts teach that seven races appear in the beginning on seven different portions of the earth. This would appear to indicate that the egos within those race-forms come from another planet in the chain. And as it is distinctly taught that an obscuration overtakes a globe when the entire race deserts it for another, it is very safe to assume the teaching to be that deserted planets go into obscuration if the races that left them have not completed all their rounds. And as the matter of obscuration as compared with *pralaya*—or total destruction —is also raised, we may keep in mind at this point that a total *pralaya* only comes when the entire seven rounds of the seven races around the seven globes is completed. The *obscuration* is similar to the sleep of man's body, making a reawakening possible; while total *pralaya* is similar to the actual death of the body of a man, followed by his ego's going into the state of *Devachan*. This agrees with the views given by H. P. B., as from the Masters, that the *Nirvâna* for the great human family is really that long period which intervenes between the total death of a planetary chain and the new birth of a new planetary chain, upon which a higher form of evolution will be started at the hour of that new birth.

When the article in July *Path* said "we must go round the whole chain of seven planets three times more before *as a race* we are perfected," the words *as a race* were intended to, as they do, point out that sub-races were not being dealt with. Sub-races grow on the planet, and not by going to other ones. Hence there is no obscuration or *pralaya* after a sub-race. As these, in their process of formation, proceed with their development upon this globe—or any other they may be on, cataclysms for that globe take place from time to time, involving either the entire mass or only a portion of it. These cataclysms are not obscurations of the globe. For the latter can only come on when the egos of the race have abandoned the globe for the purpose of continuing work on another of the same chain. And carrying on the correspondence for the purpose of illustration, those cataclysms are similar to the sicknesses and accidents which come to a man during a single lifetime. When all the necessary sub-races have been evolved, and the root, trunk, branch, twig, leaf, blossom, and fruit—seven in all—are completed, then the race, having been thus perfected as such, passes on to the next globe in the chain. This is what is involved in the sentence quoted from the July *Path*.

Confusion may be avoided by remembering that the race of which we form a part includes many sub-races, and that the term "sub-races" does not mean that a new sub-race comes on only when a preceding one has disappeared. The true Hindus and many European races are in our race, so that we and they are all sub-races. In America a new sub-race is being formed as preparation for many others, all preparing the ground for the final great race. It is only when sub-races have fully accomplished their task that they leave this earth altogether. And in saying they leave or disappear, what is meant is that the race as a physical expression goes out, not that the egos in the bodies leave this world and go to another one.

As all the egos engaged in this evolution are not in equal stages of progress, but are very varied in their development, some forward and others backward, the whole process is a matter of education for the egos. They go backward and forward in the various sub-races which are on the earth at the same time just as the development of the egos requires, in the same way as one incarnates in family after family in his own race. So that in one life one may be in an advanced sub-race in accordance with predominating qualities, but in that incarnation may bring up certain defects or generate certain causes requiring him to pass over next life to some other less progressed sub-race for the purpose of extirpating the defects or working off the causes.

In this way accurate adjustment, perfect development, regularity and roundness are all amply provided for. Classes of egos from time to time move up *en masse*, and at last no ego is left requiring the development afforded by some sub-races, and the latter then, as physical forms, begin to die away, being inhabited only by very low orders of intelligence which need no description. But as these are much lower in power than even the mere brain-matter of the forms they come into, the result is that they drag the physical race down, they are unable to give the natural brain capacity its normal expression, and that race will show all the signs of human decrepitude until its remaining members, gradually becoming curiosities in Ethnology, are at last engulfed altogether by death. This is one of the great facts in racial history not yet understood by the world. A race is both physical and spiritual. The physical body and brain require an informing intelligence of a degree of power sufficient to keep up the exact amount of tension demanded by that sort of body, and if this is not furnished the consequence will be that equilibrium is destroyed, followed in time by sterility among the females of the race, leading inevitably to extinction.

It is an obscure point, but of the highest importance. Not improbably many will reject it, but the fact of racial extinction is known, as in the case of Hottentots and others, and ordinary theories fail to show why a perfect blight falls upon some masses of people.

Returning to the great progress of the seven races, it is to be noted that when the complete seven have all finished the seven rounds the entire family of egos evolving on the seven globes commences to leave the whole chain forever, and the various globes composing it begin to die altogether. This, however, does not take place at the same time for the whole seven. They die one by one because the "human life wave" never arrives at or leaves any globe in a complete mass. Such coming and going is similar to the migration of birds from zone to zone, they being known to go in detachments until all have migrated. The advance portion of the life-wave will arrive at globe seven on its last journey, the remainder following; and thus the whole wave will be at last withdrawn from globe after globe beginning with number one or A—until the entire stream has passed out from the seventh, it being, as it were, the door of departure. It is evident, then, that globe A, being the one to be first completely abandoned, has time to throw its energies off into space for the purpose of beginning the formation of a new first-plane globe to be ready in that new chain for the incoming rush of pilgrim souls as soon as the rest between chains is over.

This is exactly what happened for the predecessors of this chain of globes, and, as our earth is a fourth-round or fourth-plane globe, it was formed in space by the energies of the old moon which is a fourth-plane globe of a former chain. For this reason the Adepts call the Moon our parent, meaning the parent of our globe. And the Moon may illustrate the question about *obscuration* and *pralaya,* as she is not in obscuration but is in her final *pralaya* and is disintegrating as quickly as nature will permit, this earth meanwhile absorbing her particles slowly from day to day while the great cycle of our evolution unerringly goes on. It has also been stated in letters from the Adepts that the well-known planet Mars is now in obscuration. This means that the body of the planet is, as it were, sleeping in space, as it rolls about the sun and has no inhabitants on it such as we. The life-wave belonging to it has passed on to the next or some other globe of its own chain, but since that wave has to return, the body of the planet does not go into pralaya, but waits for the new day. Its life as a sleeping globe is maintained by a certain subtle principle which is not publicly referred to by those who know of it, and which will not permit it to die until the whole chain of globes of which it is one has been traversed seven times, or the equivalent of seven, by the wave of life belonging to it.

[The Path, Vol. X, November, 1895, pp. 256-58]

M.—*I read in the* New York Sun *in October an editorial on the Mahâ Bodhi Society of Calcutta which designed to restore Buddha-Gayâ to the Buddhists and spread Buddhism. Although the article was full of chaff yet I thought there must be something underneath. Is that Society a Theosophical Section? Does Buddhism grow in America?*

Answer—The Mahâ Bodhi Society is, in my opinion, more of a real-estate venture, for sentiment however and not for gain. Col. H. S. Olcott is its Honorary Director and intended, as a professed Buddhist, to make great efforts towards raising the large sum needed to put the property in Buddhist hands, this being the main object. The Secretary is Dharmapala, an F.T.S. But the Society is not a Theosophical Section. It cannot be successfully held that the getting of property and a temple is Buddhism, for that religion teaches asceticism, poverty and renunciation of material things. Certainly Buddha would not have his followers waste their energies on such a venture. They did not do it in his lifetime.

Buddhism does not grow in America, though many persons call themselves Buddhists. Some doctrines, which are not only Buddhistic but also Brahmanic, have been widely spread, and it is easier to say one is a Buddhist than Brahmanical. To be a Brahmin you must be born in that sort of family; to profess Brahmanism and not be able to explain its complicated system is disgraceful. Besides this, the popular poem by Arnold, *The Light of Asia,* has given currency to the term Buddhism all over the land, whereas but few know what the other oriental religions are. The useful doctrines of both Buddhism and Brahmanism are believed in by many as a result of the wide and systematic propaganda of the Theosophical Society in America. Re-incarnation, karma, devachan and the rest, are in both religions, but to believe them does not make a man a Buddhist. And if the people knew fully the superstitions and absurdities of those two old religions they would never call themselves by either name. It cannot be possible that the Buddhism of today will ever be adopted, as such, by any western nation; but the doctrines promulgated by Theosophists will so mold the coming mind that the new religion will be a theosophical one.

Now and then there appears in some newspaper an article giving false statements about Buddhism in America. The writers have heard so much about theosophical doctrines,—which they do not understand and which they label Buddhist because, perhaps, all they ever knew of the religion they obtained from *The Light of Asia,*—that they put down all Theosophists as Buddhists. But were you to consult the agent in New York to the Buddha-Gayâ movement you would discover how few Buddhists there are here.

As another correspondent asks for the principal reason why the West will not adopt Buddhism, I will reply to that now.

One of the main teachings of Buddha was that any kind of existence is a misery. It is misery to be born either as man or deva, because this involves a perpetual series of reincarnations which may be happy or unfavorable as happens. To escape this, Nirvâna is offered. Of course I am not now speaking of other doctrines the educated may understand. This one is for the multitude. Now the western people will not accept this pessimistic view of life, and when they come to know that that is Buddhism they will not take the religion.

A.P.—Have you any idea of the proportion between the population of India and the members of the T.S. there?

Answer—There are 360 millions of people in India, and there are 90 Theosophical Societies there. As only about 40 of the latter are active we can conclude there are not 3000 F.T.S. in India. The rest of the 360 millions, except those who read English, know nothing of the Society. The major part of the people do not read English. Hence hundreds of millions are uninfluenced by theosophical propaganda. Of course it is the custom for the reports emanating from Adyar to speak of hundreds of Branches there; this is possible by counting in the hundred and more dead Branches existing only on paper—for the authorities disliked to cut off from the roll the dead ones as is done in America.

W.Q.J.

T.H.—I would like to have a concrete practice pointed out to me as something to begin with in self-discipline.

Answer—Begin by trying to conquer the habit, almost universal, of pushing yourself forward. This arises from personality. Do not monopolize the conversation. Keep in the background. If someone begins to tell you about himself and his doings do not take first chance to tell him about yourself, but listen to him and talk solely to bring him out. And when he has finished suppress in yourself the desire to tell about yourself, your opinions and your experiences. Do not ask a question unless you intend to listen to the answer and inquire into its value. Try to recollect that you are a very small affair in the world, and that the people around do not value you at all and grieve not when you are absent. Your only greatness lies in your inner true self and it is not desirous of obtaining the applause of others. If you will follow these directions for one week you will find they will take considerable effort, and you will begin to discover a part of the meaning of the saying, "Man, know thyself."

W.Q.J.

[*The Path*, Vol. X, December, 1895, pp. 289-91]

T.T.—In the November Path *there is a reply about Buddhism. May I ask whether reference was intended to the outside exoteric form of the religion or to the esoteric side?*

The answer was intended to refer solely to outer forms of Buddhism, because the esoteric teachings of Buddha, if known, would undoubtedly be found to be the same as those of Jesus and the Brahmans—since we hold that both had secret doctrines for the few. The old Jews had their secret religion—the Kabala—and Jesus, following his Jewish teachers, taught his disciples many things in private which were not recorded. But there is a good deal of evidence that that secret teaching was in all probability like Gnosticism. What Buddha secretly taught we do not know.

If all the superstitions and gross absurdities of outer Buddhism were fully known in the West you would see why it will not be adopted;

just as you would be convinced that we will not adopt Brahmanism either, with all its idolatry and superstitions.

W.Q.J.

E.M.—Has the identity of Chew-Yew-Tsâng been revealed? When I was in London the people in the T.S. center there were wild about him and some said he was an Adept. What is the truth about this?

Answer—

Chew-Yew-Tsâng was a *nom-de-plume* adopted by Mr. E. T. Hargrove, who is now lecturing for us here. He had some good ideas and sent them to *Lucifer* over that name. Many did go wild over the articles, especially its sub-editor. In time it was divulged who the author was and then the amusing part happened. The disputes about some charges in the Society were raging and Mr. Hargrove sided with the defendant. So those who had admired Chew, almost fallen at his symbolical feet, who had engrossed some of his sentences and hung them on the wall, arose quite angry at being led into praising the writing of such a young man—in fact it was a sort of reunion for the purpose of "eating crow." If there was any Adept in the matter he was in the far background and has not yet divulged himself. But it remains that the articles by Chew are well written and inspiring.

B.—Some of those who refuse to agree to our proceedings at Boston Convention are feeling hurt because in The Path *they have been slightingly referred to, as they think. Is it not better to be as kind as possible to all of them?*

Answer—

It is always best to be as kind as possible to friends and enemies, to those who are with us as to those who remain neutral. If *The Path* was unkind it sincerely apologizes for such a fault. In going over the ground after a very short struggle in which the small minority is of course beaten, the detailing of facts for information of the great constituency which could not attend the festivities, it is very natural that something unpleasant would take place—for bald facts are sometimes not agreeable. So *The Path* writer—and it was not the Editor—merely intended to point out that in some cases the bolting branch would be found to be one of those which had never been of the slightest use— in one case such a branch had been dead a year—and in others that the really earnest and devoted workers were not those who bolted after the Boston vote.

And indeed this magazine was very much milder in the matter than Col. H. S. Olcott himself. He declared it seemed as if all the best brain and energy of the American movement had gone with the vote and with that dreadful person—

W.Q.J.

P.B.—*The other evening, after a day of great activity, and being very tired, not thinking of my friend X, but rather of the passing business I had been in, I had a vision suddenly of X with whom I seemed to have a long conversation of benefit to both. Now how was this when I had not been thinking of him at all?*

Answer—

In the first place, experience shows, and those who know the laws of such matters say, that the fact of not having thought of a person is not a cause for preventing one from seeing the person in dream or vision. It makes no difference if you haven't thought of the person for twenty years.

Secondly, being wearied and much occupied during the day with absorbing business is in general likely to furnish just the condition in you for a vision or dream of a person or a place you have not thought of for a long time. But extreme and absolute fatigue, going to the extreme, is likely to plunge one into such a deep sleep as to prevent any such experience.

In consequence of bodily and brain fatigue those organs are temporarily paralyzed, sometimes, just enough to allow some of the astral senses to work. We then have a vision or dream of place or person, all depending upon the extent to which the inner astral person is able to impress the material brain cells. Sometimes it is forgotten save as the mere trace of something that took place but cannot be identified. When we are awake and active the brain has such a hold on the astral body that the latter (very fortunately) can work only with the brain and as that organ dictates. And when we fall naturally, unfatigued, into the state when it might be supposed we would have a vision, it does not come. But the pictures and recollections of the day pass before us because the brain is not tired enough to give up its hold on the astral body. Fatigue, however, stills the imperative brain and it releases its hold.

W.Q.J.

A.M.—*Who is your authority for the statement in November* Path *that there are only about 90 active branches in India of which only 40 have activity?*

Answer—

First, Mr. B. Keightley, who, as General Secretary there, reported— and it was so printed in *The Theosophist*—to the effect stated. In fact his report was even worse. Secondly, a member who had been at

Adyar many months helping with reports and accounts. He stated not much over a year ago that it was as I have said. In fact it now is a thoroughly well-known fact that the great parade of branches in India —some hundreds—is all a show, just like counting in your assets and reporting as alive a lot of long dead and valueless bonds or scrip. These other branches have long been dead and ought to have been taken off the record. But the presiding genius likes the names of back numbers so as to make a noise. We and the American public have been too long deluded about this flock of theosophical doves over there which are mere phantasms.

W.Q.J.

[The Path, Vol. X, February, 1896, pp. 353-54]

C.—I have heard some members talking about attracting elementals, and of this or that place being full of elementals. Not seeing these beings myself, and not knowing much about it, I would like to know if the phrases used are correct.

Answer—

It is quite probable that these persons never saw an elemental, and know still less, perhaps, than yourself of the subject and of the laws that may govern such entities. So do not be abashed by their assumption of knowledge. It is incorrect to talk of one place being more full of elementals than another place. We might as well say there is more of space in one spot of space than another. Elementals are everywhere, just as animalculæ fill the air; they obey the laws peculiar to themselves, and move in the currents of ether. If now and then they make themselves manifest, it does not hence follow that an additional number have been attracted to the spot, but only that conditions have altered so as to cause some disturbance.

W.Q.J.

T.C. AND F.O.R.—In some formerly published articles something is said of a future date marking the withdrawal of certain portions of the influence of the Adepts, and that those who have not gotten past the obstacles before that will have to wait until next incarnation. Is it necessary that one should be aware of having passed sufficiently far; must one be conscious of it? If so, I, for one, am "not in it."

Answer—

It is not necessary to be conscious of the progress one has made. Nor is the date in any sense an extinguisher, as some have styled it. In these days we are too prone to wish to know everything all at once, especially in relation to ourselves. It may be desirable and encouraging to be thus conscious, but it is not necessary. We make a good deal of progress in our inner, hidden life of which we are not at all conscious. We may not know of it until some later life. So in this case many may be quite beyond the obstacles and not be conscious of it. It is best to go on with duty, and to refrain from this trying to take stock and measuring of progress. All of our progress is in the inner nature, and not in the physical where lives the brain, and from which the present question comes. The apparent physical progress is evanescent. It is ended when the body dies, at which time, if the inner man has not been allowed to guide us, the natural record against us will be a cipher, or "failure." Now, as the great Adepts live in the plane of our inner nature, it must follow that they might be actively helping every one of us after the date referred to, and we, as physical brain men, not be conscious of it on this plane.

W.Q.J.

[*The Path*, Vol. X, March, 1896, pp. 385-88]

M.G.T.S.—*Will you kindly advise me in question department, how to strike the happy medium between Egoism or Egotism and the development of inner selfhood?*

Answer. This question cannot be properly answered, because you have put an indefinite question. It is not clear what you mean by a happy medium between development and the Self or Ego. The happy medium is generally between two courses. If by Egotism you mean the personal lower self, then it is said by all sages that there is continual war between it and the Higher Self until one or the other is the victor. As also what you mean by "Inner Selfhood" is indefinite, no reply based on that term, that would be useful, could be made. But if you want to know how to make a compromise, so to say, between the lower self—for that is what I assume your terms Egoism and Egotism to mean—it can only be pointed out that there can be no such truce; if attempted it would merely mean that the lower self would remain master, and the Higher Self wait for a new and better resolution. This is the state of most people, ever compromising, always allowing the lower self to have the upper hand, forever waiting for some later day when they intend to give the Higher the reins of government,—but that day will never come under such a course.

D.—*The recent death of Henry J. Newton following close on letters he sent the newspapers about the T.S. arouses the question, "Was he ever president of it, and what is there in the assertion he made that the Society was founded at his house?"*

Answer. He was its early treasurer, but never president. Like the many other spiritualists who joined and resigned quite soon, he departed also. The Society was not founded at his house. He published lately a facsimile of a pledge of secrecy in the Society signed by Mme. Blavatsky, Olcott and others, asserting this to be the beginning. This is a mistake of an old man with a bad memory. The pledge was a special one prepared in anticipation of promised wonderful revelations by a false pretender, and as the whole thing fell through, those papers were left with Newton because nobody cared for them. At the time, H.P.B. said to me that no revelations of any consequence would be made by the person, who was imposing on our spiritualistic members. Among other papers Mr. Newton had the roll, of course, because he was treasurer and used it for sending bills for dues. These documents he kept and refused to give them up to the Society. But the original minutes of organization, and other meetings, are in possession of loyal members in New York, and contradict Mr. Newton's assertion.

J.H.M.—*On page 234 of the November[1] issue it is stated that parentage is not merely for bringing an Ego into this life, but for wider and greater reasons. Please say what some of these reasons are.*

Answer. If it is held that parentage is only and solely for the purpose of furnishing a body for an Ego, then responsibility of parent to child is at an end, and the child also is relieved of all obligations and responsibilities to the parents. This view is held by some, and sad to say, by some of those F.T.S. who follow mechanical Theosophy. To my mind it is a monstrous proposition. It would also negative the doctrine of Karma and destroy the vast and wonderful continuity of things and forces relating to the human being. The child has far-reaching karmic relations with the parents, as they also with the child. The discipline and joys that come through children are karmic on both sides. If the child is a wicked one, it is the Karma of the parents also. Again, the incoming Ego requires a certain line of family so as to get the needed sort of body. In many and various ways, then, parentage can be seen to be more than a mere door to this plane.

B.R.C.—*I am unable to lecture; I cannot write good papers, and I do not seem to learn much at branch meetings. Is it any use for me to attend them?*

Answer. It must largely depend on your motive for attendance and on your actual interest. Do you go to learn or to help? If you go to learn, it is written by H.P.B. that half a dozen people meeting regularly and working harmoniously can learn more in six months than a solitary student can in two years. If you go there to help, the answer is differ-

---

1 [See *Echoes,* Vol. I, p. 470.—*Comp.*]

ent. If you believe in the power of thought, any experienced lecturer will tell you what an immense help it is to have even one intelligent and sympathetic listener; you not only give him ideas but you help also the enquirers present, by your sympathetic thought, to understand what is said. Wherever you are, you are a center of force, and it is your own fault if you are useless anywhere.

E. E. KNIGHT.—*Please inform me where I can find out about the meaning of the Society's emblem, and also about the many other signs and hieroglyphs found in our books.*

Answer. In the first volume of *The Path* (May, 1886, p. 51)[1] you will find an article on the subject of Theosophical symbolism. But in order to find out all you want it will be necessary to wade through many books, because the subject is so large and difficult. In H.P.B.'s *The Secret Doctrine* there is a great deal about symbols, and that is one of the best places to look. Your questions cover so many departments of symbolism that they could not be answered here, as proper treatment would mean the writing of a book.

W.Q.J.

R. A. FRENCH—*I have heard Theosophists condemn healing, and speak as though it were a crime. If it is true that disease is not to be healed, that physicians are hindering instead of helping the race, I should like to know.*

Answer. One invariable rule should be applied in regard to every statement made about "Theosophical teachings." Is this in accord with reason; with known facts? If not, reject it as contrary to real Theosophical teaching. This does not place reason as superior to intuition, but if a statement is made on some Theosophical subject which appears to you unreasonable, then it follows that either the statement is wrong or your understanding is wrong—and in neither case can it be true for you.

Healing is not condemned by Theosophists. It is much sought after by many of them. If your body is diseased you should go to the best physician of your acquaintance and follow his directions. Physicians who actually cure or alleviate disease are helping, not hindering, the evolution of the race. The questioner has perhaps heard a process of healing condemned, known as that of "mental science." That is condemned by some, because of its dangers and the general folly resulting from its practice. It undertakes to heal diseases without drugs and

---

[1] [*Echoes,* Vol. I, p. 11.]

without proper physicians. The mind only is used. Disaster results. But that is another matter, and as I have said, *healing* by proper and legitimate means is highly approved of by all true Theosophists.

H.

R. A. French.—*In talking with a Theosophist recently on the great crisis impending, he expressed the belief that all Theosophists would be brought through unharmed for the work of reconstruction. Has any such thing been promised?*

Answer. The "Theosophist" in question should read the February "Screen of Time" and the remarks contained therein on those who dote upon "lugubrious prophecies." And he thinks he will be saved "for the work of reconstruction?" Some people would say that he should be the first man demolished. But as regards the question: no such promise has been made, will or could be made. Very erroneous ideas seem to be entertained on the subject of this oft-quoted crisis. Some of the early Christians misinterpreted a prophecy said to have been made by Jesus and expecting the end of the world a few years after the death of their teacher. They were disappointed that it did not come. There is no need to imitate such an example and less excuse for doing so. When the crisis comes there will be time enough to study it. When the time for reconstruction comes our "Theosophist" will have his chance of being reconstructed with the rest of Nature— if he is not by then demolished. But to expect a karmic dispensation from all harm in some prophesied crisis, merely because he writes F.T.S. after his name, is a baseless and inexcusable superstition.

H.

ABRIDGEMENT OF DISCUSSIONS

Abridgement of Discussions
Upon Theosophical Subjects

[The following are discussions held at meetings of the Aryan Theosophical Society of New York. Judge's contributions are indicated by his own name or initials, as well as "The President," "General Secretary" and "X".

The following words of the young artist Leonard Lester who had recently arrived from England and who later was a resident member at the Point Loma, California, T.S. Headquarters, give an intimate touch of the atmosphere of these meetings.

"It was my great privilege to have been able to observe and note what passed at the regular Tuesday Evening meetings of the Âryan Theosophical Society, 144 Madison Ave., New York, (of which I was a member) and at which W.Q.J. presided. Regular topics of study were taken up. Speakers and writers had their say. Then at the end always W. Q. Judge would sum up, with rare and masterly wisdom, all the the ideas and teachings that had been expressed or discussed. And this point shone out. In these summings-up, emphasis and prominence *was always given to the practical ethical and spiritual message and meaning of the doctrines brought up.* Tendencies to run this way and that into exclusiveness, coldness to brotherhood, extreme intellectualism, psychic phenomena, etc., he would note, with warning or enlightening comment. And his manner and way of speaking had a simplicity and freedom from artifice, mannerisms, or attempt at eloquence, often being lit by charming humor and a smile that could never be forgotten. Modesty was like a coat of armor to him, but the calmness of true power shone through it. Those were wonderful times." *The Theosophical Forum*, April, 1948, p. 256—Comp.]

Number I

April, 1886

G.—I would like to ask how many degrees there are in the Theosophical Society, and if there are any others, who, if any one, can confer them, or how can they be obtained?

The President—I can state authoritatively that there are three degrees. The first or lowest is that in which every member is upon entering; the next is that of probationary and accepted Chelas, or disciples; and the last is that of Adepts and Mahatmas; each of these in turn has its natural divisions. The first is conferred by membership and diplomas. The second cannot be conferred *by any person, officer or otherwise,* in the Society's exoteric work, nor can the third. Those two are to be taken, so to say, by merit, and only that particular Adept in whose *ray* you are knows who is his chela.

G.—Cannot Col. Olcott or Mme. Blavatsky, or the heads of the movement here, confer the second degree?

The President—Most positively not. Persons have asked that before of Olcott and Blavatsky, and the reply has been a positive refusal and denial of power to do it.

G.—I have heard that a member of another Branch was offered the second degree by some one, either an officer or some other person.

The President—Such a proposal was highly improper. All of those who are in the second degree, when they have knowledge of it, conceal such fact; and, as I said, no official has any right in the matter. A degree so conferred would be, in fact, empty nonsense. As *Light on the Path* hints, those who reach the second degree will know it themselves, within themselves. Many work unceasingly for years not knowing from any written evidence that they are chelas.

The work of the Society is of two kinds: (*a*) Exoteric work in the world, to spread a knowledge of truth, and help all to make investigation to that end. In this work both chelas and non-chelas are engaged. It is the first degree; and anyone can take it, by asking for it and by being a person of good character. It takes in the work of all the branches of every kind, because what some choose to call "secret work" is the property of each man who pursues it. (*b*) The esoteric or secret work of the Society. This is done by adepts and their own chelas. *Without exception* this is profoundly secret, even extending to complete concealment by both adepts and chelas of what they have done. The reason is that it is all work upon the interior or soul part of the people, and chelas never say that they are chelas or that they are doing any secret work. If, for instance a chela is directed to implant in another's mind, a certain great idea, he tries to do so, but he tells no one, not even other chelas whom he may know to be such; nor do they ask him. Each proceeds on his own line of work, trying to carry out the directions he may have received. Each chela entered this so-called 2d degree because he *attained* to that moral and mental state. So it could not be conferred by any diploma, nor by any officer of any class whatever.

There are of course some chelas who are higher in mental and moral and spiritual development than other chelas. This would constitute another division among those of the 2d degree. But it is a natural division; and no amount of sentiment, or of declaration of desire, will accomplish this. The person must grow into that state, whether the growth be slow or rapid. The same differences exist among those of the highest section. Some are greater adepts than others, just as Moses appeared to be greater than the magicians of Pharaoh.

As to progress in this matter, it must follow that those progress the most who succeed in purifying their lives, their thoughts, and their motives, and who work the most unceasingly and unselfishly for others in the great cause.

It is hard to keep off the motive of working for the purpose of acquiring the reward, but it is easy to *try*, and to try to do so is absolutely necessary.

G. W. S.—A friend asked me if some chelas do not confess to others who are supposed to be higher, something like the Catholic church.

+ Decidedly not. Such a thing is extremely ridiculous. As a preceding reply said, each one has to work on his own lines and his only superior is his Guru, and even to his Guru he does not confess. It is not necessary, but must be useless. For if our ideas of the inevitableness of Karma are correct, then no amount of confessions could wipe out the Karma of our acts. Consequently such confessions would be absurd.

Confidences then are never revealed.

Question from Chicago.—"I am troubled by the idea that perhaps I am wasting time in my studies by pursuing them in the wrong direction. I do not want to fritter away the time and find after some years that all has been in the wrong direction."

R. H.—I do not see why any effort can be called wasted. All study stores up energy and there can be no waste whatever. Even study in what seems the wrong direction gives that much experience.

Col.—The only wasted time, it appears to me, would be in pursuing such powers as that of projecting the double, seeing astral forms, and so on. That does not, it would appear, develop spirituality, it is only a physio-psychical training.

+ The question could be answered better if we knew just what line of study the questioner has been and is now pursuing.

The subject of Karma was taken up, and discussion was had upon the influences which persons striving toward adeptship, had to contend with.

A. D. related the instance of a lady who said she would like to know several adepts, because "it would be so nice to have them do errands for her, recover small articles mislaid, bring coffee in Oriental cups, etc., with the aid of elementals." He thought this illustrated the false attitude in which many persons stood toward the subject, not even trying to understand the smallest of its great truths.

E. D. H.—What effect has Karma on our present struggle to better our lower nature? Is old Karma lost or mislaid, or does it enter into the matter, or are we to be governed henceforth only by that Karma which we are now making? Can old Karma be avoided?

+ The remark of Jesus is applicable here, where he desired his disciples "to be delivered from temptation." He did not desire that temptation should not come to them, but that they should be delivered from it, that is from its effects or power. Karma is not always all worked off in any one incarnation. We are now under the effects of old Karma, which we ourselves, in a past life, or in the past of this life, stored up. At the same time that we are now working Karma off, we are making new, which will rebound upon us now or in a succeeding incarnation. Our duty then to ourselves and the race, is to now make as much good Karma as we can, not devoting ourselves to, or being worried about past Karma; that is inevitable. It must come, so whatever it may be, good or bad, we now should accumulate good Karma even if we find in a few years, some terrible disaster upon us, the result of crime or error in a former life. It is certain that the life to come after this one, will not have disasters if we do right now. The most powerful of Buddha's disciples, Moggallâna, was suddenly assassinated in his later years by robbers, and Buddha did not interfere. His explanation was, that in a previous incarnation Moggallâna had committed a similar act which had not up to that time been compensated for.

Col.—I am led to believe Karma ought to be sub-divided, as: that of the body, the mind, the desires, and so on. The man himself must be the result in the ever present of all the good and evil of him in the past.

I think it can be changed and affected, (*a*) *unknowingly*, as, by climate, by family, by nationality, race, through ignorance, and by the age; (*b*) *understandingly*, by one's perceptions and judgment conjoined with will, when his mind is opened to a knowledge of Karma, for then he works with that in view. Immaturity of mind and want of clear perception of right may in this direction obstruct progress. So, until the dross is burned away, leaving only the spirit, he will have to fight many tough battles, which, however, will leave him better armed for each succeeding conflict.

+ In *Light on the Path* that is distinctly stated, and especially as to the constant fights or storms that will occur; and the silences coming among those fights and storms, are the chances for preparation.

B. X.—A thought occurs here worthy to keep. This constant struggle, up and down, surely goes on. It is easy to aspire when we feel jubilant in spirit, but not easy when we are in the depth of despondency. In the first case it is natural, for the jubilant feeling is caused by the present aspiration. If we only aspire then, the progress will be slow. But if we force ourselves to contemplation of the Supreme Soul when we are in despondency, then in the succeeding period of joy which will come, the bound upward is to a point beyond where we were before, and so the next downward rush will not be so low as the last, whereas if we leave it to itself we may for a long period never rise above, or rather never pass certain limits of this oscillation. So it is more valuable for us to aspire and to reach toward the Supreme Soul, when we are in despondency, than when we find ourselves in a highly elevated condition. We must refer to this again in another light.

Col.—Theosophists should take offence at no man, and have no *pet theories* of right for others. By helping a questioner he can build good Karma for himself. In all men is more or less of good. Nor should we despotically drive another into well doing. We should plant seeds of good. Lopping off, perforce, a branch of evil does no radical good, for the cause may still remain. So a correct view of Karma leads to a struggle with oneself in which all others are helped and affected, as we are so linked with others that any change in us must affect them.

+ The three great kinds of Karma should be well understood. That is, of our family, of our race or nation, and of the present age. It is very certain that if any of our duties are left unfulfilled, whether at death or upon renouncing the world, they will rebound on us at some time. These kinds of Karma are exhibited in the defects and good qualities of (*a*) the family, (*b*) the nation, and (*c*) the whole humanity. The first we may know and cure, (*b*) is obscure for us, (*c*) almost unknown. But all are powerful. So the rash person who rushes madly for Adepts and chelaship, unwittingly may put his head in the lion's mouth. The defects due to family Karma are strong enough to overwhelm him at the first trial, and how powerful, nay, dreadful, are the defects of his nation, all to him a blank. Here nature is cruel perhaps—no, only just— although inexorable. We first then must try to know our family defects, and by doing good Karma bring up to the front the reserved force of our past high deeds and aspirations, so that when we shall have got to a point of trial the good qualities are in sufficient strength to help us. This is what we may call "Karmic stamina." It is what Jesus meant when he said, "Lay up for yourselves treasures in heaven."

E. B. H.—I think every mental or physical fault allowed to hold its ground, insidiously leaves at every recurrence a sediment in the soul. This drags us back to earth, because of the desire which accompanied it. It would seem then that what people call fate is truly fate, but we made it and we alone can unmake it.

B. X.—That is true, and that is the whole struggle. This "fate" is Samsara, or the great wheel of rebirths, from which each alone must deliver himself.

G.—Perhaps the stress so often laid by Theosophy upon our not being anxious about the effect of our actions is really intended to prevent us occupying ourselves too much with what comes into the cognizance of our fully developed powers, lest we should not give those which are in embryo a chance to assert themselves—that, in fact, there is a different and more important effect of our actions than that generally seen, this effect being the one on which our attention should be fixed.

The danger in that case is that one may be continually thinking about what kind of Karma he is generating, which, it seems to me, would be unhealthy and abnormal and only refined selfishness—like thinking all the time of his own salvation from hellfire.

Col.—After all, but a small part of each man's total Karma is the effect of his own action; there are, besides the Karma of his own making, the Karma of the family to which he belongs, his national Karma, the Karma which results from the condition, moral, intellectual or social of the civilization in which his nature is developed, and so forth, to all of which he is subjected. Before mankind can hope to escape from the bonds of matter all these different Karmas must run down and cease to have action.

E. D. H.—Can Karma come to a head?

+ Undoubtedly, it is coming to a head all the time in life, blossoming out in the shape of thoughts, words and actions, which are themselves the seeds of future Karmic bloom and fruit. These are the lesser wheels within that greater wheel of Karma, each turn of which brings us back to the world of matter once more.

B. X.—The meaning of what is said in *Bhagavad-Gîtâ* about acting without being bound in the action, is, that we should learn to do any action because we believe it to be right, having no thought for what the consequences may be. But if we regard the consequences, then we are really acting not because we are sure of our standard of action, but with a view to some result. This inevitably binds us in the bonds of action, and results in a Karma that will bring us surely back to that kind of life. We are not to be indifferent, because that is worse yet.

We should act with the above high motive, using at same time the same amount of energy as those do who are entirely bound up in results, as the author of *Light on the Path* tells us.

As yet, we must be content with putting the state of not caring for Karma and not making Karma, as an ideal to be aspired to, for we cannot even begin the struggle without making Karma. Therefore, as a step toward a higher plane, we must try to make good Karma, and in this endeavor we should not fail to try to comprehend, through study, what we are, how we should act, what Karma really is, and how best it can be reduced, avoided, or worked off.

After all, the attitude of mind we are in when any act is performed, is more important than anything else. This is easily understood when we consider how often men do a certain thing with good intention which we cannot condemn, although others, better informed, know it to be unwise.

Number II

May, 1886.

Question from Brooklyn—I have heard that telegrams or letters signed "K. H." have been received by certain theosophists directing things to be done or lines of study to be pursued. Can they be considered genuine and from the adept named, and if so why are they not more general?

W. Q. Judge—stated his firm conviction to be, that such telegrams or messages were not genuine, and that he knew from statements made in India to him, that the Adepts do not send messages around in such a manner, and that, even with their accepted disciples, they are very chary of messages. He also said that a disciple of the adepts, whom he met in India, assured him that those Beings must not be held so cheap as they have been made by some, and the disciple (an accepted chela) declared that he would sooner cut off his hand than send a pretended message, referring also at the time, to the well-known rule in occultism that any occultist, student or adept, who directly by pretended messages or phenomena, or indirectly by mysterious assumptions or small deception, pretends to have *siddhis* (powers), or otherwise attempts to convey the idea that he has made progress in the secrets of occultism, thereby at once forfeits his progress and throws himself far back.

Col.—It seems to me also, that every one must be careful not to accuse any student of having made such an attempt at deception, because often we may feel that such attempt has been made, when in fact, the feeling is due to our own ignorance and inability to understand, or to his desire to avoid possible misconception.

After further discussion, it was decided that it is quite unlikely that any such telegrams are genuine, but are merely either a hoax, or the outcome of the vanity of the person who sent them.

A. D.—speaking on talismans said: "Admitting for the moment that talismans have real effect, we find Paracelsus and others saying that lead, which is sacred to Saturn, may be used to make a talisman which will perserve the wearer from death by means of lead. I should like to ask whether, if my life were saved from a bullet by this means, the Karmic result which would have been achieved by my being shot is avoided.

+If Karma be a Divine law governing the universe it cannot be completely wiped out by the action of a talisman, for this would require that Karma, which ceases to act only when it exhausts itself or is counteracted by opposite Karma, should be nullified and disrupted by an extraneous force. The talisman therefore must be supposed only to avert the fatal blow for the moment, and the Karmic effect will show itself in some other shape at a later period during that life, or in the next incarnation in that form or some other.

Question from Florida—In No. 1 of "Abridged Discussions" it is held that we are answerable, in effect, for the sins of the Family, the Nation and the Age. But how does this accord with the doctrine of Reincarnation?

The soul returning from Devachan to resume its Earth life, is not necessarily related to the parents with whom it takes up its abode. Now, is it just that this soul should be deprived of the fruits of his good Karma merely because he has the ill fortune to be born of wicked parents? Admitting that the race is so bound together, that no individual can do or suffer wrong without hurting others, yet it seems repellant to our sense of justice that the good should suffer. It is a misfortune to belong to an immoral family, a wicked nation, or a corrupt age, but ought the individual to be punished for this misfortune? May we not believe that he who keeps his own soul clean shall reap his due reward? Otherwise is not the incentive for goodness, wisdom and truth greatly weakened?

+In discussing this it was shown that No. 1 Abridgement did not hold that any one could be deprived of the fruit of good Karma, but that every one reaped exactly what he had sown, good or bad.

Col.—Man coming from Devachan gravitates to the family which exactly suits the Karma he has made in previous existences, and he himself in former existences helped to build up the Karma of his race and civilization; his experiences in life, moreover, are the resultant of his good and bad Karma, therefore, it seems to me, there is no injustice.

W. Q. J.—The effects of Karma can not be calculated mechanically, like weighing out a pound of sugar; for the Karma of one incarnation may appear in another under a different form, just as the sun's heat stored up in the coal is converted into flame in the furnace, reappears as steam in the boiler, changes into mechanical force in the engine, becomes electricity in the dynamo, and finally emerges as light in the electric lamp. Nor do they *always* assert themselves in the same shape or form; but they often might and do. Nor do they invariably show themselves in the incarnation immediately succeeding; their development might not occur for ten, or perhaps, one hundred lives after.

Our good and evil propensities have unknown mazes and ramifications, and they are as much a part of our Karma as are the mere effects upon our circumstances of any action, good or bad. And to these good and evil propensities, the law of science which permits one kind of energy to be converted into another under favorable conditions, must be applied; for any evil or noble element of human nature, converts itself when the conditions permit, into any other element however apparently remote. This is what is meant in *Light on the Path*,[1] where it says that the source of evil lives fruitfully in the heart of the disciple as well as in the heart of the man of desire, and that it may blossom after many hundreds of incarnations. The possibility of this blossoming, and probable conversion into some undreamed of propensity or element, is found in this, that in one life the conditions did not arise which would enable the propensity to come to the surface, and that hundreds of lives have no power to kill a seed of either good or evil which has not had its chance for growth. And the "conditions" necessary, are not alone the state of life, the family, or the age, in which we incarnate, but also the attractions we may have set up in a former life for another being or any kind of conduct.

The moment we again meet those beings or that kind of attraction, at that moment the old propensity comes to light in its original form or in some other form which may be stronger, or perhaps in two or three different kinds of mental or moral energy.

E. D. H.—If it be a fact that our progress follows the law of universal evolution, it is begging the question to say that any man suffers injustice, for his being born of bad parents or into unhappy circumstances must be considered as one of the results of his past Karma.

S. H. C.—Our sense of apparent injustice in this case, seems to come from regarding the question in the light of human justice, which requires immediate settlement, rather than of the larger divine justice which has eternity before it to set things right. If every seed that fell

---

1 [*Op. Cit.*, Pt. I, Rule 4.—*Comp.*]

on stony ground had to be compensated before the luckier ones were allowed to grow, the whole course of nature would be stopped. Providence does not strike the balance till the account of each individual is closed, but that balance is sure to be found correct.

R. H.—The adjustment of Karmic causes and effects being a matter of natural law, and of cosmic rather than human justice, it is probable that in reincarnating the spirit is attracted unconsciously to the body fitted to receive it, much as during the process of chemical combination an atom of one kind is attracted to the atom of another kind which has most affinity for it. This apparent exercise of a power of selection is seen more clearly in the faculty possessed by the various tissues to extract from the blood the particular constituents necessary for their maintenance, but in no case can it be supposed to be consciously exercised in our usual sense of the term. Were the reincarnating spirits not guided by some higher influence which makes a certain choice for each one a necessary choice, it is difficult to see how, with the competing wishes and interests that would then come into play, the millions of reincarnating spirits could find their right bodies without cross purposes and conflict.

W.—In the *Bhagavad-Gîtâ* Krishna says that he who at the moment of death utters his name goes to Him. I should like to ask whether this does not savor strongly of deathbed repentence.

Krishna.—By "the moment of death," is meant the actual moment of transition when the senses have closed to this world and not yet opened to the other. This is entirely different to the moment *before* death when the mind is filled with ideas of terrestrial origin, and the expiring sinner calls excitedly upon God to save him. When the last breath has been drawn, and, as far as spectators are concerned, all is over, a moment of intense mental activity occurs before the spirit finally leaves the body. All the past life rushes with graphic vividness before the mind, and the thoughts, emotions, and desires *which have become habitual,* arise with irresistible force. At that moment, the true moment of death, what presents itself most strongly, and forces itself out, is that which has been nearest and dearest to the heart during life— money, lust, charity, pride,—whatever, in fact, the individual has habitually made an object of pursuit and worship. For anyone, therefore, to be able to call on God at the moment of death, implies a life-long service of God, and in that sense must Krishna's saying be understood.

Col.—I am somewhat puzzled to understand whether our individual consciousness will be continued eternally. The favorite simile of a raindrop returning to the ocean seems to imply the loss of individual identity when the spirit becomes merged in the divinity.

G. W. S.—Since we have consciousness we must have come from a power which possessed that consciousness in order to give it, and when it returns whence it came it is really we who return, for our consciousness is ourselves.

R. H.—Who knows but that the rain-drop preserves in its own way its sense of identity, or memory of its drop life, although its material particles be scattered. At all events that *we* should preserve our identity forever seems to be a necessary corollary of the possession of a conscious individual indestructible spirit, and if such be the case, it does not weaken our position that, with our extremely limited mental powers, we are unable to say how it will be brought about. John Stewart Mill said that the possibility of two and two making five in some other state of existence should neither be affirmed nor denied on the strength of our present experiences and mental powers, and if material science goes so far as that, we should not be afraid to acknowledge limitation in our powers of intellectually comprehending spiritual things.

From St. Louis—Is it possible to skip an incarnation?

To skip an incarnation would be like skipping one lesson in a series. But as the subject matter taught during each incarnation, so to speak, must be learned before the individual can pass on to further development, to skip an incarnation is an impossibility and involves a contradiction. For no matter how, or in what body, or for what period of time—long or short—the ego reappears, it is an incarnation, inasmuch as *incarnation* means *coming into a body. To skip a period in Devachan* is, however, possible, but it is exceedingly exceptional, and seldom advantageous. It occurs, we are told, in two instances. First in certain rare cases when the Adepts, in order to hasten the development of a chela, aid him in passing at the moment of death into some other and younger body, which is at that instant in the act of losing its own tenant, but which is not so diseased as to prevent full recovery of health after the advent of the new vitality. Secondly in the case of the higher Lamas, when, at the death of the old Lama his spirit enters the new body while it is still unborn.

From Malden Branch, T.S., May, 1886.—The reading of the article, "Kiménis," in *The Theosophist* for April, caused a discussion on the temptations to which the student of occultism is subjected. One of the members said that *Kiménis,* or *Khimenou,* was once known to a certain student as *Kamen.* In *The Idyll of the White Lotus*[2] the name of one of the priests, who renounced his humanity in order to gain the love of his fellows, while he thenceforth loved no one in return, was *Kamen*

---

2 [Collins, Mabel, *The Idyll of the White Lotus,* with an explanation by Swami T. Subba Row, T.P.H., Adyar, several editions, 1884 on.—*Comp.*]

Baka. Had the young man who wrote his experiences with *Kiménis* been in pursuit of occult knowledge, that fair demon might have tempted him not only in the astral form, but in the body of some living woman. This is one of the twelve temptations to which, under the rites of the Egyptian mysteries, the candidate for occult advancement is subjected. Another temptation is to sell the knowledge acquired; to make use of it for the sake of gain. Whoever does this, directly or indirectly, loses his chance of advancement for the time. The Divine Wisdom cannot be prostituted to selfish ends in any way, and whoever does so becomes a black magician. All are given the chance to enter upon the Path, though they may not realize the value of the opportunity, and many fail, not knowing that they have failed. Such is the Law.

Z.—It seems to me that many who think that they would earnestly seek the light do not comprehend the true nature of the temptations to which they are continually subjected. They are looking for something unusual, something hard in the way of a trial, and think: If something of the sort would only come along, how I would show my power to stand it! At the same time, by their daily yielding to the small vexations of life they show their unfitness for meeting greater trials. Even if one who has waited long and patiently asks, "Why am I not given an opportunity, since my conduct deserves it," he shows by the very question his unfitness. As the great poet, Walt Whitman, who is full of occultism, says: "When the materials are all prepared and ready, the architects shall appear."[3] When a person loses his temper over a trifle, he is hardly likely to meet any greater temptation in the right spirit. Every time we successfully overcome even the slightest obstacle, we have made a step in our initiation into the mysteries. Let us remember that it is the unexpected that always happens in the way of trials to the novice. The devil never sends a herald to announce his coming, and when pictured as a serpent it is never as a rattlesnake. When we have learned to encounter every vexation absolutely without complaint, either internally or externally—if it disturbs us in the slightest degree within, it is just as bad as if we expressed it in words or action—then, and not till then, can we expect to be given the opportunity to take a decided step forwards. For the secret of advancement is the development of the will through its union with the Divine Will. By meeting the ordinary ills of life with unvexed soul we educate and strengthen our will, fitting us for further advancement. Humbleness, Patience and Content are the first 3 steps that lead to the door.

---

3 ["A Song of the Rolling Earth," Stanza 4, line 10, in *Leaves of Grass* (many editions).—*Comp.*]

The book entitled *Ghost Land,* familiar to many occultists, was alluded to.[4]

M. C.—I have just been reading the book for the first time. The author had undoubtedly gone far in occultism. But there are evidences of a misstep. The work is marred by the false glare of Spiritism, and it is notable how the denial of the great truth of Reincarnation is insisted upon. But the next time the author passes this way he will know more of Reincarnation, and admit that he was here before and will be again. He is an old man, and will soon desire *a new coat.* When he thinks he sees the dear friend, who gave up for him his own life, suffering among the earthbound souls and himself among the shining ones, that is self-glorification, egotism, self,—and he is mistaken. He tells more in detail concerning some great mysteries than probably any other man has yet put in print. But when he says that he himself occupied the *Seventh Seat,* that is conclusive proof that he did not, in reality, for that is a place which once occupied is never referred to by the occupant. He may have thought that he did. But there is no danger that a man can reveal the secrets of the most High. When he thinks he does, he does not. "He that exalteth himself shall be humbled." It is one of the tests that, *if a man is proud of his wisdom, he must fail.*

Number III

June—September, 1886.

E. D. W.—asked: "Is not Christianity in its purity, that is to say as taught by Jesus, much the same as Theosophy?"

X.—The religion which Jesus taught is not what the world understands by Christianity. Those who follow the real religion of Jesus think they are Christians only because they still try to combine in their minds the theology of their church with the sublime and simple ideas of their Master; and nothing could prove more clearly the moribund condition of dogmatic Christianity than the growing tendency to identify the name "Christian" with the teachings of Jesus, rather than with orthodox Christianity. The doctrines of Jesus are undoubtedly the same as those of Theosophy, inasmuch as they are the embodiment of the same high morality that all great sages have inculcated—the morality of the Ancient Wisdom Religion, which is the highest morality conceivable to mortal man. If, however, "Christianity in its purity," is to be made synonymous with the doctrines of Jesus it will be necessary to rub out nearly everything which the world has understood by Chris-

---

4 [*Ghost Land; or Researches into the Mysteries of Occultism* (Boston, 1876) by Mrs. Emma Hardinge-Britten.—*Comp.*]

tianity for 1800 years. Jesus taught that the kingdom of heaven is within men; that all men are children of one father, and therefore brothers; that man must be saved—attain to perfection—through the Comforter, the Christ, the spirit of God in his own heart, his own divine nature, and not through Jesus himself in any sense. This divine spark is man's birthright which he can either forfeit entirely or redeem and cherish, and which Jesus felt so strongly within himself that he identified his conscious principle with it. All this is pure Theosophy.

E.B.H.—It is well to have this made clear, because people are inclined to confound the phenomena generally understood as Theosophy with the philosophy of the movement. They imagine that all there is to Theosophy is to be found in its wonders, and hence suppose that the religion of Jesus and Theosophy are incompatible.

Edson H.—The doctrine of reincarnation is so different from accepted Christian theories, it is hard to convey these ideas to minds of Christians, unless they have had some instruction upon them. The moment such persons get their minds open to the fact that they are more or less bound by old ideas, they begin to make progress. Christians ought to remember that Jesus himself apparently accepted this doctrine of rebirth, as for instance, in the cases of the child born blind, and, where Jesus referred to John the Baptist as being Elias. Rev. Ed. Beecher in the book *Conflict of Ages* claims this doctrine as a Christian one.

Col.—When it shall be clearly understood that to be living a truly theosophic life includes in it the same reverence for the eternal One, the same devotion to high morality and justice, and the same love for fellowmen that Jesus inculcated, then Theosophy will begin broadly to be seen in its true light; yet the theosophic life is deeper, higher and broader than that which the Christian church ever teaches.

P. D. asked:—Ought Theosophists to send their children to Sunday School?

X—Going to Sunday School is, for the children, a social pleasure; for the parents to send them there is in this case a tribute paid to conventionality. In the absence of any similar institution on a theosophical basis it seems a tempting and easy way to dispose of the children during a few awkward hours. Much depends upon the character of the teacher, and upon the tone of the particular Sunday School. Sometimes a simple and unobjectionable morality is taught and illustrated from the Bible stories; but in those cases where the teacher offends the consciences of the children with theological dogmas it would naturally seem advisable to keep them at home, unless any bad effects of the Sunday School lessons can be counteracted by home instruction. It appears to be a choice of evils, for to keep the children at home is a punishment to them, and probably a trial to the parents, and to contradict what they hear in Sunday School would tend to puzzle the children, and to sap their faith in any teaching, for a child must be taught dogmatically and it has no criterion except personal respect for the teacher by which to choose between opposing assertions about religious matters. The dilemma shows the need of Theosophical Sunday Schools for those members who are not Christians, but in any case it is the duty of parents, when they are themselves agreed, to teach their children the fundamental truths of Theosophy, and to present to them, in such a form as the young can comprehend, whatever ideas they feel have done good to themselves. If certain doctrines have done the parents good, they should not idly allow the children to remain without them in the hope that later on the latter will find these things out for themselves.

E. B. H.—In my opinion, children can be taught by reason, and they will accept theosophical truths very readily if put before them in the true light.

Question from Los Angeles.—Many seem to feel acutely the buffeting of the world; would not a retreat, a kind of lamasery, so to speak, be of great value to such persons in their spiritual development?

R. A.—Experience proves that a lamasery which contains only students is not productive of good, and no real student retires from the world on account of weariness of life. Peace and content come only to him who tries to live each day as it is given. Wisdom and knowledge only to him who performs his duty in life. We are here to learn our lesson—to realize that all men are one, high or low, and this we cannot learn unless we live among them. Those who in this country sought seclusion in an isolated retreat would find themselves in the full glare of public notoriety. Here, the yellow robe of the ascetic, must be worn internally, not externally. Each must have his lamasery in his inner self. The effort and the money needed to establish a lamasery would be better employed in active works of charity. Self is the most dangerous of all the powers with which we have to contend, and to shut oneself up from the world for the purpose of soul development is a dangerous and extreme kind of selfishness, and he who goes off by himself to watch his soul come into blossom will see it wither and die at the roots under the blazing sun of his own selfishness.

After some discussion the views expressed by R. A. were endorsed by the meeting.

A. N. S.—asked if the Theosophical Society was a secret one, as many of his friends had put the question to him, and the President of the Board of Control had said so much in the newspaper about secrecy that he hardly knew how to reply.

The President in reply drew attention to the Report of the last Annual Convention of the Society in India, when the rule of secrecy was abolished, and the only thing required was that one desiring membership should be in sympathy with the idea of universal brotherhood. The old obligation was retained only to be used at the discretion of the Presidents of Branches. The New York Branch retains the obligation of secrecy only in regard to the signs and passwords, and their signification, a knowledge of which is imparted to a new member at the time of his initiation. But any person may become a member of the Society by making application in accordance with the Society's rules and by-laws, and need not take any obligation to secrecy, and it will then be the duty of the Society at large to admit that person as member of the Society unattached to any particular Branch.

The subject of Anger having been introduced, the Colonel said:

He who perceives a spark of the Eternal spirit in all things can have but little selfishness left in him, and he is necessarily free from attacks of Anger as distinguished from an unselfish feeling of Righteous Indignation at injury done to unprotected innocence. In all nature, animate and inanimate, he recognizes only a mass of scintilations of the Eternal Spirit, each surrounded by materiality; and this makes the doctrine of Universal Brotherhood a grand, heartfilling anthem of harmony, ever thrilling through and through him. He sees in long perspective the never ending march of evoluting progression of all things, and all tending up to the Eternal. What can anger him? He is too deeply concerned in the well-being of all to care how obscure he may be. He is too engrossed in building right principles to concern himself about himself. So flimsy is the structure of his selfishness that a blow goes through it without evoking that resistance from which anger is generated, as a spark is generated by the collision of flint and steel.

S.C.Y.—There is a floating suspicion in the Society that there exists in this country an unknown head or director of the Theosophical movement.

General Discussion.—There is strong reason to believe that such is the case, although anyone who knew it to be a fact would not be likely to declare it. It is said that although only a portion of the Brothers of the First Section were at first in favor of establishing the Theosophical Society, they have all given their adhesion to the movement now. It stands to reason, therefore, that the well-being of the Society must be a matter of common concern with the Brotherhood, and that it will employ the methods usual with it in all such cases. We should remember, however, that the mode of action of the Brothers of the First Section is to work in harmony with nature, which does not consist in arbitrary interference with the laws of cause and effect. By their unseen aid we can accomplish things which would be difficult or impossible without it, and we are apt in such cases to flatter ourselves on our achievements, like a child pulling a cart which someone unperceived is pushing from behind. It is evident that this supervision being guided by a clearer, and therefore more prophetic, perception of consequences, is apt sometimes to push things in a direction we do not want them to go, even to the extent of apparent injury; to bring on, in fact, what doctors call "a beneficent crisis;" but in all such cases our verdict, when we see afterwards how matters turn out, invariably is: "It was for the best after all."

Question from South America.—How far should such works as "Esoteric Buddhism" and "Man"[5] be taken as authoritative?

X—The writers of these books are pupil-teachers, and their works are not textbooks of Theosophy. What the Masters are now imparting are, so to speak, elementary fragments of the Ancient Wisdom religion. Much of the teaching they are now giving us is in the form of problems for ourselves to solve; but in clearly understanding the statement of those problems we learn how to solve them. Men see things and ideas in different lights, and what is proof for one mind is not proof for another. Those who are in the same "ray" as the authors above mentioned will be satisfied with their works; while to those in a different ray the books in question may perhaps appear somewhat dogmatic or fanciful, especially in points where the writers give their own inferences. In reasoning from generals to particulars it is necessary to take a birds-eye view of the field at a time when the mind has not acquired the knowledge, perhaps not even developed the faculties necessary to comprehend that part of the subject which lies beyond everyday experience. It is in endeavoring to form a clear mental picture of that unaccustomed part, that writers in Theosophy chiefly disagree with each other, and tax their readers' powers of comprehension. It should be remembered, however, that our inability to form clear and satisfactory conceptions of things which until our knowledge grows we are told we must receive as if they were provisional hypotheses, is no proof that those things are not actualities, which will be fully shown and explained to us in due time.

---

5 [*Man: Fragments of Forgotten History,* by Mohini M. Chatterjee and Laura C. Holloway-Langford; London, Reeves and Turner, 1885.—*Comp.*]

Number IV

November, 1887.

S.—I have seen various references to *"The Parent Theosophical Society,"* and would like to know the meaning of the term, and to what it is applied.

General Secretary.—At present there is no meaning in this name, and its use is a source of error; it never should have been used. If there is in existence any "Parent Society," then it is the Aryan, because its charter members are the only ones left here of the first Branch ever formed, while Mme. Blavatsky and Col. Olcott are the founders of this Branch which became the Aryan after their departure. But as the whole Society is composed of its Branches and unattached members, and as each person who joins—either through a Branch or at large—thereby becomes a member of the whole Society, there can be no "parent Society." It is advisable that this term be discarded altogether, as it has no reason for its existence and no meaning in its use.

1st Question from California.—Anatomical science teaches that the nerves of organic life, which furnish power for every vital function, have their source and center in the brain, and that the latter is the seat of the soul.

+.It seems to me that anatomical science does not teach that brain is the center of the soul, for the soul is not recognized as necessarily to be inferred from the anatomical and physiological structure.

D.—The sympathetic nerve system controls organic life. That system, as a whole, includes the heart and brain as well as the other ganglia. From this it might be inferred that the brain is not the exclusive seat of the soul, (the existence of which must of course be admitted by us), but rather that its dwelling place, as far as organic life is concerned, is in the portion of the nerve system having most to do with that life, as, for instance, the *solar plexus*. Inasmuch as the developing human germ carries its processes of organic construction to a high degree without a brain, but with more or less well defined nerve centers, we might safely conclude that the heart in that case is then the seat of the soul.

J.—The Upanishads state that the soul or self dwells in the center, or knot, of the heart. This knot of the heart is also spoken of by Mohammedan devotees. Both say that in order to know the soul the heart's knot must be unloosed. Yet we find that the Hindu yogi affirms that in order to know the soul the man's *conscious will* must pass through and become master of the different vital centers of the body, ending in one that is in the brain. This seems to give the brain a high place, but a co-operative one, because by itself it could have done nothing.

Then again many well authenticated cases show us that hearing, sight, smell, and feeling may be transferred to the stomach or even the feet—as in the hysterical patients of the Salpetriere Hospital in Paris.

Some well-versed theosophical students affirm their belief to be that the brain is only the commander who executes certain orders from the soul, which they say has its real dwelling place in the heart, while at the same time it dwells also outside of the heart.

Arjuna.—Have you reflected on that verse in the Aryan books which says that from the heart radiate various arteries—101 I think—which are said to serve for the soul's departing in different directions, and that in these arteries is a fluid of different colors, in which the soul dwells, or to which it retires when the body is asleep. They also say, I think, that that soul which can at death go out from the man through the great astral nerve, a passage going from the top of the head, will not be reborn, but knowing itself—or God—will reach salvation.

Col.—Regarding this matter, it is well to remember that all souls are not alike, and therefore would have perhaps, different places for their seat. Take, for instance, those exhibitions at spiritistic séances where sometimes a form is seen to exude from the *side* of the medium and gain consistency. Here we have an instance in which the brain seems to be ignored by a conscious, or apparently conscious, thing.

E. D. H.—I have always heard it asserted by many mediums that their "controls" told them that they took control of the body through the *spleen.* If the control had first to be obtained over the soul, the interesting query arises, is it the animal soul or the human soul of the person? The Greeks admit an animal soul, and St. Paul gives two higher principles than the body, so we may fairly ask whether, if there be two souls, one animal and the other divine, they each reside in the same spot in the body?

As for the pineal gland, it is well settled that it now has no particular function, being only a small sandy-like lump, and its assumption for the soul's place seems merely to arise from the failure of function for it. But the spleen presents just as good, if not a better, place, in which to put the soul's particular home.

W. Q. J.—Many writers of old have asserted that man had once a *third eye*, and that the pineal gland is that third eye, dead, unused, and therefore retracted to its present place. I put this idea lately before a physician of ultra materialistic ideas, and he said it was not too wild an assumption, for there are many unused organs and remains of organs in the human body which once had a function of their own.

E.D.H.—In one case I have placed my hand on the side of the medium over the spleen while being controlled, and felt a peculiar trembling there. I think it is the animal soul that is affected in those cases.

+.—Hypnotic suggestion would account for the recollection by mediums in many instances.

B.—What do you mean by "animal soul?"

E. D. H.—I use the term to make a distinction between the higher conscious soul and that part of the soul which governs mere life.

S.—I think it is the animal soul that has its seat in the solar plexus; but I do not think that the higher soul has any particular spot for its seat in the body; it is both within and without and everywhere, as I assume we are discussing the human soul as distinguished from the animal.

Dr. W.—We have first to settle what we mean by soul and spirit. The spirit in man is that which is like the divine, and the soul is outward to the inward spirit.

Mrs. G.—I have seen what has been called by some the soul, and by others the astral man, come out from a person and heard it speak; is not that the soul? And this thing has no particular spot in the body for its seat.

O. K.—If the soul has any special place in the body, it must be, I think, in the heart; for first there must arise will and desire, and the brain must be under command of the soul, but cannot say if this soul is the animal or spiritual one; and by the word "soul" I mean what is usually understood by the Christian as Soul.

G. W.—The soul does not locate itself in any particular spot; it must permeate the body, and act by and through in its different organs.

H. T. P.—To locate the soul is to materialize an immaterial thing. The body is only a manifestation of the soul. By locating it in any particular organ you are making it more material than body.

Some notes sent by Wm. Brehon, F.T.S., were then read, regarding the soul and the first chapter of the *Bhagavad-Gîtâ* in which the writer laid down the proposition that the clearest way to think of the subject was to say that the soul took upon itself one sheath, or cover, after another, beginning with the finest and ending with the body, and that in these various sheaths reside the various powers and properties ascribed to the so-called "seven principles" of Theosophical literature.

J. V.—I think this idea will aid us in clearing up the slight confusion which arises from dwelling upon a division of man into seven principles. As we admit that the seventh is spirit and therefore the whole, it would seem too much like leaving an eighth to be accounted for. But if we assume a great all pervading Higher-Self—the same as Emerson's "Over-Soul"—which assumes six manifestations more and more dense, arriving at body as the most dense, we can more easily come near the absolute truth that the *Self* is the basis for all, and thus also we may apprehend why all but that *Self* is an illusion—for to me, *illusion*, in these subjects, means "a veil."

Krishna.—I agree with J. V., and am reminded of the idea, so much dwelt on in the Upanishads, that the self—*the Higher-Self*—is the sole perceiver of all states or planes of consciousness, and therefore that which we know as the lower-self—or the "I" of most of us—must admit that it has to gradually be merged in the Higher-Self, in order to fulfil its destiny and acquire true knowledge.

C.—This then will destroy the erroneous idea that Spirit ever can be, or needs to be, developed, and show, on the contrary, that it is the lower-self which must be purified or alchemized in order that the Higher may alone be seen. It will also show that it is philosophically wrong to say that "the Higher-Self will be increasingly conscious of the lower in proportion to the extent that the latter applies itself deliberately to the task of living for the sake of the *Higher*." For if the consciousness of that task is in the Higher—as it must be—then it is the lower that gradually disappears, and, further, to say that the Higher-Self "increases its consciousness of the lower" is to reduce the greater to be included in that which is less than itself.

2nd Question from California—What became of the bodies of Moses, Elias, Jesus, and others like them?

G. W. S.—This query seems unprofitable; for if we could reply accurately, it could be of no benefit to anyone.

S. H. C.—Inasmuch as the body is a material composition subject to the laws of growth and decay, it must be the fact that these bodies decayed and dissipated in the ordinary manner, if they were not burned. But if the mystical *Something* meant by Moses, Elias, and so on, is really referred to—which I doubt—then we know that nothing could or did happen to such bodies.

Cains.—How does the Esoteric teaching bear on the doctrine of Free Will?

Col.—Whether we admit the truth of the doctrine of Free Will or not,—whether we believe that we are simply children of a life predistinct or not, this ground fact is apparent, viz: That we never make a step in advance, never live down and out an evil tendency which is within us, without what is to us a sacrifice of inclination of our lower, baser, ignorant self; a sacrifice by efforts which to our *consciousness* springs from our ego. When the youth says, "No, I will not do this thing," to his consciousness, *he* has decided, and that, too, by the sacrifice of an earthly, selfish consideration—by a sacrifice of a desire of his material self. Such a sacrifice demands self-forcing and pain or trouble, or self-imposed deprivation, and sometimes even life itself, but the suffering, the pain, the trouble, the deprivation, and the death bring man to a higher plane by *his* sufferings; and when the ego by the sufferings of self shall have at last lost its earthly nature and shall have arisen to a one-life with the universal spirit, will it matter to him whether you call his law of progress one by Free Will or one by pre-distinction? he knows "*I* chose, *I* certainly suffered; by this pain and suffering, the earth of *me* has been separated from *me*, and at last *I* am at Bliss—life with the Great Spirit; *I* received the stripes,—this advance on to the plane of God-life is *mine*."

A. N. S.—You say Mr. President, that you very much doubt if there is such a state or attribute of the mind as "Free Will," and that it is a question with you if we ever have so-called "*Free Wills*."

If one views their present status or condition from every side, that is to say, from the side of their national Karma, as well as that of their family, and the times in which they live, and their own individual Karma, we may perhaps, conclude that there is no unqualified "Free Will;" yet I cannot imagine any thought more depressing than the belief in Fate or predestination. The very rules laid down in *Light on the Path*, in the *Bhagavad-Gîtâ*, in the commands of Jesus, and in the Eightfold Path of Buddha, all imply a *freedom of choice*, which the individual may accept or reject, and the acceptance of which, we are told, will bring him ultimate happiness, and the rejection nothing but misery.

Number V

March, 1888

A mingled discussion on Karma and Self-Culture had taken place.

Dr. M.—The purification of the individual character would seem to embrace all the Society's aims. For in the realization of Universal Brotherhood as a fact, comes a realization of spiritual unity as its essence; and a grasp of the truth of spirit involves in time knowledge of its nature and workings and power. Given such sense of pervasive spirit as leads to the broadest beneficence and the loftiest endeavor, you have the germ of the principle which, in full growth, ripens to knowledge of philosophy and religion, and to the acquisition of the psychic and other powers now latent in us. Hence, I take it, the first of the Society's three aims is the greatest, as virtually including the information and the powers referred to in the others.

Anonymous.—Self-culture, as an aim, seems open to the same charge of selfishness as any other aim referring to self. As a mere personal attainment, does it differ essentially from the striving to be rich or learned or influential? On the other hand, is it possible for any one to seek self-culture only as a means to benefitting the race? If self in every form is to be discarded as a hindrance to progress, how can it be retained in the intensest of all forms—the expansion of personal gifts and powers? This seems to me a contradiction in the Theosophic scheme.

E. M. T.—I do not so see it. The very aim of such culture is to rid the person of narrow views or interests, and to enable him, not only to apprehend universal interests, but to lose himself in them. The broader the range of his sympathies and aspirations, the narrower his purely individual concerns. Besides, the spirit in which all acts are done, specially acts of charity, is a love of or homage to the Supreme, or whatever is our highest ideal, and this excludes selfishness.

Mrs. J. G.—This does not at all express my idea of charity. When I see a fellow being suffer and the wish to relieve him comes into my heart, the wish is to do away with his pain, to make him happy, and I want no other, especially no more remote, motive. Why is not the motive I have good enough in itself? If I desire to take away sorrow or confer pleasure, without any reference to myself and only for the good of another person, is not that a just and proper feeling of itself? I can't see how it would be bettered by turning away my thought from the present sufferer to a distant God and persuading myself that I am doing a kindness because of Him. And, indeed, I am suspicious of people who don't say simply that they do a right act because they want to, but say they do it for the glory of God or from thought of Him. The best proof of a God-like spirit is in God-like acts. If I have and exhibit real sympathy and helpfulness, it is because some measure of the Divine is in me,—though I may not talk of it.

E. D. Mac P.—I am not clear on this point;—How far is the production of good Karma a proper motive to good acts? If I give money or time to a charity in order that I may lay up treasure in heaven, is not this a mere investment just as truly as one in Wall Street?

General.—I think so. There seems no difference in principle between investing in Karma and investing in bonds. But *can* good Karma be thus produced? Occult writers teach that the ending of all Karma is the adept's aim, and that this is only accomplished as the causes generating it are made to end,—that is, the self-seekings, interests, desires which bind to and renew earth-lives. When these die out and the adept's wishes and will are merged in the Universal life, Karma, as a cause of rebirth, has nothing to sustain it and disappears. The desire

for good Karma is a desire for *some* Karma, whereas the highest aim
is to get rid of the necessity for any. One may say that goodness,
rather than the being good, is the goal. Charity as an investment
would not lead to either. Nor would any act, right in itself, if its object was reward. The production of good Karma is the result of good
acts, but is not a motive for them. The motive may be two-fold,—
internal, as seeking the formation of noble and God-like character;
external, as effecting benefit to others. Both may combine, the one
producing a sympathetic nature, the other a useful life. From these
good Karma will arise naturally: less so, if at all, when sought for itself.

W. Q. Judge.—Let me read you a passage from the Viśishṭādvaita
Philosophy. [Reads]. This states, as does Patanjali, that there are
three kinds of Karma,—that which is now inoperative because thwarted
by Karma of an opposite kind, that which is now operating, and that
which will operate hereafter when formed. Over the first and second
we have no control, but the third is largely within our molding
power. Now what produces a good Karma? Evidently, a good life. But
what produces a good life? As evidently, a good motive. But what
produces a good motive? Analyze one, and you will see that it springs
from two things,—true conception and a strong aspiration. We first
see the validity and beauty of spiritual truth; then we desire to as-
similate and exemplify it; from this double experience of the soul
comes the motive towards good. Towards *good*, observe; not towards
reward or happiness or self-aggrandizement in any form. Now what
maintains this motive? I should again say, two things. First, the
steadily increasing sense of the richness of spiritual attainment as contrasted with all other; second, the formation of the habit of offering
all acts, even the most trifling, as voluntary sacrifices on the altar of
life. This is a matter of growth, slow growth, but a sincere student
will find the growth possible. For if he understands that the real value
of deeds is measured by the spirit prompting them, and not the results they accomplish, he will see that a small duty discloses that spirit
as truly as a large one, and the *Bhagavad-Gîtâ* says that one's own
duty, however small, is that which we should perform. Further, this
habit is helped by fixing in the memory some pregnant sentence from
the Sacred Books. Here is one from the Upanishads:—

"Unveil, O Thou who givest sustenance to the worlds, that face of
the true sun which is now hidden by a vase of golden light! so that
we may see the truth and know our whole duty."[6]

If you will memorize this, you will find it an invaluable aid to self-
culture. It contains matter for profound thought and the stimulus to

---

6 [See *Echoes,* Vol. I, pp. 291-93 for W. Q. Judge's "Commentary on the
Gâyatrî."—*Comp.*]

the highest life. Still another thing. We need to recall the incessant caution of the *Bhagavad-Gîtâ* against action with a view to consequences. We are to concern ourselves with the quality of action, not with its results. Once more; the first of the Society's three aims seems most important because most enduring. Merely intellectual acquisitions cease with death; psychic powers do not go beyond the astral plane, and are not a permanent possession of the individuality; but any spiritual gain or power, spirit being indestructible, continues on unimpaired from one incarnation to another. I agree with Dr. M. that he who *fully* grasps the first aim has really all. Adepts acquire their vast domination over physical and astral forces as an incident in their spiritual course. It is not sought either in or for itself, but comes naturally, and is picked up, so to speak, on their way to the higher peaks of knowledge. It is not well to strive for the lesser good, but for the greater, which includes the less. All our acts, therefore, must be done without our having an interest in the result.

A. F.—I once asked an accomplished student what he judged the best and simplest prescription for Theosophic culture. He replied, "I believe the best to be that a man should read every morning *Light on the Path*, and carry out its precepts during the day." He added that a great assistance to the aspirant was to embody in a word or phrase the particular aim he had before him, and to recall it at each moment of temptation or weakness or needed endeavor. It might be "purity," "patience," "content," perhaps even "chelaship,"—whatever best expressed his need or purpose as he clearly saw it.

The caution against action with a view to consequences seems to require explanation of "consequences." Are they the logical consequences of the action, or the consequences to which the action makes himself liable? The latter should of course be disregarded, as one is to do what is right, no matter at what cost. But the logical consequences of any action are really part of the problem, and one must include them in forming judgment of its desirability. Theosophy would hardly recommend rashness, or thoughtlessness, or lack of foresight.

W. Q. Judge. — No; but I mean an adhesion to such action as, according to our lights, *on the whole* seems best, and then freedom from anxiety as to all the possible results. Every act has numberless sequences of which only the nearest can be foreseen. When these are considered wisely and the decision made, we should cease worry over possible or any effects whatever.

H. B. F. (Phila.)—We are taught that each person must develop in his own way and on his own lines. There is no one path for progress, as there is no one mold for character. But more than this, I much doubt if any one can advance faster than at a rate which all the conditions of his being make normal. Tastes, likes and dislikes, personal preferences, desires, and habits are part of each man's make-up, whether coming down from prior incarnations or an incident of this. We can outgrow them when the time comes, but can we shrivel them up or extirpate them, and, indeed, should we? The child loses interest in his toy as he becomes older, and another interest arises, fitted to his next time of life. The snake sheds its skin when the proper season arrives, and the man sheds his aims with successive stages of development. Can these changes be forced, and, if so, would they be healthful? Is not each taste or desire natural to the man when it exists, and, being natural, proper? And will it not become effete and drop away when, and only when, his general development advances beyond it? In brief, is any artificial system better than the normal one? If better, is it practicable? These considerations are strengthened by our doctrine that each man must pass through all experiences. If he curtails or mutilates any (I exclude, of course, such as are sinful or injurious to others), he lessens that experience and may have to repeat it. Surely the great experience cannot be self-mutilation.

S. H. C.—There are many replies to this—more than space admits. It is true that Nature, and therefore Occult Science, does nothing by leaps. Yet it is also true that Nature is often aided by science, and thus effects in less time and more perfectly what would otherwise require years. Plants are grafted, manured, and pruned. Breeds of animals are advantageously crossed. Men's characters may be improved by discipline and applied will. The lessons would, no doubt, be in time driven in by repeated sufferings, but no one would recommend so slow and painful a process in preference to intelligent reflection and a consequent effort after self-control. All education, as distinguished from book-study, is based upon the belief that we can, and should, work into betterment, and not merely drift into it. Theosophic culture has the same basis. It holds that development through effort is right, and that it produces a finer and stronger character, and in shorter time, than does a life without purpose; and it holds also that one may well sacrifice an inferior or transient good to a superior or permanent one. A child may give up a toy for a book, and a man may give up a pleasure for a principle. Whether either *can* do so depends upon the power of his motive. He certainly *will* not do so until the motive has grown to the needed degree of power, and in that sense it may be said that nothing can occur before its proper time; but here again comes in the doctrine of growth through effort, for motive may be developed thus. And so I should say that the question before anyone with conscious aspirations is, Whether he thinks the reasons for a vigorous Theosophic life more cogent than those for the "normal" human course, and, if so, whether he is ready to sacrifice to the greater aim the desires and habits consonant with the lesser aim.

L. B.—I should say also, as to experiences, that it is hardly meant that each man must pass through all. That is inconceivable. What is meant, I think, is that he must pass through each type, or class of experiences. One may have to be a physician in some incarnation, but not necessarily an allopath in one, a homeopath in another, and a surgeon in a third. One may learn the nature of rulership without being successively a Rajah, a President, and a Queen. So in the matters of art and emotion. I do not see that we are to be in turn poets, painters, sculptors, and musicians, though at some time we must learn the principles of all art; nor that we have to experience every shade of taste, desire, passion, but only the general quality common to all. It may very well be, then, that a time may come to each when he thinks that he has had enough of emotional interest, and would prefer, even if not without effort, to reach out after interests less perturbing and more satisfactory.

Question from California.—Does the doctrine of Karma give, through our circumstances in this life, any reliable clue to the circumstances of the preceding life or lives? In other words, can we at all conjecture what we were before being what we are?

Paul M.—I always insist that there is anyhow one such clue. The very fact that our eyes have been opened to the truths of Theosophy proves that we have somehow or somewhere acquired the right to so great a privilege. When we observe that an enormous majority of people are absorbed in purely secular interests; that, of the minority interested in super-sensual truth, most misconceive it or hold it in combination with belittling or misguiding error; and that, in our hemisphere, the number of sincere students of Theosophy is so minute as compared with the secularists or the ordinary religionists; we can hardly ascribe our being of that number to accident or to present merit. Occult Science extrudes the conception of accident, and we often find theosophic aspirations disassociated from rank, high intelligence, large culture, or strong character. The remaining explanation is that they are karmically connected with a creditable past. They imply some degree of spiritual instinct or affinity, and this so contrasts with the materialism around as to almost demand reference to an antecedent source. My contention, then, is that real interest in Theosophy is to be accounted for by good karma in a preceding incarnation. Moreover, I think this one of the most inspiring and exhilarating of thoughts. For, if my interest in the Great Truth is thus to be traced back, two things follow: 1st, I have behind me some certain mass of good Karma, and probably ended many experiences in evil which I should be sorry to repeat; 2nd, I am encouraged to believe that I am now truly on the Path, and that there is hope that my efforts will neither die down nor fail. The effect is inspiriting, whether I look backward or forward. And this view of previous karma has special value to beginners in Theosophy, who are disheartened by isolation, or by confused thought, or by the apparent futility of conflict with self. Let them understand that their interest comes from a past of good Karma, and they freshen up to cheeriness and to renewed effort.

E. D. H.—But does not such a view arouse pride? If I am now a Theosophist because hitherto a good man and a better man than my neighbors were, the elation from the fact may ruin me.

Col.—Not at all. It applies to what you were, not to what you are. What you are and what you will be depend on yourself, and you may misuse a spiritual endowment just as you may misuse any other,— beauty, talent, and so on.

* * * *—Besides, the abuse of a doctrine is no argument against its use. If the doctrine is true and is precious, we can't give it up because somebody may pervert it.

Arjuna.—We should always remember what the *Bhagavad-Gîtâ* says in the 2nd Chap., that "there is no loss or detriment to our efforts in study," and, in another place, that we "take up the thread of good Karma on each return." But I conceive it an unwise and profitless thing to try to determine what were the circumstances of previous lives.

FACES OF FRIENDS

Jirah Dewey Buck
1838-1916

Faces of Friends

[An interesting feature in *The Path* during the years 1893-94 were vignettes of some of the more prominent workers in the Movement, appearing under the title "Faces of Friends." Included here only are those signed by Judge or edited by him (unsigned), focusing mainly on his fellow-associates in America. The inclusion of a sketch by Bertram Keightley on "Jasper Niemand" draws the latter into this circle of outstanding associates of W. Q. Judge. Unless otherwise indicated the photos which accompany the articles are reproduced from the *Path* volume noted for each vignette.—*Comp.*]

Jirah Dewey Buck
(1838-1916?)

[*The Path*, Vol. VII, January 1893, pp. 319-20]

Some years ago *The Path* began to print pictures of friends and workers in the Society, but could not continue the series with regularity because of the expense. Those given were of H. P. Blavatsky, Col. H. S. Olcott, and Mrs. Annie Besant. Col. Olcott's was made from an old picture, and we purpose printing in another issue a picture of him from a late photograph showing how he looks now. Some persons object to any personal matter's appearing in a journal like *The Path*, but to see the pictures of fellow-workers who are so far away that it is unlikely we shall ever see them face to face tends to a closer sympathy and to a feeling, however slight, of acquaintance.

Dr. J. D. Buck is one of the old friends of the Society, and is the center around whom the Cincinnati Branch coalesced. He joined the T. S. in its first years. Those who know him always love him, and he has endeared himself to many members of the Society. Many years ago, as H.P.B. was just about to go on the steamer *en route* to India, she wrote him a friendly letter, using the top of a barrel for table, and telling him of her intended departure, and Dr. Buck then thought he would never see her. Later, in the year of her death, he sailed for London with Mrs. Buck and Annie Besant to make H.P.B.'s personal acquaintance. But while they were on the ocean H.P.B.'s body was deserted by its soul, and the travellers saw nothing on arriving but her empty room.

Dr. Buck was for many years the Dean of Pulete Medical College in Cincinnati, where he is still in active medical practice. His whole family are members of the Society. He was a member of the old Board of Control of the American Section, and has always been actively at work for the Society, having been several years on the Executive Committee. A valued contributor to *The Path, The Theosophist, Lucifer, and T.P.S.* series, he is known by name to nearly all of our members. His book, *A Study of Man,*[1] was written with the end in view of benefitting the Theosophical movement, and numerous small Theosophical tracts have been issued by him. As a black and white picture often misleads, we add that Dr. Buck has a light complexion and light hair; he is over six feet high, almost one of the Anakim.

[*The Path* sketch omitted mention that Dr. Buck was a practicing Homeopathic physician, having graduated from Cleveland Homeopathic College. In 1890 he was President of the American Institute of Homeopathy. He lived into the next century (d. 1916 or '17). For an idea of the variety of topics in his many books see *H. P. Blavatsky, Collected Writings,* Vol. III, p. 499—*Compiler.*]

Major General Abner Doubleday
(1819-1893)

[*The Path*, Vol. VII, March, 1893, pp. 372-74]

Major General Abner Doubleday, F.T.S., died at his home in Mendham, New Jersey, on January 26, 1893, of heart failure. He was born on June 26, 1819, at Ballston Spa, N. Y. His father served in Congress during Jackson's Presidency, and his grandfather fought at Bunker Hill and Stony Point. Abner Doubleday was graduated from West Point in 1842, and afterwards served through the Mexican war and later in the Seminole campaign. He was second in command under Major Anderson at Fort Sumter when the last war began, and sighted the first gun fired for its defense on the 12th of April, 1861. During the war he was in continuous active service, and took part in the bloody battle of Gettysburg, and in that military event he was a prominent figure. After the war a series of promotions followed until he was made

---

[1] [*A Study of Man and the Way to Health.* Cincinnati, Ohio, Robert Clarke & Co., 1889.—*Comp.*]

MAJOR-GENERAL ABNER DOUBLEDAY
1819-1893

Brevet Major General on the 13th of March, 1865. Thereafter he was stationed in the South for three years. On the 11th of December, 1873, he was retired from the active list of the U. S. Army at his own request. During succeeding years he wrote many articles relating to the war, as well as two books, *Reminiscences of Forts Moultrie and Sumter* and *Chancellorsville and Gettysburg*. His body was carried to New York, where it lay in state, and then was taken to Washington and buried in the National Cemetery, escorted by a guard of honor and receiving a military salute. This is the rough record of a noble and gentle life. The picture printed shows Gen. Doubleday as a young man.

Almost immediately after the Theosophical Society was formed he joined its ranks, attended its meetings, met Mme. Blavatsky and Col. Olcott very often, and on their arrival in India was made the President *pro tem.* here, with William Q. Judge as Secretary, January 17, 1879. He was often at our meetings, and his beautiful voice was heard many and many a time at the Aryan Branch to which he belonged. His name is the second on the roll-book of this Section. A varied experience furnished him with a fund of anecdote of many strange psychical experiences of his own, and these, told with such gentleness and sweetness, could never be forgotten. The spiritualistic journals claim him as one of their number, but as an old and deep student of theosophy he was not one of that cult but a genuine theosophist. A gift from him of over seventy books to the Aryan Branch was the nucleus for its present large library.

A translation into English of the *Dogma and Ritual of High Magic* by Eliphas Lévi was made by Gen. Doubleday, and presented to his friend, Bro. Judge, but as yet has not been published. He also translated Lévi's *Fables and Symbols*. Another Theosophical work, yet unfinished, is a complete Index and Digest of the early numbers of *The Theosophist*. Both of the last named are also in the possession of Bro. Judge.

On the 16th of May, 1879, the famous Dayânanda Saraswatî Swami wrote to the General from Meerut in India, expressing pleasure at hearing that Brother Doubleday had been made president *pro tem,* and sending him brotherly greetings: he also went on to say "I will soon send you the manuscript of three ceremonial degrees based upon Aryan Masonry which will teach western enquirers who may join the Theosophical Society the fundamental principles of primitive Aryan Philosophy". This shows, as said in a former article, that the ritual proposed for the T. S. in the early days was solely for that body and not for the Masons. The Swami further adjures all to have courage and to persevere against every obstacle.

An official letter from the Indian office signed by H. P. Blavatsky and dated the 17th of April, 1880, notified Gen. Doubleday of his election to the office of Vice-President of the Theosophical Society, and is now on file in the office of the General Secretary. After the organization of the Aryan T.S. in New York he was made Vice-President of that Branch, and continued a member of it to the day of his death. Constantly writing to the office and to members of the Society, no one can with truth say he was other than a member of the Theosophical Society, a believer in Theosophical doctrines, and one who ever tried to follow out the doctrines he believed in. It will be difficult to find another such gentle and sincere character as that of Abner Doubleday.

[The above article stands as a fine obituary to the Major-General and is attributed to Judge even though he himself is mentioned therein. It is reprinted by Sven Eek in *Damodar and the Pioneers of the Theosophical Movement,* pp. 590-92, where it is also established that Abner Doubleday was the inventor of the American game of baseball, as early as 1839.[1] In 1907 a marker was placed beside that first baseball diamond, which is now known as Doubleday Field—*Comp.*]

BERTRAM KEIGHTLEY
(1860-1945)

[*The Path,* Vol. VIII, August, 1893, p. 143]

The name of Keightley is probably as intimately associated with the Theosophical work of H. P. Blavatsky as is that of any other person, and one or other of the two Keightleys has always been working steadily in all parts of the Society's organization. The present article introduces the picture of Bertram Keightley as one of our old friends.

Bertram was born on the fourth of April, 1860, at Birkenhead, England. His father was a solicitor in Liverpool, and he also is a member of the bar. He says that his parents were both influenced to some extent by Swedenborgian thought. His education began at the Charterhouse, a famous school, was then carried on in Germany and France, and finished at Trinity College, Cambridge. There he took the degree of Master of Arts, after mathematical Tripos.

He came into Theosophy quite naturally. Having studied Mesmerism at Cambridge, that led to his reading Eliphas Lévi, and then medieval mystics and neo-Platonic writers. Later, having read Mr. Sinnett's *Esoteric Buddhism* and recognizing in it the outline of a system which would co-ordinate previous study and furnish a complete

---

1 [See *B.C.W.,* Vol. I, p. 459.—*Comp.*]

philosophy, he decided to make the acquaintance of the author. This is another proof of the value of that book. Keightley obtained an introduction to Mr. Sinnett and attended meetings of the local Lodge, and then, early in 1884, was admitted to the Society, together with Archibald Keightley and Mr. and Mrs. Cooper-Oakley, by Col. H. S. Olcott, then in England.

He first met H.P.B. at a special meeting of the London Lodge in Mr. Hood's rooms in Lincoln's Inn, H.P.B. turning up then quite unexpectedly to the astonishment of all, as they supposed her to be in Paris. I may add here that H.P.B. was in Paris just before this meeting, and suddenly informed me that she was ordered to go quickly to the London Lodge, although she was then not feeling well. Brother Keightley spent much of the spring and summer of 1884 in H.P.B.'s company in Paris and England, going with her to Germany. At the same time while in England he met me for the first time, as I was on my way to India.

In 1885 Brother Keightley was Hon. Secretary of the London Lodge until the formation of the Blavatsky Lodge upon the return of H.P.B. to London. In 1887, H.P.B. being sick at Ostende, he went over twice to that city to urge her to come to London and help them, accompanying her back to one of the suburbs of London after the second visit. In the same year he joined with Archibald Keightley and the Countess C. Wachtmeister in forming the celebrated Lansdowne Road household, where H.P.B. lived for a long time. After that he worked with Archibald Keightley, helping H.P.B. on the *Secret Doctrine* from May, 1887, until its publication.

According to a request made by H.P.B., Brother Keightley came to New York in the fall of 1889, and visited nearly the greater part of the Branches in the United States, attending the Convention at Chicago in 1890 as special delegate, returning in 1890 to Europe. Then a month afterwards, again at H.P.B.'s request, he went to India, where he was elected General Secretary of the Indian Section, which office he has held since then. While in India he visited all parts of it, and some places several times. In 1891 he came for a brief visit to London, after the death of H.P.B., returning to India shortly afterwards, and leaving India again in January, 1893. Being in London in April, 1893, he again travelled to America and was a delegate from the European and Indian Sections at the American Convention of that month. Both Bertram and Archibald Keightley have been thus associated with the Society for several years, and while Archibald has not been in India, where Bertram went so often, he has been in Australia where Bertram never went, and both of them have been several times in America, each having visited not only the Eastern but also the extreme Western Coast of the American continent. Brother

Keightley is therefore well known to a great many members, who may like once more to see his face or to show his picture to those who have heard of him. His constitution is strong, his energy very great, and his ability to deal with Theosophical doctrines has never been doubted by those who have heard him speak. As he says himself, no one can tell of the future, so that future he leaves to itself.

WILLIAM Q. JUDGE

[A more rounded and up-to-date picture of Bertram Keightley's life is to be found in *Blavatsky Collected Writings*, Vol. IX, pp. 432-35. The sketch there follows his sojourn in India, his stance in the "Judge case," as well as his later disillusionment with the T.S. under Annie Besant. He passed away in 1945. For portrait see the adjoining photograph.—*Compiler*.]

DR. ARCHIBALD KEIGHTLEY
(1859-1930)

[*The Path*, Vol. VIII, September, 1893, p. 177]

In our last we gave a picture of Bertram Keightley, and now follow with one of Archibald Keightley. Dr. Keightley was born in Westmoreland, on the 19th of April, 1859. His father was Alfred Dudley Keightley of Liverpool, who came of Swedenborgian stock, and Margaret Wakefield, whose parents were Quakers. Like Bertram, he began his education in the Charterhouse, then finished at Pembroke College, Cambridge, where he took the degree of B.A., after Natural Science Tripos. He then took the degree of B.M., licentiate of the Royal College of Physicians, London, and passed as member of the Royal College of Surgeons, England, and Master of Arts and Doctor of Medicine of Cambridge. Within the last two years he also passed the examination required in the State of New York and qualified as a physician under our law, and practiced for awhile in this city. He has also traveled a great deal, both in Europe and America, and took a long trip to New Zealand.

While in college he became interested in the phenomena of Spiritualism, as indicating unseen and unknown forces, and studied the mystical philosophical works in the library there, as well as Neo-Platonic philosophy. While engaged in this he noticed an advertisement of *Esoteric Buddhism*, bought the book, and after reading it was drawn to the subject. An introduction to Mr. Sinnett in 1884 followed, and

BERTRAM KEIGHTLEY
1860-1945

Dr. Archibald Keightley
1859-1930

Dr. Herbert A. W. Coryn
1863-1927

with others he met to study some of the letters from the Mahâtmas received by Mr. Sinnett, and then in the latter's house he met Brother Judge, who was on his way to Paris. He says he first saw H.P.B. at a meeting of the Society arranged to settle questions which had arisen in respect to the management of the movement in London, she coming over suddenly to the meeting unknown to anyone; this is the same meeting referred to at which Bertram Keightley saw her in Mr. Hood's chambers. Later he went with the party and saw H.P.B. off to India.

Later on, having a feeling with others that H.P.B.'s presence was necessary, and she being then at Ostende, he wrote jointly with others to her to come over to London and help in the work, and finally assisted her on her journey to the Capital, where she, Bertram Keightly, Dr. Keightley, and the Countess Wachtmeister joined together in a household at Norwood, which was later removed to 17 Lansdowne Road. This was in 1887, and nearly all his time was taken up then in helping in the editing and correcting of *The Secret Doctrine*. The Blavatsky Lodge and *Lucifer* were started at Norwood, but the greater part of the work was carried on at Lansdowne Road. In the following spring, at H.P.B.'s request, Dr. Keightley went to the first American Convention at Chicago, for which he started on short notice, arriving a little ahead of time, and thus being able to do some work on the Eastern Coast of America for the Society. Directly after that Convention he returned to Europe.

The following year it was proposed that he should again travel, but H.P.B. was against it for a long time. On a certain Sunday night she was opposed to it, but early the next morning at half-past six she summoned Dr. Keightley to her and asked him:

"When can you start for America?" to which he replied:

"By the next steamer," and on Tuesday night he again started for America.

On this visit he went to Chicago, Cincinnati, Boston, Washington, and Philadelphia, and on that occasion first made the acquaintance of his wife. Towards the end of the next year he traveled around the world with his sister for her health, spending six months in New Zealand. From there he went to San Francisco and visited the Branches on the Coast, doing a great deal of lecturing. Came across the continent, attended the Boston Convention in 1891, and returned to England in the summer of that year. He returned to America shortly before his marriage to Mrs. J. C. Ver Planck, and settled in New York, practicing medicine and lecturing for the Society. In the spring of 1893 he went back to England and began the practice of medicine in London.

Dr. Keightley is well known to very many Theosophists in America and is loved by them all, as his genial ways and sincere character endear him to everyone who makes his acquaintance. Very true is it that the name of Keightley is inseparably associated with our movement.

[A comprehensive outline of H.P.B.'s trusted friend and supporter is supplied in a six-page biographical entry in Vol. IX, pp. 427-32, of the *Blavatsky Collected Writings.* It includes the period after his marriage to Julia Ver Planck, their mutual support for Judge during the London trials, and subsequent literary work in the U.S.A. for many years after Judge's passing. Even though withdrawing from the reorganized T.S. in America, he contributed articles to the *Theosophical Quarterly* while continuing his successful medical career. He passed away on November 18, 1930, some 15 years after his wife.—*Comp.*]

COUNTESS CONSTANCE WACHTMEISTER
(1838-1910)

[*The Path*, Vol. VIII, November, 1893, p. 246]

Countess Constance Wachtmeister is a name so well-known to members of the Society throughout the world that her picture will certainly have a great interest. Her full name is Constance Georgina Louise de Bourbel de Montpinçon. Her parents were the Marques de Bourbel, formerly in the French diplomatic service, and Constance Bulkley, to whom she was born on the twenty-eighth of March, 1838, at Florence, Italy. The de Bourbel family is one of the most ancient in France. Originating from the southeast of France, they settled in Normandy about the year 936 A.D., and have thus a long line of ancestors, among which several were distinguished in French history, especially one Raoul de Bourbel who lived in the reign of Louis XIV.

Having lost her parents at an early age, Constance de Bourbel was sent to England to her aunt, Mrs. Bulkley, of Linden Hill, Berkshire, where she was educated and lived until her marriage in 1863 with her cousin, Count Wachtmeister, then Swedish and Norwegian Minister at the Court of St. James. There she resided for three years, when her husband was called to Copenhagen as minister to the Danish Court, and then after two years, the Count being nominated as Minister of Foreign Affairs, they took up their abode at the official residence in Stockholm. The Countess was then created a "state lady of the land" by the King, and was the last to receive this distinction as the title then became extinct. Count Wachtmeister died in 1871, and she remained in

COUNTESS CONSTANCE WACHTMEISTER
1838-1910

Sweden for several years, spending the winters in warmer climates on account of health. She has one son, the Count Axel Wachtmeister, who was born in 1865. He also is a member of the T.S., and is already well-known to members in California and other places.

In 1879 the Countess began investigations into Spiritualism, but after two years of arduous research found it both unsatisfactory and dangerous. In 1881 she joined the Theosophical Society, and ever since has been a worker for it both in and out of season, through good and evil report. H.P.B. gave her once the office of Corresponding Secretary, but that was declared null by the Council at Adyar—yet it was an honor. She was also Secretary and Treasurer of the Blavatsky Lodge, but gave those offices up to others. For a long time personally she carried on the work of the T.P.S., and revived it until it became able to run itself financially. As a close friend of H.P.B. and one who stood by that noble woman in time of great distress and anxiety both physical and social, the Countess can never be forgotten. She was privileged to see in the presence of H.P.B. and also when not near her many strange manifestations of the occult power and knowledge H.P.B. possessed, such as few have been granted. At every meeting of the Blavatsky Lodge the Countess could be seen as a familiar figure; at Conventions her presence always connected us with the days of our teacher; in private she could and often did relate what she knew of H.P.B. that was of the highest interest and value; and now she is going with Annie Besant to India, where beyond doubt her presence will prove of benefit to all who may meet her. All her work for the T.S., and it is very large and continuous, is done without having any official position, as she prefers to work for it in the ranks as an individual. She has contributed some papers and essays to Lodge work, but the book by which she will be best known is one now in hand giving an account of how H.P.B. wrote *The Secret Doctrine.*

Countess Wachtmeister is now and has been a vegetarian for fourteen years. In person she is of about the medium height, with blonde hair and blue eyes, a voice of pleasant sound, and her face has a singularly sweet expression. As a worker constantly acting she has no equal unless it be Annie Besant, as a friend of the T.S. there is no greater, as a devoted pupil of H.P.B. who is not ashamed of her teacher nor afraid of the convictions that teacher instilled—in all these she will ever be an example for every member of the Society.

[The dedication of the Countess is most clearly revealed in her own *Reminiscences*[1] which Judge refers to above as an account of how

---

1 [*Reminiscences of H. P. Blavatsky and "The Secret Doctrine"*, London, Theosophical Publishing Society, 1893; 2nd ed., Wheaton, Ill., Theosophical Publ. House, 1976.—*Comp.*]

H.P.B. wrote *The Secret Doctrine*. Details of her life are summarized on page 448 of Vol. VI of the *Blavatsky Collected Writings* where it is stated that she died in 1910.—*Comp.*]

George R. S. Mead
(1863-1933)[1]

[*The Path*, Vol. VIII, January, 1894, pp. 305-306]

George Robert Stowe Mead is the General Secretary of the European Section T.S., and works day in and day out at the Avenue Road Headquarters in London. He is an Englishman and was born in 1863. His father, Col. R. Mead, late deputy Commissioner Her Majesty's Ordnance, is a distinguished Ordnance officer. So George's childhood was spent among soldiers, sailors, cannon shot, shell, guns and bayonets. His education was obtained mostly at King's school, Rochester. At St. John's College he won school scholarship, and proper Sizarship at Cambridge. He then "went up" destined to read for mathematics supposed to be his forte. Pastors and masters said he must be a "wrangler." But he took the bit in his mouth, threw mathematics to the dogs, and read for Classical Tripos. In that he took classical honors. So far life was aimless and creedless, but unconsciously he was looking for something in life as a reality.

Having become a full-blown A.B. the query was "what to do?" He was offered a chance in an old established practice of an uncle in the law. He refused this, and while looking about taught at a large preparatory school. In 1884 when he went down for Cambridge he read *Esoteric Buddhism,* and then wrote to B. Keightley, saw Mohini, and was put on the track of Hindu philosophy, where he felt as if at home. Then he read all he could find on the subject, with no taste for phenomena, but the latter were also studied as a necessity. After three years of teaching he became restless and resolved on a new path, entering as an undergraduate at Oxford to read for classical honors and take up philosophy so as to get a fellowship and then come out for Theosophy.

After reading fourteen hours a day for five months, rest became necessary, and, the risk in the scheme seeming too great, he went to France to Clermont Ferrand and entered at a small university there, following the literary and philosophical lectures for six months. While there he was able to start many on Theosophy and Spiritualism, and had an epitome of discussions printed in French. This made a small

---

[1] Further information may be found in Vol. XII of *Blavatsky Collected Writings.*

GEORGE R. S. MEAD
1863-1933

CLAUDE FALLS WRIGHT
1867-1928

riot, pulpits preaching against Spiritualism. From there he came back to London, taught once more for a year, then left, and met H. P. Blavatsky.

Two days after H.P.B. came to London in 1887, he met her at Norwood. She as usual asked him to stop; all seemed familiar as if he had known them all his life. He spent holidays at Lansdowne Road house, working as was possible. In July, 1889, he came to work under H.P.B. for good, giving up all else. Since then there he has been, and there he also lost that great and good friend whom to know was to admire and revere. No more can be said, as life is all before him, and perhaps he is destined to work long and well for the old T.S.

Mead is strong in word and manner; his eye is bright, clear, and sincere; his voice not unusual; his devotion undoubted. About the medium height, he is built for work and to last. All that we sorrowfully confess is that his hair is just beyond the auburn, like some sunset afterglow.

Claude Falls Wright
(1867-1923)

[The Path, Vol. VIII, February, 1894, pp. 351-52]

Claude Falls Wright was born September 18th, 1867, in Dublin, Ireland. His mother is an English woman, a member of an old Cheshire family. His father was the nephew of a well-known Crimean General named Falls. He was educated at the High School in Harcourt Street, Dublin, where many well-known Irish theosophists were also taught. Preparing to enter the Civil Service in England he passed one grade, but while waiting for an appointment became an accountant in an Assurance Company. When he was eighteen years old he entered the Royal College of Surgeons to study medicine, but had not completed the first year before he heard of Theosophy through Charles Johnston. This subject then claimed his attention and he went over to London at the age of twenty to see H.P.B., afterwards asking her to advise him about going to India, to which she replied, "Do not go, but come to me and I will teach you," but saying he must first form a Branch, if possible, in Dublin. Acting on this, he gathered persons together, and finally a Branch was formed, which was opened by Brothers Judge and A. Keightley. Since then he has devoted himself entirely to the Society.

He was with H.P.B. for three years, and beside her at the time of her leaving this earth. At one time he was one of her secretaries, and at another time manager of the Duke Street Publishing Company, now the T. P. S. Almost every picture and ornament in H.P.B.'s room he put up at her request, as well as constructing many of the shelves for them. During the first and last visit H.P.B. paid to No. 17 Avenue Road, next door to the Headquarters, she leaned on Brother Wright's arm as he showed her around the place, and at the time of her death he knelt beside her holding her left hand, and as she passed away took the ring from off her fourth finger. For a long time he was also Secretary of the Blavatsky Lodge in London. After the death of H.P.B. he came to America, arriving in New York seven months to a day after that eventful hour. Since then he has been traveling about the United States, as far north as Minneapolis and south to New Orleans, working at the Headquarters in Madison Avenue when in the city of New York. A great many members of the Society are now personally acquainted with Brother Wright, and his efforts for the Branches have been productive of great benefit, not only to him but also to the organization. His efforts in the Theosophical field in America entitle him to a place in this gallery, as he has visited most of the Branches on the east coast and far to the west, lecturing in the cities visited to large audiences and helping all centers in plans and organization for the purposes of further study. His work in this direction is invaluable and not only is his coming looked for, but constant calls are made for visits. Although Claude Falls Wright is young he has an ancient look due to a slight baldness; his voice is pleasant and insinuating and his birth gives him that touch of humor which enlivens the dullest subject.

[For details on Claude Falls Wright subsequent to the Judge article, until his death by drowning on January 8, 1923, consult *Blavatsky Collected Writings*, Vol. XI, pp. 593-94.—*Comp.*]

JASPER NIEMAND
Mrs. Archibald Keightley
(Died 1915)

[*The Path*, Vol. IX, April, 1894, p. 14

A Sketch contributed by Bertram Keightley]

Among the "Friends" whose faces *The Path* has been presenting to its readers few, if any, have a greater claim to a prominent place than "Jasper Niemand." To most an unknown but dear friend, dear because of the heart-touching help and light which for many have come from the writings bearing this signature—a *nom-de-plume* as all must have known. The personality thus veiled hitherto is that of one personally

JASPER NIEMAND
(Died 1915)

very dear to many an earnest worker in the T.S.; that of Mrs. Archibald Keightley, more widely known perhaps in the ranks of the T.S. under the name of Mrs. J. Campbell Ver Planck.

Her maiden name in full was Julia Wharton Lewis Campbell, daughter of the Hon. James H. Campbell, a prominent Pennsylvania lawyer. Her father's was a highly distinguished career. He commanded his regiment during the war; served as member of the U.S. Congress for several terms; held two diplomatic commissions under President Lincoln as U.S. Minister to Sweden and Norway, and subsequently to Bogotá in South America. Her mother was Juliet Lewis, daughter of Chief Justice Ellis Lewis of the Supreme Court of Pennsylvania, a writer of verse possessing great poetical charm and value.

Mrs. Keightley's childhood was chiefly passed among the Pennsylvania mountains, and later on the continent of Europe, where she was educated and entered the Society of foreign courts at the early age of sixteen. Even then she had already developed the literary talent for which the members of both branches of her family had been noted, and had displayed for generations in the occupations of their leisure hours. Her early writings consisted of translations from the poems of the present and late Kings of Sweden, in original verse, tales and descriptions published in *Harper's Magazine*, the *Galaxy*, and other periodicals, under her own name as well as the *nom-de-plume* of "Esperance." That the work itself was of fine quality is shown by the fact that full market rates were always gladly paid for it; while the deeper tendencies in the writer's nature are seen in the fact that the spur to exertion lay in the desire to give for the helping of others, some of what she had herself *earned,* and not merely the superfluity of that wealth which the accident of birth—or Karma?—had placed at her command. The child is truly the father of the man—or woman; and how happy must she have been when feeling so early that she could already, by her own efforts, do something to lessen the misery of others?

Miss Julia W. L. Campbell (as she then was) married in 1871 Mr. Philip W. Ver Planck of New York; and six years later, in the course of a single year, she lost her husband and both sons suddenly by a most dramatic series of reverses—including dangers and losses of many kinds. Long and terrible illness followed these sudden blows.

During her recovery Mrs. Ver Planck wrote her two successful plays, "The Puritan Maid" and "Sealed Instructions," the latter having had a marked success during two seasons at the Madison Square Theater, New York, as well as throughout the country.

To turn from the outer to the inner life. By long established family custom, Mrs. Ver Planck belonged to the Episcopal Church—"The Church of England"—but she found no spiritual life there. Indeed, she had ceased to seek for any such life, content apparently with the ideals of literature and art, in a happy domestic and social circle where leisure and refined conditions permitted the cultivation of personal gifts. Yet an interior want now and then made itself felt.

One day, however, quite by chance as it were, when lunching with her close friend, Mrs. Anna Lynch Botta, the name of Madame Blavatsky was mentioned, and mentioned as that of an exposed fraud. From thence to Theosophy was but a step; Mrs. Ver Planck had never heard of either, and Mrs. Botta, whose circle comprised almost every distinguished member of society at home and abroad (that well-known circle unique in American life), invited her friend to accompany her to hear Mr. Arthur Gebhard speak on Theosophy to Mrs. Ole Bull, Mrs. Celia Thaxter, and others in the drawing room of a friend. The impression made upon Mrs. Ver Planck was so deep that she joined the T.S. within two weeks, and thenceforward began her unceasing work for Theosophy.

Living with her parents at a distance from New York she wrote for the *Path* under the names of "Julius," "August Waldensee," "J," and later on as "Jasper Niemand," as well as unsigned articles, and also corresponded with T.S. enquirers. In those days writers were so few in the Society that they had to take several names, and often one would write up the notes or finish the articles of another.

In answer to some enquirers as to the "Jasper Niemand" writings, Mrs. Keightley writes: "When I began to write articles along these lines, H.P.B. sent me a pen which I always used. The articles were and are always written in full objective consciousness, but at these times there is a feeling of inspiration, of greater mental freedom. The *Letters That Have Helped Me* were received at my Pennsylvania home. They were written for me and for Dr. Keightley—and for the use of others later on—by Mr. W. Q. Judge, at the express wish of H. P. Blavatsky. The letter which is the source of this request, and which conveys assurance of Mr. Judge's qualifications for the office of instructor, purported to be written *through* Madame Blavatsky (it begins 'Says Master'),[1] and is one of those so ably described by Col. H. S. Olcott in the *Theosophist* for July, 1893, where he says that communications from high occult sources received through H.P.B. always resembled her handwriting."

This modification of H.P.B.'s handwriting is decidedly interesting in the above-mentioned letter, whose data amply justify the manner in which "Z" is spoken of in Niemand's preface. Moreover, H.P.B. spoke of her friend Mr. Judge as the "exile" and Annie Besant wrote later on, "You are indeed fortunate in having W.Q.J. as Chief. Now that

---

1 [*Letters That Have Helped Me*, Repr., 1891 ed., Pasadena, T.U.P., 1953, Vol. I, p. 68-9, Vol. II, p. 106.—*Comp.*]

H.P.B. has gone, it is the Americans who have as immediate leader the greatest of the exiles."[1]

It is to be hoped that the Editor of *The Path*, a journal so indissolubly connected with the Theosophical writings of the subject of this sketch, will not from personal hesitation exclude from its pages information which is really a moderate statement on behalf of "Jasper Niemand" in reply to questions coming from all parts of the world. The statement would have been made earlier, were it not for a wish, on Jasper Niemand's part, to continue helpful private correspondence carried on with many persons who [were] addressed under the protection of her impersonality.

After the departure of H.P.B., Mrs. Ver Planck now and again joined the New York staff of workers as a reinforcement during Mr. Judge's prolonged absences. During one of these periods she met Annie Besant at the Boston Convention of 1891, and there began a friendship destined to evolve as link after link was formed in the chain-mutual of work. Then also was formed the T.S. League of Workers, afterwards inaugurated in Europe.

Mrs. Ver Planck continued to live with her parents in Pennsylvania until the autumn of 1891, when she married Dr. Archibald Keightley of Old Hall, Westmoreland. After a year's residence in New York they were called to England by the health of Dr. Keightley's mother.

During Annie Besant's absence in India, Mrs. Keightley has temporarily taken up a part of her work at the London Headquarters, and in consequence has been residing there for several months.

And here this sketch ends for the present. It is not for me to say more, nor to dwell upon the respect and affection which its subject has gained in her new sphere of duty. But I know that I voice the earnest wish of all in expressing the hope that many years of equally fruitful and valuable work for our beloved Cause still lie before her.

Bertram Keightley.

[Under her married name (Julia Wharton Keightley) may be found a beautiful description of her adventuresome life, in *Blavatsky Collected Writings*, Vol. IX, pp. 435-38. Apparently her birth date is unknown, but she died in 1915, some fifteen years prior to her husband. His

---

[1] The technical meaning of these titles, "Greatest of the Exiles" and "Friend of all Creatures", as employed in the East, is totally unknown in the West; the latter being a phrase that has more than once been applied, half in jest, to W.Q.J. by his intimates on account of his often enforced doctrine of "accepting all men and all things"—providing they *work* for Theosophy.—B.K.

sketch by Judge appears earlier in this section, while the "Faces of Friends" entry for Jasper appeared over Bertram's signature, not Judge's. Still we include it due to her valued connection with Judge and the important footnote concerning his cryptic title, "The Greatest of the Exiles."—*Comp.*]

ISABEL COOPER-OAKLEY
(1854-1914)

[*The Path,* Vol. IX, July, 1894, pp. 122-24]

Mrs. Isabel Cooper-Oakley is now well-known personally to Theosophists in all Sections of the Society. She is the daughter of the late Henry Cooper, C.B., Commissioner of Lahore, India, who was made the Governor of Delhi on his deathbed. She was born at Amritzar, Punjâb, India, in 1854. Her father, one of the best known men in the Bengal Civil Service, was made a "Companion of the Order of the Bath" at the early age of twenty-eight for distinguished services rendered during the mutiny in India; the Cooper Buildings in Delhi are named after him, and the "Cooper Medal" was struck for him in 1864 by the Indian Government in recognition of great and continued services in the educational questions of India, and especially in regard to the education of women. On her father's side Mrs. Cooper is descended from Baron Cooper of Paulett (Earl of Shaftsbury) and Sir William Burnaby, both old English families. Her father was a nephew of Lord Forbes of Forbes Castle in Aberdeenshire. Her mother was the daughter of Gen. Steel (who married the daughter of Prince Angelo Della Trememondo, an exiled royal family of Tuscany), one of the old families of West Cumberland, whose mother, Dorothy Ponsonby, was a niece of the Earl of Bessborough. These facts are not given by way of glorification, but for those who wish to know of a person's descent.

Mrs. Cooper-Oakley and her sister Laura passed a great deal of their early life on the Continent. At the age of twenty-three the subject of our sketch met with a severe accident and for two years was unable to walk. This enforced quiet threw all her interests into her studies, and it was during this illness in 1878 that *Isis Unveiled* was lent to her and she began her investigations into Spiritualism with its cognate subjects. Life then took a more serious aspect, and on recovering in 1879 she began to take up public questions, interesting herself in Woman's Suffrage and the Social Purity Alliance. Wishing to study

ISABEL COOPER-OAKLEY
1854-1914

philosophy more deeply, Mrs. Cooper-Oakley determined to go to Girton College, Cambridge, in order to pass through a systematic course.

In 1879 when H.P.B. was passing through London on her way to India Mrs. Cooper-Oakley just missed her. Going on with her studies she passed her "matriculation examination" in 1881 and entered Girton as a student. In 1882 she met Mr. Oakley, who was at Pembroke College, Cambridge, with Dr. Keightley, and they all began their studies together. Together with the Keightleys they wrote to Adyar in 1883 applying for membership in the Theosophical Society, but received no answer. Hearing from Mr. A. P. Sinnett in the autumn of 1883 that H.P.B. was expected in Europe, they determined to visit her upon arrival. Isabel Cooper was married early in June, 1884, to Mr. A. J. Oakley. In March Col. Olcott arrived in London, and then Mrs. Oakley, Dr. Keightley, and Mr. B. Keightley joined the Society.

During the summer of 1884 it was arranged that Mrs. Cooper-Oakley and her husband should accompany H.P.B. on her return to India, and the plan was carried out. They took a house in London where H.P.B., Dr. Keightley, and Miss Laura M. Cooper lived during September and October until the party started for India in November. On the way to India Mrs. Cooper-Oakley spent three weeks in Egypt with H.P.B. and found the period full of intense interest, as H.P.B. was a mine of deep information. Arriving at Adyar, Mrs. Cooper-Oakley says she "had every opportunity of investigating the Coulomb affair and also was an eye witness to Mr. Hodgson's investigations, besides seeing the unfair way in which the S.P.R. representative behaved to H.P.B."

H.P.B. then fell sick, and Mrs. Cooper-Oakley nursed her through a long and dangerous illness, falling sick herself afterwards and being unable to leave India when H.P.B. was ordered away in February. In May Mrs. Cooper-Oakley was sent home, arriving in the summer of 1885, when H.P.B. sent her a warm and affectionate invitation to come to Wurzburg; but owing to bad health and business affairs, Mrs. Cooper-Oakley was unable to leave London, but went to see H.P.B. as soon as the latter came to Norwood. During that summer of 1887 Mrs. Cooper-Oakley held small meetings in her rooms for inquirers, and was studying Theosophy steadily. That autumn she went to India for three months, and later in April, 1888, came back and stayed with H.P.B. in Lansdowne Road for a few weeks, and in 1889 she became one of the household staff.

Continued bad health has prevented Mrs. Cooper-Oakley from doing the work she would like to have done. In 1890 the Headquarters was moved to 19 Avenue Road; the following year H.P.B. left us and her last message for the Society was given to Mrs. Oakley the night but one before she died. At three a.m. she suddenly looked up and said "Isabel, Isabel, keep the link unbroken; do not let my last incarnation

be a failure." At the moment of H.P.B.'s death Mrs. Cooper-Oakley
was out, but received a telegram recalling her and arrived just ten
minutes late.

Since then she has been to Australia, where she worked among the
Theosophists, arousing a great deal of public and private interest and
doing much good to the Society. From there in 1893 she returned by
way of California, stopping and working there and meeting many
members. She arrived in Chicago in September, 1893, in time for the
Theosophical Congress of the World's Fair, and took part in that as a
speaker at the meetings of the Society. From there she came across to
New York and returned home to London in October with the English
and Indian delegates who had been at the Theosophical Congress. We
leave the record at this point in London where she has been at work
ever since, and hope that the future may record services to the Society
as long as she shall live.

Emil August Neresheimer
(1847-1937)

[*The Path*, Vol. IX, August, 1894, pp. 145-46]

E. Aug. Neresheimer is at present the Treasurer of the Board of
Trustees of the Aryan T.S. of New York. He is a Bavarian of Catholic
parents, and was born in Moosburg near Munich, January 2, 1847.
At Munich he graduated from a business college, and then learned
the silversmith's and jewelry trades in Switzerland, Augsburg, and
Berlin. At present he is an importer of diamonds and precious stones
in New York.

In 1868 he went to Australia, leaving there in 1870 for California.
Two years after reaching California, in 1872, he came to New York
and has been there in business ever since, taking trips to Europe very
often.

In 1886 Mr. Neresheimer heard of Theosophy from reading *Esoteric
Buddhism* which a friend had loaned him, and was particularly struck
with the information about Adepts. A foundation for this belief had
been laid by nursery tales about great and wonderful beings in India.
He had always held theories of his own about the doctrine of correspondences and of the interrelations of the ideal cosmos with the visible
universe. A study of Kant, Hegel, and Schopenhauer was made by him
to obtain a mental anchorage, but not successfully. The Theosophical
theory came like a key and a revelation, something like a formerly
known and lost philosophy. The immediate link with the Theosophical

EMIL AUGUST NERESHEIMER
1847-1937

Ernest Temple Hargrove
(Died 1939)

Society began through an abusive article in a daily paper in which were given the name and address of the Secretary in New York, on whom he at once called, and then joined the T.S. in January, 1889.

Subsequently he called on H.P.B. in London and had some conversation with her at her rooms in Lansdowne Road, but cannot claim any greater acquaintance with her. He has served on the Executive Committee of the American Section, and from his intimate acquaintance with its work and with that of its General Secretary is qualified to know what this Section is and upon what the growth of Theosophy in the United States depends. Though not a speaker or writer of facility, he is one of those strong men who give a force to those with whom they work. His face does not appear here by his own wish, but because those who know of the great assistance rendered to the work of the Society not only in wise counsel but in many another field desire that readers should see the countenance of a strong friend, a good adviser, a liberal helper, one who is not easy to find in a walk of many days.

ERNEST TEMPLE HARGROVE
(?-1939)

[*The Path*, Vol. IX, September, 1894, pp. 182-84]

This month's face is that of Ernest Temple Hargrove, who, although not known to the whole T.S., has made himself quite well acquainted with very many in the American Section. He came to the eighth Convention at San Francisco in April, 1894, travelling across the continent with the General Secretary, and after the Convention all the way up to Seattle, lecturing meanwhile at various places. For that reason and also because he is a friend, we give his counterfeit presentment.

Mr. Hargrove is the second son of James Sidney Hargrove, one of London's best known solicitors. His name has been for a long time connected with literature, several members of it being mentioned in England's *Dictionary of National Biography* as authors of considerable repute. His father's family comes from Yorkshire; on his mother's side he is Scotch, she being an Aird. The best known representative of this line is and has been for some years the member of Parliament for one of the London Constituencies. There is also a fighting streak in his veins, such men as Lieutenant General Hargrove, Governor of Gibraltar during the war in the early part of the eighteenth century, and Sir Martin Frobisher who fought against the Armada, standing to him as ancestors.

After being educated at several preparatory schools he went to
Harrow, where he is said to have spent most of his time reading novels,
but at this date he does not regret it. When eighteen years of age he
left Harrow and studied for the diplomatic service; was then offered
the choice of going to Cambridge University or traveling abroad.
Choosing the latter he went to Australia and visited Tasmania, making
a long tour through New Zealand, where some time was spent among
the Maories, returning home by way of Ceylon. Considerable time was
spent in the office of a charter accountant where he was sent to get a
general idea of business. He then decided to become a barrister, and
is now a member of the Middle Temple.

Mr. Hargrove first heard of Theosophy during the time of the great
discussion in the London *Daily Chronicle*. Being at a seaside holiday
resort, he saw a placard on a wall with the large heading "Theosophy"
advertising a lecture by Mrs. Besant. He did not go to the lecture,
but by seeing the word "Theosophy" his whole inner and outer life
was changed. Books were then bought on the subject, and he was
admitted as a member-at-large without even having the acquaintance
of another member. Since then most of his days and a good many of
his nights have been spent at the London Headquarters, helping in the
General Office with correspondence, with the *Vahan*, with certain
Lucifer reviews, and lecturing at various lodges. He was also Treasurer
of the Blavatsky Lodge. Since he was nine years old he has travelled
a great deal in Europe and other places, and thus has had most of the
edges knocked off his distinctive character as an "insular Englishman".
To prove this he says he is a great reader of *The Path* and that he has
learned more from it than from other sources. For the Society he has
written under various *noms de plume*, but not under his own name.
He stands six feet two in his stockings, but having grown rather fast
he thinks he is rather weedy but hopes under the action of Karma he
may fill up in time.

James Morgan Pryse
(1859-1942)

[*The Path*, Vol. IX, June, 1894, pp. 90-91]

James Morgan Pryse is our head printer, and he with his brother
John must remain immortal among our annals. He came with his
brother to New York in July, 1888, and enabled the editor of *The Path*
to start the Aryan Press for the printing of much needed Theosophical
literature.

JAMES MORGAN PRYSE
(1859-1942)

Brother Pryse was born in New London, a suburb of Cincinnati, Ohio, August 14th, 1859, and is of Welsh descent. His father was a Presbyterian minister in Cincinnati, where James spent his childhood. Both father and mother were born in Wales. It may be noted that Pryse is also the name of the recent Grand Druid of Wales. Being a minister's son, James went from place to place in America, taking a high-school course and preparing in Latin, Greek, and the like, for a college in Crawfordsville, Ind. Ill health, overstudy, and trying to do three years' work in a little over one spoiled these plans, and Brother Pryse began to read law. At 17 he was ready for the bar, but not caring to spend four years as a clerk he went to Red Cloud, Nebraska, to the frontier. There for a while he ran a photograph gallery, but sold it out and entered a printing office, learned that business, edited a country paper, and with his brother John published other papers in various towns. They started an office at Anaconda, Montana, sold that out and began a paper at Prescott, Michigan, and St. Paul, Minnesota. From there he went to Florida, and then up to Minnesota, where in January, 1886, he gave up printing and was admitted to the bar in the Circuit Court for the Eighth District of the State.

Intending to practise law he went to Lacrosse, Wisconsin, but took a position as telegraph editor on the *Republican Leader* instead. Becoming what the Americans call "disgruntled" with all things, he joined a socialistic colony going to Sinaloa, Mexico. A year was spent at Hammonton, New Jersey, doing the printing for the colony and helping to organize. While there he got into correspondence with Mrs. VerPlanck, who is now Mrs. A. Keightley, and resolved to work for the T.S. instead of for socialism. Brother Pryse had never taken to any religion nor joined a church, and was too familiar with psychic phenomena to be in sympathy with naturalism, yet took no interest in mere spiritualism, its phenomena being of no use and the utterances of its spirits being nonsense. He had been studying Fourier while holding to pantheism and reincarnation, and the instant he met Theosophy recognized it as that for which he sought. Then began a study of *Isis,* of *The Path,* of all that could be found on Theosophy, as well as an invaluable correspondence with Mrs. VerPlanck. In July, 1887, he joined the T.S. at Los Angeles, and met there again his brother, by that time also full of Theosophy. From there both went to Peru and back to Panama, and from there to New York.

In August, 1889, Brother Pryse went to London to start the printing office there named the H.P.B. Press, wherein the machinery is American. There he is still at work night and day. He has wandered over most of the States of the U.S., keeping himself foot-free for a possible work in the future. He and his brother cannot be erased, and while our books are read, though no printer's name is on them, yet the soul and the work of James M. Pryse are in them. That he is a printer of the highest ability no one can deny, that he is a man who has unselfishly worked for the T.S. is a fact that is recorded in the unimpeachable books of Karma. We show his counterfeit presentment.

F

G

egoic stature in the Manvantara,
345
on evolution of globe chain,
406 fn.

Justice:
in doctrine of Karma, 64. 130,
131, 148
not apart from mercy, 147
and self-styled "Karmic
Agents," 310

K

Kabalah:
Hebrew, on word, 213
holds key to occult numbers, 217
secret teaching of the Jews, 413

Kabalists, refuse to divulge
psychic experiences, 63

Kali-Yuga:
length of, 244
Black Adepts premature in, 244,
399
White Adepts preceded, 244,
399
seeds of black magic in, 244

Kâma:
-Mânasic forms are pictures, 235
entanglement of ego in, 287
and sympathy, 314
coalescence with astral body
after death, 322

Kâma-loka:
victims of violent death prolonged in, 266
Is it purgatory? 267
suffering in, 267, 290
recognition of friends in, 290,
317
state is still quite physical, 293,
317
many different states of, 317
a state in which some are unaware that they are dead, 317

Kâma-Rupa:
in normal cases dissipates, 266,
404

of suicides and violent deaths,
266
drawn by mediums into séances,
266, 336, 404
separation of higher triad from,
267
suffering of the, 267-68
how Manas separates from,
267-68
how it is formed, 321-22
can gravitate to animal kingdom, 404

Kardec, Allan (pseud. of Rivail,
Hippolyte Leon Denizard, 1803-
1869), denied theory of reincarnation, 318

Karma:
Law of Compensation, 64, 129,
130-31, 395, 431
of beggary, 64-65
of inflicting pain, 65-66, 300
ethical law of causation, 129,
152, 432
in Christian scriptures, 129,
130-31, 153, 427
as justice with mercy, 148, 233,
325
explains class differences, 152
moral and spiritual, 171, 327,
334-35, 395, 430-31
material agents of, 214
Lipikas and, 215
rules entire universe, 215, 259,
391, 430
"not interferring" with, 224,
232-33, 269-70, 388-89, 426,
439
includes altruistic acts, 232-33,
334-35, 388
forgiveness and, 232-33, 310-11
on entering the occult path, 250-
51
Is it destiny? 257, 270, 432
governs astrology, 259
Adepts themselves *are*, 270
of diseases from previous life,
277
balance-sheet of, 280-81, 316,
325-26, 334-35, 431-32